WALTZING THROUGH EUROPE

Waltzing Through Europe

Attitudes towards Couple Dances in the Long Nineteenth Century

Edited by
Egil Bakka, Theresa Jill Buckland, Helena Saarikoski, and Anne von Bibra Wharton

https://www.openbookpublishers.com

© 2020 Egil Bakka, Theresa Jill Buckland, Helena Saarikoski and Anne von Bibra Wharton. Copyright of individual chapters is maintained by the chapters' authors.

This work is licensed under a Creative Commons Attribution 4.0 International license (CC BY 4.0). This license allows you to share, copy, distribute and transmit the text; to adapt the text and to make commercial use of the text providing attribution is made to the authors (but not in any way that suggests that they endorse you or your use of the work).

Attribution should include the following information:

Egil Bakka, Theresa Jill Buckland, Helena Saarikoski and Anne von Bibra Wharton (eds.), *Waltzing Through Europe: Attitudes towards Couple Dances in the Long Nineteenth-Century.* Cambridge, UK: Open Book Publishers, 2020, https://doi.org/10.11647/OBP.0174

Copyright and permission for reuse of many images included in this publication differ from the above. Copyright and permissions information for images is provided separately in the List of Illustrations.

In order to access detailed and updated information on the license, please visit https://doi.org/10.11647/OBP.0174#copyright

Further details about CC BY licenses are available at https://creativecommons.org/licenses/by/4.0/

All external links were active at the time of publication unless otherwise stated and have been archived via the Internet Archive Wayback Machine at https://archive.org/web

Updated digital material and resources associated with this volume are available at https://doi.org/10.11647/OBP.0174#resources

Every effort has been made to identify and contact copyright holders and any omission or error will be corrected if notification is made to the publisher.

ISBN Paperback: 978-1-78374-732-0
ISBN Hardback: 978-1-78374-733-7
ISBN Digital (PDF): 978-1-78374-734-4
ISBN Digital ebook (epub): 978-1-78374-735-1
ISBN Digital ebook (mobi): 978-1-78374-736-8
ISBN XML: 978-1-78374-737-5
DOI: 10.11647/OBP.0174

Cover image: *A Drunken Scene in a Dancing Hall with a Sly Customer Eyeing a Young Girl* (1848). Coloured etching by G. Cruikshank, after himself. Wellcome Collection, CC BY 4.0. Cover design: Anna Gatti.

Contents

Preface		vii
1.	The Round Dance Paradigm *Egil Bakka*	1
2.	The State of Research *Egil Bakka*	27
3.	A Survey of the Chapters in the Book *Egil Bakka*	53
4.	The Waltz at Some Central European Courts *Egil Bakka*	63
5.	The Polka as a Czech National Symbol *Daniela Stavělová*	107
6.	Decency, Health, and Grace Endangered by Quick Dancing? The New Dance Style in *Bohemia* in 1830 *Dorota Gremlicová*	149
7.	Reception of Nineteenth-Century Couple Dances in Hungary *László Felföldi*	177
8.	The Waltz among Slovenians *Rebeka Kunej*	239
9.	Dancing and Politics in Croatia: The *Salonsko Kolo* as a Patriotic Response to the Waltz *Ivana Katarinčić and Iva Niemčić*	257
10.	Waltzing Through Europe: Johann Strauss (the Elder) in Hamburg and Altona in 1836 *Jörgen Torp*	283

11. Continuity and Reinvention: Past Round Dances in Present Estonia   317
    Sille Kapper

12. The Ban on Round Dances 1917–1957: Regulating Social Dancing in Norwegian Community Houses   343
    Egil Bakka

13. Dance and 'Folk Devils'   375
    Mats Nilsson

14. Nostalgia as a Perspective on Past Dance Culture in Finland   395
    Helena Saarikoski

15. A Twenty-First Century Resurrection: The *Potresujka*, the Croatian Polka Tremblante   417
    Tvrtko Zebec

List of Illustrations   433

Contributor Biographies   449

Index   453

Preface

This collection of essays is the result of several meetings, conducted over many years, of the international research group, the Sub-Study Group on Round Dances — 19th Century Derived Couple Dances. Operating within the Study Group on Ethnochoreology, under the auspices of the International Council on Traditional Music (ICTM), this collective was launched in 2002 at the 22nd Symposium of the Study Group on Ethnochoreology, Szeged, Hungary. It was initiated by Norwegian ethnochoreologist and dance historian Egil Bakka, who not only remained as its secretary and chair throughout but also led this research and editorial project.

The initial meeting was held in Prague (3–6 April 2003) and hosted by Daniela Stavělová and Dorota Gremlicová at the Academy of Performing Arts. The participants were: Anca Giurchescu, Anna Starbanova, Dalia Urbanavičienė, Daniela Stavělová, Dorota Gremlicová, Egil Bakka, Elsie Ivancich Dunin, Eva Kröschlova, Iva Niemcic, László Felföldi, Mats Nilsson, Rebeka Kranjec, and Theresa Buckland. Grażyna Dąbrowska and Aenne Goldschmidt contributed material to the meeting, even though they were not able to be present.

The group elected to work on and contribute material to four parallel tracks:

1. Analysis and classification of round dance movement patterns, including musical parameters.
2. Dancing masters/dance teachers and their material on round dances.
3. Political, ideological and socio-cultural discourses on round dances.
4. Organisational contexts for round dances.

Work continued on all four tracks at each of the subsequent meetings (2002–2016) with the intention to publish a monograph. It became clear, however, that track three presented the most fruitful theme to prioritise for publication of shared findings.

This edited collection could not have been realised without the generous help and support of a number of different colleagues and institutions in hosting our meetings which enabled work to be shared in person and our discussions to progress. These include: The Academy of Performing Arts, Prague, Czech Republic, April 2003, May 2011, December 2012; The Council for Protection of Ethnic Culture, Vilnius, Lithuania, October 2003; Elsie Ivancich Dunin in her home in Zaton in the Dubrovnik area, Croatia, June 2004; The Institute of Ethnology of the Academy of Sciences in Prague, September 2004; The Folk Dance Department of the Hungarian Academy of Sciences in Budapest, June 2005; The Institute of Ethnomusicology, Scientific Research Centre of the Slovenian Academy of Sciences and Arts in Ljubljana, April 2006; The Academy of Performing Arts, Prague, Czech Republic, October 2007; The Tanzarchiv, Leipzig, February 2007; The Voivodeship House of Culture in Kielce, Poland, November 2009; Institut za etnologiju i folkloristiku in Zagreb, Croatia, October 2009; The Council for the Protection of Ethnic Culture, Vilnius, Lithuania, May 2012; and the Institute of Ethnomusicology of the Scientific Research Centre of Slovenian Academy of Science and Arts, November 2016. Participants also took advantage, where practicable, of the symposia and conferences held by the parent Study Group on Ethnochoreology and the ICTM. In 2005, the Sub-Study Group gave a panel presentation on selected research outcomes to date at the 38th World Conference of the ICTM.

In addition to the authors and editors listed as contributors to this volume, several other members from the Study Group on Ethnochoreology have attended meetings and contributed to the research project. We would like to thank Aenne Goldschmidt, Anca Giurchescu, Anna Starbanova, Eva Kröschlova, Gediminas Karoblis, Grażyna Dąbrowska, Judy Olson, Kateřina Černíčková, Katerina Silna, Lisa Overholser, Marianne Bröcker, Mirko Ramovš, Vaida Naruševičiūtė, and Volker Klotsche.

Our grateful thanks are due to the Faculty of Humanities, Norwegian University of Science and Technology (NTNU) and to the Norwegian

Council for Traditional Music and Dance for their generous financial assistance in supporting the publication of this project.

We also wish to express our appreciation to the International Council for Traditional Music and the Study Group on Ethnochoreology for the organizational framework in which we have carried out our research and for granting us permission to use its logos on this publication.

Throughout the book, links and QR codes allow readers to view samples of the dances discussed. In order to access these recordings, follow the links or scan the QR code which appears alongside the relevant link. The editors want to stress that the many video examples given are a selection of what is available on the internet, we have not had the means to take material from specialised archives. We have selected material that gives an impression of the dance forms. It may not always do justice to the forms in terms of historicity, or quality of dancing. For more video links and further discussion, please see the additional resources tab on the listing for this book on Open Book Publisher's website (https://www.openbookpublishers.com/product/995).

Egil Bakka, Theresa Buckland, Helena Saarikoski, and Anne von Bibra Wharton

1. The Round Dance Paradigm

Egil Bakka

This book explores the European phenomenon of rotating couple dances, such as the Waltz and the Polka, which, for much of the nineteenth century, were collectively known as round dances. My introduction is divided into three sections: the first presents a brief survey of round dances as dance structures and forms, proposes terminological approaches, and discusses how the dances were situated historically and geographically. The second section reviews the current state of knowledge and research with reference to selected principal works, before the third and final section introduces and contextualises the new studies of round dances that constitute the main body of this book.

Structures and Forms — Geography and History

Round dances are a group of dances that rose to fame with the Waltz around 1800 and stayed in fashion until the end of the nineteenth century. Although they had lost their fashionable status by the twentieth century, some of these dances remained popular in many countries alongside the new African-American[1] dances such as the Tango and Foxtrot throughout the twentieth century. The round dance group includes dances such as the Waltz, the Polka, the Mazurka, and the Schottische, many of which are recorded in the manuals of dancing masters, but there are also forms that developed and spread independently from the masters.[2] Much of the material about these dances is available to us

---

1. I use the term American to mean dances with influences from both North and South America.
2. Henning Urup, Henry Sjöberg, and Egil Bakka, eds, *Gammaldans i Norden*: *Komparativ analyse av ein folkeleg dansegenre i utvalde nordiske lokalsamfunn — Rapport*

through their continued practice, as well as in documentation, such as films, mainly from the twentieth century. This can augment historical sources. We contend that the round dance group has a profile that allows us to delimit and study it as a relatively cohesive phenomenon in terms of structure and form. The way it is situated historically and geographically also contributes to its cohesiveness.

This does not mean that the term 'round dance' exists wherever these dances are performed; nor are they always understood as a group. The aim of this section is to describe and discuss this contended cohesiveness and to enable the reader to understand the various dance practices whose reception is scrutinised in this book. The authors are all European and write about European countries, and, for the sake of making the task manageable, the book is restricted to Europe. There is a vast amount of material about round dance forms outside Europe, as well as non-European descriptions of and reactions to them. They spread very rapidly to the Americas and Australia but also to other parts of the world that had large diasporas or populations of European descent. However, this discussion lies outside the scope of the present volume.

Structure of the Material

Round dances as considered here constitute a repertoire of social dances practised in most countries of Europe, and our diverse group of contributors generally write about the countries from which they come.

To name cultural elements is a very complex process, not least when colloquial terms and expert terminology meet in a historical context. To describe and discuss a large body of dances, it is necessary to establish sharp and well-defined terminology. What we propose here does not aim to be universally applicable, but it will offer a way of defining, thinking about and understanding the movement material[3] we are going to discuss.

---

    fra forskningsprosjekt (Dragvoll: Nordisk forening for folkedansforskning, 1988), p. 282.

3 Movement material refers to the movement patterns that can be observed when people dance, and which have been stored on film, in notation or in descriptions, and can therefore be studied.

Dance Type — Realisation — Concept — Event

The term *dance type* will be used to mean a movement pattern that reoccurs during the social dances of a community. Typically, this refers to the dances in a local repertoire, for instance, the Waltz, the Polka, the Mazurka, and the Schottische. The community members conceive each reoccurrence as a realisation of the same dance and usually identify the pattern by a name, 'they dance the Waltz again'. In simple terms, the dance types in a local community are the dances for which the locals have names. By starting at this level, and the names used in such a context, we have a concrete and precise point of departure for developing grounded definitions.

The community members will often consider similar dance forms in other communities as the same dance type as theirs. Researchers can base similar contentions upon more careful analysis, with more systematic tools to survey larger amounts of data. Then they can use the term *dance type* in their research terminology, considering many local dance types to belong to a regional dance type in order to systematise variation within a geographical area. In Norway, the local types of Mazurka on the eastern side of the country are distinctively different from the local types in other areas, so they represent different regional types. *Waltz*, *Vals* or *Walzer* might be the name for an item in a local repertoire, but it can also be used as a research term for an internationally known dance type with shared characteristics and patterns of variation.

The term *realisation* will be used for the actual dancing of a certain local dance type. So, when Peter dances a local Polka type three times at a dance party, and considers them all to be the same Polka, he has danced three realisations of the local Polka. The term *dance concept* will be used to mean 'the potential of skills, understanding, and knowledge that enables an individual or a dance community to dance that particular [local dance type] and to recognise and relate to each particular realisation of it'.[4] It is Peter's dance concept (his skills and knowledge

---

4 Egil Bakka, Bjørn Aksdal, and Erling Flem, *Springar and Pols. Variation, Dialect and Age. Pilot Project on the Methodology for Determining Traditions Structures and Historical Layering of Old Norwegian Couple Dances* (Trondheim: Rådet for folkemusikk og folkedans, The Rff-Centre, 1995), p. 21.
Georgiana Gore and Egil Bakka, 'Constructing Dance Knowledge in the Field: Bridging the Gap between Realisation and Concept', in *Re-Thinking Practice and Theory. Proceedings Thirtieth Annual Conference. Cosponsored with CORD. Centre*

about the Polka) that enables him to dance the Polka in accordance with his own and his fellow dancer's understanding of what a Polka is. The concept usually includes variations, so that even if Peter dances a bit differently each time, he and the others still consider it to be the local Polka.

The dance parties are typical examples of *dance events* for social dancing, and when we talk about the reception of the round dances, we do not refer to the dance movements or music as independent 'texts' standing on their own. The places, occasions, intentions and whole layout of their realisation make up the complete texts with which we must engage, as argued by Owe Ronström.[5] This book will focus on events at which a group defined by their social class, their geographical situation or regular interaction of other kinds come together to dance for pleasure or to fulfil their social duties. There are, of course, dance events that treat dance theatrically, and dance events where theatrical elements and non-theatrical dancing merge in many ways. Our focus here is on dance events that do not split the practitioners formally into audience and performers. Here, realisations play out through named dances, and, in accordance with the conventions of the ruling dance concepts, their constraints can operate differently. At the dancing master's ball, the master tries to impose his conventions and a strict layout as best he can, but when the peasants dance outdoors, the realisations are still based upon valid dance concepts and the layout of conventions. The latter might be more flexible and less strict, and the consequences for breaking some of them might be less, but they still depend upon the unwritten norms of the group in question.

Dance Form — Dance Paradigm

The term *dance form* will be used to mean the total content of movement and music, of a dance realisation or a local dance concept or dance type, including all the constituent elements and their interrelations.

National De La Danse, Paris 21–24 June 2007, ed. by Ann Cooper Albright (Patin: Society for Dance History Scholars, 2007), pp. 93–97. Egil Bakka and Gediminas Karoblis, 'Writing *a Dance*: Epistemology for Dance Research', *Yearbook for Traditional Music*, 42 (2010), 109–35.

5   Owe Ronström, 'It Takes Two — or More — to Tango: Researching Traditional Music/Dance Interrelations', in *Dance in the Field: Theory, Methods and Issues in Dance Ethnography*, ed. by Theresa Buckland (Basingstoke: Macmillan, 1999), pp. 134–44.

We will apply the term *dance paradigm* to the phenomenon we are investigating, i.e., round dances. I originally proposed to use this term to signify a set of basic and constitutive conventions that govern the organisation of a specific kind of dancing and provide an ongoing basis for its practice.[6] I suggest that the following criteria constitute a new dance paradigm:

1. When a set of conventions for the design and organisation of dancing are so radically different from what is already in use that they are perceived as something completely new in the place where they take root.
2. When the set of conventions is stable enough to remain in use over a long period of time, for instance half a century, and is inspirational and fruitful enough to give rise to a large number of dances.
3. When a group of characteristics can be used to define which dances belong to the paradigm, although no characteristic is necessary or sufficient to include all dances of the paradigm (polythetic classification).[7]
4. Not all dance forms necessarily belong to a specific paradigm. Each realisation needs to be assessed to determine whether it is an instance of a certain paradigm.

This book deals with a dance paradigm that conquered a large number of European dance floors and dance spaces and became dominant during the nineteenth century: the round dance.

Oskar Bie divided the history of European fashionable dancing—as promoted by the dancing masters—into three eras: Italian styles held sway until the early seventeenth century; French and English dances were dominant until the beginning of the nineteenth century; and, finally, German and Slavic styles were preeminent until the start of the twentieth century. This model has certain similarities with our paradigm model, in that we argue the round dances sprang from German and

---

6 Egil Bakka, 'Dance Paradigms: Movement Analysis and Dance Studies', in *Dance and Society: Dancer as a Cultural Performer*, ed. by Elsie Ivancich Dunin, Anne von Bibra Wharton, and László Felföldi (Budapest: Akadémiai Kiadó, 2005), pp. 72–80.

7 Egil Bakka, 'Typologi og klassifisering som Metode', in *Nordisk folkedanstypologi: En systematisk katalog over publiserte nordiske folkedanser*, ed. by Egil Bakka (Trondheim: Rådet for folkemusikk og folkedans, 1997), pp. 7–16 (p. 7).

Slavic roots in the nineteenth century.[8] Common roots or origins could, in fact, be seen as another criterion for dance paradigms, although we do not adopt it here.

In conclusion, we deal with the round dances as social dances, whether in the ballrooms of the upper classes, in the hands of the dancing masters or at the parties among the lower classes, and the term *dance type* links them to their concrete use at any kind of dance party. We then place large numbers of similar dance types into groups at regional or international level, in order to survey the material. The third level is the paradigm, and we do not use terms such as dance families or dance genres in a specific way.

It seems often to be assumed that dances either develop thanks to an inventive genius, or else one established dance form metamorphoses into the next. When studying the often-mythical stories of origin, as well as the written sources that describe how new dances come into being at certain points in time and space, it is easy to reach such a conclusion. However, when we dig into the actual movement structures of which dances consist, we see reoccurring basic elements and techniques that shape the paradigm. Some of these have generative potential: that dancers discover and use to create new variants, new types and, eventually, perhaps even new paradigms. The couple-turning technique I shall discuss next represents this kind of generative potential.

Characteristics of the Round Dance Paradigm

The contributors to this book started out with a working definition, based on a small set of tentative criteria, to delimit the core of the round dance genre. The aim was to try to identify essential material — such as descriptions, films and notations — and to find similarities across Europe, rather than differences. These were the preliminary criteria upon which we agreed:

1. One couple can realise a complete version of a dance.
2. Couples turning along a circular path is a major characteristic of round dances.

---

8   Oskar Bie, *Der Tanz* (Berlin: J. Bard, 1919), p. 132.

3. Couple-turning in which both partners face each other is a major characteristic of round dances.
4. Our focus will be on unregulated[9] dances with many melodies. We consider one-melody/regulated (sequence) dances to be a separate group, outside but nonetheless connected to the round dances, and we do not look closely at dances of this type.[10]

Fig. 1.1 Video: The folk-dance group Springar`n at Ås, Norway dancing the Waltz to Enebakk Spelemannslag. Note how the couples dance counter-clockwise on an approximately circular path: this is typical for round dances. 'Vals og Folkedanslaget Springar`n sin avslutning i HD format', 7:08, posted online by Svein Arne Sølvberg, *Youtube*, 12 May 2010, https://www.youtube.com/watch?v=LolpphyIWS8

Fig. 1.2 Victor Gabriel Gilbert, *The Ball or an Elegant Evening*, c.1890, showing couples dancing on a mostly circular path turning counter-clockwise. Wikimedia Commons, Public Domain, https://commons.wikimedia.org/wiki/File:Une_soir%C3%A9e_%C3%A9l%C3%A9gante_par_Victor_Gabriel_Gilbert_(A).jpg

---

9   We use 'regulated' to mean dances in which the elements have a fixed order and fixed length and in which each element is always performed to a specific part of the melody.
10 Egil Bakka, Minutes from Meeting 2 of Project, [unpublished], 2003.

Fig. 1.3 Video: The Klapptanz is a typical one-melody dance found in similar versions in many countries; this example is performed by a folk-dance group in Brazil wearing traditional German or Austrian dress. 'Klapptanz', 1:20, posted online by Stefan Ziel, *Youtube*, 17 August 2009, https://www.youtube.com/watch?v=aJ6CVIAn5u0

Fig. 1.4 The Hombourg Waltz, with characteristic sketches of family dancing, 1818. The two couples show the position of the feet when waltzing. Coloured engraving, British Cartoon Prints Collection (Library of Congress), Wikimedia Commons, Public Domain, https://upload.wikimedia.org/wikipedia/commons/1/1d/The_Hombourg_waltz%2C_with_characteristic_sketches_of_family_dancing_LCCN2006688900.jpg

The subtlest criterion is point three, which stresses the couple-turning as a key element. These couple-turning patterns require that the partners place themselves more or less face to face, and it is critical that the right foot of each partner is placed between the feet of the other and that the left foot remains on the outside. While dancing, the couple may hold their upper bodies slightly to one side of each other. Depending on how closely they are dancing, the right foot might not be placed squarely between their partner's feet, but at a small distance from the space. This precise foot placement is crucial for the basic turning technique: dances in which the partners turn with both feet on one side of their partner fall into another category, The Czardas, a dance described by László Felföldi in Chapter Seven, a very interesting example of a dance related but not belonging to the round dances according to this criterion.

This said, the central criteria are intended to function with the flexibility of polythetic[11] classification. Twenty-first-century digital technologies make dance documentation available and analysable. This enables the writing of the history, not only of dancing, but also of dances. Then, classification of dances in a modern, updated version will be vital.

Fig. 1.5 Couples dancing on a circular path moving slowly counter-clockwise. Photo from Bangsund, Norway, 1981. Photo by Egil Bakka, CC BY 4.0.

---

11   Polythetic is a central term for classification in many disciplines such as archaeology or biology. It is not used much in dance research, but it is vital for working with a large amount of material. 'Relating to or sharing a number of characteristics which occur commonly in members of a group or class, but none of which is essential for membership of that group or class'. Oxford University Press, 'Polythetic', *Lexico.com* (2019), https://www.lexico.com/en/definition/polythetic

The Main Dance Types of the Round Dance Paradigm

The movement content of the different dance types belonging to the round dance paradigm is not the subject of this book, even if some of the chapters deal with certain aspects of it. Nonetheless, a basic comprehension of the different dance types, their characteristics, their names and how they are related is necessary. It is not possible to discuss the reception of round dances without distinguishing the different types, since they were not received in the same way and at the same time in each country. For this reason, there will be only a short discussion about the movement content of the main types of the paradigm in the book itself, but a broad selection of video links is given to illustrate various examples of the types.

Dance histories discussing round dances have mainly been based on sources from high society and the work of dancing masters.[12] Round dances, however, have also had an important place in the dance repertoires of the lower classes. The dances taught by dancing masters were certainly used by the lower classes, but so were dances that the dancing master hardly ever touched. There is, in other words, an important part of the round dance paradigm that has been ignored in most discussions about its history. I argue that if we explore the full scope of the paradigm, new light will be shed upon its genesis as well as upon its further development, migration and reception. There is not space here to examine more comprehensively the form and structure on which these contentions are based: a deeper study will follow in later publications.

The round dance paradigm had its roots in a kind of dancing called 'Walzen', or 'Walzen und Drehen' (waltzing and turning). These terms were used in German lands from at least the last third of the eighteenth century.[13] They were even mixed into the *zwiefacher*, as seen in Fig. 1.6.

---

12   Philip John Samprey Richardson, *The Social Dances of the Nineteenth Century in England* (London: H. Jenkins, 1960); Mary Clarke and Clement Crisp, *The History of Dance* (London: Random House Value Pub, 1981); Walter Sorell, *Dance in its Time* (Garden City, NY: Anchor Press/Doubleday, 1981).

13   Walter Salmen, *Geschichte der Musik in Westfalen, Bis 1800* (Kassel/Basel/London/New York: Bärenreiter, 1963), p. 33; Christian Heinrich Theodor Schreger, *Kosmetisches Taschenbuch für Damen zur gesundheitsgemässen Schönheitspflege ihres*

As Christian Heinrich Theodor Schreger explains, the moderate, easy, effortless, moral dancing at not too crowded, draft-free places, preferably in small circles of friends and family under the eyes of a watchful elder, belongs to the appropriate movements of this age. That does not include the bacchanical 'Walzen und Drehen', whirling until the dancer falls about, nor the wild, unruly flying around in the 'Schleifer', in the rapid, fiery Schottische, or in the shattering 'Hopsanglaise' on public dance floors, especially when the ball is opened [with this kind of dancing] at once after the meal.¹⁴

Fig. 1.6 Video: A programme about a dance that mixes steps of Walzen und Drehen danced to melodies which mix bars of the Waltz and the Polka. 'Woher kommt der Zwiefache? Verzwickter Tanz', 12:00, posted online 27 February 2016, *BRMediathek*, https://www.br.de/mediathek/video/woher-kommt-der-zwiefache-verzwickter-tanz-av:584f862a3b467900119cdb27

From the expression alone, it is not clear if people at this time used the two terms about distinctively different forms or as interchangeable names for more or less the same thing. The dancing master Johann Heinrich Kattfuss claims that *'Walzen, Drehen, Ländern'* (waltzing, turning and Ländler dancing) have no difference in the steps, and he gives a description of the Waltz.¹⁵ There is, however, a dance manual from Ernst Chr. Mädel that describes the Dreher,¹⁶ and the description coincides with, for instance, the description by Rudolph Voss¹⁷ and with

---

    Körpers durchs ganze Leben, und in allen Lebensverhältnissen (Nürnberg: Schrag, 1812), p. 62.
14 Schreger, *Kosmetisches Taschenbuch*, p. 62.
15 Johann Heinrich Kattfuss, *Taschenbuch für Freunde und Freundinnen des Tanzes von Johann Heinrich Kattfuss* (Leipzig: Graff, 1800), p. 149, https://books.google.co.uk/books?id=-GYNAQAAIAAJ&printsec=frontcover&source=gbs_ge_summary_r&cad=0#v=onepage&q&f=false
16 Ernst Chr Mädel, *Anfangsgründe Der Tanzkunst* (Erfurt: Verlag des Werfassers, 1801), pp. 175, 141.
17 Rudolph Voss, *Der Tanz und seine Geschichte*, ed. by Kurt Petermann (Leipzig: Zentralantiquariat der Deutschen Demokratischen Republik, 1977 [1868]), p. 336.

those in Aenne Goldschmidt's book.[18] The latter is an authoritative survey of German folk dance. There is also a description of the Waltz from 1806 from the Baltic dancing master Ivensenn, which coincides with later descriptions and contemporary practice of the Waltz as a social dance.[19]

Fig. 1.7 Young couples waltzing, 1802. Aquatint, 117 x 18.5 cm. From John Dean Paul, *Journal of a Party of Pleasure to Paris in the Month of August, 1802* (London: Cadell & Davies, 1802). Probably the earliest known picture of the Waltz. Wellcome Collection, CC BY 4.0, https://wellcomecollection.org/works/stggecfr

---

18   Aenne Goldschmidt, *Handbuch des deutschen Volkstanzes: Textband* (Berlin: Henschelverlag Kunst und Gesellschaft, 1967), p. 177.

19   Many dance historians have credited an English dancing master for having published the first professional description of the Waltz: Thomas Wilson, A Description of the Correct Method of Waltzing, th e Truly Fashionable Species of Dancing (London: Sherwood, Neely, and Jones, 1816). However, in 1806, the Baltic dancing master Ivensenn had already published a manual with a long discussion and description of the Waltz: Dietrich Alexander Valentin Ivensenn, *Terpsichore: ein Taschenbuch für Freunde und Freundinnen des Tanzes in Liv-Cur-und Ehstland* (Riga: [n.p.], 1806).

1. The Round Dance Paradigm 13

Fig. 1.8 Eadweard Muybridge, *A Couple Waltzing*, colour lithograph presented in a phenakistoscope, 1893. This is a representation of an older description of a Waltz, using one of the short-lived technologies designed to create moving images at the end of the nineteenth century.[20] Wikimedia Commons, Public Domain, https://commons.wikimedia.org/wiki/File: Eadweard_Muybridge%27s_phenakistoscope,_1893.jpg

These descriptions, made by people who were trained dancers, show that the Dreher and the Walzer are at the core of two clearly different dance techniques, even if both have the characteristics of the round dance paradigm.[21] A Nordic project, which I shall discuss further, also made a distinction between the two, and named them '*eintaktssnu*' (one-measure turning, in which the couple turns 360° during one measure of the music), which corresponds to the Drehen technique, and '*totaktssnu*' (two-measure turning, in which the 360° turn takes place over two measures of music), which corresponds to the Walzen.[22] This is still the case: the techniques are still practised today.[23]

The waltzing in 3/4 as well as 2/4 has one turn across two bars of music, which means that six paces can be used. According to Goldschmidt's survey of German folk dance, Drehers, there is a Zweischrittdreher, or

---

20 A GIF of the phenakistoscope in motion can be viewed on Wikimedia: https://commons.wikimedia.org/wiki/File:Phenakistoscope_3g07690d.gif

21 It is difficult to say what Kattfuss means with his statement, since he sees a similarity between different ways of dancing, but does not say that they are all the same.

22 Urup, Sjöberg, and Bakka, *Gammaldans i Norden*, p. 250. The notation of duple time music requires additional rules to be followed, for the definition to work out.

23 Egil Bakka, Interview with Richard Wolfram and Herbert Lager, researchers/ experts of Austrian folk dance (Video at the Norwegian Centre for Traditional Music and Dance: Rff Vu 41)' Vienna, 17 October 1985'

Zweitritt with a full turn on two beats, a Dreischrittdreher, with a full turn with three beats, and even more variants.[24] There is quite a dramatic difference between the Waltz and the Dreher principles in terms of speed and effort. Voss suggests that Zweischrittdreher 2/4 was probably the wildest and most notorious dance of the sixteenth and seventeenth centuries.[25] In addition, the musical metre of the Waltz could be duple as well as triple.[26] The same is true for Dreher.[27]

The Waltz in 2/4 usually had an addition to its name: Ecossaise Walzer, Hopwaltz, Hamburger Waltz etc.[28] It is important to note that when the Waltz is criticised for its quick turning and even for hopping, the antagonism may have been directed at the Waltz in duple time, rather than the Waltz in triple time. The latter was softer, due to the relationship between the dance and the music and its less extreme vertical patterns.[29] There are, of course, many variations of the Waltz as well as of the Dreher, but the basic differences described above are based on technical principles and seem to have remained core throughout at least two centuries. Nearly all the elements of couple-turning found in round dances are built upon either 'Walzen' or 'Drehen'or both, and couple-turning is the most central building block in the paradigm.

---

24 It is worth noting, however, that the term Dreher comes from German and rarely from Austrian sources. Goldschmidt, *Handbuch des deutschen Volkstanzes*, p. 177.

25 Rudolph Voss, *Der Tanz und seine Geschichte* p. 336; Zweitritt is a form where the dancer makes a full turn with two steps, as in Danish Svejtrit.

26 Franz Magnus Böhme, *Geschichte des Tanzes in Deutschland: Darstellender Theil* (Breitkopf & Härtel, 1886), p. 145; Egil Bakka, 'The Polka before and after the Polka', *Yearbook for Traditional Music*, 33 (2001), 37–47, https://doi.org/10.2307/1519629; Friedrich Albert Zorn and Alfonso Josephs Sheafe, *Grammar of the Art of Dancing, Theoretical and Practical: Lessons in the Arts of Dancing and Dance Writing (Choreography)*, ed. by Alfonso Josephs Sheafe (Boston, MA: Heintzemann Press, 1905), p. 233

27 Rudolph Voss, *Der Tanz und seine Geschichte* pp. 336, 339; Goldschmidt, *Handbuch des deutschen Volkstanzes*, p. 177.

28 Egil Bakka, 'The Polka before and after the Polka', 37.

29 The *svikt* curve in a triple Waltz has a long and a short *svikt*, and hardly any elevations, whereas the duple Waltz probably had two or three *svikts*, included more elevations, and was danced at greater speed. For an explanation of *svikt* analysis see Egil Bakka, 'Analysis of Traditional Dance in Norway and the Nordic Countries', in *Dance Structures. Perspectives on the Analysis of Human Movement*, ed. by Adrienne L. Kaeppler and Elsie Ivancich Dunin (Budapest: Akadémiai Kiadó, 2007), pp. 105–12 (p. 108).

1. The Round Dance Paradigm

Fig. 1.9 Video: film showing, first, 2/4 waltzing or the Polka (Hamborgar), then 3/4 waltzing (Vals) from a regional competition in Western Norway. 'Pardans runddans. Hamborgar og vals. Kvalik. Vestlandskappleiken 2015', 5:52, posted online by Jostedalsvideo, *Youtube*, 11 October 2015, https://www.youtube.com/watch?v=C2ZQAIyYWe8&feature=youtu.be

Fig. 1.10 Video: film showing Snoa, a couple dance from Sweden, as presented by the Israeli Noa-am folk dancers. The couple-turning is Zweischrittdreher or Zweitritt. 'Snoa', 1:49, posted online by Folkdance Noa-am, 18 March 2018, *Youtube*, https://www.youtube.com/watch?v=_RXbbAeqXuE

Fig. 1.11 Video: film showing Dreischrittdreher. It is taken from a course in German dance taught by Ralf Spiegler at the Grand Bal de l'Europe at Saint Gervais in 2013. The music is provided by the group Aelixhir. 'Aelixhir — Atelier de Dreischrittdreher avec Ralf Spiegler', 2:48, posted online by Lionel Thomas, 14 August 2013, https://youtu.be/qPxHcmGEpRY?t=81

The consistency and stability of the difference between 'Walzen' and 'Drehen' is significant for our understanding of the paradigm, and of the dance types related to it.[30] Moreover, there is also a dramatic difference in how polite society received the two techniques of the paradigm.

Boycott of Dreher Forms

The dancing masters from the early nineteenth century onwards seem to have eschewed the challenging and rapid turning of the Dreher dance types. From the 1820s onwards, they explored and developed the Waltz principle in most manuals. However, the Dreher technique had clearly not yet fallen into obscurity, since it is either defined or mentioned by some dance historians of the nineteenth century.[31] At the same time,

---

30 In turn, *'Walzen und Drehen'* influenced the development of many Nordic folk dances. Since, however, this is not the topic of the present book, I shall not discuss it in detail.

31 Wilson, *A Description of the Correct Method of Waltzing*; Eduard Friedrich David Helmke and Kurt Petermann, *Neue Tanz- und Bildungsschule* (Leipzig:

dance histories prioritised ballroom dancing and theatre dance, and ignored the dancing which only belonged to the lower classes. This means that a significant part of the round dance paradigm was more or less absent from the dancing masters' repertoires, as reflected in their manuals and their teaching repertoires. This absence of Dreher-based dances among dancing masters is also confirmed by a project on round dances in the Nordic countries.[32] The project found two streams of influence on the Nordic dancing: the dance masters' repertoire, with 'Walzen' (waltzing) at the core; and the 'Drehen' (turning) that spread without their assistance. 'Drehen' diffused mostly across the north, and less so in the south.

The Dreher remained an important traditional dance in Germany. The so-called 'Dreischrittdreher', particularly the version in 3/4 time, was taken up in traditional dance contexts in Poland as *Powolniak* and in the Nordic countries, it can be recognised as part of the Danish *Jysk på næsen*; as *Hamburska* or *Hambo* in Sweden; and as a part of S*pringdans* and *Mazurka* in Norway.[33] The 'Zweischrittdreher' (in 2/4) is found in the Danish *Svejtrit*; in Sweden as *Snoa*, and in Norway as the *Rull*.

Fig. 1.12 Video: the Polish dance Powolniak with Dreher technique in 3/4 time. 'Powolniak', 1:24, posted online by Dom Tańca, 12 January 2013, *Youtube*, https://www.youtube.com/watch?v=Vy3mxGQBhiM

Fig. 1.13 Video: Skansens folkdanslag, a folk group from Stockholm dances the Hambo, a Dreher technique in ¾ metre. 'Hambo', 1:16, posted online by Skansens Folkdanslag, *Youtube*, 9 October 2013, https://www.youtube.com/watch?v=fif8Zt1ir70

Zentralantiquariat der Deutschen Demokratischen Republik, 1982); Theodor Hentschke and Kurt Petermann, *Allgemeine Tanzkunst: Theorie und Geschichte: antike und moderne (gesellschaftliche und theatralische) Tanzkunst und Schilderung der meisten National-und Charaktertänze*, 12 vols (Leipzig: Zentralantiquariat der Deutschen Demokratischen Republik, 1836–1986).

32   Urup, Sjöberg, and Bakka, *Gammaldans i Norden*, p. 282.
33   Bakka, ed., *Nordisk Folkedanstypologi*.

Fig. 1.14 Video: Ami og Håkon Dregelid are dancing the Rull at the annual national competition in Vågå. 'Sff: Ami og Håkon Dregelid — Vossarull', 1:59, posted online by Norwegian Centre for Traditional Music and Dance, Trondheim, *Youtube*, 15 June 2011, https://www.youtube.com/watch?v=f3c4mUeMFCEor

Fig. 1.15 Video: This dance includes couple-turning. Recording from Thybal i Aarhus Folkemusikhus. 'Ture i svejtrit, Vals+ — MVI 1892', 15:58, posted online by Jørgen Andkær, *Youtube*, 28 October 2016, https://www.youtube.com/watch?v=iaN37z6cbXk

The Galop, the Polka and the Schottische

The first round dance that became fashionable after the different types of the Waltz was the Galop. Voss sees it as a derivation from popular dance material, for instance the 'Rutscher',[34] which was only a simple type of sideways dancing. Later, in order to stress that it was developed into a round dance with Waltz turning, dance historians called it the Galop-Waltz.[35]

The term Waltz was used more and more for the 3/4 Waltz only. In the 1840s, a form similar to the 2/4 Waltz was presented, first in Prague and later in Paris, under a new name — the Polka. This became the standard name for any kind of 2/4 Waltz.[36] Finally, the Schottische or Rheinlender arrived in the Nordic countries after 1860. However, because this dance had elements of Dreher technique, it was not considered appropriate in the ballrooms of the Norwegian upper classes until the last decades of the century.[37] A small pocket book for dancers describes the steps with the following caveat: 'Rheinlænder has previously only been seen in less fashionable venues, but since it lately has won its place in the best circles, the author believed he should include it'.[38]

34　Voss, *Der Tanz und seine Geschichte*, pp. 340, 369.
35　Zorn and Sheafe, *Grammar of the Art of Dancing*, p. 771.
36　Bakka, 'The Polka before and after the Polka'; Zorn and Sheafe, *Grammar of the Art of Dancing*, p. 233.
37　Urup, Sjöberg, and Bakka, *Gammaldans i Norden*, p. 278.
38　Carl Teilman, *Danse-Bog: Anvisning til at danse Polonaise, Vals, Galopade, Polka, Rheinländer* (Christiania: Damm, 1882), p. 37, translation from Danish by Egil Bakka.

Fig. 1.16 Johann Christian Schoeller, *Der große Galopp von Joh. Strauß*, 1839. Copper engraving. Wikimedia Commons, Public Domain, https://commons.wikimedia.org/wiki/File:Strauss_I_-_Wiener_Scene_-_Der_gro%C3%9Fe_Galop.jpg

Mazurka Types

Oscar Bie discusses how a number of dances in lively triple time are inspired by Polish national dances, and mentions the Redowa, a Czech dance that was much discussed and criticised in Prague, as Dorota Gremlicová explores more fully in Chapter Six. Bie also describes the Tyrolienne and the Polka-Mazurka,[39] a Polka done in triple time that appeared in Paris in the late 1840s.[40] All these dances appear to have

---

39 Bie, *Der Tanz*, p. 235.
40 Egil Bakka, 'Rise and Fall of Dances', in *Dance, Gender, and Meanings: Contemporizing Traditional Dance. Proceedings from the 26th Symposium of the ICTM Study Group on Ethnochoreology 2010*, ed. by Elsie Ivancich Dunin, Daniela Stavělová, and Dorota Gremlicová (Praha: Akademie Ved Ceské Republiky (Etnologický Ústav), pp. 274–80.

been based on elements of the Polish national dance, Masur. This was danced by couples in complex formations reminiscent of a contra dance, whereas the dances listed above stand out as round dances because the couples did not depend on each other for formations. The Mazurka types do not appear much in discussions of the round dance paradigm. Dances identified as Czech and Polish were hardly as politically problematic as the German Waltz throughout Slavic lands, and as they were spread through the aristocracy, they did not have the lower-class flair of the Waltz in Germany.

I have chosen the dances above based my own judgement of which were the most widespread types belonging to the paradigm of round dances. For practical reasons, I have restricted my discussion to material in the English, French, German and Nordic languages.

Fig. 1.17 G. Munthe, *En Østlandsk St. Hansaften*. Lithograph from Chr. Tønsberg, *Billeder af Norges Natur og Folkeliv* (Christiana: Tønsberg, 1875). Owned by Egil Bakka, CC BY 4.0.

Dance Names and Imputed Origins

A large number of dance names seemingly attribute particular geographic origins to the dance, such as countries, regions or cities. Examples include the Allemande, the Deutscher, the Hamburger, the Hamburska, the Berliner, the Steierisch, the Tyrolerienne, the Schottische, the Ecossaise, the Françoise, the Polka, the Polonaise, the Krakowiak, the Masur, the Varsovienne, the Warschauer, the English, the Anglaise, the Trondhjemmer, the Bergenser, etc. This reference to the origin (or reputed origin) of a dance accords with a common understanding, shared by dancing masters and dance historians in the nineteenth century, that dances were thoroughly marked by their place of origin and could not be performed as well in other places. For example, here is the explanation of the German dancing master Eduard Friedrich David Helmke (1794–1879):[41]

> *Diversity of dances.* Almost every nation has its own dances, in which its character is also reflected. Many dances from foreign nations have become popular here, but their national origins are rarely obvious, and their aesthetics, that are only maintained by this national character, are lost; therefore, even the most beautiful dance of a foreign nation rarely speaks to us. [...] Imagine but the proud, saucy Spaniard alongside the humble, honest German, and the voluptuous Spanish woman against a pure German girl! What a difference!? The flaming tulip and the white lily, [...] the tulip can never become lily, and the latter can never become tulip. It is like this with the dancers too: the pure German girl will never present herself in Spanish dances in the same way as real Spanish woman [...].

Helmke continues that he sees the Minuet as French and the Waltz as German — that is, he sees the 'slow' Waltz as German, but he claims that the 'Eccosaise-Waltzer' is Scotch (as the name suggests), and he also mentions the Vienna Waltz, the Russian Waltz, and the Bavarian Galop-Waltz. Helmke is well aware that dances are spreading and being taken up in new countries, but in his opinion, they lose something when danced outside their place of origin.

---

41 Helmke and Petermann, *Neue Tanz- und Bildungsschule*, p. 109. Translation from German by Egil Bakka.

Even a limited study of dance names reveals the variability and the complexity of the relationship between a dance name and the movement pattern to which it refers. In some cases, there is stability — through time as well as space — between the dance name and the movements. By the time the Waltz was well established, there was great consistency between its movement patterns when it was danced socially — and its name. In some cases, a name is kept across languages: for example, the name Polonaise, the French word for Polish, is used for the same movement pattern in many countries, and even though the Swedes and Norwegians have dances they call Polish (*Polska — Pols(k) dans*), they keep the term Polonaise for the solemn processional dance, whereas *Polska/Polskdans* refer to very different dances. The German city Hamburg inspired the term Hamburska and eventually Hambo, which are triple time dances in Sweden. In Norway, *Hamborgar* (Waltz) and, in a few cases, *Hambor* or even *Hambo* refers to a Polka, or, according to late-eighteenth-century terminology, a Waltz in duple time. The very convoluted development of dance names can be observed in source material of which we have precise knowledge. This can also help us to understand some basic principles for the naming of dances, even in the more distant past.

Fig. 1.18 Video: Slangpolska från Skåne, Sweden (possibly danced in the USA), a Polska not influenced by the Dreher. 'Slangpolska från Skåne', 2:26, posted online by Steve Carruthers, *Youtube*, 5 May 2010, https://www.youtube.com/watch?v=Ces253nl19U&t=63s

Fig. 1.19 Video: Anbjørg Myhra Bergwitz and Audun Gruner-Hegge dance the Polsdans fra Finnskogen, which includes Dreher turning, at a national competition in Norway. 'Polsdans fra Finnskogen 1', 2:55, posted online by Atle Utkilen, *Youtube*, 23 August 2015, https://www.youtube.com/watch?v=hB1RJaVBBRk

Fig. 1.20 Video: High school graduation performance of a Polonez (Polonaise). 'Polonez Gimnazjalny 2015', 15:16, posted by Telewizja internetowa Gminy Nadarzyn, *Youtube*, 28 May 2015, https://www.youtube.com/watch?v=3zVnVaGiQv0

Fig. 1.21 Video: The HälsingeHambon Final at the World Cup in Hambo. 'HälsingeHambon Final 2010', 4.50, posted online by meriksson84, *Youtube*, 30 August 2010, https://www.youtube.com/watch?v=nJYwODr8700&list=RDnJYwODr8700#t=28

Fig. 1.22 Video: Leiv Fåberg and Johanna Kvam are dancing the Hamborgar at Dølaheimen, Jostedal, in Norway in 1997. Music by Liv Fridtun. 'Leiv Fåberg og Johanna Kvam. Hamborgar', 2.37, posted online by Jostedalsvideo, *Youtube*, 28 November 2015, https://www.youtube.com/watch?v=kGenW4UV2vs

In conclusion, the dances we are discussing have been used in many different contexts throughout Europe since at least the 1770s. They generally conquered the dance floors of all social classes, but how and when varies from case to case. There are some exceptions: for example, in the Easternmost Balkan countries we can surmise that round dances hardly spread beyond urban people belonging to the upper classes, but since none of our authors are from these countries, we have not been able to establish this for certain. According to Felföldi in Chapter Seven of this volume, the exception probably holds true even for Hungary.

Bibliography

Andersson, Göran, Egil Bakka, Gunnel Biskop et al., *Norden i dans*: *Folk, fag, forskning* (Oslo: Novus, 2007).

Bakka, Egil, 'Rise and Fall of Dances', in *Dance, Gender, and Meanings*: *Contemporizing Traditional Dance. Proceedings from the 26th Symposium of the ICTM Study Group on Ethnochoreology 2010*, ed. by Elsie Ivancich Dunin, Daniela Stavělová, and Dorota Gremlicová (Praha: Akademie Ved Ceské Republiky (Etnologický Ústav), 2012), pp. 274–80.

——, 'Analysis of Traditional Dance in Norway and the Nordic Countries', in *Dance Structures. Perspectives on the Analysis of Human Movement*, ed. by Adrienne L. Kaeppler and Elsie Ivancich Dunin (Budapest: Akadémiai Kiadó, 2007), pp. 105–12.

——, 'Dance Paradigms: Movement Analysis and Dance Studies', in *Dance and Society*: *Dancer as a Cultural Performer. Re-Appraising Our Past, Moving into the Future*, ed. by Elsie Ivancich Dunin, Anne von Bibra Wharton, and László Felföldi (Budapest: Akadémiai Kiadó, 2005), pp. 72–80.

——, 'The Polka before and after the Polka', *Yearbook for Traditional Music*, 33 (2001), 37–47, https://doi.org/10.2307/1519629

——, 'Typologi og klassifisering som metode', in *Nordisk folkedanstypologi*: *En systematisk katalog over publiserte nordiske folkedanser*, ed. by Egil Bakka (Trondheim: Rådet for folkemusikk og folkedans, 1997), pp. 7–16.

——, Interview with Richard Wolfram and Herbert Lager, researchers/experts of Austrian folk dance (Video at the Norwegian Centre for Traditional Music and Dance: Rff Vu 41), Vienna, 17 October 1985.

Bakka, Egil, Bjørn Aksdal, and Erling Flem, *Springar and Pols. Variation, Dialect and Age. Pilot Project on the Methodology for Determining Traditions Structures and Historical Layering of Old Norwegian Couple Dances* (Trondheim: Rådet for folkemusikk og folkedans, The Rff-Centre, 1995).

Bakka, Egil, and Gediminas Karoblis, 'Writing *a Dance*: Epistemology for Dance Research', *Yearbook for Traditional Music*, 42 (2010), 109–35.

Bie, Oskar, *Der Tanz* (Berlin: J. Bard, 1919).

Böhme, Franz Magnus, *Geschichte des tanzes in Deutschland*: *Darstellender theil* (Leipzig: Breitkopf & Härtel, 1886).

Clarke, Mary, and Clement Crisp, *The History of Dance* (London: Random House Value Pub, 1981).

Goldschmidt, Aenne, *Handbuch des deutschen Volkstanzes*: *Textband* (Berlin: Henschelverlag Kunst und Gesellschaft, 1967).

Gore, Georgiana, and Egil Bakka, 'Constructing Dance Knowledge in the Field: Bridging the Gap between Realisation and Concept', in *Re-Thinking Practice* and Theory. Proceedings Thirtieth Annual Conference. Cosponsored with CORD. Centre National de la danse, Paris 21–24 June 2007, ed. by Ann Cooper Albright (Patin: Society for Dance History Scholars, 2007), pp. 93–97.

Helmke, Eduard Friedrich David, and Kurt Petermann, *Neue Tanz- und Bildungsschule* (Leipzig: Zentralantiquariat der Deutschen Demokratischen Republik, 1982).

Hentschke, Theodor, and Kurt Petermann, *Allgemeine Tanzkunst: Theorie und Geschichte: antike und moderne (gesellschaftliche und theatralische) Tanzkunst und Schilderung der meisten National-und Charaktertänze*, 12 vols (Leipzig: Zentralantiquariat der Deutschen Demokratischen Republik, 1836–1986).

Ivensenn, Dietrich Alexander Valentin, *Terpsichore: ein Taschenbuch für Freunde und Freundinnen des Tanzes in Liv-Cur-und Ehstland* (Riga: [n.p.], 1806).

Kattfuss, Johann Heinrich, *Taschenbuch für Freunde und Freundinnen des Tanzes von Johann Heinrich Kattfuss* (Leipzig: Heinrich Gräff, 1800), https://books.google.co.uk/books?id=-GYNAQAAIAAJ&printsec=frontcover&source=gbs_ge_summary_r&cad=0#v=onepage&q&f=false

Mädel, Ernst Chr, *Anfangsgründe der Tanzkunst* (Erfurt: Verlag des Werfassers, 1801).

Oxford University Press, 'Polythetic', *Lexico.com* (2019), https://www.lexico.com/en/definition/polythetic

Richardson, Philip John Samprey, *The Social Dances of the Nineteenth Century in England* (London: H. Jenkins, 1960).

Ronström, Owe, 'It Takes Two — or More — to Tango: Researching Traditional Music/Dance Interrelations', in *Dance in the Field: Theory, Methods and Issues in Dance Ethnography*, ed. by Theresa Buckland (Basingstoke: Macmillan, 1999), pp. 134–44.

Salmen, Walter, *Geschichte der Musik in Westfalen Bis 1800* (Kassel/Basel/London/New York: Bärenreiter, 1963).

——, *Grundriss einer Geschichte des Tanzes in Westfalen* (Münster: Aschendorff, 1954).

Schreger, Christian Heinrich Theodor, *Kosmetisches Taschenbuch für Damen zur gesundheitsgemässen Schönheitspflege ihres Körpers durchs ganze Leben, und in allen Lebensverhältnissen* (Nürnberg: Schrag, 1812).

Sorell, Walter, *Dance in its Time* (Garden City, NY: Anchor Press/Doubleday, 1981).

Teilman, Carl, *Danse-Bog: Anvisning til at danse Polonaise, Vals, Galopade, Polka, Rheinländer* (Christiania: Damm, 1882).

Urup, Henning, Henry Sjöberg, and Egil Bakka, eds, *Gammaldans i Norden: Komparativ analyse av ein folkeleg dansegenre i utvalde nordiske lokalsamfunn — Rapport fra forskningsprosjekt* (Dragvoll: Nordisk forening for folkedansforskning, 1988).

Voss, Rudolph, *Der Tanz und seine Geschichte* (Leipzig: Zentralantiquariat der Deutschen Demokratischen Republik, 1977).

Wilson, Thomas, *A Description of the Correct Method of Waltzing, the Truly Fashionable Species of Dancing* (London: Sherwood, Neely, and Jones, 1816).

Zorn, Friedrich Albert, and Alfonso Josephs Sheafe, *Grammar of the Art of Dancing, Theoretical and Practical: Lessons in the Arts of Dancing and Dance Writing (Choreography)*, ed. by Alfonso Josephs Sheafe (Boston, MA: Heintzemann Press, 1905).

2. The State of Research

Egil Bakka

A comprehensive body of literature deals fully or partly with round dances, and particularly with the Waltz. There are works that deal with the form and structure of the dances based on first-hand knowledge, such as manuals from dancing masters. Many surveys describe the history of round dances, often as part of broader projects. These are often built upon the compilation and study of scattered excerpts from a large variety of historical documents, such as diaries, letters, memoirs, newspapers etc. A large number of these excerpts recur in various books to justify different arguments, and sometimes with conflicting interpretations. There are also studies of the music that accompanied the round dance, which discuss the dance form and the historical context. The moral and medical criticism of, and resistance to, the round dances, and particularly the Waltz, is a recurrent theme that is also central to this book.

Writers in the field range from the dancing masters of the nineteenth century, dance historians belonging to quite different professions, and more typical academic researchers from the late twentieth and early twenty-first centuries. In the survey that follows, I shall concentrate more on the knowledge made available than on the research methodologies, both because this was the main focus of the researchers themselves, and because it is the dominant interest of the present book.

Works on Dance Form and Structure

The manuals of the dancing masters contain discussions about and, eventually, descriptions of, round dances from the very beginning of the nineteenth century,[1] well into the twentieth century.[2] These are not research publications, but since experts who could dance (as well as teach the dances) wrote many of them, they are trustworthy sources for the forms of dance enjoyed by the educated classes from the nineteenth century onwards.[3] The writers' skills in analysis and description vary, however. Additionally, many writers copied their descriptions from each other, particularly if they did not have first-hand knowledge and/or were putting together encyclopaedias or surveys, rather than descriptions for their dance pupils.[4] Such weak points are not always easy to identify.

At the beginning of the twentieth century, around a century after the dancing masters' first descriptions of round dances, pioneers in different European countries started to collect what they called folk dances. These were similar to the dances in the collections of the dancing masters, again written by experts who knew and could teach them. The aim was to prevent the characteristic dances of each nation from being lost, and to enable groups and organisations to use them.

In western Europe, round dance types constituted a major part of the rural dance repertoire, but the collectors found that these dances were mostly too common, too new and too simple to be included in the

---

1   Johann Heinrich Kattfuss, *Taschenbuch für Freunde und Freundinnen des Tanzes von Johann Heinrich Kattfuss* (Leipzig: Heinrich Gräff, 1800), http://books.google.com/books?id=-GYNAQAAIAAJ; Ernst Chr. Mädel, *Anfangsgründe der Tanzkunst* (Erfurt: Verlag des Werfassers, 1801), p. 175; Dietrich Alexander Valentin Ivensenn, *Terpsichore: ein Taschenbuch für Freunde und Freundinnen des Tanzes in Liv-Cur-und Ehstland* (Riga: [n.p.], 1806).

2   Lucile Svae, *Kortfattet selvinstruktør i moderne dans: første bok på norsk om den moderne selskapsdans undervist ved landets danseskoler*, ed. by Hjalmar Svae (Oslo: [n.p.], 1947).

3   Eduard Friedrich David Helmke and Kurt Petermann, *Neue Tanz-und Bildungsschule* (Zentralantiquariat d. Deutschen Demokratischen Republik, 1982); Franz Anton Roller, *Systematisches Lehrbuch der bildenden Tanzkunst und körperlichen Ausbildung von der Geburt an bis zum vollendeten Wachthume des Menschen: ausgearbeitet für das gebildete Publikum, zur Belehrung bei der körperlichen Erziehung und als Unterricht für diejenigen, welche sich zu ausübenden Künstlern und zu nützlichen Lehrern dieser Kunst bilden wollen und herausgegeben bei Gelegenheit des dreihundertjährigen Jubiläums der Königl. Preuss. Landesschule Pforta* (Leipzig: Zentralantiquariat d. DDR, 1989); Bernhard Klemm, *Katechismus der Tanzkunst: Ein Leidfaden für Lehrer und Lernende* (Leipzig: Weber, 1855).

4   Gustav Desrat and Charles Nuitter, *Dictionnaire de la danse, historique, théorique, pratique et bibliographique, depuis l'origine de la danse jusqu'à nos jours* (Paris: Librairies-imprimeries réunies, 1895); Franz Magnus Böhme, *Geschichte des Tanzes in Deutschland: Darstellender Theil*, 2 vols, I (Leipzig: Breitkopf & Härtel, 1886).

manuals. As a result, if any material about round dances is included in these manuals it is, at best, very uneven and selective.[5]

The development of folk dance manuals throughout the twentieth century is too large a subject to discuss here. The simplest and most widespread versions of round dances were not particularly attractive to these manuals, but forms with round dance elements as part of more complex structures were well represented; Tvrtko Zebec discusses this point further in Chapter Fifteen of this volume. It was not until the 1970s that there was any interest in collecting even the simple round dances, at least in the Nordic countries.[6] One notable exception is a work of academic standard by the Finnish amateur folk dance collector Yngvar Heikel, who collected and systematically published all the material his informants could show him, even their loose references to dances. His book is therefore a unique work from the first half of the twentieth century, giving us a survey of the whole dance repertoire of several generations in the Swedish region of Finland.[7] A study from the Nordic countries, could, however, be seen as a continuation of the early folk-dance collections, using modern techniques, at the end of the twentieth century. In 1983, the Nordic Association for Folk Dance Research began a research project on the Nordic repertoire of round dances, and some results from this project have served as a basis for the delimitations in Chapter One.[8]

---

5 Gertrud Meyer, *Tanzspiele und Singtänze* (Leipzig: Teubner, 1923); Cecil J. Sharp, *The Country Dance Book* (London: Novello and Company, Ltd., 1909); Anna Helms, *Bunte Tänze* (Leipzig: Hofmeister, 1913); Raimond Zoder, *Altösterreichische Volkstänze*, 4 vols, I (Vienna: Österreichische Bundesverlag, 1921); Klara Semb, *Norske folkedansar II. Rettleiding om dansen* (Oslo: Noregs Ungdomslag, 1922); Gustaf Karlson, *Svenska Folkdanser*, ed. by Svenska Folkdansringen (Stockholm: Svenska Folkdansringen 1923); Foreningen til Folkedansens Fremme, *Beskrivelse af gamle danske folkedanse* (Copenhagen: Foreningen til Folkedansens Fremme, 1901).
6 Göran Karlholm and Inger Karlholm, *Gamla danser från Härjedalen, Jämtland, Ångermanland* (Oviken: Eget forlag, 1974); Egil Bakka, *Danse, danse, lett ut på foten: Folkedansar og songdansar* (Oslo: Noregs boklag, 1970), p. 204; Egil Bakka, Brit Seland, and Dag Vårdal, *Dansetradisjonar frå Vest-Agder* (Kristiansand: Vest-Agder Ungdomslag, 1990), p. 287.
7 Yngvar Heikel, *Dansbeskrivningar. I: Finlands svenska folkdiktning* (Helsingfors: Svenska litteratursällskapet i Finland, 1938).
8 The project uses the term *Gammaldans* [old-time dance], the colloquial term at that time in Sweden and Norway. The delimitation of the project is the same as used here under the term round dances.

The aim of the project was to survey the main features of the genre in terms of patterns of variation, type division, structure and form.[9] It began by filming social dances in twelve Nordic communities that had round dances at the core of their repertoire, and in which the transmission was not dominated by organised teaching from the folk dance movement or dancing schools. It concentrated on the age groups for whom round dances were the most important part of their dance knowledge. We documented two communities in each of the six countries: Denmark, Finland, Faroe Isles, Iceland, Norway and Sweden.[10] The scope of the study was intended to include all the main types of Nordic round dances.[11]

Fig. 2.1 Project meeting in the Nordic Association of Folk Dance Research at the Finnish Literature Society in Helsinki, 2002. From left, Mats Nilsson, Anders Christensen, Gunnel Biskop Pirkko-Liisa Rausma, Egil Bakka, Henning Urup, Göran Andersson. Photo by Esko Rausmaa, CC BY 4.0.

---

9   *Gammaldans i Norden: Rapport frå forskningsprosjektet: komparativ analyse av ein folkeleg dansegenre* i *utvalde nordiske lokalsamfun*, ed. by Henning Urup, Egil Bakka, and Henry Sjöberg (Dragvoll: Nordisk Forening for Folkedansforskning, 1988).
10 The Faroe Isles are part of Denmark but are geographically and culturally distinct.
11 Urup, Bakka, and Sjöberg, *Gammaldans i Norden*, p. 15.

2. The State of Research

A selection of two hundred and ninety-nine dance realisations was used for video publication, but the total material was considerably larger.[12] During the fieldwork, interviews were undertaken that showed round dancing was a popular and well-known dance genre in many Nordic communities, particularly among people who were more than fifty years old when the study took place. Attitudes towards round dances, however, were not a particular focus of the investigation. The material was surveyed, and examples of all different types of round dances documented in each of the countries were selected for detailed analysis and comparison. The results showed that the dances contained five different types of motives: turning motives; promenade motives; on-the-spot motives; resting motives; and special motives.[13] There were four main types of musical metre and a number of different step patterns. The project shows a cohesion in structure and motives, which supports the idea of considering round dances as a dance paradigm. The project also investigated nineteenth-century manuals from Nordic dancing masters,[14] as well as other historical source material, and concluded with estimations of when the different round dances were established in the Nordic countries.[15]

By comparing the descriptions from the dancing masters' manuals with the forms in our fieldwork material, we saw that some of the forms were very close to the descriptions in the manuals of the dancing masters.

---

12   Several or many couples participated in each of the realisations.
13   Urup, Bakka, and Sjöberg, *Gammaldans i Norden*, p. 249. The term 'motive' is a conventional term for the structural analysis of dance, and it means a movement sequence. See Egil Bakka, 'Analysis of Traditional Dance in Norway and the Nordic Countries', in *Dance Structures. Perspectives on the Analysis of Human Movement*, ed. by Adrienne L. Kaeppler and Elsie Ivancich Dunin (Budapest: Akadémiai Kiadó, 2007), pp. 105–12.
14   Jørgen Gad Lund, *Terpsichore, eller: En Veiledning for mine Dandselærlinger til at beholde de Trin og Toure i Hukommelsen, som de under mig have gjennemgaaet* (Mariboe: C. G. Schultz, 1823); Fredrik Alexander Gjörcke, *Anvisning att inom möjligaste korta tid och utan serskild undervisning grundligt lära alla nu brukliga sällskapsdansar: Med upplysande teckningar. Genomsedd och ändamålsenlig befunnen Af F. A. Gjörcke* (Stockholm: Östlund & Berling, 1850); Paul Petersen, *Danse-Album* (Copenhagen: [n.p.], 1884).
15   This builds upon the assumptions that the round dance forms mostly spread to the Nordic countries from other European countries, particularly Germany: Egil Bakka, 'Rise and Fall of Dances', in *Dance, Gender, and Meanings: Contemporizing Traditional Dance. Proceedings from the 26th Symposium of the ICTM Study Group on Ethnochoreology 2010*, ed. by Elsie Ivancich Dunin, Daniela Stavělová, and Dorota Gremlicová (Praha: Akademie Ved Ceské Republiky (Etnologický Ústav), 2012), pp. 274–80.

Some forms, however, particularly those that included rapid turning, were not mentioned at all in the manuals; these were forms that existed independently of dancing masters. They were probably considered improper at the balls of the higher classes but were still popular among the lower classes.[16] This was a consistent feature throughout the large amount of Nordic material.

Fig. 2.2 The publications resulting from the project *Gammaldans i Norden*, 1988. Photo by Egil Bakka, CC BY 4.0.

---

16   Urup, Bakka, and Sjöberg, *Gammaldans i Norden*, p. 282.

Fictional Accounts

While the descriptions of the dancing masters are essential sources to understand the round dances in terms of their form and structure, novels and fiction are important to understand the reception of, and attitude to, the dances. We will take as an example the famous novel by Johann Wolfgang von Goethe (1749–1832), *Die Leiden des jungen Werthers* [The Sorrows of Young Werther] (1774), which is one of the earliest sources that describes how the budding paradigm of round dances was received in the south-eastern parts of today's Germany.[17]

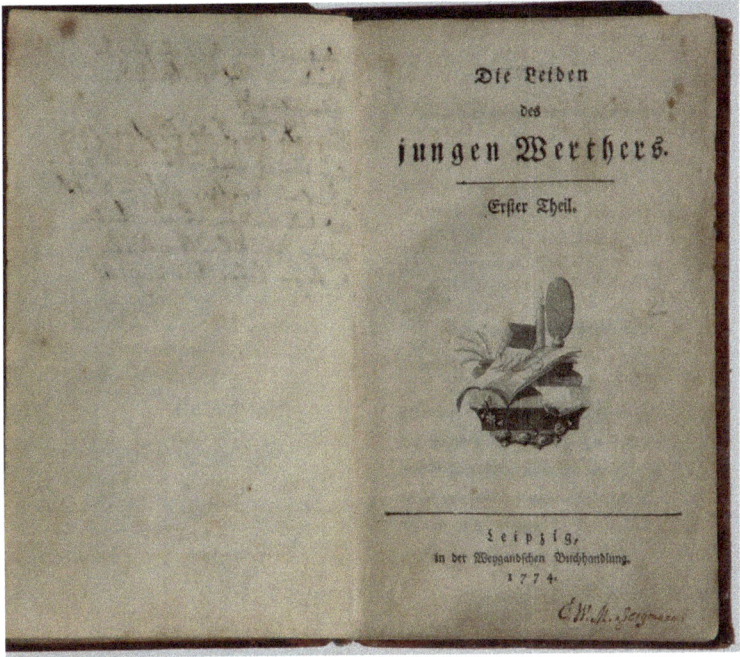

Fig. 2.3 Title page of Johann Wolfgang von Goethe's *Die Leiden des jungen Werthers*, Part 1 (Leipzig: Weygand, 1774). Wikimedia Commons, CC BY 3.0, https://commons.wikimedia.org/wiki/File:-1-_Die_Leiden_des_jungen_ Werthers._Erstdruck.jpg

---

17   Johann Wolfgang von Goethe, *Die Leiden des Jungen Werthers* (Leipzig: Weygand, 1774). There are a number of novels from the second half of the eighteenth century presenting the Waltz in a social environment, which provide a good illustration of its reception; for instance: Sophie von La Roche, *Geschichte der Fräulein von Sternheim: von einer Freundin Derselben aus Originalpapieren und Andern Zuverlässigen Quellen Gezogen Theil 2* (Carlsruhe: Schmieder, 1777).

Goethe belonged to the bourgeoisie, but he knew the dance repertoire of the lower classes. He also gained access to aristocratic circles, becoming ennobled in 1782. As a keen dancer, he was able to join in at any dance event. He and his sister received their first instruction from their father, who taught them the Minuet, and later Goethe learned 'das Walzen und Drehen'[18] while he was in Strasbourg as a student from 1770.[19] Most likely, Werther's lively stories about dance events are based on Goethe's own experiences from Strasburg and other places where he stayed or visited during the period from 1770–1774.

Goethe's description of the Waltz is unusually rich for fiction at this time, and tells us much about the reception of the new dance. On the one hand, he gives a very romantic description of a dancing couple and the feelings the dance inspires in the young man. On the other, since the Waltz allowed a dubious intimacy, the young man is torn by jealousy. The degree to which this was a romantic construction established by novelists, or an aspect of the Waltz that often played out in reality, is hard to establish.

The novel takes place among the bourgeoisie and lesser nobility, but in the beginning the class distinctions are not so visible and the young people at the dance event seem to be socially equal. When Werther begins work in the house of a nobleman, however, he experiences humiliating episodes in which he is excluded because of his lower-class status. It also turns out that the girl he falls in love with is a member of the lesser nobility, and he is not good enough for her. Since the novel is so clearly based on Goethe's personal experiences, and many incidents and characters seem to have been taken from real life, it is reasonable to believe that the dancing, the dance event and the relationships between the young people can also be taken as historical evidence. The novel describes an environment in which class distinctions are latent, but do not affect the dancing and social life of young people of the 'educated classes'. It gives an impression that the young people learned to dance among themselves, and that the influence of dancing masters was not very strong, even if it was most likely present. The lower classes, however, are visible only as servants and peasants. There is no hint as to

---

18 'Waltzing and turning'.
19 Walter Salmen, *Goethe und der Tanz: Tänze, Bälle, Redouten, Ballette im Leben und Werk* (Hildesheim: Olms, 2006), p. 138

whether new dances might be exchanged between the higher and lower classes in this environment.

The Battle of 'Origin'

Writers on round dances have used much space and energy to pursue questions that might colloquially be phrased as: 'Where do they come from?' or 'To whom does this dance belong?' This interest is based on the idea that a dance has a place of origin, where it was invented and where it is danced in a way that cannot be easily copied by outsiders, as the quotation from Helmke in chapter one shows. Often this place of 'origin' is considered to have a kind of ownership of the dance, which has created intense disputes. Daniela Stavělová's contribution in Chapter Five of this book examines how such ideas came about in the Czech lands. The idea that a country or a region had characteristic dances is idealised and simplified, but it nonetheless has roots in reality. It was the basis for presenting a character's nationality through the character dances in ballets of the eighteenth and nineteenth centuries, and it underlies the folk dance movement of the late nineteenth and twentieth centuries. Fashionable dances such as round dances were probably well established in particular regions or countries before they rose to fame and began to spread.[20]

The idea that a country's character is reflected in its dances conflates dance and national pride, but this tendency is sometimes at odds with the references to origin in the dance names themselves. The Czechs consider the Polka their national dance, even if the name refers to Poland; likewise the Swedish consider the 'Polska' to belong to them.[21] It seems that a nation or a group will name a new dance after the place from which they believe it to come: even if it goes on to develop into something very particular to its new home, the dance keeps its original name, with its reference to elsewhere.

The struggle over origin is not based only on the name of the dance: there is, for instance, a long-lasting dispute between French and German dance historians about the origin of the Waltz. The Franco-German

---

20 See, for instance, Stavělová's chapter in this book (Chapter Five).
21 Polka is the Czech word for a Polish girl, or dance, whereas Polak is the word for a Polish man. A 'Polska' is the Swedish word for a Polish woman, dance or melody.

historian and anthropologist Remi Hess wrote a voluminous book in which he argues that the Waltz is a derivation of the French Volta,[22] which was popular in European courts during the period 1550–1650.[23]

Fig. 2.4 [Anonymous, possibly Marcus Gheeraerts], *Queen Elizabeth I Dancing La Volta with Robert Dudley, Earl of Leicester*, c.1580, Wikimedia Commons, Public Domain, https://commons.wikimedia.org/wiki/File:Robert_Dudley_Elizabeth_Dancing.jpg

Thoinot Arbeau described the dance in 1589[24] and there are several interpretations available on the internet, one clearly based on Arbeau and a looser version in a feature film in which Queen Elizabeth I of England, played by Cate Blanchett, is dancing (see Fig. 2.6).

A large number of dance historians have taken their side in the debate on whether the Waltz has German or French origin, and Hess gives detailed references to this whole discussion. Hess is connected to France as well as to Germany, but usually French dance historians

---

22 Rémi Hess, *Der Walzer: Geschichte eines Skandals* (Hamburg: Europäische Verlagsanstalt, 1996). The book first appeared in French.
23 Selma Jeanne Cohen and Dance Perspectives Foundation, *International Encyclopedia of Dance*, 6 vols, VI (New York: Oxford University Press, 1998), p. 349.
24 Thoinot Arbeau, *Orchésographie: Méthode et théorie en forme de discours et tablature pour apprendre á danser, battre le tambour* (Genève: Editions Minkoff, 1972), p. 63.

argue that the Volta is the origin of the Waltz, whereas the Austrians and Germans argue that it is a German dance and vehemently reject the French claim. One of the earliest supporters, perhaps even the source of the idea that the Waltz grew from the Volta, was the dancing master Gustave Desrat (born c.1830)[25] who published several books. Therefore, the feud is nearly two hundred years old.[26] Hess gestured towards the politics that were involved when he proposed that the participants should listen to authors from neutral countries.

Fig. 2.5 Video: 'Contrapasso Historical Dance Ensemble: Volte (Lavolta)', 1:34, posted online by E. Contrapasso, *Youtube*, 19 February 2012, https://www.youtube.com/watch?v=AvaGvUoorlE

Fig. 2.6 Video: Volta from the film *Elizabeth* (1998). 'Coronation Banquet — Elizabeth Dance', 2.44, posted online by gozala00, *Youtube*, 16 May 2007, https://www.youtube.com/watch?v=5rXpNtXNOrI&feature=youtu.be

As I have indicated earlier, I take the 'German side'. There are two different understandings of the concept of origin involved here. On the one hand, there is the argument that a dance practised for a long time in a certain place belongs to that place, and that ancient roots elsewhere do not take away that ownership. On the other, there is the suggestion that certain ways of dancing have 'old origins' and the place where a technique or principle came into being is the birthplace of the dance. Both arguments have some validity. It is a fact that dance forms and dance practices move and spread from one place to another. The problem is the pursuit of an ultimate origin of a dance, a notion which is essentially a myth. The German art historian and publicist Oskar Bie has

---

25 Christian Declerck, *G. DESRAT a désormais un prénom* (21 May 2008), http://maitre-a-danser.blogspot.no/2008/05/g-desrat-desormais-un-prenom.html
26 Desrat and Nuitter, *Dictionnaire de la danse*, p. 370.

argued against the simplistic idea that there was an originary moment when a dance was first invented.[27] Certainly, traditional social dances are unlikely to have a precise point of genesis, and it is more probable that new forms arise when existing dances are mixed, when triggered by new impulses, or from some novel twist gaining popularity.[28] The idea that the Volta was the predecessor of the Waltz seems to have developed in the second half of the nineteenth century. Nobody apparently made the connection in the first century of Waltz history, and, in any case, the Volta was out of use long before the Waltz appeared. The mooted connection is based on an alleged similarity in form and musical metre, but such a resemblance can easily be found between dances that are not connected at all, so the likelihood of a connection is very slim.

The Austrian folk dance researcher Richard Wolfram (1901–1995) was a strong voice in defending the Austrian claim to be the place of origin of the Waltz. He argued vehemently against the assertion that the Waltz was 'gesunkenes Kulturgut', or that the higher classes had supplied the models for the Waltz and even the Ländler forms through the Allemande, a description of which was first published in France in 1769. He also disagreed that the Waltz was invented in the theatres for the operas and ballets.[29] He supported his views with studies undertaken in diasporic Austrian communities located in what we know today as Ukraine and Romania. These communities emigrated from Austria in 1732 and 1775, and had continued to dance their Austrian Ländler well into the twentieth century. The newer Allemande or a Waltz from an opera could therefore not be the basis for the Ländler.[30]

Even if there are different ideas about the origin of the Waltz, there is hardly anyone who disputes that the dance became famous in Vienna,

---

27 Examples of such arguments include the suggestion that the Waltz was first presented at the Opera *Una cosa rara*, Oskar Bie, *Der Tanz* (Berlin: J. Bard, 1919), p. 228; or the suggestion that a rural Czech maid invented the Polka step, Mark Knowles, *The Wicked Waltz and Other Scandalous Dances: Outrage at Couple Dancing in the Nineteenth and Early Twentieth Centuries* (Jefferson, NC: McFarland, 2009), p. 196.
28 Egil Bakka, 'Rise and Fall of Dances', p. 274.
29 Simon Guillaume and Jacques La Hante, *Almanach dansant, ou, positions et attitudes de l'Allemande: Avec un discours préliminaire sur l'origine et l'utilité de la danse* (Paris: Chez l'auteur rue des Arcis, 1769), https://gallica.bnf.fr/ark:/12148/btv1b8626149j/f41.item.zoomin
30 Richard Wolfram, *Die Volkstänze in Österreich und verwandte Tänze in Europa* (Salzburg: Müller, 1951).

due to the many compositions for the Waltz and for many other round dances written by the celebrated musicians who lived there, such as Wolfgang Amadeus Mozart, Joseph Haydn, Joseph Lanner, and, first and foremost, the Strauss family. The influence of Strauss the Elder is more fully explored in Chapter Ten of this book, where Jörgen Torp discusses the impact of his concert tours. In the early twentieth century, nostalgic, nationalistic descriptions of the old Vienna were prevalent, and can be read as evidence of the heritagisation and branding processes to which the Viennese Waltz and Viennese culture were increasingly subject.[31] The Nazi regime banned African-American dances, so the Waltz was danced more frequently as a consequence, but the regime did not promote it directly. Hitler personally had no liking for ballroom dancing and refused to learn to waltz or to dance in public.[32] In the twenty-first century, however, the Viennese ball made it onto the Austrian UNESCO list of Intangible Cultural Heritage, but the organisers of one of the balls listed were accused of having neo-Nazi sympathies and the balls were taken off the list again.[33]

The German musicologist Walter Salmen has contributed substantially to dance history, particularly the history of the German-language area; a number of his publications offer historical source material about iconography. He discusses the role of dance in the lives of Goethe and Mozart, and writes about the dancing masters.[34] The Austrian musicologist Monika Fink's work *Der Ball* is also valuable in this regard.[35]

---

31 Hess, *Der Walzer*, p. 41. Fritz Klingenbeck, *Unsterblicher Walzer: die Geschichte des deutschen Nationaltanzes* (Vienna: W. Frick, 1943); Joseph August Lux, *Der unsterbliche Walzer Altwiener Tanz und Lied* (Munich: Holbein, 1921), p. 99; Fritz Lange, *Der Wiener Walzer* (Vienna: Verlag d. Volksbildungshauses Wiener Urania, 1917).

32 Sherree Owens Zalampas, *Adolf Hitler: A Psychological Interpretation of His Views on Architecture, Art, and Music* (Bowling Green, OH: Bowling Green State Univ. Popular Press, 1990) p. 114.

33 'Unesco streicht "Wiener Ball" aus Weltkulturerbe-Liste', *Die Presse*, 19 January 2012, https://www.diepresse.com/725035/unesco-streicht-wiener-ball-aus-weltkulturerbe-liste

34 Walter Salmen, *Grundriß einer Geschichte des Tanzes in Westfalen* (Münster: Aschendorff, 1954); Walter Salmen, *Tanz Im 19. Jahrhundert* (Leipzig: VEB Deutscher Verlag für Musik, 1989); Salmen, *Goethe und der Tanz*; Walter Salmen, *Der Tanzmeister: Geschichte und Profile eines Berufes vom 14. bis zum 19. Jahrhundert* (Hildesheim: Olms Goerg AG, 1997); Walter Salmen, *Mozart in der Tanzkultur seiner Zeit* (Innsbruck: Ed. Helbling, 1990).

35 Monika Fink, *Der Ball: Eine Kulturgeschichte des Gesellschaftstanzes im 18. und 19. Jahrhundert* (Innsbruck: Studien Verlag, 1996).

Fig. 2.7 The Allemande. From Simon Guillaume, *Almanach dansant ou positions et attitudes de l'Allemande* (Paris: Chez l'auteur rue des Arcis, 1769). Wikimedia Commons, Public Domain, https://commons.wikimedia.org/wiki/File:Guillaume_Almanach.jpg

Recent Austrian research on the Waltz has been undertaken by the cultural historian Reingard Witzmann, who has published several substantial works on its early history and prehistory. In her monograph *Der Ländler in Wien* her main aim is to discuss the movement and music content of the Ländler and Deutscher dances, which are considered to be predecessors of the Waltz.[36] She contextualises the dance material by discussing the dance life of Vienna in this period, including dance venues, dance parties and dance musicians. Witzmann has also contributed to the anthology *Zur Frühgeschichte des Walzers*, a celebration of the two-hundredth anniversary of the Viennese Waltz. She also discusses its choreo-musical aspects and scrutinises dance descriptions to tease out the progression from the Ländler and the Deutscher Tanz to the Waltz.[37]

---

36 Reingard Witzmann, *Der Ländler in Vienna: ein Beitrag zur Entwicklungsgeschichte des Wiener Walzers bis in die Zeit des Wiener Kongresses* (Vienna: Arbeitsstelle f. den Volkskundeatlas in Österreich, 1976).

37 Reingard Witzmann, 'Magie der Drehung — Zum Phänomen des Wiener Walzers von der Aufklärung zum Biedermeier', in *Zur Frühgeschichte des Walzers*, ed. by Thomas

Music-Dance Relationship

The American researcher Eric McKee published a monograph in 2012 comparing the music-dance relationship of the Minuet and the Waltz. The core of his work is the influence of the social context of dance on the dance music compositions of Johannes Sebastian Bach, Wolfgang Amadeus Mozart, Johann Strauss I, Joseph Haydn, Joseph Lanner, and Frédéric Chopin. He points to some similarities between the Minuet and the Waltz, such as their shared triple metre and what he calls the two-bar hypermetre, in which the pattern of the dance steps takes two bars of music. He does not claim that the Waltz derives from the Minuet, and supports the understanding that the Minuet is a typical creation of *l'ancien régime*, whereas the Waltz has its roots in the dancing of the lower classes, and rose to fame as a dance of the bourgeoisie.[38]

Sevin H. Yaraman's book *Revolving Embrace: The Waltz as Sex, Steps, and Sound* discusses the Waltzes that were composed in the tradition of western art music. She claims, however, that a study of the Waltz as music cannot be abstracted from the Waltz as dance, which she also takes seriously. She discusses the technical characteristics of the dance steps and dance holds, and combines them with some of the written sources about the reception of the Waltz in the early nineteenth century to situate the totality of dance and music.[39]

These studies are based on music and dance history, and depart from the written musical score and general descriptions of the Waltz. It would have been interesting to see these supplemented with studies using ethnomusicological and ethnochoreological methods and perspectives, looking at performance practices that can still be studied live today. This has not been done before, would be worthwhile in itself, and would shed new light on historical questions.

Nussbaumer, Franz Gratl and Ferenc Polai (Innsbruck: Wagner Innsbruck, 2014), pp. 9–31.

38 Eric McKee, *Decorum of the Minuet, Delirium of the Waltz: A Study of Dance-Music Relations in 3/4 Time* (Indiana University Press, 2012).

39 Sevin H. Yaraman, *Revolving Embrace: The Waltz as Sex, Steps, and Sound* (Pendragon Press, 2002).

Moral and Health Issues

In 1569, the German writer Florian Daul wrote an entire book as a warning that men *'verdrehten'* women while dancing — that is, they turn them until they lose their reason or senses. This protest against a couple-turning dance in the German lands is, perhaps, evidence of a precursor to round dances.[40] A large number of pamphlets and articles were produced in Europe over the centuries, striking out at new dance genres or dance paradigms. Claims of immorality were supported by arguments about health risks, and the dance masters pointed to norms of etiquette, decency and distinction. The following material has been useful for, and welcomed by, dance historians as first-hand sources about and illustrations of the reception of dance forms, and lately several books have been written about the topic.

The dancing master had to strike a difficult balance between, on the one hand, ignoring or condemning dances that his clientele did not find acceptable, and on the other, not losing out by failing to teach the new and fashionable dances. The dancing master Andreas Schönwald offered a solution to this dilemma, saying that his aim at Freiburg University in 1807 was to teach the students to dance the very popular Waltz *decently* — in contrast to the (indecent) style of the general public.[41]

The dancing masters found support from many sources in their condemnation of new dances. Medical professionals would warn that they were threatening to the dancer's health, causing exhaustion or dizziness. A book review in a medical magazine summarises a discussion on contemporary dance and states:

> The dances that could be accepted and recommended even by the strictest dietitians and moralists have pretty much disappeared from our dance halls. The wild hopping dance of the Waltz degenerated into even more wildness, and other billy-goat jumps have replaced [the acceptable dances].[42]

---

40 Florian Daul, *Tantzteuffel: Das ist, wider den leichtfertigen, unverschempten Welt tantz, und sonderlich wider die Gottßzucht und ehrvergessene Nachttäntze* (Leipzig: Zentralantiquariat der DDR, 1984).
41 Salmen, *Der Tanzmeister*, p. 72.
42 This is most likely a reference to the 2/4 metre Waltz (a Polka type of dance), which can include hopping and becomes much wilder than the softer 3/4 Waltz, at least as we know the dances today. Georg Wilhelm Sponitzer, *Das Tanzen in pathologisch moralischer Hinsicht erwogen* (Berlin: Friedrich Maurer, 1795); *Medicinisch Chirurgische*

2. The State of Research

Fig. 2.8 Daniel Hopfer, copper engraving, c.1500. German peasants celebrating. We see a dance in which most couples are moving forward on a path that is not a full circle. One couple close to the tree are in a tight embrace, which might be interpreted as couple-turning, supporting the idea that this is not a new technique in the German lands. Wikimedia Commons, Public Domain, https://commons.wikimedia.org/wiki/File:Kulturbilder_489.JPG

Almost all of these discussions are about the upper classes, but the linking of dancing with drinking, gambling, and prostitution among the lower classes probably colours attitudes to dancing even among the upper classes. It is questionable, however, whether moral and health issues were really the most burning concerns of the dancing masters. There seems to be a subtext underlying the distinction between the different social groups: the educated classes needed to behave decently in order to stand out from the supposedly vulgar and uncivilised ways of the lower classes. The construction of an embodied class distinction was at the core of the justification of the dancing masters' profession and kept their services in demand.

Mark Knowles' book *The Wicked Waltz and Other Scandalous Dances: Outrage at Couple Dancing in the Nineteenth and Early Twentieth Centuries* is one of the recent studies on moral issues. Knowles starts with the Waltz and the round dances, but also examines an interesting selection of twentieth-century dances. The main focus is the balance between moral attempts to eradicate or limit the new dances, and the enthusiastic reception they nonetheless received. He contextualises the material by

Zeitung, 11 February 1797, p. 174, http://anno.onb.ac.at/cgi-content/anno?aid=mcz&datum=17971102&seite=14

looking at fashions, trends and societal developments, using the ample sources available in English.⁴³

The contemporary written sources characterising the Waltz and commenting upon its reception are extremely diverse, and a large number of questions remain open. Who is writing or giving information? Do his or her views represent a majority or an extreme minority? Is the source taken from fiction? Is it a hoax taken up by a large number of newspapers? Is it a report of a unique event written by an eyewitness? Is it written at the time the described phenomenon happened, or is it an old memory or a generalisation based more on popular discourse rather than on personal memories?

Now, to be fair, some of the most concrete and simple of these questions can be deduced from the sources themselves, or might even be commented on by the authors. To situate the dancing, the dances and the dancers that feature in any quotation within their full social context is an enormous task.

Fig. 2.9 George Cruikshank, *The Drunkard's Children. Plate I*, 1848. A series of eight images depicting various vices and their consequences, of which this is the first. Cruikshank's text to this image reads: 'Neglected by their parents, educated on the street, and falling into the hands of wretches who live upon the vices of others, they are led to the gin shop, to drink at the fountain which nourishes every species of crime'. We see the pimp in the picture waiting to recruit the daughter. Wellcome Collection, CC BY 4.0, https://wellcomecollection.org/works/utfd99fy

---

43 Knowles, *The Wicked Waltz*, p. 1.

A Contextualised Dance Study

An example of how to achieve this can be found in Theresa Jill Buckland's book *Society Dancing: Fashionable Bodies in England 1870–1920*. Buckland focuses on the dancing of the so-called 'Society' or the 'Upper Ten (Thousands)', the cream of the English aristocracy with the Royal family at its helm.[44] Using extensive source material, Buckland takes the readers to the ballrooms and describes the dance events and their contexts, their rules and etiquette. She introduces the ladies and gentlemen attending, and the expectations of how they should embody their gendered roles. She also discusses the dance repertoire and dance forms based on concrete and practical knowledge of the material. She describes the slowly changing practices in the ballroom and connects these with broader changes in the politics, economy, and mindset of the country. She also contextualises the dancing of 'society' by comparing it with the practices of the lower classes. Further works of this kind would enable the writing of dance histories for longer periods to be based on firm ground.

Another valuable contribution would be an analysis of dance forms based on what is left of concrete practice, be it in ballroom dancing, in folk dances or in the character dance of the classical ballet. The descriptions in historical sources from people who mastered these dances at various points in history would be an additional source for such a work, although these are difficult to interpret on their own. Such a contribution is necessary in order to critically evaluate the endlessly repeated characteristics that are often chosen from sources incompatible in time as well as in space.

The Dance of Power

The Swiss historians Rudolf Braun and David Gugerli published a book on the power of dance and the dances of the powerful in 1993.[45] The book spans the period from 1550 to 1914, and is rich in quotations and

---

44 Theresa Buckland, *Society Dancing: Fashionable Bodies in England, 1870–1920* (New York: Palgrave Macmillan, 2011).
45 Rudolf Braun and David Gugerli, *Macht des Tanzes — Tanz der Mächtigen. Hoffeste und Herrschaftszeremoniell, 1550–1914* (Munich: Verlag C. H. Beck, 1993).

paraphrases of sources, tying the development of dances and dancing to developments in the arts, military training, the uses of the body and to societal developments in general. The authors do not seem to have any expertise in the technical aspects of dance, and rely on dance names and the conventional understanding of the sources when it comes to the form of dances; they do not refer much to music characteristics either. The book has four main chapters: the dancing queen (Elizabeth I of England), the dancing king (Louis XIV of France), the dancing bourgeois, and the dancing imperialists. The third chapter is mainly about the Waltz; it does not have a hero as do the first two, but concentrates on the late acceptance of the Waltz at the German courts. There was no one in this period who stood out as a dancing ruler, or at least they did not use the Waltz to symbolise their power. On the contrary, the Waltz was banned at the main German courts long after it was accepted in the best circles of society.

Round Dancing and the Dancing Masters

Let us now take a very broad and long perspective on some of the major dance paradigms of the aristocracy in Western and Central Europe during the last five centuries. It seems reasonable to assume that the aristocracy mostly used the same dance material as the lower classes during the Middle Ages, before the time of the dancing masters. The distinction then would not be in the dance forms, but in style, dress, music etc. Later, during the Renaissance and Baroque periods, the dancing masters would create ballets and masques at many courts. They even invented social dances for use at courts, and these stood out from the repertoire of the lower classes. The dancing masters might take inspiration from the dances of the peasants of rural regions, but their codification and adaption of these dances would militate against direct similarity.[46] This may be the reason why traces from the noble dances invented or codified at the courts do not seem to be represented to the same degree as the chain dances and the contra dances in the traditional dance material throughout Europe. Even if the contra dances were said

---

46   Many dance historians repeat a claim that that the Minuet is based upon the Branle de Poitou; see discussions by Jean-Jacques Rousseau, *Le dictionnaire de musique de Jean-Jacques Rousseau: Une édition critique* (Bern: Peter Lang, 2008).

to have distant lower-class roots, the creativity of the dancing masters was dominant. This can be seen from the wealth of contra dances in manuals by dancing masters all the way from the English Playford, to the early twentieth-century descriptions, to the many books referred to in this chapter. That they spread to the lower classes can be seen from their presence in the folk dance manuals referred to above.

Then around 1800, the round dances came fully into fashion. These dances came from the lower classes and posed new challenges to the dancing masters. Previously, they had worked with the dances their profession had created, codified or choreographed for the courts and upper classes. Now they had to consider whether and how their customers valued dances from other social classes. I have not seen claims or evidence that dancing masters played a central role in bringing Waltzing into fashion. It seems that they took these dances on when the demand for them became powerful. Round dances therefore have a different relationship to courts and power, since they were not created or codified for the upper classes by the dancing masters. These dances slowly made their way to the upper classes in ways comparable to the journeys of the 'nouveaux riches'. They also did not have the structural richness of the contra dances, so they could not be adapted as easily to new choreographies. When, however, the dancing masters saw they needed to deal with the round dances, they faced the challenge of adapting them to the mechanics and strategies of class distinction.

Bibliography

Arbeau, Thoinot, *Orchésographie: Méthode et théorie en forme de discours et tablature pour apprendre á danser, battre le tambour* (Genève: Editions Minkoff, 1972).

Bakka, Egil, 'Rise and Fall of Dances', in *Dance, Gender, and Meanings: Contemporizing Traditional Dance. Proceedings from the 26th Symposium of the ICTM Study Group on Ethnochoreology 2010*, ed. by Elsie Ivancich Dunin, Daniela Stavělová, and Dorota Gremlicová (Praha: Akademie Ved Ceské Republiky (Etnologický Ústav), 2010), pp. 274–80.

——, 'Analysis of Traditional Dance in Norway and the Nordic Countries', in *Dance Structures. Perspectives on the Analysis of Human Movement*, ed. by Adrienne L. Kaeppler and Elsie Ivancich Dunin (Budapest: Akadémiai Kiadó, 2007), pp. 105–12.

——, *Danse, danse, lett ut på foten*: *Folkedansar og songdansar* (Oslo: Noregs boklag, 1970).

Bakka, Egil, Brit Seland, and Dag Vårdal, *Dansetradisjonar frå Vest-Agder* (Kristiansand: Vest-Agder Ungdomslag, 1990).

Bie, Oskar, *Der Tanz* (Berlin: J. Bard, 1919).

Böhme, Franz Magnus, *Geschichte des Tanzes in Deutschland*: *Darstellender Theil*, 2 vols (Leipzig: Breitkopf & Härtel, 1886).

Braun, Rudolf, and David Gugerli, *Macht des Tanzes — Tanz der Mächtigen. Hoffeste und Herrschaftszeremoniell, 1550–1914* (Munich: Verlag C. H. Beck, 1993).

Buckland, Theresa J., *Society Dancing*: *Fashionable Bodies in England, 1870–1920* (New York: Palgrave Macmillan, 2011).

Cohen, Selma Jeanne, and Dance Perspectives Foundation, *International Encyclopedia of Dance*, 6 vols (New York: Oxford University Press, 1998).

Daul, Florian, *Tantzteuffel*: *Das ist, wider den leichtfertigen, unverschempten Welt tantz, und sonderlich wider die Gottßzucht und ehrvergessene Nachttäntze* (Leipzig: Zentralantiquariat der DDR, 1984).

Declerck, Christian, *G. DESRAT a désormais un prénom* (21 May 2008), http://maitre-a-danser.blogspot.no/2008/05/g-desrat-desormais-un-prenom.html

Desrat, Gustav, and Charles Nuitter, *Dictionnaire de la danse, historique, théorique, pratique et bibliographique, depuis l'origine de la danse jusqu'à nos jours* (Paris: Librairies-imprimeries réunies, 1895), https://archive.org/details/dictionnairedela00desruoft

Fink, Monika, *Der Ball*: *Eine Kulturgeschichte des Gesellschaftstanzes im 18. und 19. Jahrhundert* (Innsbruck: Studien Verlag, 1996).

Foreningen til Folkedansens Fremme, *Beskrivelse af gamle danske folkedanse* (Copenhagen: Foreningen til Folkedansens Fremme, 1901).

Fredrik Alexander Gjörcke, *Anvisning att inom möjligaste korta tid och utan serskild undervisning grundligt lära alla nu brukliga sällskapsdansar*: *Med upplysande teckningar. Genomsedd och ändamålsenlig befunnen Af F. A. Gjörcke* (Stockholm: Östlund & Berling, 1850).

Goethe, Johann Wolfgang von, *Die Leiden des Jungen Werthers* (Leipzig: Weygand, 1774).

Guillaume, Simon, and Jacques La Hante, *Almanach dansant, ou, positions et attitudes de l'Allemande*: *Avec un discours préliminaire sur l'origine et l'utilité de la danse* (Paris: Chez l'auteur ruë des Arcis, 1769), https://gallica.bnf.fr/ark:/12148/btv1b8626149j/f41.item.zoomin/

Heikel, Yngvar, *Dansbeskrivningar. I*: *Finlands svenska folkdiktning* (Helsingfors: Svenska litteratursällskapet i Finland, 1938).

Helmke, Eduard Friedrich David, and Kurt Petermann, *Neue Tanz-und Bildungsschule* (Leipzig: Zentralantiquariat d. Deutschen Demokratischen Republik, 1982).

Helms, Anna, *Bunte Tänze* (Leipzig: Hofmeister, 1913).

Hess, Rémi, *Der Walzer: Geschichte eines Skandals* (Hamburg: Europäische Verlagsanstalt, 1996).

Ivensenn, Dietrich Alexander Valentin, *Terpsichore: ein Taschenbuch für Freunde und Freundinnen des Tanzes in Liv-Cur-und Ehstland* (Riga: [n.p.], 1806).

Karlholm, Göran, and Inger Karlholm, *Gamla danser från Härjedalen, Jämtland, Ångermanland* (Oviken: Eget förlag 1974).

Karlson, Gustaf, *Svenska Folkdanser*, ed. by Svenska Folkdansringen (Stockholm: Svenska Folkdansringen 1923).

Kattfuss, Johann Heinrich, *Taschenbuch für Freunde und Freundinnen des Tanzes von Johann Heinrich Kattfuss* (Leipzig: Heinrich Gräff, 1800), http://books.google.com/books?id=-GYNAQAAIAAJ

Klemm, Bernhard, *Katechismus der Tanzkunst, ein Leitfaden für Lehrer und Lernende* (Leipzig: Weber, 1855).

Klingenbeck, Fritz, *Unsterblicher Walzer: die Geschichte des deutschen Nationaltanzes* (Vienna: W. Frick, 1943).

Knowles, Mark A., *The Wicked Waltz and Other Scandalous Dances: Outrage at Couple Dancing in the 19th and Early 20th Centuries* (Jefferson, NC: McFarland, 2009).

La Roche, Sophie von, *Geschichte des Fräulein von Sternheim Von einer Freundin derselben aus Original-Papieren und andern zuverlässigen Quellen gezogen Theil 2* (Carlsruhe: Schmieder, 1777).

Lange, Fritz, *Der Wiener Walzer* (Vienna: Verlag d. Volksbildungshauses Wiener Urania, 1917).

Lund, Jørgen Gad, *Terpsichore, eller: En Veiledning for mine Dandselærlinger til at beholde de Trin og Toure i Hukommelsen, som de under mig have gjennemgaaet* (Mariboe: C. G. Schultz, 1823).

Lux, Josef August, *Der unsterbliche Walzer Altwiener Tanz und Lied* (Munich: Holbein, 1921).

Mädel, Ernst Chr., *Anfangsgründe Der Tanzkunst* (Erfurt: Verlag des Werfassers, 1801).

McKee, Eric, *Decorum of the Minuet, Delirium of the Waltz: A Study of Dance-Music Relations in 3/4 Time* (Indiana: Indiana University Press, 2012).

Medicinisch Chirurgische Zeitung, 11 February 1797, p. 174, http://anno.onb.ac.at/cgi-content/anno?aid=mcz&datum=17971102&seite=14

Meyer, Gertrud, *Tanzspiele und Singtänze* (Leipzig: Teubner, 1923).

Petersen, Paul, *Danse-Album* (Copenhagen: [n.p.], 1884).

Roller, Franz Anton, *Systematisches Lehrbuch der bildenden Tanzkunst und körperlichen Ausbildung von der Geburt an bis zum vollendeten Wachthume des Menschen: ausgearbeitet für das gebildete Publikum, zur Belehrung bei der körperlichen Erziehung und als Unterricht für diejenigen, welche sich zu ausübenden Künstlern und zu nützlichen Lehrern dieser Kunst bilden wollen und herausgegeben bei Gelegenheit des dreihundertjährigen Jubiläums der Königl. Preuss. Landesschule Pforta* (Leipzig: Zentralantiquariat d. DDR, 1989).

Rousseau, Jean-Jacques, *Le dictionnaire de musique de Jean-Jacques Rousseau: Une édition critique* (Bern: Peter Lang, 2008).

Salmen, Walter, *Goethe und der Tanz: Tänze, Bälle, Redouten, Ballette im Leben und Werk* (Hildesheim: Olms, 2006).

——, *Der Tanzmeister: Geschichte und Profile eines Berufes vom 14. bis zum 19. Jahrhundert* (Hildesheim [etc.]: Olms, 1997).

——, *Mozart in der Tanzkultur seiner Zeit* (Innsbruck: Ed. Helbling, 1990).

——, *Tanz Im 19. Jahrhundert* (Leipzig: VEB Deutscher Verlag für Musik, 1989).

——, *Grundriß einer Geschichte des Tanzes in Westfalen* (Münster: Aschendorff, 1954).

Semb, Klara, *Norske folkedansar II. Rettleiding om dansen* (Oslo: Noregs Ungdomslag, 1922).

Sharp, Cecil J., *The Country Dance Book* (London: Novello and Company, Ltd., 1909).

Sponitzer, Georg Wilhelm, *Das Tanzen in pathologisch moralischer Hinsicht erwogen* (Berlin: Friedrich Maurer, 1795).

Svae, Lucile, *Kortfattet selvinstruktør i moderne dans: første bok på norsk om den moderne selskapsdans undervist ved landets danseskoler* (Oslo: [n.p.], 1947).

'Unesco streicht "Wiener Ball" aus Weltkulturerbe-Liste', *Die Presse*, 19 January 2012, https://www.diepresse.com/725035/unesco-streicht-wiener-ball-aus-weltkulturerbe-liste

Urup, Henning, Egil Bakka, and Henry Sjöberg, eds, *Gammaldans i Norden: Rapport frå forskningsprosjektet: komparativ analyse av ein folkeleg dansegenre i utvalde nordiske lokalsamfun* (Dragvoll: Nordisk Forening for Folkedansforskning Dragvoll, Norway, 1988).

Witzmann, Reingard, 'Magie der Drehung — Zum Phänomen des Wiener Walzers von der Aufklärung zum Biedermeier', in *Zur Frühgeschichte des Walzers*, ed. by Thomas Nussbaumer, Franz Gratl, Ferenc Polai (Innsbruck: Wagner Innsbruck, 2014), pp. 9–31.

——, *Der Ländler in Vienna: ein Beitrag zur Entwicklungsgeschichte des Wiener Walzers bis in die Zeit des Wiener Kongresses* (Vienna: Arbeitsstelle f. den Volkskundeatlas in Österreich, 1976).

Wolfram, Richard, *Die Volkstänze in Österreich und verwandte Tänze in Europa* (Salzburg: Müller, 1951).

Yaraman, Sevin H., *Revolving Embrace: The Waltz as Sex, Steps, and Sound* (Hillsdale, NY: Pendragon Press, 2002).

Zalampas, Sherree O., *Adolf Hitler: A Psychological Interpretation of His Views on Architecture, Art, and Music* (Bowling Green, OH: Bowling Green State Univ. Popular Press 1990).

Zoder, Raimund, *Altösterreichische Volkstänze*, 4 vols (Vienna: Österreichische Bundesverlag, 1921).

3. A Survey of the Chapters in the Book

Egil Bakka

Most of this book is comprised of case studies from European countries that, during the late eighteenth and the first half of the nineteenth centuries, were not the independent states they are today. They were more or less clearly defined provinces or parts of empires or kingdoms.[1] Dance histories have, to a large extent, been written on the basis of material from the large, prestigious centres of Europe, written in the dominant languages. The contributions in this book present sources from a larger selection of languages, and we hope to broaden perspectives on how the round dances were received throughout other parts of Europe. There is, however, one exception: Chapter Four by Egil Bakka deals with round dancing at a number of European courts. This chapter is intended to link the other case studies in the book to the practices and discourses of larger countries which, although not the focus of this collection, are significant in the overall history of how round dances were received even at the top level.

It is most logical to group the chapters according to the century with which they mostly deal, and this is the approach we have taken in this volume. This approach tends to group sections according to the source material used, as well as topics and perspectives covered. Some chapters focus on the first half of the nineteenth century, others on the twentieth or even twenty-first centuries. There are, of course, excursions forwards or backwards in time, and Chapter Eight by Rebeka Kunej considers both centuries more or less equally.

---

1   These include Croatia, Czech Republic, Estonia, Finland, Hungary, Norway, and Slovenia; the exceptions are Hamburg/Germany and Sweden.

© Egil Bakka, CC BY 4.0   https://doi.org/10.11647/OBP.0174.03

Comparing the groups of chapters that deal with each period, those concentrating mostly on the nineteenth century (Chapter Five by Daniela Stavělová, Chapter Six by Dorota Gremlicová, Chapter Seven by Lászlò Felföldi, Chapter Nine by Iva Niemčić and Ivana Katarinčić, and Chapter Ten by Jörgen Torp) are based on published material, literary works, newspaper articles, or the reports and works of historians. The chapters dealing with the twentieth century (Chapter Eleven by Sille Kapper, Chapter Thirteen by Mats Nilsson, and Chapter Fourteen by Helena Saarikoski) are to a larger extent based on material from folklorists, ethnologists or collectors from the folk-dance revival. This material was generally collected and published in the twentieth century, and sources on dance from such experts would not usually reach back to the early nineteenth century. One chapter is mainly about the twentieth century but utilises historical sources other than folklore material (Chapter Twelve by Bakka), and the study dealing mostly with the twenty-first century uses near-contemporary sources with an ethnographic fieldwork angle (Chapter Fifteen by Tvrtko Zebec).

The rejection of, or resistance to, round dances is a theme pertinent to most of the period in which they were practised and performed, and most chapters discuss or refer to it. During the early nineteenth century there were complaints about the risks to dancers' health caused by the rapid turning and exhausting speed. There were also references to the indecency of the close embrace and claims that the wild turning was inappropriate, particularly for ladies of polite society, as discussed by Gremlicová in Chapter Six. In the early twentieth century, however, round dances were no longer considered to be so provocative. The new African-American-derived dances were far more troubling; they were choreo-musical forms rooted in ragtime and jazz, giving rise to dances such as the One-Step and the Foxtrot. Another controversial, but popular, South American form was the Tango. These forms are not covered here in their own right since they do not fall under our definition of round dances.

Still, dancing in general — and thereby also round dances — was attacked by religious lay movements, and moral panic over dance arose from time-to-time based on reports or rumours about drinking, fighting and sexual promiscuity, as explored by Nilsson and Bakka.

3. A Survey of the Chapters in the Book 55

Fig. 3.1 Alexander Altenhof, *Europe in 1812: Political Situation before Napoleon's Russian Campaign*. Map of Europe in 1812, immediately prior to the end of the Napoleonic wars and the many changes that took place in 1814. Wikimedia Commons, CC BY 3.0, https://commons.wikimedia.org/wiki/File:Europe_1812_map_de.png

Another recurrent theme is how national movements could embrace dances as national symbols or reject them as a harmful foreign influence, and there are examples of both attitudes in this book in the chapters by Stavělová, Gremlicová, Felföldi, Niemčić and Katarinčić, and myself. In cases of rejection, we see that new dances were created to serve as national symbols at the balls of the elite.

The second part of the nineteenth century was a period when round dances became more established and discussions about their role were less heated, and perhaps therefore less common. In the early part of the twentieth century, round dances received stiff competition from the African-American-derived dances, and slowly faded from the dancing masters' repertoires. At the same time, the folk-dance revival grew to become an important factor in the field of dance. Folk dance collectors mostly ignored the round dances, considering them to be too simple and too recent to merit preservation or cultivation. However, they remained central to the repertoire of 'dancing crowds',[2] and were therefore practised throughout the twentieth century in places where the influence of the new African-American-derived dances was not so strong. Several of the chapters deal with round dances in this period, when they were still controversial enough in many places to be either criticised or banned. They also aroused nostalgic feelings, as Saarikoski explores, and had different kinds of local revivals or resurrections parallel to, or even in competition with, the more elitist folk-dance revival, as discussed by Zebec.

Fig. 3.2 Theeuro, *Location Map of Armenia Within Europe*, 2010. The home nations of the authors in this book. Image by Egil Bakka, based on Wikimedia Commons, Public Domain, https://commons.wikimedia.org/wiki/File: Europe_map_armenia.png

Chapters on the Early Nineteenth Century

The earlier part of my introduction does not discuss the early history and reception of the two Slavic-derived branches of round dancing, the Polka and the Mazurka types. It is therefore very convenient that the two chapters by our Czech colleagues do just that.

---

2   Egil Bakka, 'Class Dimensions of Dance Spaces: Situating Central Agents Across Countries and Categories', in *Nordic Dance Spaces: Practicing and Imagining a Region*, ed. by Karen Vedel and Petri Hoppu (Farnham: Ashgate, 2014), pp. 129–58 (p. 131).

Stavělová (Czech Republic) discusses how the Polka was established as a Czech national symbol during the middle of the nineteenth century. She analyses a large number of sources that discuss the Polka, tracing the dance from its appearance in Czech national circles in the 1830s to its success in Paris in the 1840s. She discusses its consolidation as a Czech symbol through the work of music composers such as Bedřich Smetana in the second part of the century, arguing that it was first and foremost the name of the dance that carried political meaning: Polka as a cultural product fulfilled this goal to a lesser extent. In this way, Stavělová offers a detailed discussion of how the myth of the Polka became a significant aspect of Czech national culture.

Gremlicová (Czech Republic) provides a detailed analysis of newspaper discussions of dance. She shows how a text of the kind that is often read as evidence of resistance to new dances can be contextualised: she identifies the people behind it, and the political and cultural contexts to which they belonged. Gremlicová takes the Redowa as an example of the dances mentioned in newspaper discussions: a dance that has Slavic roots, just as the Polka does, and possesses the basic characteristics of the Mazurka types. By means of the newspaper sources, Gremlicová explores the reception of the Redowa in the Czech Republic.

Felföldi (Hungary) offers a broad survey of the Hungarian dance repertoire as it stood when the round dances began to spread into Hungary from neighbouring countries, and how they were met as a foreign influence that the ethnochoreologists did not engage with. He continues by presenting a catalogue that samples the variety of the rich Hungarian sources, which are currently unavailable in other languages. Describing the sociocultural and political context that nourished the substantial resistance to round dances in Hungary, Felföldi discusses the appearance of *Csárdás* as an alternative national dance. It has a clear similarity to the round dances, as opposed to the alternatives arising in other countries, and Felföldi discusses these similarities and differences, and the context from which the dance arose.

Kunej (Slovenia) surveys the sources for knowledge about the Waltz in her country. She follows the Waltz from its first appearance in Slovenian sources in the early nineteenth century until the early twenty-first century, and shows how it is still popular, particularly in the countryside. Her chapter presents an overview of how one dance type finds its place among other dance types, and how it survives changing influences.

Katarinčić and Niemčić (Croatia) portray the situation around 1830 when round dances arrived in Croatian cities and started to appear in the source material. They demonstrate the tension between national loyalties and the attraction of the fashionable dances imported from abroad, and how solutions were found to satisfy and combine the two streams of influence through the creation of the *Salonsko Kolo*. This dance is performed by couples forming large and complex formations reminiscent of the Polonaise, the Mazurka or contra dances. Katarinčić and Niemčić's article concludes with a discussion of the convoluted paths of this dance through history into the twentieth century, including how it moves back and forth between first and second existence, and how it also survives among diasporic communities of Croatians.[3]

Torp (Germany) is the only author who focuses on music. He examines how local newspapers in the Hamburg region can throw light on the concert tours of the Viennese composer Johann Strauss the Elder in the 1830s. Strauss was known as the King of the Waltz, and Torp investigates how new music spread during this period, arguing that the dissemination of music also has relevance for dance.

Chapters on the Early Twentieth Century

While the early and mid-nineteenth century was a period when round dances were still developing, by the early twentieth century they were more stable and consolidated. The main context in which dancing took place was still the informal dances of ordinary people who paid no attention to cultivating dance forms — 'the dancing crowds'.[4] This context has always been the most significant, because this is where many round dances have continued to be practised up to the present day. At typical social dance events, round dances dominated, even if African-American forms such as Tango, Foxtrot, and, later, rock 'n' roll slowly also gained their places. The dancing of the upper classes and the dance schools laid the foundations of ballroom dancing, along

---

3 Felix Hoerburger, 'Once again: On the Concept of "Folk Dance"', *Journal of the International Folk Music Council*, 20 (1968), 30–32, https://doi.org/10.2307/836068

4 Egil Bakka, 'Class Dimensions of Dance Spaces', p. 131.

with African-American-derived forms. The dance teachers developed standard forms for competition, and the Waltz was the only round dance that was taken up there. The third context for development was the folk-dance movement, which mostly cultivated more complex dances with firmer structures rather than the simple and loosely structured round dances (as Kapper also explores). Still, many of the folk-dance forms had music, steps and turning techniques in common with round dances, and the Waltz or the Polka were often part of more complex structures.

Kapper (Estonia) focuses mainly on the twentieth century, basing her discussion on information from folk dance collectors and researchers connected to the folk-dance movement. She surveys round dance forms described or referred to as part of this information, and discusses the relationship between round dances and other dances in a local community, particularly if that community was known as a stronghold of traditional dance. She also refers in brief to the folk-dance movement. In this way, she includes two of the groups mentioned above: the 'dancing crowds' and the folk dancers, and discusses the place round dancing has within each.

Nilsson (Sweden) addresses the moral outcries against dance as a phenomenon, which are levelled against most kinds of new dancing. He discusses the concepts of moral panic and 'folk devils', referring to a number of international research publications in the process. Nilsson concludes with a question about how adaptable these concepts are in contemporary studies. When dealing with the older source material, it can be difficult to distinguish between individual outcries and a moral panic, which is defined as including larger groups. Such panics can disappear without leaving many traces.

Saarikoski (Finland) bases the core of her article on ethnological archive material produced in the course of an inquiry in 1991 about the dancing on so-called pavilions or at outdoor dancing venues in the middle of the twentieth century. Accounts of the post-World-War-II period predominate, and Saarikoski finds nostalgia to be the primary attitude displayed as elderly people look back on their youth and happy memories of dancing. The dance repertoire was a mix of round dances and African-American-derived dances, and the distinction between the styles did not seem to be important to the dancers.

In my own chapter (Norway), I discuss, and contextualise, the banning of round dances by one of Norway's largest youth movements for about forty years from 1917. I show how the three popular movements that built assembly houses had conflicting attitudes towards social dancing, and dealt with it in different ways. The Liberal Youth Movement, which imposed the ban, gave a variety of reasons, first among them being that it destroyed interest in popular enlightenment, which was the main aim of the movement. The movement also did not consider round dances to be folk dances, and therefore held them to be of less national and educational value. However, only the lay Christians strongly rejected round dances as having a sinful and morally corrupting effect.

Zebec (Croatia) surveys and contextualises the place of round dances, and particularly the Polka, in the twentieth-century Croatia. He shows how the folk-dance movement largely ignored or even rejected the round dances as new and foreign. He then portrays the revival of a 'shaking' kind of Polka that has a history in the region, but only rose in popularity as late as the twenty-first century. The peculiar aspect of the revival is that it seems to have arisen independently of the folk-dance movement, among the 'dancing crowds'.

This book demonstrates how a dance genre grew from different roots and sources in Central Europe, being moulded into the form of individual couple dances in which the couples turn on their own axis along a circular path. The contributions show how these dances spread quickly across most parts of Europe, receiving similar criticisms of the risks to moral and physical health they supposedly posed, and a varied reception according to their perceived national value and other mechanisms of distinction. The fact that large parts of Europe are not covered here is to some degree coincidental, but it also shows that round dances are not considered traditional or rooted enough to be interesting to most researchers. This might be the case in the Balkans, for instance. The round dances, in any case, represent the largest export of European-derived social dances to other parts of the world, comparable only to the export of the European-derived theatrical dance. Round dances and round-dance-derived dances outside Europe are obvious areas where future researchers can build on this publication.

Bibliography

Bakka, Egil, 'Class Dimensions of Dance Spaces: Situating Central Agents Across Countries and Categories', in *Nordic Dance Spaces: Practicing and Imagining a Region*, ed. by Karen Vedel and Petri Hoppu (Farnham: Ashgate, 2014), pp. 129–58.

Hoerburger, Felix, 'Once again: On the Concept of "Folk Dance"', *Journal of the International Folk Music Council*, 20 (1968), 30–32, https://doi.org/10.2307/836068

4. The Waltz at Some Central European Courts

Egil Bakka

As discussed above (see Chapters 1 and 2), many of the books written about round dances circle around the outcries that these dances are morally unacceptable because of the tight embrace of, and closeness to, the opposite sex. The arguments include the view that the dances make women defenceless, that they are open to abuse, and that they are harmful to women's health. On the other hand, there are reports about dance crazes, endless enthusiasm, and, finally, in the later stages, nostalgic praise of the Waltz as a cornerstone of dance tradition and polite dancing.[1]

This chapter proposes that there are other perspectives that may not be so explicitly present in the source material but that still deserve to be discussed; one of these is the dimension of class. If we assume that round dances were folk dances which somehow became fashionable, they would, at the beginning, have been seen by the elite as lower-class and vulgar. Accepting them would therefore threaten the social distinction of the upper classes. The class journey of some of these dances is therefore in many ways parallel to that of the bourgeoisie in this period. Another perspective is offered by the stereotypes about neighbouring countries and the feelings and attitudes that members of the higher classes in the different countries had towards each other. Dances could be seen as foreign and marked by the negative qualities

---

[1] Theresa J. Buckland, 'Edward Scott: The Last of the English Dancing Masters', *Dance Research: The Journal of the Society for Dance Research*, 21 (2003), 3–35, https://doi.org/10.3366/3594050

of another nation, or they could be seen as highly fashionable or exotic due to the status of that country. The relationships between the empires and the nations they ruled were a key factor in how the round dances were seen, which is particularly apparent within the Austro-Hungarian Empire. The national movements promoting Hungarian and Slavic languages and cultures would take different stances to different round dances, depending on whether they were seen as national or foreign.

Much research and historiography has concentrated on the dancing queen and the dancing king of earlier centuries. In the era of round dances, no dancing ruler has been canonised. The rulers still had their attitudes and relations to dancing, be they negative or positive. The influence of non-dancing rulers is also an interesting topic in dance history. In this chapter, I will present quick sketches of some main courts and rulers in the period of the Waltz. The idea is to exemplify alternative readings of attitudes to the dances, questioning the arguments about health and morality mentioned above.

This book presents chapters with detailed discussion of the reception of, and attitudes towards, round dances in various countries, many of which, at that time, were not independent. This chapter, however, offers a backdrop to unify the more diverse accounts that make up the main part of the book, surveying the reception of the round dances at some Central European courts. These were comparable environments that also interacted with each other, which lends a cohesiveness to the survey. The source material is anecdotal, and taken from the courts in Vienna, Berlin, Paris, London, and Saint Petersburg.[2] The concluding proposals and interpretations will hopefully be taken up by new studies that scrutinise unpublished, more substantial sources from the courts to further improve our knowledge of this period.

An important problem in dealing with German sources from the late eighteenth to the early twentieth century is the fragmentation and complexity entailed by the division of political power in the country we now know as Germany, and the difference in attitudes to dance exercised by the different rulers. The number of courts changed from time to time, as did the influence of the different monarchs and princes. Several

---

2   Moscow was the capital city of Russia before 1732 and after 1917.

princesses and princes from small German courts became consorts for monarchs at the larger courts, as discussed below.

There were, however, two main centres of political power in the German lands in the eighteenth and nineteenth centuries: the Austrian court[3] in Vienna and the Prussian court in Berlin. The reception of the round dances at these courts does not reflect what happened in other classes of society, nor necessarily other German courts, but it still conveys the attitudes and motivations that lay behind the scepticism or bans of the round dances.

The Prussian Court

During the 1770s and 1780s, when we can assume the Waltz was spreading and establishing itself in the German lands, Frederick II, also known as Frederick the Great (1740–1886),[4] was king in Prussia. He and his queen consort had separate courts. His court comprised mainly men, a circumstance that did not favour social dancing. In his famous letter on education, the king mentions dance only twice, as a female activity, superficial, and unimportant.[5]

The attitude to dance at the Prussian court hardly changed during the short reign of the next royal couple, Frederick William II and Queen Frederica Louisa (1786–1797). During their reign, just before the woman who was to become the next queen of Prussia, Louise (1776–1810),[6] married into the royal family, she and her sister danced the Waltz at a ball of the Prussian court, defying the prohibition against it. The queen consort, their mother-in-law to be, was shocked and refused to allow her own daughters to dance it.

---

3   From 1868 known as the Austro-Hungarian court.
4   Friedrich der Große.
5   Gustav Berthold Volz, *Historische, militärische und philosophische Schriften, Gedichte und Briefe*, with illustrations by Adolph von Menzel (Köln: Anaconda, 2006).
6   King Frederick William II kept company with other women than the queen, making court life irregular. See Wikipedia contributors, 'Frederick William II of Prussia', *Wikipedia, The Free Encyclopedia*, 13 November 2019, https://en.wikipedia.org/wiki/Frederick_William_II_of_Prussia

Fig. 4.1 Postcard from Lith. Kunstanstalt Heinr. & Aug. Brüning. Hanau, 1901, on the occasion of the two-hundredth anniversary of the Prussian monarchy, picturing its kings between 1701 and 1901.[7] Wikipedia, Public Domain, https://de.wikipedia.org/wiki/Datei:200_Jahre_Preussen.jpg

---

7   The Waltz period started in Frederick the Great's reign (second row, first from left). The second king, Frederick William II, had a queen who banned the Waltz; the third

4. The Waltz at Some Central European Courts

Fig. 4.2 Anna Dorothea Lisiewska, *Portrait of a Princely Family*, c.1777. oil on canvas, National Museum in Warsaw. The picture shows Frederick William II of Prussia with his family. This was the family Louise married into; her husband-to-be is the first from the left. Wikimedia Commons, Public Domain, https://commons.wikimedia.org/w/index.php?title=File:Lisiewska_Portrait_of_a_Princely_family.jpg&oldid=237421193

The Crown Princess Louise soon acquired a striking popularity, partly due to her friendliness to ordinary people. The royal couple bought the Paretz estate out to the countryside, where every year they held an 'Erntefest' for the villagers, and participated in rural dancing.[8] This closeness to the countryside and to ordinary people was unusual for royals at that time, but it hardly changed the dancing practices at the court. Queen Louise died in 1810, after harsh times during the Napoleonic wars, which in many ways marked Prussia. Her husband Friedrich Wilhelm III was said to have little understanding for music and the arts, and Louise had to accommodate herself to the etiquette and protocol at the very stiff Prussian court.[9] Louise herself, however, reported in her diary that she danced a Waltz with the Russian emperor Alexander I, when she and her husband met with him in Memel,

---

    king, Frederick William III, was married to Queen Louise who danced the Waltz, and he attended the Vienna Congress. On the third line we find Wilhelm II who is celebrated in the middle, to the left his grandfather Wilhelm I and to the right his father, who ruled less than a year before dying.

8   Eilhard Erich Pauls, *Das Ende der galanten Zeit: Gräfin Voss am preussischen Hofe* (Lübeck: O. Quitzow, 1924), p. 157.

9   Gertrude Aretz, *Königin Luise* (Paderborn: Salzwasser-Verlag Gmbh, 2013).

Lithuania in 1802.[10] There is no mention of her husband dancing, but the Russian emperor was very popular with both of them for his kindness. Goethe's mother remembers in a letter to his son in 1806 that Queen Louise visited with her brother in 1790 and that they enjoyed the brief freedom from the stiff court etiquette, singing and dancing the Waltz.[11] In other words, the dancing of the Waltz was not a problem in itself, but to dance it at court balls was not permitted.

Fig. 4.3 An engraving by J. Fr. Bolt of a painting by J. C. Dähling, *Die Gartenlaube* [The Garden Arbor], 1883. Copper engraving. Reception of the Emperor Alexander I at Memel by their majesties Frederick William and Louise of Prussia in Memel, 1802. Wikimedia Commons, Public Domain, https://commons.wikimedia.org/wiki/File:Die_Gartenlaube_(1883)_b_785.jpg

Felix Eberty (1812–1884) grew up in Berlin in a bourgeois Jewish family and remembered that during his youth, 'dancing was seen as a frivolous French amusement that was detested in the aftermath of the

---

10 Aretz, *Königin Luise*, loc 1068.
11 Katharina E. Goethe, *Briefe — Band II* ([n.p.]: Tradition Classics, 2012). Aretz, *Königin Luise*, loc 2065, loc 118.

liberation war [1813]'.¹² Eberty also refers to his aunt Hanna, 'who when she was young had been an attractive partner for the French officers ¹³ who preferred to invite her for "Ekossaise" and "C". The Waltz and the Galop are newer, even if the Minuet already was about to die'.¹⁴

Fig. 4.4 Heinrich Anton Dähling, *Friedrich Wilhelm III and His Family*, 1806. Wikimedia Commons, Public Domain, https://commons.wikimedia.org/wiki/File:Friedrich_Wilhelm_III._und_seine_Familie.jpg

It seems that Louise's little revolt as crown princess did not have any effect, and that the prohibition of the Waltz remained at the Prussian court until its end in the early twentieth century. We do not have sources

---

12   Felix Eberty, *Jugenderinnerungen eines alten Berliners* (Berlin: Hertz, 1878), p. 181, https://books.google.co.uk/books?id=IW7omnNaArAC&pg=PP7&source=gbs_selected_pages&cad=2#v=onepage&q&f=false. Translated from the German by Egil Bakka.
13   This will probably have been during the French occupation of Prussia in the early nineteenth century.
14   Eberty, *Jugenderinnerungen eines alten Berliners*, p. 106.

to confirm that the Waltz was banned throughout this period, but it seems that the Prussian king, Louise's husband, avoided the Waltz at the Vienna congress in 1814, together with the Austro-Hungarian emperor. The next two Prussian kings were strict and serious, and the last of them, Wilhelm I (1797–1888) had an aversion against dancing ministers, and criticised Otto von Bismarck (1815–1898) and his other ministers for dancing.[15]

Fig. 4.5 Anton von Werner, Coronation of Wilhelm I as Emperor of Germany in Versailles, oil on canvas, Otto-Von-Bismarck-Stiftung, 1885. Wikimedia Commons, Public Domain, https://commons.wikimedia.org/wiki/File:Anton_von_Werner_-_Kaiserproklamation_in_Versailles_1871.jpg

Additionally, we have firm evidence about William II's practice in an account from his daughter, Princess Victoria Louise (1892–1980). This makes it likely that there was a more or less continuous ban on the Waltz all the way up to World War II, as Braun and Gugerli also assume.[16]

---

15 Anna Ebers, *Das Bismarck-Buch* (Paderborn: Salzwasser-Verlag Gmbh, 1909), p. 72.
16 Rudolf Braun and David Gugerli, *Macht des Tanzes — Tanz der Mächtigen: Hoffeste und Herrschaftszeremoniell, 1550–1914* (Munich: Verlag C. H. Beck, 1993); Viktoria

4. The Waltz at Some Central European Courts 71

Fig. 4.6 Postcard of Wilhelm II and his family, 1912. His daughter Victoria Louise is the furthest woman on the right. Wikimedia Commons, Public Domain, https://commons.wikimedia.org/wiki/File:Kaiser_Wilhelm_II_Familie_main35.jpg

Duchess Victoria Louise relates her own experiences at the court balls of her father, Emperor Wilhelm II, where she first 'came out' in society in 1910:

> The court ball was basically not a celebration of jubilant merriment but an act of representation. [...] For the young people the dance was nevertheless the main point. Dance is, however, not dance, for sure the present day's youth would hesitate to describe the figures, chains and steps that were danced by the court community by this name. There were the Minuets, Gavottes, Francaises, Lancers, Polonaises and Quadrilles. Some of these dances were already [a] hundred years or more of age. My father valued their continued practice, and even decided that this or that dance should be reintroduced.[17]

Lily Braun (1865–1916) — a lady who was twenty-seven years older and frequented the Berlin court — confirms this, reporting in her memoirs that in her childhood, when she attended the dance school for

---

Luise, Herzogin, *Im Glanz der Krone* (Göttingen: Göttinger Verlagsanstalt, 1967); Pauls, *Das Ende der galanten Zeit*, p. 157.
17 Viktoria Luise, *Im Glanz der Krone*, p. 210. Translated from the German by Egil Bakka.

children connected to the court, the Waltz was not taught because it was considered inappropriate and therefore forbidden.[18] This was during the reign of Wilhelm I, so we can assume that he maintained the ban on the Waltz. At a later stage, she relates episodes when she and her partner forgot about the prohibition and danced the Waltz regardless. Somebody present commented that the Waltz was only forbidden because nobody knew how to dance it; the couple was praised for their dancing and allowed to dance once more.[19]

The Prussian court even had a 'court Waltz', which 'was not more or less a Viennese Waltz, much more a kind of Galop'.[20] 'The Viennese Waltz was not considered to be suitable for the court at official balls. It was forbidden to dance it in the presence of the Emperor and Empress'. When the Emperor entered the dance hall, the Viennese Waltz was interrupted.[21] Eduard von der Heydt (1882–1964), just ten years older than Victoria Louise, confirms and expands on her account:

> In answer to my question, why an experienced dancer of [the] Waltz was not allowed to turn to the left, I was told that their Majesties had the opinion that it would look untidy; everyone should turn in unison to the right.[22] The so-called Court Waltz at the official court balls was a Waltz in Galop tempo, and descended from the time of the old Wilhelm [I]. The impression of the 'prudishness' of the Empress Augusta[23] came from her court ladies [...] from whom she was inseparable.[24]

Theresa Buckland discusses the unpopularity of reversing in British high society in the late nineteenth century, even though the Waltz was fully accepted.[25] Lily Braun also confirms the ban on the Waltz at the Berliner court in her childhood in the 1870s, stating that the children

---

18   Lily Braun, *Memoiren einer Sozialistin* (Altenmünster: Jazzybee Verlag, 2012), p. 48.
19   Braun, *Memoiren*, p. 204.
20   Viktoria Luise, *Im Glanz der Krone*, p. 213.
21   Ibid., p. 215.
22   Theresa J. Buckland, *Society Dancing: Fashionable Bodies in England, 1870–1920* (Houndmills, Basingstoke, Hampshire; New York: Palgrave Macmillan, 2011), p. 64 refers to the same restriction at the British court, where it was called reversing.
23   Wilhelm I and his Empress Augusta were Wilhelm II's grandparents, and the grandson took over after an interregnum of only ninety-nine days of his parents. Wilhelm II was chosen to follow in the footsteps of his grandfather's authoritarian style.
24   Eduard von der Heydt and Werner von Rheinbaben, *Auf dem Monte Verità: Erinnerungen und Gedanken über Menschen, Kunst und Politik* (Zürich: Atlantis, 1958), p. 100.
25   Buckland, *Society Dancing*, p. 64.

learned the Polka and the Francaise, but not the Waltz; the latter was prohibited as inappropriate even at children's balls at the court.[26]

The new dances imported from the Americas, such as the Tango, were even more strictly banned. The Kaiser issued orders that no one should dance a Tango or Turkey Trot at the season's balls, nor 'go to the house of any person who, at any time, whether officers were present or not, had allowed any of these new dances to be danced'.[27]

Wilhelm II's revival of old dances at his court had a nostalgic flair, in harmony with his wish for a splendour and grandeur that he could only find modelled in the past. Lily Braun reports how the Minuet was revived for a court ball, and how historical costumes were also made to grace the event.[28] It is paradoxical that this occurred at the same time as the budding folk dance movement. There are similarities as well as differences between the revivals, but it is difficult to ascertain whether there is any explicit connection between the two.

Fig. 4.7 Adolph von Menzel, *Das Ballsouper* [Dinner at the Ball], oil on canvas, Alte Nationalgalerie, 1878. Menzel was close to the Prussian court circles, so this is probably a realistic representation of a meal at a court celebration in the late 1870s. Wikimedia Commons, Public Domain, https://commons.wikimedia.org/wiki/File:Adolph_Menzel_-_Das_Ballsouper_-_Google_Art_Project.jpg

---

26 Braun, *Memoiren*, p. 48.
27 Giles MacDonogh, *Prussia: The Perversion of an Idea* (London: Sinclair-Stevenson, 1994).
28 Braun, *Memoiren*, p. 210.

The Austro-Hungarian Court

From a twenty-first-century perspective, one would expect that the court in Vienna would have accepted and even embraced waltzing quite early. There are, however, sources that show the opposite, that the Waltz was forbidden at official court balls until the late nineteenth century.

It has been repeatedly claimed that there is a Waltz in the Opera *Una Cosa Rara*, with music by the composer Vicente Martín y Soler (1754–1806) (see Fig. 4.8) and libretto by Lorenzo Da Ponte (1749–1838).[29] The German dance historian Oskar Bie argues against earlier claims that this was the first Waltz to be performed,[30] but in our context the event might have some relevance. The opera had a tremendous success at its premiere at the Royal Burg Theatre in Vienna in 1786, during the reign of Joseph II (1780–1790).[31] The monarch (b. 1741-d. 1790) promoted music and dance, and seemed to have directly engaged with the staging of the opera. He is said to have insisted on the carrying through of the staging, when the musicians complained about the music.[32]

Fig. 4.8 Video: 'Martín y Soler: Una cosa rara (opera completa)', 2:45:45, posted online by Classicus Musicalis, *Youtube*, https://www.youtube.com/watch?v=TtSFzFoUCoc&t=8251s. This historically informed production was directed by Francisco Negrin, and was filmed at the Drottningholm Court Theatre of Sweden in 1993, with Nicholas McGegan leading the Drottningholm Court Theatre Orchestra. The dance scenes we are referring to start at 2:35:46, and the dance in question does not look like a Waltz.

Joseph II had strong ideas about fostering a more egalitarian society, and was radical in his care for the lower classes. He lifted censorship and curtailed the powers of the aristocracy and the Church. Presenting a dance of the lower classes on the stage might have harmonised well with his attitudes. The opera might therefore have contributed to making the Waltz more acceptable among the upper classes of Vienna.

---

29   Lorenzo Da Ponte and Vicente Martín y Soler, *Una Cosa Rara*, 17 November 1786, http://www.librettidopera.it/cosarara/a_02.html
30   Oskar Bie, *Der Tanz* (Berlin: J. Bard, 1919), p. 228.
31   John Platoff, 'A New History for Martín's "Una Cosa Rara"', *The Journal of Musicology*, 12 (1994), 85–115 (p. 85), https://doi.org/10.1525/jm.1994.12.1.03a00050
32   Ibid., p. 88.

4. The Waltz at Some Central European Courts 75

There are, however, no signs in the libretto, nor in the scores, of the word Waltz or similar terms. There is a melody that is definitely Waltz-like in recent recordings of the music, and here the libretto says: 'scene nineteen: The above-mentioned [the actors already on stage]; enter Lille, and Ghita dressed without jackets with a little guitar etc. Two villagers bring out chairs adorned with flowers and offer them to the queen and the prince'.[33] Then follows a tribute to the queen, sung by the villagers and their soloists. This is the melody that sounds like a Waltz, but no dancing is mentioned. After a while, when the Waltz melody is finished, the village hero and heroine are dancing. At the end, there is a scene ('Finale II (Seghidiglia)') in which the hero and the heroine are still dancing, but this dance is said to be a *Seghidiglia*.

A second early source dates from 1801–1802, when the castrato singer Luigi Marchesi (1754–1814) visited the court in Vienna and came to be on very friendly terms with the Empress Maria Theresa (1772–1807), granddaughter of the famous Maria Theresa. Her mother, Maria Caroline, Queen of Naples was worried about his visit, saying that her daughter even danced Waltzes and Polkas[34] with Marchesi.[35] We cannot tell from the text if the main problem is the man or the dancing. Nonetheless, it shows that royals and members of the court might learn modern dances of their time, even if the rulers or the keepers of etiquette did not allow them in the official court context.

Firm evidence for the ban on the Waltz comes from the Vienna Congress. At least two sources suggest that Waltzes were played only when the Emperor Francis I (reigned 1804–1835) and the Prussian King had left the ball (see below). It is not likely that court practices changed during the reign of the next emperor (1835–1848), the epileptic and weak Ferdinand I. In an account of an unusually merry ninth anniversary party at the court in 1839, even his empress Maria Anna is said to have danced, 'although she during her eight previous years at the court never took so much as a step of the Waltz'.[36]

---

33 Da Ponte and Martín y Soler, *Una Cosa Rara*, http://www.librettidopera.it/zpdf/cosarara_bn.pdf. Quote translated from the Italian by Egil Bakka. There may of course exist other librettos or similar sources where a Waltz is referred to.
34 The term Polka is an anachronism, probably due to Rice's translation.
35 John A. Rice, *Empress Marie Therese and Music at the Viennese Court, 1792–1807* (Cambridge, UK: Cambridge Unversity Press, 2007), p. 58.
36 Egon Caesar Conte Corti, *Vom Kind zum Kaiser Kindheit und erste Jugend Kaiser Franz Josephs I. und seiner Geschwister* (Munich: Graz, 1951), p. 167.

The last Austrian emperor to enjoy a lengthy reign, Francis Joseph I (1830–1916) is reported to have been an elegant and eager dancer as a child and a young man.[37] Even from his court there is, however, an anecdote about the ban on the Waltz:

> The Waltz, which Strauss and Lanner have made popular, was for a long time not considered appropriate even at the Viennese court. A beautiful story is told from the court ball, where the Waltz finally was danced for the first time. The young people present were entranced by the high-flown ring [of the music] and defied the directives. For the general adjutant (1887–1917) of the Emperor Francis Joseph, the Count [Eduard von] Paar, this seemed a sacrilege, a crime committed against the untouchable laws of the ceremonial. With indignation, he hastened to his master. 'Your Majesty, in there they are playing the Straussian Waltz'. The Emperor slowly looked up at him and asked: 'Well, does it give the people joy, then?' and when the count affirmed, added: 'If it gives them joy, then let them continue'.[38]

Fig. 4.9 Josef Kreutzinger, *Porträt der Familie des österreichischen Kaisers* [Portrait of the Family of the Austrian Emperor], c.1805. Oil on canvas. Pictured are Franz I, later hosting the Vienna Congress, his queen Maria Therese, who danced with Marches, and the boy on the far left was to become Emperor Ferdinand I. Wikimedia Commons, Public Domain, https://commons.wikimedia.org/wiki/File:Josef_Kreutzinger_-_Kaiserliche_Familie.jpg

---

37 Corti, *Vom Kind zum Kaiser*, pp. 155–56.
38 Viktoria Luise, *Im Glanz der Krone*, p. 215. Translated from the German by Egil Bakka.

Fig. 4.10 Engraving after Richard Cosway, *The Italian Castrato Singer Luigi Marchesi*, 1790. National Portrait Gallery, London. He was a highly respected artist and a charming personality. Wikimedia Commons, Public Domain, https://commons.wikimedia.org/wiki/File:Luigi_Marchesi.jpg

Several persons at the court in Vienna wrote diaries or memoirs in which dance names such as the Quadrille, the Cotillion and the Francaise are mentioned, but not the Waltz.[39] In February 1874, Francis Joseph visited the Russian court; the Prince and the Princess of Wales as well as the Danish Crown Prince were also there. A report from a ball tells us that some round dances had been danced before the emperor entered. Then the emperor sat, watching two Quadrilles, before leading a Polonaise and leaving early with his court. We see the same pattern in several sources: the Waltz seems not to have been danced in the presence of the emperor, even if this was not explicitly stated or commented upon.[40]

Fig. 4.11 Wilhelm Gause, *Hofball in Wien*, 1900. Historisches Museum der Stadt Wie. The nobility greets the Emperor Francis Joseph at a Court Ball in Vienna. Wikimedia Commons, Public Domain, https://commons.wikimedia.org/wiki/File:Wilhelm_Gause_Hofball_in_Wien.jpg

---

39 Mária Festetics, *Das Tagebuch der Gräfin Marie Festetics: Kaiserin Elisabeths intimste Freundin*, ed. by Gudula Walterskirchen and Beatrix Meyer (St. Pölten, Salzburg, Vienna: Residenz Verlag, 2014), pp. 152, 2550, 4325; Marie Valerie von Osterreich, *Das Tagebuch der Lieblingstochter von Kaiserin Elisabeth 1878–1899*, ed. by Martha Schad and Horst Schad (Munich: Langen Muller, 1998), p. 108. It is possible that the Cotillion included Waltz or other round dances.

40 Francis Joseph I, Emperor of Austria-Hungary, *Seiner Majestät des Kaisers Franz Joseph I von Österreich Reise nach Russland im Monate Februar 1874* (Vienna: Kaiserlich-Königlichen Hof- und Staatsdruckerei, 1874), pp. 62–63, http://catalog.hathitrust.org/api/volumes/oclc/1624904.html

There may well be sources that say the Waltz was not really banned at the court in Vienna, or that the material presented above is weak. The main point is that it challenges the impression that there was no reservation in the acceptance of the Waltz, and causes us to ask from where the resistance in court circles against the Waltz came. It is also striking to note that extensive searches have hardly resulted in any political cartoons or satirical pictures produced in the German lands in the late eighteenth and early nineteenth centuries. In contrast, such pictures can be found in abundance in France and the United Kingdom in the same period.

The British Court

The reluctance to waltz at the main German courts is not mirrored at the court in London, where Queen Victoria (1819–1901) is reported to have danced Quadrilles and the Waltz at her fourteenth birthday. She was an accomplished and eager dancer into her old age.[41]

The British royal family was tightly connected to Germany in the eighteenth and early nineteenth centuries. On the male side, the King of Hanover ascended to the British throne as George I in 1714. This established a personal union of the thrones that lasted until 1837 through the reigns of five monarchs. George III, Queen Victoria's grandfather, was the first of them to be born and raised in Britain. On the female side, Queen Victoria's grandmother Queen Charlotte, her mother Princess Victoria, and the queen consorts of her two uncles and predecessors on the throne were all princesses from smaller German courts. Even Victoria's husband was German. English cartoons mocking royals and their German background are plentiful (see Fig. 4.12).

In fact, righteous indignation and personal malice may have been partly responsible for Lord Byron's satire 'The Waltz' (1812), yet its uneven tone, a mixture of humour and bitter mockery, and its many Regent-baiting and anti-Hanoverian allusions, both pointed and hidden, convey the anti-Germanic sentiments of an outraged English patriot as much as they do the grievances of an infirm celebrity or a puritanical

---

41 Helen Rappaport, *Queen Victoria: A Biographical Companion* (Santa Barbara: ABC-CLIO, 2003), p. 113.

poet.⁴² Implicit in the poem is a running attack upon the Germanic invasion of English life and letters under the first four Georges; the Germanophobia found in the poem, however, is largely an extension of the poet's violent antipathy to the Waltz-loving Prince Regent.⁴³

Fig. 4.12 James Gillray, *Monstrous Craws, at a New Coalition Feast*, 1787. Etching with aquatint. King George III dressed as an old woman, the Queen, and the Prince of Wales seated around a basin perched on the laps of the king and queen; they eagerly spoon the contents, representing gold coins, into their mouths. Pouches hanging from their necks like goitres are full, except for that of the Prince of Wales, whose pouch is empty. The gate to the treasury, in the background, is open. Wikimedia Commons, Public Domain, https://commons.wikimedia.org/wiki/File:Monstrous_craws,_at_a_new_coalition_feast.jpg

---

42 Byron suffered from a deformity of his right foot, giving him a limp and making dancing difficult for him.
43 The later King George IV (1762–1830).

Fig. 4.13 Thomas Phillips, *Portrait of Lord Byron in Albanian Dress*, 1813. Oil on canvas. Government Art Collection at the British Embassy, Athens. Lord Byron, was a leading British Romantic poet. Wikimedia Commons, Public Domain, https://commons.wikimedia.org/wiki/File:Lord_Byron_in_Albanian_Dress_by_Phillips,_1813.jpg

Waltz: An Apostrophic Hymn was written in the fall of 1812, when Byron's hatred of the Prince had become so intense that it coloured all his thinking about Germany:[44]

> Although inspired by personal malice against the Regent, Byron's satire nevertheless accurately gauges the growing resentment in England against the German cast of English life. The frequent and malicious thrusts at the corpulent George IV reflect the attitude of many patriotic Englishmen who looked upon the corpulent George IV as the complete embodiment of German vulgarity and depravity, despite his attempts to reject his German ancestry.[45] The Waltz, 'this fiend of German birth, destitute of grace, delicacy, and propriety',[46] met with hostile opposition right from the time it was first danced at Almack's in about 1812. Loyal Englishmen shuddered when they thought about its perverting effects upon English manners and morals.[47]

The strong attacks on the Waltz as German and vulgar did confirm that the British court already danced it, probably long before 1812, but this was the time when it began to gain acceptance. The elderly royal couple at this time, King George III and Queen Charlotte, who reigned from 1760 to 1820, were dancers, not least the queen,[48] but they belonged to the Minuet generation.[49] At a small party in 1778 we are told that the royal children made a small dance performance of a Minuet.[50] In 1811, their son became regent due to his father's illness, and he was the Waltz-lover whom Byron hated. He remained in power as regent, and ruled as King George IV from 1820. At his death in 1830, his brother William IV took over and, finally, in 1837, their niece Queen Victoria came to the

---

44 William Childers, 'Byron's "Waltz": The Germans and their Georges', *Keats-Shelley Journal*, 18 (1969), 81–95 (p. 82).
45 Thomas Creevey, *The Creevey Papers*, ed. by Sir Herbert Maxwell (New York: E. P. Dutton, 1904), p. 47.
46 Mosco Carner, *The Waltz* (London: Parrish, 1948), p. 20.
47 Childers, 'Byron's "Waltz"', p. 82.
48 Walley Chamberlain Oulton, *Authentic and Impartial Memoirs of Her Late Majesty, Charlotte, Queen of Great Britain and Ireland: Containing a Faithful Retrospect of Her Early Days, Her Marriage, Coronation, Correspondence, Illness, Death, Funeral Obsequies, &c. &c. Interspersed with Occasional Anecdotes of the Royal Family, and Other Illustrious Personages. Including various Interesting and Original Particulars, Never before Published* (London: J. Robins and Co., Albion Press, 1819), p. 68.
49 Queen Charlotte came to Britain in 1761, probably too early for her to have learnt any Waltz at home.
50 John Van der Kiste, *George III's Children* (New York: The History Press, 2013), p. 18.

throne. There is, in other words, no sign of scepticism of the dance in the British royal family during this period, and with the family's close connections to smaller, probably more liberal courts in Germany, they could easily learn to Waltz. One of Queen Caroline's[51] ladies in waiting reports rather viciously about a ball soon after Caroline's arrival in Britain to marry the crown prince George (later George IV) in 1795. She states that it was 'very difficult to get together personages sufficient to make up a ball', and that another German princess was not sufficiently attractive:[52]

> But what was my horror when I beheld the poor Princess enter, dressed en Venus, or rather not dressed, further than the waist. I was, as she used to say herself, 'all over shock'. A more injudicious choice of costume could not be adopted; and when she began to Waltz, the *terrae motus*[53] was dreadful. Waltz she did, however, the whole night, with pertinacious obstinacy; and amongst others whom she honoured with her hand upon this occasion, was Sismondi.[54] These two large figures turning round together were quite miraculous. As I really entertained a friendship for the Princess, I was unfeignedly grieved to see her make herself so utterly ridiculous.[55]

From these accounts we can assume that the crown prince, as well as the crown princess, knew the Waltz already well before their wedding in 1795.[56] Unlike the main German courts, the English royalty probably took up the Waltz well before the upper classes. The scepticism of their German background, the lack of respect for the couple's looks and lifestyles, and the criticism of their separation and bitter fights made it difficult for the English aristocracy to accept them, but nothing could stop the Waltz.

---

51 Caroline of Brunswick (1768–1821).
52 Charlotte C. Bury, *Diary Illustrative of the Times of George the Fourth, Interspersed with Original Letters from the Late Queen Caroline, and from various Other Distinguished Persons* (London: H. Colburn, 1838), p. 85.
53 'Movement of the earth' [earthquake].
54 A Swiss historian who visited London in 1894–1895.
55 Bury, *Diary Illustrative of the Times*, p. 85.
56 He was thirty-two and she was twenty-seven, and they probably established their dance repertoire at the latest in their early twenties.

Fig. 4.14 George Cruikshank, *Merry-Making on the Regent's Birthday*, 1812. Print shows George, the Prince Regent, dancing and drinking at a lavish party with the wife of a man who sits with a dejected look on his face and holding a sheet of paper, 'Order of the day', which lists 'Breakfast — 2 to be HUNG at Newgate' with lunch, dinner and tea schedules followed by 'Supper — German fling, d [penny] sausage with bread, cheese & kisses &c &c, Dancing all night', with his feet resting on sheet music titled 'The black joke', while behind him stand two demon-like figures playing French horns, alluding to his present cuckold condition. Through an opening in the palace is a view of a gallows and poor persons seeking relief. Wikimedia Commons, Public Domain, https://commons.wikimedia.org/wiki/File:Merry_making_on_the_regents_birth_day,_1812_LCCN2003689159.tif

An article by William Childers discusses the early reception of the Waltz in England: [...] 'the year 1812 has been called "The Year of the Waltz"'.[57] Reminiscing about the introduction of the Waltz into the West End of London in 1812, Thomas Raikes describes its impact upon society: 'No event ever produced so great a sensation in English society as the introduction of the German Waltz. [...] Old and young returned to school and the mornings were now absorbed at home in practising the figures of a French Quadrille or whirling a chair round the room to learn the step and measure of the German Waltz'.[58] A second commentator

---

57 Peter Quennell, *Byron: The Years of Fame* (London: Reprint Society, 1943), p. 78.
58 Quoted in introduction to George Gordon Byron, *Waltz, an Apostrophic Hymn* (London: S. Gosnell, 1812), p. 476, https://en.wikisource.org/wiki/The_Works_of_Lord_Byron_(ed._Coleridge,_Prothero)/Poetry/Volume_1/The_Waltz

on the English rage for Quadrilles and dancing parties is Lady Caroline Lamb, who was especially fond of the dance: 'we had them in the great drawing-room at Whitehall. All the *bon ton* assembled there continually. There was nothing so fashionable'.[59]

A battle was fought with moral indignity against the new fashion. At the same time, an excited, frivolous enthusiasm arose. The two sides probably did not influence each other much; they were somehow incompatible as two sides of an argument. The critique of the first was partly political, aimed at German domination and a perceived lack of royal style; partly it was based in issues of morality and distinction. The second may have found its inspiration in reports from Paris that the Waltz was in fashion there, and from an exotic visit to London by the elegantly waltzing and good-looking Russian Tsar in 1814 (see the section below, 'The Russian Court').

Fig. 4.15 George Cruikshank, *Longitude and Latitude of St Petersburgh*, 1813. A caricature of Countess Lieven waltzing at Almack's. Countess Lieven was the one of the lady patronesses of Almack's and was the wife of the Russian Ambassador. (St Petersburg was then the capital of Russia.) Wikimedia Commons, Public Domain, https://commons.wikimedia.org/w/index.php?search=Waltzing+at+Almacks%2C+George+Cruikshank+&title=Special%3ASearch&go=Go#/media/File:Almack%27s_Longitude_and_Latitude.jpg

---

59   Byron, *Waltz*, I, 476.

The French Court

The French Revolution that started in 1789 obviously influenced the French court decisively in the decades that followed. It does not seem likely that the Waltz was even in question at the court during the old regime. German research has pointed to the Ländler as a basis for the Waltz, and a French dancing master published a version of the Allemande with figures very similar to those of the Ländler as early as 1769.[60] The music he offers is 2/4, and the French seem to look at the pre-revolutionary Allemande and the Waltz as two very different phenomena. The French author Antoine Calliot (1759–1839) describes in retrospect the dancing and the dancing masters during and after the revolution in a book published in 1827. He witnessed the last years of the old regime, the revolution, Napoleon's reign, and the restoration, and his text seems to betray a sympathy for the old regime.

Fig. 4.16 Carle Vernet, a depiction of a couple dressed in French formal court styles, 1973. Detail from the series of the *Incroyables et Merveilleuses* [the incredible men, and the marvellous women], who were members of a fashionable aristocratic subculture in Paris during the French Directory (1795–1799). They held hundreds of balls and started fashion trends in clothing and mannerisms. This couple are dressed in the fashion *l'ancien régime*, showing a contrast to the new mentality of the revolution. Image scanned by H. Churchyard from Blanche Payne's *History of Costume* (New York: Harper & Row, 1965), Wikimedia Commons, Public Domain, https://commons.wikimedia.org/wiki/File:1793-1778-contrast-right.jpg

---

60   Simon Guillaume and Jacques La Hante, *Almanach dansant, ou positions et attitudes de l'Allemande: Avec un discours préliminaire sur l'origine et l'utilité de la danse* (Paris: chez l'auteur ruë des Arcis, 1769), https://gallica.bnf.fr/ark:/12148/btv1b8626149j/f41.item.zoomin

4. *The Waltz at Some Central European Courts* 87

Fig. 4.17 John Cassell, *Sans Culottes dancing the Carmagnole*, 1865. Image from *Cassell's Illustrated History of England*, Volume 5 (London, Paris, & New York: Cassell Petter & Galpin, 1865), p. 613. The *sans-culottes* were people of the lower classes, militant partisans of the French Revolution, and this was their dance and song in particular at that time. Wikimedia Commons, Public Domain, https://commons.wikimedia.org/wiki/File:P613_SANS_CULOTTES_DANS_THE_CARMAGNOLE.jpg

During the terrible days of the revolutionary government, since the male and female Jacobins[61] were the only ones who danced, the great masters of the Minuet and Gavotte and Allemande found themselves condemned to a fatal rest of their bourse and forced to give place to Masters of an inferior order. [...]

After 9 Thermidor,[62] joy and dancing were renewed with even more brilliance and among even more people, since they had been banned for such a long time. Then there was not a single young girl who did not hurry to take lessons in an art so uniquely suitable for making oneself distinguished in public and private gatherings.

The dancing masters ran in all directions, their violins under their arms or under their coats, to go and teach their charming art from house to house and they did not return home before night, panting, tired and all covered in sweat. It was at this same time, when so many families deplored the tragic death of their leaders and of what that was most precious to them, that we saw dances established on the ground of the old cemetery Saint Sulpice. The dance teachers were more in vogue than ever during the consulate and the empire.[63] The court, the palaces the hotels, the residential schools of young ladies, the houses of bankers, in short, all doors were opened to them and all the beauties rushed to them to receive their lessons. It was a complete revolution in the choreographic art. Dancing masters occupied themselves in inventing new figures, new steps and new 'contredanses', or in borrowing from abroad what their genius could not invent, in order to instil trust in their skills and strengthen their reputation.

In this way the 'Walse', heavily executed by the male and female dancers from Germania, was imported to France to the despair of mothers and husbands. This lascivious dance was for many years the most fashionable dance at the grand houses and among the bourgeois. Today it is no longer much in use except in the most common balls and in the taverns.[64]

---

61 Led by Robespierre, the left-wing Jacobins, supported by the *sans-culottes* of the Parisian working class, established a revolutionary dictatorship, the Reign of Terror.
62 On nine Thermidor, year II (27 July 1794), there was a parliamentary revolt that led to the fall of Maximilien Robespierre. The revolutionary fervour and the Reign of Terror then collapsed.
63 The French Revolution is considered to have ended in 1799 when Napoleon overthrew the Directorate. He established power during the Consulate period (1799–1804). Then came Napoleon's empire (1804–1814/15).
64 Antoine Caillot, *Mémoires pour servir à l'histoire des moeurs et usages des Français: depuis les plus hautes conditions, jusqu'aux classes inférieures de la société, pendant le règne de Louis XVI, sous le Directoire exécutif, sous Napoléon Bonaparte, et jusqu'à nos jour*, 2 vols (Paris: Dauvin, 1827), II: pp. 247–49, https://gallica.bnf.fr/ark:/12148/bpt6k6378010q.texteImage. Translated from the French by Egil Bakka.

Even if Napoleon did take dance lessons in his youth, in Paris as well as in Valence, he never became a skilled dancer.[65] An episode reported by the French imperial family around 1810 gives an impression of their relaxed attitudes to the Waltz. At the time of this episode, Napoleon's two sisters, his adopted son, and the lover of his oldest sister are all in their late twenties, except the lover who is around twenty-five, a good-looking, cocky army officer well known for his audacity. This man insists that he wants to dance a Waltz with the hostess, who is his mistress, even if the next dance on the programme is a 'contredanse'. The viceroy, Napoleon's son, is about to dance with the other sister and calmly asks the conductor to keep to the programme, smoothing over the scandalous behaviour of the lover. The problem does not seem to be the Waltz, but that a nobody dares to interfere with the programme.[66]

An anecdote from a writer whose mother worked for the Empress Josephine may not be true in detail, but is still realistic in its basic points. In 1810, Napoleon is waiting to receive his new wife from Austria. His niece says that all Germans want to dance the Waltz, and as a good husband he should be ready to dance it with his wife. Napoleon admits that he is not good at it, but tries to dance with his niece who knows the dance well. He manages to dance some rounds, quite awkwardly, but becomes so dizzy that he has to sit down, saying that his wife will have to be content that he dances the Monaco with her. This is a simple Contradance he knows.[67] Napoleon understands that he needs to dance sometimes, but he recognises his lack of skill, which is mentioned in several sources.[68]

---

65 John Holland Rose, *Napoleon: Lefnadsteckning efter nya källor*, trans. by Ernst Lundquist, 2 vols (Stockholm: Hugo Gebers Förlag, 1907), I: p. 115.
66 Georgette Ducrest, *Mémoires sur l'impératrice Joséphine, sur la ville, la cour et les salons de Paris sous l'Empire* (Paris: Georges Barba, 1863), p. 74, https://gallica.bnf.fr/ark:/12148/bpt6k6310101z.texteImage
67 Emile Marco de Saint-Hilaire, *Napoléon au bivouac, aux Tuilleries et á Sainte-Hélène anecdotes inédites sur la famille et la cour imperiale* (Bruxellès: Meline, Cans, 1845), p. 159, http://books.google.com/books?id=rZUvAAAAMAAJ
68 Gertrude Aretz, *Napoleon und die Gräfin Maria Walewska* (Hamburg: Severus Verlag, 2013), p. 25; Louis Constant Wairy, *Mémoires de Constant, premier valet de chambre de l'Empereur, sur la vie privée de Napoléon, sa famille et sa cour* (Paris: Ladvocat, 1830), p. 271.

Fig. 4.18 Ivan I. Terebenev, Russians teaching Napoleon to dance, etching, Bodleian Library, 1979. Translation of caption: 'You tried to make us march; we now will make you dance'. Napoleon's dancing is more often shown figuratively than in a real-life context. Wikimedia Commons, CC BY 4.0, https://commons.wikimedia.org/wiki/File:Bodleian_Libraries,_Russians_teaching_Napoleon_to_dance-_Napoleon_Bonaparte_premier_consul_s%27est_rendu_%C3%A0_Notre_Dame_pour_y_entendre_la_Saint.jpg

Jean-Michel Guilcher in his very advanced study of the French Contradance describes how the social importance of dance varied through the decades after the revolution, and how the prominence of highly ambitious and advanced dancing by the few gave way to a far more relaxed attitude that enabled everybody to join in.[69]

In summary, there is little, if any, sign of any condemnation of the Waltz at the French court during Napoleon's reign. He was a parvenu ruling half of Europe, and, being a mediocre dancer, to see dancing skills as a distinction valued at court was not in his interest; likewise, it is hard to believe that issues of morality were of any concern for him.

---

69 Jean-Michel Guilcher, *La contredanse et les renouvellements de la danse Française* (Paris: Mouton., 1969), p. 160–61.

The Russian Court

If one seeks to find a dancing European ruler from the early nineteenth century, the Russian emperor Alexander I (1777–1825) would be a very good candidate. He reigned from 1802–1825 and contemporary sources from court circles in other countries are full of praise for his kindness, friendliness, good looks and dancing skills.[70] German newspapers reported on his impact, and how he charmed the English ladies and boosted the popularity of the Waltz during his visit to London in July 1814.[71] He is said to have introduced the Waltz in the famous Almack's with one of the patrons there, the Russian Countess van Lieven.[72]

The old 'Oberhofmeisterin' at the Prussian court, Sophie von Voss, reported on her visit to the Russian court in St. Petersburg in January 1808. She danced the Polonaise several times, even with the emperor.[73] Whether the Tsar avoided the Waltz out of respect for the Prussian guests, or the Prussian protocol keeper avoided mentioning the Waltz, is hard to tell. The German philologist, Aage Ansgar Hansen-Löve, sums up the arrival of the Waltz:

> In Russia, the transition from typical aristocratic court dances like the Minuet to the repertoire of social dances, such as the Mazurka and the Waltz, took place at the beginning of the 19th century. It happened in the course of a new wave of appropriation and is to be understood as a new break from tradition. So, the introduction of the bourgeois Waltz took place during the Napoleonic wars at the court of the tsar.[74]

---

70 Gertrude Aretz, *Königin Luise* (Paderborn: Salzwasser-Verlag Gmbh, 2013), loc 3037; Sophie Marie von Voss, *Neunundsechzig Jahre am preußischen Hofe: Aus den Erinnerungen der Oberhofmeisterin Sophie Marie Gräfin von Voss* (Berlin: Berlin Story Verl., 2012), p. 188.

71 *Friedensblätter: Eine Zeitschr. für Leben, Litteratur und Kunst* (Vienna: Schaumburg, Schallbacher, Mayer, 1814), p. 165, https://books.google.co.uk/books?id=-YhPAA AAcAAJ&printsec=frontcover&source=gbs_ge_summary_r&cad=0#v=onepage &q&f=false

72 Ibid; Judith Lissauer Cromwell and Dorothea Lieven, *A Russian Princess in London and Paris, 1785–1857* (Jefferson NC; London: McFarland & Co., 2007), p. 41.

73 Voss, *Neunundsechzig Jahre am preußischen Hofe*, p. 346.

74 Aage Ansgar Hansen-Löve, 'Von der Dominanz zur Hierarchie im System der Kunstformen zwischen Avantgarde und Sozrealismus', *Wiener Slawistischer Almanach*, 47 (2001), 7–36 (p. 7). Translated from the German by Egil Bakka.

Fig. 4.19 Gerhard von Kügelgen, *Dorothea, Princess of Lieven*, 1801. Oil on canvas. Private collection. A Russian noblewoman and wife of the Russian ambassador to London, 1812 to 1834. Wikimedia Commons, Public Domain, https://commons.wikimedia.org/wiki/File:Gerhard_ von_K%C3%BCgelgen_-_Portrait_of_Princess_Dorothea_von_Lieven_ (1801).jpg

It seems that the Waltz was introduced quickly and very early at the Russian court. Probably Alexander I knew it even before he became Tsar in 1802, since the Prussian Queen Louise reports in her diary that she danced the Waltz with him that year.[75] It is worth noting that his grandmother Catherine the Great (1729–1796), who brought him up, was herself raised in a princely house in Germany. She was inspired by

---

75 Aretz, *Konigin Luise*, loc 1068.

European influences in the arts, and gave Alexander a tutor who taught him English in addition to the standard foreign languages at that time, French and German.[76] Alexander's mother Maria Feodorovna (Sophie Dorothea of Württemberg 1759–1828) arrived in Russia in 1776, so even if his grandmother probably did not know the Waltz from Germany, his mother may well have known it. According to the German Johann Joachim Bellermann, who visited the Russian court in 1781–1782, she loved dancing, but he only mentions the Waltz as a German dance and not as something that was danced in Russia at that point.[77] Maria Feodorovna and her husband also undertook a grand tour of Europe starting in 1781, which lasted more than a year. During this tour they would certainly have encountered the Waltz, and the royal party would most likely have picked up new dances. Dancing masters may have contributed to their knowledge, but this was before the first descriptions of the Waltz by the dancing masters.

Hansen-Löve's idea that the change from the Minuet to the Waltz was a change from aristocratic to bourgeois dance at the Russian court transfers a pattern that may have relevance in Western Europe to a context in which it hardly fits. The Minuet and the Waltz were foreign dances, just as the country dances were. Russian histories do not refer to any Russian bourgeoisie that would have the strength to influence the culture at the court in this period. It is hard to believe that the Waltz would make any big difference there, and the 'Mazurka' mentioned is hardly a round dance, but rather the aristocratic Polish Mazur with its complex group formations. The most aristocratic dance around 1800 may have been the Polish Polonaise, with its pompous walking around the dance floor in royal and aristocratic style, which did not require dancing skills. Alexander was much in favour of the Polonaise (see below), and it is more likely that the Russian court contributed to its spread in Germany than vice-versa.

---

76 Wikipedia Contributors, 'Alexander I of Russia', *Wikipedia, The Free Encyclopedia*, 24 November 2019, https://en.wikipedia.org/wiki/Alexander_I_of_Russia; Adrien-César Égron, *Vie d'Alexandre Ier, Empereur de Russie, suivie de notices sur les Grands-Ducs Constantin, Nicolas et Michel par A. E. [Égron.]* (Paris: F. Denn, 1826), p. 210.

77 Johann J. Bellermann, *Kurzer Abriß der Rußischen Kirche nach ihrer Geschichte, Glaubenslehren und Kirchengebräuchen: aus Bemerkungen über Rußland in Rücksicht auf Wissenschaft, Kunst, Religion, und andere merkwürdige Verhältnisse* (Erfurt: Keyser, 1788), pp. 327, 345, https://reader.digitale-sammlungen.de/de/fs1/object/display/bsb10782010_00005.html

94   *Waltzing Through Europe*

Fig. 4.20 Gerhard von Kugelgen, *The Emperor Paul I with his Family*, oil on canvas, Pavlovsk State Museum, 1800. This was painted a few years after Catherine the Great died, during the short reign of her son Paul I and his wife Maria Federovna. The young man standing first from the left at the back of the group is their son Alexander I who two years later became the Emperor of Russia. Wikimedia Commons, Public Domain, https://commons.wikimedia.org/wiki/File:Family_of_Paul_I_of_Russia.jpg

Fig. 4.21 Dmitry Nikolaevich Kardovsky, Ball at the Assembly Hall of the Nobility in St Petersburg, 1913. The ball was held to celebrate the 300th anniversary of the Romanov family in 1913. Organisers tried to revive the tradition with a ball in Old Billingsgate Hall, London. It might be seen as a parallel to the revival attempts at the Prussian court at the same time. Wikimedia Commons, Public Domain, https://commons.wikimedia.org/wiki/File:Ball_at_20s_by_Kardovsky.jpg

Courts of Europe Meet: The Vienna Congress, 1814–1815

After Napoleon Bonaparte was defeated and forced to abdicate in the spring of 1814, the famous Congress of Vienna was summoned in September the same year. It was renowned for its sumptuous balls and its social life, and a congress diary was published in the *Friedensblätter* [Peace Magazine]. This tells us about the arrivals of the celebrities, such as ministers, diplomats and top military officers, but particularly royalty. The kings of Denmark and Württemberg arrived early and the Russian emperor and empress and the Prussian king some days later, as did the king and queen of Bavaria. The Austrian emperor and empress hosted the congress and many glittering events. France and England were represented only by diplomats, and the Swedish regent Bernadotte is also not mentioned. The *Friedensblätter* stresses a personal friendship between the king of Prussia, the emperor of Russia, and the emperor of Austria-Hungary, and describes one of the balls:

Fig. 4.22 Johann Peter Krafft, *Declaration of Victory After the Battle of Leipzig, 1813*, 1839. Oil on canvas. Deutsches Historisches Museum. Tsar Alexander I, Emperor Francis I and Friedrich Wilhelm III are receiving the message that they have defeated Napoleon. They were later the three top Royal figures at the Vienna Congress. Wikimedia Commons, Public Domain, https://commons.wikimedia.org/wiki/File:1839_Krafft_ Siegesmeldung_nach_der_Schlacht_bei_Leipzig_1813_anagoria.JPG

> On the 9th October, there was a court ball — a 'Redoute paré' [masked ball] for 4000 participants. It started at 8pm, and at 10pm a procession of the made their entrée, led by the emperors and kings. The usual dances stopped at the royal entrance, and were succeeded by a March with trumpets. Then the music changed to a Polonaise, in which many of the highest-ranking members of the ball participated. The dance consisted of free quick walking[78] to the hand of a lady of the gentleman's choosing. Then the dancers progressed in a long line through the length of the ballroom and in many directions, and made many smaller or longer breaks. The Russian Emperor Alexander was the soul of this dancing; he and other high-ranking guests initiated the Polonaise throughout the evening. This continued until midnight, when many of the older, most high-ranking people had left, and staff served exclusive refreshments. Around three o'clock in the morning the dancing began again and then particularly the Waltz was favoured.[79]

The French Count Garde-Chambonas wrote detailed memoirs from the congress. He gives a parallel description of a court ball, probably the same, and confirms the royal entrance and the Polonaise, which he characterises as inevitable. He also says that the orchestra started playing Waltzes after the 'departure of the "souverains"'.[80]

This organising of the court balls, with the Polonaise danced while two German rulers were present, seems to have been typical at the congress. There are more comments about this:

> Notwithstanding the variety of musical forms advertised as the Russian emperor's favorites [sic.], Alexander's preferred terpsichorean exercise seems to have been the Polonaise. Despite the name, this dance had a dual function in the period almost as Russian national music and official Romanov court music. It was the Polonaise, rather than the Waltz, that most characterized Congress ballrooms.[81] Waltzing did go on, and one could say quite a bit about it in connection with the Congress, but its distinguishing dance was actually the Polonaise, considered at the time the epitome of aristocratic elegance.[82]

---

78 In German, '[...] freyen raschen Gange'.
79 *Friedensblätter*, p. 190.
80 Auguste Louis Charles, Comte de La Garde-Chambonas, *Fêtes et souvenirs du congrès de Vienne, tableaux des salons, scènes anecdotiques et portraits, 1814–1815* (BruXElles: Société typographique belge, A. Wahlen, 1843), p. 75, https://books.google.co.uk/books?id=pf0LAAAAYAAJ&printsec=frontcover&source=gbs_ge_summary_r&cad=0#v=onepage&q&f=false
81 Brian E. Vick, *The Congress of Vienna Power and Politics After Napoleon* (Cambridge, MA: Harvard University Press, 2014), p. 88.
82 Vick, *The Congress of Vienna*, p. 51.

 Fig. 4.23 Video: Polonaise at the Pushkin Ball, 2011. The ball is held in honour of Aleksandr Pusjkin 1799–1837 in Catherine Palace in Tsarskoe Selo (in Pushkin, near St. Petersburg). 'Polonaise (Pushkin Ball 2011)', 4:51, posted by Khasanov1988, *Youtube*, 19 October 2011, https://www.youtube.com/watch?v=o3e1OH1BpjA

The wife of the Danish ambassador complained that the dancing was dull at the ball given by the Danish king, the Polonaises were not amusing, and the other dances too short. The Danish king and the Russian emperor continued to dance through the night, so that their staff worried about their health. Most of the royals mentioned above were in their forties; the hostess, the empress of Austria-Hungary was the youngest at twenty-seven, followed by the Russian empress and emperor at thirty-five and thirty-seven.

Fig. 4.24 Jean Godefroy, after Jean-Baptiste Isabey, *Delegates of the Congress of Vienna*, 19th c. Wikimedia Commons, CC BY 3.0, https://commons.wikimedia.org/wiki/File:Congress_of_Vienna.PNG

Garde-Chambonas also reports from several other balls: the Russian ball offered a performance of traditional Russian dances, and then Russian and Polish ballroom dances were performed, such as the Mazur.[83] At the ball given by the principal British diplomat's wife, her husband, Lord Castlereagh, a man in his mid-fifties, showed off his English dancing: but the sight of him 'dancing a "Gigue" with his big frame, lifting his long thin legs in time to the music, was more of a spectacle than an entertainment'.[84] There is no report of a ball hosted by the Prussian king, and the Austro-Hungarian emperor presented a Venetian ballet at one of the balls he hosted.[85] One wonders if the banning of the Waltz at the German courts was mainly an issue of distinction, to keep up the court standards of *l'ancien régime* in France. If so, they would try to retain old dances such as the Minuet, focus on ballet, and avoid the round dances of the bourgeoisie. Even the presentation of 'national dances' given by other countries was apparently absent.

Fig. 4.25 Forceval, *The Congress*, 1814–1815. Vinck Collection, National Library, Paris. A caricature of the Vienna Congress. In the centre, Austria, Russia, and Prussia are represented by their three rulers, balancing on tip-toes. To the left, Talleyrand is observing, leaning against the wall, and next to him the British Lord Castlereagh hesitates. The two people on the right represent smaller nations. Wikimedia Commons, Public Domain, https://commons.wikimedia.org/wiki/File:Forceval-Congr%C3%A8s_de_Vienne_1814-815.png

---

83   La Garde-Chombonas, *Fêtes et souvenirs du congrès de Vienne*, p. 448.
84   Ibid., p. 431. Translated from the French by Egil Bakka.
85   La Garde-Chombonas, *Fêtes et souvenirs du congrès de Vienne*, p. 36.

Summary

Popular twentieth-century histories of dance, offering broad accounts of the development of particular dances, often suggest that England and France took a long while to accept the Waltz after it had already been established in Germany. The English pioneer of the history of ballroom dancing, Philip J. S. Richardson, writes in his well-referenced dance history: '[the Waltz] was first seen at Almack's about 1812, introduced in all probability by travelled aristocrats, who had seen it on the Continent where, as was to be the case in England, it met with very strenuous opposition'.[86] The Austrian-American dance critic and professor Walter Sorell writes: 'The list of the Waltz's condemnations is endless. England did not accept this dance before 1812, and for a long time it was forbidden in many parts of Europe. France, whose cultural reign was identified with the past, was most strongly opposed to the new dance; its dance teachers, of course, disapproved of it most vehemently'.[87]

This understanding seems commonsensical, and all the condemnations seem to offer a strong support. Therefore, it is paradoxical that my discussions above about the Waltz at the main European courts suggests more or less the opposite. The German courts prohibited the dance, whereas other courts had few reservations about it. Of course, what happened at court did not represent what happened in the rest of the country, not necessarily even among the aristocracy. It is, however, questionable whether resistance to the Waltz can be measured by the number of indignant statements. More relevant would be the influence and power that the protesters had. Indignation is also salacious, and therefore well suited to spice up more sober source material, and might be somewhat overrepresented in dance histories. It could also be argued that dance enthusiasts hardly bothered to take moral indignation seriously and that they ignored condemnations and prohibitions that were not enforced. Therefore, the lack of replies does not mean that most people were in agreement. Indignation and acceptance or enthusiasm are not expressed in comparable ways, and acceptance is rarely explicitly

---

86   Phillip J. S. Richardson, *The Social Dances of the Nineteenth Century in England* (London: H. Jenkins, 1960), p. 63.
87   Walter Sorell, *Dance in Its Time* (Garden City, NY: Anchor Press/Doubleday, 1981), p. 205.

expressed. Finally, most people cared little about the arrival of new dances; they would just adopt them when they were needed.

We have seen that the Waltz was probably prohibited at the two main German courts through the nineteenth century. That does not mean that it was prohibited in the smaller courts, in any of the states, or even at all court events in Berlin or Vienna. The British crown prince and princess, however, seem to have favoured and danced the Waltz fifteen years before it became acceptable among the British upper classes. They were criticised for this, because, not only did the dance have connections with Germany, but they themselves had strong ties to Germany, which many leading people in Britain disliked. France had undergone a dramatic revolution, and overturned a monarchy that had been a model for court life. That style and the most demanding of the old court dances were not relevant any more during Napoleon's reign. There were, of course, dance teachers and members of the aristocracy who regretted the loss of the old style and the old dances, and disliked the new. There is, however, no evidence that Napoleon, who did not master the Waltz, even hesitated to accept it. Finally, the Russian court was very open to European influences: Catherine II and several other German princesses had married into the court, and teachers from Germany and France taught their children. During the first two decades of the nineteenth century, the Russian emperor, true to his upbringing, was renowned as the most sociable, good-looking and skilled dancer of the Waltz among European monarchs.

The round dance paradigm had two parallel sets of impulses; those transmitted by the dancing masters, the 'Walzen'; and a set that existed among the lower classes, particularly in the Nordic countries, the 'Drehen'. The first type of dance is well represented in most European countries, and is relatively stable in terms of form. The second type did not seem to achieve recognition in polite society, even if German dance experts mention it during the decades before and after 1800. This type reverted to folk culture and influenced the Nordic countries heavily and Poland to some degree. The Schottische was, as far as I know, the only dance with Dreher elements that spread through most of Europe.

Much of the literature presented about round dances is about their origin, the precursors to the Waltz, before exploring how this dance grew to fame and spread. Several books also emphasise the resistance to and the outcry against the Waltz as immoral and harmful to health, particularly for young ladies. This introductory chapter has considered material about the European courts and their reception of the Waltz. The sources are not much more than a small selection of anecdotes, so the intention is obviously not to rewrite the history of the Waltz and the round dances. It is, however, an attempt to propose some new readings and some new perspectives, toning down earlier scholarly attention on the noisy cries about morals and health, and questioning their influence.

There are the stereotypes about relationships between neighbouring countries, which tend to colour attitudes to the neighbour's dances. There are rulers' conflicting ideals about how to be distinguished from their subjects, competing with a wish from some of them to be close to the people. Within this complex tangle of influences there is also the question of 'national' dances, that is, dances that originate from the country itself, adapted for use as the social dances of the upper classes. This kind of national dance is particularly typical in Poland. The desire to copy the most prestigious examples of foreign culture faced some competition from the national romantics, but not necessarily at court level.

Finally, one must consider the style and 'personality' of rulers and their courts, and their ideals. During the first decades of the nineteenth century, in the aftermath of the French Revolution, *l'ancien régime* was no longer the model for aristocratic social life, at least not in France. Napoleon increased the pomp and splendour at court throughout his reign, and the Bourbon Restoration tried to return to the past with little success. France lost its unquestioned leadership in matters of courtly fashion.

The sources from Napoleon's court do not reveal any direct reservations about the Waltz, even if Antoine Calliot is nostalgic about the masters of the old dances and their distinction, and slightly critical of the Waltz and the 'heavily dancing' Germans who brought it. The nostalgia for *l'ancien régime* did not seem to hinder the acceptance of the Waltz, which conquered France in less than a decade with the approval of her ruler and his court.

The English court, which had kings of German descent, also did not seem to have had any second thoughts about the German Waltz. The queen-to-be learned the dance from a young age and practised it with her German cousins when they visited. How typical and widespread was the dislike Lord Byron voiced for the 'German' king and the German Waltz, it is difficult to say. Byron's anger seemed as much rooted in politics and a personal grudge against a regent of German descent as in moral issues.

It is even possible that it was the Russian Tsar, rather than the German relatives of the royal family, who made the Waltz fashionable among the English upper classes. The Tsar's Waltz with Queen Louise of Prussia in 1802 suggests its very early acceptance in Russia. In some ways Alexander I and Queen Louise were the waltzers who had a particular aura during the first decades of the nineteenth century.

If we are to believe that the Waltz was banned for some one hundred years at the main courts of its place of origin, Germany, this is a striking situation. A deeper analysis is needed first to confirm that situation, and secondly to suggest the explanation for it. Finally, we must look into questions of distinction, of balance between foreign and national ideals and perhaps even of the personalities of rulers and the ambiance of courts.

Bibliography

Friedensblätter: Eine Zeitschr. für Leben, Litteratur und Kunst (Vienna: Schaumburg, Schallbacher, Mayer, 1814), https://books.google.co.uk/books?id=-YhPAA AAcAAJ&printsec=frontcover&source=gbs_ge_summary_r&cad=0#v=on epage&q&f=false

Aretz, Gertrude, *Königin Luise* (Paderborn: Salzwasser-Verlag Gmbh, 2013).

——, *Napoleon und die Gräfin Maria Walewska* (Hamburg: Severus Verlag, 2013).

Johann J. Bellermann, *Kurzer Abriß der Rußischen Kirche nach ihrer Geschichte, Glaubenslehren und Kirchengebräuchen: aus Bemerkungen über Rußland in Rücksicht auf Wissenschaft, Kunst, Religion, und andere merkwürdige Verhältnisse* (Erfurt: Keyser, 1788), https://reader.digitale-sammlungen.de/de/fs1/object/display/bsb10782010_00005.html

Bie, Oskar, *Der Tanz* (Berlin: J. Bard, 1919).

Braun, Lily, *Memoiren einer Sozialistin* (Altenmünster: Jazzybee Verlag, 2012).

Braun, Rudolf, and David Gugerli, *Macht des Tanzes — Tanz der Mächtigen. Hoffeste und Herrschaftszeremoniell 1550–1914* (Munich: Verlag C. H. Beck, 1993).

Buckland, Theresa J., *Society Dancing: Fashionable Bodies in England, 1870–1920* (New York: Palgrave Macmillan, 2011).

——, 'Edward Scott: The Last of the English Dancing Masters', *Dance Research: The Journal of the Society for Dance Research*, 21 (2003), 3–35, https://doi.org/10.3366/3594050

Bury, Charlotte C., *Diary Illustrative of the Times of George the Fourth, Interspersed with Original Letters from the Late Queen Caroline, and from various Other Distinguished Persons* (London: H. Colburn, 1838).

Byron, George G., *Waltz, an Apostrophe Hymn* (London: S. Gosnell, 1812), https://en.wikisource.org/wiki/The_Works_of_Lord_Byron_(ed._Coleridge,_Prothero)/Poetry/Volume_1/The_Waltz

Caillot, Antoine, *Mémoires pour servir à l'histoire des moeurs et usages des Français: depuis les plus hautes conditions, jusqu'aux classes inférieures de la société, pendant le règne de Louis XVI, sous le Directoire exécutif, sous Napoléon Bonaparte, et jusqu'à nos jour*, 2 vols (Paris: Dauvin, 1827), https://gallica.bnf.fr/ark:/12148/bpt6k6378010q.texteImage

Carner, Mosco, *The Waltz* (London: Parrish, 1948).

Childers, William, 'Byron's "Waltz": The Germans and their Georges', *Keats-Shelley Journal*, 18 (1969), 81–95.

Corti, Egon Caesar Conte, *Vom Kind zum Kaiser Kindheit und erste Jugend Kaiser Franz Josephs I. und seiner Geschwister* (Munich: Graz, 1951).

Cromwell, Judith L., *Dorothea Lieven: A Russian Princess in London and Paris, 1785–1857* (Jefferson, NC; London: McFarland &Company, 2007).

Ducrest, Georgette, *Mémoires sur l'impératrice Joséphine, sur la ville, la cour et les salons de Paris sous l'Empire*, 2 vols (Paris: Georges Barba, 1863), https://gallica.bnf.fr/ark:/12148/bpt6k6310101z.texteImage

Ebers, Anna, *Das Bismarck-Buch* (Paderborn: Salzwasser-Verlag Gmbh, 1909).

Eberty, Felix, *Jugenderinnerungen eines alten Berliners* (Berlin: Hertz, 1878), https://books.google.co.uk/books?id=IW7omnNaArAC&pg=PP7&source=gbs_selected_pages&cad=2#v=onepage&q&f=false

Égron, Adrien-César, *Vie d'Alexandre Ier, Empereur de Russie, suivie de notices sur les Grands-Ducs Constantin, Nicolas et Michel par A. E. [Égron.]* (Paris: F. Denn, 1826).

Festetics, Mária, *Das Tagebuch der Gräfin Marie Festetics: Kaiserin Elisabeths intimste Freundin* (St. Pölten, Salzburg, Vienna: Residenz Verlag, 2014).

Franz Joseph, *Seiner Majestät des Kaisers Franz Joseph I von Österreich Reise nach Russland im Monate Februar 1874* (Vienna: Kaiserlich-Königlichen Hof- und Staatsdruckerei, 1874), http://catalog.hathitrust.org/api/volumes/oclc/1624904.html

Goethe, Katharina E., *Briefe — Band II* ([n.p.]: Tredition Classics, 2012).

Guilcher, Jean-Michel, *La contredanse et les renouvellements de la danse française* (Paris: Mouton, 1969).

Guillaume, Simon, and Jacques La Hante, *Almanach dansant, ou, positions et attitudes de l'Allemande: Avec un discours préliminaire sur l'origine et l'utilité de la danse* (Paris: Chez l'auteur ruë des Arcis, 1769), https://gallica.bnf.fr/ark:/12148/btv1b8626149j/f41.item.zoomin/

Hansen-Löve, Aage Ansgar, ‚Von der Dominanz zur Hierarchie im System der Kunstformen zwischen Avantgarde und Sozrealismus', *Wiener Slawistischer Almanach*, 47 (2001), 7–36.

Heydt, Eduard von der, and Werner von Rheinbaben, *Auf dem Monte Verità: Erinnerungen und Gedanken über Menschen, Kunst und Politik* (Zürich: Atlantis, 1958).

La Garde-Chombonas, Auguste Louis Charles, Comte de, *Fêtes et souvenirs du congrès de Vienne, tableaux des salons, scènes anecdotiques et portraits, 1814–1815* (Bruxelles: Société typographique belge, A. Wahlen, 1843), https://archive.org/details/ftesetsouvenirs01gardgoog/page/n9

MacDonogh, Giles, *Prussia: The Perversion of an Idea* (London: Sinclair-Stevenson, 1994).

De Österreich, Marie Valerie von, *Das Tagebuch der Lieblingstochter von Kaiserin Elisabeth 1878–1899*, ed. by Martha Schad and Horst Schad (Munich: Langen Muller, 1998).

Oulton, Walley C., *Authentic and Impartial Memoirs of Her Late Majesty, Charlotte, Queen of Great Britain and Ireland.* (London: Printed and published by J. Robins and Co., Albion Press, 1819), https://babel.hathitrust.org/cgi/pt?id=uva.x002531799&view=1up&seq=1

Pauls, Eilhard Erich, *Das Ende der galanten Zeit: Gräfin Voss am preussischen Hofe* (Lübeck: O. Quitzow, 1924).

Platoff, John, 'A New History for Martín's "Una Cosa Rara"', *The Journal of Musicology*, 12 (1994), 85–115, https://doi.org/10.1525/jm.1994.12.1.03a00050

Ponte, Lorenzo Da, and Vicente Martín y Soler, *Una Cosa Rara*, 17 November 1786, http://www.librettidopera.it/cosarara/a_02.html

Quennell, Peter, *Byron: The Years of Fame* (London: Reprint Society, 1943).

Rappaport, Helen, *Queen Victoria: A Biographical Companion* (Santa Barbara: ABC-CLIO, 2003).

Rice, John A., *Empress Marie Therese and Music at the Viennese Court, 1792–1807* (Cambridge, UK: Cambridge University Press, 2007).

Richardson, Philip J. S., *The Social Dances of the Nineteenth Century in England* (London: H. Jenkins, 1960).

Rose, John Holland, *Napoleon: Lefnadsteckning efter nya källor*, trans. by Ernst Lundquist, 2 vols (Stockholm: Hugo Gebers Förlag, 1907).

Saint-Hilaire, Emile M. de, *Napoléon au bivouac, aux Tuilleries et á Sainte-Hélène anecdotes inédites sur la famille et la cour imperiale* (Bruxellès: Meline, Cans, 1845), http://books.google.com/books?id=rZUvAAAAMAAJ

Sorell, Walter, *Dance in Its Time* (Garden City, NY: Anchor Press/Doubleday, 1981).

Van der Kiste, John, *George III's Children* (New York: The History Press, 2013).

Viktoria Luise, Herzogin, *Im Glanz der Krone* (Göttingen: Göttinger Verlagsanstalt, 1967).

Volz, Gustav Berthold, *Historische, militärische und philosophische Schriften, Gedichte und Briefe*, with illustrations by Adolph von Menzel (Köln: Anaconda, 2006).

Voss, Sophie Marie von, *Neunundsechzig Jahre am preußischen Hofe: Aus den Erinnerungen der Oberhofmeisterin Sophie Marie Gräfin von Voss* (Berlin: Berlin Story Verl., 2012).

Wairy, Louis C., *Mémoires de Constant, premier valet de chambre de l'Empereur, sur la vie privée de Napoléon, sa famille et sa cour* (Paris: Ladvocat, 1830).

Wikipedia Contributors, 'Alexander I of Russia', *Wikipedia, The Free Encyclopedia*, 24 November 2019, https://en.wikipedia.org/wiki/Alexander_I_of_Russia;

——, 'Frederick William II of Prussia', *Wikipedia, The Free Encyclopedia*, 13 November 2019, https://en.wikipedia.org/wiki/Frederick_William_II_of_Prussia

5. The Polka as a Czech National Symbol

Daniela Stavělová[1]

Wikipedia defines the Polka as follows: 'originally a Czech dance and genre of dance music familiar throughout all of Europe and the Americas. It originated in the middle of the 19th century in Bohemia, now part of the Czech Republic'.[2] Many people outside the Czech Republic will probably believe that the Polka was born somewhere in the Czech lands; some might even have heard that a maidservant devised the Polka in her free time on a farmyard.[3] But what if it comes from Poland after all? 'Not at all; the Polka is ours!', say the French. 'We gave it the form in which it became world famous, and no one is really interested in what preceded this'.[4] As explored below, encyclopedias from different countries fail to give clear evidence about whether or not the Polka is a Czech dance.[5]

It is not intended that this chapter provoke arguments about the Czech origins of the Polka. Nor does this chapter aim to offer more evidence in favour of its roots and social derivation. This has already

---

1 This investigation was conducted under the research initiative of the Institute of Ethnology of the Czech Academy of Sciences AVOZ 68378076. The first version of the text was published in Czech: Daniela Stavělová, 'Polka jako český národní symbol', *Český lid*, 93 (2006), 3–26.
2 Wikipedia contributors, 'Polka', *Wikipedia, The Free Encyclopedia*, https://en.wikipedia.org/wiki/Polka
3 Jan H. Brunvand, *American Folklore: An Encyclopedia* (New York: Routledge, 2006) p. 1207.
4 Argus, 'Chronique', *La Semaine des Familles*, 18 (11 October 1884), pp. 159–60.
5 The doubts about whether the Polka is Czech or not are partly based on the name, which seems to refer to Poland, but, in any case, the Polka has never had a clear choreographic structure as it combines the features of cosmopolitan drawing-room dances (the Écossaise, the Galop, the Waltz).

© Daniela Stavělová, CC BY 4.0 https://doi.org/10.11647/OBP.0174.05

been analysed in great detail by Czech music historian Zdeněk Nejedlý.[6] Rather, the questions it addresses are: why do the Czech people keep taking the Polka for a Czech folk dance and national dance, and where does this myth come from? What makes the Polka Czech? Is there any distinction between a Polka and a Czech Polka? Is there any difference between 'folk' Polka and 'national' Polka? This chapter discusses how the Polka came to represent the Czech values of modern times, and how it also coexisted with regional patriotism, on the one hand, and Pan-Slavism, on the other.

Fig. 5.1 Polka, watercolour from Petr Maixner, published in the ethnological journal *Český lid*, 12 (1903), p. 93. All rights reserved.

---

6   Zdeněk Nejedlý, *Bedřich Smetana 4. díl. Česká společnost* (Prague: Hudební Matice Umělecké Besedy, 1925).

The Polka has been the subject of expert debate in the Czech lands ever since it appeared, as is described in detail by Nejedlý. The huge amount of sheet music that exists for the Polka and the numerous records in nineteenth-century fiction, newspapers, memoirs, and other sources testify to the widespread popularity of the Polka among all strata of society. The Polka appeared in the nineteenth century, and was at its height of popularity in this period. However, it has remained popular and enjoys a preeminent position among Czech cultural practices, as it is considered to be *national heritage*. No-one in the Czech Republic would doubt these days that the Polka is a Czech folk dance: for example, it is performed by the whole village in Bedřich Smetana's famous nineteenth-century opera, *The Bartered Bride*. Even those Czech people with no interest in opera whatsoever will have seen this piece at least once in their lifetimes.

Nejedlý draws upon a number of historical sources that present reliable evidence about the historical context of the Polka and its origin.[7] The Polka is thought to have emerged from Czech patriotic circles initially established in smaller regional towns. This chapter investigates the historical and descriptive dimensions of Nejedlý's work, in order to consider the Polka as a social phenomenon, as part of a broader analysis of the development of the Polka as a Czech national symbol. Indeed, it took some time for Czech society as a whole to accept it as such, and for the Polka itself to take on this ideal form. What was the basis of the Polka as a dance, and which of its features were seen as characteristic of the Czech national movement? What other conditions were involved in its establishment as a Czech symbol? Questions like these make us think of the Polka not only as a dance but — first and foremost — as a process running hand in hand with socio-cultural and ideological-political contexts — in other words, the Polka is a text growing out of these contexts. By admitting that the Polka was established as a Czech national symbol, we have to ask questions such as when, for whom,

---

7   Ibid. In his book, Nejedlý relies on intensive research into the press, including magazines and papers such as *Květy, Česká včela, Dalibor, Bohemia, Wiener Theater-Zeitung*; he also draws upon diaries, memoirs, and letters written by individuals involved in the national movement, such as V. V. Tomek, J. J. Langer, J. K. Tyl, I. I. Sreznevsky, and K. Vinařický. In turn, Nejedlý provides a detailed analysis of the musical form of the Polka in compositions by Czech teachers and others, while his book includes a list of the Polka's dance compositions.

how, under what conditions, and for what reasons was it established as a Czech national symbol? A further question is why the Polka achieved its status as *the* Czech national dance. Or was it the other way round: did the Polka first become popular, and only later become Czech?

Dance as Cultural Text

In order to answer these questions, it is necessary to define the conditions in order to reflect the whole context. This holistic approach to dance requires a notion called *cultural text*,[8] according to which dance is defined as a coherent and dynamic aspect of culture, bringing together the ethnochoreological and anthropological approaches to the subject. According to cultural text theory, the socio-communicative meaning of dance fills the process with the quality of text. Dance texts are not only choreographic structures, but also integral functions that combine social interaction with the concrete dance elements, depending on the type of communication involved. In this process of communication, dance does not work separately: it includes non-choreographic features such as gestures, facial expressions, music, speech, costumes, social rules and knowledge of the surrounding space. These components have a hierarchical structure, being interactively interlinked within a meaningful dance process with variable social contexts.[9] Dance as a multi-dimensional cultural text is not separate from other texts belonging to a particular social group; all the texts remain in mutual dependence, retaining an active relationship with the wider socio-cultural context. There are numerous examples of dance being a constitutive part of various activities — not only in entertainment, but also in politics, military life, and so on.

Dance is a symbol that possesses power and is able to bring about change. It is accepted as such and performed by dancers as a kinesthetic, affective and mental representation; not only does it reflect society

---

8   The concept of 'cultural text' was introduced by Yuri Lotman in his work on cultural semiotics; see Ann Shukman, 'Lotman: The Dialectic of a Semiotician', in *The Sign. Semiotics around the World*, ed. by Richard W. Bailey, Ladislav Matejka, and Peter Steiner (Ann Arbor, MI: Slavic Publications, 1980), pp. 19–206.

9   Anca Giurchescu, 'The Power of Dance and its Social and Political Uses', in *Yearbook for Traditional Music*, 23, ed. by Adrienne L. Kaeppler, Dietmar Christensen, and Stephen Wild (2001), 109–22 (p. 110), https://doi.org/10.2307/1519635

but, more importantly, it produces some kind of meaning any time it is performed. It is important to realise that dance is always part of some context or other, and, therefore, it depends on socio-cultural conditions, aesthetic rules and on the role it is expected to play.[10] The power of dance is expressed in an active dance act, and it is crucial to understand that this involves the whole performance, including the performers and spectators, rather than simply the dance itself. Having such power, dance can be used to structure, support or even modify the social system according to the ideology of the particular group and to its socio-political interests.[11]

The notion of folk culture[12] as an ideological concept that appears alongside growing national consciousness is not an unknown pheonomenon. In such cases, folk culture establishes the existence of the nation through language and common history, often manipulating traditional symbols in order to import the past into the present. However, the presence of foreign influences, and their contamination with local features, tends to be erroneously interpreted during reconstructions of the past. Symbols, therefore, likewise tend to be manipulated in political processes. My research, through this approach, aims to discover:

- which socio-political group determines and selects 'authentic' and representative products of traditional culture;
- for what purpose they do so;
- what selection criteria they use to do so;
- and what characteristics are applied in order to create an ideal symbol.

---

10   Ibid., p. 110.
11   Ibid., p. 113.
12   This concept was introduced in the Czech area in 1778–1779 through the work of the German philosopher J. G. Herder's (1744–1803) *Volkslieder* and, in particular, through his *Ideen zur Philosophie der Geschichte der Menschheit* (1784–1791) which was soon adopted as a manifest of the Slavic enlightenment. Herder stressed the role of traditional songs as proof of a nation's existence as well as differentiating between *Volk* and *Pöbel* (nation and plebs). The aesthetic values attributed by him to the production of the singing people, opposed to the crying plebs, made the word *Volk* acquire a more emblematic meaning. Inspired by Herder intellectuals leading the Czech national movement started discussing *national* songs, dances, etc., where the term 'national' signalled the emblematic features of their country's traditional culture.

The New Myth about the Czech Nation

The Polka is known to have played a crucial role in establishing Czech national identity. The dance may have arisen from Czech patriotic circles whose members were men of letters, active in public, political and cultural life. These people had an important role in the national movement and their literary works helped to create the Czech nation and its identity. Their goal — as Vladimír Macura puts it in *The Czech Dream* — was to shape Czech identity in a manner typical of the revival period.[13] They knew identity was a *cultural* fact; it became valid only after it had become a cultural fact, and, as such, had been incorporated into the network of other cultural facts, past and present. There would always be dance involved at the social events, discussions, parties, and balls held by these Czech. As early as the 1830s, dance had become an important tool of national promotion;[14] a genuine boom in national promotion arrived in the 1860s when the choreographic, musical, literary and visual aspects of the Polka were being established.

The establishment of the concept of the Polka against the background of the Czech national movement is comparable to the creation of myths. Roland Barthes has argued that *myth* is a combination of false evidence, and a kind of language. In his *Mythologies*, Barthes describes myth as a semiological system, and suggests that it is most important to look for significations. In this system, myth is a type of speech, and, therefore, anything can become a myth. Myth is subject to discourse rules. Its definition is not based on what it says, but how it speaks.[15] Thus, any object can mutate from its closed, mute existence into an oral state, ready to be accepted by society as something embellished, something adapted to a certain type of consumption, something that has been given a clear social status that complements the pure material it was in the very beginning. What gives the Polka the status of myth is the contradiction between the signified — which was, in a certain period of

---

13 Vladimír Macura, *Český sen* (Prague: Knižnice dějin a současnosti, 1998).
14 This was a time when a group of patriotic members of the intelligentsia attempted to persuade the members of their ethnic group that they belong to a nation which has its value and the right to the same attributes as nations that had existed for a long time. See the work of the Czech historian Miroslav Hroch, *Vnárodním zájmu* (Prague: Knižnice dějin a současnosti, 1999), pp. 15–16.
15 Roland Barthes, *Mytologie* (Prague: Dokořán, 2004), p. 107.

time, its musical-choreographic structure and cultural origin — and the signifier, which is the name of the dance, which was expected to be a symbol of Czech national identity.

Initially, the name 'Polka' — referring to Polish origin — did not cause any confusion. It was only later that it was found rather contradictory, when it became necessary to justify the name at a time when the Polka was supposed to demonstrate attitudes and political beliefs.

As noted above, the name of the dance[16] emerged from the patriotic Czech intelligentsia who — in using the name Polka — expressed their sympathy with the Polish revolutionary movements of the early 1830s.[17] The fact that the name is feminine in grammar is no coincidence. It refers to *Amazonia*, a woman in arms, a popular symbol of European culture for several centuries, which became especially topical in mid-nineteenth-century Czech society. The literary historian Vladimír Macura considers that the appeal of *Amazonia* lies in the double-sided nature of the motif, combining typical feminine features — such as humility, tenderness, sensibility and charm — with opposing masculine attributes, such as defiance, power, pugnacity, courage and might.[18] As the nineteenth century saw the revival of Czech culture, this general stereotype of 'female warriors' became a new symbol of revolutionary change to the existing order. The semiotics also changed as the focus shifted from a real person playing such a role, to the expectations, ideas and meanings given to the symbol. Not surprisingly, there were a number of dances newly designed for national or social events in the nineteenth century that had names that were feminine in grammar: for example,

---

16 There is an important example of how the patriotic circles sang and later danced Polish folk songs based on famous Czech melodies — the songs are included in F. L. Čelakovský's collection called *Slovanské národní písně* of 1822–1827. In J. J. Langer's 1835 article which appeared in the magazine Časopis českého muzea, an important periodical of the Czech national movement, we read: '...people began dancing and singing in the following way: dancers and their partners make a row; the singer in front of the musicians, the rest behind him; when the singer has sung the first half of the Krakowiak dance, every one repeats it; then comes the other half. Then other dances (Třasák, Břitva, Kalup) are performed in the same way: once the dance is over, everyone stops, and someone starts a new song etc. In a place in the Hradec Králové region, the pattern is different and called Polka, and it may be more like the genuine krakowiak'. Translated from the Czech by David Mraček. Josef Jaroslav Langer, 'České krakováčky', in *Bodláčí a růže* (Prague: Státní nakladatelství krásné literatury, hudby a umění, 1957), p. 211.
17 Nejedlý, *Bedřich Smetana*, p. 338
18 Macura, *Český sen*, p. 81.

Sousedská, Skočná, Dupavá, and *Slovanka*.[19] Significantly, a female warrior was frequently found in fiction and therefore understood as part of a long historical tradition. The symbol had its roots in Czech mythology (where female warriors such as Šárka and Vlasta appear) and did not clash with the contemporary ethical and social position of women.[20]

Another argument in favour of the Czech origin of the Polka and its role in the creation of Czech national identity was the fact that Slavic traditions were high on the agenda. Czech identity was frequently defined by the Czech intelligentsia as something extraordinary. No wonder that the strategic emphasis on the unique Czech character included not only the European aspect — which was sometimes strongly rejected — but also the Slavic context to which the Czech world can refer. It is important to distinguish the two contexts, as the European context included German culture and institutions to which the Slavic attributes stood in opposition. Czechs are different from Germans, belong to a different, Slavic world with a different past and — most importantly — a different future.[21] The Slavic tendencies are visible in how the Polka was established: first, the name; second, the way it was visualised by Petr Maixner in his collection of allegoric drawings showing Czech dances.[22] Dances like *Skočná, Hulán,* and *Obkročák* are shown by a couple dressed in folk costumes with gestures characteristic of folk dance, whereas the Polka has different features. The couple's stature is comparable to that typical of contemporary ballroom dancers; they are dressed in pseudo-folk clothes: her hair is styled in a long ponytail, she wears wrap-up sandals and a town dress with imitation embroidery; he is dressed in a festive black coat called a *čamara* which, again, had a certain symbolic meaning for Czech people.[23] Clearly, the Polka is given the status of a *national dance*: whereas the other three dances have features typical of Czech folk traditions, the Polka comes out of patriotic town circles which promoted Slavic ideas.

---

19 See Nejedlý, *Bedřich Smetana*, p. 341
20 Ibid., p. 87.
21 Ibid., p. 66.
22 This was published in the ethnological journal, *Český lid*, in 1903, at p. 92.
23 Čamara [chamara] refers to a man's festive black coat with a collapsible collar and a number of buttons on the lace. Originally, it was part of a Polish garment. In the Czech lands, it was worn especially in the second half of the nineteenth century as an expression of Czech patriotism and of an inclination towards the idea of Slavic reciprocity.

The Polka myth was established as part of the political and ideological discourse of the intelligentsia who developed the concept of Czech national identity. The conflict between the signifier and the signified is even more profound when further investigation reveals the historical actualities of the signified. Discrepancies may have existed between, on the one hand, how the Polka was really performed, how it was danced (and by whom and on what occasions), and on the other hand, how society (who exactly?) spoke and thought about it on the other.

Polka Fever in the Czech Lands

It is important to realise that the rhythms and choreographic structure did not carry the major symbolic meaning of the Polka in the beginning. There is no recorded evidence to suggest that anyone in the 1830s really thought about what they danced; what mattered was that a dance called the Polka demonstrated the attitudes of the town bourgeoisie — which had just began to develop — by introducing simple pleasure without the conventions typical of previous ballroom dances. These patriotic circles intended to achieve internal independence as a liberal 'new bourgeoisie', rather than to strongly promote Czech patriotism. In addition, the Polka was something they had created themselves, as opposed to the Waltz, which initially had helped to foster the unconventional spirit of young townspeople but soon came to be considered as something foreign. The Polka, therefore, was exactly what the town bourgeoisie demanded: it demonstrated their worldview no matter what its constituent elements were.

The fact that the Polka had not yet become a specific political or national symbol might well have enabled its massive expansion throughout society. Although the expansion began in the Hradec Králové region, as a number of reports prove, it is very likely that the Polka had become popular in other Czech regions — both urban and rural — well before it virtually engulfed Prague in 1838.[24] There is evidence for this in the list of twenty-three Czech dances (without descriptions) from the Litomyšl county, made when Ferdinand V was crowned King of the Czech lands

---

24 Nejedlý, *Bedřich Smetana*.

in 1836.²⁵ Its title is in German — *Verzeichniss der auf der Herrschaft Leutomischel üblichen Volkstänze* — and it included the following dances:

Třinožka, also called *Drimajka* — *Wopice* — *Kráwa* — *Slepička* — *Mráz* — *Nadiwajna* — *Woštěpačka* — *Zeman* — *Trakač* — *Baborak* — *Polka* — *Drátař* — *Sekejn* — *Furiant* — *Kocour* — *Salat* — *Placawá* — *Kozel* — *Trám* — *Kdyby moje byla* — *Jsem rad, že jsem dostal mladou ženu* — *Šupák* — *Hulán*.²⁶

Except for some of the dances, whose names are difficult to decode, they are all found in later collections of folk songs and dances. The fact that this list of folk dances — the oldest printed one — includes the Polka supports the hypothesis that, wherever there were active patriotic circles in small towns, the Polka had so much value that it was automatically adopted by villages as well. Also, it may well be that the choreographic structure of the Polka as danced in towns had so much in common with village folk dances that the name was given to a practice that had been there for some time. In any case, the regions of East Bohemia, the Central Labe Region, and the Jizera Region were the venues of major patriotic promotion. Towns with a population of over one thousand had various cultural unions, in addition to intense trading activity and good transport possibilities.²⁷

By 1838, Prague had been engulfed by the Polka in dance halls and elsewhere. Josef Kajetán Tyl's 1839 article entitled *Pražané ve Hvězdě* [Prague people at the Hvězda Park] supports the fact that there was no ball, no social event, no outing, without the Polka, and it was danced both inside and outside, by the young and the old, Czechs and Germans alike.²⁸ 'Instead of saying Good Morning or Good Evening, people will

---

25   Hannah Laudová found the list when searching the archives for evidence on a popular festivity held at Invalidovna, Prague, and Brno-Lužánky on the occasion of Ferdinand's crowning ceremony. The records of the Czech and Moravian governing bodies gave H. Laudová numerous details on the preparation and background of these festive events. The Brno Province Presidential Office produced a file called *Krönungsceremoniel S. M. des Kaiser Ferdinand V. und I. M. der Kaiserin Maria Anna zu Prag im Jahre 1836* which contains a list of guests attending a wedding ceremony in Litomyšl and a list of dances that were planned to be performed. There is evidence that the dances were carefully rehearsed for this purpose. See Hannah Laudová, 'Další pramen ke studiu českých lidových', *Český lid*, 44 (1957), 273–74.

26   Hannah Laudová, *Další pramen*, p. 274.

27   Jiří Kořalka, *Češi v Habsburské říši a v Evropě 1815–1914. Sociálně historické souvislosti vytváření novodobého národa a národnostní otázky v českých zemích* (Prague: Argo, 1996), p. 92.

28   Nejedlý, *Bedřich Smetana*, p. 348.

greet each other with "Have you heard of the Polka?", or "Have you danced the Polka?"and the answer is: "Oh, the Polka currently occupies all my free time"', wrote Josef Proksch — who later became Smetana's tutor — in his diary, going on to say that the Polka had come to Prague from some of the rural areas.[29] Writer Václav Vladivoj Tomek gives a nice example of this in his memoirs. Although he went to live in Prague, Tomek stayed in touch with his home town of Hradec Králové as he regularly went there to spend his holidays. This is his account of his visit in February 1837 to a ball in Prague: 'Little nimble as I was, I was still one of the best dancers of the ball: for I could dance the Polka, which was little known in Prague back then, although it was very popular in the Hradec Králové region. Not even half of the dancers at the ball could dance the Polka'.[30]

But what were the characteristics of the Polka in the 1830s and early 1840s, what were its music and choreographic features, and what was the difference between the Polka in the town and in the village? There are almost no contemporary descriptions of the dance or detailed reports about how the Polka was danced in the Czech lands, except for accounts that say it was similar to some other dances to which it may have been related or with which it might have shared features. In addition to Josef Jaroslav Langer's account of the Czech *krakowiaks* (see footnote 16, above), another person who asserted that the Polka was close to Třasák [shake-dance][31] was the poet and collector of folk songs Karel Jaromír Erben,[32] who, in the magazine Česká včela [Czech Bee], wrote his account of the summer in 1831 when he visited Třesovice in the Hradec Králové region:

> The pub was very crowded; it was almost impossible for us to take a seat at a table. In the middle of the room about ten couples were dancing right next to each other in a modest circle, with some more couples dancing gently in the circle. The dancing was moderate and pleasant to watch. The dancers were skipping lightly and with no rustling in a regular two-four time to a simple tune — to spice things up, the band played it in G at one time or in C at another. 'What is the dance called?' I asked my friend. 'And what is its place of origin?' 'It is only danced here in Třesovice',

---

29 Ibid. Translated from the Czech by David Mráček.
30 Ibid., p. 359. Translated from the Czech by David Mráček.
31 The name of the dance *Třasák* is derived from the Czech word 'třásti' — to shake.
32 Karel Jaromír Erben, 'Ještě něco o polce', *Česká včela*, 11 (1844), 304.

replies Mr B, 'and in other villages of this county, and so it is called Třasák'. Keen lovers will remember that the tune is identical with the one once known as Polka throughout the Czech lands — thus, the Polka is nothing but a new name for Třasák, the latter gradually becoming almost identical with Gallopade; therefore many dancers or even composers do not see any difference between the Polka and the Gallopade.[33]

A description of how the Polka was danced in towns is given by Ivan Izmail Sreznevsky who stayed in Prague in the 1840s; in order to be invited to Czech balls, he had to be accepted into the Czech intelligentsia by showing he knew something about the Polka.[34] In a letter to his mother living back in Charkov, Ukraine, Sreznevsky gives an account of how the Polka was danced in Prague, expressing hope she would like this 'Prague Waltz':

> Polka is the same as the Waltz, only a lot faster, in 2/4 time. It is either played *piano* — which is very quietly, or *forte* — very strongly. This is extremely attractive for the dancers. Let Ms Fanny and Anna Andreevna have a go: the position of hands is different than in an ordinary Waltz: the gentleman has the palms of both his hands under the lady's elbows and the lady's arms hold the gentleman's so that her palms touch his elbows. Is that clear? Sometimes this version is danced: with one arm akimbo, the gentleman uses his other arm to embrace the lady, like in an ordinary Waltz; the lady has one arm akimbo, too. You need to dance very, very quickly.[35]

Although Sreznevsky does not report on the step parametres, he gives some important indications. Interestingly, Sreznevsky compares the Polka to the Waltz, which is no coincidence, as the Polka's close relationship to the Waltz is commented on in later accounts of the Polka, in the guides by dance masters Henri Cellarius and Eugène Coralli,[36] who taught in Paris.

---

33 This source had not been known until Jiří Horák drew attention to it in his paper on Erben's collection of Czech folk songs: Jiří Horák, 'Erbenova sbírka českých písní lidových', *Národopisný věstník českoslovanský*, 7 (1912), 6–7. In recent years, the importance of Erben's findings was highlighted by Martina Pavlicová, *Lidový tanec v Českých zemích. Sondy do historiografie, ekologie a metodologie* (Brno: FF MÚ, 1992), pp. 24–27.

34 When in Prague, Sreznevsky wrote frequent letters to his mother in Charkov, and these were published by V. Lamanskij as 'Putěvi pisma I. I. Sreznevskego k materi jego', in the journal *Živaja Starina*, cited after Nejedlý, *Bedřich Smetana*, p. 345.

35 Cited in Nejedlý, *Bedřich Smetana*, p. 345.

36 His way of dancing the Polka is depicted in a guidebook by MM. Perrot and Adrien Robert, *La Polka enseignée sans maître, par MM. Perrot et Adrien Robert, d'après M. Eugène Coralli de l'Académie royale de musique* (Paris: Aubert, 1844).

In their descriptions, *waltzing* — turning in couple position — was one of the figures used in the Polka, and it was this that made it different from other ballroom dances at that time. In Sreznevsky's account, the Polka is different from the Waltz because of its 2/4 time, very quick speed, and dynamic contrasts in the accompanying music.

Ethnochoreologist Egil Bakka, who has conducted research on dances which later became the Polka in the Nordic countries, highlights the relationship between the Polka in its early stage and the Waltz in his article on 'The Polka before and after'. He argues that the first dances called Waltzes in Norway were in 2/4 time, and the label Polka was adopted as one of the names for a type of dance in which the couple turns round regularly while going in a circle in two metrically different stages. Apart from the official Polka, the most popular dances of this type included *Hamborgar* (as in Hamburg Waltz), *Hoppvals*, *Skotsk* and the Galop.[37] This supports the hypothesis that fashionable new dances may have been adopted in different ways in different socio-cultural contexts. The fact that the Polka mingled with the Waltz and they later became separate dances again was due to other factors that gave the Polka the role that it was expected to have in different contexts.

It is feasible to say that in the 1830s, the Polka became a symbol in the patriotic circles of small rural towns, whereas in the wider social context of the Czech-German society living in the Czech lands — no matter how it was danced — it remained more a demonstration of a newly developing town society with democratic principles, rather than a symbol of Czech nationalism. It was not only in the Czech lands that the former lower classes managed to carry out independent activities; the Polka played a major role in this process. In France, for example, the poet Théophile Gautier reports that there were arguments about how to dance the Polka in Paris in 1844, with different opinions evident in the different social classes in France: the conservative aristocratic circles preferred the slower speed typical of ballroom etiquette, whereas democratic younger generations were in favour of the livelier version which — they said — expressed spontaneous joy. As Gautier put it, there was a clash of aristocratic and democratic principles.[38]

---

37   Egil Bakka, 'The Polka before and after the Polka', *Yearbook for Traditional Music*, 33 (2001), 37–47, https://doi.org/10.2307/1519629
38   Cited in Nejedlý, *Bedřich Smetana*, p. 353.

Whose Polka?

The need to define the Polka in its choreographic and musical aspects became urgent once the Polka was adopted as a symbol of the mentality of patriotic activists. In the early 1840s, as a more self-confident group of nationalists emerged (František Ladislav Rieger, Karel Havlíček Borovský, František Palacký), there was a stronger political edge to national promotion. New Czech associations — or social meetings called *Beseda* in Czech — were established, which had been preceded by the first Czech balls. Most of the patriots knew very well how important it was to hold meetings where they could sing, recite poems, and dance. Although dance was considered only as entertainment by some people, they knew it had the potential to bolster their national vision and attract great masses of people.[39] No less importantly, as the promotion of this vision reached its peak, the Czech language could not possibly be the major symbol or manifestation of nationality. German maintained its preeminent position as the language of officialdom, trade and culture, and many Czech patriots knew German better than Czech because grammar schools, comprehensive and specialised secondary schools as well as universities taught only in German up until the early 1860s. The process of making patriotic society more Czech was a difficult one, and non-verbal tools had to be used. Therefore, cultural items such as clothing or dance had the potential to play a crucial role.[40] It is therefore no coincidence that some famous politicians or writers, such as J. K. Tyl and F. L. Rieger, helped organise the first Czech balls.

Josef Kajetán Tyl gives a thorough account of the message and purpose of these events in the magazine *Vlastimil*:

> You may have heard about them or even been to one of them, dear readers. Well, they have made a lot of noise in Prague and elsewhere for the last four or five years. It is a little bit funny to hold Czech balls and social events in the Czech lands — it sounds as if the French or Turks held their own events here from time to time — though the name is convenient and important. You know very well there are people — and there were even more of them not long ago — who do not actually know who they

---

39 Dorota Gremlicová, 'Tanec a český národní program', *Národopisná revue*, 11 (2001), 93–95.
40 Mirjam Moravcová, *'Národní oděv roku 1848': Ke vzniku národně politického symbolu* (Prague: Academia, 1986).

are. They were born in Bohemia, received education here, and eat Czech bread now; but they fail to think they are Czech and to support the Czech traditions; some of them are even proud and glad to deny their Czech blood. In order to make such people wake up and make them think they are expected to always use their natural language so that the true Czechs can enjoy themselves without looking down on these 'semi-Czechs', we have set up these Czech balls, social events where people dance and do other noble things such as singing and poem-reciting. These events were first held in Prague in 1840 and 1841, and their nice design made them so popular that more and more people sign up for them and they have so far spread across the country.[41]

J. K. Tyl thought the Czech world was isolated from all disturbing 'foreign' influences: revolutions, combats, female emancipation, social conflicts, and so on. His rejection of such foreign influences can be seen in his play called *Jiříkovo Vidění* [Jiřík's Vision], and, indeed, he rejected the Waltz fever that set in at the beginning of the nineteenth century, countering this Germanic influence by renaming the Waltz the *Houpavá* [Swing Dance].[42]

However, the Polka enjoyed a special status at balls and social events, where it was declared to be genuinely Czech — at the first Czech ball it was performed four times, whereas the Waltz was played only three times and the Gallopade only twice. This was because the Polka was the only dance that could be differentiated from the contemporary cosmopolitan repertory of ballroom dances. By being accepted as a Czech product, it fulfilled the idea of nationalism that puts *nation* as the highest of human values. It was part of the concept of Czech patriotism that strictly distinguished between *we* and *they*, thus differentiating between the Czech country and foreign countries and states.[43] Still, it was necessary to come up with convincing proof that the Polka really was of Czech origin. And since its existence in a society consisting of various nations had not proved this, evidence was sought in Czech folk traditions. In order to say the Polka was national in the sense of political, its folk or rural origin had to be proven. The news that the Polka had

---

41 Cited in Čeněk Zíbrt, *Jak se kdy v Čechách tancovalo*, 2nd edn (Prague: Státní nakladatelství krásné literatury, 1960), p. 294.
42 Nejedlý, *Bedřich Smetana*, p. 356.
43 Stanislav Brouček, Jiří Cvekl, Václav Hubinger et al., *Základní pojmy etnické teorie*, *Český lid*, 78 (1991), 273–57.

existed in Czech villages long before it was first given that name and that it had mingled with dances peculiar to these places (*Třasák*, *Maděra*) helped to form a group consciousness of belonging to a nation. There was a debate[44] about the origin of the Polka in the early 1840s in the press, and it was part of the ideological-political discourse running in magazines like *Květy* [Flowers] and *Česká Včela*; this discourse was a critical institution of the national movement. Rather than its musical and choreographic features, it was the discourse based on *we* as opposed to *the others* that gave the Polka a symbolic position in society.

Tip Toe-Heel, Entire Foot

The first printed compositions of the Polka from the late 1830s played an important role in the process of myth-formation. These versions were thought to best represent the Polka — i.e., what was accepted by society and matched the contemporary dance standards. At the same time, they helped to spread this official, representative version of the Polka. The the first printed compositions of the Polka were by F. M. Hilmar, a teacher working in Kopidlno near Jičín, and it was there that he played with a band in the early 1830s. He recalls that the local people danced *Maděra*, or *Nimra*, whose motifs he used in his accompanying music.[45] The Polkas he printed soon became popular with the guests of national balls, and social events like *besedy* or *merendy*, since they were exactly what the organisers thought a dance should be, and they played the role they thought a dance should play. The best known Polka, called 'Esmeralda', from 1838, soon gained popularity in the Czech lands and beyond.[46] From its musical structure, it is evident that Hilmar was inspired by

---

44 This debate was started by a story about the discovery of Polka by a servant Anna Chadimová-Slezáková who danced in 1830 a curious new dance in the courtyard of the house she has been working in the small town of Kostelec nad Labem, which was later called as Polka. It became so interesting for onlookers that the local teacher Josef Neruda put it in scores and the servant had to teach the people how to dance it. See in Alfred Waldau, *Böhmische Nationaltänze* (Prague, 1859), pp. 40–41; Zíbrt, *Jak se kdy v Čechách tancovalo*, pp. 319–21. This story was soon put in doubt by the argument that a social dance cannot be invented by one person as well as it has to grow up from the society. See Václav Antonín Crha, 'F. M. Hilmar a jeho vztah k polce', *Dalibor* (1860), 100.

45 Ibid.

46 Nejedlý, *Bedřich Smetana*, p. 362.

the melody that accompanied the dance, called *Maděra*; for example, the frequent semiquaver figures with a group of semiquavers at the end of the movements, which could have given the Polka the *small-stepped* feel when played more slowly.[47] In Hilmar's Polkas, these figures had various positions, always at a different quaver of the bar; triplets were frequently placed in the first quarter of the bar, followed by sharply scored quavers in the second bar.

We do not know how Czech people danced Hilmar's Esmeralda, but it may help to think about the origin of his music that accompanied the folk dance called *Maděra*. There are no descriptions of dances from that time, but the collection of folk songs and dances by Vycpálek, made mainly in the 1880s and based on old people's memories, says a great deal about their active dancing careers, i.e. from the 1830s to the 1860s.[48] For example, *Maděra* is accompanied with the melody *Strejček nimra koupil šimla* from the Rychnov region in East Bohemia:

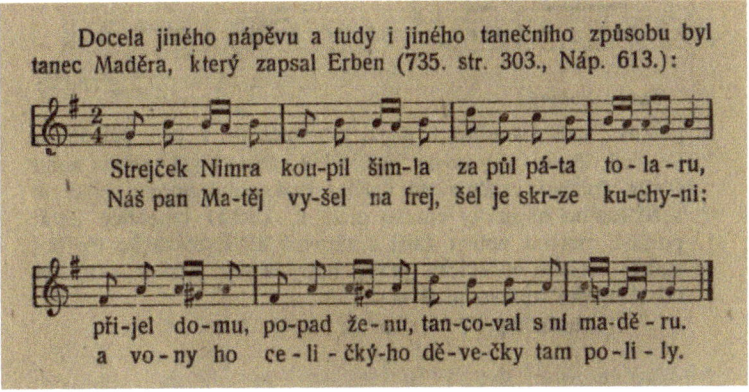

Fig. 5.2 *Maděra* in the collection of folk dances from Josef Vycpálek, *České tance* (Praha: B. Kočí, 1921), p. 105, CC BY.

---

47 Little steps and a free tempo were often highlighted by Czech patriots: for example, in his article entitled 'Moje procházka s dvěma umrlýma', Josef Kajetán Tyl complained that the dancers: '...began to change the nice playful Polka with little steps into "greyhound" gallopade'. Cited after Nejedlý, *Bedřich Smetana*, p. 346.

48 Josef Vycpálek, *České tance* (Prague: F. Topič, 1921).

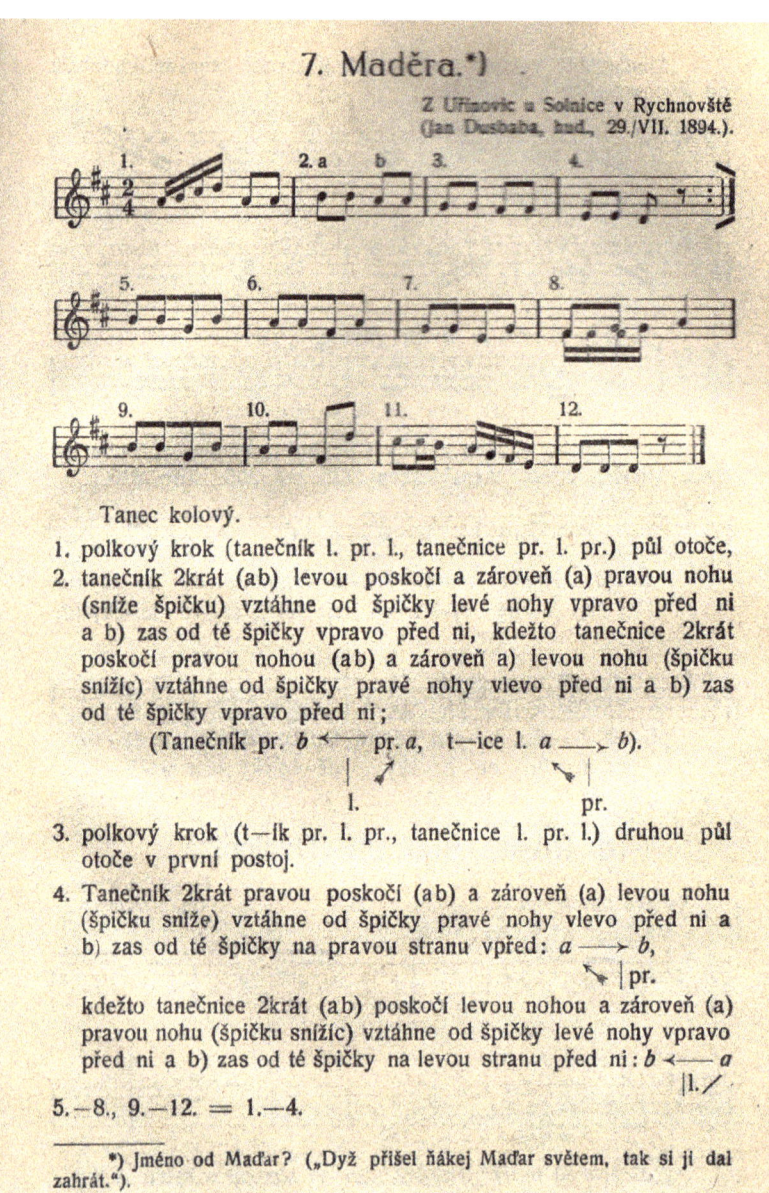

Fig. 5.3 *Maděra cpálek* in the collection of folk dances from Josef Vycpálek, *České tance* (Praha: B. Kočí, 1921), p. 106, CC BY.

There is an interesting comparison to be made with dances that Vycpálek places in the same category as *Maděra* and, apart from a similar rhythm and melody, they have almost identical dance descriptions:

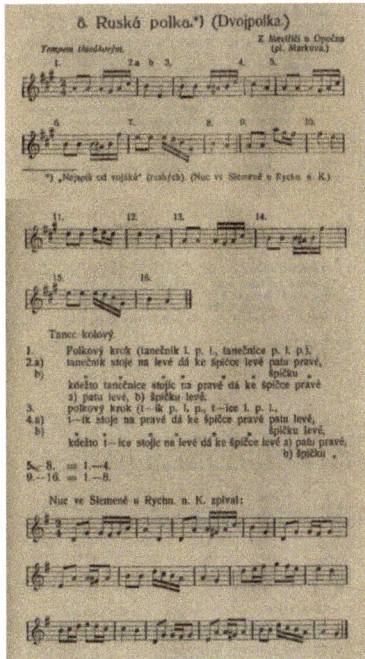

Fig. 5.4 'The Russian Polka (Double-Polka)' in the collection of folk dances from Josef Vycpálek, *České tance* (Praha: B. Kočí, 1921), p. 106, CC BY.

What *Maděra*, the Russian Polka and the Double-Polka have in common is that they are usually danced with Polka steps based on the heel-tip toe motif — '*tip toe-heel, entire foot…*', go the lyrics of a folk song. So in two bars the entire Polka step includes a changing step with a slight swing whenever the foot touches the ground, in addition to a heel-tip toe or a tip toe-heel motif.[49] The swing demands a free tempo, which is necessary if the melody is broken down into semiquavers. In addition to a slow tempo, all examples share a slight swing in the step choreography.

---

49   The tip toe of the foot means here to touch the ground with the end of toes, especially with the big toe. A tip toe-heel or heel-tip toe motif is considered as the typical changing of the heel and tip toe in touching the ground as a flex and pull of the foot.

Another dance worth noting is *Tramlam-Polka*, though it has a slightly different rhythm, as this dance is the 'renamed Třasák'. The name comes from the French word *trembler* ('to shake', or *třásti* in Czech) and it was used in Paris in the late 1840s for the Polka Tremblante, but the notation contains an *obkročák* dance motif[50] with a shake or even a jump whenever the dancers are ready to step forward, as it helps the couple turn round:

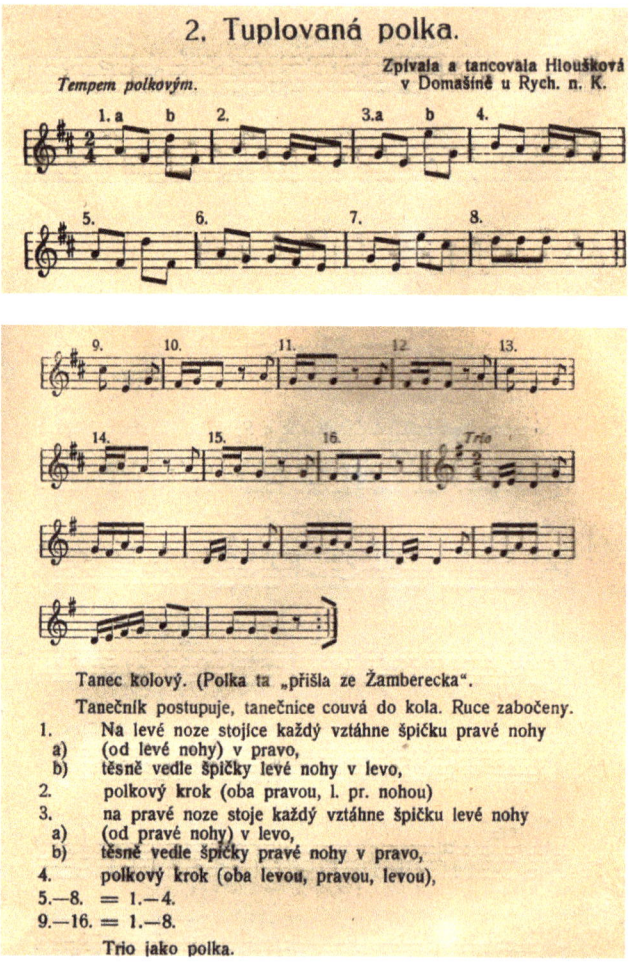

Fig. 5.5 'The Double-Polka' in the collection of folk dances from Josef Vycpálek, *České tance* (Praha: B. Kočí, 1921), p. 94, CC BY.

---

50 *Obkročák* — the name of the dance motif is derived from the method of dancing in a straddle position.

Fig. 5.6 *Tramlam-Polka* in the collection of folk dances from Josef Vycpálek, *České tance* (Praha: B. Kočí, 1921), p. 107, CC BY.

The names of dances also reveal interesting facts. *Maděra*, for instance, refers — through its name and the note of the researcher who recorded the dance—to Hungarian origins (or *Maďar* in Czech); the Russian Polka must have had something to do with Russia.[51] Whatever their origin, the swinging step and the heel-tip toe motif seemed to become symptomatic and do not clash with Josef Kajetán Tyl's 'Polka with little steps' (see footnote 45, above), especially when danced to the music of Hilmar's 'Esmeralda'.

---

51 The person who recorded *Maděra* said: 'Maybe the name comes from Hungary?' and he quotes the person whom he interviewed about the dance: 'Whenever a person from Hungary came along, he had this dance played'. With respect to *Russian Polka*, he gives this quote: 'Most probably from [Russian] soldiers'.

Pas Bohémien, or 'How Gypsies Dance'

The promotion and focus on certain values during the establishment of national identity, and the stronger pressure on a more national consciousness, led, in the early 1840s, to greater promotion of the Czech Polka abroad, as it was intended to represent and promote the Czech nation. The Czech press took on that role, and magazines such as *Květy* and *Česká Včela* reported on how enthusiastically the Czech Polka was accepted in Paris. The reports feature one particular name, that of Johann Raab,[52] a dance master of the Prague Estates Theatre; a Paris correspondent of the Wiener Theater-Zeitung in 1840 reported Raab's guest performance of a piece called *The Golden Axe* at the Théâtre Ambigu, during which Raab danced the Polka. The report also featured in *Květy*:

> The dance admired by the Paris audience so much is no Polish Polka but the favourite Polka danced by our dance-loving boys and girls. Polka, the Czech national dance, when performed by Raab, caused general surprise and gained noisy admiration. The French will now hopefully say they know how 'Gypsies' dance![53]

We do not know how Raab danced the Polka. The only thing we know is that — as in Prague in 1838 when the performance was first held — he and his partner performed dressed in Czech folk costumes (see Fig. 5.7) accompanied by his own composition of the Polka.[54] The audience in both

---

52 The question is to what extent a German dance-master knew about the patriotic message of this 'mission'. He did say in Paris that he was a connoisseur of the Czech Polka, which he said he had found in Czech rural areas and had cultivated for the drawing rooms, but it may just as well be that he had purely utilitarian goals, as teaching the *right* Polka was an extremely profitable job in Paris in 1844: the trick was to use clever advertising to promote his instructions. This way, he could earn quite a fortune. See Nejedlý, *Bedřich Smetana*, pp. 352–54.

53 Cited after Nejedlý, *Bedřich Smetana*, p. 357. The connotation of the French term *bohémiens* which indicate the Roma led to the confusion with the Czech country Bohemie (la Bohême) which could be thus understood as a place where the Roma live. Translated from Czech by David Mraček.

54 The composition was published as *Neue Polka* in Prague in 1839 by the M. Berry Publishing House, together with a Polka by Hilmar of the same name and a few more dances in a collection of Galops. It has a sophisticated form; the initial part is in 3/4 time, the other 2/4-time part contains a trio and a coda, as was usually the case with such early Polkas.

cases responded — as the press put it — with enthusiastic ovations.[55] It seems unlikely that the audience was attracted by this very artificial musical composition coming from the category of cosmopolitan Galops; rather, what made an impact on the audience here was the folk feel to it, emphasised by the costumes and the contemporary social role of the dance.

Raab made another visit to Paris in 1844, giving more lectures on *the right* Polka. Although the press in Prague produced some enthusiastic reports on Raab's representation of the Polka, some of the Paris media reporting in 1844 on the Polka's arrival in Paris are surprisingly much more tentative.[56]

The introduction to the guide *La Polka*,[57] for example, fails to give a clear background as to the origin of the Polka, alluding to an exotic story of how, on his way from Africa, Hippollitus the painter had to make a stop by the river Danube somewhere near Belgrade: dressed as an Egyptian prince and accompanied by a local Hungarian man, he visited a local dancing event. He saw the local people dance with spurs on their boots and bagpipes playing; the dancers turned round every now and then by taking a round turn without letting go of each other. The author went on to analyse the Polka and its origins, taking into consideration how it was danced by Hungarians, Russians, and Poles: he concluded that the Polka was danced in the whole of Germany, particularly in 'La Bohême', which could refer to Bohemia (or the Czech lands), or the regions where Roma Gypsies lived, since the French word carried both of these meanings. The Polka's arrival in Paris is depicted metaphorically as the arrival of a inconspicuous Pole in a town that soon welcomed him with enthusiastic acclaim.

The French were not overly concerned with the origin of the Polka, since their 'Polka nationale' had left the village for the town in order to become genteel, and was soon accepted as French. In turn, the first performances of the Polka at the Paris Opera by Coralli (see Fig. 5.8) in a kind of folk costume did not contradict the notion that the dance could have come from virtually anywhere.

---

55   Cited after Nejedlý, *Bedřich Smetana*, pp. 357–58.
56   Ibid.
57   Perrot and Robert, *La Polka enseignée sans maître*.

Fig. 5.7 Title page by J. Brandard of the score for *The Bohemian Polka* by Hermann Louis Koenig, 1847. Lithograph. The bare feet of the woman, and the man's earring, may hint at gypsy style. Source: *The Bartered Bride*, Royal Opera House programme, 10 December 1998, p. 25. Wikimedia Commons, Public Domain, https://commons.wikimedia.org/wiki/File:Bohemian_Polka.jpg#/media/File:Bohemian_Polka.jpg

5. *The Polka as a Czech National Symbol*   131

Fig. 5.8 Eugène Coralli and Mlle Maria dancing in particular costumes at the Paris Opera, picture in the guide *La Polka enseigné sans maître par MM. Perrot et Adrien Robert* (Paris: Aubert, 1845), p. 10. Private archive of Dorota Gremlicová, all rights reserved.

Three years later, the dance master of Paris, Henri Cellarius, the author of the dance guide *The Drawing-Room Dances*, published in 1847, said the Polka was simply French because it was the good French taste that made it into something that the world would accept.

The kind of Polka Raab performed and taught in Paris remains to be investigated. It is interesting to note, however, that the guide *La Polka*[58] contains Polka figures of ten different kinds (e.g., waltzing) including a description and a drawing of *pas bohémien*. Both the description and the drawing (see Fig. 5.9) make it clear that it is a heel-tip step combined with a changing step.

---

58 This was a guide for the general public, instructing them how to learn Polka even without a dance master. The guide used the same method that the dance master Eugène Coralli was using in Paris at that time.

Fig. 5.9 'Pas bohémien', picture in the guide *La Polka einseignée sans maître par MM. Perrot et Adrien Robert* (Paris: Aubert, 1845), p. 58. Private archive of Dorota Gremlicová, all rights reserved.

Cellarius describes this dance, too, although he suggests that it should be abandoned. Instead, he prefers a simple Polka with the basic motif of a changing step with impromptu variations in a fast tempo *di Marcia*, which he says makes the Polka even more lively and spontaneous.

What, or who, for that matter, was *pas bohémien* associated with? Was Raab a messenger in Paris describing the (Hungarian) Maděra, Russian Polka, and so on, as coming from the Czech rural areas, or from patriotic Czech social events held in towns? If so, it is very likely that he exported Polka in the form that was performed at dance events held in Prague in the early 1840s. With clever advertising, he could make a fairly good living in Paris. No less importantly, Raab helped the Polka return to the Czech lands, as the magazine *Květy* reported in 1842:

> Having made an irresistible appeal to so many minds and legs in the drawing-rooms of Paris and London since last year's Carnival, the

Polka — our wonderful countrywoman — has now returned to the place of her origin, although not as a village woman wearing a close-fitting costume but as a lady dressed in a long silk dress, and is now known as *'polketa en colonne'*. Travelling across Europe, she was accompanied and guided by Mr Raab, an expert on dancing. Giving lectures to all keen dancers in his flat, this dance master is now busy emphasising all Polka's virtues in a way which gives you a good grasp of this dance within six hours — that is at least what is offered to the general public in Mr Raab's special Czech advertisement.[59]

Fig. 5.10 J. Raab and Mlle Valentine dancing Polka at the Théâtre Ambigu Paris. Private archive of Dorota Gremlicová, all rights reserved.

---

59 Cited in Zíbrt, *Jak se kdy v Čechách tancovalo*, p. 325.

Dance as a National Programme — Polka on the Go!

The early 1860s brought favourable conditions for social activities independent of the state. Czech national associations were being established to a huge extent in Czech towns: almost every town had its *Beseda*. Sokol, a physical culture association with a tradition lasting to this day, was founded in 1862; there were open-air meetings, camps which brought together the small-town bourgeoisie and farmers as well as workers. There was a new element to the political life of the Czech nation, and it was supposed to unify society under the banner of a national movement. It was a Quadrille dance called *Česká Beseda* printed in 1863, danced a year before by the famous poet Jan Neruda at a public ball. It is no coincidence that it was Neruda who helped the author of the music, Ferdinand Heller, and the dance master Karel Link to establish the dance. Being a promoter of social events, Neruda realised how well dance could help revive and strengthen national consciousness. Arne Novák, for example, reports on Neruda's adoration of dance in general:

> Neruda, called jokingly and reproachfully a dance master, had little understanding for music, which was everything for Smetana. It was in dance that Neruda found the impressive power that laymen associate with music, one that tears humans out of reality, bringing them closer to the primeval soul of the universe.[60]

Also, even before *Česká Beseda* appeared, Neruda had published his first essay on dance in the magazine *Obrazy života* in 1859; called '*České národní tance*' [Czech national dances]. The paper even deals with some of the theoretical aspects of dance.[61] Later, Neruda proposed that the journalist Alfred Waldau should produce the first comprehensive paper on dance in Bohemia.[62] All this testifies to his real interest in dance and to his endeavour to grasp its national message. He studied dance in detail and understood the potential that dance could have in society under some specific conditions. His essays on the national message of dance have no doubt effected how the Polka was understood; Neruda considered

---

60   Arne Novák, 'Bedřich Smetana a Jan Neruda', in *Studie o Janu Nerudovi*, ed. by Arne Novák (Prague: F. Topič, 1919), pp. 112–26 (p. 114).
61   Jan Neruda, *České národní tance* (Prague: Nová osvěta, 1956).
62   Alfred Waldau, *Böhmische Nationaltänze* (Prag: Verlag Herman Dominikus, 1859–1860).

the Polka *the* Czech dance.⁶³ He claimed that the Polka's liveliness and natural joy reflected the nation's renaissance and its triumphant arrival in towns from Czech villages — as shown in *Balada o polce* [The Ballad of Polka] with the refrain of *Polka jede!* [Polka on the go!] — symbolised the influx of renewed strength from folk rural regions into towns, and helped better communicate the concept of national identity.

Fig. 5.11 Portrait of Jan Neruda by Jan Vilímek from *České album, sbírka podobizen předních českých velikánů* (V. Praze: Jos. R. Vilímek, [n.d.]). Wikimedia Commons, Public Domain, https://commons.wikimedia.org/wiki/File:Jan_Vil%C3%ADmek_-_Jan_Neruda.jpg#/media/File:Jan_Vil%C3%ADmek_-_Jan_Neruda.jpg

---

63 It was reflected by ethnochoreologist Martina Pavlicová, 'Postavy z dějin české etnochoreologie (Jan Jeník z Bratřic, Václav Krolmus, Josef Jaroslav Langer, Jan Neruda)', *Národopisná revue*, 2 (1992), 156–64.

It is evident from his poems that Neruda was very critical about *national identity*. He said, with bitter scepticism, that the Czech nation was 'a soulless goose, lacking manly courage, a non-nation, a mere group of scoundrels, more of a dreaming, sleeping, dead-alive nation than one that is waking up'.[64] The motif of dreams and sleep is actually a frequent metaphor for national paralysis during the period of national revival. By initiating the patriotic movement, the sleeping nation was *woken up*; the direct participants in the process of emancipation considered themselves *awakened* whereas those who refused to demonstrate their Czech identity publicly were *sleepy*. Neruda thought it necessary to visibly demonstrate a sign of identity; therefore he wore a *čamara*, a festive black coat with a symbolic meaning, and thought it absurd that anyone who spoke Czech and was obviously Czech failed to declare this by carrying any visible sign.[65] Dance, he thought, was one of these visible signs. The meaning he associated with dance is obvious from a number of his newspaper columns, and Neruda understood dance was a source of energy, awakening and introspection:

> A great role is played by dance rhythm. It is the rhythm that mirrors our own identity, unconscious, far from our egotism; in sounds we hear ourselves and identify with them, becoming fiery, wildly fast, less dignified, nicely merry just like the sounds. We give up our personality, enthused by the sound and movement of our whole being. Without music, dance would have no such ideal feeling to it, and we would feel no variety of moods.[66]

The lack of expression in dancing is something Neruda associated with a lack of national enthusiasm. In his study of 1869 *O tanci* [On dance], Neruda says, with disillusionment: 'And what about our dance? Dancers only walk rather than dance in Quadrille and *Beseda*, shuffle rather than dance in Polka and Gallopade, both of which need a fast tempo; there are hardly any good dancers, perhaps fast ones, those with healthy lungs or those who ignore their tuberculosis'.[67]

---

64 See footnote 60.
65 See Macura, *Český sen*, pp. 42, 44.
66 Jan Neruda, 'O tanci. Rozjímání dle velmi učených lidí' in *Dílo Jana Nerudy VIII. Studie krátké a kratší I. Uspořádal M. Novotný* (Prague: Kvasnička a Hampl, 1923), pp. 165–89 (p. 199).
67 Ibid., p. 166.

Therefore, Neruda's participation in the establishment of *Česká Beseda* was a key factor as Neruda made sure that this Quadrille contained dances selected carefully, according to their potential to carry a message. By being modified into something that would meet certain expectations, the dances were manipulated in their symbolic value, and, at the same time, it was important to think about the form that could be accepted by society at that time. The Polka enjoyed a fairly large place within *Česká Beseda*; it appears in two different forms there, modified into a Quadrille dance, which may have been what society wanted most — there is also the Polka's return from Paris as 'polketa en colonne':

Fig. 5.12 Polka, from a booklet describing the dance *Česká Beseda* (*Česká Beseda*, ed. by J. Fiala, J. Prokšová-Evaldová, M. Malá, J. Vokáčová, and H. Livorová, p. 10), CC BY.[68]

---

[68] Cited in the second edition of *Česká beseda s nápěvy se slovy všech jednotlivých písní a popis tanců*, ed. by J. Fiala, J. Prokšová-Evaldová, M. Malá, J. Vokáčová, and H. Livorová (Prague: Komenium, 1947).

I-B-1　　　　　　　　　　　　　　　　　　　　　　　POLKA

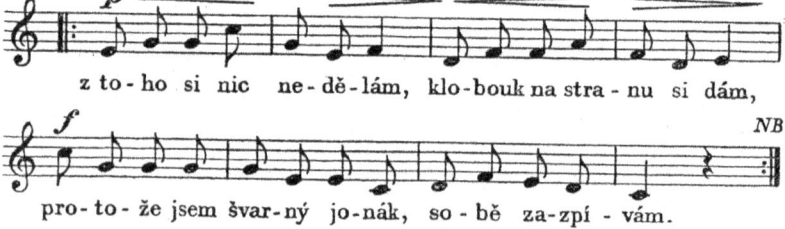

(2) Zelená je švarná barva,
　　lásky barva je;
　　černooké děvče hezké
　　už mne miluje:
　　[: upřímně mne miluje,
　　štěstí mnoho slibuje,
　　až se domů z vojny vrátím,
　　že bude moje.:]

(3) Já už sedím na mém věrném,
　　vraném koníčku;
　　přiveďte mně, kamarádi,
　　mou holubičku:
　　[: ať se se mnou rozžehná,
　　bílou ruku mi podá,
　　přes pole mne vyprovodí
　　holubička má.:]

NB. Repetice platí jen pro zpěv mimo Besedu.

Fig. 5.13 Polka, from a booklet describing the dance Česká Beseda (Česká beseda, ed. by J. Fiala, J. Prokšová-Evaldová, M. Malá, J. Vokáčová, and H. Livorová, p. 6), CC BY.

The first of these two forms is a Polka in a slower tempo in the Hilmar-style and with the heel-tip motif called Double-Polka. In the other form, the couple steps forward with a changing step in various dimensional formations to a livelier marching tempo. In other words, this is a meeting point of two musical and choreographic types of Polka — one that was composed by village teachers at a slower tempo, the other more down-to-earth, played by military bands, based on Gallopades. And, as they are modified into Quadrilles, they come to play a representative role in Czech patriotic circles.

Having been printed, *Česká Beseda* easily spread across all social classes both in towns and in rural areas, and soon became a universal instrument raising awareness about national cultural values. Dancing *Česká Beseda* meant showing publicly one's national consciousness.

However, the Polka began to lose its initial significance,[69] and it was Neruda again who called for its return. In his column '*O taneční hudbě*' [On Czech Dance Music], printed in the daily *Národní listy* in 1885, Neruda exhibited his anxiety about the weakening national consciousness and lack of enthusiasm in society. He called for the return of the times when the Polka had engulfed the dance halls of Prague, making people look forward to the future with joy and take an active role in social life:

> It is high time we had our own Prague king — not a king of Waltz, but a king of Polka. Ever since Komzak held the position of a civilian bandmaster, there had always been two kings on the Prague throne, Svoboda and Procházka. You would hardly find more loyal subjects than the people of Prague. Every time notices stuck on street corners announced that Svoboda and his band of artillery soldiers were about to give a concert on one of the islands of Prague introducing a new Polka, the island would always be overcrowded. Everyone would look forward to the new Polka, tension was growing, and as the desired music started the entire crowd would break into merry whispering. Suddenly, all went quiet. Heads nodded in time with the music, every single foot would pound on the ground, every single face would brighten up, smiling.[70]

He may have realised the power of a dance that is able — under certain conditions — to wake people up and bring them together in the name of an ideal. As enthusiasm for the Polka was decreasing in Prague, Neruda called for its renaissance, as part of a wave of new energy and enthusiasm for the national programme which — he thought — society failed to demonstrate visibly enough.

In the meantime, the Polka had lost some of its ability to be a symbol, as simplifications to its choreographic structure had made it more similar to other cosmopolitan drawing-room dances accompanied by numerous musical compositions. The form had become simpler: the

---

69　Gremlicová, *Tanec a český národní program*, p. 95.
70　Jan Neruda, 'O taneční hudbě', in *Studie vážné i humoristické II* (Prague: F. Topič, 1919), pp. 155–59 (p. 158).

couple danced around the room in one step in an increasing tempo. Patriots inevitably saw such modifications as a weakening of the national features of the dance, and therefore new symbols were sought. There was more and more demand for older folk dances of Czech origin and of various forms. 'Why do we have so many Polkas and Waltzes?', asked the composer Leoš Janáček in his article of the same name published in the daily *Lidové noviny* in 1905, commenting on the simplification of something that had changed from more structured choreography into mere couple-turning:

> The reason why we have about 300 different dances in Moravia is that neither Waltz nor Polka had been special folk dances; instead their choreographic motif (turning) was only one of the motifs in the more structured dances. Now, this has changed: only two dances are danced — Polka and Waltz — but they may be accompanied by a terrible amount of musical compositions.[71]

Some of the guides to national dances published on the occasion of the Czech-Slavic Ethnologic Exhibition do not put the Polka among these dances.[72]

What Makes the Czech Polka Czech?

In the 1860s, the Polka was given the position of an ideal national symbol in the works of Bedřich Smetana: in particular, his opera *The Bartered Bride*, which was composed when the composer was asked to produce a national comic opera. It is important to realise that the dances of Polka, Furiant and Skočná were included in the opera as late as its French version, composed three years after the Prague premiere of 1869 for the purposes of guest performances on international stages. The Polka included in the performance was supposed to be danced and its spontaneous joy was meant to reflect the life of Czech villages.

---

71 Leoš Janáček, 'Proč máme tolik polek a valčíků? in *Fejetony z Lidových novin*, ed. by J. Racka, A. Nováka, V. Helferta, and L. Firkušného (Brno: Krajské nakl. v Brně, 1958), p. 72.
72 Tomeš Geisselreiter, *Návod k tančení Národních tancův, upravil Ph. Mg. Tomeš Geisselreiter. 1. a 2. díl* (Prague: Fr. A. Urbánek, 1895).

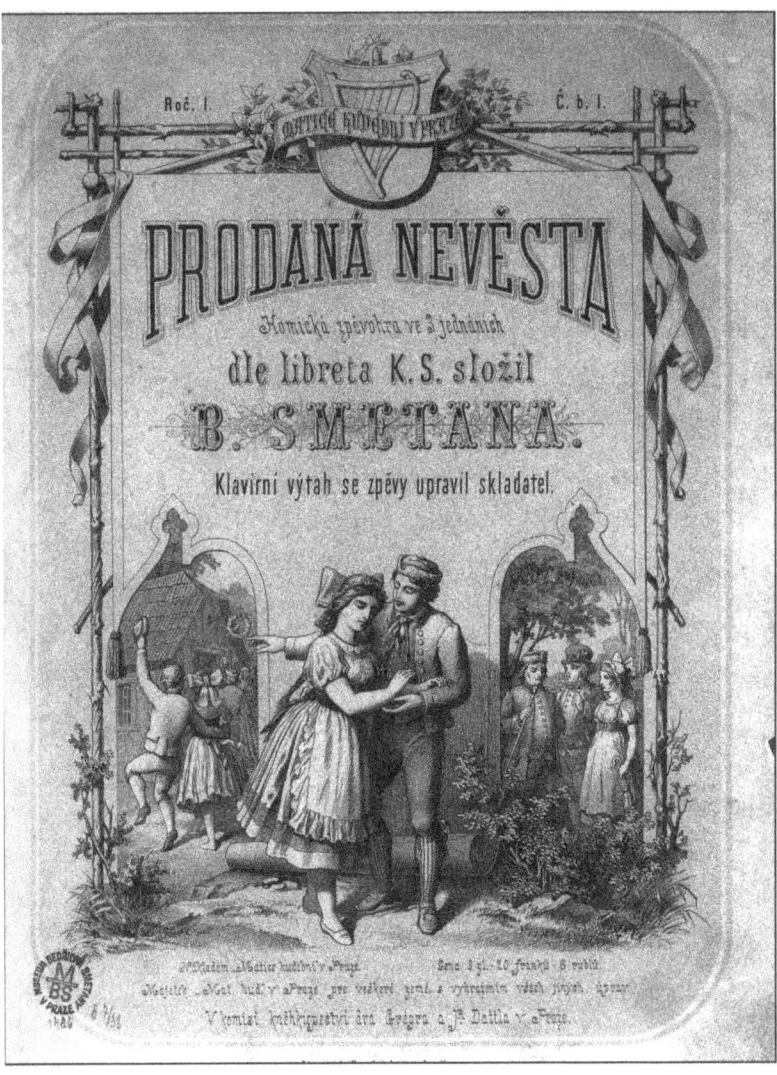

Fig. 5.14 Smetana's *The Bartered Bride*, title page of the first edition of the piano reduction (1872). Bedřich Smetana, *La Fiancée vendue. Avant Scène Opéra No. 248* (Paris: Premières Loges, 2008). Wikimedia Commons, Public Domain, https://commons.wikimedia.org/wiki/File:BarteredBridePianoReduction.jpg#/media/File:BarteredBridePianoReduction.jpg

This chapter does not seek to analyse the links to and dependencies on the folklore background, nor to discuss the concept of national music, which is dealt with by numerous essays anyway.[73] Instead, it investigates the ways in which Smetana used his experience with Czech patriotic ballrooms, and which features of folk tradition he thought were representative of Czech national Polka. Even though the musical form of the Polka is dealt with here, the significant point is that it was produced for the purpose of dance.

The Polka as present in *The Bartered Bride* is a summary of the previous changes to the formal content of the dance and its concept. What was reflected here was Smetana's experience with performing Hilmar's Polkas — which he frequently performed during the student meetings called *merenda* — as well as his familiarity with the dancing conventions of that time. His Polka in *The Bartered Bride* brings together several of the typical Polka types — Hilmar-style graceful Polka in a free tempo, *třasák*-style [shake-dance] rhythm figures leading to *Polka tremblante*, as well as a special rhythmic structuring similar to the Galop in a very lively tempo. However, these are absolutely not quotations of folk motifs, but a special principle of the metro-rhythmic structure, with the 2/4 rhythm as a basic sign. He used this to clearly distinguish the Polka from the 'foreign' Waltz in triple metre and to build upon Skočná melodies typical of Czech folk songs.[74] Smetana's Polka in *The Bartered Bride* is a product of artistic work, but its role as a national symbol, which it was assigned due to the overall effect of *The Bartered Bride*, made a substantial contribution to the social discourse at a time when national identity was being established. Consequently, this Polka became the final product of the hunt for an ideal form of Czech Polka as a national symbol.

---

73   See Mirko Očadlík, *Tvůrce české národní hudby Bedřich Smetana* (Prague: Práce, 1949); Jan Racek, *Idea vlasti, národa a slávy v díle B. Smetany* (Prague: Hudební matice Umělecké besedy 1947); Rudolf Pečman, 'K problému národní hudby v Evropě a v českých zemích', *Opus musicum*, 9 (1977), 8–13.

74   Nejedlý, *Bedřich Smetana*, pp. 362–84.

Summary

The Polka came to manifest the Czech values of modern times, which also coexisted with regional patriotism, on the one hand, and Pan-Slavism, on the other. It helped create national consciousness at a time when the attribute *national* could only be given to items that originated in local Czech villages, disregarding the fact that even these places were faced with various cultural influences, with some features migrating out and others being brought in. First and foremost, the name of the dance carried political meaning; the Polka as a cultural product fulfilled this goal to a lesser extent. When the Polka was being established as a Czech national symbol, some external signs played a major role as well. The choice focused not on those that would be of genuinely local origin, but on those that could be accepted as Czech by society at that time. In the process of manipulating with signs, the main purpose was to distinguish them from the *foreign* ones; in other words, from those able to directly harm anyone called *ours*. Therefore, the heel-tip step and the swinging changing step, supported by the appropriate metro-rhythmic structure and tempo, became the representative features of the Czech Polka, and they went on to play this role despite the conventions of dance halls developing in a different way. This helped deepen the clash between the signified and the signifier, and further improved the ideal form of the myth of the Czech Polka, which was the product of the endeavour of Czech patriots and artists. By reaching its ideal form, the myth started to deviate from the Polkas danced by society — from Polkas linked to particular places, Polkas of a local, regional or even cosmopolitan nature. The meaning and social use of the dance kept changing; the myth of the Polka had become a constant value of Czech national culture. Even the myth, however, must be seen as a fusion of social, cultural and ideological-political, as well as artistic, perspectives.

Fig. 5.15 Video: Final in the regional competition for Česká Lípa in Czech Polka for children, ballroom style. 'Česká polka — finale Česká Lípa dupen 2012', 1:37, posted online by Lenka čermáková, *Youtube,* 22 April 2012, https://www.youtube.com/watch?v=oYiaywtlQxU

Fig. 5.16 Video: Dance TV from the Czech Television showing clips of Polka, many group choreographies, and teaching the dance. 'Polka', 14:35, posted online by An000b, *Youtube*, 24 October 2011, https://www.youtube.com/watch?v=LiIxtj0wtcA

Additional Video Resources

Video: Dance instruction for basic Polka. 'Základní taneční — Polka', 1:46, posted online by tkclassic, *Youtube*, 5 October 2010, http://www.youtube.com/watch?v=r_Ceds7iX5U&feature=related

Video: A Polka choreography with many couples dancing to a brass band, seen from above. 'Taneční — polka', 1:11, posted online by 162591419, *Youtube*, 24 December 2010, http://www.youtube.com/watch?v=HjEso6JyBX0&NR=

Video: A program on Polka in a series broadcast on Česká televize. 'Taneční-Polka', 0:49, posted online by broxwille, *Youtube*, 14 October 2007, http://www.youtube.com/watch?v=WNeXUhE6-a4

Video: Young people dancing Polka to accordion music in a dance school. 'TANEČNÍ VRDY — Polka III'., 0:36, posted online by brunetkabbb, *Youtube*, 21 October 2007, http://www.youtube.com/watch?v=Vg_J5Gm2NMY&feature=related

Video: 'A rather messy Polka', with young people dance the steps on different beats of the music. 'tročku chaotická polka', 1:35, posted online by snowboardackaaa, *Youtube*, 23 November 2008, http://www.youtube.com/watch?v=NRzbKWpiLkc

Video: A dance course where the instructor teaches and demonstrates Polka. '2. závěrečná prodloužená cún česká polka', 0:27, posted online by Tuan Lai, *Youtube*, 11 December 2010, http://www.youtube.com/watch?v=L5KeZqPuZzg

Video: Dance competition for children dancing Polka. 'Taneční soutěž — polka', 1:38, posted online by adejkak, *Youtube*, 28 September 2010, http://www.youtube.com/watch?v=VR6Hg408Dbs

Video: Folk dancers in traditional costumes dance Polka with figures. 'Czech Polka', 1:56, posted online by pjacko1017, *Youtube*, 25 April 2009, http://www.youtube.com/watch?v=AunRWB_dmiM&feature-related

Video: A couple dancing a Victorian-era Polka in period clothing. 'Polka/Excerpt from How to Dance Through Time, Vol. 5, Victorian Era Couple Dances',

0:58, posted by DancetimePublication, *Youtube*, 12 March 2009, http://www.youtube.com/watch?v=ajxfQk_zbjM

Video: Vejvodova band plays the well-known Polka tune Rosamunde (music only). 'Škoda lásky — Vejvodova kapela', 2:49, posted online by rudolfo6666, *Youtube*, 14 May 2010, http://www.youtube.com/watch?v=jyI9Pj4CEdE&feature=related

Video: Karel Gott, famous Czech singer, performing a Polka with dancers on a television show. 'Škoda lásky', 1:45, posted online by benetomm, *Youtube*, 25 December 2007, http://www.youtube.com/watch?v=8x6KOE0HowA&feature=related

Video: Recreational folk dancers in America dancing Doudlebska Polka. 'Doudlebská Polka', 3:53, posted online by Roy Butler, *Youtube*, 15 November 2008, http://www.youtube.com/watch?v=Y9gmBrAwtPo&feature-related

Video: Dancers in German costumes dancing Doudlebska Polka. 'Doudlebská Polka — Tyrolsko', 2:30, posted online by born2danz, *Youtube*, 17 August 2009, http://www.youtube.com/watch?v=nf7O7Lzt8Oo&feature=related

Bibliography

Argus, 'Chronique', *La Semaine des Familles*, 18 (11 October 1884), pp. 159–60.

Barthes, Roland, *Mytologie* (Prague: Dokořán, 2004).

Bakka, Egil, 'The Polka before and after the Polka', *Yearbook for Traditional Music*, 33 (2001), 37–47, https://doi.org/10.2307/1519629

Bradáč, Josef, *Ze zašlých časů. Několik starých českých polek, jež sebral a pro klavír upravil Jaroslav Bradáč* (Prague: Hudební matice Umělecké Besedy, 1921).

Brouček, Stanislav, Jiří Cvekl, Václav Hubinger, et al., 'Základní pojmy etnické teorie', *Český lid*, 78 (1991), 273–57.

Brunvand, Jan H., *American Folklore: An Encyclopedia* (New York: Routledge, 2006).

Cellarius, Henri, *La danse des salons*, 2nd edn (Paris: chez l´auteur, rue Neuve-Vivienne, 49 et chez principaux libraires, 1849).

——, *The Drawing-Room Dances* (London: E. Churton, 1847).

Crha, Václav Antonín, 'F. M. Hilmar a jeho vztah k polce', *Dalibor* (1860), 100.

Erben, Karel Jaromír, 'Ještě něco o polce', *Česká včela*, 11 (1844), 304.

Fiala, J., J. Prokšová-Evaldová. M. Malá, J. Vokáčová, and H. Livorová, *Česká beseda s nápěvy se slovy všech jednotlivých písní a popis tanců* (Prague: Komenium, 1947).

Geisselreiter, Tomeš, *Návod k tančení Národních tancův, upravil Ph. Mg. Tomeš Geisselreiter. 1. a 2. díl* (Prague: Fr. A. Urbánek, 1895).

Giurchescu, Anca, 'The Power of Dance and its Social and Political Uses', *Yearbook for Traditional Music*, 23, ed. by Adrienne L. Kaeppler, Dietmar Christensen, and Stephen Wild (2001), 109–22, https://doi.org/10.2307/1519635

Gremlicová, Dorota, 'Tanec a český národní program', *Národopisná revue*, 11 (2001), 93–95.

Horák, Jiří, 'Erbenova sbírka českých písní lidových', *Národopisný věstník českoslovanský*, 7 (1912), 6–7.

Hroch, Miroslav, *V národním zájmu* (Prague: Knižnice dějin a současnosti, 1999).

Janáček, Leoš 'Proč máme tolik polek a valčíků?', in *Fejetony z Lidových novin*, ed. by J. Racka, A. Nováka, V. Helferta, and L. Firkušného (Brno: Krajské nakl. v Brně, 1958), p. 72.

Kořalka, Jiří, Češi v Habsburské říši a v Evropě 1815–1914. Sociálně historické souvislosti vytváření novodobého národa a národnostní otázky v českých zemích (Prague: Argo, 1996).

Langer, Josef Jaroslav, 'České krakováčky', in *Bodláčí a růže* (Prague: Státní nakladatelství krásné literatury, hudby a umění, 1957), p. 211.

Laudová, Hannah, 'Další pramen ke studiu českých lidových tanců', *Český lid*, 44 (1957), 273–74.

Macura, Vladimír, *Český sen* (Prague: Knižnice dějin a současnosti, 1998).

Mirjam Moravcová, *'Národní oděv roku 1848': Ke vzniku národně politického symbolu* (Prague: Academia, 1986).

'Národopisné studie našich Umělců' [n.a.], *Český lid*, 12 (1903), 87–93.

Nejedlý, Zdeněk, *Bedřich Smetana 4. díl. Česká společnost* (Prague: Hudební Matice Umělecké Besedy, 1925).

Neruda, Jan, *České národní tance* (Prague: Nová osvěta, 1946).

——, 'O tanci. Rozjímání dle velmi učených lidí', in *Dílo Jana Nerudy VIII. Studie krátké a kratší I. Uspořádal M. Novotný* (Prague: Kvasnička a Hampl, 1923), pp. 165–89.

——, 'O taneční hudbě', in *Studie vážné i humoristické II* (Prague: F. Topič, 1919), pp. 155–59.

Novák, Arne, 'Bedřich Smetana a Jan Neruda', in *Studie o Janu Nerudovi*, ed. Arne Novák (Prague: F. Topič, 1919), pp. 112–26.

Očadlík, Mirko, *Tvůrce české národní hudby Bedřich Smetana* (Prague: Práce, 1949).

Pavlicová, Martina, *Lidový tanec v Českých zemích. Sondy do historiografie, ekologie a metodologie* (Brno: FF MÚ, 1992).

——, 'Postavy z dějin české etnochoreologie (Jan Jeník z Bratřic, Václav Krolmus, Josef Jaroslav Langer, Jan Neruda)', *Národopisná revue*, 2 (1992), 156–64.

Pečman, Rudolf, 'K problému národní hudby v Evropě a v českých zemích', *Opus musicum*, 9 (1977), 8–13.

Raab, Johann, *Neue Polka. Prager Lieblings-Galoppen für das Pianoforte, č. 70* (Prague: Nákladem Marca Berry, 1839).

Racek, Jan, *Idea vlasti, národa a slávy v díle B. Smetany* (Prague: Hudební matice Umělecké besedy, 1947).

Perrot, MM., and Adrien Robert, *La Polka enseignée sans maître, par MM. Perrot et Adrien Robert, d´après M. Eugène Coralli de l´Académie royale de musique* (Paris: Aubert, 1844).

Shukman, Ann, 'Lotman: The Dialectic of a Semiotician', in *The Sign. Semiotics around the World*, ed. by Richard W. Bailey, Ladislav Matejka, and Peter Steiner (Ann Arbor, MI: Slavic Publications, 1980), pp. 19–206.

Stavělová, Daniela. 'Polka jako český národní symbol', *Český lid*, 93 (2006), pp. 3–26.

Tyl, Josef Kajetán, *Od nového roku do postu. Kus pražského života*, ed. F. Strejček (Prague: F. Topič, 1926).

Tomek, Václav Vladivoj, *Paměti z mého života.* (Prague: F. Řivnáč, 1904–1906).

Vycpálek, Josef, *České tance* (Prague: F. Topič, 1921).

Waldau, Alfred, *Geschichte des böhmischen Nationaltanzes* (Prague: Kath. Gerzabek, 1861).

——, *Böhmische Nationaltänze* (Prague: Verlag Herman Dominikus, 1859–1860).

Wikipedia contributors, 'Polka', *Wikipedia, The Free Encyclopedia*, 11 March 2020, https://en.wikipedia.org/wiki/Polka

Zíbrt, Čeněk, *Jak se kdy v Čechách tancovalo*, 2nd edn (Prague: Státní nakladatelství krásné literatury, hudby a umění, 1960).

——, 'Zprávy o polce v první polovici věku 19', *Národní listy*, 197 (1894), 45.

6. Decency, Health, and Grace Endangered by Quick Dancing? The New Dance Style in *Bohemia* in 1830

Dorota Gremlicová

Newspaper articles constitute significant contemporary sources for discourses on dance. This chapter examines two such sources, offering detailed analysis of the texts, the authors, their background and the cultural and political climate they represent. The sources, consisting of a letter and a reply, discuss what the leading authorities of the time saw as positive and negative aspects of dancing, and together they redress the balance of the frequently one-sided outcries against dance as a danger to morality, decency and health.

Discussions about Dance in the Newspaper *Bohemia*

In February 1830, there appeared in the newspaper *Bohemia*, printed in Prague, a series of articles dealing with various aspects of Carnival, including dancing. Two of them were written in the form of a letter and a response, and their authors reacted to the dancing practices of the time, citing in particular *Reydowak*, a fashionable dance of the contemporary repertoire.

The *Bohemia* was published as a free supplement to the newspaper *Prager Zeitung* from 1828 to 1835 with the subtitle *Unterhaltungsblätter für gebildete Stände* [Paper of Amusement for Educated People]. It later became an independent newspaper, one of the most influential German newspapers published in Bohemia until World War Two. In 1830, the supplement largely offered information on culture, theatrical and musical events, society life, curiosities, and sometimes also stories, travel experiences and depictions of foreign countries and their customs and culture. Political events were reported only occasionally, and when they were, it was for their more 'amusing' aspects.[1]

The first article, a letter addressed to the author of the column 'Prager Novitäten' [Prague Novelties] in *Bohemia*, was published on 7 February under the title 'Sendschreiben' [the Letter] (hereafter, referred to as the Letter). It covered the whole of page four under the heading 'Theater und geselliges Leben' [Theatre and Social Life]. After transcription from the Gothic script, it is slightly longer than two pages of A4 and is signed only with the initials 'A. M.'.[2]

The author begins by complimenting his addressee, dancing fashion whom he describes as an expert on Carnival matters. He says he is writing because he wishes to clarify his own opinion on some features of the, as he feels confused by conflicting impressions. On the one hand, he was touched by the statement in an article published previously in *Prager Zeitung*,[3] which claimed that current dancing practices would have to become a subject for the 'health police'. The young ladies would need special lung capacity to tackle the popular 'Extra-Touren',[4] or else the turns might lead them directly to the cemetrey. The author referred to by his initials A. M. draws contrasting pictures of a seventeen-year-old girl dancing in February in the arms of her partner with red cheeks, out of breath, with her dress flying around her, and then in May, dying in her room from the effects of this activity. His anxiety was deepened by the poet Harro Harring (see below) who had expressed a hostile attitude towards *Reydowak*. Harring described the dance as the main offender in a general decline of good manners, and on this basis he

---

1   *Bohemia, Unterhaltungsblätter für gebildete Stände* [n.a.], 3 (1830), http://kramerius.nkp.cz/kramerius/PShowVolume.do?it=0&id=14191
2   Anton Müller, 'Sendschreiben. Theater und geselliges Leben', *Bohemia, Unterhaltungsblätter für gebildete Stände*, 17 (7 February 1830), pp. 3–4, section 'Prager Novitäten'.
3   *K. K. privat, Prager Zeitung* [n.a.], 15.18 (31 January 1830), http://anno.onb.ac.at/cgi-content/anno?aid=pag&datum=18300131&zoom=33
4   It is not clear exactly what the 'Extra-Touren' was.

denounced the whole nation of Bohemia for its sensuality. The author of the Letter does not want to accept such a harsh opinion, but, at the same time, he believes that the quick dancing lacks grace, while the behaviour of the dancing couples mixes unusual intimacy in public with a degree of indifference once the dance has finished.

On the other hand, he sees dancing as the only opportunity for girls to move more freely in public. He names three fields in which dance provides a counterbalance to their everyday life: girls spend all their time sitting or standing by the fire, while sewing, playing the piano, in the theatre, or in a coach. They are always watched by the eyes of their mothers and aunts so that girls can not be closer than three metres to their beloved; wearing a ball-dress, each girl feels better and prettier than in her everyday clothes.

In summary, the author of the Letter wants to find a balance between permissiveness and extreme severity in his attitude to dance manners. He identifies the topics of discussion: the danger to health including the threat of death, the loss of grace caused by the quickness of the dancing; and the level of intimacy versus polite public behaviour. At the centre of all these considerations he places the girls who dance.[5]

The Answer, entitled 'Antwort auf das Sendschreiben des Herrn Rezensenten in Nr. 17 dieses Blattes' [Response to the Letter of Mr Reviewer in No. 17 of this Paper] (hereafter, referred to as the Answer), appeared in *Bohemia* five days later, on 12 February in No. 19 in the same section of the newspaper (*'Theater und geselliges Leben'*). After transcription, the length is three A4 pages, and it is signed by Julius Max Schottky (with the polite ending formulated 'Mit Liebe und Hochachtung Ihr Julius Max Schottky', i.e. 'With Love and Respect Your J. M. Sch.').[6]

The author begins by saying that the question addressed to him in the Letter is one of the 'great questions of the century'. In his opinion, dance is a very influential phenomenon of the time in which they are living, and it affects not only the ballroom but also family relations and the whole of public life. Firstly, he reacts to the rebuke of the quickness

---

5 Müller, 'Sendschreiben', pp. 3–4.
6 Julius M. Schottky, 'Antwort auf das Sendschreiben des Herrn Rezensenten in Nro. 17 dieses Blattes', *Bohemia, Unterhaltungsblätter für gebildete Stände*, 19 (12 February 1830), pp. 3–4.

of dancing and reminds readers that in everyday life people travel at similar speed in many fields. If steam engines, quick carriages, express messengers exist, there is no reason to fear the quick Waltz and quick dancers, he writes. And moreover, he sees a tendency to accelerate the speed of dancing even more.

To balance this conciliatory attitude, Schottky continues with a sad tale he had heard about a young lady who made a bet with her partner at a ball that she could dance longer than he. Eight times she flew through the hall dancing the Galop, then she drank a glass of cold water; the next day she fell ill, and several days later she died. For Schottky, this represented the dark side of contemporary modes of dancing.

The author also reflected on the criticism of *Reydowak* (the Redowa) by Harro Harring, mentioned in the Letter. He describes his own experiences of this dance. When he saw it for the first time, he was alarmed by the lack of grace and charm. The girl drew so closely and passionately towards the man that one could see the imprints of his buttons on her face. Schottky even published a critical reaction to this indecent dancing fashion. However, thanks to a friend, a 'real' gentlewoman, he later changed his mind. While dancing *Reydowak* with her, he realised that the problem lies not in the dance but in the manner of dancing; one can dance *Reydowak* either nicely and tastefully, or dirtily and cheaply. It depends on the personality of the dancer. This statement concludes the article.

The Context of the Articles

In the year 1830, Prague and the whole of Bohemia belonged to the Austrian Empire. Prague had approximately 100,000 inhabitants. The Czech national movement was already underway, but it touched only a small part of society — the educated Czech middle-class circles. The majority of inhabitants felt German by nationality: that is why the newspaper *Bohemia* was printed in German, although some Czech magazines already existed. Public life was cultivated mainly in German, but the Czech language was slowly finding its place in the theatre, the sciences and so on. During the course of 1830, the national movement accelerated in a number of ways: the *Sbor Muzejní pro řeč a literaturu českou* [The Committee of the Museum for Czech Speech and Literature] was established, and student Karl Schneider organised a leaflet campaign for the national freedom of the Czech people.[7] Some of the first public manifestations of the Czech nation in Prague were Czech balls, which started in the late 1830s. At first, they were private balls organised by Josef Kajetán Tyl; the first real public Czech ball was held in the Convict Hall in 1840. The idea that national aims could be successfully supported by dancing events such as public balls relates to the issues explored in the Letter and the Answer — the social significance of dancing.

The arts and culture of both Germans and Czechs living in the Czech lands at that time were especially influenced by the Biedermeier style, as was the case in the other countries that belonged to the Holy Alliance — Prussia, Austria and Russia. This movement was connected with the political era of the so-called Restoration, the consolidation of the political situation within the Austrian Empire and across Europe after the Napoleonic wars and the Congress of Vienna in 1815. The era is characterised by political conservatism on one side, and the slow establishment of bourgeois culture on the other. In the Austrian Monarchy, and especially the Czech lands, the period from the Vienna Congress to the Revolutions of 1848 is often seen as a time of growing conflict between the conservatism of the government and its attempts to resist the new tendencies — a constitution, civil liberties, freedom of speech etc. — inspired by the French Revolution, and the public desire for social and political change. Biedermeier style can be explained as a reaction to this social tension and it focused on matters of everyday life, encouraging moderation in behaviour and feelings.[8]

The Austrian Empire stood at the centre of these conservative political powers. On 25 October 1820, the Congress of the Holy Alliance, which took place in the Moravian town of Opava (Troppau), discussed a plan of action against revolutionary movements in Europe. Opposition to this political centralisation can be seen in the interest of Bohemian intellectuals in events in Greece, such as the uprising against the Turks in 1821, the independence of Greece in 1830, and especially the revolution in Poland in 1830, which was a topic of great significance for Czechs.

---

7 Jitka Lněničková, *České země v době předbřeznové: 1792–1848* (Prague: Libri, 1999).
8 Jiří Štaif, *Obezřetná elita: Česká společnost mezi tradicí a revolucí 1830–1851* (Prague: Dokořán, 2005).

Characteristics of the Authors and Authorities

The initials A. M. under the Letter belong to *Bohemia*'s reviewer, Anton Müller.[9] He studied classical languages and aesthetics at Prague University and taught at the Gymnasium in Jičín and Písek. In 1819, he was invited to the University in Innsbruck as a lecturer of classical languages and aesthetics. In 1823, thanks to the intercession of Count Karel Chotek, the Tyrolean governor, he started to teach history of philosophy, aesthetics, pedagogy, ethics, and, later, also Greek and Latin philology at Prague University. He did not write any books; he was especially active as a journalist for *Prager Zeitung* and between 1828 and 1843 for *Bohemia*. He wrote long reviews of performances in the Estates Theatre, critiques of exhibitions, concerts, and books and referred to public events.

Müller was German but had many relationships with Czech intellectuals who circulated around František Palacký, a historian and politician, who was the leading figure of the Czech national movement. He paid attention, for instance, to Czech folk songs in an article in the magazine of the Museum (now the National Museum), as well as in his lectures. As a writer, he used themes from Czech mythology, for example, in the story *Horymir and his Steed Šemík*. He based his aesthetic opinions on Classicism: the works of Wolfgang Amadeus Mozart and Christoph Willibald Gluck demonstrated for him the pinnacle of perfection. He believed in some basic rules of artistic creativity, and in his reviews compared the specific artistic event with these ideal norms. After 1830, his aesthetic thinking changed slightly under the influence of the circle around Josef Proksch, a musician with progressive artistic opinions, and later the private teacher of the Czech composer Bedřich Smetana. In this circle, Müller acquainted himself with the thoughts of Georg Wilhelm Friedrich Hegel, which influenced his aesthetic thinking, while earlier he was probably more familiar with Johann Georg Sulzer and his encyclopaedic work *Allgemeine Theorie der Schönen Künste* [General Theory of Fine Arts] (1771–1774).[10] The Letter discussed in this chapter

---

9   Born on the 6 or 8 July 1792. Osečná u Mimoně died on the 5 or 6 January 1843 in Prague.

10 Sulzer, Johann G., 'Tanz', in *Allgemeine Theorie der schönen Künste in Einzeln, Nach alph. Ordnung der kunstwörter... Abgehandelt* (Leipzig: M. G. Weidmann, 1773–1775), pp. 747–51.

perhaps mirrors the start of the shift in Müller's opinions, and his budding doubts about formerly held truths. In the 1830s, a growing openness to new phenomena can be discerned in his reviews.[11]

In the Letter, Anton Müller names as his 'authority' the North Frisian/German poet, painter and 'professional' revolutionary Harro Harring.[12] From 1821, Harring supported the Greek fight for freedom, and in 1828 he visited Prague in an attempt to intervene on behalf of the Greek revolutionary Alexander Ypsilanti, who was imprisoned in the fortress Theresienstadt.[13] After the failure of this effort, he escaped to Munich, and later stayed in Poland, Rio de Janeiro, and New York. He participated in the revolutionary events in Leipzig and Braunschweig in 1830 and in North Frisia in 1848. The last years of his life were spent on the island of Jersey where he committed suicide. He knew George Gordon Byron, Heinrich Heine and Giuseppe Garibaldi. According to Müller, Harring wrote and published in Prague a poem dealing with *Reydowak*.[14] In this poem, mentioned earlier, he expressed a deep distaste for the dance, which he saw as an affront to decency and even as a reflection of the sensuality and luxuriance of the whole nation.[15] This opinion seemed too strict to Müller and he convinced Harring to strike out the offensive words before printing. Müller asked Schottky, to whom he addressed his Letter, if his defence of *Reydowak* against Harring was justified. Harring's dismissal of the dance fashion symbolised by *Reydowak* is reminiscent of the opinion of that other 'revolutionary' poet, Byron, in his poem 'The Waltz'.[16]

A person of local importance is also mentioned in the Letter: Sebastian Willibald Schiessler,[17] active as a writer (who wrote novels as well as books on economics, topography, and amusement), an amateur piano player, and a composer. In 1830, Schiessler published a book in Prague

---

11 Jitka Ludvova, et al., *Hudební divadlo v českých zemích: Osobnosti 19. století* (Prague: Divadelní ústav: Academia, 2006).
12 Harro Paul Harring was born on 28 August 1798 in Ibenshof by Wobbenbüll, North Frisia. He died on the 15 May 1870 in Saint Helier, Jersey.
13 Terezín in Czech.
14 This poem has not yet been identified.
15 Müller, 'Sendschreiben', pp. 3–4.
16 George G. Byron, 'Waltz, an Apostrophic Hymn' [1812], *Wikisource*, 7 February 2013, http://en.wikisource.org/wiki/The_Works_of_Lord_Byron_(ed._Coleridge,_Prothero)/Poetry/Volume_1/The_Waltz
17 Born on 17 July 1791 in Prague, died on 15 March 1867 in Graz.

under the title *Carnevals-Almanach*, a compilation of information dealing with Carnival in history and the present. There are also short poems that provide characteristics of fashionable dances, music scores for dancing, and the first descriptions of these social dances printed in Bohemia. No similar book appeared in in Bohemia over the following decades, and it was connected with the excited interest in dancing that was also evident in newspapers during 1830. The book includes *Reydowak*, but only in the form of several musical scores; there is no description of movement.[18]

The author of the Answer, as previously mentioned, was Julius Maximilian Schottky.[19] He was active as a writer, publishing books on historical topics from Bohemia, the life story of Nicolo Paganini or past and present Prague. In January 1830 in his column 'Prager Novitäten' [Prague Novelties] in *Bohemia*, he published articles dedicated to the theme of Carnival, hence Müller addressed him as a Carnival expert. In his Answer to Müller's Letter, Schottky did not cite authorities, relying only on information known by hearsay from his acquaintances.

Fig. 6.1 Excerpt from music for *Reydowak* by Ch. W. Schiessler, published in his *Carnevals-Almanach für das Jahr 1830* (Prague: C. W. Enders, 1830), http://kramerius.nkp.cz/kramerius/MShowMonograph.do?id=24112. Josef Vycpálek, *České tance* (Prague: B. Kočí, 1921), p. 47.

Anton Müller and Julius Max Schottky almost certainly knew each other; the exchange of the Letter and the Answer in the pages of *Bohemia* seems

---

18   Sebastian W. Schiessler, *Carnevals-Almanach für das Jahr 1830* (Prague: C. W. Enders, 1830), http://kramerius.nkp.cz/kramerius/MShowMonograph.do?id=24112

19   Born in 1794, died in 1849.

scripted, manufacturing an opportunity to have a public discussion about an attractive topic.

Dance Forms Mentioned in the Discussion

In the two texts, four dances are explicitly named: the Galop, *Reydowak* (in the more Czech form known also as *Reydowák*), *Reydowačka*, and the quick Waltz. *Reydowak* receives the bulk of the attention, but all the dances are used as examples of dances at a fast tempo, and as illustrations of the debate on ballroom fashion of the time. We have some evidence of the contemporary popularity of these dances in Prague. They were included in the social dance events repertoire as seen on dance programmes. For instance, a programme from the ball in the Convict Hall held on 26 January 1829 included the following dances: the Polonaise, the Deutscher, the Galop, the Ländler, *Reydowak*, the Waltz, the Cotillion, and *Schlußdeutsch*. At the ball held in the hall of the Spa at the Kleine Seite (in Czech Malá Strana) on 18 February in the same year, the programme of dances was exactly the same.[20]

Fig. 6.2 Invitation card to balls held in the Convict Hall in Prague between 1810–1820, still a popular place for dancing in 1830 (the building is in the background). Zdeněk Míka, *Zábava a slavnosti staré Prahy* (Prague: Nakladatelství Ostrov 2008), p. 128.

---

20 Dance programme of the ball in the Convict Hall 26.1.1829 and in the hall of the Spa at the Kleine Seite 18.2.1829. Archive of the National Museum, the Collection of J. Dušek, Inv. Nro. 1710/11, 1715/8.

The popularity of the Waltz and the Galop lasted throughout the nineteenth century, as in other European countries. *Reydowak* was also popular for some time across Europe and the USA, usually under the name of the Redowa. In the Czech lands, it slowly disappeared in the years following 1830, a phenomenon that was particularly notable among Germans; unfortunately, there are insufficient dance programmes in the archive to understand this process more accurately. Certainly, however, the order of dances from the first Czech ball[21] in 1840 does not include *Reydowak*, indicating that this dance was not popular even among Czechs. Both dance programmes from 1829 show the composition of the repertoire. The exact movement differences between the Ländler, the Deutscher and the Waltz are not clear, as no detailed descriptions of these three dances as practised in the Czech lands exist from this period. The Deutscher is most likely the older, slower form of the Waltz. The reference to the Waltz almost certainly means the Viennese Waltz, the quicker version of the dance, which came into fashion after the Viennese Congress. The Ländler most probably included the arm movements that were typical of this form.

With respect to *Reydowak*, Bohemian descriptions from the period are also not available. In *Carnevals-Almanach* by Schiessler, musical scores for *Reydowak* are included: one as the closing part of the Kegelquadrille (the Skittle-Quadrille), named *Reydowak* (in 3/4) by the composer Joseph Triebensee, the orchestra leader of the opera in the Prague theatre. As an independent number, there is *Reydowak* (in 3/8) with Reydowaczka (in 2/4) by S. W. Schiessler, the editor of the *Almanach* himself.[22] This music was later reprinted in various sources, as well as in the most important collection of Czech folk dances by Josef Vycpálek (published in 1921 under the title České *tance*). Among the several dances described in words, *Reydowak* is not included in the *Almanach* (in the case of the Kegelquadrille, which is described, *Reydowak* is left without explanation). *Reydowak* can be found in the part of the *Almanach* entitled 'Tanz-Vignetten', including two-line stanzas dedicated to the particular dances

---

21 This was the first public ball organised by Czech patriotic circles to support the Czech national movement. More in Čeněk Zíbrt, *Jak se kdy v Čechách tancovalo: Dějiny tance v Čechách, na Moravě, ve Slezsku a na Slovensku Od nejstarší doby až do konce 19. století se zvláštním zřetelem k dějinám tance vubec* (Prague: F. Šimáček, 1895), pp. 306–34, https://archive.org/details/jak_se_kdy_v_cechach_tancova-zibrt

22 Schiessler, *Carnevals-Almanach*.

created by Schiessler. Here also are the Minuet, the Waltz, the Quadrille, the Mazurka, the Galop, *Reydowak* and *Reydowaczka*, the Cotillion, *Schnellwalzer*, the Ecossaise, and *Kehraus*. For *Reydowak* and *Reydowaczka* the text is as follows: 'Wenn mein Name nicht schon verriethe, welch Land mich geboren/ Wahrlich, ich würde mich scheu'n, ihn zu verkünden der Welt'.[23] This does not in any case deal with the movement patterns of the dance or with the dance style.

Fig. 6.3 Video: the Stanford Vintage Dance Ensemble and Academy of Danse Libre performs their winning the Redowa at the Spoleto Festival, Italy 2011. Reconstruction/choreography by Richard Powers. 'Stanford at Spoleto Festival: Winner's Redowa', 2:08, posted online by Jason Anderson, *Youtube*, 17 July 2011, https://www.youtube.com/watch?v=fzSRDv3f0-8

References to the dance in the Czech lands appeared from the beginning of the nineteenth century. One musical score for *Reydowak* is included in the manuscript collection of folk songs *Böhmische Nationalgesänge und Tänze* by Thomas Anton Kunz, created before 1830, but there is no description of the movement.[24] Jan Jeník z Bratřic provides interesting details in his memoirs.[25] He mentions the connection between two contrasting dances: *Reydowak* and *Reydowaczka*. Contrary to the later evolution of the two dances, he states that the *Reydowaczka* (in even metre) was played more slowly than *Reydowak* (in odd metre). This corresponds to the characteristics of *Reydowak* as the quick dance in Müller's Letter. But another notice from 1833 speaks of the slow *Reydowak* and quick, 'crackpot' *Reydowaczka*,[26] which again casts doubts on the preceding information. The evidence by Kunz and Bratřic also supports the note by Müller, that *Reydowak* came to the dance hall from the rural environment (employing the metaphor of a field flower being replanted in the greenhouse of the dancing hall).[27]

---

23 'If my name did not already betray the country that gave birth to me/ Truly, I would be afraid to announce it to the world'. Translation from German by Dorota Gremlicová. Ibid., p. 297.
24 Thomas Anton Kunz, *Böhmische Nationalgesänge und Tänze* (Prague: Ústav pro entnografii a folkloristiku AV ČR, 1996)
25 Zíbrt, *Jak se kdy v Čechách tancovalo*, pp. 356–57.
26 Čeněk Zíbrt, *Jak se kdy v Čechách tancovalo: Dějiny tance v Čechách, na Moravě, ve Slezsku a na Slovensku Od nejstarší doby až do konce 19. století se zvláštním zřetelem k dějinám tance vubec* (Prague: Státní nakladatelství krásné literatury, hudby a umění, 1960), p. 272.
27 Müller, 'Sendschreiben', pp. 3–4.

Fig. 6.4 'The Redowa Waltz: A new Bohemian waltz as danced in the Parisian saloons and taught by Monsieur Jules Martin', c.1846. The Redowa waltz seemed to have become popular even in America. Jerome Robbins Dance Division, The New York Public Library Digital Collections, Public Domain, https://digitalcollections.nypl.org/items/9fae00f0-3386-0131-f0f9-58d385a7bbd0

Böhmische Nationaltänze [Bohemian National Dances] by Alfred Waldau (1859)[28] includes some commentary on the dance and its character. He included *Reydowak* among the round dances with changes and figures (*Rundtänze mit Abwechslungen und Figuren*), and mentioned its popularity not only among ordinary people but also in higher society

---

28 Alfred Waldau, *Böhmische Nationaltänze. Culturstudie* (Prague: Hermann Dominikus, 1859), http://www.libraryofdance.org/manuals/1859-Waldau-Bohmische_(Goog).pdf

during the 1840s; he also described its later decline and return to the villages.²⁹

The dance was used as one component of the Quadrille *Česká Beseda*, created in 1863, in the third Tour of the third Figure. The description of the *Reydowak* step, given by the creator of this national Quadrille, Karel Link, stressed the specific rhythm of the movement created by a prolonged first step (one-and-a-half beats in the 3/4 metre) and the sliding movement of the tip of the toe in the first and third step of each bar.³⁰ The connection between *Reydowak* and *Česká Beseda* prolonged its life considerably in the Czech ballroom context, and could have influenced its acceptance in German circles, too. But in books such as the German manual of 1881 by the Moravian dancing master Adam Reichert, *Reydowak* is not included.³¹

Fig. 6.5 The ballroom dance *Česká Beseda*, Sokolské šibřinky in Beroun. '"Česká Beseda" — Vystoupení skupiny "Beseda" Jitky Bonušové — Beroun 23/03/13', 14:51, uploaded by Ludmila Sluníčková, *Youtube*, 27 March 2013, https://www.youtube.com/watch?v=Pmrh_0uhLX8

Descriptions of *Reydowak* appeared later in the nineteenth century in technical dance manuals from various countries, reflecting its fashionable nature (the dance went by the name of the Redowa abroad). It was popular not only in the ballroom but also in the theatre — the dance appeared in some operas. It is included in the books by Henri Cellarius,³² by Coulon³³ and in the *Guide Complet de La Danse* by Philippe

---

29 Alfred Waldau, *Böhmische Nationaltänze: Eine Kulturstudie* (Prague: Vitalis, 2003), p. 27.
30 Karel Link, *Beseda: Český salonní tanec* (Prague: Nakladatel A. Storch syn, 1882).
31 Adam Reichert, *Die moderne Tanzkunst von ästetischen und theoretischen Standpunkte* (Olmütz: Selbstverlag, 1881).
32 Henri Cellarius, *The Drawing Room Dances* (E. Churton: London, 1847), pp. xi., 140 (pl. VII), http://www.libraryofdance.org/manuals/1847-Cellarius-Drawing_Room_(LOC).pdf
33 Eugène Coulon, *Coulon's Hand-Book; Containing all the Last New and Fashionable Dances* (London: Jullien & Co., 1860), http://www.libraryofdance.org/manuals/1860-Coulon-Hand-Book_(LOC).pdf

Gawlikowski, printed in Paris in 1858.[34] Both *Reydowak* and *Reydowaczka* (as 'Die Redowa/La Redowa' and 'Die Redowaczka/La Redowaczka') are included in the dance manual by Bernhard Klemm, *Katechismus der Tanzkunst*, published for the first time in 1855 (and then in many further editions), which was very influential in the German-speaking countries. Klemm describes the characteristic movement in both dances as jumping, and he compares the step of *Reydowak* with the pas de Basque in ballet.[35] Klemm states the speed of *Reydowak* to be M. M. 88 for one quarter, which is valuable information. In the case of *Reydowaczk*, such details are missing.

Link´s *Česká Beseda*[36] and Klemm´s *Katechismus der Tanzkunst*[37] nevertheless only partly reveal the vivid character of these dances in the Prague ballrooms of 1830. Between 1830 and 1855 (Klemm´s description), or 1863 (*Česká Beseda*), dancing style changed. This had less effect on the dances in 3/4 metre based on the Waltz than on those in 2/4 metre, including probably *Reydowaczka*. In 1830, the Polka was still not practised as a social dance in Prague, although in some form it already existed outside the city, especially in East Bohemia.[38] The fashion for the Polka started in Europe in the 1840s. It is therefore difficult to ascertain what *Reydowaczka* looked like in the year 1830. Probably it was based on the Galop, the most popular 2/4 dance of that time, and it did not include the double turning of the couple, typical for the Polka (and linked later with *Reydowacka*, as it is found in some Czech sources from the second half of the nineteenth century). Klemm mentions the connection between *Reydowaczka* and the Galop, and according to him, its basic step is *pas chassé*.

Klemm also provides information on some typical additional movements and motifs; namely, in *Reydowak*, he describes the alternation of the turning and progressing around the circle using the pas de Basque steps, and halting and moving forwards and backwards using the same

---

34 Philippe Gawlikowski, *Guide Complet De La Danse* (Paris: Taride, Libraire-éditeur, 1858), pp. 59–61, http://www.libraryofdance.org/manuals/1858-Gawlikowski-Guide_Complet_(LOC).pdf

35 Bernhard Klemm, *Katechismus der Tanzkunst: Ein Leitfaden für Lehrer und Lernende nebst einem Anhang über Choreographie 7 Aufl* (Leipzig: J. J. Weber, 1901) pp. 148–9, http://books.google.com/books?id=XkpKAAAAYAAJ

36 Link, *Beseda*.

37 Klemm, *Katechismus der Tanzkunst*, pp. 149–57.

38 Daniela Stavělová, 'Polka jako český národní symbol', *Český lid*, 93 (2006), 3–26.

step without turning; this halting was done at the man's instigation. The same principle is also used in *Reydowaczka*.[39] As *Reydowak* is included in *Česká Beseda* as a part of the Quadrille, it is limited only to the basic step motif, without any additional movements.

Another Czech description can be found in the book by František Dlouhý, *O historickém vývoji tance a jeho kulturním významě. Český tanec národní* [On the Historical Evolution of Dance and its Cultural Significance: The Czech National Dance], published in 1880. He mentions some features of *Reydowak* that Klemm also notes: the returning in the movement around the circle (three times turning and progressing by Waltz steps forward, then one backward) and balancing on the spot (which can happen at any time according to the decision of the dancing couple). In the case of *Reydowaczka* (*Rejdovačka*), he states only that it is danced in Polka rhythm.[40]

The description of *Reydowak* in a social dance manual by Josef Pohl from the end of the nineteenth century is not very clear: he states that the dancers do not embrace each other, they hold each other with crossed hands, the lady walks backward, the gentleman faces in her direction, and they move in the characteristic '*rejdování*' manner (*lenken, umwenden* or *herumtreiben* in German), alternating this movement by balancing on the spot.[41]

Reydowak was included in many social dance manuals printed in Bohemia from the end of the nineteenth and beginning of the twentieth centuries, and in the folk songs and dance collections from the twentieth century. But the dance programmes from the public balls of the second half of the nineteenth century do not include the dance. It could have been part of the curriculum in the dance schools, but it was not a living element of the repertoire of the balls as an independent dance, only as a part of the *Česká Beseda*.

The movement structure of the dance probably changed in the course of time and in different contexts. Often, as we have seen, the characteristic movement pattern of *rejdování* (*herumtreiben*) is mentioned. The concept

---

39 Klemm, *Katechismus der Tanzkunst*, pp. 149–57.
40 František Dlouhý, *O historickém vývoji tance a jeho kulturním významě; Český tanec národní* (Prague: F. A. Urbánek, 1880), pp. 47–8.
41 Josef Pohl, *Úplný tanečník: soubor všech tanců s návodem naučiti se jim* (V Praze: Frant. Bačkovský, 1899), pp. 43–4.

is not etymologically clear; the German word can be translated as 'to drive to and fro' or 'to drive around'. The Czech verb *rejdovat* had a special meaning connected to the movement of a boat during anchoring, approaching its berth; it is connected to the German term for the anchorage: 'die Reede'. It indicates movement with (small) changes of direction (as the boat tries to hit the mooring). In his dictionary, Josef Jungmann connects the Czech term *rejdovat* with the notion of driving with the back of a car slightly at an angle.[42] In dance, *rejdování* could be performed by several different movements: by alternative turning (directing) of the couple slightly to the right and left, by the alternation of moving forward and backward, by balancing inside and outside the circle, either while moving in space or staying (almost) on the spot. It was typical for the specific movement motifs to be executed by each dancing couple at will, so that couples were independent and the course of the dance was not uniform and strictly fixed. This feature could give the dance the symbolic aspect of being free from rules and conventions.

The Play of Opinions

In the Letter and the Answer, we find several categories of thoughts and evaluation dealing with dances, dance fashion and social behaviour. The majority are not new. Some of them repeatedly appeared from the Renaissance onwards, either in the dance manuals or other texts, for instance, medical or moralising treatises. Some of them were connected specifically with the dance forms of the Waltz type and the dancing etiquette of bourgeois culture in the eighteenth and nineteenth centuries. The manner in which the Letter and the Answer reflect these things is affected by the local atmosphere, mentality, and the historical background of the Czech lands; the discussion is not only nuanced by these things, but also by personalities and the opinions of individuals who conducted the debate.

The Bohemian society of the 1830s represented specific circumstances, influenced by the growing Czech national movement, the political dependence of the country on the Austrian Monarchy, the strong

---

42 Josef Jungmann, *Slownjk česko-německý* (Prague: Knjžecj arcibiskupská tiskárna, Josefa wdowa Fetterlowá, 1837), p. 822, http://kramerius.nkp.cz/kramerius/handle/ABA001/183651

impact of the Napoleonic Wars not only in the material sphere (military engagements on the territory of Moravia and Bohemia, namely the battle of Austerlitz/Slavkov in 1805 and the battle of Chlumec in 1813) but also mentally and spiritually by strengthening censorship, limiting public behaviour (especially political activity) and the propagation of liberal, 'Republican' ideas. During 1830, a process of recovery and the relaxation of restrictions on public life began, in which dance events played an important role as public social activities. The whole period from the Napoleonic Wars until the Viennese revolution in March 1848, followed by a similar affair in Prague, is labelled 'Pre-March Time' by historians and understood as a relatively stable period but with some noticeable events, among them mainly the revolutionary year of 1830. Czech society was deeply affected by the revolution in Poland, since it experienced a sense of connection and solidarity with another Slavonic nation, but this happened in November 1830, long after the debate analysed in this chapter. Nevertheless, from the beginning, the year 1830 marks an obvious turning point: prior to this, the atmosphere seemed to be moderate, muted, and sleepy, while preference for the private sphere of life and conservative feelings held sway; afterwards, life started to become more vivid, optimistic, and active, more public, more progressive in opinions and attitudes, and more individualistic.[43]

The change that happened around the year 1830 was also visible in the artistic, aesthetic field. The beginning of the nineteenth century is connected in Bohemia mainly with the Biedermeier style, which was embraced by people belonging to the bourgeoisie (but also accepted by the aristocracy). Biedermeier is usually understood as the art of home interior design, applying the arts to create an intimate, private mood. More recent interpretation of the Biedermeier movement has tended to rethink its meaning, widening its application into more cultural and artistic spheres, rather than seeing it as some passive, private, closed, spiritual, and artistic phenomenon. Instead, emphasis is placed upon the achievement of balance between real life and ideals, upon searching for an equilibrium in mind, and harmony between the notion of liberty and the responsibility of the individual. The main tool for achieving this was the concept of moral sense (as formulated, for instance, by the German

---

43   Lněničková, *České země v době předbřeznové*.

philosopher Johann Friedrich Herbart).⁴⁴ This approach corresponds with the importance of questions of morality that are also expressed in the Letter and the Answer. The discussion about dance fashion held in *Bohemia* in 1830 stands on the edge of two types of cultural life and ways of thinking in the Czech lands.

Fig. 6.6   V. R. Grüner, 'Carneval in Prague', ca.1829. Zdeněk Míka, *Zábava a slavnosti staré Prahy* (Prague: Nakladatelství Ostrov, 2008), p. 123.

---

44   Miloš Havelka, 'Byl Herbart filosofem biedermeieru? Herbartův pokus o realistickou akceptaci zdvojenosti člověka a světa', in *Biedermeier v českých zemích. Sborník příspěvků z 23. ročníku symposia k problematice 19. století, Plzeň, 6.–8. března 2003*, ed. by Helena Lorenzová and Taťána Petrasová (Prague: Koniasch Latin Press, 2004), pp. 25–37.

One topic discussed in the debate between Anton Müller and Julius Max Schottky is the impact of the contemporary way of dancing on health, especially that of young women. Commentaries dealing with this topic had appeared already in Renaissance dance manuals and medical literature. According to Alessandro Arcangeli's interpretation, the Renaissance physicians shared, in general, the notion of the prophylactic benefit of dancing when performed in a 'controlled' way. Dance balances body and mind, it gives people the ability to move harmoniously, it strengthens the body, especially the legs, and it can even serve as a cure, for instance for melancholy. The desirable way of dancing formulated by these sources is to dance in a very calm manner, without any wild movements, after dining, performed in harmony and measure following the music. They also articulated the more problematic attributes of dance, which could have the contrary influence not only on one's health and physical state but principally on one's moral being: violent movements and excessively quick whirling might cause loss of balance or dizziness, which meant also a loss of the balance of one's mind, a loss of dignity, and other undesirable outcomes. They also differentiated between dance situations: they believed it was most appropriate to dance in the open air, not to hold a ball in a closed dusty room that was noisy and crowded, as was customary. But, instead of dancing for their health, they noticed that people danced more for their pleasure.[45]

Many of these opinions crop up repeatedly in various types of texts dealing with dance until the nineteenth century. In the first third of the nineteenth century in Bohemia, as in other German-speaking countries, there were popular instructions on how to achieve a long, healthy and happy life, formulated for instance by Christoph Wilhelm Hufeland in his book *Die Kunst das menschliche Leben zu verlängern*, known later as *Makrobiotics*, first published in 1796.[46] He did not write specifically about dance, but he named among misdemeanours that could shorten life the diseases caused by unreasonable actions. Violent and uncontrolled dancing could easily be such a dangerous activity. His successor Wilhelm

---

45 Alessandro Arcangeli, 'Dance and Health: The Renaissance Physician's View', *Dance Research*, 18.1 (2000), 3–30, https://doi.org/10.3366/1291009
46 Helena Lorenzová, 'Dietetika duše. K praktické filosofii (estetice) osvícentsví a biedermeieru', in *Biedermeier v českých zemích. Sborník příspěvků z 23. ročníku symposia k problematice 19. století, Plzeň, 6.–8. března 2003*, ed. by Helena Lorenzová and Taťána Petrasová (Prague: Koniasch Latin Press, 2004), pp. 38–48.

Bronn in his *Kalobiotik* (1835) formulated a more joyous picture of a suitable way of life and recommended a rich social life including dance events and physical activities. A truly happy life has to be, nevertheless, moral, too.[47] The authors of the Letter and the Answer likewise vacillated between these two points: dance as a danger, and dance as a joyful phenomenon. Both Müller and Schottky remind the reader about the sad accident of a young girl, who apparently died after of her behaviour during a ball. Such stories are nothing new or rare at this point in time. From the end of the eighteenth century, warnings that dancers (mainly girls) could die as a result of quick, violent dancing, because they became sweaty, caught a chill, drank too much cold water, and thus fell ill with pneumonia or tuberculosis, frequently appeared in newspapers and dance treatises. This danger was, according to the opinions of authors of these texts, connected especially to specific dances: the Waltz (the Deutscher), the Galop, and, in our newspaper debate, *Reydowak*. In the Czech lands, as early as 1789 Bernard Specht had written in his treatise *Ueber Anstand, Schönheit und Grazie im Tanz* about the profits of dancing (strengthening of the body, becoming lighter, more pliable, developing a more natural movement when walking) and its dangers (exhaustion, tuberculosis and death).[48] And still in 1838, Christian Länger (and many other European authors before and after), in his dance manual *Terpsichore*, repeated similar warnings about the danger of death from tuberculosis because of overly enthusiastic dancing (or rounds of dance that were too quick and too long).[49] Several reports of such accidents appeared in the Prague newspapers in the 1830s, not only involving young girls but also gentlemen.[50] Later, during the nineteenth century, this theme of illness and death slowly disappeared, replaced by more emphasis on the positive impact of dance on health, as in the book by Prague dancing master Karel Link in 1872.[51] In the debate in *Bohemia*, Müller also tried

---

47 Lorenzová, 'Dietetika duše'.
48 Bernard Specht, *Ueber Anstand, Schönheit und Grazie im Tanz. Nebst einem Vorschlage zur allgemeinen Balltracht* (Prag: J. J. Diesbach, 1789).
49 Christian Länger, *Terpsichore: Ein Taschenbuch der neuesten gesellschaftlichen Tänze* (Würzburg: Etlinger'schen Buchhandlung, 1838), http://www.libraryofdance.org/manuals/1838-Langer-Terpsichore_(BSB).pdf
50 Tereza Babická, 'Německá taneční kritika v Praze ve 30. letech 19. Století' (unpublished thesis, Academy of Performing Arts in Prague, 2011), p. 52.
51 Karel Link, *Tanec se stanoviska theoretického a aesthetického* (Prague: Knihkupectví J. Nowotný, 1872), pp. 4–6.

to ameliorate the sad story of the dead girl by contrasting it with the fact that dancing was almost the only opportunity for greater physical activity for girls from the middle-class families.[52]

The theme of the dangerous pace of some popular dances was closely connected in the debate with questions of endangering health; these two aspects were usually understood as being linked. According to the traditional view, quick dancing risked uncontrolled, passionate, and wild behaviour, and so it was an additional aspect of moral impropriety. Speed was accompanied by the close (indeed, too close) embrace of the couple, and with whirling, which was often mentioned in connection with the Waltz. For Anton Müller, 'in the bacchantic fast running', grace[53] is lost. While a horse can be beautiful while galloping at its fastest pace, a girl cannot (A. M. 1830).[54] Julius Schottky was less strict in his Answer and viewed the popularity of quick dances in a wider perspective. He saw the speed and tempestuous nature of the flight that was typical for the dances of his time as a parallel to the vigour of that era, when everything was as fast as a mountain stream: steam and machines, quick carriages, quick print machines, quick typewriters.[55] In such a world, quick dancers could also exist, he said. His words imply that his evaluation was not negative; he understood this quickness as joined with happiness, the joy of life, a mood that would be positive for human living and society.[56] He was not alone in holding this point of view at that time; similar opinions can be seen in Bronn's *Kalobiotik*.[57] But there were also opposing voices, like that of Czech writer Jaroslav Langer. In the mid-1830s, Langer wrote to condemn the quick (wild) dances that came from the villages to the towns and even abroad (*Reydowak*, among

---

52 Müller, 'Sendschreiben'.
53 Grace was one of the most important qualities for him also in the case of theatrical dancing, as seen in his theatre reviews published also in the newspaper *Bohemia*. Babická, *Německá taneční Kritika*.
54 Müller, 'Sendschreiben'.
55 In respect to carriages, Schottky either has in mind express mail stagecoaches, which started to go from Prague to Vienna in 1823 and shortened the travel from three days to thirty-seven hours, or the new horse-drawn trams, the first lines of which were opened in 1827 (from České Budějovice to Linz) and in spring 1830 (so called Lány horse-drawn rail).
56 Schottky, 'Antwort auf das Sendschreiben'.
57 Wilhelm Bronn, *Für Kalobiotik, Kunst, das Leben zu verschönern, als neu ausgestecktes Feld menschlichen Strebens: Winke zur Erhöhung und Veredelung des Lebensgenusses* 1 (Vienna: Gerold, 1835).

others) and did not bring any credit to the nation. He also repeated the connection between quick dancing and the danger of death.[58] Schottky and Langer therefore represented a polarisation in the Bohemian society of that time. Schottky's standpoint was closer to the view of the young intellectual generation, especially students, who were also the typical participants in such rapid dancing.

Fig. 6.7 Entrance ticket to the charitable ball of the Institute of the Poor held in the hall of the Spa in Prague, 20 January 1830. Zdeněk Míka, *Zábava a slavnosti staré Prahy* (Prague: Nakladatelství Ostrov 2008), p. 128.

---

58 Jaroslav Langer, 'České prostonárodní obyčeje a písně, [1834]', in *Spisy Jaroslava Langera*, 2 vols (Prague: Vídeň, 1861), II, 75.

The third field for discussion identified by Müller and Schottky was that of morals and of the place of dance in social life. The manner in which they argued shows a mixture of 'universal' and 'local' aspects and standpoints; those shared universally among European middle-class intellectuals, as well as those distinctive to Bohemian circumstances. Among the relatively universal ideas was the opinion that the mode of dancing, including posture and movement, mirrors or expresses the moral character of an individual. This idea was precisely formulated, for example, by Johann Georg Sulzer in the entry on dance in his encyclopaedia.[59] His thoughts were also very influential in Bohemian-German circles, including upon Anton Müller, the aesthetician. From this point of view, we can understand the commentary by Müller about the overly intimate behaviour of couples dancing the Waltz.[60] And Schottky expressed the same way of thinking in his conclusion: it was not the dance itself, but the personality of the dancer and his or her morals that ultimately decided the moral message of the particular dance.[61]

Together with the idea of personality transposed into dance movement, Müller mentioned another aspect of contemporary dancing behaviour, which we can call 'published intimacy'.[62] It is connected with the tendency of bourgeois society to differ between several spheres of life: the sphere of the state, the public space of the citizen's community, and the private (intimate) space of family. Each of these spheres had appropriate behaviour and rules, a specific 'culture'.[63] Dances like the Waltz, in which the couple came together inside a closed space with very intimate, personal feelings, made it possible to break the limits of the public sphere by embracing, touching a person of the opposite sex who was not a relative. These attributes of the Waltz provoked both enthusiasm and distaste from the beginning of the social life of this dance. Johann Wolfgang Goethe in his novel *Die Leiden des jungen Werthers* [The Sorrows of Young Werther] saw in it the sign of belonging to an unofficial circle of 'new' bourgeois people capable of deep feelings,

---

59 Sulzer, 'Tanz'.
60 Müller, 'Sendschreiben'.
61 Schottky, 'Antwort auf das Sendschreiben'
62 Dorota Gremlicová, 'Tělo, nebo sen? Romantický tanec 19. století', in *Tělo a tělesnost v české kultuře 19. století, Sborník příspěvků z 29. ročníku symposia k problematice 19. století, Plzeň, 26.-28. února 2009*, ed. by Taťána Petrasová and Pavla Machalíková (Prague: Academia, 2010), pp. 168–75.
63 Štaif, *Obezřetná elita*, pp. 92–93.

represented by the leading figures of Lotte and Werther.[64] He also exactly expresses the intimate atmosphere of the dance, the enclosing of the couple and their isolation from the other 'world': 'we revolved around each other like the (cosmic) spheres'.[65] The opposite opinion was voiced a little later by Byron, who, in his poem 'The Waltz', denounced the dance mainly from a moral point of view.[66] Anton Müller did not add anything new to these polarised opinions. Rather, he reflected weakened concern about the moral aspect of such dances. It seems that this 'published intimacy' was, in his time, experienced less and less by dancing people as something important and symbolic: while dancing, the couple showed provocative 'public tenderness', but when the dance was finished, the dancer would indifferently throw his lady off. In fact, with understanding and sympathy, Müller commented on the fact that, for girls, dancing gave a rare opportunity to experience the nearness of a young man, to touch him without any rebuke, although he also expressed his doubts about the borderline of proper public behaviour and personal liberty, a theme of concern to both German and Czech intellectuals at the time.[67] The fact that girls and women are placed at the centre of these ideas seems to correspond with the new tendency of the time to include women more in Bohemian public life.[68]

The debate in the newspaper *Bohemia* on the topics of health, the rapidity of the dancing, and its moral aspects, was a stimulus for contemplation of cultural and social spheres. It is clear that for the authors of the Letter and the Answer, dance could serve as a basis for such considerations. Schottky wrote directly, that 'if dance belongs still among the most influential phenomena of our days, its consequences are not limited only to the dance hall, but they also touch on family and public lives'. He opened his Answer with this statement, and it forms the basis for his subsequent thoughts. He tried to keep this overall perspective and to focus on this symbolic meaning of dance in contemporary Bohemian society.[69]

---

64 Johann Wolfgang von Goethe, *Die Leiden des jungen Werthers* (Leipzig: Weigand, 1774), p. 38.
65 'Und da wir nun gar an's Walzen kamen, und wie die Sphären um einander herum rollen'. Translated from the German by Dorota Gremlicová.
66 Byron, 'Waltz'.
67 Müller, 'Sendschreiben'.
68 Štaif, *Obezřetná elita*, p. 93.
69 Schottky, 'Antwort auf das Sendschreiben'.

Conclusion

As already stated, the basic mood of the exchange of opinions between Müller and Schottky is amicable; they searched for a balanced attitude to the phenomena with which they dealt. Nevertheless, in this attempt at harmony, a desire for joyful, liberal behaviour in dance that was currently missing in real life can also be detected. As noted above, in contemporary Czech historiography, the period of the 1830s is understood as a time of social and cultural change. This shift had political and mental aspects. After the Congress of Vienna in 1815, which concluded the period of the Napoleonic Wars, society in the Austrian Empire was under very strict state control; it was forbidden to express any progressive, liberal or republican thoughts, not only in public but also for example in private correspondence. People were vigilant; many of them accepted 'state' opinion that prohibited such revolutionary movements or thoughts. This atmosphere also created some mental barriers against accepting cultural phenomena, including dance. The notions of liberty and equality were reflected diffidently and cautiously, in a limited way. [70]

At the end of the 1820s, however, intellectual circles in Bohemia, both Czech and German, were more and more influenced by the liberal movement in other European countries, especially in the parts of Germany close to its territory, such as Saxony, for instance. Alongside this, some change in mentality began in bourgeois circles, which resulted in greater courage to think about human rights, liberty and self-expression, and about the value of novelties in material as well as spiritual aspects of life.[71] In this light, the conclusions of Müller and Schottky effectively herald the development of public life in the 1830s. As members of local intellectual circles, they show that dance could be an appropriate element of public behaviour, capable of acting as a model example.

---

70 Miroslav Hroch, *Na prahu národní existence: touha a skutečnost* (Prague: Mladá fronta, 1999).
71 Štaif, *Obezřetná elita*, pp. 40–43.

Bibliography

Arcangeli, Alessandro, 'Dance and Health: The Renaissance Physician's View', *Dance Research*, 18.1 (2000), 3–30, https://doi.org/10.3366/1291009

Babická, Tereza, 'Německá taneční kritika v Praze ve 30. letech 19. Století' (unpublished thesis, Academy of Performing Arts in Prague, 2011).

Bohemia, Unterhaltungsblätter für gebildete Stände [n.a.], 3 (1830), http://kramerius.nkp.cz/kramerius/PShowVolume.do?it=0&id=14191

Bronn, Wilhelm, *Für Kalobiotik, Kunst, das Leben zu verschönern, als neu ausgestecktes Feld menschlichen Strebens: Winke zur Erhöhung und Veredelung des Lebensgenusses* 1 (Vienna: Gerold, 1835).

Byron, George G., 'Waltz, an Apostrophic Hymn' [1812], *Wikisource*, 7 February 2013, http://en.wikisource.org/wiki/The_Works_of_Lord_Byron_(ed._Coleridge,_Prothero)/Poetry/Volume_1/The_Waltz

Cellarius, Henri, *The Drawing Room Dances* (E. Churton: London, 1847), http://www.libraryofdance.org/manuals/1847-Cellarius-Drawing_Room_(LOC).pdf

Coulon, Eugène, *Coulon's Hand-Book; Containing all the Last New and Fashionable Dances* (London: Jullien & Co., 1860), http://www.libraryofdance.org/manuals/1860-Coulon-Hand-Book_(LOC).pdf

Dlouhý, František, *O historickém vývoji tance a jeho kulturním významě*; *Český tanec národní* (Prague: F. A. Urbánek, 1880).

Gawlikowski, Philippe, *Guide complet de la danse* (Paris: Taride, Libraire-éditeur, 1858), http://www.libraryofdance.org/manuals/1858-Gawlikowski-Guide_Complet_(LOC).pdf.

Goethe, Johann Wolfgang von, *Die Leiden des jungen Werthers* (Leipzig: Weigand, 1774).

Gremlicová, Dorota, ‚Tělo, nebo sen? Romantický tanec 19. století', in *Tělo a tělesnost v české kultuře 19. století, Sborník příspěvků z 29. ročníku symposia k problematice 19. století, Plzeň, 26.-28. února 2009*, ed. by Taťána Petrasová and Pavla Machalíková (Prague: Academia, 2010), pp. 168–75.

Havelka, Miloš, 'Byl Herbart filosofem biedermeieru? Herbartův pokus o realistickou akceptaci zdvojenosti člověka a světa', in *Biedermeier v českých zemích. Sborník příspěvků z 23. ročníku symposia k problematice 19. století, Plzeň, 6.–8. března 2003*, ed. by Helena Lorenzová and Taťána Petrasová (Prague: Koniasch Latin Press, 2004), pp. 25–37.

Hroch, Miroslav, *Na prahu národní existence: touha a skutečnost* (Prague: Mladá fronta, 1999).

Jungmann, Josef, *Slownjk česko-německý* (Prague: Knjžecj arcibiskupská tiskárna, Josefa wdowa Fetterlowá, 1837), http://kramerius.nkp.cz/kramerius/handle/ABA001/183651

K. K. privat, *Prager Zeitung* [n.a.], 15.18 (31 January 1830), http://anno.onb.ac.at/cgi-content/anno?aid=pag&datum=18300131&zoom=33

Klemm, Bernhard, *Katechismus der Tanzkunst: Ein Leitfaden für Lehrer und Lernende nebst einem Anhang über Choreographie*, 7th edn (Leipzig: J. J. Weber, 1901), http://books.google.com/books?id=XkpKAAAAYAAJ

Kunz, Thomas Anton, *Böhmische Nationalgesänge und Tänze* (Prague: Ústav pro entnografii a folkloristiku AV ČR, 1996)

Länger, Christian, *Terpsichore: Ein Taschenbuch der neuesten gesellschaftlichen Tänze*. (Würzburg: Etlinger'schen Buchhandlung, 1838), http://www.libraryofdance.org/manuals/1838-Langer-Terpsichore_(BSB).pdf

Langer, Jaroslav, ,České prostonárodní obyčeje a písně. [1834]', in *Spisy Jaroslava Langera*, 2 vols (Prague: Vídeň, 1861), II, 75.

Link, Karel, *Tanec se stanoviska theoretického a aesthetického* (Prague: Knihkupectví J. Nowotný, 1872).

Link, Karel, *Beseda: Český salonní tanec* (Prague: Nakladatel A. Storch syn, 1882).

Lněničková, Jitka, *České země v době předbřeznové: 1792–1848* (Prague: Libri, 1999).

Lorenzová, Helena, 'Dietetika duše. K praktické filosofii (estetice) osvícentsví a biedermeieru', in *Biedermeier v českých zemích. Sborník příspěvků z 23. ročníku symposia k problematice 19. století, Plzeň, 6.–8. března 2003*, ed. by Helena Lorenzová and Taťána Petrasová (Prague: Koniasch Latin Press, 2004), pp. 38–48.

Ludvová, Jitka, et al., *Hudební divadlo v českých zemích: Osobnosti 19. století* (Prague: Divadelní ústav: Academia, 2006).

Míka, Zdeněk, *Zábava a slavnosti staré Prahy* (Prague: Nakladatelství Ostrov 2008).

Pohl, Josef, *Úplný tanečník: soubor všech tanců s návodem naučiti se jim* (V Praze: Frant. Bačkovský, 1899).

Reichert, Adam, *Die moderne Tanzkunst von ästetischen und theoretischen Standpunkte* (Olmütz: Selbstverlag, 1881).

Schiessler, Sebastian Willibald, *Carnevals-Almanach für das Jahr 1830* (Prague: C. W. Enders, 1830), http://kramerius.nkp.cz/kramerius/MShowMonograph.do?id=24112

Specht, Bernard, *Ueber Anstand, Schönheit und Grazie im Tanz. Nebst einem Vorschlage zur allgemeinen Balltracht* (Prag: J. J. Diesbach, 1789).

Stavělová, Daniela, ,Polka jako český národní symbol', *Český lid*, 93 (2006), 3–26.

Sulzer, Johann G., ,Tanz', in *Allgemeine Theorie der schönen Künste in Einzeln, Nach alph. Ordnung der kunstwörter... Abgehandelt* (Leipzig: M. G. Wiedmann, 1773–1775), pp. 747–51.

Štaif, Jiří, *Obezřetná elita: Česká společnost mezi tradicí a revolucí 1830–1851* (Prague: Dokořán, 2005).

Vycpálek, Josef, *České tance* (Prague: B. Kočí, 1921).

Waldau, Alfred, *Böhmische Nationaltänze: Eine Kulturstudie* (Prague: Vitalis, 2003).

——, *Böhmische Nationaltänze. Culturstudie* (Prague: Hermann Dominikus, 1859), http://www.libraryofdance.org/manuals/1859-Waldau-Bohmische_(Goog).pdf

Zíbrt, Čeněk, *Jak se kdy v Čechách tancovalo: Dějiny tance v Čechách, na Moravě, ve Slezsku a na Slovensku Od nejstarší doby až do konce 19. století se zvláštním zřetelem k dějinám tance vubec* (Prague: Státní nakladatelství krásné literatury, hudby a umění, 1960).

——, *Jak se kdy v Čechách tancovalo: Dějiny tance v Čechách, na Moravě, ve Slezsku a na Slovensku Od nejstarší doby až do konce 19. století se zvláštním zřetelem k dějinám tance vubec* (Prague: F. Šimáček, 1895), https://archive.org/details/jak_se_kdy_v_cechach_tancova-zibrt

7. Reception of Nineteenth-Century Couple Dances in Hungary

László Felföldi

Introduction

The aim of this chapter is to give an account of the appearance and reception of round dances[1] — also known as nineteenth-century couple dances — in Hungary.[2] Since these dances did not stand out as a paradigm with a separate name in Hungary, we first need to identify them within the broader Hungarian dance repertoire. The fact that research on social dances in Hungary has focused on the older forms makes this difficult. Round dances were mostly seen as too new and too foreign to be deemed worthy of documentation and research. The task therefore remains to identify them among the dance forms practised in Hungary and to contextualise them in the socio-cultural and political circumstances of the first half of the nineteenth century.

Having briefly delimited and situated the dance material in question, we are faced with a great amount of material from a broad range of very different sources. Moreover, only a small amount of this material has been published in languages other than Hungarian. In order to achieve the task, we have set ourselves, a selected corpus of the most important

---

1 For a definition of this group of dances: see the Introduction (Chapter 1) to this volume.
2 In the time-frame of this research, Hungary was a country of ca.300,000 square kilometres, with 14,000,000 inhabitants belonging to the Austrian Empire. See János Csaplovics, *Gemälde von Ungarn* (Pest: Hartleben, 1829).

sources is presented here in the form of an annotated catalogue. This catalogue aims to demonstrate the variability and richness of the relevant sources, but also serves as a reference for the last part of this chapter, which discusses issues of reception, the rivalry between Hungarian and foreign dances, and the cultural climate in that context. The rise of a Hungarian counterpart to the foreign round dances is one of the main conclusions. The catalogue material is mainly selected from existing literature about this topic in Hungary, supplemented with results produced by the present research.[3]

Following the catalogue, there is a discussion of the *Csárdás* as a Hungarian reaction and response to the round dances. On the one hand, we will see that the *Csárdás* does not fall entirely within the definition of round dances. On the other hand, it was clearly inspired by them, making it a national replacement.

Finally, the chapter maps the changing political contexts and climate during the nineteenth century, which created the framework for the tension that existed among ordinary people between dancing the foreign and the national dances.

Our point of departure is the identification of the dance repertory in Hungary. At the outset of the nineteenth century, the repertory of dances practised in Hungary was extraordinarily diverse, reflecting the multiplicity of ethnic groups and socio-cultural conditions of the country.[4] This was a result of the political, socio-economic and cultural changes taking place in the region during the eighteenth century.[5] Since changes continued at an accelerated rate in the nineteenth century, dance paradigms changed rapidly under their influence as well.

Lower-Class Dances

It is first worth addressing the traditional dance forms of the lower classes, mainly the peasantry. For instance, these include Hungarian *Verbunk*; *Csárdás*; *Kanásztánc* (swineherd dance); *Boricatánc*; Slovakian

---

[3] Comparison with other countries was beyond the scope of this study.
[4] András Gergely, ed., *Magyarország története a 19. században* (Budapest: Osiris Kiadó, 2005).
[5] See in detail in a later section of this chapter headed 'Socio-Political and Cultural Contexts of Nineteenth-Century Couple Dances in Hungary'.

Frisska; *Odzemok*; Serbian *Kolo*; Croatian *Kumpania*; Romanian *Lunga*, *Minitelu*, and *Căluş*; German *Német*, Ländler, *Landaris*, and *Steirisch*; and finally, Ruthenian *Kolomejka*. Soldier dances, as a multi-ethnic phenomenon inherited from the eighteenth century, were gradually fading from the repertoire. Women singing as an accompaniment to round dances among Hungarians were rarely mentioned by the sources, and researchers paid little attention to them.[6] Until the middle of the nineteenth century, this traditional dance repertoire was shared by both the local nobility and, to an extent, the aristocracy.

In multi-ethnic regions, people learned dances from each other, which in turn became an integral part of their own dance repertory. This process was hastened by the fact that the practise of traditional dance types was not limited to particular ethnic groups or countries. The spread of dances and melodies was likely a result of factors like migration, common service in the imperial army, extensive family relations and seasonal work by rural people in distant provinces. For example, the melody of the 'Németes' (German) or 'Landaris' (Landler) dance was, according to the evidence, popular among Széklers in the 1840s and beyond due to Hungarian soldiers serving in the Tirol.[7] (See Musical Source No. 4).

National Dances for the Upper Classes

Numerous historical sources mention *Magyar Tánc* (Hungarian dance), *Nemzeti Tánc* (national dance), *Nemeses Tánc* (a nobleman's dance), *Néptánc* (folk dance), *Körmagyar* (round Hungarian), and *Magyar Csárdás* (Hungarian *Csárdás*), which were used as nationalistic social dance forms by the nobility to symbolise patriotic feelings. They were also favoured by the less populous, multi-ethnic middle classes who exhibited an anti-Habsburg sentiment, and who had a kind of 'Hungarus'

---

6   Ernő Pesovár, *A magyar tánctörténet évszázadai: Írott és képi források* (Budapest: Hagyományok Háza, 2003); Ernő Pesovár, *Tánchagyományunk történeti rétegei: A magyar néptánc története* (Szombathely: Berzsenyi Dániel Főiskola, 2003); György Martin, 'Népi tánchagyomány és nemzeti tánctípusok Kelet-Közép-Európában a XVI–XIX. században', *Ethnographia*, 95 (1984), 353–61.

7   Marián Réthei Prikkel, *A magyarság táncai* (Budapest: Studium, 1924), p. 233. See Musical Source No. 4.

identity in terms of country rather than ethnic allegiance.[8] There are several references to these dances in the first half of the nineteenth century. They were made by foreign and Hungarian authors alike, but the only detailed description, from which we can reconstruct the dance, was published by Kilányi in Hungarian and in German, in his reference book *Körtánc*.[9] Little by little, the popularity of these dances spread to every social circle in contemporary Hungary. 'Hungarian dance' as a kind of social or national dance form had an impact on traditional couple dances, leading mainly to changes in their structural and musical features. Moreover, the name 'Hungarian dance' or 'Hungarian *Csárdás*' was also adopted, replacing various previously-used local dance names like the following: *Kutyakopogós* (dog tapping, *Kuferces* ('horse-coper', a faster *Csárdás*), *Darudübögős* (crane stamping etc.[10] *Körtánc* (*Körmagyar* and several other choreographies, such as *Társalgó* or *Vigadó* were composed by Hungarian dance masters and theatre dancers especially for the purposes of national and social expression. As such, they enjoyed only temporary fame. Most of them were soon forgotten, and, instead, the free improvisatory, 'non-regulated' forms prevailed under the name *Magyar Tánc* (Hungarian dance).[11]

---

8   György Martin, 'Az új magyar táncsatílus jegyei és kialakulása', *Ethnographia*, 88 (1977), 39; György Martin, 'Népi tánchagyomány és nemzeti tánctípusok', 361. Ambrus Miskolczy, '"Hungarus Consciousness" in the Age of Early Nationalism', in *Latin at the Crossroads of Identity: The Evolution of Linguistic Nationalism in the Kingdom of Hungary*, ed. by G. Almási and L. Šubarić (Leiden, Netherlands: Brill, 2015), pp. 64–93.

9   Lajos Kilányi, *A Kör-tánc mellyet Szőllőssi Lajos a pesti nemzeti színház táncművészének tanítása után Minden táncrész könnyen felfogható rajzolatával és magyarázatával terjedelmesen előadta Kilányi Lajos nemzeti és balettánc oktató, a nemzeti színház tagja 6 rajzolattal és egy zenemű melléklettel. Der Kör-Tanz. Erste Ungarische National-Quadrille, Erfunden Von Ludwig Szőllősi... Beschrieben Von L. Kilányi... Mit Abbildungen... und Einer Beigabe Der National-Musik* (Bécs: Wagner, 1845).

10 Martin György, 'Tánc és társadalom: Történeti táncnévadás-típusok itthon és Európában', in *Történeti Antropológia*, ed. by Hofer Tamás (Budapest: MTA Néprajzi Kutatócsoport, 1984), pp. 152–64.

11 The terms 'regulated' and 'non-regulated' were used in the contemporary social discourse; e.g. in the description given by August Ellrich, a German traveller, in 1831. See Written Source No. 4.

International Fashion Dances

The so called *Divattáncok* or *Módi Táncok* (fashion dances) disseminated by the dance masters and danced as social dances in urban, middle-class and aristocratic circles were clearly differentiated from the above-listed dance forms. They appear in Hungary in sources from the 1790s, and they include *Némettánc* (German dance), *Németes* (Germanic), *Voltzerisch*, *Walzer*, *Keringő* (Hungarian translation of *Walzer*, meaning 'whirling'), *Kalupáda* (the Galop), *Lengyel Tánc* (Polish dance), the Mazurka, the Polka, *Francia Tánc* (French dance), the Quadrille, and the Cotillion. To a lesser extent, *Csárdás* as a Hungarian national dance with a social dance function was also integrated into this group of nineteenth-century couple dances. In everyday discourse, they were seen as a 'new' fashion, reflecting the changing social taste and the political orientation of the different social classes.

Dancing Masters and Choreographies for the Stage

In the first half of the nineteenth century in Europe, we witness the appearance of 'wandering' dance masters and dancers, who created choreographies for show and stage performances. Generally, the choreographies had a fantasy name (e.g. Devil Dance, Highwayman Dance, Turkish Group), but it was also popular to name them after their form, or profession, or nationality. For instance, in a dance-drama titled *Az elrabolt hölgy vagy a szerencsés összetalálkozás a fogadóban* ['The kidnapped lady, or a lucky meeting in the pub'] played in 1835 in Buda, the following choreographies were performed by the two pantomimic parts choreographed by Hungarian dance master Szőllősy Szabó Lajos: *Ugrós Tízes Tánc* ['Jumping dance with ten dancers'], *Kettős Csikós Tánc* ['Horseherd duet by men'], *Magános Tánc* ['Solo male dance'], *Ideális Magános Tánc* ['Ideal solo dance'], and *Végső Körtánc* ['Final round dance'].[12]

In 1845, Hungarian dance master Veszter Sándor and his company gave guest performances in provincial towns and in the National

---

12 Klára B. Egey, 'Szinpadi táncművészetünk fejlődése a reform korban és a szabadságharc első szakaszában', in *A magyar balett történetéből*, ed. by Vályi Rózsi (Budapest: Művelt Nép, 1956), pp. 32–46 (p. 41).

Theatre in Pest with the following dances: *Krakovianka*, *Kozák Kettős* ['Kozak duet'], *Magyar Nemes Tánc* ['Hungarian noble dance'], *Sváb Tánc* ['Swabian dance'], *Komoly Kettős* ['Honourable duet'], and *Csárdás*.[13]

At the National Theatre in 1846, in the ballet comedy *Markotányosnő és a postalegény* ['Madam canteen-keeper and the young postman'] by Arthur Saint Leon, the company performed dance pieces such as 'A Markotányosnő Tánca' ['Dance of the canteen-keeper'], 'Nagy Négyes Tánc' ['The great *pas-de-quatre*'], 'Német Nép-Körtánc' (German round folk dance), and 'Redowa-Polka' (original Czech folkdance). These were choreographed by Arthur Saint Leon, and the music composed by Caesar Puigni.[14]

According to the theatrical posters and the reports in the periodicals, the contemporary audience of the theatres could watch dances like *Spanyol Tánc* (Spanish dance), *Tarantella*, *Jota*, *Kínai Tánc* (Chinese dance), the Mazurka, the Galop and Polka, danced both by foreign and Hungarian dance companies in Hungary.[15]

Round Dances in the Nineteenth- and Twentieth-Century Literature

As presented above, we can determine a group of new, fashionable couple dances that appeared in Hungary from the 1790s onwards as social, recreational, representational, or stage dances. Among them, we can define some dance types that are partly of German, partly of Slavic (Polish-Czech) and partly of French origin, and show the characteristic features of the nineteenth-century couple dances listed in the Introduction to this volume The following part of this chapter focuses on these dances in particular. We introduce the results of the research in Hungary so far, and provide a selection of the most relevant sources.

The first signs of a scholarly way of thinking about dance and about the newly fashionable dances can be found in the writings published in the periodicals of the first half of the nineteenth century, parallel with and shortly after the appearance of these dances in social life.

---

13   B. Egey, 'Szinpadi táncművészetünk fejlődése', pp. 67–68.
14   Ibid., p. 59.
15   Ibid.

The main topics of the contemporary discourse among the first 'experts' (journalists, actors, writers, historians, etc.) were the national characteristics of the Hungarian dances, and the features differentiating them from the so called 'foreign' dances. The laconic remarks and short descriptions regarding the 'foreign' dances were summarised by Réthei Prikkel Marián (1871–1925) in his book, *A magyarság táncai* [Dances of Hungarians] published in 1924. He dedicated to them two separate chapters: 'Hungarians and the foreign dances' and 'Fight against the foreign dances'. Réthei's ideas about the connection between social dances in the Hungarian dance culture are presented in the introduction of his book:

> I imagine the dances of Hungarians as a tree, the trunk of which is constituted by the folk dances, that is the ancient, original way of their dancing. The branches of the tree represent those peculiar dances which grew out from the trunk, or foreign dances 'merged' into the trunk and transformed into Hungarian. Besides, we may find dances which grow beside the tree, neither coming from it, nor being merged into it. I cannot omit either of them from the book, because historical data prove that they became fashionable among Hungarians, although their character could not become Hungarian.[16]

In the aforementioned chapters, Réthei collects and evaluates all the historical evidence available to him in connection with the European fashion dances spreading in Hungary. The nineteenth-century couple dances are represented by twelve items of data. Four of them date back to the end of the eighteenth century and the others to the first decades of the nineteenth. The short remarks, musical notes, iconographic materials, epic poems, and political writings listed by Réthei were part of a nationwide social discourse about the 'Hungarian dance' that lasted more than a century. Additionally, he supplemented the historical data with valuable ethnographic information about the spreading of these dances among the peasantry in Hungary during the second half of the nineteenth century. As a result, these parts of his book became more complex and scholarly than any other previous writing on this topic. However, we have to take into consideration that Réthei was himself

---

16 Réthei, *A magyarság táncai*, pp. 2–3. Translation from the Hungarian by László Felföldi.

biased by the ideas of nineteenth-century patriots — the authors of these sources — and his book was also dedicated to this issue.

From the beginning of the twentieth century, dance historians Emil Haraszti (1887–1958), Olga Szentpál (1895–1968), Rózsi Vályi (1907–1997), Edit Kaposi (1923–2006), László Maácz (1929–1998), Klára B. Egey (1910-?70), and Iván Vitányi (1925-?), paid some attention to nineteenth-century couple dances. As for the music of these dances, historian Bence Szabolcsi has contributed substantially to the research on this topic.[17] Among dance historians, Olga Szentpál and Edit Kaposi did most to promote more comprehensive, in-depth analysis of the source material, notably with Olga Szentpál's book *A Csárdás: a magyar nemzeti társastánc a 19. század első felében* [*Csárdás*: The Hungarian national social dance in the first half of the nineteenth century]. Published in 1954, it provides more than one hundred historical sources (texts, pictures, musical notes) about *Csárdás*, which has a similar history to the nineteenth-century couple dances and in some sense belongs to the same class as these. Due to the nature of the historical sources, the book constitutes a treasure trove of evidence about nineteenth-century couple dances as well. That is to say, in many of the written documents, *Csárdás* is characterised by comparison with the Waltz, the Polka, the Galop, and so on; 'foreign' dances that competed with the Hungarian national dance in the ballrooms. Although the evaluation of these dances is negative, with careful interpretation, researchers can gain good information about these so-called 'foreign' dances: their popularity, socio-cultural features, and the particular ways they were danced. Olga Szentpál focused on *Csárdás*. She did not place special emphasis on the study of the Waltz, the Polka, and the others, but she did collect material that proved to be useful for further research. In the 1950s, members of the research group on Historical Social Dances of the State Ballet Institute in Budapest, headed by Olga Szentpál, made several reconstructions based on dance masters' books. From the nineteenth century they chose 'Valse à trois temps' and the Polka from Henry Cellarius' manual *La Danse des Salons* (published in Paris in 1847). The scientific reconstruction based on these two dances was published in *Táncművészeti Értesítő* [Bulletin

---

17   Bence Szabolcsi, *Népzene és történelem* (Budapest: Akadémiai Kiadó, 1954).

of the Dance Arts] in 1956.[18] It served both educational and scientific purposes. Reconstructions contributed to the precision of the formal-structural features of these dances. Foreign dance historians enriched the literature, such as Tobias Norlind with his article, published in Hungary, on the history of the Waltz and the Polka, dedicated in honour of Zoltán Kodály's sixtieth birthday in 1943.[19]

From the 1970s to the 1990s, Edit Kaposi's research focused on the history of social dances; the activities of dancing masters; dance masters' books; the life and career of nineteenth-century Hungarian dancers and dance masters; and scenes of dancing in theatres and ballrooms. Her comprehensive articles address the history of European and Hungarian dance teaching as a craft from the fifteenth to the twentieth century. They give a wide panorama of the topic, with numerous interesting details contextualised in the political, social and cultural situation of the period.[20] With the critical analysis and publication of the social dance literature — mainly dance masters' books (not only by Hungarians) — she created a firm basis for the further investigation of this field of research.[21] Being based in ethnography in Budapest University, she was sensitive to the socio-cultural relatedness and cross-cultural features of the social dances, and in her field research she paid special attention to them.

In the 1950s, György Martin and Ernő Pesovár studied social dances and their derivatives among the lower classes in a wider historical and geographical framework. Among others, Ernő Pesovár dealt with social dances (also from the nineteenth century) and their affinity

---

18 Olga Szentpál, 'Keringő és polka a a 19. században. Táncrekonstrukció Cellarius táncmester leírása alapján', in *Táncművészeti Értesítő*, ed. by Morvay Péter (Budapest: Magyar Táncművészek Szövetsége, 1956), pp. 73–89.

19 Tobias Norlind, 'Adatok a keringő és a polka történetéhez', in *Emlékkönyv Kodály Zoltán 60. születésnapjára* ed. by Gunda Béla (Budapest: Magyar Néprajzi Társaság, 1943), pp. 189–94.

20 Edit Kaposi, 'Egy híres táncos önéletírása: Szőllősy Szabó Lajos', *Táncművészet*, 4 (1955), 154–56; Edit Kaposi, 'Adalékok az európai és a magyar táncmesterség történetéhez', *Tánctudományi Tanulmányok*, 1969–1970 (1970), 16–194; Edit Kaposi, 'Kiegészítő adatok az európai táncmesterség történetéhez', *Táncművészeti Értesítő*, 9 (1973), 34–37, 87–91; Edit Kaposi, 'Szőllősy Szabó Lajos élete és munkássága (1803–1882)', *Tánctudományi Tanulmányok*, 1978–1979 (1979), 145–88.

21 Edit Kaposi, 'A magyar társastánc szakirodalom forráskritikai vizsgálata I.', *Tánctudományi Tanulmányok*, 1984–1985 (1985), 177–94; Edit Kaposi, 'A magyar társastánc szakirodalom forráskritikai vizsgálata II.', *Tánctudományi Tanulmányok*, 1986–1987 (1987), 50–75.

to (or isolation from) the couple dances practised in Hungary.[22] He revised the previous understanding of the genesis of the Csárdás by a reinterpretation of the historical couple-dance sources from the end of the eighteenth and the first half of the nineteenth century.[23] He paid special attention to the impact of Polish dance on life in the first half of the nineteenth century.[24] I myself contributed to this research with the discovery of some new historical documents and the reinterpretation of some lesser known ones related to the nineteenth-century social dances.[25] Martin put more emphasis on determining the place of the dances (deriving from the nineteenth-century couple dances and practised in local communities in the twentieth century) in the system of Hungarian folk dances. In his classification, Martin created a special category for them, beyond the old and new stylistic layers. He claims:

> We rank the dances of foreign origin (mostly of Western European, noble, bourgeois or dance-master's-school origin, which were practised in some strata of the peasantry, in one generation or more, temporarily and regionally) into a mixed layer of the Hungarian dance culture. The criterion belonging to this stylistic layer is not simply their obvious foreign provenance, but the limited degrees of their assimilation, folklorisation and spreading. These dances preserved their original form, and music of their own. Their style is totally different from that of our old- and new-style dances.[26]

Ferenc Pesovár (Ernő's Pesovár younger brother) also contributed to the topic by the presentation of historical forms of dance mastery and

---

22 Ernő Pesovár, *A magyar páros táncok* (Budapest: Planétás, 1997).
23 Ernő Pesovár 'A *csárdás* kialakulásának szakaszai és típusai', *Ethnographia*, 48 (1985), 17–29; Pesovár, *A magyar páros táncok*; Pesovár, *A magyar tánctörténet évszázadai*; Pesovár, *Tánchagyományunk történeti rétegei*.
24 Ernő Pesovár, 'A lengyel táncok hatása a reformkorban', *Néprajzi Értesítő*, 47 (1965), 159–77.
25 László Felföldi, 'Táncábrázolások az abszolutizmus és kiegyezés korabeli kottás kiadványok címlapjain', in *Magyarországi kottacímlapok* (1848–1867), ed. by Szabó Júlia (Budapest: Argumentum, 2000), pp. 13–23; László Felföldi, 'Tánctörténet', in *Magyar kódex*, 6 vols, ed. by Szentpéteri József (Budapest: Kossuth, 1999–2001), I, 269–71; László Felföldi, 'Picturing Hungarian Patriotism: Bikkessy Album Imaging Dance', in *Imaging Dance: Visual Representation of Dancers and Dancing*, ed. by Barbara Sparti and Judy Van Zile (New York: Georg Olms Verlag, 2011), pp. 181–94.
26 György Martin, *Magyar tánctípusok és táncdialektusok* (Budapest: Népművelési Propaganda Iroda, 1970), p. 40. Translated from the Hungarian by László Felföldi.

dance events.²⁷ Historical anthropologist Tamás Hofer assisted dance researchers to contextualise these phenomena in the socio-cultural changes of the eighteenth and nineteenth centuries.²⁸

Among lexicons related to dance, the *Színészeti Lexikon I–II* [Theatrical Lexicon] published in 1930²⁹ deserves most attention. Pálfy György, dance historian and writer of ten to fifteen entries on the Waltz, the Polka, the Mazurka, the Galop, the Ecossaise, and the Cotillion, used the available international and Hungarian literature, though unfortunately without detailed references. He dedicated a separate entry to the social dances, which he named 'Modern Szóló Táncok' [Modern solo dances] and in which he gives an overview of the socio-cultural background and changing mentality behind the social dances in comparison with stage dance, modern dance and sport. Other professional lexicons (*Balett lexikon*, *Magyar táncművészeti lexikon*)³⁰ published in the twentieth century paid less attention to these dance forms, except for the Ethnographic Lexicon. Ernő Pesovár and Ferenc Pesovár, writers of the entries on nineteenth-century couple dances in the *Hungarian Ethnographic Lexicon*, volumes 1–5 (1978–1982),³¹ group them under the name 'Bourgeois social dances' or 'Bourgeois fashion dances'. They give relatively detailed information about their history and ethnographic features (spreading, social function in the local communities, activity of dance masters etc) in Hungary.

In the twentieth and twenty-first centuries, young dance researchers became more interested in the investigation of nineteenth-century couple dances.³² Hopefully, this will lead to the formation of a separate

---

27 Ferenc Pesovár, 'Táncmesterek a szatmári falvakban', *Tánctudományi Tanulányok*, 1959–1960 (1960), 309–22; and Ferenc Pesovár, *A magyar nép táncélete* (Budapest: Népművelési Propaganda Iroda, 1978).
28 Tamás Hofer, 'A magyar népi kultúra történeti rétegei és európai helyzete', in *Martin György emlékezete* ed. by Felföldi László (Budapest: Magyar Művelődési Intézet, 1993), pp. 341–51.
29 *Színészeti lexikon*, 2 vols, ed. by Németh Antal (Budapest: Győző Andor kiadása, 1930).
30 Horst Köegler, *Balett lexikon* (Budapest: Zeneműkiadó, 1977); *Magyar táncművészeti lexikon*, ed. by Dienes Gedeon (Budapest: Planétás, 2008).
31 *Magyar Néprajzi Lexikon*, 5 vols, ed. by Ortutay Gyula (Budapest: Akadémiai Kiadó, 1978–1982).
32 Dóka, Krisztina, '19. századi társastáncok a magyar paraszti táncklutúrában', *Tánctudományi Közlemények*, 2 (2014), 49–66; Kavecsánszky, Máté, 'Társastáncok a magyar paraszti közösségben a 19–20. században', in *Notitiae Iuvenum: Tanulmányok Ujváry Zoltán 75. születésnapjának tiszteletére*, ed. by Kiri Edit, Kovács László Erik, and

research field on this topic. The hundred or so documents discovered and published so far (one third from between 1790–1850) and the scientific knowledge accumulated in these books and articles may be a good basis for this.

Selected and Annotated Source Catalogue

The next passage contains documents representing the most characteristic types, and thematic groups, of sources about nineteenth-century couple dances. Written texts, such as public or scientific papers, reports on balls, personal letters, dance masters' books, or literature, are the most common. Iconographic material, like engravings of dance events or portrayals of the Waltz, the Polka, the Mazurka, or the Quadrille on, for example, the front page of the printed musical scores, is not so widespread, but this makes it all the more interesting to researchers. There is also a collection of musical scores, both with and without text. The written sources and the titles of other kinds of documents were translated by the author.

Written Sources

No. 1: Description of a Ball in Pest (Fragment) from 1790

(Gvadányi, József) *Egy falusi nótáriusnak budai utazása, melyet önnön maga abban esett viszontagságaival együtt az elaludt vérű magyar szivek felserkentésére és mulatságára e versekbe foglalt* [A Village Clerk's Journey to Buda, Put into Verse in Order to Refresh and Entertain 'Sleepy' Hungarian Hearts, Including his Adventures on the Way] [n.a.] (Pozsony és Komárom: Wéber Simon Péter, 1790), p. 29.

> *A táncok többnyire álla keringésből*
> The dances consisted mostly of whirling,
> *forgószél port mint hajt, olyan tekergésből,*
> like a whirlwind driving dust,
> *gondoltam: virradtig sok meghal ezekből,*

Szilágyi Judit (Debrecen: DE-BTK HÖK, 2007), pp. 199–242; Máté Kavecsánszki, *Tánc és közösség*, Studia Folkloristica et Ethnographica 59 (Debrecen: Debreceni Egyetemi Kiadó, 2015).

I thought: they would die at dawn,
Guta következik a fej-szédülésből.
from a stroke caused by dizzyness.

Az én iffiúm is közöttök fetrengett ,
My son was whirling among them,
Egy csínos lyánkával, mint többi, keringett,
with a nice girl like the others.
Izzadt vólt; mondotta, mindjárt vesz más inget.
He sweated so heavily, that he had to
úgy is tett, hogy éppen csúf táncnak vége lett.
change his shirt at the end of this ugly dance.

Kérdém: — 'Uram! ugyan mi neve e táncnak?
I ask: — 'Sir, what is the name of this dance?
Mert egyszer, keringős hogy lett ökröm, annak
Once my ox was ill, it was whirling
szint ilyen tánca vólt, mint itten forganak,
like the people are whirling here.
Az is csak keringett, itten sem ugranak'.
It was similarly whirling without jumping'.

Felelt: — ,Uram! hívják eztet voltzerisnek,
Answer: — 'Sir, its name is: voltzerish.
Voltzen kallót tészen, s természete ennek
Valzen means wool mill, which
szűntelen forgani, mint malomkeréknek,
turns endlessly like a mill-wheel.
kalló-tánc ez tehát, melybe keringenek.
Namely, it is Kalló-tánc, where they turn.

'Higgye az úr nékem, hogy lészen az nagy kár,
'Believe me, Sir, it is unfortunate
hogyha el nem megyen, egy voltzerist nem jár,
if you do not dance a voltzerish.
Ama dáma olyan könnyű, mint a madár,
that lady is so light, like a bird,
vigye el: mert látom, hogy csak az úrra vár'.
take her; she is waiting only for you'.

'Uram! bolondgombát még sohase ettem,
'Sir, I am not crazy. I have never danced,
mint a bódúlt marha, nem is keringettem;
like a dazed cattle; I have not been whirling.
Ha táncoltam, tehát igaz táncot tettem,

> If I ever danced, I did a real dance,
> *melyből a fejembe szédűlést nem vettem.*
> which did not make my head dizzy'.

Comments: The writer of this epic poem, József Gvadányi, a Hungarian poet (1725–1801), is a representative of the radical nationalist lower nobility. His work (first published in 1790) is a good example of the initial reception the new fashionable dance — Voltseris (Hungarian pronunciation: Valtserish) — received when it came from Vienna. The main hero of the poem is attending a ball held in Pest, in Hét Kurfürst *fogadó* (a restaurant with hotel and a ballroom, named 'dance palace') where the multi-ethnic dancers came from the middle classes and the aristocratic circles. He evaluates the Valceris from the perspective of a village man having his first experience of it in the town. He characterises it with vulgar words and describes it in an ironic way. The dancers, among them his son, are portrayed in similar tone. In addition, he gives a detailed, realistic description of the ballroom, the dancers and their dresses. He emphasises the intensive whirling and jumping as the main features of the dance, and also mentions the '*Kontradanz*' [contradance] elsewhere in the poem.

No. 2: Comparison of German, French, and Hungarian 'National' Dances in a Poem of Classical, Metrical Style from 1811

Dániel Berzsenyi, 'A táncok' ['Dances'], in *Berzsenyi Dániel összes versei*, ed. by Merényi Oszkár (Budapest: Szépirodalmi Könyvkiadó, 1982), p. 134.

> *Nézd a tánc nemeit, mint festik játszi ecsettel*
> Perceive the various dances, how they mirror, with playful brush,
> *A népek lelkét s nemezetek ízleteit.*
> The folks' soul and the nations' taste.
> *A német hármas lépéssel lejtve kering le,*
> The German is whirling with triple steps
> *S párját karja közé zárja s lebegve viszi.*
> He embraces his partner and carries her as if floating.
> *Egyszerű a német mindenben, s csendesen örvend,*
> The German is simple in everything, having fun silently,
> *Egyet ölel mindig, s állhatatos szerető.*
> He always embraces the same women and is a faithful lover.

A gallus fellengve szökik, s enyelegve kacsingat,
The Gallic jumps high-flown with flirting winks,
Párt vált, csalfa kezet majd ide, majd oda nyújt:
He changes partner, with deceitful hands here and there:
Ez heves és virgonc, örömében gyermeki nyájas
He is passionate and agile, delighted at everything, like a child.
Kényeiben repdez, s a szerelmbe' kalóz.
He flatters in high spirits, and he is a pirate in love.
A magyar egy Pindár: valamerre ragadja negéde,
The Hungarian is a Pindar: when his enthusiasm takes him
Lelkesedett tűzzel nyomja ki indulatit.
His feelings burn like fire.
Majd lebegő szellő, szerelemre olvad epedve,
Then he melts into longing for love, like a soft breeze
S buja hevét kényes mozdulatokba szövi;
And he weaves his enthusiasm into delicate movements.
Majd maga fellobbanva kiszáll a bajnoki táncra
Then he gets to martial dance
(Megveti a lyánykát a diadalmi dagály),
(The woman is taken by the fighting spirit as well)
S rengeti a földet: Kinizsit látsz véres ajakkal
The earth quakes under his feet: You see a 'Kinizsi' with bloody lips
A testhalmok közt ugrálni hőseivel.
Jumping among the dead bodies together with his heroes.
Titkos törvényit mesterség nem szedi rendbe,
Its secret rules are not tamed by dance masters,
Csak maga szab törvényt, s lelkesedése határt.
Only the dancer creates rules, and his enthusiasm inscribes limits.
Ember az ki magyar tánchoz jól terme, örüljön!
He, who has talent for Hungarian dance, let him be glad!
Férfierő s lelkes szikra hevíti erét.
His blood is filled with manliness and sparks of zeal.

Comments: Dániel Berzsenyi (1775–1836), a Hungarian poet, represents the educated and creative landowners who participated actively in cultural and political life. His aim in this poem is to depict and emphasise differences in the characteristic features of German, French and Hungarian ways of dancing. He intended to show how dances harmonise with the national character of different peoples. The German way, with its triple basic step, whirling character and 'simple' structure might describe the Waltz — the German national dance — which was already well known in Hungary in 1811, at the time of the genesis of the poem. French people were famous for their Quadrille, contra dance, Galop, and Cotillion, executed in a passionate, agile and delightful way as regulated, collective couple dances. The Hungarian way of dancing is represented as a free, unregulated solo male and couple dance with high emotions in a rapturous mood. It was known as the national dance of Hungarians inside and outside Hungary. By mentioning Pindaros (Pindar in the poem), the Greek poet (c. 522/518–422/438 BC), famous for his passion for dance and dance songs, Berzsenyi refers to the similar zeal for dance on the part of the Hungarians. Recalling Kinizsi Pál's dance on the battle field in 1478 against the Turkish army, he confirms the heroic character of the Hungarian national dance.[33]

No. 3: Journalistic Feuilleton Concerning the Characteristic Features, Social Position, and Necessity for Regulation of the 'Magyar Nemzeti Tánc' [Hungarian National Dance]

Balla Károly, 'A' Magyar nemzeti Tánczról' [On Hungarian National Dance], *Tudományos Gyűjtemény*, 7 (1823), 85–106.

...A' honnan a mái pallérozott nemzetek, kiknek tánczok eleinte szinte darabos és rendetlen vala, annyira igyekeztek tánczaikat kipallérozni 's határok közé szorítani, hogy többnyirő a' maga tökéletessége grádusát már már mindenik elérte; 's bár az emberiségbe oltott tarkaságon való kapás, az idegen tánczokat is járatja velek; de mindeniknek önnön táncza azelső, ' s egy sincs ki benne ne büszélkedne. Annyival inkább minél bizonyosabb az, hogy az idegen nemzetek szokásainak követéséből, minden csalatás nélkül sokat veszt 'a Nemzetiség; és csak az látszik legtisztább nemzetnek, kinek nyelve, öltözete, törvénye és szokása a' többi Nemzetekétől leginkább különböznek.

Az idegen Quadril't, Cotilliont, Ecossoisét, Mazúrt 's t. e' f. gúnyolni nem célom: mivel azok a Nemzeti muzsikákhoz lévén alkalmazva, a' hangoknak megfelelnek, de dicsérnem is bajos, ha csak előbb meg nem mutatnám, hogy a' szeles test-fintorgatások a' lélek' nemes tüzének külső jelei. Hogy azonban ezeknek táncolása, némi-nemű hozzájok hasonló nyomot hágy a lélekben is, azt némely mazúrkás ifjaink tapasztaltatják, kikben a' nemzeti fő bélyeg már már lengeség. Annyival inkább, hogy ezen tánczokhoz Medvenadrág vagyis Bolondon (pantallon), Csizma

---

33 Pesovár *A magyar tánctörténet évszázadai* p. 95. Pál Kinizsi (1413?-94) was a famous general in the service of the Hungarian army in the fifteenth century.

helyett holnap czipő: nyakravaló helyett vörös Schal; és kalap helyett
főkötő kívántatván, még akkor sem fogja az eltanúlt gyermek felhúzni
a sarkantyús csizmát és mentét, ha a' magyar nemes név' elvesztésével
ijesztgetik.³⁴

[...] megilletődve tapasztalám egy magyar faluba, midőn egy
kegyetlen bőgős a' kemencze torkán egy német nótát, a'gatyás és
rásaszoknyás köztársaság pedig a' német tánczot nyaggatták. Mit csinálsz
Zsiga! mondám, miért nyomorgatjátok a levegőt? A sötét képű prímás,
ki már verejtékezett a' nehéz munkába: Kegyelmes Uram! úgymond, a'
Nagyságos földes Uraktól tanulták paraszt Uramék őkelmék. Szemébe
inték ekkor a Falu urának; ki elkomolyúlt; s' 20 forintot adott az igazság
szembe való mondásáért. — A Lagzi számára pedig 50 fltot ajándékozván:
kifordúltunk; hogy már a magyar paraszt is mit csinál — s ki ennek az
oka? — azon töprenkedve.³⁵

[For the civilised nations of today, their own dance is best and they are
all proud of it; they tried to regulate their dance and keep it within limits,
so that it could reach perfection, and they dance the foreign dances as
well, following the natural human instinct to be fond of diversity. It is
becoming more and more evident that practising the customs of the
foreign nations, without a doubt, harms a nation; and only that nation
seems to be immaculate, whose language, costume, law and customs are
most different from the others.

I do not want to make fun of the foreign Quadrille, Cotillion,
Ecossoise, Mazur, since they are well applied to their national music,
but I can hardly praise them, unless I first prove that their windy 'body-
grimacings' are expressions of the fire of their soul. We may experience
it in the case of our youngsters who subscribe to mazur-mania, whose
national mark has almost already disappeared. What is more, for these
dances, people have to wear *medvenadrág* [Bear-trousers] or *bolondon*
[pants]; put on shoes instead of boots; instead of a necktie they wear a
red *schal* [scarf] and instead of the hat, they have the bonnet; and these
spoiled young men cannot be forced to put on boots with spurs and
mente [a short fur-lined coat], even if they are threatened with the loss of
their noble 'Hungarian' name.

[...] I was surprised in a Hungarian village, that on the top of
the oven an ugly bass player is playing German music, and that the
're-public'³⁶ in *gatya* [white linen culottes] and in *rasha* [half-linen type
of textile] skirts are aping the German dance. 'What are you doing,
Zsiga?' — I ask — 'Why do you afflict the air?' The dark-faced primate

---

34 Pp. 86–87.
35 P. 95.
36 That is, the dancers.

sweating because of the hard work, says: 'Your Excellency! The peasant "excellencies" learn it from the honourable landlords'. I looked at the landlord of the village inquiringly. He frowned, and gave twenty *forints* to the primate for telling the truth. Moreover, he presented fifty *forints* to the participants of the wedding, and at last we left the place meditating on what the peasants were doing, and who can be blamed for it.]

Comments: Balla Károly (*mándi*) (1792–1873) is a poet, writer and publicist, correspondent of numerous journals and newspapers in Hungary and in Vienna, who dealt with very diverse topics, from socio-cultural matters to economic and political issues. His article, published in the *Tudományos Gyüjtemény* (Scientific Collection, a monthly periodical published between 1817 and 1941), is a kind of polemic essay about the problems with the Hungarian national dance. As we can see from the above quotation, he was of the opinion that Hungarians ought to regulate their national dance after the model of the other nations in Europe. He raises the question of the responsibility of the national elite for the increasing decline of their traditional dances among the peasant communities, in favour of the foreign, fashionable dances.

No. 4: Characterisation of the Hungarian Dance Compared to the Contemporary Fashion Dances Coming from Abroad (Fragment) from 1831

August Ellrich, *Die Ungarn wie sie sind. Charakter-Schilderung dieses Volkes in seinen Verhältnissen und Gesinnungen* (Berlin: In der Fereins Buchhandlung, 1831), pp. 142–3.

> Schritte, Toure, Bewegungen, Attitüden sind willkürlich, dem Genie, dem Geschmacke der Tanzenden überlassen. Man schreitet nicht in regelmässigen, abgezirkelten Schritten, eins, zwei, drei und vier, auf und nieder wie im Menuett, es ist nich das monotone Drehdichum des Walzers, es ist ein freier, durch irgend eine Idee belebter Tanz. Die Leute macht nie bummere Gesichter als da sie Menuet Tanzen oder walzen, und das ist natürlich: Mann siecht nie belebtere, geistvollere Menschenäntliche, als im ungarischen Tanze, und das it wieder ganz natürlich, denn der ungarische Tanz ist Poesie, der Walzer, Das Menuett sind mechanische Gewerbe. Der Mechaniker kann ein Automat machen, welches vortrefflich Menuet tanzt und übertrefflich walzt, aber er kann keines machen, welches ungarisch tanzt, oder eine Arie komponirt [...] Das Minenspiel solcher ungarisher Tänzer ist eben so admirable als das Spiel ihrer Füsse.

[Dancers execute their steps, turnings, movements, attitudes according to their own talent and taste. This is not regulated, reserved stepping: one, two, three and four, up and down, as in the Minuet, and not incessant turning like the Waltz; this is a free dance in which an idea is living. People do not make such silly faces as they do when dancing the Minuet or the Waltz, and this is self-evident. Faces are never and nowhere so vivid and enthusiastic as in the Hungarian dance, and this also obvious, because the Hungarian dance is poetry; the Waltz and the Minuet are mechanical products. An engineer is able to make a robot that dances the Minuet and the Waltz in a splendid way, but he cannot make one for the Hungarian dance and cannot compose such music. [...] The facial expressions of these Hungarian dancers are as magnificent as the movements of their legs.]

Comments: August Ellrich (whose real name was Albin Johann Baptist von Meddlhammer, 1777–1838) was a German writer and traveller, who gave detailed accounts about the culture and way of life of the Austrian Monarchy, including Hungary. He paid special attention to dances, and to the theatrical life of Hungary. He appreciated the freedom and poetic quality of Hungarian dance, in contrast to the regulatedness and mechanic features of the Menuett and the Walzer. Some other foreign travellers who noticed the distinctiveness of Hungarian dances include George Johann Kohl (1808–1878), a German geographer;[37] Arthur Patterson (1835–1899), an English writer and teacher of the English language;[38] Victor Tissot (1845–1917), a French writer of Swiss origin;[39] Margaret Fletcher (1862–1943), an English writer and religious activist;[40] and, finally, Albert Czerwinski, a dance historian who also witnessed dances when he happened to be in Hungary, and wrote about them in the same style as Ellrich and the others.[41]

---

37 Kohl, Georg Johann, *Hundert Tage auf Reisen in den östereichischen Staten* (Dresden und Leipzig: in der Arnoldische Buchhandlung, 1842).
38 Arthur Patterson, *The Magyars: Their Country and Institution* (London: Smith, Elder and Co., 1869).
39 Victor Tissot, *La Hongrie: De l'Adriatique au Danube: Impressions de voyage* (Paris: Plon, 1883).
40 Margaret Fletcher, *Sketches of Life and Character in Hungary* („New York: Macmillan and Co, 1892).
41 Albert Chervinszki, *Geschichte der Tanzkunst bei den cultivirten Volkern* (Leipzig: Velagbuchshandlung von J. J. Weber, 1862).

No. 5: On the Differences between Hungarian and 'Modish' Dances. Fragment from a Letter Sent by Dániel Berzsenyi, Poet and Nobleman, to Count István Széchenyi, Politician and Patriot, written in Nikla, 1830

Published in Berzsenyi Dániel, Összes Művei [The Complete Works of Daniel Berzsenyi] collected by Oszkár Merényi (Budapest: Szépirodalmi kiadó 1956), p. 688.

> [...] A mi táncaink nem két-három gyermekes lépdelésbül állanak, mint a mostani módi táncok, melyeket egy-két napon belül megtanulunk, harmadikon pedig egyforma, gyermekes, lelketlen volta miatt meg is ununk; hanem olyan célerányosak, hogy azoknak tanulása egész ifjúságunkban dolgot adott, s aesthetiás természeteik szerint olyan kedvesek, hogy azok bennünk passzióvá válnak, s azáltal a barátságnak, nyájasságnak ösztönei lesznek. S tapasztaljuk, hogy azokkal fogy a barátság, mert saját táncainkat elfeledtük; az idegent pedig nem szeretjük, s megszűnt muzsikánk. Ez pedig a görögöknél nagy szó vala, s annyit tett, mint a legfőbb oskolának — a társalkodásnak romlása.
>
> [[...] Our dances do not consist of two or three childish steps, as do the fashionable dances of today, which we learn in one or two days, and on the third day we get bored of them because of their shallow, childish character. Our dances are so purposive that we make ourselves master them throughout all of our youth; and because of the aesthetic nature of our dances, they are so good for us that they become our passion, and with that comes the motivation to make friendships and good relationships with others. Now we realise that good relations are coming to an end, because we have forgotten our dances; we do not like the foreign ones; our music has disappeared. And this was a significant word for the Greeks, and it meant the destruction of the supreme school — the social life.]

Comments: As this letter proves, national dance was a theme in the correspondence among the cultural and national elite (mainly noblemen). Count István Széchenyi (1791–1860), a landowner, politician, and outstanding figure of the political and cultural life in Hungary, was an expert on the economy and finance. However, as an educated aristocrat and patriot, his field of interests also covered literature, philosophy, and several socio-cultural questions as well. Dániel Berzsenyi (1776–1836) was a poet and writer dealing with the

Harmony thesis of the classical Greek philosophers, and he intended to apply this to the fields of the Hungarian language and literature, music, and dance. His ideas were explained in detail in his essay 'Poetai harmonistica' in 1833. In his opinion, in the world of arts, the only constant component is Harmony, regardless of whether the artistic piece is the product of Classicism, Romanticism or something else. His letter to Széchenyi reflects this mentality.

No. 6: Short Presentation of Some National Dances in Europe with Arguments for Their Correspondence with National Characters. Opinion about the Regulation of the National Social Dances from 1841

Vahot Imre, 'Nemzeti társastánczunk, tánczzenénk és öltözetünk ügyében' ['About our Social Dance, our Dance Music and our National Costume'], *Athenaeum*, 2 (1841), 859–62.

> [...] milly szépen mutatkozik a tánczok külön féle nemeiben minden egyes nép és nemzet sajátos jelleme; mennyire érdekes például a quadrilleben egyszerre megismerni a franczia heves, könnyű, finom, udvarias jellemét, a walzerben a német bárány kedélyét, gyáriasan egyidomú, fáradságos, de czéltalan életét, a tarantelltánczban az olasz dühét, a mazurban a lengyel örökös éber lelkesedését, a bonekkatánczban a szép görög nők fölötte víg természetét, vagy az Európába is áthurczolt bayaderek eleven testmozgásaiban a hindu nép magasztos vallásosságát.[42]
>
> [...] Nincs itt egyéb kérdés, mint az: valljon úgy amint meg volt kezdve, tovább is minden szabály nélkül s csak természetesen tánczolják azt, vagy kissé rendbe szedve? — Mindenesetre ez utóbbit kell választani, mert a puszta természetesség ugyan magában szép is lehet, a művészi természetesség még szebb. Azonban nemzeti társastáncunk szabályozása csak olly feltételek alatt engedhető meg, ha az által eredeti sajátosságából, egyszerű szépségéből legkissebet sem veszt, s holmi feszes, cifra torzfigurákkal el nem rontatik, sőt ellenkezőleg, ha könnyű hajlékony természeténél fogva, a szábályzó által oly széppé alakíttatik, hogy művészi becsben valamennyi társastánczot felülmúlja.[43]
>
> [[...] It is so nice, how the individual character of each people and nation are represented in the different varieties of dance. How interesting, for

---

42   P. 859.
43   Pp. 860–61.

example, to discover the passionate, easy, gentle and polite nature of the French in the Quadrille; the lamb-like temperament and tedious, tiresome but aimless life of the Germans in the Walzer; the fury of Italians in the *Tarantella*; the constant burning enthusiasm of the Polish people in the Mazur; the cheerful nature of the nice Greek women; or the exalted piety of the Hindu people in the lively movements of the *bayadères*, who were forced to come to Europe.

[...] The only question here is whether it (Hungarian social dance) should be executed as before, without any rules, naturally, or in a slightly regulated form? At any rate, the latter should be chosen, because mere naturalness might be nice in itself, but artistic naturalness is even more beautiful. Regulation of our national social dance could be permitted only under conditions which do not deprive it of even the smallest part of its original features and simple beauty, and if it is not spoiled with strange, deformed figures; on the contrary though, it might also be spoiled if the regulator, knowing its easy, flexible character, makes it so excessively beautiful that it surpasses all the other social dances in artistic qualities.]

Comments: Vahot Imre (1820–1879) was a public-spirited Hungarian lawyer, writer, dramatist, editor of periodicals and one of the main figures of the cultural life of the middle of the nineteenth century. He published his polemic writing on the matter of national dances, music and costume in the *Athenaeum*, the most influential periodical of political opposition that was active between 1837 and 1843. It was the mouthpiece of the urban middle-class people who had characteristic national anti-Habsburg feelings, and criticised the ideas of the aristocrats. His ideas became very popular for almost a decade, and inspired the Hungarian dance, musicians and other members of the cultural elite to create art in this spirit.

No. 7: Description of the Csárdás (Chardash) Dance and Dance Music Compared with Other Fashion Dances, Written by Arthur J. Patterson

Arthur J. Patterson, *The Magyars: Their Country and Institutions*, 2 vols (London: Smith, Elder and Co., 1869), I, Chapter 9, pp. 195–96.

> This dance is a peasant's dance, yet I do not know that I have ever seen it danced better or with more spirit than in middle-class circles in the

country. Since the policy taken up by the Viennese Government after the revolutionary war drove the greater part of the Hungarian aristocracy into opposition to the court, this dance has been admitted into the balls of the *haute voleé* in Pest. But like other European aristocracies, the Hungarian is too denationalised and too self-conscious to surrender itself wholly to the enthusiasm which is the soul of this dance. Well as the countesses and baronesses dance, one misses, in their *csárdás*, the *abandon* of the wives and daughters of their stewards and attorneys. A lady who had been educated at Vienna said to me, «*Je n'aime pas le* csárdás; *pour le danser bien il faut être très-coquette*».

But it would be indeed inexcusable were I here to omit to notice the musicians, upon whom so much of the Hungarian's enjoyment depends. In Hungary 'no amusement without the gypsy' has passed into a proverb. In some of the principal balls of the Carnival at Pest, where the *csárdás* alternates with dances of more European celebrity, two bands are provided, one of Bohemians, the other of gypsies. As long as it was a question of quadrilles, waltzes, &c., the Tshekhs were the performers; but as often as the turn of the *csárdás* came round, they remained quiet, and the music was given by the swarthy children of India.

Comments: Arthur J. Patterson (1835–1899) was a writer, university professor and correspondent for several British journals and newspapers. Between 1862 and 1867 he stayed in Hungary and collected material for his book *The Magyars*, published in 1869 in London. This short passage from the detailed description of the *Csárdás* shows that he paid much attention to the socio-political and ethnic relations of the country. He emphasises that, although it is a peasant-dance, it became popular among middle-class people, and it temporarily became widely favoured by the aristocracy as well. He mentions only the 'unregulated' form of the *Csárdás*, which could be explained by the domination of the free, improvisatory form in the 1850s and 1860s. He depicts the situation in the big balls of Pest, where the organisers hired two kinds of music bands: Bohemian musicians for the Quadrille, the Waltz and other dances of 'European celebrity', and gypsy bands for the *Csárdás*.

Iconographic Material

Fig. 7.1 Pollencig József, *Grosser Ball bey Sv. Kőnigh Hoheit de Palatins Ofen den 11ten Februar 1795* [Great Ball held by His Royal Highness of Palatine], 11 February 1795. Paper and gouache, 282 x 408 mm. Szépművészeti Múzeum, Budapest, Index number: 1930–2188. Image courtesy of Szépművészeti Múzeum.

Comments: This picture portrays a ball of aristocrats, with a great number of participants in a luxurious, spacious room, decorated with rococo ornaments and magnificent chandeliers. The orchestra is located on a high pulpit in the left foreground (presumably ten fiddlers and flutists, noticeably not gypsies.) The space in front of the musicians is almost empty, so we can clearly see the closest dancers (three to four couples) and the onlookers (around twenty people, men and women who are standing, talking or sitting by the wall). The other participants are covered. We can distinguish only their heads in the picture, so we cannot positively say that they are dancing. The first dancing couple on the right-hand side is embracing each other in a face-to-face position. The right arm of the man is above the woman's arm, and his hand touches her waist from the back. The left arm of the woman is under his, and her hand is placed on the same part of the man's body. They hold each other with their other hand in a so-called Walzer position.

The other two couples are holding each other with their arms in a side-by-side position. The women's arms are above the men's, and they hold their skirts with their other hands, as if they could stop the skirts from flying too high while turning. The costume of the participants is the fashionable 'Hungarian' aristocratic one. Some of the men are carrying swords, which would have been a curious sight for the visitors coming from abroad. Two figures in the front wear costumes like those of the lackeys in Vienna. One of them seems to be engaged with the musicians and the other with the dancers. The artist, Pollencig József (1763–1823), painter and engraver on copper, lived in Pest from 1787 to 1795. During his stay, he worked as an illustrator for periodicals and so he may have had direct experiences of the portrayed events. He was not a talented painter, but he was appreciated for commemorating the social life and architecture of Buda and Pest.

Fig. 7.2 Unknown artist, *Bál a kis Redoute-ban* [Ball in the small Redoute], c.1830. Coloured lithography. Historical Museum, Metropolitan Gallery in Budapest. Image courtesy of Budapesti Történeti Múzeum.

Comments: The unknown artist portrays an aristocratic ball in luxurious (in the so-called Small Redoute) in Pest. The ballroom is decorated with classical half-columns, ceiling frescos, magnificent curtains, and both standing and hanging chandeliers (it was built between 1829 and 1832 in the Classical style). Musicians (about ten men with string and wind instruments) are playing on a gallery in the middle of the back wall. The event is not too crowded, with about twenty-five couples standing or sitting on benches or chairs around the room. In the foreground of the picture, around eight couples are situated facing the musicians, as if they are having a rest or waiting for the next dance. Women are sitting on chairs and men are standing behind or beside them talking to each other. In the background of the room, with their backs to the musicians (presumably Czechs), there stand five to six couples. Presumably, they are dancing, holding each other by the arm in a side-by-side position. From the left side, the men hold their partners by their left arm on their left side, and by their right arm on their right side. The men stand with their legs apart (in the second position). The participants' costumes are of a new international fashion with trousers (pantaloons), shoes and jackets (presumably neckties). In the foreground, the central man wears a '*frakk*' or tail-coat.

Fig. 7.3 Max Felix von Pauer, *Pest-Budai bál* [Ball in Pest-Buda]. From the collection: Original Skizzen aus Ungarn, 1837–1839. Paper and ink, 110 x 16 mm. Metropolitan Szabó Ervin Library of Budapest (FSZK). János Jajczay, *Pest-Budai figurák a múlt század 30-as éveiből. Max Félix Pauer rajzai a Fővárosi Könyvtárban* (Budapest: Stadtbibliothek, 1941), pp. 9–10. Image courtesy of Fővárosi Szabó Ervin Könyvtár, Budapest.

Comments: The author of the picture is Max Felix von Pauer (1804-?), a German-born draughtsman and architect from Bavaria. He spent several years as an architect in Hungary in the 1830s. It was his pastime to commemorate contemporary Budapest through his drawings. He was interested mainly in the representatives of the lower social strata. As an artist, draughtsman, and architect, he did not idealise his experiences. His pictures are like his technical drawings: precise, naturalistic displays of the subject without any particular artistic ambitions. The black-and-white ink drawing here portrays a lower-middle-class ball, in a solidly decorated small hall, with a mixture of participants. Based on their costumes, we assume that some of them are soldiers, tradesmen, merchants, clerks, and servants. Judging by their movements, we presume that half of the twenty-five guests are dancing and half of them are talking or looking at the dancers. There are ten people on the high pulpit at the back wall of the hall, the majority of them being musicians: a violinist, a viola player, a bassist, a clarinettist, a drummer, and some other people who cannot be identified. The dancers (six couples) are moving around counter-clockwise in the room, which is graphically indicated by the artist with a broken curved line on the floor. Three of them (one on each side and one at the back) dance in a sideways position and hold each other by their inner arm. The women's arm is under her partner's. She puts her hand on the man's waist; he holds her back at the shoulder blade. One couple in the middle consists of two women. The taller woman keeps her right hand on her own hip from the back, while the shorter woman embraces her partner at her shoulder-blade. Presumably they are dancing around. The couple on the right side at the back are dancing face-to-face with each other without physical contact. Both are concentrating on their leg movements. She rests her hands on her hips, and he keeps his left hand in the pocket of his trousers, his other hand not being visible. The role of the couple in the middle at the back (with the man wearing a fur coat) is unclear. It seems as if they are turning away from each other. It may also be the case that the woman is dancing alone. It is remarkable that some of the female participants wear spurs as well as the men. One of the male dancers has a pipe in his mouth.

Fig. 7.4 Unknown artist, *Tánciskola* [Dance school], 1845–1846. Lithography. Historical Museum, Metropolitan Gallery in Budapest. Ignácz Nagy, *Magyar titok* [Hungarian secret] (Pest: Hartleben Konrád Adolf, 1845–1846), p. 258. Image courtesy of Budapesti Történeti Múzeum.

Comments: This picture is an illustration from a novel by Ignácz Nagy (1810–1854), first published in 1845 in Pest. The event is happening in a petit-bourgeois milieu in Pest. The small room in the flat of the dance master serves to teach fourteen people (seven women and seven men). The rest of the people in the middle of the picture are the fiddler, who is the dance master himself; the clarinettist, from the neighbouring flat; and the author of the novel, standing at the door. They are portrayed in an ironic style with their shabby costumes, grotesque movements and ridiculous grimaces. The dancers are divided into two lines, facing each other. There seem to be four men and three women on the left side, and three men and four women on the right side. They are learning a French dance (a kind of contra dance) as the author informs the readers. He writes, on page 258:

> Francia tánczot tanultak és nem magyart, s én ezért egyáltalán nem bírok neheztelni, mert ennek valóban nem annyira a tánckedvelők az okai, mint magok a tánczkedvelők tanítói, vagyis a magyar tánczmesterek, akik a szép magyar tánczot annyira kiferdíték, a magyar zene eredeti jelleméből, hogy lábficamítás nélkül, alig lehet azt már eljárni. Mintha bizony tagrángásokban szépség rejlenék.

[They learnt a French dance and not Hungarian, but I cannot blame the dancers for it, because, to tell the truth, it is not the dancers but the teachers that are at fault for it, the dance masters themselves, who so deformed the nice Hungarian dance from the original of the Hungarian music that it can not longer be executed without spraining one's foot. As if jerking one's body were nice.]

Irony is created by the surroundings — the empty, plain room — if we think of the pomp of the ballrooms. The writer continues, on page 261:

A két város hemzseg ily táncziskolától, s a reményteljes lyánykák, [...] csapatonként barangolnak a művészet efféle csarnokaiban.

[The two towns (Buda and Pest) are filled with these dance schools, and the hopeful young girls [...] go around in troops in these halls of art.]

Fig. 7.5 A playbill of the opera *Hunyadi László* composed by Ferenc Erkel, 'father' of the Hungarian national opera. Textbook written by Béni Egressy. The opera was premiered in the National Theatre in Pest, in 1844. The original playbill belongs to the collection of the Széchenyi István State National Library.

Comments: *Hunyadi László* is the opera composed by Ferenc Erkel (1810–1893), creator of the Hungarian national opera, as a genre. As conductor of the National Theatre, he was familiar with the operas by Cherubini, Auber, Bellini, Rossini, and Donizetti and he considered their style as a model for his compositions. He tried to amalgamate it with the style of verbunkos and the Hungarian traditional songs of that period. This happened also in the case of other masters, for example, the German Flotow, or the Polish Moniuszko, or the Czech Smetana, the Russian Glinka, who all respectively combined the musical characteristics of their own nation with Italian and/or French and German traditions. *Hunyadi László*, Erkel's second opera premiered in 1844 in the National Theatre in Pest, is one of his best composition embodying his aspiration. The dance scene, named 'Csárdás', inserted into the Act 3 of the opera, titled 'Ármány' (Intrigue), mirrors the same ambitions followed by Tóth Soma, the probable choreographer as well. The kinetic style of the dance modelled that of the 'Első Magyar Körtánc' mentioned in later in this chapter. (In 1850, the title was changed to 'Palotás', which means 'in the palace' in sketchy translation.) At that time the dance scenes were integral parts of the operas, but they were rarely parts of the plot. They were inserted separately between two Acts or added to the end of the opera. In contrast, Erkel tried to give dramatic significance to the dance. Hunyadi László and Mária Garay, the main figures of the opera, are celebrating their forthcoming wedding with their young friends in the garden of the palace, while inside the palace, the king and his landlords are weaving a conspiracy for arresting and executing László. This situation gives the dance huge emotional charge. Since then, 'Palotás' has become very popular independently from the opera. It frequently plays the role of opening dance of national significance at the balls and other dance events, even today.

7. Reception of Nineteenth-Century Couple Dances in Hungary 207

Fig. 7.6 The Polka Mazur, on the front-page of the publication with musical notes, 1864. 150 x 90 mm. Kränzchen-Souvenir, *Polka Mazur für pianoforte von kapellmeister Josef Dubez* (Pest: Rózsavölgyi & Comp., 1862). Image courtesy of the Library of the Liszt Ferenc Music Academy, Budapest.

Comments: The picture illustrates a piece of music issued by the most popular music publisher (Rózsavölgyi & Comp.) in Hungary. The music of the Polka Mazur was composed in Vienna by Johann Dubez (1828– 1891) (not Josef Dubez, as printed), the famous Austrian composer and virtuoso music player. The artist (or graphic designer) is not indicated on the front page, but we assume that it was Vilmos Tatzelt, the so-called 'resident graphic designer' for the publisher between 1860 and 1864. The picture portrays an evening ball from the perspective of the open gates of a restaurant or hotel, the location of the dance. We can see the garden of the restaurant with some guests just arriving, and others sitting at the tables on both sides under the trees. The dance might occur inside the building (which has a colonnade and a tympanum in the classical style, and a flag on the top of the roof). Some people might be dancing outside as well, under the trees on the left-hand side, but we cannot be sure because of the small size of the image (115 x 90mm). The whole picture is framed by a decorative wooden construction similar to a greenhouse, and the text crowds around the picture. The publication serves as a ball gift (*kränzchen-souvenir*), as is written on the top of the front page. In the 1860s, these kinds of musical publications — with light dance music in an easy piano forte arrangement — were very popular and appropriate for making music at home. The dance music that was published most often was *Csárdás*, but the Polka, the Polka Mazur, the Mazurka, the Waltz, and the Quadrille featured as well. This fashion came from Vienna, and it was fostered by the appearance of music publishers with more modern techniques in Hungary.

Musical Sources

No. 1: Rábaközi stajer tánc [Styrian Dance[44] from the Rábaköz Region, a North-Western Region of Hungary], 1813.

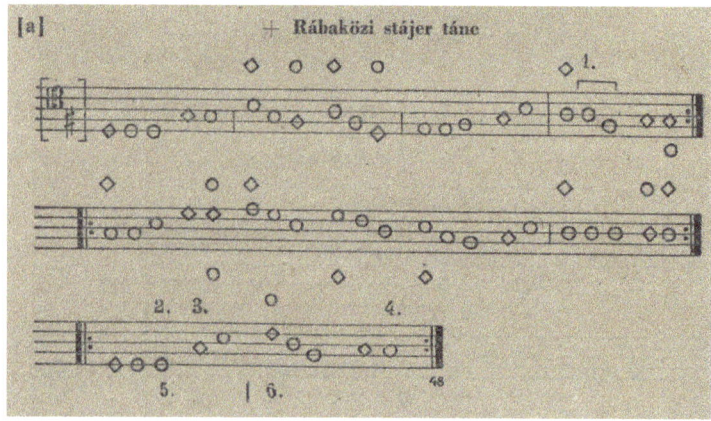

Fig. 7.7 Pálóczi Horváth Ádám, Ó és új mintegy Ötödfélszáz énekek, *ki magam csinálmánya, ki másé* [450 Old and New Songs, Composed by Myself and Others] (Budapest: Akadémiai Kiadó, 1953), pp. 172–73 (notes) and 528–29 (lyrics).

44　The Styrian was a dance name but was also used to refer to Austrians during this period. Given the poetic, political, and often allegorical nature of these songs by Pálóczi Horváth Ádám, the allusional quality in my translation has been retained beneath each line of the original Hungarian text.

Lyrics:

Hát, Isten néki! kapjunk rá, szokjunk rá a német táncra;
Let it be! Let us take to, let us turn to the German dance;
Bécs után úgyis minket ver a fegyver a szolgaláncra;
After Vienna it is our turn to be chained as slaves by this weapon;
A táncmester nem ismeri, nem méri a mi hangunkat,
The dancing master does not know the sound and measure of our music,
Csosztatót vér, ne pengessük hát, vessük el sarkan(t)yúnkat.
He plays shuffling music, so we stop jingling our spurs, we cast them away.

Szánd meg, Árpádom! szánd unokádat!
My Árpád, feel pity for your grandchildren!
Tartsd meg ez vérrel szerzett hazádat!
Keep your homeland obtained by blood.

Már a Rábán túl a nagy sas, a kakas körme mivé tett?
What was the great eagle, the nail of the cock doing with us over the Rába (river)?
Stájer tánc végzi a manifestummal kezdett minétet;
The Styrian dance ends the Minuet which was begun by the manifesto;[45]
Nyalka csizmám elrombolja a pór szolga-saru formára;
The servant deforms my smart (male) boots into sandals,
Fűzött topányom elszabta francia cipő-kaptára.
He cut my (female) footwear badly like a French shoe.

Szánd meg Árpádom, szánd unokádat,
My Árpád, feel pity for your grandchildren!
Tartsd meg ez vérrel szerzett hazádat.
Keep your homeland obtained by blood.

---

45   The manifesto refers to that written by the Hungarian aristocracy against Napoleon when he attacked Hungary in 1809.

No. 2: Ekuzén felel Napóleon [Napoleon answers for the Écossaise], 1813.[46]

Fig. 7.8 Pálóczi Horváth Ádám, Ó és új mintegy Ötödfélszáz énekek, ki magam csinálmánya, ki másé [450 Old and New Songs, Composed by Myself and Others] (Budapest: Akadémiai Kiadó, 1953), pp. 173 (notes), 529 (lyrics).

Lyrics:

> *Nem Minétre lépek én, Szökni szoktam Ekuszénn,*
> I do not step for the Minuet, I jump for the Écossaise,
> *Sok tsatám', vitéz nevem' Ez nyerette meg velem:*
> I earned victory and fame in battles:
> *Sőt ez adta Thrónusom', Bétsi Herczeg Asszonyom':*
> I gained my throne and my princess from Vienna:
> *Szerszem elme, friss kezek Által épül a Remek.*
> The masterpiece is made by a sharp mind and quick hands.
>
> *Nem Minét hozá tehát A 'Stájer litániát;*
> Thus, the Styrian litany was brought not by the Minuet;
> *De mind e jó Magyarom! Mind Ipam, mind Sógorom;*
> But all of you my dear Hungarians, together with my father in law and my brother in-law;
> *Hogy velem ki szálltatok, Ekuszét ugrottatok:*
> You jumped the Écossaise when you came against me:
> *'S ki fitzamla lábatok, Bankóra szorúltatok:*
> And you sprained your leg, and you became in need of money:
>
> *Tudsz e Sánta! érzeni? — Sorsod' az elébbeni*
> And now, what can you feel, lame-footed? Your life had been determined
> *Sok erőltetés, kozák, 'S kontra táncz határozák.*

---

[46] The speaker in this allegorical poem, in which dance forms symbolise nationalities, is Napoleon, and the poem is addressed to the Hungarians.

7. Reception of Nineteenth-Century Couple Dances in Hungary

by earlier being forced to do the Cossack and the Contra dance.
Meg tsomósodott a' vér, Megrekedt az aranyér:
Your blood went lumpy, your haemorrhoids became blocked:
A' Podagra meglepett, Bétsi-bankó-lábra tett.
You were riddled with gout, but the money from Vienna revived you.

Már neked tsak Stájer jó; Mellyben nints mutatio:
Only the Styrian is good for you, which has no variation:
Szokj hozzá szegény Nemes! Másra nem vagy érdemes;
Get used to it, poor Noblemen! You do not deserve any other!
Egy 's közös a' Musikás, Egy a' szála, táncz se más.
You have only one musician, who plays for everybody for the same dance in the common hall[47]
Ha tsak egy régi lejtő Nem lesz a' bú felejtő.
Unless we dance an old *Lejtő* [Hungarian dance] to comfort us.

No. 3: Magyar Táncz [Hungarian dance], 1813, ad notam Vissza-nevetés [sung to the melody entitled Laughing Back, or Answer by Laughter][48]

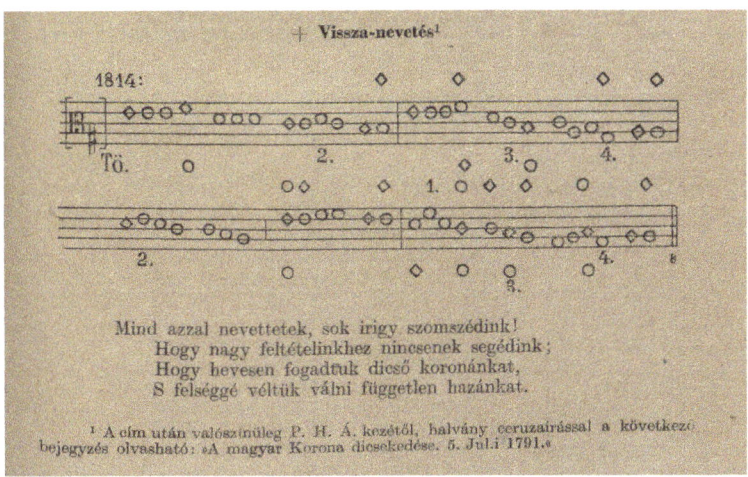

Fig. 7.9 Pálóczi Horváth Ádám, Ó és új mintegy Ötödfélszáz énekek, *ki magam csinálmánya, ki másé* [450 Old and New Songs, Composed by Myself and Others] (Budapest: Akadémiai Kiadó, 1953), pp. 131 (notes), 265 (lyrics).

---

47 The musician here, symbolically speaking, is the Habsburg Monarchy.
48 *Magyar Táncz* is the name of the song which is sung to the popular melody *Vissza-nevetés*.

Lyrics:

> *Azt mondják, hogy nem illik a tnc a magyarnak,*
> They say that dancing does not suit the Hungarian,
> *Nem ha neki butyogót s fél nadrágot varrnak,*
> It is true, if they sew knickerbockers and short trousers for him,
> *De pengő sarkantyúnak, kócsagtollas főnek,*
> But our dance suits the jingling spurs and the cap with egret feather,
> *Illik, gyönygyös pártának, Magyar fejkötőnek.*
> And it suits the pearly headdress and the Hungarian bonnet.
>
> *A franc tánc mind negédes, mind szeles a német,*
> French dances are all affected, the German ones are giddy,
> *Nincsen mutációja, mind egyrül varr hímet,*
> They have no variety; they sew the figure only on one side,[49]
> *Melancholis az anglus szövevényes tánca,*
> The entangled dance of the English is melancholic,
> *Csak az ugrós magyar tánc a Szent Dávid tánca.*
> Only the jumping Hungarian dance is worthy of Saint David's dance.

Comments to Nos. 1–3: The author of the three songs is Pálóczi Horváth Ádám (1760–1820), a poet, writer, and collector of songs at the turn of the eighteenth century and in the early years of the nineteenth. He came from a family headed by an educated Protestant (Helvetian) priest. His career was that of a community-minded patriot and a so-called 'honoratior' — working as a lawyer, engineer and deputy of the parliament. Scholars of Hungarian music history and literature remember him primarily because of his collection of traditional and popular songs, which aimed to preserve the old Hungarian songs at the turn of the eighteenth century and in the early years of the nineteenth. Additionally, he wrote poems himself and 'applied' music to them in a similar style to the collected songs. His collection was ready for publication in 1813, but, because of its political, anti-Habsburg content, it was prohibited. The entirety of the material, with texts and melodies together, was only published in 1953 as a critical source publication. The three songs presented here are closely related to dance. On the one hand, the texts written by the author mention several dance names

---

49   Appropriate dress was important to the performance of Hungarian dances. Foreign fashions in dress and dance did not, the poet claims, suit them. Combining here the symbolism of dancing and embroidery to represent each nationality, the poet scorns the lack of variety and simplicity of German dances.

(Steierish, the Minuet, the Écossaise, Cossack, contra dance, and *Lejtő*, a Hungarian couple dance) and the manner of dancing them. On the other hand, the melodies are adaptations of contemporary dance songs — the first and the second are based on German dance songs, the second, presumably on the music of a Hungarian jumping dance. They were popular as political songs, and, in some areas of Hungary, also as dance music. This is why Pálóczi was chased by the police. The musical transcription he made does not indicate the tempo, the rhythm or the bars. He used old-fashioned, simple techniques for writing music, but it can still be interpreted to a limited degree. Pálóczi's musical transcriptions are therefore very useful sources for music history, dance history and literature.

No. 4: The Accompanying Music for the "Dance Németes (Landaris) 48 előtt a határőrző székelyeknél" [Germanic Landler before 1848, by Székler Frontier Guards at the Tirolean Border] (Without Lyrics), Early Nineteenth Century.

Fig. 7.10 Réthei Prikkel Marián, *A magyarság táncai* [Dances of Hungarians] (Budapest: Stúdium, 1924), pp. 232–33.

Comments: The dance melody — 'Németes' (German), or 'Landaris' (Lendler) — was discovered by Imets Fülöp Jákó (1837–1912), a Roman Catholic priest, canon, dean, teacher, and historian of the Széklers in Transylvania in the last third of the nineteenth century. He sent it to Réthei Prikkel Marián (1871–1925), a philologist, ethnographer and teacher of the Benedict order, who was about to write his monograph, *Dances of the Hungarians*. Imets informed Réthei that this Landaris dance melody dated back to the first half of the nineteenth century, when the Széklers served in the Austrian army in Tirol as frontier guards. It became so popular among Széklers that they played it even at the beginning of the twentieth century. The melody is set down for a forte piano, in a 'Tempo di Mazurka' signature with a dotted rhythm. It consists of two parts in 3/4, and concludes with a short 'codetta' or refrain in 2/4 (or 4/4). Both parts are repeated twice. This musical source represents the survival of an early dance fashion, part of a local, isolated community's dance repertory.[50]

Nos. 5–7: Printed Music Scores for Nineteenth-Century Couple Dances from the 1850s to the 1860s

No. 5: *Pest-Ofner Polka für pianoforte von Kéler Béler Kapellmeister* [Polka from Budapest, for Pianoforte by Conductor Kéler Béler] (Budapest: Rózsavölgyi et Co Cinkography, 1858). Composed by an unknown master. 33 x 26 cm. Dedication: Hern Franz von Jurkovits. Press: Lorber. Collection: Liszt Ferenc Zeneművészeti Egyetem Központi Könyvtára, Rézkarc gyűjtemény 3068 [Central Library of The Liszt Ferenc Academy of Music, Rézkarc collection 3068].

No. 6: *Deux valses pour le Piano, composées par Charles Thern, à Mademoiselle Andorine de Kiss* [Two Waltzes for the Piano, Composed by Charles Thern for Mademoiselle Andorine de Kiss] (Budapest: Lauffer and Stolp, c.1860s). Budapesti Állami Zenekonzervatórium 4530. M/42411-ik [Budapest National Music Conservatory, 4530.M to M/42411].

---

50 Lajos Kiss, 'A bukovinai székelyek tánczenéje', *Tánctudományi tanulmányok*, 1 (1958), 67–88.

No. 7: *Huszár-négyes (Hussar-Quadrille). Zongorára szerzé és Ő nagysága Schiller Lajos a 11ik Würtemberg herceg huszár ezred ezredese s' parancsnoka, cs.k. Kamarás Úrnak és több magas rendek Vitézének mély tisztelettel ajánlja unokaöccse Schiller Gyula. (Nyomás) Wagner Józsefnél Pesten.* [Hussar-Quadrille Composed for Piano and Dedicated with High Respect by Gyula Schiller to Lajos Schiller, Colonel of the Würtenberg Hussar Regiment No 11, Imp. and Roy. Chamberlain and Owner of Other High Decorations. Printed in Pest, by József Wagner.] (Budapest: József Wagner, c.1860s).

Socio-Political and Cultural Contexts of Nineteenth-Century Couple Dances in Hungary

The nineteenth century in Hungary was a period of rapid, radical, and irreversible changes in the field of socio-political and cultural life. At the beginning of the century, the country was a subordinated kingdom of the Austrian Empire, isolated from Western European standards of living. At the end of the century, it was a powerful member of the Austro-Hungarian Empire, celebrating the millennium of its statehood and representing its values in Europe. These changes were induced by violent fights between conservative and liberal forces and against Austrian oppression, fuelled in parallel by the ideas of the Enlightenment, nationalist movements, and the French Revolution. The main transitional impetus was the transformation of the feudal social structure, which increased the dominance of the bourgeoisie and resulted in national independence.[51] Each of the political powers consented to the common aim — the construction of a national culture — in the fields of language, literature, music, fine arts and others, including dance. But they could not agree on how to realise this. It depended on the significance they attached to the past or the future, to tradition or modernity. It was not a simple task in a multi-ethnic, rural country with so many different religions.

'Ungern ist Europa in kleinen' ('Hungary is a small version of Europe') — wrote János Csaplovics (1780–1847), a Slovakian-born

---

51 In researching these socio-political questions, I have relied on Gergely, ed., *Magyarország története a 19. században*.

Hungarian lawyer and scientist, in his book *Gemälde von Ungern* [Paintings of Hungary] in 1822.[52] The small urban population (teachers, clerks, clergy etc.) was German, Serbian, Greek, Armenian, Slovakian and Jewish, and they shared anti-Habsburg feelings and the political aspirations of the Hungarians.[53] They favoured national music and dance as the most visible symbols of their sympathy. But the radicalisation of Hungarian national policy in the 1830s and 1840s, which led to the suppressed revolution and civil war, made them disappointed and disillusioned. In the second half of the nineteenth century, due to the migration of rural populations to the towns, the number of urban inhabitants grew considerably. Pest and the other big urban areas became the scenes of large-scale assimilation and embourgeoisement of the population. Hungarian social dance and nineteenth-century couple dances had a significant role in this process by creating a common 'kinetic language' for social communication in the towns. Members of the political elite came from a small, educated, multi-ethnic aristocratic group (about 600–700 families), and from the populous society of Hungarian noblemen (not aristocrats) with an average-to-low standard of living (130,000–140,000 families out of the approximately 14 million inhabitants of the country). They were the most active agents of social change, including the liberation of the serfs and the renunciation of the old privileges of noblemen. At the same time, they contributed a great deal to the creation and propagation of the new Hungarian national culture, which was the symbolic capital of a strong Hungarian identity. Dance and dance music, besides language, literature, music, national costumes, fine arts, and so on, were an integral part and the most attractive elements of these identity symbols, which they used successfully in their political practice. Through the rejection of German dances in ballrooms and the contrasting acceptance of French and Polish dances, ball participants expressed their political sympathies, or lack thereof.

---

52   Not just because of richness of the natural sources — but also because of its population — Hungary is Europe in miniature; because all the peoples, languages, religions, occupations, cultures of Europe find their home here. See Csaplovics, *Gemälde von Ungarn*, p. 13.

53   This phenomenon is called Hungarus Consciousness. See Ambrus Miskolczy, 'A hungarus-tudat a 19. században', *Limes* 4 (2009), 71–96.

The assistants of the political elite propagating these new fashions were the dance masters, predominantly of German, Austrian, Czech, and Hungarian origin, and the musicians, mainly Czech, Jewish, and Gypsy. Over the course of the nineteenth century, teaching dance became a very popular 'profession'. Until the establishment of the Association of Dance Teachers in Hungary in 1891, anybody (from tailors and barbers, to shoemakers) could teach dance without a certificate. Dance masters were eager to disseminate the most fashionable knowledge in the field of dance. In Hungary, the first dance master's books were published in the last decades of the nineteenth century. The first to contain descriptions of nineteenth-century couple dances (*Keringő*, the Hungarian for the Waltz; the Polka; the Mazurka; and the best-known international choreographies) is *Rajta párok táncoljunk* [Let us, couples, dance], by Sándor Lakatos, which was published in Nagykanizsa in 1871. Before this, dance masters used books that had been published abroad.[54]

Some of the most efficient media for disseminating new dance fashions were the theatres. In the first half of the nineteenth century, dances appeared as interludes between two acts or as closing sequences for plays. These were short choreographies, as we read on the playbillspresented in the selected sources of this chapter (see Fig. 7.5). Later, dance became part of the dramaturgy, and there were examples of dance dramas choreographed in several acts. This was the case among the wandering theatrical troupes, in the so-called 'stone-theatres' in the towns, in the private theatres of the big landowners and in the theatres of schools maintained by the different churches and religious orders. The whole dance history of nineteenth-century Hungary was dominated by the rivalry between the German and the Hungarian theatres, which ended with the closure of the German theatres (which staged plays in German) all over Hungary in the 1890s, and the simultaneous rising prosperity of the Hungarian ones.

Similarly, important resources for the promotion of nineteenth-century fashionable dances (both Hungarian and international) were the products of the print media. The history of the press in

---

54 For instance: Henri Cellarius, *La danse des salons* (Paris: J. Hetzel, 1847); Bernhard Klemm, *Katechismus der Tanzkunst* (Leipzig: J. J. Weber, 1855, 1869, 1876); and Friedrich Albert Zorn, *Die Grammatik der Tanzkunst* (Leipzig, J. J. Weber, 1887).

nineteenth-century Hungary was similar to that of the theatre. Both of them suffered because of the propagating politics of the Austrian government. Both of them were controlled by strict censorship. In 1830, there were only ten journals and weekly papers published in Hungarian altogether, but their number had increased to eighty-six by 1848–1849. During this period of time, the most popular literary, artistic and fashion journals — *Honderű* (1843–1848), *Honművész* (1830–1843), *Pesti Divatlap* (1844–1848), and *Életképek* (1843–1848) — were most interested in social events, theatre performances and balls. This can be explained by the fact that they were the organs of the Hungarian middle classes and the liberal aristocracy. Additionally, almost every journal and weekly paper dealt from time to time with the matter of contemporary social dances. As the articles written by Károly Balla and others in the *Tudományos Gyűjtemény* [Scientific Collection] (see Written Source No. 3) prove, national dances were treated as a key theme in professional writings. We can read essays propagating the Hungarian language, music, dance, and costume, but the most frequent 'genre' was the written accounts of the balls. They celebrate *Csárdás* — the Hungarian social dance — but they pay attention to the international ones as well, though frequently with a negative undertone. For instance, in 1832 in *Honművész*,[55] the authors write about the dance event in Pest in the Seven Prince-Electors Hotel where the ball was opened with a Hungarian dance performed by one young man. Apart from him, there were no other Hungarian dancers — so all the other dances were Strauss Waltzes, German Quadrilles, Galops etc. The frequency of the Hungarian dances, the number of dancing couples, and the increasing use of the Hungarian language and national costumes during the balls sensitively indicate the ongoing changes in the political situation.

Csárdás as a 'Nineteenth-Century Couple Dance'

'*Csárdás*', or 'Hungarian *Csárdás*', first appears in 1835 as the name of a ballroom dance. It has a kind of romantic undertone; its name suggests that it comes from the remote provincial inns (*csárda*).

---

55   *Honművész* [n.a.], 2 (1834), 37.

Hasznos Mulatságok, a popular weekly paper in 1829 explains the motivation behind this name: '...Fájdalom, még csak félpallérozású magyar vásrosokban is a magyar nemzeti táncot hiába keressük, de az együgyű falusiak társaságában és a magyar kocsmákon csalhatatlanul feltaláljuk' ('Alas, we are searching for the Hungarian national dance in vain, even in the half-educated Hungarian towns, but we may find them for sure in the society of the simple-minded village people or the Hungarian pubs').[56] In 1844, *Regélő Pest Divatlap*, a similar type of publication, writes: '...a Csárdás vagy más néven néptánc [...], ez éppen és ugyanaz, melyet vasárnaponként az utolsó falusi csárdában is megláthatni pórleányok által táncolni' ('*Csárdás*, or any other such folk dance [...] is just the same as those you can see every Sunday in the last village inn').[57]

In time, the name '*Csárdás*' was used for different kinds of dances: the 'regulated' ballroom dances based on the aforementioned traditional dances, which were inherited from the previous generations or learnt from experts. The 'regulated' ballroom dance choreographies with complicated structures had their own names — *Körtánc, Társalgó, Vigadó* — but, functionally, they belonged to the group named 'National ballroom dance', or '*Csárdás*' in short. At the same time, it was the name of the fashionable printed (or not printed) 'folksy' musical compositions used as accompanying music for these dances, or, more commonly, as music to be listened rather than danced to.[58] Traditional dances practised mainly by the peasantry and partly by the noblemen were designated by the name '*Csárdás*' as well, as a fashionable symbol of 'Hungarian-ness'. Gradually, the name became widely used.

Having clarified the origin of the name and identified its meaning, it is illuminating to follow the career of the Hungarian national ballroom dance though the nineteenth century.

---

56   *Hasznos Mulatságok* [n.a.], 13 (1929), 154.
57   *Regélő Pesti Divatlap* [n.a.], 3 (1844), 127.
58   Felföldi, 'Táncábrázolások'.

1790–1830

In this period, the absolute rule of the Habsburgs was at its zenith. Dance life in the urban context was dominated by foreign (German, French and Polish etc.) dances. Foreign dance masters propagated their own international repertoire. Around the turn of the eighteenth and the beginning of the nineteenth centuries they began to create dance choreographies in 'Hungarian' style. Their areas of activity were predominantly Vienna, Pressburg and Budapest and their ambition was to make 'Hungarian' dance acceptable as a national ballroom dance. These regulated, male solo and couple dances met with serious criticism from the Hungarians (see, e.g. Written Source No. 3). In parallel with this process, foreign travellers and visitors to Hungary discovered special features of the Hungarian way of dancing that differed from the other European fashionable dances. They found it exotic and expressive of the romantic attitude of the age. They appreciated the capacity for individual self-expression within it. This excerpt from a short description of the Hungarian dance, written by a German officer in 1792, illustrates the contemporary *Verbunk* and the quick couple dance, which was named *Magyar Tánc* [Hungarian dance]. He saw it danced at a noble wedding in Hungary near Pest:[59]

> The ungarischer Tanz charakterisiert so ganz einen Menschen der sich frei und ungebunden fühlt, indem der Tänzer mit nachlässiger Bewegung des oberen Teils seinen Körpers, mit den Füssen willkürliche Wendung macht, solange er für sich allein tanzt, als er will, und dann, wenn es im einfällt, seine Tänzerin nimmt und sie ganz ungekünstelt von der Rechten zur Linken und der Linken zur Rechten umdrecht.
>
> [In fact, Hungarian dance characterises such a man, who feels himself free and uncontrolled, since he turns his leg at his pleasure, moving his upper body carelessly; he dances alone as long as he will, he takes his partner when it comes to his mind and he turns her around from right to left and from left to the right in an entirely unsophisticated way.]

---

59 Réthei, *A magyarság táncai*, p. 287.

Fig. 7.11 An iconographic illustration of the dancing style described above, by Czech-born painter Georg Emmanuel Opitz (1775–1841), *Táncoló Magyarok* [Dancing Hungarians], early nineteenth century. Paper, gouache, 478 x 361 mm. Magyar Nemzeti Múzeum, Történeti Képcsarnok T. 7136. Image courtesy of Magyar Nemzeti Múzeum.

1831–1848

In Hungarian history, this is known as the Reform Age, which was preceded and triggered by the political events of the 1820s. The radicalisation of the Hungarian nationalist movement, and the democratic revolution induced by the unfavourable political situation for the Austrian Empire, resulted in significant socio-cultural changes in the country. Hungarian dance became a kind of political demonstration and effective medium for representing patriotic feelings. This atmosphere was favourable for the development of Hungary's own democratic, national dance culture. The aim was to create a 'national social dance' form that would be marketable in European social life, and expressing national characteristic features perfectly. From 1835 its name became *Csárdás* and gradually it developed into a two-part (slow and quick) couple dance. The previous *'verbunk'* and *'friss'* was absorbed in the new dance type.[60]

In the contemporary printed media, we witness a long and intensive discussion about the character of the Hungarian national dance among the experts and the public. The basic question was whether to regulate the movements as western European nations did, or to permit them to stay unregulated and preserve the features of the traditional dances (see Written Source No. 6).

It seemed that one of the best solutions was to compose a standard, regulated form based on the figures and features considered to be the most characteristic of the traditional dances practised at that time. Several Hungarian dance masters tried to create such dances, but only one of them survived to the present day in written form: the *Körtánc*. The music was composed by Márk Rózsavölgyi (1788–1848), and the choreographer of the dance was Lajos Szőllősy Szabó (1803–1882).

---

60   Pesovár, 'A *csárdás* kialakulásának szakaszai'.

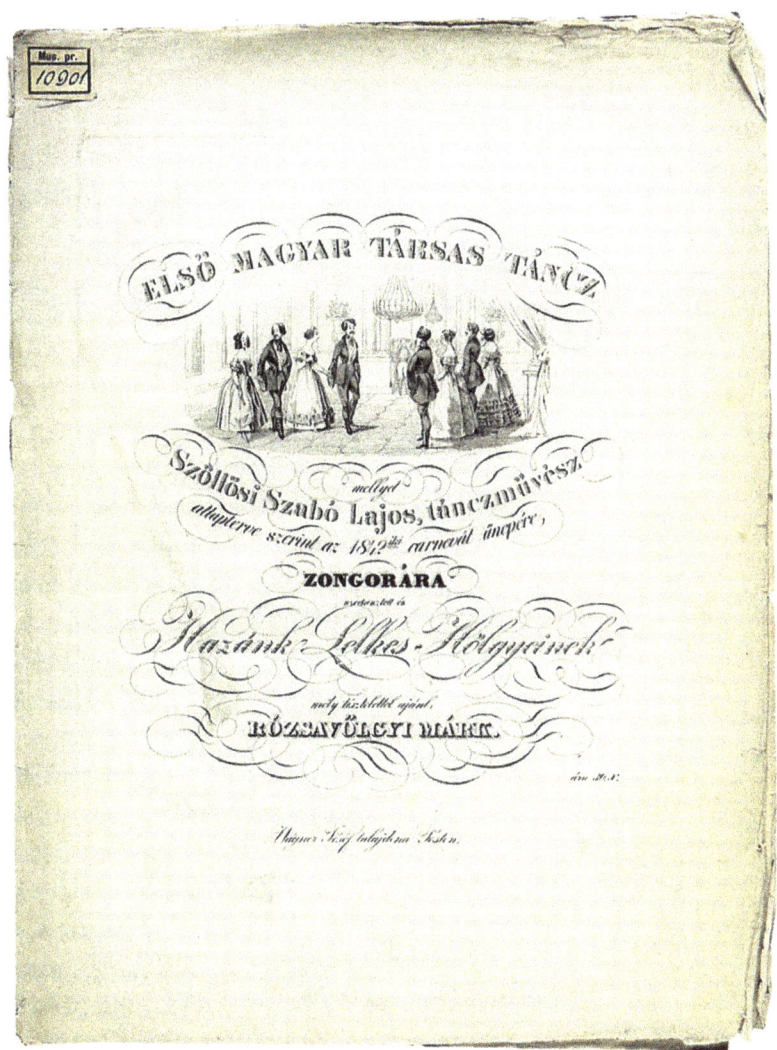

Fig. 7.12 Márk Rózsavölgyi, *Első magyar társas tánc* [First Hungarian Social Dance]. The front page of the publication of the accompanying music, from Szentpál Olga, *A csárdás* (Budapest: Zeneműkiadó, 1954), p. ix.

The text reads as follows:

> Első Magyar társas tánc mellyet Szőllősy Szabó Lajos táncművész allapterve szerint az 1842-iki carneval ünnepére zongorára szerkesztett és hazánk lelkes hölgyeinek mély tisztelettel ajánl Rózsavölgyi Márk. Pest.
>
> [First Hungarian Social Dance constructed on the basis of Szőllősi Szabó Lajos' draft, set for piano and dedicated to the enthusiastic young man of our homeland by Rózsavölgyi Márk, for the occasion of the Carnival in 1842. Pest].

The dance and dance music together were published in Vienna in 1845 in Hungarian, and in German with textual description and graphic illustration by Lajos Kilányi (1819–1861), Hungarian dancer, dance master, and choreographer:

> A Kör-táncz mellyet Szőllősi Lajos a' pesti nemzeti színház táncművészének tanítása után Minden tánczrész könnyen felfogható rajzolatával és magyarázatával terjedelmesen előadta Kilányi Lajos nemzeti és balettánczoktató, a nemzeti színház tagja. 6 rajzolattal és egy zenemű melléklettel. Der Kör-Tanz. Erste Ungarische National-Quadrille, Erfunden Von Ludwig Szőlősi... Beschrieben Von L. Kilányi... Mit Abbildungen... und Einer Beigabe Der National-Musik.[61]
>
> [Circle dance taught by Szőllősi Szabó Lajos, dancer of the National Theatre in Pest, presented by Kilányi Lajos, teacher of national and ballet dance, member of the National Theatre, with its easily comprehensible graphic transcription and detailed explanations. Six drawings and one musical supplement.]

Kilányi's dedication in the introduction of the dance master's book was written in the spirit of the general contemporary understanding of the relation of dance to the national character of the nations:

> Egy nemzet jelleme 's táncza közti szoros viszony kétségbe vonhatatlan, a' német rajongó ömlengése 's ismert állhatatossága magát keringőben élénken tükrözi; — a' frank heves és állhatatlan természete tánczában megismerhető, — 's a magyar táncz deli, keleti és szép mozdalatai, nemde nemzeti jellemünk hű tolmácsai [...] E jelen munkácska czélja a' magyar táncz tanulását világosan és lépéseinek módját oly érthetőleg

---

61 Kilányi, *A Kör-táncz*, p. 2.

előadni 's lerajzolni, a'mennyire ezt leírni 's írásból elsajátítani lehetséges. Pest Őszhó 20-án 1844, Kilányi.[62]

[The close relationship between the character and the dance of a nation is unquestionable; the Germans' passionate enthusiasm and well-known steadfastness is well shown in their Waltz, the hot-tempered and flighty nature of the Franks is recognisable from their dance, and the gallant, oriental and nice movements of Hungarian dance are a faithful indicator of our national character [...] The aim of this small work is to present, as clearly as possible, how to learn and perform the Hungarian dance using words and drawings. Pest, the 20 October, 1844, Kilányi.]

For illustration we present here one page of the graphic drawings on the first part of the dance from the book published by Kilányi.

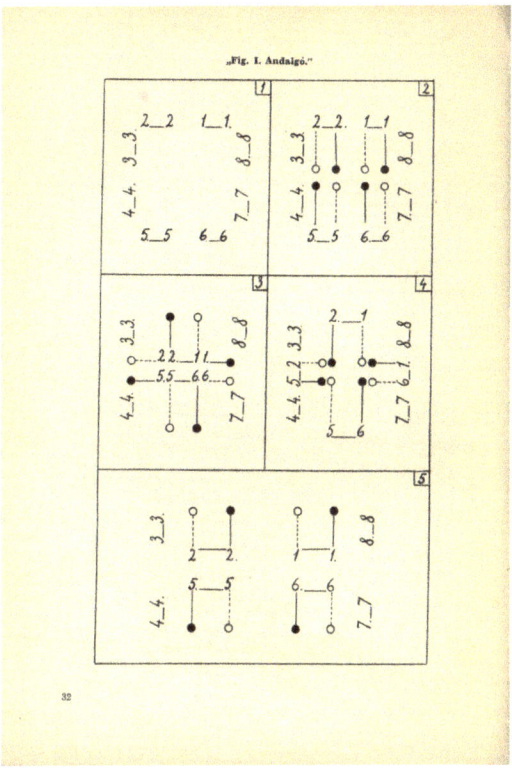

Fig. 7.13 Lajos Kilányi, *Andalgó* [Promenade], 1844. Image copied from Szentpál Olga, *A csárdás* (Budapest: Zeneműkiadó, 1954), p. 32.

---

62 Ibid.

Szőllősy, who named his dance simply 'Hungarian Quadrille', used 'Les Lancieres' as an example for how to structure the dance. Changing partners while dancing, alternating the male and female parts, rotating the individual and collective parts, varying the floor pattern and returning back to the starting position at the end of each part — these are all characteristic elements of the contra dances in *Körtánc*. But the differentiation of the men's and women's movements, and the selection of local dance figures proposing different methods of execution and dancing behaviour, shows that the choreographer endeavoured to preserve the character of the Hungarian dance. *Körtánc* soon became very popular all over Hungary, in Transylvania and abroad. Dance events for the middle classes and the aristocracy also took place. They danced the Körtánc several times during the ball and followed it with the Waltz, the Polka, the Mazurka, the Galop, the Quadrille, and other fashionable dances from Vienna. Travelling dance groups performed it in Milan, Munich, London, and Paris with much success. Its accompanying music, whose author was an educated and talented musician, contributed very much to its acceptance.

Some years later, the regulated couple dance was in competition with the unregulated free couple dance for the dominant position in dance life. But from the second half of the 1840s the latter, with the name *Csárdás*, became the generally accepted social dance even in the provincial towns. According to much evidence, *Csárdás* as a ballroom dance changed in some ways compared to the traditional *Csárdás*, but it preserved its main traditional features. Mosonyi Mihály (1815–1870), composer and musicologist, remembers *Csárdás* of his youth in the 1830s, when he was forced to dance the Walzer and the Galop in order to be accepted in his community. He draws attention to the inter-generational character of *Csárdás*:

> A Csárdás valóban a szabadság táncának nevezhető [...] Hasonló az egy forgó lángoszlophoz melynek alakja szűntelenül változik. [...] Nem olyan ez, mint a keringő vagy a zepperpolka, mely egymáshoz köti a táncolókat. A Csárdásban épp olyan szabad a nő, mint a férfi, s csak kölcsönös akarat mellett egyesülnek, sőt ez esetben is apró ingerkedésekkel ellensúlyozhatják egymást; ha a lovag elveszti táncosnőjét a sokaságban, táncolva s kedélyesen keresi fel ismét. E táncban minden mozdulatot kellemessé lehet tenni, s semmiféle 1-ére,

2-me sat. féle positiók nem korlátozzák az illető szabadságát. Ha néha éltesebb urak is [...] sorakoznak e táncban az ifjak mellé, ez nem hogy nevetséges lenne, de még inkább emeli annak szépségét s új életre költi a kedveket; mit a keringő vagy polkára vonatkozólag éppen nem lehet elmondani, mert ez esetben csak mosolygó vagy gúnyarcokkal találkozhatni. Ha pedig valami házi-ünnep alkalmával még a nagyanyák és a nagyapák is egyet-kettőt fordulnak, akkor a kép még méltóságosabb alakot ölt...[63]

[The *Csárdás*, really can be named as the dance of freedom [...] It looks like a flaming column continuously alternating its form. [...] It is not like the Waltz and Polka, which bind the dancers together. In the *Csárdás*, the woman is as free as the man; they unite only by their mutual wish, accompanied with tiny alluring gestures as a kind of compensation. If he lost his partner in the crowd, he would find her with dancing steps in a merry manner. In this dance you may make every movement in a pleasant way, no first, second etc. positions limit your freedom. If sometimes elderly men joined the dance of the young dancers, it would not be ridiculous, it would even contribute to the beauty of the dance and would increase the high spirits; it is not the same as the Waltz and Polka: such a case would result in smiling and mocking. And if, during some family event, grandmothers and grandfathers made one-two turns in the dance, the picture would be even more dignified.]

1849–1867

This was the last period of Austrian Absolutism, which began with the total control and oppression of all kinds of 'Hungarian' political ambitions, leading the Hungarian political elite into passive resistance. However, from 1859, because of the deterioration of the political conditions of Austria due to its relations with England, France, Italy and Russia, the Habsburgs were forced to compromise with Hungary. This happened, finally, in 1867, and most of the Hungarians' demands were fulfilled. In this positive political atmosphere, the depoliticisation, denationalisation and embourgeoisement of social life accelerated significantly. Consequently, *Csárdás* began to lose its role as a national symbol.

---

63   Mihály Mosonyi, 'Két népies *csárdás*', *Zenészeti lapok*, 1 (1860–1861), pp. 186–87.

1867–1918

This was the period of Dualism, with the establishment of the Austro-Hungarian Monarchy. The compromise of 1867 between Austria and Hungary animated social life considerably. Plenty of new civil society organisations (unions, associations, societies, clubs) came into being. It led to the establishment of the first association of the dance masters in Hungary in 1891. Most influential dance masters began to publish dance books in the Hungarian language.[64] They built on the practice of the German and French dance masters. Instructions for teaching the *Keringő*, the Polka, the Mazurka, *Sottis* etc. were borrowed from them. The common name for round dances in Hungarian was 'Körvonat Táncok' or 'Túr Táncok' (Tour dances). Generally, Hungarian dance masters confessed the impossibility of teaching *Csárdás* because of its free, improvisatory character. Notwithstanding, at the end of the nineteenth century we can find short, simplified, easily memorised dance compositions in the Hungarian dance masters' books, which became popular in the countries of the Austro-Hungarian Monarchy. Their name was 'Magyar Szóló' (Hungarian male solo and 'Magyar Kettes' (Hungarian couple dance), not *Csárdás*, although 'Magyar Kettes' belonged to the *Csárdás*-type category of ballroom dances. During this period, visitors coming from abroad turned from the urban, national ballroom dances to the dances of the peasantry, and published several detailed descriptions of them (see Written Source No. 7).[65]

During the period of Dualism, the Csárdás and Hungarian ballroom dances of the same type (e.g. 'Palotás', or 'For the palace') appeared again in ballrooms, or at midnight as a kind of 'national five minutes' in the program of the ball. Gradually, it became an empty display of 'Hungarian-ness' in the ballrooms.

---

64   Sándor Lakatos, *Rajta párok táncoljunk!: Tánckedvelők könyve* (Nagykanizsa: Waidits József, 1871); P. Pál Róka, *A táncművészet tankönyve* (Nagykőrös: Ottinger Kálmán kiadása, 1900); Kaposi, 'A magyar társastánc szakirodalom I.'; Kaposi 'A magyar társastánc szakirodalom II'.

65   Patterson, *The Magyars*, pp. 195–96; Tissot, *La Hongrie*, pp. 199–200; Fletcher, *Sketches of Life*, pp. 95–96, 110–12.

Fig. 7.14 Front page of the musical publication of *Palotás* [For the Palace], composed by the Hungarian composer and pianist Bertha Sándor (1843–1912). Budapest: Khor & Wein könyvnyomdája, 1864. Lithograph, 31 x 26 cm. Liszt Ferenc Zeneművészeti Egyetem Könyvtára, 50.471.

Having presented the career of *Csárdás* throughout the nineteenth century, we now summarise those features which make it both similar to, and different from, other nineteenth-century round dances:

1. They both originated from traditional dance forms, which expressed a mixture of democratic and Romantic dedication to the lower social classes, who preserved 'ancient' cultural elements.

2. As far as their function is concerned, they serve the purpose of social amusement.

3. Dancers of the nineteenth-century couple dances more or less shared the ideology of 'national character', as well as notions of Romanticism. Moreover, *Csárdás* became a strong national symbol for the Hungarians, used for democratic aims and serving as a kind of political demonstration in the context of the Austrian Empire.

4. Round dance practice and events worked in the nineteenth century as catalysts for the accelerating social changes in Europe, promoted mainly by the populous bourgeois, who were its most active agents. In Hungary, because of the low level of embourgeoisement, the leading force came from the middle stratum of the nobility.

5. While European round dances gained international fame and spread across the continent, the international popularity of *Csárdás* was limited.

6. Regarding the structure, improvised, free forms exist universally, but the regulated sets are less frequent in *Csárdás* compared to other European dance forms.

7. *Csárdás* is constructed from two parts, one slow and one quick. Both are of even rhythm. In European one-part round dances, even and odd pulsation is alternating, according to their different types.

8. Concerning the proxemic features, close connection between the partners, who embrace each other, dominates in European forms, while, in *Csárdás*, the dancers are either more loosely connected or move without holding each other.

9. The leading and initiating role being ascribed to the men is a general tendency in both European forms and in *Csárdás*, but women have more room for individual creativity in the latter.
10. Both types have the general tendency to prescribe a specific floor pattern, advancing counter-clockwise in a round formation. However, free forms are predominant in *Csárdás*, which allows a freer use of the space.
11. The division of movement types according to gender is one of the main characteristic features for *Csárdás* dancers, which is not necessarily true for the European round dances.
12. Whirling is a basic movement type for each of these dance forms, but in *Csárdás*, it is used only in certain special parts of the dance dedicated to whirling.[66]
13. In *Csárdás*, typical inter-generational restrictions are missing. Elderly people may participate in the dance freely, together with the young dancers. This is far less accepted in the European ballroom dances.
14. Family relations between the partners are not restricted, e.g. mothers may dance together with their sons, or men will dance with their female relatives. This was not the case for other nineteenth-century round dances.
15. Both *Csárdás* and the European round dances have a great repertory of accompanying music, with great rhythmic diversity and variation in their musical features. This did not only serve a dance purpose, since people also enjoyed these pieces by listening to them and playing them in family circles as 'dance music'. This was promoted by the modern newspaper habit of facilitating the mass reproduction of the musical scores, and the growing popularity of the music.

---

66   Patterson, *The Magyars*, pp. 195–96.

Conclusion

This chapter has presented an account of the emergence and reception of a particular dance paradigm in Hungary: the nineteenth-century round dances. I have identified them in the general dance repertory practised in Hungary, and contextualised them in the socio-cultural and political circumstances of the first half of the nineteenth century. My additional goal was to compare the main characteristic features of the European round dances with those of the Hungarian *Csárdás*, in order to define its local and international (global) uniqueness.

I am aware that the selected corpus of sources presented here, and the existing knowledge that has accumulated so far in the literature, is not enough to make far-reaching conclusions. Nonetheless, they establish some preliminary proposals for future research. The reception and acceptance of the nineteenth-century round dances were determined by various criteria, from which two groups emerge: a) practical; and b) ideological.

a) From the point of view of ordinary practice, people either rejected or accepted the new dances because they were unusual and, until then, unknown. They contained new movement techniques (e.g. constant turning, maintaining a straight upper body) and affected the body differently than the former dances had done (e.g. sweat, dizziness, shortness of breath). They required different behavioural patterns (e.g. to emphasise or conceal gendered behaviour, to express enthusiasm and strong feelings, or to use the dance for light amusement — see Written Source No. 1).

b) As far as ideological criteria are concerned, the rejection or acceptance of the new dances was closely connected to political ideologies and related to nationalist, social, and ethnic sentiment. For instance, Polish dances were popular in Europe because of the country's political situation in the nineteenth century. In contrast, German (Austrian) dances and dance masters were disliked in Hungary, because of bad political relations with the Austrian Empire.⁶⁷ Each of the written sources selected in this chapter reflects this mentality.

We can agree with Ernő Pesovár's ideas about the global, international features of the changes in dance history during the nineteenth century. He claims:

> The emergence of the new traditional and national style in Hungary, reflecting the change of taste in dance culture, is not an isolated phenomenon, but part of that comprehensive historical process taking place in Europe. The common feature of this new period in dance history is that the modern forms unfolded organically from the earlier traditions, determining the future of traditional dance and the characteristic features of the new national social dances. These traditional-national styles and social dances, with a variety of roots in Europe (to the north and west of the Carpathian basin) developed in interaction with each other and resulted in forms to some degree similar to each other. The best examples are the Mazurka, the Polka and the Waltz, which were rooted really in earlier traditional forms, and they were significant not only as traditional and national dances, but as widely popular ballroom dances.⁶⁸

In his article about the history of *Csárdás*, Pesovár draws attention to the inter-relatedness of the traditional, national and ballroom dances in nineteenth-century Europe, and their roots in the earlier traditional forms. He emphasises that changes in Hungarian dance culture happened in harmony with wider global tendencies, conditioned by local possibilities and capabilities.

Martin also emphasises the embeddedness of the changes in Hungarian dance culture in nineteenth-century historical processes at a regional and European level. His propositions and conclusions about the creative endeavours of the Hungarian national ballroom dances are important contributions to the research:

> By the end of the 1820s, the demand for the creation and dispersal of a nationally-based social dance culture was growing. At the beginning of the century, even the dignified slow dance was emphasised at the expense of the swirling, *friss* [high-tempo] dance. However, national

---

67 In vain, because German dances were already widely spread when the radicalisation of the nationalist movements began.
68 Pesovár, 'A *csárdás* kialakulásának szakaszai', p. 17. Translated from the Hungarian by László Felföldi.

dances, which correspond to the earlier forms, are consciously linked with certain western and neighbouring dance forms, and they also seek domestic historical antecedents and analogies to them (Slow Palotás' slow dance in the palace, Polish dance). Our nobility and our citizens tried to make the national dance acceptable, following the example of currently politically sympathetic Polish and French dance cultures. This innovative endeavour smothered the Austrian-German dance and music culture, because this nation had impeded our independence efforts. But its effects could not have been avoided by the proximity of the linguistic boundary, the direct, constant fashion influences and the presence of significant German citizenship that recently became Hungarian.[69]

My chapter has attempted to deepen the knowledge accumulated so far in Hungary with the presentation and analysis of some specific examples. Written, pictorial and musical sources are ordered chronologically, showing the local individuality of the global historical process. On the basis of these we may conclude that dances (traditional, national, social) are very significant elements of national self-identification, and an important part of national memory. What is more, self-identification is closely connected with the picture that other nations create of us, and with how we depict others' dances. The historical trajectory of Hungarian dance culture can be understood only in comparison with that of others.[70] Dance and music sources have already been discovered, but not exploited enough from the point of view of national self-understanding and critical evaluation of the cultural 'image' created so far.

The identification and comparison of the many diverse source materials may enable us to understand the global changes in dance that were taking place in the nineteenth century. To mention only a few:

a) The popularity of the so-called 'deli', 'daliás', 'délceg' [tight, straight, erect] posture of the upper body (unlike the curved body posture, kneeling, beating the ground etc.). This was a new kind of fashionable technique for holding one's body, which was probably propagated by the dance masters before becoming the norm in national, ballroom and traditional as well. It is mentioned in most of the written sources in this chapter.

---

69 Martin, 'Az új magyar táncstílus jegyei', p. 42.
70 György Martin, 'East-European Relations of Hungarian Dance Types', in *Europa et Hungaria: Congressus Ethnographicus in Hungaria*, ed. by Ortutay Gyula (Budapest: Akadémiai Kiadó, 1965), pp. 469–515; Pesovár, 'A *csárdás* kialakulásának szakaszai'.

b) The disappearance or declining popularity of the exclusively men's — and exclusively women's — dances, and the dominance of the mixed-couple dances in the ballrooms. In the nineteenth century, this was an ongoing process in Hungary and in Eastern and Central Europe. It was brought about by Western dance fashions and the mentality that considered couple dance as an ideal dance form.

c) The detachment and growing role of 'social entertainment' as a special social activity (the pleasant use of leisure time), and dance as a more and more frequent form of entertainment, mainly in an urban context. This was unlike the traditional culture in rural areas, where dance had not yet become a separate, segregated form of entertainment — rather, it was an integrated part of social life. The encounter between these two mentalities in Hungary, where a great part of the nobility also shared the traditional way of life, brought about political tension among both the promoters and the opponents of the new dance fashion — the nineteenth-century couple dance.

Bibliography

Bakka, Egil, 'Dance Paradigms: Movement Analysis and Dance Studies' in *Dance and Society: Dancer as Cultural Performer*, ed. by Elsie Dunin, Anne von Bibra Wharton, and László Felföldi (Budapest: Akadémiai Kiadó, 2005), pp. 72–80.

Balla, Károly, 'A Magyar nemzeti Táncról', *Tudományos Gyűjtemény*, 7 (1823), 85–106.

B. Egey, Klára, 'Színpadi táncművészetünk fejlődése a reform korban és a szabadságharc első szakaszában', in *A magyar balett történetéből*, ed. by Vályi Rózsi (Budapest: Művelt nép, 1956), pp. 32–46.

Cellarius, Henri, *La danse des salons* (Paris: J. Hetzel, 1847).

Csaplovics, János, *Gemälde von Ungarn* (Budapest: Hartleben, 1829).

Czerwinski, Albert, *Geschichte der Tanzkunst bei den cultivirten Volkern* (Leipzig: J. J. Weber, 1862).

Dienes, Gedeon, ed., *Magyar táncművészeti lexikon* (Budapest: Planétás, 2008).

Dóka, Krisztina, '19. századi társastáncok a magyar paraszti tánckultúrában', *Tánctudományi Közlemények*, 2 (2014), 49–66.

Ellrich, August, *Die Ungarn wie sie sind: Charakter-Schilderung dieses Volkes in seinem Verhältnissen und Gesinnungen* (Berlin: Vereins Buchhandlung, 1831).

Felföldi, László, 'Picturing Hungarian Patriotism: The Bikkessy Album', in *Imaging Dance: Visual Representation of Dancers and Dancing*, ed. by Barbara Sparti and Judy Van Zile (New York: Georg Olms Verlag, 2011), pp. 181–94.

——, 'Tánctörténet', in *Magyar Kódex*, 6 vols, ed. by Szentpéteri József (Budapest: Kossuth, 1999–2001), I, 269–71.

——, 'Táncábrázolások az abszolutizmus és kiegyezés korabeli kottás kiadványok címlapjain', in *Magyarországi kottacímlapok (1848–1867)*, ed. by Szabó Júlia (Budapest: Argumentum, 2000), pp. 13–23.

Fletcher, Margaret, *Sketches of Life and Character in Hungary* (New York: Macmillan and Co, 1892).

Gergely, András, ed., *Magyarország története a 19. században* (Budapest: Osiris, 2005).

Haraszti, Emil, *A tánc története* (Budapest: Magyar Szemle Társaság, 1937).

Hofer, Tamás, 'A magyar népi kultúra történeti rétegei és európai helyzete', in *Martin György emlékezete: Visszaemlékezések és tanulmányok születésének hatvanadik évfordulójára*, ed. by Felföldi László (Budapest: Magyar Művelődési Intézet, 1993), pp. 341–51.

Kaposi, Edit, 'Bálok a régi Pest-Budán', *Táncművészet*, 1 (1991).

——, 'A táncmesterség és a 19–20. századi társastánckultúra nemzeti vonásai hazánkban és Európában', in *Népi kultúra és nemzettudat*. ed. by Hofer Tamás (Budapest: A Magyarságkutató Intézet kiadványa 1990), pp. 105–20.

——, 'A magyar társastánc szakirodalom forráskritikai vizsgálata II.', *Tánctudományi Tanulmányok*, 1986–1987 (1987), 50–75.

——, 'A magyar társastánc szakirodalom forráskritikai vizsgálata I.', *Tánctudományi Tanulmányok*, 1984–1985 (1985), 177–94.

——, 'Szőllősy Szabó Lajos élete és munkássága (1803–1882)', *Tánctudományi Tanulmányok*, 1978–1979 (1979), 145–88.

——, 'Kiegészítő adatok az európai táncmesterség történetéhez', *Táncművészeti Értesítő*, 9 (1973), 34–37, 87–91.

——, 'Adalékok az európai és a magyar táncmesterség történetéhez', *Tánctudományi Tanulmányok*, 1969–1970 (1970), 16–194.

——, 'Egy híres táncos önéletírása: Szőllősy Szabó Lajos', *Táncművészet*, 4 (1955), 154–56.

Kavecsánszki, Máté, *Tánc és közösség*, Studia Folkloristica et Ethnographica 59 (Debrecen: Debreceni Egyetemi Kiadó, 2015).

——, 'Társastáncok a magyar paraszti közösségben a 19–20. században', in *Notitiae Iuvenum: Tanulmányok Ujváry Zoltán 75. születésnapjának tiszteletére*, ed. by Kiri Edit, Kovács László Erik, and Szilágyi Judit (Debrecen: DE-BTK HÖK, 2007), pp. 199–242.

Kilányi, Lajos, *A Kör-táncz mellyet Szőllősi Lajos a' pesti nemzeti színház táncművészének tanítása után Minden tánczrész könnyen felfogható rajzolatával és magyarázatával terjedelmesen előadta Kilányi Lajos nemzeti és balettáncz-oktató, a nemzeti színház tagja. 6 rajzolattal és egy zenemű melléklettel. Der Kör-Tanz. Erste Ungarische National-Quadrille, Erfunden Von Ludwig Szőlősi Lajos. Beschrieben Von L. Kilányi Lajos. Mit Abbildungen... und Einer Beigabe Der National-Musik* (Vienna: Wagner 1845).

Kiss, Lajos, 'A bukovinai székelyek tánczenéje, La musique de Danse des 'Székely' de Bukovinie', *Tánctudományi Tanulmányok*, 1 (1958), 67–88.

Klemm, Bernhard, *Katechismus der Tanzkuns* (Berlin: J. J. Weber, 1855, 1869, 1876).

Kohl, Georg Johann, *Hundert Tage auf Reisen in den östereichischen Staten* (Dresden und Leipzig: in der Arnoldische Buchhandlung, 1842).

Köegler, Horst, *Balettlexikon* (Budapest: Zeneműkiadó, 1977).

Lakatos, Sándor, *Rajta párok, táncoljunk!: Tánckedvelők könyve* (Nagykanizsa: Waidits József, 1871).

Maácz, László, *A magyar néptánc színpadi pályáfutása a XIX–XX. században* (Budapest: Népművelési Intézet, 1976).

Martin, György, 'Tánc és társadalom: Történeti táncnévadás-típusok itthon és Európában', in *Történeti antropológia*, ed. by Hofer Tamás (Budapest: MTA Néprajzi Kutatócsoport, 1984), pp. 152–64.

——, 'Népi tánchagyomány és nemzeti tánctípusok Kelet-Közép-Európában a XVI–XIX. században', *Ethnographia*, 95 (1984), 353–61.

——, 'Táncdialektusok és történeti táncdivatok', in *Előmunkálatok a Magyarság Néprajzához 7*, ed. by Paládi-Kovács Attila (Budapest: Akadémiai Kiadó, 1980), pp. 139–45.

——, 'Az új magyar táncstílus jegyei és kialakulása', *Ethnographia*, 88 (1977), 39.

——, *Magyar tánctípusok és táncdialektusok* (Budapest: Népművelési Propaganda Iroda, 1970).

——, 'East-European Relations of Hungarian Dance Types', in *Europa et Hungaria: Congressus Ethnographicus in Hungaria*, ed. by Ortutay Gyula (Budapest: Akadémiai Kiadó, 1965), pp. 469–515.

——, 'Magyar tánctípusok kelet-európai kapcsolatai', *Az MTA Irodalomtudományi Osztályának Közleményei*, 21 (1964), 67–96.

Miskolczy, Ambrus, 'A hungarus-tudat a 19. században', *Limes*, 4 (2009), 71–96.

——, '"Hungarus Consciousness" in the Age of Early Nationalism', in *Latin at the Crossroads of Identity: The Evolution of Linguistic Nationalism in the Kingdom of Hungary*, ed. by G. Almàsi and L. Šubarić (Leiden, Netherlands: Brill, 2015), pp. 64–93.

Mona, Ilona, ed., *Magyar zeneműkiadók és tevékenységük, 1774–1867*, 2nd edn (Budapest, MTA Zenetudományi Intézet, 1989).

Mosonyi, Mihály, 'Két népies *Csárdás*', *Zenészeti lapok* (1860–1861), 186–87.

Németh, Antal, ed., *Színészeti lexikon I–II.* (Budapest: Győző Andor kiadása, 1930).

Norliond, Tobias, 'Adatok a keringő és a polka történetéhez', in *Emlékkönyv Kodály Zoltán 60. születésnapjára*, ed. by Gunda Béla (Budapest: Magyar Néprajzi Társaság, 1943), pp. 181–94.

Ortutay, Gyula, ed., *Magyar Néprajzi Lexikon I–V.*, 5 vols (Budapest, Akadémiai Kiadó, 1978–1982).

Patterson, Arthur, *The Magyars: Their Country and Institutions* (London: Smith, Elder and Co. 1869).

Pesovár, Ernő, *A magyar tánctörténet évszázadai*: Írott és képi források' (Budapest: Hagyományok Háza, 2003).

——, *Tánchagyományunk történeti rétegei: A magyar néptánc története* (Szombathely: Berzsenyi Dániel Főiskola, 2003).

——, *A magyar páros táncok* (Budapest: Planétás, 1997).

——, 'A *Csárdás* kialakulásának szakaszai és típusai', *Ethnographia*, 96 (1985), 17–29.

——, 'A lengyel táncok hatása a reformkorban', *Néprajzi Értesítő*, 47 (1965), 159–77.

Pesovár, Ferenc, *A magyar nép táncélete* (Budapest: Népművelési Propaganda Iroda, 1978).

——, 'Táncmesterek a szatmári falvakban', *Tánctudományi Tanulányok*, 1959–1960 (1960), 309–22.

Réthei Prikkel, Marián, *A magyarság táncai* (Budapest: Stúdium, 1924).

Róka, P. Pál, *A táncművészet tankönyve* (Nagykőrös: Ottinger Kálmán kiadása, 1900).

Szabolcsi, Bence, *Népzene és történelem* (Budapest: Akadémiai Kiadó, 1954).

Szentpál, Olga, 'Keringő és polka a 19. században: Táncrekonstrukció Cellarius táncmester leírása alapján', *Táncművészeti Értesítő* (1956).

——, *A Csárdás: A magyar nemzeti társastánc a 19. század első felében* (Budapest: Zeneműkiadó vállalat, 1954).

Tissot, Victor, *La Hongrie: De l'Adriatique au Danube: Impressions de voyage* (Paris: Plon, 1883).

Vályi, Rózsi, *A táncművészet története* (Budapest: Zeneműkiadó, 1969).

Vitányi, Iván, *A tánc* (Budapest: Gondolat, 1963).

Zorn, Friedrich Albert, *Die Grammatik der Tanzkunst* (Leipzig: J. J. Weber, 1887).

8. The Waltz among Slovenians

Rebeka Kunej[1]

Introduction

The Slovenian language has no equivalent term for round dances (literally translated as *okrogli plesi*). Therefore, a Waltz is defined only as a couple dance, which can be danced in a circle; but the typological category round dance is not used at all. This chapter examines round dances in Slovenia, focusing on the Waltz as folk dance. The analysis of Waltz dance forms, which forms the central part of this chapter, is based on collected material (written descriptions and labanotation scores) about the Waltz as folk dance in archives of the Institute of Ethnomusicology ZRC SAZU in Ljubljana. The Waltz material is based on the field research of a handful of researchers who conducted their research mostly in the second half of the twentieth century, with the intent of providing information about the folk dance of the past.[2] Consequently, their research created an impression of folk dance that was limited to the end of the nineteenth century and the first half of the twentieth century.

Today, the established Slovenian name for a Waltz is *valček* [a small roller] with other terms only rarely used. In the past, several expressions were used to denote the Waltz. The most common among them, e.g. *valc*,

---

1   This article was written as part of the research programme *Research on Slovenian Folk Culture in Folklore Studies and Ethnology*, No. P6–0111, funded by the Slovenian Research Agency.
2   Ethnochoreologists (e.g. Marija Šuštar, Tončka Marolt, Mirko Ramovš) were focused more on the rural inhabitants (and their dance tradition), and less on other social classes of the population in the towns, arguing that the majority of the Slovenian population, until the Second World War, belonged to the peasantry.

valcer, bolcar, indicate yet more clearly the connection with the German name *Walzer*, and the very origins of the dance. From an etymological standpoint, its German origins are indisputable. *Walzer* derives from the German verb *walzen*, originally meaning 'to travel', as in the German expression 'auf der Walz' ('travelling on the job'), and later on meaning 'to turn', as in Germ. 'sich walzen'.[3] Nowadays, a dance named *valček* is a simplified, impoverished and modified form of the Viennese Waltz, and is one of the most common and widespread dance forms. The Waltz, with its 3/4 beat, represents an alternative to the equally widespread Polka, which is danced in 2/4. Together, they are staples of many dance parties, especially in the countryside, where half of the Slovenian population lives. In the context of today's ballroom dancing, dance schools and so-called *international standard dances*, the two types of Waltz are usually separated: *dunajski valček* [Viennese Waltz] and *angleški valček* [English Waltz], also called *počasni valček* [slow Waltz; known in the English-speaking world as the basic Waltz].

The Beginnings in the Slovenian Lands

The Waltz probably emerged in Slovenia at the end of the eighteenth century, or, at the latest, at the beginning of the nineteenth century. Like other dances, the Waltz was introduced to Slovenia by travelling craftsmen, soldiers, students and intelligentsia.[4] Since the Second World War, this particular dance has mostly been researched as a part of folk dance culture in rural areas, and largely overlooked as a part of dance culture in urban areas. Most of the ethnographic data on the previous centuries, especially the nineteenth century, relates to the rural environment, and less to the urban.

The concept of moral panic and 'folk devils'[5] provides an appropriate context for the introduction of the Waltz among Slovenians. Initially, in towns and cities, the Waltz was considered immoral. Furthermore,

---

3 Otto Schneider, *Tanzlexikon: der Gesellschafts-, Volks- und Kunsttanz von der Anfängen bis zur Gegenwart mit Bibliographien und Notenbeispielen* (Vienna: Verlag Brüder Hollinek; and Mainz: Schott Verlag, 1985), pp. 594–95.
4 Mirko Ramovš, 'Valček kot slovenski ljudski ples', *Traditiones*, 32/2 (2003), 33–49 (p. 36).
5 Stanley Cohen, *Folk Devils and Moral Panics: The Creation of the Mods and Rockers*, 3rd ed. (New York: Routledge, 2009). See also Chapter 13 in this volume.

because the affection felt for the Waltz stemmed in part from its German origins (it was seen as appealingly modern, rather than traditional), it was often associated with the ethnic issues of the time, and the struggle for the cultural and political autonomy of the Slovenian people.[6] In 1884 the periodical journal *Slovan* included the following statement:

> The Germans claim the Waltz is their national dance. The Waltz is not aesthetically pleasing, certainly immoral. I mention this because some in our country are in love with this dance, about which General Sherman's wife wrote a book exclusively about that dance. It would be better to accustom ourselves to the '*kolo*' [circle] dance, which is also popular in our country.[7]

However, some decades later, the Tango appeared as a new 'folk devil' and object of moral panic, and the Waltz was reconsidered as a model of elegance and morality. Hence, in December of 1913, a great controversy ensued over the Tango in the Slovenian press. Judgments in newspapers were very contradictory, depending on whether they belonged to the liberal or conservative circle. For example, the newspaper *Slovenski narod* published an article in which an anonymous author compared the history of the cherished Waltz with the new Tango. Its author glorifies the Waltz, describing it as 'lovely' and the 'happy Waltz', while describing the strong resistance to the dance upon its arrival, despite it not being

---

6   From the fourteenth century to 1918, the Slovenians lived under the rule of the Habsburg dynasty. The exception was the period 1805–1813, when the Slovenians settled in territory that was part of the autonomous Illyrian Provinces of Napoleon. After a short French interregnum, which contributed significantly to greater national self-confidence and Slovenian awareness of their own rights, Slovenian lands were once again included in the Austrian Empire. German remained the main language of culture, administration and education well into the nineteenth century. The interest in Slovenian language and folklore grew in the 1820s and 1840s, and, by the end of the nineteenth century, Slovenians had established a standardised literary language, and a thriving civil society. The period 1848–1918, the so-called Slovenian National Awakening, was marked by a demand to unite all Slovenians in a common state. After the First World War and the dissolution of the Austro-Hungarian Empire, the Slovenians joined the Slavs to form the state of Slovenians, Croats and Serbs, and, eventually, the kingdom of Serbs, Croats and Slovenians, which was renamed the kingdom of Yugoslavia in 1929. Slovenians whose territory fell under the jurisdiction of neighbouring states such as Italy, Austria and Hungary in that period, joined the majority of Slovenians after the Second World War, when Slovenia became part of the Socialist Federal Republic of Yugoslavia. In June 1991 Slovenia declared its independence.
7   'Razne novice' [n.a.], *Slovan* (13 March 1884), p. 88. Translated from the Slovenian by Rebeka Kunej.

clear whether the resistance was specifically Slovenian or spread across wider European territory.[8] The article asserts that when the Waltz first appeared, it had been described as a 'dance deserving persecution', 'dance of sensuality', 'a mark of adultery', 'certain damnation for the Christian soul'.[9] The bishops had written pastoral letters against the dance, and theology scholars had argued, using the Church Fathers' writing that the Waltz was of pagan origin and was a manifestation of a godless view of life. The article further points out that, at the time of the Waltz's arrival, despite priests having a great influence over people, their attempted repression of the Waltz was ultimately unsuccessful.

The first Slovenian dance master's book, *Slovenski plesalec* (*Slovenian Dancer*, 1893), by Ivan Umek, discussed the Waltz in comparison to other dances. He classified it as *navadni ples* [an ordinary dance that is usually danced independently of other couples, as opposed to *sestavljeni plesi* [compound dances], that require a number of couples to be danced successfully (e.g. the Quadrille). He called the Waltz *valček* and *valjček* but also *walzer*, and mentioned that the Waltz could be danced in more ways than any other dance. The most common type he called *valjček na šest korakov* [the Waltz in six steps], and quoted the well-known variations — *francoski, laški in štajerski* [French, Italian and Styrian Waltz] — that differ in speed, step mode and motion.[10]

In his later book *Moderni plesalec* [Modern Dancer] (1904), where he discusses *navadni plesi* [ordinary dances] under the section '*Valček*', he comments that the Waltz is not an exacting dance; however, it takes time to learn it well. Umek added a relatively detailed description of the Waltz, which included sliding steps.[11] In the same chapter there is also a section on '*Slovanski valček*' [Slavic Waltz], which contains a description of a dance composed by Umek himself on the occasion of the opening of *Narodni dom* [Slovenian National] in 1904 in Trieste. His *slovanski valček* includes figures of *pas balancé* in the first part, whereas the second part

---

8   'Tango' [n.a.], *Slovenski narod* (6 December 1913), p. 9. Translated from the Slovenian by Rebeka Kunej.
9   Ibid.
10 Ivan Umek, *Slovenski plesalec: zbirka raznih narodnih in navadnih plesov* (Trst: self-published, 1893), p. 7.
11 Ivan Umek, *Moderni plesalec: zbirka raznih narodnih in drugih najnovejših, navadnih in sestavljenih plesov* (Trst: self-published, 1904), p. 11.

of the dance is a Waltz.¹² At the end of his book, Umek provides statistics on how many dance masters there are in the world, as well as details of the time he judged necessary to learn a particular dance. Here, Umek argues that it is necessary to dance the Waltz fifty times to dance it well, and a hundred times to dance it very well. It is necessary to dance the Polka twenty-five times, and it takes thirty attempts to dance the Mazurka well.¹³

The first evidence of the Waltz as a folk dance can be found in the responses to a questionnaire,¹⁴ initiated by Archduke John of Austria, which was sent out to all the recruiting districts of the Duchy of Styria between 1811 and 1845. The response was poor. Of the eleven questionnaires that were returned from Slovenian areas, three relate significantly to dance. The completed questionnaires for Fala and Studenice, dated 1812, state that the most widespread dances in these regions are *die Deutsche Tänze* [German dances].¹⁵ It is not certain whether this includes the Waltz, but we can assume that it does, because the Waltz was often called *Deutcher* or *Deutche Tanz* among Slovenians. The responses from Hrastovec, dated 1815, mention *der Deutche Walzer*

---

12   Umek, *Moderni plesalec*, pp. 17–18.
13   Ibid., p. 60.
14   The main purpose of the survey conducted in the 1811–1845 period was to collect data about the 'statistical-topographic' features of the Duchy of Styria in the first half of the nineteenth century. Questionnaires for the collection of topographic materials were first sent out in 1811 by the Archduke John of Austria to recruiting districts, however, the response was poor. Twenty years later, the Archduke's work was continued by his secretary, Dr Georg Gött, an archivist and librarian, whose efforts proved more successful — he also sent the questionnaires to manors, tax municipalities, parishes, etc. The questionnaire answers were collected c.1843 and are kept in the Styrian Provincial Archives (present-day Austria). The questionnaire results were also published in two books (1840, 1841), however, only responses for the German-speaking part of Styria were included. The 'Slovenian section' (the section referring to the Slovenian-speaking population) was omitted. The efforts of Slovenian ethnologists for the 'Slovenian section' to be acquired by the Institute of Slovenian Ethnology ZRC SAZU bore fruit and, since 1980, photocopies have thus been available in the Institute's archives. Approximately 150 years after the answers were collected, ethnologist Niko Kurent translated them, made a selection and published the compilation in four volumes (1985–1993), thus providing a wide circle of interested individuals with access to the responses, which are written in the Gothic alphabet.
15   Niko Kuret, *Slovensko Štajersko pred marčno revolucijo 1848*, part 1, vol. 2 (Ljubljana: Slovenska akademija znanosti in umetnosti, 1987), p. 145.

[the German Waltz].[16] Certainly, the interviewer from Hrastovec knew the Waltz as the *Walzer* and was aware of its German origin.

Early evidence of the Waltz can also be found in the answers to a circular on dress culture, festivities and dance that was sent out to the five district offices of the Ljubljana district before the intended visit of Emperor Ferdinand in 1838. Based on these responses, it seems that it was the intention to arrange a presentation of the unique traditions belonging to people in the countryside. While the visit itself never occurred, the responses to the circular still survive. While the answers are quite short, they nonetheless give some image of the dancing at that time. Written down by the German administrators, they reveal that dancing was common at the time and that the Waltz, in addition to other German dances, had already replaced the local dances. The Waltz continued to be most commonly referred to as *der Deutsche Tanz* [the German Dance] (among fourteen villages) or *der Deutche* [the German] (thirteen villages), but often also as the *Walzer* (ten villages) or just as *Walzen* [dancing Waltz] (three villages). A remark by one interviewer, who has put *Walzer* in brackets next to the word *Deutche*, clearly indicates that the *Deutsche* was an alternate name for the Waltz.[17]

Unfortunately, there is no exact data on the Waltz as a folk dance in the second half of the nineteenth century, even though it was undoubtedly already firmly established in the repertoire of rural musicians, and danced at village public festivities and private dance parties. It is evident from the data from before the First World War (taken from various sources, including newspapers and archival material) that, by then, the Waltz had become one of the most popular dances. In the 1907 'Questionnaire on Folk Songs, Music and Dances', the Waltz was usually not considered a 'folk' dance, but categorised as an 'ordinary' dance.[18] This reflects the opinions of priests, teachers and other state officials, who were mostly involved in formulating the responses to this nationwide survey. Response to that questionnaire was lacking, however. Only seventy-seven examples of completed questionnaires are kept in the archives of the Institute of Ethnomusicology ZRC SAZU,

---

16   Niko Kuret, *Slovensko Štajersko*, part 2, vol. 1. (1993), p. 85.
17   Ramovš, 'Valček', 36–37.
18   Ljubljana, Institute of Ethnomusicology ZRC SAZU Archives, Collection of the OSNP (GNI OSNP), *Povpraševalne pole*.

and, of those, only eighteen listed dances by name. Seventeen of those questionnaires also include the Waltz, described mostly as *valček* (ten times), but also *valcer* (four times), and *valcar, bolcer, tajč* (once).

Choreological Aspects of the Waltz as a Folk Dance

During the interwar period, as well as after the Second World War, the Waltz and the Polka were undoubtedly among the most popular dances in Slovenia. A diverse picture of the Waltz in Slovenia (presented below) has been created primarily on the basis of field research conducted by the Institute of Ethnomusicology's associates after the Second World War, the results of which present the Waltz as performed at the end of the nineteenth century and beginning of the twentieth. The basic materials used below are dance notations (Kinetography Laban) from the Institute of Ethnomusicology ZRC SAZU Archives.[19]

According to the sources and documents, different varieties of the Waltz became established in the countryside and survived at least until the Second World War. It can therefore be claimed with great certainty that among Slovenians the Waltz was danced in three main ways:

1. *valček s prestopanjem* [Waltz with shift steps];
2. *valček z menjalnim korakom* [Waltz with the change step];
3. *dvokoračni valček* [two-step Waltz].

1. Waltz with Shift Steps [*Valček s prestopanjem*]

One of the oldest forms of the Waltz in Slovenia includes shift steps [*prestopanje*]. In two measures, the couple makes six steps of equal duration using the whole foot, and, at the same time, makes one turn (L R L / R L R). The male dancer usually starts with his left foot and the female with her right foot, although the other way around is also possible. The couple turns clockwise, moves forward, and then moves counter-clockwise in the circle (see Fig. 8.1).

---

19 Ljubljana, Institute of Ethnomusicology ZRC SAZU Archives, Dance Collection (GNI Pl). Cf. Ramovš, 'Valček', 39–44..

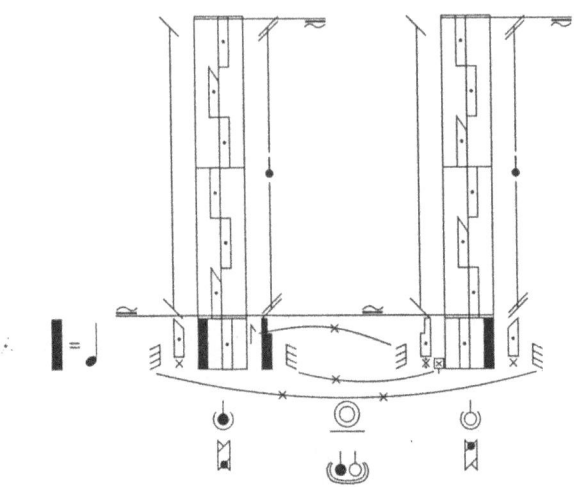

Fig. 8.1 *Valček s prestopanjem* [Waltz with shift steps], 2003. © Institute of Ethnomusicology ZRC SAZU. Drawing by Mirko Ramovš.

The form with shift steps probably evolved from one of the figures of the *štajeriš* [Styrian] that was danced in a very similar way as the Waltz. The couple takes an ordinary dance position (closed position), characteristic of the Waltz: standing face to face, the man holds the woman at the waist with his right hand, the woman places her left hand on his right shoulder, and the man's left hand holds the woman's right hand stretched out at the height of her shoulders. The couple then turns on the spot. The Waltz was danced in the same manner as the *štajeriš* described above, except that the couple moved forward during the turns. In the variation from Brezovica pri Buču,[20] the couple stamped their feet on the ground at the end of each eighth measure of the Waltz's melody, similar to the *štajeriš*. This was called *potrkan valček* [stamping Waltz]. There were two unique variants of the Waltz with shift steps:

- *potresavka* [shaking, trembling Waltz] was danced in western parts of Slovenia, where the steps were accompanied by the shaking of the body;[21]

---

20 GNI Pl 642.
21 Cf. GNI Pl 944.

- and *ta nizki bolcar* [the low Waltz] from southern parts of Slovenia,[22] in which the first step of each measure was made with bent knees.

Today the Waltz with shift steps [*prestopanje*] is very rarely danced.

2. Waltz with the Change Step [*Valček z menjalnim korakom*]

The most frequently danced Waltz form involves one turn being made with two change steps [*menjalna koraka*], L R L / R L R. The second step in each measure is made as a change step on the ball of the foot. As in the previous variant, the male dancer starts with his left foot and the female with her right, although it is also possible to dance it the other way around. They turn clockwise and dance counter-clockwise around the circle (see Fig. 8.2).

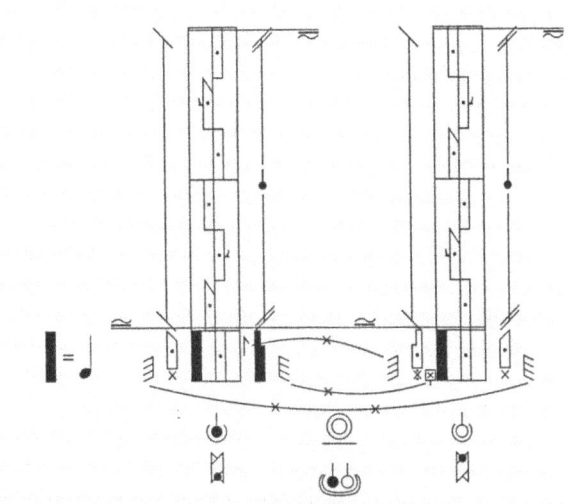

Fig. 8.2 *Valček z menjalnim korakom* [Waltz with the change step], 2003. © Institute of Ethnomusicology ZRC SAZU. Drawing by Mirko Ramovš.

---

22 Cf. GNI Pl 228.

This variant is still the one danced the most, except that moving in the circle is no longer as intensive or is absent altogether. The changing steps could be performed with some stylistic specialties. For example, if the first step is made with a bent knee[23] it is called *ta nizki bolcar* [the low Waltz]. Or if the first step is made with a slide of the free foot, the dance is named *podrsan valček* [the sliding Waltz].[24] In the variant from the eastern part of Slovenia,[25] named *pemišvalček* [Bohemian Waltz], the couple performs the first part of the dance along the circle while holding each other only with one hand, or not at all. In the second part of the dance, they dance in the ordinary dance position, on the spot.

3. Two-Step Waltz [*Dvokoračni valček*]

If the change-step Waltz was too difficult for the less skilled dancers, they preferred dancing a simpler form of Waltz called *dvokoračni valček* [two-step Waltz], which appears in three different variants.

The First Variant

The first variant could be called *drseči valček* [the sliding Waltz]. Its characteristic is that in the first step (performed with a preliminary slight bend of the knee) on the first beat in each measure, the toes of the free foot slide to the supporting leg. On the second beat in each measure, the supporting foot lifts to the ball and the free foot touches the floor with its toes. On the third beat in each measure, the entire foot of the supporting leg is placed on the ground and the leg makes a shallow squat, thus making the free foot ready for the next step: L (R), R (L). The male dancer usually starts with his left foot, the female with her right, but this is not a hard and fast rule. The turning of the couple is not as intensive as in the change-step Waltz (2), and there is no consistency around the circle (See Fig. 8.3). The Waltz is still danced in this way. One of the sliding Waltz variants is *ta nizki bolcar* [the low Waltz] from Carinthia,[26] but it is known in other parts of Slovenia as well. It is danced

---

23 Cf. GNI Pl 222.
24 Cf. GNI Pl 1201.
25 GNI Pl 858.
26 GNI Pl 1023.

with a distinctive tremble of the knees on the upbeat and on the third beat in each measure but without the sliding of the free foot and rising to the ball with the supporting foot on the second beat.

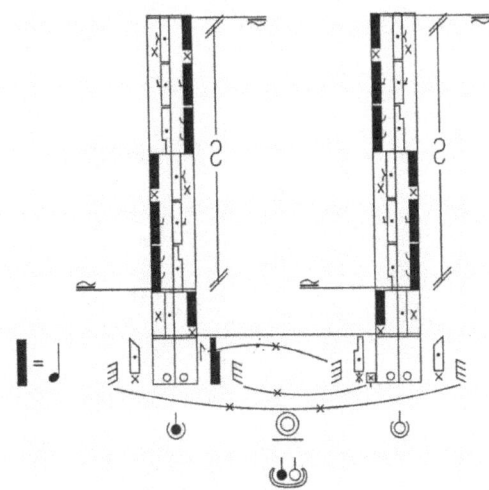

Fig. 8.3 *Drseči valček* [the sliding Waltz], 2003. © Institute of Ethnomusicology ZRC SAZU. Drawing by Mirko Ramovš.

The Second Variant

The second variant is sometimes called *poskočni valček* [gambolling, springing Waltz].[27] Because of the high hops it includes, it was also called *ta visoki valcer, ta visoki bolcar* [the high Waltz]. The couple makes a step on the first beat in each measure, on the second beat jumps up, and, on the third beat, jumps down on the same foot as they started with, contracting the free foot in the meantime: L-L / R-R (the male dancer usually starts with his left foot, the female with her right). With two gambolling steps, the couple makes one turn clockwise and dances counter-clockwise in the circle. The older position of the hands is characteristic of this variant of the Waltz: the male dancer grasps his partner's waist with both hands, and she places both hands on his shoulders (see Fig. 8.4). The variant danced by Slovenes in the Austrian

---

27   Cf. GNI Pl 1022.

part of Charintia[28] is unusual: the male dancer leans on his partner during the jumps (and claps with his feet while he is in the air, as if he were trying to kill a fly). Because of this foot movement the dance is called *muhe pobujat* [killing flies]. The *poskočni valček* [springing Waltz] has been forgotten, and is no longer danced. It can only be seen in performances by folklore dance groups.

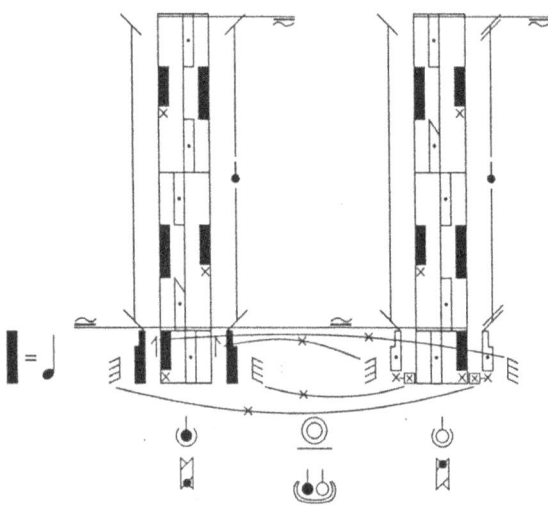

Fig. 8.4 *Poskočni valček* [gambolling, springing Waltz], 2003. © Institute of Ethnomusicology ZRC SAZU. Drawing by Mirko Ramovš.

The Third Variant

The third variant is relatively rare. It is similar to the second variant (the springing Waltz) except that the couple does not hop, but lifts to the balls of their feet on the second beat, and lowers themselves down again on the third beat, which looks like vertical swaying (up and down): L / R. The male dancer begins with his left foot and the female with her right, but the beginning position is not fixed. The couple turns clockwise (two steps make one turn) and dances counter-clockwise in the circle,

---

28   GNI Pl 1025.

or dances on the spot (see Fig. 8.5). In some places, this variant was performed with a tremble of the knees on the first beat and named *mulcertanc*.[29] In the eastern part of Styria, this Waltz form developed into a specific dance with typical fixed melodies (e.g. *Na oknu glej obrazek lep*,[30] *dvojni valček*).[31]

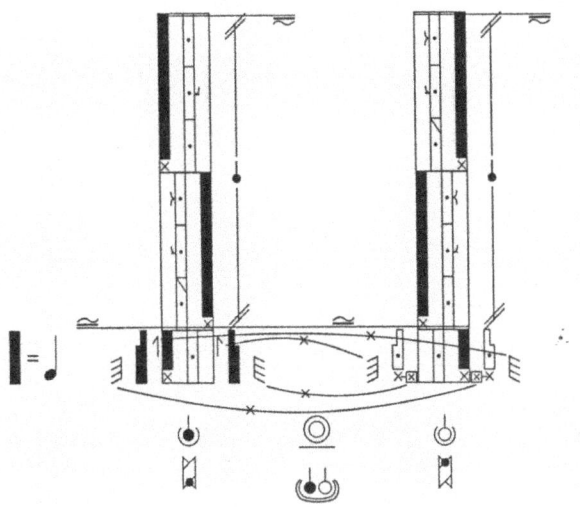

Fig. 8.5 Third variant of *dvokoračni valček* [two-step Waltz], 2003. © Institute of Ethnomusicology ZRC SAZU. Drawing by Mirko Ramovš.

The above variations of the Waltz were danced autonomously: couples danced it with the same dance steps as long as they wanted or the music lasted, revolving around their own axis and moving forward.

The Waltz could also be a segment of other folk dances, as in these two instances:

1. The other dance takes on all the steps (changing steps) and posture of the Waltz but retains its own structure (for example: *štajeriš* [Styrian] from Lahov Graben pri Jurkloštru, *malender* from

---

29 GNI Pl 456.
30 GNI Pl 856.
31 GNI Pl 859.

Dule, and *neubayerisch* from Dule (which is known as *Moja dečva je djawa*)).

2. The Waltz becomes a part of another dance, and the second part of the dance includes figures or a walk around the circle accompanied by singing or by dance music (for example: *mašarjanka, ta potrkan tajč, ta potrkana, majpajeriš, mrzulin, kmečki valček, Fsaka ftica je vesela*, and *špacirbolcar*). The change-step Waltz or the shift-step Waltz was used most frequently, which was danced clockwise or counter-clockwise in the circle, on the spot, in some cases also with jigs around the circle (*ta potrkana, špacirbolcar*).

The Waltz was also danced as a part of a game in which the dance partner was chosen with a cushion, a mirror or a chair, or as a part of a game with alternating dance partners. In such cases, the Waltz was danced only by a dancer who chose a partner; other participants would watch, or run in the circle. In dance games with alternating dance partners, all participants waltzed, but the Polka was more common in these games than the Waltz.

When the Waltz became the most popular dance in the rural dance repertoire, it also acquired a ritual function previously held by the *štajeriš* [Styrian] at weddings.[32] Still today, but to a lesser extent, the Waltz is reserved as the honorary dance of the bride and groom at their wedding celebration (their first dance at midnight or even before it), or as the solo dance of marrying couples. The Waltz still has an important role at many wedding celebrations (if the celebration also includes dance), in both rural and urban areas.

Although the Waltz was a well-known dance among the Slovenian population in the nineteenth and twentieth centuries, it never became a part of national identity; it has never become a 'typical Slovenian'. This is perhaps due to it being considered too European (and German), and thus not distinctively Slovenian. On the other hand, perhaps it was considered *too* Slovenian, too widespread and well-known to be able to meet the criteria to place it on a national pedestal.

---

32 Author's field research at *Ohcet*, Grosuplje (Slovenia), 30 August 2003, and at *Ohcet*, Lesce na Gorenjskem (Slovenia), 26 June 2004.

Conclusion

In the countryside the Waltz is still popular.[33] There is a tendency to simplify the dance steps or to substitute simpler steps, resulting in the gradual extinction of more difficult ones. The change-step Waltz or the two-step Waltz (usually the sliding Waltz) are mostly danced by the less skilled dancers, while other variants introduced above have actually been forgotten. Sometimes, the crowded dance floor does not permit dancing counter-clockwise in a circle. Therefore, couples dance anywhere on the dance floor, with each couple dancing in an invisible small circle, so their turning is not as intensive either. They usually turn clockwise; only proficient dancers turn counter-clockwise in the ordinary dance position. The old dance position, in which the male dancer holds the female at her waist with both hands and she places both hands on his shoulders, has been abandoned.

Fig. 8.6 Maturantski ples elite dance at graduation event in Maribor, 17 March 1962. Photo by Danilo Škofič (1962). Wikimedia Commons, Public Domain, https://commons.wikimedia.org/w/index.php?search=Maturantski+ples+&title=Special%3ASearch&go=Go#/media/File:Maturantski_ples_v_Mariboru_1962_(5).jpg

The so-called *dunajski valček* [Viennese Waltz] and *angleški valček* [English Waltz] still feature at important social dance gatherings, such

---

33 Author's field research at *Gasilska veselica*, Vrzdenec (Slovenia), 24 June 2012.

as at graduations,[34] or at big public dance events, such as *Maturantska parada* — the Quadrille Dance Parade.[35]

Regarding contemporary observations of various dance events and their analysis, it can be concluded that the golden age of the Waltz has already passed. As presented above, its diversity in performance has lessened and its social role is increasingly replaced by other social dances, which have a shorter tradition among Slovenians.

Fig. 8.7 Video: The annual *Maturantska Parada* — the Quadrille Parade — that was danced by more than 500 graduates in Ljubljana on 23 March 2014. 'MATURANTSKA PARADA — 2014 — QUADRILLE PARADE', 6:36, posted online by Tomaz Ambroz, *Youtube*, 28 May 2014, https://www.youtube.com/watch?v=QoSOpu4Y58w

The author's field research took place at:

Gasilska veselica [Volunteer Fire Brigade's Festivity], 24 June 2012 in Vrzdenec, Slovenia.

Ohcet [Wedding Party], 30 August 2003 in Grosuplje, Slovenia.

Ohcet [Wedding Party], 26 June 2004 in Lesce na Gorenjskem, Slovenia.

Maturantski ples [Graduating Dance], 9 May 1995 in Ljubljana, Slovenia.

Maturantska parada [Quadrille Dance Parade], 20 May 2011 in Ljubljana, Slovenia

Maturantska parada [Quadrille Dance Parade], 22 May 2009 in Ljubljana, Slovenia.

Bibliography

Archival Sources and Field Research

Ljubljana, Institute of Ethnomusicology ZRC SAZU Archives, Collection of the OSNP (GNI OSNP), Povpraševalne pole.

Ljubljana, Institute of Ethnomusicology ZRC SAZU Archives, Dance Collection (GNI Pl).

---

34 Author's field research at *Maturantski ples,* Ljubljana (Slovenia), 9 May 1995.
35 Author's field researches at *Maturantska parada,* Ljubljana (Slovenia), 22 May 2009 and 20 May 2011.

Secondary Sources

Cohen, Stanley, *Folk Devils and Moral Panics: The Creation of the Mods and Rockers*, 3rd edn (New York: Routledge, 2009).

Kuret, Niko, *Slovensko Štajersko pred marčno revolucijo 1848*, 2 vols (Ljubljana: Slovenska akademija znanosti in umetnosti, 1987–1993).

Ramovš, Mirko, 'Valček kot slovenski ljudski ples', *Traditiones*, 32/2 (2003), 33–49.

——, *Polka je ukazana: plesno izročilo na Slovenskem*, 7 vols (Ljubljana: Kres, 1992–2000).

'Razne novice' [n.a.], *Slovan* (13 March 1884), p. 88.

Schneider, Otto, *Tanzlexikon: der Gesellschafts-, Volks- und Kunsttanz von der Anfängen bis zur Gegenwart mit Bibliographien und Notenbeispielen* (Vienna: Verlag Brüder Hollinek; and Mainz: Schott Verlag, 1985).

'Tango' [n.a.], *Slovenski narod* (6 December 1913), p. 9.

Umek, Ivan, *Moderni plesalec: zbirka raznih narodnih in drugih najnovejših, navadnih in sestavljenih plesov* (Trst: self-published, 1904).

——, *Slovenski plesalec: zbirka raznih narodnih in navadnih plesov* (Trst: self-published, 1893).

9. Dancing and Politics in Croatia: The *Salonsko Kolo* as a Patriotic Response to the Waltz[1]

Ivana Katarinčić and Iva Niemčić

During the period of Croatian national revival, the Illyrian movement (1830–1948), dance halls became one of the key places where Illyrians gathered, and dance became one of the ways they promoted their ideas. This chapter will discuss these aspects, as well as how dances themselves had a role in the political life of Zagreb. We trace the arrival of the Waltz in the Croatian ballrooms and compare it with the appearance of the *Salonsko Kolo* (Fig. 9.1). *Salonsko Kolo* was an indigenous urban dance composed of figures and formations, which sprang up as a patriotic reply to the foreign Waltz. In order to express resistance to foreign influences, dance entertainments proclaimed and promoted national colours, national fashion, and patriotic verses, and it was in this environment that the Croatian or Slavonic *Kolo*-dance was born. We will trace its arrival, its spread, and its coexistence with other dances at balls, and we will also examine the survival of the Waltz and *Salonsko Kolo* until the beginning of the twentieth century.[2]

The *Salonsko Kolo* slowly fell into obscurity in urban ballrooms in Croatia. However, because its original purpose was to express national

---

1   A similar version of this chapter was first published in 2016/2017, as Iva Niemčić and Ivana Katarinčić, 'Croatian Couple Dances from 19th Century till the Present Day: The Waltz and Salonsko Kolo', *Porte Akademik. Journal of Music and Dance Studies*, 14/15 (2016/2017), 147–60.
2   All translations from Croatian sources throughout this chapter were produced by Nina Vrdoljak.

identity, it was taught and danced among Croatian expatriates. Unlike the *Kolo*, the Waltz successfully resisted the ravages of time and political upheavals, penetrated all levels of society, and is still danced today. We will first discuss dance venues, in order to demonstrate how the frequency with which dance socials were organised was connected with the discovery of appropriate dance venues. We will then examine dance events in the social context of nineteenth-century Zagreb, presenting their role and influence on Zagreb social life over a period of major political turmoil.

Fig. 9.1 Video: Goran Knežević reconstructed the performance of *Slavonsko Kolo*. Veterani KUD-a Croatia — "hrvatsko salonsko kolo"', 7:50, posted online by fudoooo1, *Youtube*, 7 May 2017, https://www.youtube.com/watch?v=OA9D5Zt94HQ; and 'Goran Knežević- Hrvatsko salonsko kolo, FA Ententin, 1. FFK — Zagreb, 2003', 7:48, posted online by Goran Knežević, *Youtube*, 21 July 2013, https://www.youtube.com/watch?v=J8LOIffuy_0

Dance Venues in Zagreb

In the newspapers describing Zagreb life and customs, dances from the end of the eighteenth century were noted only in passing or were briefly mentioned. The daily newspapers of the nineteenth century, however, are a rich source of information about dance.[3] With the rise of the noble

---

3   *Narodne novine*, and its literary supplement *Danica horvatsko, slavonska, dalmatinska*, in particular, included a host of reports on the time and place of the occasion of a particular dance, along with reports in which one could read about the number of people present at the dance, the order and protocol of the dances on the programme, and even the atmosphere at the dance venues. *Narodne novine* [National newspaper] was created in Zagreb in 1835 under the title *Novine horvatske* [Croatian newspaper]; from 1836 to 1843, it was titled *Ilirske narodne novine* [Illyrian national newspaper]; while from 1843, as the Illyrian name was banned, it became *Narodne novine*. It is still published today as the *Official Gazette of the Republic of Croatia* (Antun Vujić, 'Narodne novine', in *Hrvatski leksikon*, vol. 2 (Zagreb: Naklada Leksikon, 1997), p. 160). *Danica horvatsko, slavonska, dalmatinska* was a literary paper with cultural and educational aims; it began in 1835 as a weekly supplement to *Novine horvatske*. It was a medium of linguistic standardisation and cultural and political integration. It came out in Zagreb from 1835–1849, in 1853, and from 1862–1867 (Antun Vujić, 'Danica', in *Hrvatski leksikon*, vol. 1 (Zagreb: Naklada Leksikon, 1996), p. 234).

and aristocratic families during the mid-eighteenth century, dances in Zagreb largely took place in the noble Upper Town aristocratic mansions, in the homes of the Zagreb nobility.[4] Since dance entertainments were a novelty in the social and entertainment life of Zagreb at that time, they were met by opposition, criticism and condemnation. Baltazar Adam Krčelić characterised these first dances as 'a temple of lust' and 'nest of promiscuity'.[5] Describing the 'living pictures' that were an integral part of eighteenth-century dance events, he criticised 'the debauchery and lasciviousness with which a man frolicked with the women, so that his legs were between the women's legs, with one leg between the legs of one woman, and the other between the legs of another'.[6] However, dance entertainment quickly became fashionable, and constituted the main activity in the social lives of the ruling Zagreb classes. Wanting to be 'distinguished, everyone yearned [to be] at a dance ball or in the theatre':[7]

> At the end of the eighteenth century and during the nineteenth, the Croatian lands were divided territorially[8] and under the great political and thus inevitably the social influence of Buda, Vienna, and Prague. On the other hand, young intellectuals, for their part, educated at European universities, spread the influence of the Slavic lands and their common political ideas, particularly the attainment of economic autonomy (by the abolition of the feudal order) and political autonomy (by the restoration of authority to the national institutions and support for the use of the native Croatian language) from the Habsburg Monarchy. The age of the Croatian national revival, the Illyrian movement (1830–1848), was a period of the awakening of national consciousness rejection of the foreign and promoting of the native language, customs, music, song and thus also — dance. During those years in Zagreb, the Illyrians tried to ensure

---

4   Cf. Zvonimir Milčec, *Galantni Zagreb* (Zagreb: Mladost, 1989), p. 16; Nada Premerl, 'Ples kao oblik društvenog života u prošlosti Zagreba', in *Iz starog i novog Zagreba*, vol. 5, ed. by Ivan Bach, Franjo Buntak, and Vanda Ladović (Zagreb: Muzej grada Zagreba, 1974), pp. 139–50 (p. 139); Baltazar Adam Krčelić, *Annue ili historija 1748–1767* (Zagreb: Jugoslavenska akademija znanosti i umjetnosti, 1952).
5   Baltazar Adam Krčelić, *Annue ili historija*, pp. 129–30.
6   Ibid.
7   Dragutin Hirc, 'Stari Zagreb', *Zbornik III. Programa Radio-Zagreba*, 17 (1987), 97–155.
8   At the time, Croatia was part of the Habsburg Empire and had a divided administration. The *Banate* of Croatia was under the administration of the Croatian *Sabor*, or Parliament; the Military Borderland, or *Krajina*, was under the direct authority of the Court Military Council in Vienna; while Dalmatia and Istria were administered by the Viennese Court.

that the 'national spirit' took hold in the everyday festive life of Zagreb. Even previously, the popular dance evenings and balls had been slightly changing their musical and dance content. Along with the 'European' social dances, 'national' dances were being included more frequently.[9]

Dance events and dance entertainments, in the social context of the major political turmoil of Zagreb in the nineteenth-century, had a significant influence on Zagreb's social life. During the period of Croatian national revival (1830–1848), dance halls became important places for the Illyrians to gather, and one of the forums in which they could promote their ideas. One of the main goals of the movement was the struggle to use the Croatian language in public and private life, raising national awareness and to lift the Croatian spirit. Dances became a platform for expressing patriotism and promoting national ideas. In order to express resistance to the imposition of foreign influences, dance entertainments proclaimed and promoted national colours, national fashion and patriotic verses, and it was in this atmosphere that the Croatian or Slavonic *Kolo*-dance was born. It was those Illyrians who, utilising the *Kolo* and insisting upon it as an articulation of the indigenous and the national, introduced this circle dance into the Zagreb mansions and salons.

Fig. 9.2 Dragutin Weingärtner, *Meeting of the Croatian Parliament, 1848*, 1885. Session of the Croatian Parliament of 4 July 1848, at which the parliamentary deputies sought means for the defence of their homeland and the arming of the Croatians for a war of independence. Wikimedia Commons, Public Domain, https://commons.wikimedia.org/wiki/File:Dragutin_Weing%C3%A4rtner,_Hrvatski_sabor_1848._god.jpg

---

9   Dubravka Franković, 'O muzičkom životu Hrvatske tragom oglasnika ilirske štampe', *Iz starog i novog Zagreba*, vol. 6, ed. by Franjo Buntak (Zagreb: Muzej grada Zagreba, 1984), pp. 169–78 (pp. 169–74).

Until the Illyrian movement, when social classes were brought closer together in opposition to foreign influences, the dance entertainments were largely detached — that is, held separately for the citizenry and for the nobility. The citizenry organised their own *'purger* dances'[10] that were held in taverns and cafés. From records of the payment of community tariffs for those events, we learn that several 'balls' with hundreds of visitors were held at various taverns in a single Carnival season around the year 1780. These events were held in taverns on the central Lower Town square.[11] There were several inns on the southern side of Zagreb's Harmica, where 'they ate and drank day and night, danced, sang, to the music of a bass and tweedle *gusle*, and made a lot of noise'.[12] When organising Carnival dances, 'the aristocracy in Zagreb organised its entertainment exclusively for themselves at smallish venues, while the citizenry did so at the newly-built shooting range, in a small hall without sufficient comfort'.[13] A Zagreb café proprietor, Pley,[14] stood out as an organiser of Carnival celebrations, arranging dances for the nobility and for the citizenry. In 1786, he hired the great hall of the Vojković mansion (at 9 Matoš Street)[15] for 'refined dances', and the City Council hall for entertainments for the citizenry. During that season, Pley held thirty events, which were attended by some 2,500 guests.[16]

The majority of dances were organised at Carnival time, when more freedom was permitted than was customary. Croatian lands historically belonged to the Catholic Church, and the religious calendar typically dictated the time of social gatherings that included dancing. It was customary in the villages to dance at various times of the year (apart from during Lent and Advent, when dancing took place only exceptionally and not in public), since beliefs were bound up with the

---

10 People originally from Zagreb are called *Purgeri*.
11 Igor Karaman and Ivan Kampuš, *Tisućljetni Zagreb* (Zagreb: Školska knjiga, 1994), p. 146.
12 Dragutin Hirc, 'Stari Zagreb', 138.
13 Mijo Krešić, *Autobiografija* (Zagreb: Tisak Dioničke tiskare, 1898), p. 69.
14 Unfortunately, the source does not provide the first name of this individual.
15 All the streets mentioned in this chapter are situated in the centre of Zagreb, Croatia's capital. Zagreb's streets and squares are specified so that dance venues can be traced.
16 Karaman and Kampuš, *Tisućljetni Zagreb*, p. 146. According to the official 1819 census, Zagreb had just over 9,000 residents at that time (Franjo Buntak, *Povijest Zagreba* (Zagreb: Matica hrvatska, 1996), p. 641).

performance of dances. For example, the villagers danced to influence the outcome of the harvest in order to repel evil spirits from the villages, the houses, people, the domestic animals and the like; or they danced to mark particular dates (name days, for example). Dances were regularly performed on Christmas Eve, in the season from Palm Sunday[17] to Whitsuntide,[18] and on other occasions, which would have been fairly uncommon in Zagreb.[19] The social life of the citizens of Zagreb at the end of the eighteenth century — apart from during special and/or Carnival periods[20] — took place largely within a domestic environment, amongst the circle of family and friends. The months during which the Carnival took place were fairly cold, so dancing required an indoor venue. In other words, no appropriate public venues existed at which the people of Zagreb could meet, chat and enjoy themselves in their free time.[21] At the end of the eighteenth century, steps began to be taken to solve this problem of space, since this problem afflicted not only the citizens of Zagreb, but also the theatre companies operating there between 1780–1860.[22]

When the Clarissa Convent[23] passed into city administration after the disbanding of the Order of St Clare (1782), the first public theatre

---

17 Palm Sunday is the Sunday before Easter.
18 The feast day that commemorates the descent of the Holy Ghost upon Christ's disciples, fifty days after Christ's Resurrection.
19 Ivan Ivančan, *Narodni plesni običaji u Hrvata* (Zagreb: Hrvatska matica iseljenika, Institut za etnologiju i folkloristiku, 1996), pp. 103–04.
20 There were also exceptions, and we know that some entertainment was organised in Zagreb in connection with exceptional events. For example, in September 1842, the 600th anniversary of the declaration of the Golden Bull (the name of the charter by which Zagreb became a free royal city in 1242) was celebrated for three days. The third day of the celebrations ended with a great ball in all the auditoria of the theatre (Nada Premerl, 'Društveni život u sjevernoj Hrvatskoj kao dio preporodnog nacionalnog programa', in *Hrvatski narodni preporod 1790–1848*, ed. by Nikša Stančić (Zagreb: Muzej za umjetnost i obrt, 1985), pp. 135–45 (pp. 136–37)). During the visit of Emperor Franz Joseph I in 1852, a dance was held in the Hall and the national *Slavonsko kolo* was performed (Franjo Bučar, 'O posjeti Franje Josipa I. godine 1852. u Zagrebu', *Narodna starina*, 9 (1930), 323–25 (p. 324)). These events can, in some cases, be given the significance of (political) rituals (Tvrtko Zebec, *Krčki tanci* (Zagreb-Rijeka: Adamić; Institut za etnologiju i folkloristiku, 2004), pp. 54–61).
21 Vanda Ladović, 'Oslikani ciljevi građanskog streljačkog društva', in *Iz starog i novog Zagreba*, vol. 5, ed. by Ivan Bach, Franjo Buntak, and Vanda Ladović (Zagreb: Muzej grada Zagreba, 1974), pp. 127–38 (p. 127).
22 Slavko Batušić, 'Osnova za prvo kazalište u Zagrebu', in *Iz starog i novog Zagreba*, vol. 5, ed by. Bach, Buntak, and Ladović, pp. 107–12 (p. 108).
23 In Opatička Street (today's City of Zagreb Museum).

auditorium for holding dances and other performances in Zagreb was established.[24] When Count Ante Pejačević had a large mansion built in 1796, he included a dance hall along with a stage and auditorium.[25] After Count Pejačević's death, Count Antun Amadé de Varkonyi[26] became the new owner of the theatre in 1807.[27] Count Amadé gave the theatre its name, while Maksimilijan Vrhovac, then Bishop of Zagreb (1787–1827), put up the necessary money.[28] Dance entertainments and theatre productions performed by the travelling German companies were held in that hall until the beginning of the 1830s.[29] However, the Amadé Theatre became unsuitable for the more ambitious theatre undertakings, and too small for large dances.

Using money he had won in the lottery, the Zagreb merchant Kristofor Stanković made a cash gift to Zagreb to erect the first permanent theatre building. With the building of the theatre on St Mark's Square, Zagreb received its first public dance hall, while a few years later in 1837, when the shooting gallery at Tuškanac was built, the Zagreb Marksmen Society held dances there that brought together the 'patriotic' public.[30] The Society arranged dances so that the shooting range, and the social hall situated next to it, soon became the social hub of Zagreb in that period, and it was to remain so for decades.[31]

As the middle classes became economically and politically stronger, especially with the appearance of Illyrians on Zagreb's social scene, the social life of the city became significantly more exciting. The growing middle class took over the organisation of social events, seeking newer and larger public venues where entertainments and dances could be held.

---

24 Pavao Cindrić, 'Trnovit put do samostalnosti (do 1860)', in *Enciklopedija Hrvatskoga narodnoga kazališta u Zagrebu*, ed. by Pavao Cindrić (Zagreb: Naprijed — Hrvatsko narodno kazalište u Zagrebu, 1969), pp. 13–75 (pp. 26–27).
25 Nada Premerl, 'Ples kao oblik društvenog života u prošlosti Zagreba', in *Iz starog i novog Zagreba*, vol. 5, ed. by Bach, Buntak, and Ladović (Zagreb: Muzej grada Zagreba, 1974), pp. 139–50 (p. 139).
26 Antun Amadé de Varkonyi (1757–1835), Royal Chamberlain and Great County Prefect of Zagreb.
27 At Demetrova Street.
28 Pavao Cindrić, 'Trnovit put do samostalnosti (do 1860)', p. 35.
29 Karaman and Kampuš, *Tisućljetni Zagreb*, p. 180.
30 Premerl, 'Ples kao oblik društvenog života u prošlosti Zagreba', p. 139.
31 Ladović, 'Oslikani ciljevi građanskog streljačkog društva', pp. 127–28.

In 1846, the Illyrians bought a building called the Mansion,[32] and converted it into the National Hall. Meetings were held and dances arranged in the main hall. Various revivalist and cultural activities, as well as other social events, were held at the National Hall, so that it soon became the focal point of the cultural, entertainment and political life of Zagreb.[33]

The Hungarian Society then bought the Amadé Theatre (mentioned above) in 1845, as a counter-balance to the Illyrian National Hall. It was renamed the Casino, and dance evenings were held there regularly. The Casino and the shooting range became rivals of sorts in organising larger and more attractive dance evenings, particularly during the time of the Croatian national revival.

The Zagreb public had an awareness of Illyrian ideology, and the efforts of the Illyrians to promote the nation — in their language, mode of attire and national colours. However, at that time, Zagreb society was still inclined towards the traditional, foreign, largely Viennese fashion and the Viennese school, even in certain minor aspects of manners that were not in keeping with the national spirit, but were commonplace and thus widely accepted. Nonetheless, resistance and even hostility to what was Hungarian and Austrian was clearly manifested in Zagreb. The shooting range and the Casino, as representatives of national convictions on the one hand, and a pro-Hungarian stance on the other, were at the forefront in expressing mutual hostility and competitiveness in preparing and organising dances.

The Croatian National Revival and Dance Balls in the Nineteenth Century

The appearance of social dance in Europe was linked to the growth of the larger European cities, and conditioned by the development of trade and crafts. Social and/or city dances made their way to Zagreb

---

32 The Mansion had been built a few years previously in 1838 at 18 Opatička Street (now the Institute of the Croatian Academy of Sciences and Art) by the architect Bartol Felbinger, who was the most important native architect in the first half of the nineteenth century and leading representative of Classicist architecture in Zagreb and continental Croatia.

33 Karaman and Kampuš, *Tisućljetni Zagreb*, p. 182.

from these European cities, leaving their first known traces during the eighteenth century. During the nineteenth century, these dances further changed in form and significance. Popular social dances, like the Minuet and the Cotillion, because of their numerous complex forms and steps, gave way to simpler and merrier dances in the nineteenth century. The Waltz, the Polka, the Galop, the Quadrille and the Mazurka were danced at social balls. In the nineteenth century, and during the Illyrian movement, couple dances that originated from folk dances (indigenous peasant dances) intertwined with foreign couple dances that arrived in Zagreb dance halls.

The Waltz was the most dominant and most interesting nineteenth-century dance. It was performed as a social, national and stage dance and it can be found in all the dance programmes preserved at Zagreb City Museum.[34]

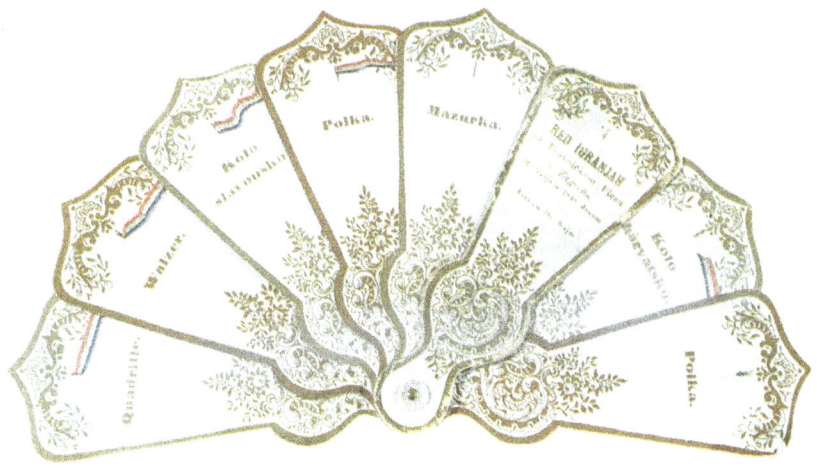

Fig. 9.3 Dance programs preserved at the Museum of the City of Zagreb, with permission from the Zagreb City Museum.

---

34 The Zagreb City Museum is now home to more than two hundred different examples of the dance programmes. The oldest example is from a lawyers' ball and dates from 1838. The last is a dance programme with a list of dances from the journalists' ball from 1935 (Premerl, 'Ples kao oblik društvenog života u prošlosti Zagreba', p. 141).

Although it was the most popular dance, the Waltz was constantly subject to criticism since, apart from the overly bold (for the time) physical closeness of the dance partners, its non-Slavic origins were held against it.[35] Particularly during the Illyrian period, the Viennese Waltz carried significant German associations, and therefore there was a certain degree of hostility directed towards it.[36] As a result of the 'fervent struggle against the seductive Viennese Waltz, which our ladies defended with persistent pleas and melancholic sighs', a resourceful Count Jurica Oršić ordered Croatian melodies to be performed in 3/4 time, and thus 'patriotism was satisfied, and the Waltz was still played'.[37]

An article published in 1840 in the newspaper *Danica*, by an unknown author, describes the Carnival in Zagreb. He notes that there are 'all-new Waltzes and *Kalops*, this year composed in unusually large numbers by native composers, full of folk Illyrian tunes, and accepted with excitement by our folk'.[38] In an article entitled 'Letošnje poklade u Zagrebu' ['This Year's Carnival in Zagreb'], Ljudevit Vukotinović wrote that there were entertainments at the Casino and certain private houses, although he himself did not attend these, since he did not want to visit places 'where patriotism disappears'.[39] At the same time, he gave prominence to the role of the Zagreb Marksmen Society, whose balls were 'the most important; they had a clear significance to everyone: that this ball was being held in Zagreb, in a land where the Slavs live'.[40] He emphasised that the folk circle dance *Narodno Kolo*, which slowly became a part of the Zagreb dance repertoire, 'was performed every time and, apart from that, the hall was decked out in national colours, the notices were in the national language everywhere, various national

---

35 On the pervasive popularity of the Waltz, as well as the Waltz crossing the boundaries of acceptable behaviour, see Mark Knowles, *The Wicked Waltz and Other Scandalous Dances: Outrage at Couple Dancing in the 19th and Early 20th Centuries* (Jefferson, NC: McFarland & Co., 2009).

36 Antonija Kassowitz-Cvijić, 'Nekoć na svečanom balu', *Jutarnji list* (20 February 1927), pp. 19–22.

37 Premerl, 'Ples kao oblik društvenog života u prošlosti Zagreba', p. 140.

38 'Prošaste poklade kod nas u Zagrebu' [n.a.], *Danica Ilirska*, 11 (14 March 1840), 43–44.

39 Ljudevit Vukotinović, 'Letošnje poklade u Zagrebu', *Danica Ilirska*, 9 (11 March 1843), 39–40.

40 Ibid., 40.

melodies were played, and the ladies and girls, the men and the youths, competed in speaking in the national language only'.[41]

Since the structure of the circle dance — which connected the dancers and thus incorporated individuals into a community — perfectly suited the patriotic ideology of the Illyrians concerning the unity of Slavic peoples, *Narodno Kolo* became the dance symbol of the unity of South-Slav peoples.[42] *Narodno Kolo*, which later became known as *Salonsko Kolo* (Fig. 9.1), emphasised the cultural identity of the Croatians in opposition to the other popular social dances of the nineteenth century, such as the Waltz and the Polka.[43] Thus, certain dance figures performed by peasants during village festivities — along with some of the steps from the folk circle dance — slowly entered Zagreb ballrooms as a part of the dance repertoire at the Illyrian masked balls.[44] Still, it is highly unlikely that middle-class society would have accepted *Narodno Kolo* in its original choreographic and musical form. It is no wonder, therefore, that the choreographed round dance appeared.[45] In this way, *Kolo* cannot be called a folk dance *per se*, but a salon dance with figures partly based on Slavonian folk dance.[46] Although *Kolo* was accepted with joy and open arms, few could dance it. *Narodno Kolo* was performed at a ball in Zagreb in 1840 by an unknown society 'wearing folk costumes who were led into the ballroom by the pipers'.[47]

This marks the beginning of the merging of couple dances based on folk dances with foreign couple dances, and their coexistence up until the present day at rural parties and urban balls.

A short article by Vukotinović, issued in *Danica* during Carnival on 27 January 1842, mentions a ball entitled 'folk evening ball', held in Zagreb.[48] In this article, Vukotinović criticises the title 'folk evening ball',

---

41 Ibid., 40.
42 Stjepan Sremac, 'Ples u suvremenim pokladnim običajima u Hrvatskoj', *Narodna umjetnost*, 25 (1988), 143.
43 Elsie Ivancich Dunin, '"Salonsko kolo" as Cultural Identity in a Chilean Yugoslav Community (1917–1986)', *Narodna umjetnost*, 2 (1988), 109–22.
44 Dubravka Franković, 'Uloga ilirske štampe u muzičkom životu Hrvatske od 1835. do 1849., II dio: od 1840. do 1843. godine', *Arti musices*, 8.1 (1977), 5–54; 'Prošaste poklade kod nas u Zagrebu', 43.
45 Stjepan Sremac, 'Ples u suvremenim pokladnim običajima u Hrvatskoj', 143.
46 Dunin, '"Salonsko kolo"', 110.
47 'Prošaste poklade kod nas u Zagrebu', 43–44.
48 Ljudevit Vukotinović, 'Salon u Zagrebu', *Danica Ilirska*, 6 (5 February 1842), 23.

and wonders what the term 'folk' means in this context.[49] He suggests that folk refers to a set of rules among people, including particular customs, folk costumes and language. However, at this 'European ball, the costumes are European, and the customs are too, which we are all familiar with under the term *etiquette*'.[50] Still, Kolo attracted the most attention, since, according to Vukotinović, it was being introduced into the salon for the first time.

We will briefly outline the different terms used across time for the *Kolo*. It can give some perspective about its moving through different classes. There is not much information given about the choreographer .of the *Kolo* — a young army officer named Marko Bogunović. He called it *Slavonsko Kolo*. However, since young Illyrians wanted the Croatian circle dance, he also choreographed *Hrvatsko Kolo*. The music for both *Slavonsko* and *Hrvatsko Kolo* was composed by Vatroslav Lisinski.[51] *Dvoransko Kolo* became a general term for *Narodno*, *Hrvatsko* and *Slavonsko Kolo* (Fig. 9.1). Later, *Salonsko Kolo* was also often used, or just *Kolo*, which remained on the dance repertoire in Croatian cities until the Second World War.[52] According to Višnja Hrbud-Popović, by using the term *Dvoransko Kolo*, Franjo Kuhač 'precisely indicated its specific character in accordance with the established rules for that kind of dance' and emphasised the difference between the performance of *Narodno Kolo* and its interpretation for balls in middle-class and aristocratic circles.[53] Kuhač describes *Narodno Kolo* as 'finer than folk, but still such that folk people could recognise characteristics in that elegant circle dance, which they could perform in their simple circle dance'.[54] If we look at the very structure of *Kolo*, it can be seen that it is a couple dance in which different

---

49 In 'O folklorizmu', Maja Bošković-Stulli observes that Vukotinović noticed the relevant characteristics of folklore at the Illyrian folk balls (Maja Bošković-Stulli, 'O folklorizmu', ZNŽO, 45 (1971), 165–86).
50 Vukotinović, 'Salon u Zagrebu', 23.
51 Vatroslav Lisinki (1819–1854) was the first Croatian professional musician, who also laid the groundwork for the national movement in Croatia, especially opera, solos, orchestral performances, and choral music.
52 Franjo Kuhač, *Vatroslav Lisinski i njegovo doba: Prilog za poviest hrvatskoga preporoda* (Zagreb: Matica hrvatska, 1904), p. 30; Sremac, 'Ples u suvremenim pokladnim običajima u Hrvatskoj', 144.
53 Višnja Hrbud-Popović, 'Kolo hervatsko: Das kroatische Kolo kao društveni ples prema opisu iz 1848', *Narodna umjetnost*, 27 (1990), 199.
54 Franjo Kuhač, 'Ples i plesovna glazba', *Prosvjeta, List za zabavu znanost i umjetnost*, 1 (1893), 5–7.

dance figures are performed. The number of dance figures and couples differ depending on the source; generally, there are seven dance figures for *Slavonsko Kolo*, and six for *Hrvatsko Kolo*.[55]

In addition to *Narodno Kolo*, there was also the Cotillion, the Quadrille and the Polka, which were danced once or twice at every ball. However, at Carnival in 1843, the Waltz was the most popular. As a great patriot, Vukotinović was surprised and found the answer in the simplicity of the Waltz:

> …it does not cause many worries and requires just a little bit of attention. When a man holds his partner tight and starts turning recklessly, just as they turn once, they can turn ten times or a hundred times…[56]

This is probably the first description of the Waltz in Croatia.

The memoirs of Dragutin Rakovac, a Croatian writer, translator and journalist, record an interesting letter sent to Dragutin from his friend Stjepan Pejaković,[57] who mentions a Slavic ball in Vienna at Carnival on 4 February 1844. Pejaković reports that, since he had been unable to bring Illyrian musicians with him, it was questionable how the *Kolo* could be performed. However, an otherwise unknown individual named Mr. Brlić saved the day; he had danced the *Kolo* in Zagreb and knew the necessary figures. He taught eight Illyrian boys and eight Slavic girls how to dance the *Kolo*, and selected accompanying music from folk songs for the orchestra to play. The *Kolo* was performed by eight couples twice that evening, though it was announced only once on the repertoire, next to the all-pervasive Polka and Waltz. There were more than four hundred guests at the ball, and, when the *Kolo* was played, only eight newly-taught couples danced, whereas the other dances were performed by roughly one hundred couples.[58]

Dance balls were a crucial element of any party. In order for them to develop and function effectively, professional dance teachers and dance schools became necessary. A dance teacher, Alojzije Deperis, arrived from Trieste with the intention of teaching 'both indigenous and foreign

---

55 Compare Višnja Hrbud-Popović, 'Kolo hervatsko', 199–209.
56 Ljudevit Vukotinović, 'Letošnje poklade u Zagrebu', *Danica Ilirska*, 9 (11 March 1843), 36.
57 Stjepan Pejaković (1818–1904) was a well-known Croatian publicist and politician.
58 Emil Laszowski and Velimir Deželić, 'Dnevnik Dragutina Rakovca', *Narodna starina*, 3 (1922), 302–03.

dances'.[59] Albert Dragoner, a 'Horvat Varaždinec'[60] [a Croatian from Varaždin], became known as a result of his advertisement, in which he emphasised his sound knowledge of all European and national dances.[61]

Pietro Coronelli, an Italian ballet master, was the first permanent dance teacher to come to Zagreb. He arrived in 1859, at the invitation of Baron Ambroz Vranyczany, to undertake the teaching of his daughter, Klotilda. Coronelli soon expanded his activities, and, as well as his work in the theatre, he gave lessons to the public both in group courses and privately. Coronelli's advertisement for the teaching of dance came out in *Pozor* in 1860. He played an active part in the teaching and affirmation of social dances right up until his death in 1902, when his daughter Elvira continued to teach dance with the help of her sister Bianca.[62]

It can reasonably be assumed that the dance teachers who arrived in Zagreb from European cities were the main, decisive factor in the dissemination of the European dances, which became fully adopted in Zagreb.[63]

In February 1847, a gala ball was held to celebrate the opening of the Zagreb ballroom at *Narodni dom*, where the dancing of the *Kolo* 'was followed by the usual European dances'.[64] An anonymous author writing in *Danica* argues that, to compensate for the fact that the balls cannot be limited to native dances, it would be favourable to have 'native folk music for the European dances'.[65] While there are many articles written in *Danica* about music for Waltzes and Polkas by native

---

59 Stjepan Sremac, 'Folklorni ples u Hrvata od "izvora" do pozornice' (unpublished doctoral thesis, University in Zagreb, Faculty of Humanities and Social Sciences, Zagreb Institute of Ethnology and Folklore Research, 2001), p. 45.
60 Varaždin is a city not far from Zagreb.
61 *Narodne novine* [n.a.], 71 (1847).
62 Sremac, 'Ples u suvremenim pokladnim običajima u Hrvatskoj', 144–45.
63 The dissemination and popularity of the *Kolo*-dance was also boosted by the booklet in pocket-book format, written by an unknown author, which was sold under the dual-language title *Kolo hervatsko-Das kroatische Kolo* (*Narodne novine* [n.a.], 12 (1848)). The booklet was probably the first in a series of several descriptions of the *Kolo*-dance that were published. Kuhač utilised this booklet in compiling his description of the *Courtiers Kolo*, which he published in a paper that came out in *Vienac* in 1872 (Franjo Kuhač-Koch, 'Dvoransko kolo', *Vienac*, 4 (1872), pp. 58–61; 7 (1872), pp. 106–07; 8 (1872), pp. 123–24; 9 (1872), pp. 138–40; 10 (1872), pp. 154–55; 11 (1872), pp. 170–72).
64 'Svečano otvorenje dvorane zagrebačke u narodnom domu' [n.a.], *Danica Ilirska*, 7 (13 February 1847), 51–52.
65 Ibid.

composers, giving a patriotic flavour to popular European dances, we have concluded it was more likely that at the balls those dances were performed with the original music by foreign composers. At the end of the author's discussion of dance, the article makes a remark that suggests the merging of urban and rural dances took people by surprise: 'who could imagine several years ago, that our *Kolo* would be introduced to elegant balls!'[66] The next article was written by Bogdan Kuretić, and it concerned the Slavic ball held in Vienna, also in February 1847, which hosted Czechs, Croatians, French, Germans, Russians, and very few Poles. Here, Kuretić suggested that *Kolo* and the accompanying music should adapt more to the balls by becoming more 'European' and less distinctively Slavic, so that, like the Polka, they could grow in popularity across Europe.[67]

The Zagreb City Museum's collection of dance programmes contains a fan from the lawyers' ball, which took place on 12 February 1848. The fan has eight wings and each wing has one dance written on each side. As an anonymous author describes in an article in *Danica* in 1848, 'The beautiful fans (*fächer*) for ladies were elegantly embroidered with names of dances on each side, containing the list of dances before and after midnight'.[68] Thus, on the aforementioned fan from the Zagreb City Museum's collection, we can observe the dance repertoire of the lawyers' ball: *Horvatsko Kolo*, the Polka, the Quadrille, *Walzer*, *Kolo Slavonsko*, the Polka, the Mazurka.[69] The anonymous author in *Danica* reports that the prominent place in the repertoire was reserved for 'folk dances', and there were four of them — '*Kolo Horvatsko*, *Kolo Slavonsko*, the Polka and the Mazurka' — which collectively 'express in the clearest way the importance of folk for those who call those dances the native ones'.[70]

In turn, in Zagreb, the Polka, the Waltz and the Quadrille are contrasted with three folk dances performed — *Kolo Horvatsko*, *Kolo Slavonsko* and the Mazurka, all connected by a common Slavic element.

---

66 Ibid.
67 Bogdan Kuretić, 'Dopis o slavjanskome balu u Beču', *Danica Ilirska*, 9 (27 February 1847), 36.
68 'Pravnički bal' [n.a.], *Danica Ilirska*, 8 (19 February 1848), 32.
69 Premerl, 'Ples kao oblik društvenog života u prošlosti Zagreba', 143.
70 'Pravnički bal', 32.

Seen as one, these three dances are like a piece of art by a famous artist. *Slavonsko Kolo* brings the *allegro*, *Horvatsko Kolo* brings the *adagio*, and the Mazurka brings a brilliant, concluding *vivace*.[71]

As reported in another article in *Danica*, a ball took place at the beginning of March 1848, and more than 1,200 guests attended.[72] Apart from the citizens of Zagreb, there were also guests from Varaždin, Križevci, Jastrebarsko, Koprivnica, and Petrinja. The ball was very joyful, and lasted till the morning light. Clergy, soldiers, and nobility all enjoyed it equally. The article reports that 'the ball started as usual, with *Kolo Horvatsko* which alternated several times with *Kolo Slavonsko*'.[73] While other dances are not mentioned in the article by their name, it is clear from this reference that *Horvatsko* and *Slavonsko Kolo* were performed alternately several times at the most visited ball that year. *Kolo Horvatsko* and *Kolo Slavonsko* became fixtures at many balls in Zagreb and across Croatia, but also, for example, in Vienna at Slavic balls, where such dances, as a social couple dance, had equal status to that of the Waltz, Polka and Mazurka.

The frequency of dance socials was primarily linked to long-term efforts to seek out appropriate dance venues. As we have outlined in this chapter, while dancing took place initially in taverns, inns, private houses and the mansions of the Zagreb aristocracy, the efforts to build a theatre and other premises for holding dances eventually culminated in the foundation of various institutions, which undertook the organisation and arrangement of dances at their premises and solved the problem of where to dance.

An essential change that took place during the time of the National Revival was the increasingly close connection between all the Zagreb classes at dances. Groups of people from diverse social and economic backgrounds were linked in the struggle for attainment of national awareness. This period also marks the beginning of the merging of couple dances based on folk dances with foreign couple dances, and their coexistence, till the present day, at rural parties and urban balls.

---

71   Ibid.
72   'Gradjanski bal', [n.a.], *Danica Ilirska*, 11 (11 March 1848), 48.
73   Ibid.

Epilogue: Further Reverberations and Comparisons

Kuhač provides some interesting, contemporary contemplations on dance at the end of the nineteenth century, though his initial intention was not to conduct research into dance, but rather, to write about music.[74] He discusses the breakthrough of urban couple dances into the tradition, connecting this breakthrough with the beginning of the emancipation of women.

> In modern Waltzes and Polkas, each part has two motifs — not just two different melodious motifs but also two different rhythmical motifs. One is for the male dancer, the other is for the female dancer. This new structure perfectly matches the present spirit of the times in which every woman seeks emancipation and wants to think with her own brain, speak her own mind and act independently. In the past, women willingly agreed with their husbands, and gladly confirmed what their husbands said [...] It is different with our *Kolo*, which doesn't represent the conversation between two persons, but the conversation of the whole society. [...] If someone in that society says something clever, it is repeated by men and women, the young and the old. A composer has to see all that and bear it in his mind.[75]

In about 1910, the Waltz was still the most prevalent dance at balls. At an average European ball, every fifth dance would be reserved for Polka, Quadrille or Mazurka, and the rest were Waltzes.[76] In her paper on masked balls in Zagreb at the beginning of the twentieth century, Aleksandra Muraj points out that simpler couple dances like the Waltz, the Polka and the Mazurka dominated, but the Croatian circle dances were performed as well.[77]

It is worth returning briefly to *Horvatsko* and *Slavonsko Kolo* (Fig. 9.1). After publishing a detailed choreographic description of the ballroom *Slavonsko Kolo* in *Vienac* in 1872, which undoubtedly encouraged the spreading and preservation of *Kolo*, Kuhač stopped dealing with it altogether. The terms *Horvatsko Kolo* and *Slavonsko Kolo* do not appear

---

74   'I didn't see all the dances, I noted down music only for some of them, but the ones I saw, I described them as much as I could, being an amateur in that field' (Kuhač, 'Ples i plesovna glazba', 35).
75   Kuhač, 'Ples i plesovna glazba', 108.
76   Sremac, 'Ples u suvremenim pokladnim običajima u Hrvatskoj', 147.
77   Aleksandra Muraj, 'Poklade u Zagrebu (1900–1918.)', *Narodna umjetnost*, 41.2 (2004), 205–34 (p. 212).

in any subsequent articles. At the end of the nineteenth century, we do, however, encounter the term *Hrvatsko Salonsko Kolo*, which survived until World War Two. It was described by Pietro Ortolani (1936)[78] after watching the performance in Dubrovnik on St. Vlaho's Day. In his description, we learn that *Kolo* was rarely performed, and gradually started sinking into oblivion. According to all the available information, Stjepan Sremac concludes that, after the Illyrian movement, *Horvatsko Kolo* was completely forgotten, whereas *Slavonsko Kolo* changed its name into *Hrvatsko Salonsko Kolo* and gradually lost its national symbolism. It nonetheless continued to live at balls until World War Two, during which it too disappeared.[79] Unlike *Kolo*, the ever-popular and charming Waltz successfully resisted the ravages of time and all political upheavals, penetrating all social layers, and is still danced today.

The two *Kolos* from urban ballrooms were unable survive in their newly choreographed form, and slowly fell into obscurity in Croatia. They did not even manage to spread beyond the city limits and penetrate the rural tradition. However, because of their original purpose — to express national identity — they were successfully taught and danced in Chile among Croatian expatriates there. For example, in 1917, in Antofagasta, the Gjuro Roić taught his fellow Croatians how to dance during a period in which it was important to express Croatian/Slavic identity, in contrast to Austrian identity. The same was true in 1941, during the Nazi invasion. Apart from 1917 and 1941, *Salonsko Kolo* was not danced in Chile until the 1950s, when Roić taught the second and third generation of the Croatian expatriates. It became particularly prominent during periods in which there was political turmoil in their ancestors' homeland.[80]

Andriy Nahachewsky, writing about the concept of the 'second existence' of folk dance, mentions as an example *Salonsko Kolo* and Croatian expatriates in Chile.[81] Nahachewsky outlines how the 'first

---

78 The Ortolani unpublished typewrittcn manuscript is located at the Institute of Ethnology and Folklore Research in Zagreb, Croatia.
79 Sremac, 'Folklorni ples u Hrvata od "izvora" do pozornice', p. 49.
80 See Dunin, '"Salonsko kolo"', 122.
81 Andriy Nahachewsky, 'Once Again: On the Concept of "Second Existence" Folk Dance', in *Dans Müsik Kültür, ICTM 20th Ethnochoreology Symposium Proceedings 1998*, ed. by Frank Hall and Irene Loutzaki (Istanbul: International Council for Traditional Music Study Group on Ethnochoreology and Boğaziçi University Folklore Club, 2000), pp. 125–43 (pp. 137–40).

existence' of *Salonsko Kolo* has its roots in Slavonian folk dances and salon Quadrilles. Then, as the 'second existence', there is Bogunović's choreography of *Salonsko Kolo*, as described in detail by Kuhač. Finally, during political turmoil in Croatia (in 1917 and 1941), Roić teaches the Croatian expatriates in Chile that same *Salonsko Kolo*. In that period in Croatia, *Salonsko Kolo* began to be danced less and less frequently. So, *Salonsko Kolo*, in all the above-mentioned examples, promoted predominantly a national character, which was consciously accentuated in every performance. In the 1980s, in dance performances of the *Kolo* among emigrants of Croatian descent in Antofagasta entitled *Davi Ćiro*, Nahachewsky observes the return of *Salonsko Kolo* to its 'first existence' among the Croatian expatriates. He argues that the context of the performances of *Davi Ćiro* mirror the context of the 'first existence' of *Salonsko Kolo*, because dancers are no longer interested solely in the authenticity and originality of the dance, but have incorporated it into their everyday social life. According to Ivancich Dunin, *Davi Ćiro* had never been performed spontaneously as a part of social dance life, but the choreography was learnt and meant to be performed exclusively on stage.[82] Despite the fact that at that time dancers in South America were probably not concerned about the authenticity and originality of the choreography, since it was performed exclusively on stage, it is difficult to discuss its so-called 'first existence'. During the Homeland War,[83] *Salonsko Kolo* again became the symbol of national identity among expatriates, and was performed with this express purpose. In this way, as Nahacheswky asserts, *Salonsko Kolo* again enters into a 'second existence'.[84]

Nancy Lee Chalfa Ruyter describes how Dick Crum[85] learnt one version of the choreography for *Dvoransko Kolo* from Coronelli's daughter in the 1950s, and used Kuhač's notes to reconstruct the choreography and put it on stage at the University of California in 1984. It was performed

---

82 From personal communication with Elsie Ivancich Dunin.
83 The Homeland War or the Croatian War of Independence was fought from 1991 to 1995.
84 In 1999 in Zagreb, according to Coronelli's interpretation and Kuhač's music, "Dr. Ivan Ivančan", Zagreb folklore company, introduces the Croatian *Salonsko Kolo* into their repertoire (Sremac, 'Folklorni ples u Hrvata od "izvora" do pozornice', p. 49).
85 An American choreographer, researcher and dancer who rendered the traditional dances of the Balkans popular in America.

by his students and the members of the International Folklore Society. Ruyter illustrates how the tradition of the Croatian *Dvoransko Kolo* was transferred from its homeland across to American soil, and outlines its independent development and life among the Croatian diaspora and lovers of Balkan dance.[86]

Salonsko Kolo (Fig. 9.1) can be compared to the Czechs' national dance, *Česká Beseda* in terms of its historical development. Despite the fact that the Polka is considered the Czechs' national dance, *Česká Beseda* was first introduced to the society and danced in 1862. The term *Česká Beseda* was the common label of urban gatherings of Czech nationalistic circles in the nineteenth century, parallel with the Illyran movement in Croatia. Despite being composed of figures from folk dance, it belongs to an urban ballroom dance context. From the very beginning, it was learned and performed at balls in cities. The choreography for *Česká Beseda* remains in practice until the present day, unlike *Salonsko Kolo*. The sheer size of its national character can be observed in the fact that communities of the Czech minority (people of Czech origin living in Croatia or elsewhere) across Croatia are gathered in societies called *Česká Beseda*. In turn, Czech minorities, in their communities across the globe, learn and perform *Česká Beseda*. In doing so, they affirm their national identity. [87] In the 1850s, the Hungarians also choreographed their national dance, which is called Palotás. It is a couple dance with six figures based on folk dance. Nowadays it is performed only on stage.[88]

It is worth to notice that the Croatian *Salonsko Kolo* was created in 1842, twenty years before a similar Czech choreography, and fifteen years before the Hungarian version of their choreographed national dance. Comparative analysis of those dances will be left to future research.

Unlike the choreographed national dances (such as *Salonsko Kolo*), the Waltz and Polka, which have their roots in folk dance and which were also adapted to city ballrooms, returned successfully to their national tradition in their new form, not merely reverting to the form in which

---

86 Nancy Lee Chalfa Ruyter, '*Dvoransko kolo*: From the 1940s to the Twentieth Century', in *Balkan Dance. Essays on Characteristics, Performance and Teaching*, ed. by Anthony Shay (Jefferson, NC: McFarland & Co., 2008), pp. 239–49.
87 We thank Daniela Stavélova for the information about *Ceská Beseda*.
88 We thank László Felföldi for this information.

they originated. They live successfully in the context of ballroom dances at balls. In other words, they have returned to their 'first existence'.

***

The Waltz and Polka are dances that successfully resisted the passage of time, surviving all repertoire and structural changes in the development of ballroom dancing in the nineteenth and twentieth centuries. They concurrently belonged to both urban and rural dance repertoire. Sremac suggests that they owe such popularity and resistance to the structure of their dance elements, which are firmly rooted in the Croatian dance tradition and practice. For example, Polka steps can be found in many Croatian dances, whereas the Waltz continued Mazurka tradition and the tradition of other simple triple-metre dances. The simplicity and choice of the appropriate accompanying music have greatly facilitated the learning and spreading of the Waltz and Polka.[89] Therefore, the Waltz and Polka cannot be explained in simple terms even in Croatia. We cannot pinpoint the exact time when they began to be danced at certain locations, but we can say when they began to be danced as the Waltz and Polka. Already in the first half of the twentieth century the Waltz and Polka were put on trial in the rural tradition, at least for stage performances organised by *Seljačka Sloga* [Peasant Harmony], a society who organised different performances and folklore festivals. In this period, *Seljačka Sloga* was thus responsible for the definition of folk culture, the authority of knowledge concerning this culture, and the presentation of this culture beyond the local community. Since *Sloga*'s perception of folk culture was based on traditional, domestic, and rural[90] practices, the performances of the native dance repertoire were dependent on this perception. Likewise, the principle of performing exclusively Croatian and rural dance was strictly obeyed; at festivals, the performance of foreign and middle-class dances like Polka, the Waltz, *Csárdás* and so on, was forbidden. Despite large, important, strictly regulated festivals obeying these rules, certain groups at less important

---

89 Sremac, 'Ples u suvremenim pokladnim običajima u Hrvatskoj', 152.
90 Naila Ceribašić, *Hrvatsko, seljačko, starinsko i domaće: Povijest i etnografija javne prakse narodne glazbe u Hrvatskoj* (Zagreb: Institut za etnologiju i folkloristiku, 2003), p. 75.

festivals managed to introduce a part of foreign local practice by dancing Polka and the Hungarian *Csárdás*.[91]

Thus, popular social dances of the nineteenth century, despite various prohibitions and criticism, continue to be danced in cities and villages until the present day. In the twentieth century, while the Waltz was replaced by many new, modern dances, it is still taught in different ballroom dance schools across Europe, and is still danced on formal occasions, mostly by senior couples. It also endured in rural areas, which had accepted the Waltz only when it reached peak popularity elsewhere, and, today, it is danced in these areas as a folk dance.[92]

If you ask someone in Croatia today if they know what the Waltz and Polka are, they will definitely give an affirmative answer. They might not know the exact execution of the steps, but when they hear the first strokes of music, the body moves by itself and either dances the Waltz or Polka, with only a few mistakes. Today in Croatia, Polka is much more widespread than the Waltz in folk tradition, and the Waltz is still considered an elegant dance. The Waltz today has pride of place at almost every Croatian wedding, as the opening dance of newlyweds, taking them into their new life together.[93] The Waltz and Polka are danced across generations, as parts of the repertoire at parties both for the middle-aged and elderly, or at mixed parties, like weddings.

Fig. 9.4 Video: A Waltz performed at the Birthday ball at Dani grada Karlovca [Karlovac City Days], starting at time code 8:25. 'Dani grada Karlovca 2012 (07–3): Rođendanski bal — valcer', 13:24, posted online by MaPisKA047, *Youtube*, 13 August 2012, https://www.youtube.com/watch?v=-wH873n5EU4

First attempts to dance the Waltz also feature at graduation balls. It is interesting to note that, at graduation balls in the Czech Republic, high-school graduates sometimes dance other dances apart from the Waltz, e.g. disco dances, and also perform *Ceška Beseda* which they practice

---

91 Ibid., p. 144.
92 Desmond F. Strobel, 'Waltz', in *International Encyclopedia of Dance*, vol. 6, ed. by Selma Jeanne Cohen (New York: Oxford University Press, 1998), pp. 359–62.
93 Zorica Vitez, *Hrvatski svadbeni običaji* (Zagreb: Golden marketing, 2003), p. 191.

9. The Salonsko Kolo as a Patriotic Response to the Waltz

specifically for that occasion. In contrast, at Croatian graduation balls, young people never perform *Salonsko Kolo*.

On New Year's Day in 2005, inspired by the traditional New Year's Eve concert in Vienna, the second New Year's Eve concert at Croatian National Theatre (HNK) took place. It was entitled *Valceri, polke i druge špelancije* [Waltzes, Polkas and Other Adventures] and conducted by Siniša Leopold. As the title of the concert indicates, popular ballroom dances like the Waltz and Polka came to a prominent position, followed by interpreted Croatian folk dances, marches, some classical evergreens and similar items. The concert featured performances from Croatian Radiotelevision Symphony Orchestra, visiting soloists and ballet dancers from HNK, folk dancers from *LADO* ensemble, and modern and ballroom dancers. Due to the popularity of the concert (tickets sold out, and it was watched by a huge number of people live on TV), it continued to be held on every New Year's Day, with the intention to become traditional as well. Once again, we are able to watch ballroom couple dances at social and cultural gatherings — specifically, Waltzes, Polkas, and traditional couple dances.

Fig. 9.5 Video: *Valceri, Polke i druge špelancije* [Waltzes, Polkas and Other Adventures], 2016. New Year's Concert by HRT Tamburitza Orchestra. Waltz at timecode 1:15; Polka at 7:00 and 1:07:18. 'Valceri, Polke i druge špelancije 2016', 1:18:08, posted online by Hrvatska radiotelevizija, *Youtube*, 7 July 2017, https://www.youtube.com/watch?v=pnhihJ7Lab0

Mirko Ramovš, who writes about the Waltz in Slovenia, asks a popular question: What is it about the Waltz that enabled it to become, and remain, one of the favourite dances of different social groups and generations?[94] Before and after the arrival of the Waltz, different dances were performed, and many of them are not danced anymore, or have been completely forgotten, but the Waltz is still alive. It did not lose its initial charm, nor did its structure change. Ramovš sees its longevity as a result of its accompanying music, and specifically its 3/4 time signature, which produces joy, pleasure and positive energy among dancers and

---

94 Mirko Ramovš, 'Valček kot slovenski ljudski ples', *Traditiones*, 32.2 (2003), 33–49 (p. 47).

audience alike. Moreover, in order to dance the Waltz, it is not necessary to have exceptional dance skills. It is possible to learn it quickly because it doesn't have figures, which require hours to be learnt. It is also possible to simplify the step further, without losing its characteristic wave-like movement. At first, the close embrace of dancers was the cause of much criticism and lack of acceptance, but, later, the very same embrace was likely the cause of its spreading and popularity until the present day.

The example of almost every Croatian wedding shows that couple dances are still very popular, and suggests that we will likely see the Waltz ceaselessly turning on the dance floor, resisting influxes of newly fashionable dances and continuing through social turmoil.

Bibliography

Batušić, Slavko, 'Osnova za prvo kazalište u Zagrebu', in *Iz starog I novog Zagreba*, vol. 5, ed. by Ivan Bach, Franjo Buntak, and Vanda Ladović (Zagreb: Muzej grada Zagreba, 1974), pp. 107–12.

Bošković-Stulli, Maja, 'O folklorizmu', *ZNŽO*, 45 (1971), 165–86.

Bučar, Franjo, 'O posjeti Franje Josipa I. godine 1852. u Zagrebu', *Narodna starina*, 9 (1930), 323–25.

Buntak, Franjo, *Povijest Zagreba* (Zagreb: Matica hrvatska, 1996).

Ceribašić, Naila, *Hrvatsko, seljačko, starinsko i domaće: Povijest i etnografija javne prakse narodne glazbe u Hrvatskoj* (Zagreb: Institut za etnologiju i folkloristiku, 2003).

Cindrić, Pavao, 'Trnovit put do samostalnosti (do 1860)', in *Enciklopedija Hrvatskoga narodnoga kazališta u Zagrebu*, ed. by Pavao Cindrić (Zagreb: Naprijed — Hrvatsko narodno kazalište u Zagrebu, 1969), pp. 13–75.

Dunin, Elsie Ivancich, '"Salonsko kolo" as Cultural Identity in a Chilean Yugoslav Community (1917–1986)', *Narodna umjetnost*, 2 (1988), 109–22.

Franković, Dubravka, 'O muzičkom životu Hrvatske tragom oglasnika ilirske štampe', *Iz starog i novog Zagreba*, vol. 6, ed. by Franjo Buntak (Zagreb: Muzej grada Zagreba, 1984), pp. 169–78.

——, 'Uloga ilirske štampe u muzičkom životu Hrvatske od 1835. do 1849., II dio: od 1840. do 1843. godine', *Arti musices*, 8.1 (1977), 5–54.

'Gradjanski bal' [n.a.], *Danica Ilirska*, 11 (11 March 1848), 48.

Hirc, Dragutin, 'Stari Zagreb', *Zbornik III. Programa Radio-Zagreba*, 17 (1987), 97–155.

Hrbud-Popović, Višnja, 'Kolo hervatsko: Das kroatische Kolo kao društveni ples prema opisu iz 1848', *Narodna umjetnost*, 27 (1990), 199–209.

Ivančan, Ivan, *Narodni plesni običaji u Hrvata* (Zagreb: Hrvatska matica iseljenika, Institut za etnologiju i folkloristiku, 1996).

Karaman, Igor, and Ivan Kampuš, *Tisućljetni Zagreb* (Zagreb: Školska knjiga, 1994).

Kassowitz-Cvijić, Antonija, 'Nekoć na svečanom balu', *Jutarnji list* (20 February 1927), pp. 19–22.

Knowles, Mark, *The Wicked Waltz and Other Scandalous Dances. Outrage at Couple Dancing in the 19th and Early 20th Centuries* (Jefferson, NC: McFarland & Co., 2009).

Krčelić, Baltazar Adam, *Annue ili historija 1748–1767* (Zagreb: Jugoslavenska akademija znanosti i umjetnosti, 1952).

Krešić, Mijo, *Autobiografija* (Zagreb: Tisak Dioničke tiskare, 1898).

Kuhač, Franjo, *Vatroslav Lisinski i njegovo doba*: *Prilog za poviest hrvatskoga preporoda* (Zagreb: Matica hrvatska, 1904).

——, 'Ples i plesovna glazba', *Prosvjeta, List za zabavu znanost i umjetnost*, 1 (1893), pp. 5–7; 2 (1893), pp. 35–38; 3 (1893), pp. 59–63; 4 (1893), pp. 82–84; 5 (1893), pp. 106–108.

Kuhač-Koch, Franjo, 'Dvoransko kolo', *Vienac*, 4 (1872), pp. 58–61; 7 (1872), pp. 106–07; 8 (1872), pp. 123–24; 9 (1872), pp. 138–40; 10 (1872), pp. 154–55; 11 (1872), pp. 170–72.

Kuretić, Bogdan, 'Dopis o slavjanskome balu u Beču', *Danica Ilirska*, 9 (27 February 1847), 35–36.

Ladović, Vanda, 'Oslikani ciljevi građanskog streljačkog društva', in *Iz starog i novog Zagreba*, 5, ed. by Ivan Bach, Franjo Buntak, and Vanda Ladović (Zagreb: Muzej grada Zagreba, 1974), pp. 127–38.

Laszowski, Emil and Deželić, Velimir, 'Dnevnik Dragutina Rakovca', *Narodna starina*, 3 (1922), 283–312.

Milčec, Zvonimir, *Galantni Zagreb* (Zagreb: Mladost, 1989).

Muraj, Aleksandra, 'Poklade u Zagrebu (1900.–1918.)', *Narodna umjetnost*, 41.2 (2004), 205–34.

Nahachewsky, Andriy, 'Once Again: On the Concept of "Second Existence" Folk Dance', in *Dans Müsik Kültür, ICTM 20th Ethnochoreology Symposium Proceedings 1998*, ed. by Frank Hall and Irene Loutzaki (Istanbul: International Council for Traditional Music Study Group on Ethnochoreology and Bogaziçi University Folklore Club, 2000), pp. 125–43.

Narodne novine [n.a.], 12 (1848).

——, 71 (1847).

Niemčić, Iva, and Katarinčić, Ivana 'Croatian Couple Dances from 19th Century till the Present Day: The Waltz and Salonsko Kolo', *Porte Akademik. Journal of Music and Dance Studies*, 14/15 (2016/2017), 147–60.

'Pravnički bal' [n.a.], *Danica Ilirska*, 8 (19 February 1848), 32.

Premerl, Nada, 'Društveni život u sjevernoj Hrvatskoj kao dio preporodnog nacionalnog programa', in *Hrvatski narodni preporod 1790–1848.*, ed. by Nikša Stančić (Zagreb: Muzej za umjetnost i obrt, 1985), pp. 135–45.

Premerl, Nada, 'Ples kao oblik društvenog života u prošlosti Zagreba', in *Iz starog i novog Zagreba*, vol. 5, ed. by Ivan Bach, Franjo Buntak, and Vanda Ladović (Zagreb: Muzej grada Zagreba, 1974), pp. 139–50.

'Prošaste poklade kod nas u Zagrebu' [n.a.], *Danica Ilirska*, 11 (14 March 1840), 43–44.

Ramovš, Mirko, 'Valček kot slovenski ljudski ples', *Traditiones*, 32.2 (2003), 33–49.

Ruyter, Nancy Lee Chalfa, '*Dvoransko kolo*: From the 1940s to the Twentieth Century', in *Balkan Dance. Essays on Characteristics, Performance and Teaching*, ed. by Anthony Shay (Jefferson, NC: McFarland & Co., 2008), pp. 239–49.

Sremac, Stjepan, 'Folklorni ples u Hrvata od "izvora" do pozornice' (unpublished doctoral thesis, University of Zagreb, Faculty of Humanities and Social Sciences, Zagreb Institute of Ethnology and Folklore Research, 2001).

——, 'Ples u suvremenim pokladnim običajima u Hrvatskoj', *Narodna umjetnost*, 25 (1988), 137–74.

Strobel, Desmond F., 'Waltz', in *International Encyclopedia of Dance*, vol. 6, ed. by Selma Jeanne Cohen (New York: Oxford University Press, 1998), pp. 359–62.

'Svečano otvorenje dvorane zagrebačke u narodnom domu' [n.a.], *Danica Ilirska*, 7 (13 February 1847), 51–52.

Vitez, Zorica, *Hrvatski svadbeni običaji* (Zagreb: Golden marketing, 2003).

Vujić, Antun, 'Narodne novine', in *Hrvatski leksikon*, vol. 2 (Zagreb: Naklada Leksikon, 1997), p. 160.

——, 'Danica', in *Hrvatski leksikon*, vol. 1 (Zagreb: Naklada Leksikon, 1996), p. 234.

Vukotinović, Ljudevit, 'Letošnje poklade u Zagrebu', *Danica Ilirska*, 9 (11 March 1843), 39–40.

——, 'Salon u Zagrebu', *Danica Ilirska*, 6 (5 February 1842), 23–24.

Zebec, Tvrtko, *Krčki tanci* (Zagreb-Rijeka: Adamić; Institut za etnologiju i folkloristiku, 2004).

10. Waltzing Through Europe: Johann Strauss (the Elder) in Hamburg and Altona in 1836

Jörgen Torp

This chapter reflects upon the distribution of Waltz music in urban environments. As Derek B. Scott wrote in his *Sounds of the Metropolis*:

> Unlike rural types of music, it was produced for urban leisure-hour consumption (urban social dance). That being so, it had the advantage of being more readily available for audiences elsewhere, since cities were beginning to share much in common in the nineteenth century.[1]
>
> [...] Urban popular styles were not as marked by their places of production as rural styles. Cities were much more like each other than were rustic areas.[2]

The cities were connected via media and via traffic networks, as I have previously shown with regard to the importance of port cities around and before 1900.[3] Nevertheless, each city also had its own particular places and environments, unique in the political world of that time. Therefore, it makes sense to investigate case studies that are historically and locally limited. This chapter does so, taking as its focus a two-week window in October 1836 in Hamburg (and Altona).

---

1 Derek B. Scott, *Sounds of the Metropolis: The 19th Century Popular Music Revolution in London, New York, Paris and Vienna* (New York: Oxford University Press, 2008), p. 122.
2 Ibid., p. 138.
3 See Jörgen Torp, *Zur Entwicklungsgeschichte urbaner Popularmusik unter besonderer Berücksichtigung des Tango rioplatense* (unpublished master's thesis, University of Hamburg, 1989), and *Alte atlantische Tangos: Rhythmische Figurationen im Wandel der Zeiten und Kulturen* (Hamburg: LIT Verlag, 2007).

Introduction: Strauss's Orchestra Tours in the 1830s

The Waltz is a music and dance genre that reached its zenith in nineteenth-century Vienna. Other, more rural regions may have played a role in the early development of the Waltz going back to the eighteenth century,[4] but — at least in regard to the development of musical composition — the Waltzes of the Viennese composers became the most famous and popular throughout the nineteenth century, both in Vienna itself, and on an international level.

However, in the case of the Waltz, it would not be sufficient to write its history by only focusing on a certain region or city. One should also take into account its geographical dissemination. As happens readily with urban popular music and dance genres, the dissemination of the Waltz was widespread on an international, and, eventually, intercontinental level. In turn, this dissemination was comparatively quick, in accordance with the growing possibilities of a rapidly industrialising world.[5]

The Waltz dance and Waltz music may both have had their own, independent means of dissemination, but the dissemination of the music certainly influenced the dissemination of the dance and vice versa. The editing and printing of notated musical works developed quickly.[6] Moreover, the live performances of musical pieces by touring musicians was also an evolving factor that had an important impact.

4　See Reingard Witzmann, *Der Ländler in Wien. Ein Beitrag zur Entwicklungsgeschichte des Wiener Walzers bis in die Zeit des Wiener Kongresses* (Vienna: Arbeitsstelle für den Volkskundeatlas in Österreich, 1976).

5　With regard to Hamburg and Altona, we find, as early as 1806, the little waltzes by the young Friedrich Kuhlau (1786–1832): 'Hamburgischer Favorit-Walzer' and 'Altonaischer Favorit-Walzer' (see Jørgen Erichsen, *Friedrich Kuhlau, Ein deutscher Musiker in Kopenhagen*: *Eine Biographie nach zeitgenössischen Dokumenten* (Hildesheim: Olms, 2011), pp. 50ff).

6　According to the division of media into four groups proposed by Werner Faulstich, written and print media are 'secondary media' (1. primary media: media of man (theatre), 2. secondary media: written and print media, 3. tertiary media: electronic media, 4. quaternary media: digital media), see Werner Faulstich, 'Einführung', in *Grundwissen Medien*, ed. by Werner Faulstich, 5th edn (Munich: Fink, 2004), p. 9. However, Faulstich describes as secondary media only various forms of literary media, and does not include music (or dance). The importance of print media for the spread of music is well described in Peter Wicke's cultural history of popular music (Peter Wicke, *Von Mozart zu Madonna*: *Eine Kulturgeschichte der Popmusik* (Frankfurt am Main: Suhrkamp Verlag, 2001)). Here, Wicke particularly draws attention to the invention of lithography by Alois Senefelder (1771–1834) leading to the first lithographic reproduction of a notated musical piece in 1796.

10. Johann Strauss (the Elder) in Hamburg and Altona in 1836

Fig. 10.1 Josef Kriehuber, *Johann Strauss the Elder*, 1835. Lithograph. Wikimedia Commons, Public Domain, https://commons.wikimedia.org/wiki/Category:Johann_Strauss_I#/media/File:Strau%C3%9FVaterLitho.jpg

Johann Strauss the Elder (1804–1849) began touring with a full orchestra, using new means of transport, such as the steam train and steam ship.[7] The first of such travels was a short trip to Pest (Budapest) in early November 1833, which he meditated on immediately in his Op. 66: the Waltz *Emlék Pestre — Erinnerung an Pesth*.[8] In the following years, he organised more distant and longer expeditions.

In October 1834, he travelled with an orchestra of thirty musicians to Berlin, where he played in several concerts and balls in November.

---

7   See, for example, Norbert Linke, *Musik erobert die Welt oder Wie die Wiener Familie Strauß die Wiener Familie Strauß die 'Unterhaltungsmusik' revolutionierte* (Vienna: Herold, 1987).

8   See also the comments in Max Schönherr and Karl Reinöhl, *Johann Strauss Vater: Ein Werkverzeichnis* (London: Universal Edition, 1954), pp. 99–101.

On the way back to Vienna, he played in Leipzig, Dresden and Prague, arriving back in Vienna in mid-December.[9]

Leaving Vienna again the following year on 30 September 1835, with an orchestra of twenty-six musicians, Strauss toured Munich, Augsburg, Ulm, Stuttgart, Heilbronn, Karlsruhe, Heidelberg, Mannheim, Mainz, and Wiesbaden, Frankfurt am Main, Hanau, Offenbach, Darmstadt, again Frankfurt, and Heidelberg, Wurzburg, Nuremberg, Regensburg, and Passau, playing altogether at twelve balls and twenty-seven concerts, coming back via Linz to Vienna on 22 December.[10]

The journey of 1836 was even longer, beginning in early September in Prague, where he played during the festivities of the coronation of the (Habsburg) king and queen of Bohemia. From there, he and his orchestra travelled to Leipzig, Halle, Magdeburg, Brunswick, Hanover, Bremen, Hamburg, Oldenburg, again Bremen, Osnabruck, Munster, Amsterdam, The Hague, Rotterdam, Düsseldorf, and Elberfeld, Cologne, Aachen, Liège, Brussels, and Antwerp, again Liège, and Aachen, Duren, Bonn, Koblenz, and Regensburg. He arrived back in Vienna on 30 December. During this voyage of four months, the largest number of events were held in Hamburg, Brussels, and The Hague.[11]

The longest tour — lasting over a year — was the one that established Strauss's international fame. He and his orchestra toured to France (principally Paris), Belgium, and Great Britain (principally London). He left Vienna in early October 1837, and finished this long journey by returning to Vienna shortly before Christmas in December 1838.[12] He arrived sick, having caught influenza during the cold winter days in December. He was very busy thereafter during Carnival season of 1839,[13]

---

9   See Linke, *Musik erobert die Welt*, pp. 109–12, and also the comments to Strauss's Op. 78 (the Waltz *Erinnerung an Berlin*) and Op. 79 (the Waltz *Gedanken-Striche*) in Schönherr and Reinöhl, *Johann Strauss Vater*, pp. 117–22.

10 See Schönherr and Reinöhl, *Johann Strauss Vater*, p. 132. Schönherr and Reinöhl write about this journey in their comment on Strauss's Waltz Op. 84, *Heimath-Klänge*, but also the *Reise-Galopp*, Op. 85, and the Waltz *Erinnerung an Deutschland*, Op. 87, may be of interest in this respect.

11 See Schönherr and Reinöhl, *Johann Strauss Vater*, pp. 140–42 and their additional remarks to the *Krönungswalzer* Op. 91, and in Linke, *Music erobert die Welt*, pp. 121–29 (chapter 15, 'Das erste Reise-Orchester der Welt').

12 This voyage is described in Linke, *Musik erobert die Welt*, pp. 130–36.

13 From January 1838 to January 1839, Strauss presented his Opp. 100–05, beginning with the Galop *Der Carneval von Paris* (Op. 100), the Waltz *Paris* (Op. 101), the *Original-Parade-Marsch* (Op. 102), the Waltz *Huldigung der Königin Victoria von*

but finally collapsed at the end of Carnival, and the doctors prescribed long-lasting and complete rest.[14] He did not appear recovered until 1 May of that year, playing his new *Taglioni-Walzer*, Op. 110, in the dance hall of the famous venue *Sperl*,[15] and in 1839 he took only a very short trip to Brno between 3–5 September.

In the following ten years, until his death in September 1849, Strauss continued touring, but never again as intensively and extensively as before. For that reason, one may focus on the time span from 1833 to 1838 (respectively from Op. 66 to 105 of his 251 numbered musical works), since this was the period in which the circulation of Waltz music through live events performed by Strauss and his orchestra was expanding.

Hamburg Newspaper Coverage of Strauss's Visit in Hamburg, 1836

Strauss's and his orchestra's stay in Hamburg (and Altona) in 1836 is a good starting point to gain insight into the reception of Strauss's music during his tours. Firstly, the two weeks between 2–16 October — when he and his orchestra musicians were guests in the hotel *Zum König von England* at Neuer Wall — are not too lengthy to outline here. Secondly, Hamburg was an important stop in his 1836 tour. It was, moreover, an important place for reflection on German as well as international affairs, and several newspapers and journals were based there, allowing one to retrieve information in respect to Strauss's concerts, and their political and cultural circumstances.

The journals I reviewed for 1836 are as follows:[16]

1. *Staats und Gelehrte Zeitung des Hamburgischen unpartheiischen Correspondenten* (henceforth abbreviated as *Correspondent*).[17]

    Großbritannien (Op. 103), the *Boulogner-Galopp nach Motiven aus der Oper Die Botschafterin von D. Auber* (Op. 104) and the Waltz *Freuden-Grüße* (Motto: 'Überall gut — in der Heimath am besten'), his Op. 105.
14 Schönherr and Reinhöhl, *Johann Strauss Vater*, p. 169.
15 Ibid., pp. 170–72.
16 All direct quotations from the journals are translated from the German by Jörgen Torp.
17 The *Hamburgischer Correspondent* was successor to the *Holsteinischer Correspondent* (founded 1712), when the latter moved from Schiffbek to Hamburg in 1731; see

2. *Neue Zeitung und Hamburgische Adreß-Comtoir-Nachrichten* (henceforth abbreviated as *NZ*).[18]

3. *Priviligirte wöchentliche gemeinnützige Nachrichten von und für Hamburg* (henceforth abbreviated as *PgN*).[19]

4. *Königlich priviligirte Altonaer Adreß-Comtoir-Nachrichten* (henceforth abbreviated as *Altonaer Nachrichten*).[20]

5. *Der Freischütz*.[21]

For Strauss's second stay in Hamburg, in 1847, I consulted the following journals:

1. *Der Freischütz*.

2. *Börsen-Halle*: *Hamburgische Abend-Zeitung für Handel, Schiffahrt und Politik*.[22]

My intention in reading these old journals went slightly beyond a desire to explore the bare notes and comments on Strauss's concerts. I was interested to find further information about the circumstances of the period and place, and also to acquire some information about the dance.[23] However, although some notes regarding dance could be

---

Ernst Baasch, *Geschichte des Hamburgischen Zeitungswesens von den Anfängen bis 1914* (Hamburg: Friederichsen, de Gruyter & Co., 1930), pp. 3ff. In 1836, it appeared from Monday to Saturday and — like the *NZ* and the *PgN* — consisted of eight pages with three columns per page.

18 This newspaper was the result of the 1826 fusion of the *Neue Zeitung* and the *Hamburgische Adreß-Comtoir-Nachrichten*, both founded in 1767 (Baasch, *Geschichte des Hamburgischen Zeitungswesens*, pp. 8–11 and p. 49).

19 The *PgN* appeared first in 1792 (see Baasch, *Geschichte des Hamburgischen Zeitungswesens*, p. 11).

20 A small newspaper from Hamburg's neighbour city Altona. In 1836, it appeared twice a week on Wednesdays and Saturdays with four pages each.

21 *Der Freischütz* appeared weekly on Saturdays from 1825 (Baasch, *Geschichte des Hamburgischen Zeitungswesens*, p. 53). It had eight pages in 1836 and 1847 with two columns per page in 1836 and three columns in 1847.

22 The *Börsenhalle* appeared since 1805 (Baasch, *Geschichte des Hamburgischen Zeitungswesens*, p. 14). In 1847, it was a daily newspaper (Monday to Saturday) of four pages.

23 I will not describe here the full content and composition of these journals and newspapers, their political or their entertainment ambitions, and their ups and downs. During the time of the French (Napoleonic) occupation, most newspapers disappeared in 1811, and reappeared in 1813 and 1814. In many regards, the cultural importance of Hamburg reached its peak in the second half of the eighteenth

found in the journals, only very little can be related directly to Strauss's balls. Finally, this study cannot be more than a pilot with respect to the overall topics of the interregional and international spread of Waltz music, set against the backdrop of the relation between the music and the performance of the dance.

According to Max Schönherr and Karl Reinöhl,[24] the dates of concerts and balls given by Strauss and his orchestra in Hamburg and the nearby city of Altona in 1836 are the following:

Monday 3 October: Concert in the Apollosaal

Wednesday 5 October: Concert in the Museumssaal (Altona)

Thursday 6 October: Concert in the Apollosaal

Sunday 9 October: Ball in the hotel Zur alten Stadt London

Monday 10 October: Private concert in Ottensen (outside Altona)

Tuesday 11 October: Concert in the Stadtheater

Wednesday 12 October: Ball in the Museum of Altona

Thursday 13 October: Concert in the Stadtheater

Friday 14 October: Private concert in Ottensen

Saturday 15 October: Concert in the Stadttheater

These dates are generally reliable, as Schönherr and Reinöhl consulted the diary of Johann Thyam, a clarinettist in the Strauss orchestra in the years 1835 to 1838, who provided logistical information regarding the Strauss tours: 'departure and arrival times, transportation customs and tax adjustments with respect to luggage and the time squandered as a result, accommodation in diverse cities and finally the staged concerts and balls as well as their venues'.[25] Unfortunately, Thyam does not give information on the programmes, performers or attendance at the events.

---

century. The French occupation was a hard blow, from which Hamburg recovered only very slowly.

24 Schönherr and Reinöhl, *Johann Strauss Vater*.
25 Schönherr and Reinöhl, *Johann Strauss Vater*, p. 129.

Fig. 10.2 Johann Poppel, *Das Stadttheater in Hamburg* (after C. A. Lill), published by Berendschenschen Buch & Kunsthandlung, Hamburg, c.1842. The Hamburg Stadttheater was one of the venues where Strauss played. Wikimedia Commons, Public Domain, https://commons.wikimedia. org/wiki/File:Hamburg_Stadttheater_c1842.jpg

The programme of pieces performed in the Hamburg concerts of 1836 can be partly reconstructed from the longer reviews of concerts on 3 October[26] and 11 October.[27] Other newspaper entries inform us about the co-programme of theatre pieces, in which the concerts were embedded. Not every event of the ten listed above was announced beforehand in the journals. The daily newspapers (*PgN* and *Correspondent*) announced only the five concerts given in the Apollosaal and the Stadttheater in Hamburg. The *Altonaer Nachrichten* did not mention any appearance by Strauss, but included interesting announcements of dance teachers and of seasonal balls. Only *Der Freischütz* (No. 42, 15 October) lists the first eight of the ten concerts given by Strauss in Hamburg and Altona, and we find in this short article only a sentence about the two balls.

It is not possible to reconstruct from these sources a concrete plan of how the tour was organised, but they give a strong impression that much of the organisation was last-minute, indeed 'improvised', in comparison with current standards. It appears that Strauss had arranged beforehand for only one concert in the Apollosaal. This concert was announced at the

---

26 Published in *PgN*, No. 237, 5 October, and in *Der Freischütz*, No. 41, 8 October.
27 *PgN*, No. 244, 13 October.

end of September for 1 October, and postponed to 3 October, for Strauss arrived in Hamburg on 2 October. Later events, which led to a stay for two weeks altogether, were arranged during his stay, probably due to the success of the earlier concerts, although there were harsh comments directed at the organisers about how overcrowded these concerts were, especially the first concert: there were far too many tickets sold (sold at the set price of 2 marks and 8 schillings, in Hamburg currency).

Early information about Strauss's tour was printed in Hamburg newspapers on Monday 26 September, in the *PgN* (No. 229, p. 4): a short message of one sentence saying that 'the Waltz virtuoso Strauß gave a *humoristisch musikalische Abend-Unterhaltung* [humoristic-musical Evening-Entertainment] in Brunswick with his own orchestra on the 24th'.[28] On the last page of this very issue (No. 229, p. 8) we are informed that 'passing through to Holland and France capellmeister Strauß from Vienna will have the honour of giving a *humoristisch musikalische Abend-Unterhaltung* in the Apollosaal with his orchestra of twenty-nine musicians on Saturday 1 October. Bookings of tickets at 2 marks 8 schillings will be accepted in the music store of Mister A. Cranz'. On the following two days (Tuesday 27 September, No. 230, p. 8, and Wednesday 28 September, No. 231 p. 8), we find a similar message, adding that the concert will start at seven o'clock in the evening. The notice that Strauss was giving a concert in Hamburg, in nearly the same wording as in the *PgN* (No. 229), was published in the *NZ* from 26 and 27 September, and in the *Correspondent* (No. 230) from Wednesday 28 September. On Wednesday evening, the *NZ* reports that Strauss and his troupe turned up in Hanover on 26 September and wanted to give a concert there on 27 September. On Thursday 29 September, two of the daily newspapers *PgN* (No. 230, p. 8) and *Correspondent* (No. 231, p. 8) published a correction, signed by Strauss himself, apologising that 'through unforeseeable travel hindrances with his orchestra' it will be impossible to give the concert (*Abend-Unterhaltung*) on 1 October, but it 'will take place irrevocably' on Monday, 3 October. The *PgN* confirms the date of 3 October in the following numbers (Friday, Saturday, and finally Monday).

---

28 I was unable to find any information in the Hamburg newspapers about the voyage of Strauss predating 26 September.

The *Correspondent* did not repeat the announcement of the concert before 3 October (No. 234). In the same issue, a longer article from Hanover was also published, written on 28 September, containing a report about Strauss's there (in Hanover):[29]

> The famous Waltz-king, Joh. Strauß, arrived suddenly like lightning in the night. Yesterday the whole city was on the move. In the evening nearly 1400 people (including the gallery) gathered for his concert in the hall of the Ballhof. There has never before been a gathering of such size in this country. What Strauss, with his orchestra, thirty members in number, accomplish, is close to incredible. His most original compositions deserve the attention of experts as well as laymen; his diverse subjects — such as sledgings, battles, military subjects, storms, tempests, etc. — are expressed in tonal paintings, and the music composed for the most abstract of subjects astonishes the audience for its faithful evocation, as well as for the skilful playing of the instruments. His Waltzes are unsurpassable. The applause was rapturous. Tomorrow, the 29th, he will give his second and last concert, then travel straightway to Bremen, where he will give a concert on the first of October. From there he proceeds to Hamburg, where he intends to arrive in the evening of October the second. The viceroy who for some weeks has been dwelling at his hunting château at Rothenkirchen, is expected here with his Serene family tomorrow for Strauss's concert.[30]

The daily newspapers regularly published reports from hotels listing the arrival of guests ('Angekommene Fremde'), as well as details concerning where these guests were travelling from. On Monday evening, 3 October, the *NZ* (No. 235, p. 4) briefly reported the arrival of 'Mr. Johann Strauß, capellmeister, together with twenty-eight members, from Bremen, *König von England*' (the name of the hotel where Strauss had checked in). On Tuesday morning, 4 October, the *PgN* (No. 236) gave the same notice. In the same issue, the *PgN* also announced a further Strauss concert in the Apollosaal on 'Thursday, 5 October [sic]'. The *Correspondent* (No. 239) followed a day later, on Wednesday the fifth, with the announcement of the second concert in the Apollosaal taking place on Thursday the sixth. The same issue also informs its readers about the accommodation of 'Mr. Johann Strauß, Kapellmeister from Vienna in *Zum König von England*'.

---

29 Newspaper articles from other places took time to reach Hamburg, and therefore are marked as 'delayed' according to the distance and the circumstances of communication.

30 *Correspondent*, No. 234, p. 6.

Further, all the members of the orchestra are listed by name (p. 7).³¹ A day before, on 4 October, the *NZ* (No. 236, p. 4) afforded a short overview of the days of Strauss's arrival and stay: Strauss had arrived on 2 October in Hamburg, 'coming from Bremen, where he had given on October the first a concert in the Schauspiel-Haus'. He gave 'his already-announced concert' on 3 October in the Apollosaal, but the spacious venue 'was not large enough' for the quantity of people, who 'wished to listen to the much-reviewed Waltz-king. Just as it was the case in Bremen [...] the demand for tickets could not be met, even by half'. Nevertheless, Strauss and his company 'won high praise for [their] performances from all those who attended' the concert.

Finally, the article gives some insight into the somewhat improvisational way in which Strauss planned his tour:

> About the departure of the artist from here to London, nothing seems to be determined. In any case, he will stay until the coming week, as, according to reports, he has entered into an engagement to appear with his musicians at a ball arranged at the 'Hôtel zur Alten Stadt London' next Sunday [9 October].³²

For its part, *PgN* (No. 237, p. 4), in the issue dated Wednesday 5 October, includes one of the two long reviews of Strauss's first given on Monday 3 October (the other one appeared in *Der Freischütz* on 8 October). The review can be divided into four parts.

The first is introductory, noting that finally Strauss, described here as 'the well-known reformer of dance music', appeared in Hamburg — 'as has already been the case in so many other German cities' — 'to earn fame and money'. Strauss had the advantage of travelling with his own orchestra, so that he would not have to find local musicians in a foreign city. Moreover, his orchestra would have been so accustomed to playing together, that rehearsals would have seemed unnecessary, although the composition — according to the anonymous reviewer — were 'music-entertainments' of the 'light, cheerful, pleasingly trifling' kind, so that merely *ripienists* rather than *virtuosos* were needed to perform them.

---

31 'die Herren G. Jegg, F. Amon, J. Famberger, A. Hohnstatt, J. Babel, E. Pauli, E. Fuchs, G. Fistl, J. Fichter, J. Loschdorfer, L. Thauer, J. Thyam, J. Drabsch, F. Styaßny, J. Benesch, J. Woitischek, C. Schalta, L. Hofinger, F. Bödl, J. Erber, J. Janofsky, J. Fink, M. Stark, J. Moser, L. Hanglmann, F. Zöhrer, J. Liebe und Demois. Elise Zöhrer'.

32 *NZ*, No. 236, p. 4.

The second part describes very roughly the programme of musical pieces in the concert played on 3 October, beginning with an overture from Auber's opera *Die Falschmünzer* (in French: *Le serment, ou Les faux-monnayeurs*, which premiered in Paris on 1 October 1832); it was very well played, as the reviewer confirms, although this overture would have been 'executed by our orchestra of the Stadttheater with similar precision'. The 'Waltzes and potpourris' that followed, with their 'electric enchantment', were nothing new, since these compositions had 'naturally' already made their way to Hamburg. The music of 'esprit and humour' would certainly improve by being conducted and played by the orchestra of the composer himself.

In the third part, the anonymous author of the article writes with ironic distance about a male singer (Mr. Stark) who sings the *cavatina* of Isabella in Giacomo Meyerbeer's opera *Robert le diable* (written and premiered in 1831) in high voice; and a female singer (Demoiselle Zöhrer) who sings the first aria of Georges Brown in Boieldieu's opera *La Dame blanche* (of 1825) in a deep voice. The final section describes the unpleasant circumstances in which the concert took place: it was overbooked and extremely crowded, and those who finally got a place in the front hall could not see anything.

An appendix states that it is hard to understand why, in the early announcements, an important place like Hamburg was described only as a station to be passed in transit, and repeats the 'irresponsible discourtesy' (*unverantwortliche Unhöflichkeit*) towards the audience of selling tickets when there is not enough space for all, a mistake made not by 'Mr. Strauss's, but by his 'local friends' (in Hamburg).

In the same issue, Strauss announces another concert in the Apollosaal for Thursday 6 October. Additionally, it is stated that only a moderate number of tickets will be sold to avoid overcrowding.

Finally, the Wednesday newspaper (No. 237, p. 8) prints an anonymous query about whether it would not be agreeable to Strauss 'to please the friends of his art with his ingenious recitals also in the Stadttheater'.

The review of the same concert in the weekly *Freischütz* is not written by an admirer of Strauss's music, but gives an overview of pieces played in the programme. The reviews of these pieces are, however, very unbalanced in length, and the pieces of most interest for the study of

Waltzes are only mentioned in one sentence, without further analysis or discussion. The author, writing under the pseudonym Wahrlieb, begins with a question in French: *Tous les genres sont bons?*[33] He declares that he is not a friend of Strauss as a composer, nor of the Waltz genre at all. He lauds, however, the performance of the musicians playing together. He also mentions all the eight pieces on the programme, which was comprised of two sets of four numbers. The first part began with the overture of Auber's opera *Le serment* (1832), followed by Strauss's *Philomelen-Walzer* (1835, Strauss's Op. 82). Thirdly, the audience heard the previously-mentioned *Cavatina* of Meyerbeer's *Robert le diable*, and the first part concluded with the potpourri *Ein Strauß von Strauß* (1832, Op. 55). The second part opened with Strauss's Waltz *Die Nachtwandler* (then a comparatively new work written in 1836, Op. 88), followed by the aforementioned aria of Boieldieu sung by 'Mamsell Zöhrer'. Another potpourri or *quodlibet* followed, *Der Musikalische Wortwechsel*, a work by Strauss without an opus number written in 1833. Finally, the orchestra played *Walzer-Guirlande*, a combination of several parts of favourite Strauss Waltzes. Since Strauss published two such garlands before 1836, I am not sure whether Wahrlieb refers to the first (Op. 67 from 1834) or the second one (Op. 77 from 1835). After briefly mentioning that the concert was overcrowded, the review ends with a preview for the following Sunday evening, 9 October, when Strauss and his orchestra would play for a dance event in the hotel Alte Stadt London.

The balls are mentioned, but the journals do not pay as much attention to these as to the concerts. This is understandable, since, at that time, music journalism had already developed as criticism of musical works (opuses) and performances. The question remains as to why the balls were not advertised to the same extent as the concerts were, especially because advertisements of private balls and dancing

---

33 I could not discover the identity of the person behind the pseudonym 'Wahrlieb'. Eduard Beurmann (1804–1883) in his book *Skizzen aus den Hanse-Städten* (on Lübeck, Bremen, and Hamburg), published in 1836, wrote that 'Kapellmeister Wahrlieb' regrettably had died, and that his successor was a writer of much lesser quality (see Eduard Beurmann, *Skizzen aus den Hanse-Städten* (Hanau: Friedrich König, 1836), pp. 181 ff., https://reader.digitale-sammlungen.de/de/fs1/object/display/bsb10018583_00005.html). Indeed, the following issues of the *Freischütz* do not include information signed by Wahrlieb about further Strauss's concerts. It may be that 'Wahrlieb' had died shortly after having written his article on Strauss's first concert in Hamburg.

were quite usual in the newspapers. Apart from that, the Strauss balls seem to be outnumbered here by his concerts. Strauss acted here as a businessman: his works were printed by the famous Vienna publishers Diabelli in 1827 and Haslinger from 1828. He had seen the success of Paganini's concerts in Vienna in 1828, wrote and published his *Walzer (à la Paganini)*, Op. 11, in the same year and began to take entrance fees.[34]

On Friday, 7 October 1836, Strauss advertised in the *PgN* (No. 239) a 'third and last' *Humoristische und Musikalische Abend-Unterhaltung* for the following Saturday evening in the Apollosaal, wrote that he would be taking his leave and thanked Hamburg's public for the warm reception. There is no document that evidences him giving this concert, but on Saturday he again published a message in the same journal, saying that — according to the requests and wishes of the public — he had arranged with the administration of the Stadttheater to give a concert on Tuesday 11 October. The newspaper also announced this concert, adding that the evening would open with a one-act comedy (*Die Verräther*), and would include a one-act farce (*Drei Frauen auf einmal*) as the entr'acte between the two sets of the concert.

On Wednesday 12 October, the newspapers notified readers that the last concert by Strauss would take place on Thursday 13 October, but, on Thursday, it was announced that this concert was actually a penultimate one.

Finally, on Friday and Saturday, a final concert was again announced for Saturday 15 October, and this third of the three concerts by Strauss performed in the Stadttheater was indeed the last time Strauss's music was played by himself and his orchestra in Hamburg in 1836.

The *PgN* published a second concert review on Thursday 13 October (No. 244, p. 4) of the first concert in the Stadttheater (given on Tuesday 11 October). It is much shorter than the first review featured in this newspaper, and partly repeats what was mentioned before. Again, it seems that the concert was overcrowded, so some people had to leave and wait for the next one. An excellent performance, especially that given by the brass section, is mentioned. The prejudice that northern German 'character' would not be receptive to these humorous, trifling (*bloß scherzhaft tändelnd*) compositions had to be abandoned, since Strauss — contrary to his original intention — was willing to prolong his stay for some time in the city. The same day (13 October), two short, dignified poems of gratitude, signed by

---

34   See Schönherr and Reinhöhl, *Johann Strauss Vater*, pp. 29–32.

an anonymous M., were published in the *NZ* (No. 244), one dedicated to 'Capellmeister Strauß', the other to the members of the band.

Der Freischütz published in its following weekly issues (15, 22, and 29 October Nos. 42, 43, 44) some pieces of information concerning Strauss. The first was a brief summary of the first eight events that Strauss had previously held in Hamburg. Strauss would be 'listened to, danced to, and even eaten to' (people could picnic during the concert in Ottensen in the saloon of Sir Rainville). The *tempi* of the music played at the ball are described as somewhat quick, and therefore physically demanding for the dancers. The second (22 October) describes the last two concerts in the Stadttheater as well-attended and the performance as excellent, laced with humour, and received with sonorous applause. On the 29 October, two weeks after Strauss's departure, the journal declared the state of health in Hamburg to be very good: except for the circulation of some fever (Strauß- and Lanner-fever).[35]

Fig. 10.3 Charles Wilda, *Der Ball*, 1906. Lanner is the violin player on the left, Strauss is the player on the right. Wikimedia Commons, Public Domain, https://commons.wikimedia.org/wiki/File:Charles-Wilda_Joseph-Lanner-und-Johann-Strauss_1906.jpg

---

35 Mentioning the state of public health was not unusual in nineteenth-century Europe, especially in times of cholera epidemics. The cholera epidemic of 1831, spreading from India via Russia, extracted a heavy cost, with many deaths in Europe. In 1836, the newspapers reported on cholera in Prague, the first stop of Strauss's tour. Even at the end of the nineteenth century, in 1892, Hamburg suffered an epidemic in which thousands of people died; see the comprehensive study by Richard J. Evans, *Death in Hamburg: Society and Politics in the Cholera-Years 1830–1910* (Oxford: Oxford University Press, 1987).

Strauss and Other Musicians

On 17 October, an announcement appeared in the *PgN* (No. 247), written by the owner of the Apollo-Theater, E. F. D. Wilckens. He declared that, in order to satisfy requests from several sides, there will be a weekly music entertainment under the name of *Apollo-Soirée*, like those in Vienna and imitated in other places. An orchestra of thirty members will play under the direction of the famous Conrad Berens (1801–1857), beginning on Wednesday 19 October. On that Wednesday, one could read in the same newspaper a programme of the musical pieces that Berens and his orchestra would perform: overtures of *Die diebische Elster* (*La gazza ladra*) by Rossini (1792–1868); *Jelva* (Yelva) by Carl Gottlieb Reissiger (1798–1859); *Iris-* and *Huldigung-Walzer* by Strauss; and *Lock-Walzer* and *Die Neapolitaner*, the newest Waltzes by Joseph Lanner (1801–1843). Such events can certainly be regarded as a prompt reaction to Strauss's appearance in Hamburg, although, in an older issue of the *PgN* (No. 196, p. 4), dated 18 August 1836, we find a short review of the first *Musikalische Abend-Unterhaltung* in the open air of the Tivoli garden with 'the most pleasing melodies of Strauss, Lanner, Labitzky', alternating with military music. A composition by Berens himself is singled out, a Galop from *Die Hugenotten* (the Huguenots), Meyerbeer's latest opera, which premièred in 1836. Such entertainments were held regularly, as long as the weather allowed open air events, and we find announcements for another 'große, musikalische Abend-Unterhaltung à la Strauss und Lanner' ('great musical evening entertainment à la Strauss and Lanner') at the *Elbpavillon* (*PgN*, No. 225, 21 September), a sixth 'große, musikalische Abend-Unterhaltung à la Strauss und Lanner' in the garden of G. L. Salje (*PgN*, No. 231, 28 September), and the last one for this season in the same place on Saturday 8 October. Another musical director, August Martin Canthal (1804–1881), played with a large orchestra several times a week in the *Privat-Verein an der Alster*, performing works by Lanner (22 September), by Reissiger and Canthal (24 September), Lanner and Weber (26 September), Auber and Lanner (6 October), or even the same works Strauss had in his current concert repertoire of that time, like *Ein Strauss von Strauss, großes Potpourri* (8 October).

Lanner and Strauss were also explicitly mentioned in the announcements of the music shops that were lending or selling musical scores. August Cranz's *Musikalienhandel* announced the newest Waltz by Lanner, *Die Neapolitaner* (Op. 107), on 20 September, published originally by Pietro Mecchetti in Vienna less than a month before. Also, on 7 October, B. S. Berendsohn announced Strauss dances 'in all arrangements' (*PgN*, No. 239, p. 8). Schuberth and Niemeyer again announced 'Strauß's complete Waltzes and Galops, for pianoforte, two-handed, four handed, for one flute, one guitar, one violin, and for orchestra, Lanner likewise, at fixed prices; further: all overtures, potpourris, Waltzes and galops, namely the compositions of Strauß, Lanner and Canthal, are in great number and in all arrangements on offer at our house' (*PgN*, No. 234, p. 8, 1 October).

Joh. Aug. Böhme likewise announced the sale of the newest dances by Joh. Strauß (*NZ*, No. 235, 3 October); he mentions fifty-five numbers, and lists in detail the last fifteen of these, ending with *No. 55 Die Nachtwandler* (Strauss's Op. 88, first announced by Tobias Haslinger in Vienna, 13 September, in the *Wiener Zeitung*).

In summary: the works of Strauss (and Lanner) were available in several arrangements in at least four different places, and shortly after they were first announced by the publishers in Vienna.

Strauss and Lanner were, by far, the two names most often mentioned in the context of published (dance) music in the 1830s. Later somewhat overshadowed by the Strauss sons, especially by Johann Strauss the Younger (1825–1899), they (Strauss the Elder and Lanner), in their time, themselves overshadowed other dance musicians, many of whom today are either completely unknown to us, or are known to us only by name, and not by their music. A source-critical catalogue of works of Lanner did not appear before 2012. There, the editor, Wolfgang Dörner, wrote very concisely about Lanner's forerunners, contemporaries and successors, 'most [of whose] compositions are lost and only from a very few compositions are more than just the titles delivered to posterity'.[36] According to Dörner, only one of these composers could maintain an appreciation comparable to Lanner and Strauss: Franz Morelly (1809–1859), who — interestingly, in respect to the spread of dance

---

36 Wolfgang Dörner, *Joseph Lanner — Chronologisch-thematisches Werkverzeichnis* (Vienna: Böhlau 2012), p. 26. Translated from the German by Jörgen Torp

music — lived in Bombay, India for most of the 1840s and 1850s. Outside Vienna, one should mention: in Karlovy Vary (known in German as Karlsbad), the 'Bohemian Waltz-King' Joseph Labitzky (1802–1881, Czech: Josef Labický); in Paris, Philippe Musard (1792–1859), '*le Napoléon du quadrille*'; and, in Copenhagen, the 'Strauss of the North', Hans Christian Lumbye (1810–1874). The naming of 'Kings' shows that only a few composers dominated the field, in contrast to concepts about 'folk music' or 'folk dance'.

Publishing Waltzes with opus numbers led to their presentation as musical works for performance in concerts. On the one hand, this resulted in them being viewed as distinct from other types of dance music and musicians. On the other hand, there was an increasing tendency to discuss Strauss's music as merely 'entertaining' (*unterhaltend*) rather than 'serious' (*ernst*) music. This gave rise to the enduring German differentiation between so-called 'U-' (*Unterhaltende*) and 'E-Musik' (*Ernste Musik*), similar to the English categories of 'light music' or 'popular music' versus 'art music' or 'classical music'.

Excursus: Serious vs. Entertaining Music

Around 1800, Romantic thinkers began to formulate quasi-religious claims about musical composition. As a result, music history portrayed the development of 'Classical' music in Vienna from Haydn to Mozart and, finally, Ludwig van Beethoven. These three are already mentioned as the masters of instrumental music in E. T. A. Hoffmann's (1776–1822) review of Beethoven's Fifth Symphony, published in the *Allgemeine musikalische Zeitung* in 1810, where Beethoven is described as a deeply Romantic composer. In his time, the significance of Beethoven was not undisputable, but already in the 1820s, Beethoven, not least according to the reception of Adolf Bernhard Marx (1795–1866), founder and editor of the *Berliner Allgemeine Musikalische Zeitung*, became an unquestionable genius of the musical *avant garde*.[37] The philosopher and music theorist Johann Amadeus Wendt (1783–1836)[38] adopted the conceptualisation of

---

37   See Elisabeth Eleonore Bauer, *Wie Beethoven auf den Sockel kam. Die Entstehung eines musikalischen Mythos* (Stuttgart: Metzler, 1992).
38   Wendt died on the 15 October in Göttingen, on the day Strauss gave his last concert in Hamburg in 1836.

a Classical period in music in his work *Ueber den gegenwärtigen Zustand der Musik besonders in Deutschland und wie er geworden* of 1836.[39] He wrote there about the trio ('*Kleeblatt*') of Mozart, Haydn and Beethoven,[40] and summarises 'that exactly with Beethoven a great era is brought about, an era in which secular music climbed to the peak of its energy and significance'.[41] As secondary masters of symphonic instrumental music, Wendt mentions Andreas and Bernhard Romberg (both worked for some time in Hamburg), Louis Spohr, Johann Wenzel Kalliwoda, George Onslow, and Peter Josef von Lindpaintner.[42] After describing music for solo instruments, Wendt closes his overview of instrumental music with a remark about *military music* (which, as a specific genre, would cease to exist in his time), and about 'dance compositions'. He writes: 'Of dance compositions, however, one does not know that they would ever have gained such widespread fame as those bearing the names of Strauß or Lanner'.[43] Strauss and Lanner, again, are singled out here in the same sentence as the only names connected with dance music, and merely with dance music. The writing of music history is already framed around a very few composers, and above all is enthroned the 'monumental genius' of Beethoven: 'With original freedom his monumental genius burst the barriers, which the symmetrical treatment of compositions had for him'.[44]

This understanding paralleled the advent of fictional Beethoven literature, beginning with stories by Johann Peter Lyser (1804–1870), Ernst Ortlepp (1800–1864) and Richard Wagner (1813–1883).[45] In 1834, as Egon Voss observed, Lyser began writing fictional books about Beethoven, initiating this trend.[46] The story Lyser tells concerns Beethoven's youth, and culminates in a visit to Mozart in Vienna,

---

39   (Johann) Amadeus Wendt, *Ueber den gegenwärtigen Zustand der Musik besonders in Deutschland und wie er geworden. Eine beurtheilende Schilderung* (Göttingen. Dieterichsche Buchhandlung 1836).
40   Ibid., p. 3.
41   Ibid., p. 1.
42   Ibid., pp. 8–10.
43   Ibid., p. 21.
44   Ibid., p. 6.
45   See Egon Voss, 'Das Beethoven-Bild der Beethoven-Belletristik. Zu einigen Erzählungen des 19. Jahrhunderts', in *Beethoven und die Nachwelt. Materialien zur Wirkungsgeschichte Beethovens*, ed. by Helmut Loos (Bonn: Beethoven-Haus, 1986), pp. 81–94.
46   Ibid.

thereby suggesting a concept of music history in which Beethoven is the successor to Mozart.[47] Ortlepp, whose screed on Beethoven was published in 1836, presented highly Romantic ideas of Beethoven, as a lonely outsider who condemned money, who worked superhumanly for his art, and, while he was misunderstood in his own time, was destined to be appreciated in the future.[48] In Wagner's *A Pilgrimage to Beethoven* (written in 1840, and published in 1841), a poor artist plans to visit Beethoven in Vienna. To earn money for the voyage, he tries to make a name for himself by composing Galops and Potpourris, which he feels ashamed about. Creating serious music is a clearly formulated ideal, one that seems more appropriate to the Northern regions of Germany than to the Viennese surroundings of Beethoven. Wagner depicts Beethoven saying: 'I often lose patience with the people of Vienna. They listen daily to too much poor stuff to be in the mood — for any considerable length of time — to take up serious work in a serious manner'.[49] Beethoven, according to Wagner's fiction, imagines having a better life composing Galops, for if he continues in this way, he will always live in want.[50] Non-fictional biographical reminiscences of Beethoven were also published at that time — Ferdinand Ries's and Gerhard Wegeler's *Biographische Notizen über Ludwig van Beethoven* appeared in 1838, Anton Schindler's *Biographie von Ludwig von Beethoven* in 1840[51] — as well as portrayals of Beethoven's works, such as that of Hermann Hirschbach (1812–1888) focusing on the late string quartets, published in 1839, in which even Haydn and Mozart's music is described as listenable and entertaining

---

47 Johann Peter Lyser, 'Beethoven', in *Beethoven. Zwei Novellen von Johann Peter Lyser und Ernst Ortlepp*, ed. by Paul Bülow (Lübeck: Antäus 1924), pp. 8–41 (originally published in *NZ*, 17 July-7 August 1834).

48 Ernst Ortlepp, 'Beethoven', in *Beethoven. Zwei Novellen von Johann Peter Lyser und Ernst Ortlepp*, ed. by Paul Bülow (Lübeck: Antäus, 1924), pp. 43–72.

49 Richard Wagner, 'Eine Pilgerfahrt zu Beethoven ', in *Richard Wagner. Ausgewählte Schriften und Briefe*, ed. by Philipp Werner (Frankfurt am Main: Fischer, 2013), pp. 27–53 (originally published in *Abend-Zeitung*, 30 July-5 August 1841), 1900 edition available at https://archive.org/details/einepilgerfahrtz00wagn. 'Deutsche Ernsthaftigkeit' (German seriousness) as opposed to French 'légèreté' ('französische Leichtigkeit') in poetry was already a topos representing the national character in the eighteenth century, see Jörg Echternkamp, *Der Aufstieg des deutschen Nationalismus (1770–1840)* (New York: Campus, 1998), p. 122.

50 Wagner, 'Eine Pilgerfahrt zu Beethoven', p. 51.

51 However, Schindler's biography of Beethoven has proved to be partly fictional.

'without difficult contemplation'. Hirschbach writes in favour of intellectual work and against 'the hedonism of most music enthusiasts'.[52]

Such a digression about the reception of Beethoven's work might not seem essential in a chapter on Waltz music. It is important to recognise though that in the writing of music history, entertainment-orientated music was depreciated such that dance music (not to mention dance itself) has been left out of the discourse. Moreover, the authors of the works quoted here were close contemporaries of Strauss, and were writing in a post-Beethoven period. Other voices, like that of Heinrich Heine (1797–1856), were seldom heard. Heine wrote: 'Beethoven urges the spiritual art to sound the agony of the phenomenal world, the annihilation of nature, which terrifies me in a way I cannot hide, although my friends shake their heads about it'.[53] Such views were widely overlooked until recent times, for example, in Jan Caeyers's biography of Beethoven.[54]

With regard to Strauss's success in Pest (Budapest) in November 1833, the correspondent of the *Theaterzeitung* (Vienna) described Strauss as 'the Mozart of the Waltzes, the Beethoven of the Cotillions, the Paganini of the Galops, the Rossini of the potpourris'.[55] In an indirect response, an article by Johann W. Hofzinser in the journal *Der Sammler* in December stated that Strauss's compositions should be called fabrications rather than works.[56] According to Norbert Linke, this, together with other

---

52 Hermann Hirschbach, 'Ueber Beethoven's letzte Streichquartette', *Neue Zeitschrift für Musik*, 11 (1839), 5–6.
53 Heinrich Heine, 'XXXIII' (Paris, 20th of April 1841), in 'Lutetia — Erster Teil', http://www.heinrich-heine-denkmal.de/heine-texte/lutetia33.shtml.
54 Jan Caeyers, *Beethoven. Der einsame Revolutionär. Eine Biographie* (Munich: Beck, 2012), originally published as *Beethoven. Een Biografie* (Amsterdam: De Bezige Bij, 2009). Caeyers quotes from Heine's article, but from a shortened version of it, in which a critique of Beethoven's biographer Anton Schindler is given, but not of Heine's remarks about Beethoven. In regard to Johann Strauss the Elder and his music, Caeyers musters only belittling words: such music pleases the senses, but does not make demands of the mind (p. 16), is meant for superficial consumption (p. 593), is fabricated, easily comprehensible, rhythmical according to the dizziness of dance (p. 598), and suitable only for hedonistic ignoramuses (p. 599). Caeyers' solid biography of Beethoven here remains partial just at the point at which he opens his perspective towards politics and quality of life.
55 Quoted from Linke, *Musik erobert die Welt oder Wie die Wiener Familie Strauß die Wiener Familie Strauß die 'Unterhaltungsmusik' revolutionierte*, p. 104
56 See Schönherr and Reinhöhl, *Johann Strauss Vater*, pp. 99–101.

articles, was 'the first publicly held discussion regarding entertainment music'.[57]

Dance and Dance Music

There were different preferences within the Waltz genre too, with regard to both the dance music and the dance itself. Schönherr and Reinöhl quote Moritz Gottlieb Saphir, who distinguished between public balls, masquerade balls (*redoutes*), society balls, house balls, picnics and *Schnackerlballs*.[58] The orchestras of that time, and the venues in which they played, were also different. Lanner or Strauss, Morelly or Faistenberger, Hablawetz or Wanzenböck: the latter (Hablawetz and Wanzenböck) played in smaller locations, but there was no overcrowding and therefore more space to dance.[59]

Announcements with respect to dance in Hamburg in 1836 are mainly to be found in two newspapers: the *PgN* (Hamburg) and the *Altonaer-Nachrichten* (Altona). These announcements refer to balls and to dancing classes. However, there is no information about which dances were performed at the balls, or which dance forms were taught

---

57 Linke, *Musik erobert die Welt*, p. 104. The term *Unterhaltung* [entertainment], however, was also in use for 'classical' music during the whole period: Musikalische Abendunterhaltungen [evening entertainments] were held under this name in Vienna as part of the Gesellschaft für Musikfreunde [Society of Friends of Music] between 1818 and 1840, in which string quartets, in particular, played an important part; see Ingrid Fuchs, 'Zur Wiener Kammermusiktradition zwischen Schubert und Brahms', in *Brahms' Schubert-Rezeption im Wiener Kontext*, ed. by Otto Biba, Gernot Gruber, Katharina Loose-Einfalt, and Siegfried Oechsle (Stuttgart: Franz Steiner, 2017), pp. 33–49. The unwillingness to denominate Waltzes as works and Strauss and Lanner as capellmeisters is already noted in a letter by Chopin to his teacher Josef Elsner in January of 1831 — see Chopin's *Briefe* (Letters), ed. by Krystyna Kobylanska (Frankfurt am Main: Fischer, 1984), p. 116 — and also Schönherr and Reinöhl, *Johann Strauss Vater*, p. 71. Lanner, however, was not accepted in 1830 as a member of the Viennese Tonkünstler-Societät (Musician Society), because of being a dance musician, see Frank Miller, *Johann Strauss Vater. Der musikalische Magier des Wiener Biedermeier* (Eisenburg: Castell, 1999), p. 98.

58 See Schönherr and Reinöhl, *Johann Strauss Vater*, p. 22. Unfortunately, neither Schönherr and Reinöhl (nor Linke) in the book(s) quoted here give the bibliographical references. They are probably discussing Moritz Gottlieb Saphir's (1795–1858) journalistic work. This work is so copious that it is very difficult to find the passage to which Schönherr and Reinöhl refer. In regard to Saphir, they refer to the *Wiener Theaterzeitung*, a journal founded by Adolf Bäuerle (1786–1859), for which Saphir wrote at times.

59 Schönherr and Reinöhl, *Johann Strauss Vater*, p. 23.

in the classes. Altona, as well as Hamburg, was part of the German Confederation (1815–1866). Hamburg was a Free (and Hanseatic) City; meanwhile, Altona was under the rule of the Danish king. The distance between the city boundaries of Hamburg (Millerntor) and Altona (Nobistor) was only about 1.5 kilometres.[60]

A comparison of the size of the two cities (see Fig. 10.4) may mislead the observer. Hamburg was a much bigger and more populous city, with a population of around 134,000 inhabitants in 1836, in contrast to the 27,000 of Altona.

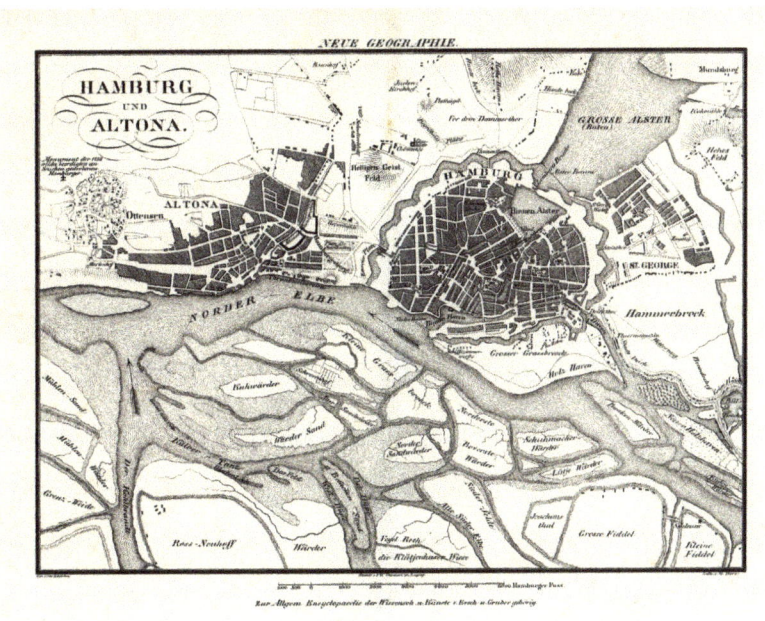

Fig. 10.4 Wilhelm E. A. von Schlieben, Map of Hamburg (in the East) and Altona/ Ottensen (in the West) in 1833, https://www.christian-terstegge.de/ hamburg/karten_umgebung/files/1833_neue_geographie_300dpi.jpeg. Image courtesy of Christian Terstegge, Public Domain.

Several balls were announced in Altona. At the end of September and at the beginning of October, there were several vintage and harvest festivals, including balls. Regular subscriber's balls (*Abonnentenbälle*)

---

60 South of the river Elbe, the city of Harburg (today also part of Hamburg) fell under a different political authority, the king of Hanover. Hamburg and Altona were unified in 1937.

also announced opening balls for the winter season. At the same time, advertisements appeared for dance classes by the dance teachers G. Hennig, J. Katzenstein, August von Wobeser-Rosenhain, and a certain J. Sch.

It is not clear exactly what kind of dancing was taught. J. Sch. announced common dance teaching (*Altonaer Nachrichten*, No. 78, 28 September 1836), G. Hennig 'dance art for adults' (*Altonaer Nachrichten*, No. 75, 17 September 1836, p. 333), J. Katzenstein taught according to 'the newest rules of the ballet master Tescher [1812–1883] from Vienna' (*Altonaer Nachrichten*, No. 75, 17 September 1836, p. 333), and A. von Wobeser-Rosenhain came over from Kiel as a Royal (Danish) Academic dance teacher to announce his classes for adults and children (see *Altonaer Nachrichten*, No. 81, 8 October 1836). He also publicised his arrival in Altona in the *PgN* (No. 231) of Hamburg on 28 September, and announced the beginning of the classes on 1 October. Other dance teachers also announced themselves in the *PgN*, especially in the issue of 28 September: J. H. C. Lindhorst, H. W. Voss, and A. C. Töpfer (a ballet dancer). Some balls are also announced there, but to a slightly lesser extent than in Altona. Additionally, however, there are several announcements of dance music, some of them illuminated by special gas lighting or 'brilliant Venetian theatre illumination' (*PgN*, No. 225, p. 9, 21 September 1836).[61] A special ball with *Harmoniemusik*, i.e. music played by a brass band, was announced for 20 October. Here, again, Strauss's Vienna was the model, as the advertisement says explicitly: 'humoristic-musical Evening-Entertainment à la Strauß and Lanner' (*PgN*, No. 250, p. 8).

Circumstances

Living composers of so-called 'serious' musical works are not often mentioned in the Hamburg newspapers of early autumn 1836, insofar as their work is not listed in the programme of concerts and operas played at that time in Hamburg, or in the announcements of music shops selling

---

61 Such a 'Venetian illumination' is also connected with the name of Johann Strauss. A brightly illuminated Venetian Night in the open-air Augarten took place on 29 July 1833, see Schönherr and Reinöhl, *Johann Strauss Vater*, pp. 96ff., repeated the following year on 21 July 1834, ibid., pp. 111ff.

musical scores. We find some brief news items in the *Correspondent*: about the concerts of Franz Lachner (1803–1880) in Munich, who was capellmeister there from 1 July (*Correspondent*, No. 234, 3 October); about Felix Mendelssohn (1809–1847), who had returned from his journey to Leipzig, now married to the daughter of a reformist preacher in Frankfurt (*Correspondent*, No. 238, 7 October); or about the first opera by a female composer in France, *Le mauvais oeil* of Loïsa Puget (1810–1889) (*Correspondent*, No. 244, 14 October).

The political affairs of September and October 1836, in Germany and elsewhere, were widely reported. Most of the space was taken up by the revolutionary chain of events in Spain and Portugal, which were communicated via Paris (this appeared in the Hamburg newspapers up to three weeks later than the actual events). Later in October, the German veterans of the Napoleonic Wars from 1813 were still remembered in news outlets.

The most remarkable technical innovations of the time were already under way: gas lighting and the transport revolution, comprising steamships on rivers and oceans, and the invention of the railway.[62] Superficially speaking, railway and steamships do not seem to have much to do with music and dance. They are intimately linked to them, however, when it comes to the dissemination of products and the interchange of goods and ideas, modes and fashions. Strauss did not only use new industries to spread his music, but also included them as part of his very compositions (as, for example, in the *Railway Pleasure Waltzes*). In this context, *Hansjörgel*'s comment about naming Waltzes is understandable: 'I think about: Heaver and Hoaver, Swinger, Fire in Every Corner, Electrifying Waltzes, Feet Steam Engine, or something similar'.[63] The dynamics of the Waltz are comparable to the dynamics of technically advanced locomotion movements, with both developing in parallel. What was later called the Biedermeier period was also a time of rapid technological change, from the late 1820s, which occurred alongside the evolution and dissemination of Strauss's Waltzes.

---

62 Further developing technical innovations of the later 1830s were electric telegraphy and the daguerreotype.

63 *Komische Briefe des Hansjörgels von Gumpoldskirchen*, a monthly Austrian journal, appearing from 1832–1851. Quoted according to Schönherr and Reinöhl, *Johann Strauss Vater*, p. 93: 'I denket mir für so was: Heber und Schweber, Antaucher, Feuer in allen Ecken, Electrisir-Walzer, Fußdampfmaschin' oder so was'.

Gas lighting on the streets was first tested in London in 1807–1808 and came into general use from 1814. Vienna followed in 1818. Other German cities that adopted gas lighting at this time were Hanover (1825) and Berlin (1826), while Hamburg instituted gas lighting as street light in 1845. Aiming to provide European cities with gas lighting, the London-based *Imperial Continental Gas Association* (ICGA) was founded in 1824. The *NZ* (No. 246) of 15 October published the arrival of (George William) Drory (1803–1879), co-director of the ICGA, in Aachen for negotiating the gas lighting for the city.[64] The newspaper also reported that Mr Drory had previously established gas lighting in Amsterdam, Ghent, Lille, and Harlem. Illumination also played a growing role in the locations chosen for concerts and balls, as these were often evening or night events.

Fig. 10.5 Jacob Petersen, *The Steamship Frederik den Siette*, 1838. Landesmuseum, Schleswig, Germany. Frederik den Siette was the first steamship built in Denmark. Wikimedia Commons, Public Domain, https://da.wikipedia.org/wiki/Jacob_Petersen_(maler)#/media/Fil:Ship_Frederik_den_Siette_by_Jacob_Petersen.jpg

---

64   Gas lighting illuminated the streets of Aachen from September of 1838.

With respect to new developments in transport, a regular steamboat crossing the river Elbe between Hamburg and Harburg began in 1829, although intercontinental overseas travel by steamboat had not yet begun.[65] Shorter distances between Kiel and Copenhagen were already done by the steamship *Caledonia* in 1819, and in 1836 the *NZ* (15 October) announced the steamship *Frederik den Siette* was to leave Kiel for Copenhagen on (all) Saturdays. A longer article from the day before (*NZ*, No. 245, 14 October) discussed the advent of 'steamboating on the ocean' (p. 2): 'The steamships will change the contacts of the people with whom they move [or socialise]'.

The railways were also on the horizon. The first railway connection, built between Liverpool and Manchester, opened in 1830. Five years later, the first German railway connected Nuremberg with Fürth. In Austria, the railway between Vienna and Deutsch-Wagram opened in 1837. In July 1836, Strauss's first 'Railway Festival' (*Eisenbahnfest*) took place, for which he composed the *Railway Pleasure Waltzes* (*Eisenbahn-Lust-Walzer*), Op. 89.

A long article *Ueber Eisenbahnen und das Interesse Hamburgs* from Friedrich List's (1789–1846) *Railway-Journal* (*Eisenbahn-Journal*) of 1835 was republished in three parts in the *NZ* (No. 230) of 27 (No. 232) and 29 September, and 5 October 1836 (No. 237). Since the early 1830s, there were plans for a railway connection from Hamburg to Lübeck at the Baltic Sea, but it would have had to cross parts of Denmark, and the Danish did not accept these plans, so the line was not built before the 1860s. The first Hamburg railway was connected with Bergedorf (on Hamburg ground, between 1844 and 1846 extended to Berlin), planned by William Lindley (1808–1900) in 1838 and opened in May 1842, during the great fire of Hamburg (5–8 May), when it transported firemen rather than guests, and evacuated those who had lost their homes. The Danish, for their part, built a railway between Kiel and Altona, which opened in 1844. This demonstrates the political dimensions of national and international connections: Altona (as well as Hamburg) was part of the German Confederation with its many member states and a territory that extended south to Trieste and Ljubljana (Laibach). At the same time,

---

65 The US sailing ship 'Savannah' had an additional paddle steam engine, when it crossed the Atlantic in 1819 (without cargo and passengers), but most of the journey was powered by sail.

it was also part of the Danish *helstaten* (1773–1864),[66] which included Iceland, Greenland, the Faroe Isles, some oversea colonies, and (until 1814) Norway.[67] As for Hamburg, it had the power to negotiate shipping and trade treaties that connected German economies with overseas countries.[68] Finally, south of the Elbe, a railway connection from Harburg to Hanover was planned in the 1830s, which opened between Hanover and Celle in 1845, and between Celle and Harburg in 1847.[69]

---

66 Some maintain that the period of *helstaten* began in 1814 with the treaty of Kiel, others allude to the treaty of Zarskoje Selo (near St. Petersburg in Russia), 1773. On the treaty of Kiel see *Der Kieler Frieden 1814. Ein Schicksalsjahr für den Norden*, ed. by Sonja Kinzler (Neumünster/Hamburg: Wachholtz, 2014).

67 Thomas Hill remarks that the nineteenth-century period of *helstaten* was viewed negatively by Danish national romantics. However, this would not have been the case in the eighteenth century, when patriotism was very different from the nineteenth-century nationalism it became. A professor in Kiel, Dietrich Hermann Hegewisch (1740–1812), for example, wrote in 1784: 'Love your fatherland to bits; and what is your fatherland? All countries of the King; Denmark, Norway, Holstein and Iceland, not a single one excluded' (Dietrich Hermann Hegewisch, *Über die gegenseitigen Pflichten verschiedener unter Einem Oberhaupte vereinigter Nationen*, 2nd edn (Eckardt: Altona, 1784), p. 5). Hegewisch quoted this sentence from a work by the Danish-Norwegian historian Peter Frederik Suhm (1728–1798); see Peter Frederik Suhm, *Danmarks, Norges og Holstens Historie i Udtog, til den studerende Ungdoms Tjeneste* (Copenhagen: L. Simmelkjaer, 1776), https://archive.org/details/historienafdanm00suhmgoog/page/n9/mode/2up. See also Silke Göttsch, 'Grenzziehungen — Grenzerfahrungen. Das Beispiel Schleswig-Holstein und Dänemark 1800–1860', in *Grenzen and Differenzen. Zur Macht sozialer und kultureller Grenzziehungen*, ed. by Thomas Hengartner and Johannes Moser (Leipzig: Leipziger Universitätsverlag 2006) pp. 383–94, who argues, along with Suhm, that national differentiation was still not problematised. Hegewisch, for his part, considered that the period characterised by nationalism (*Nationalhass*: national hate) lay in the past, and his time would be happier for everybody (Hegewisch, *Über die gegenseitigen Pflichten*, p. 9). More unusual, particularly in the German context, is the comprehensive study of Jörg Echternkamp, who describes differences as well as continuities between eighteenth-century patriotism and nineteenth-century nationalism in three parts (1770–1800, 1800–1820, 1820–1840): Echternkamp, *Der Aufstieg des deutschen Nationalismus*.

68 The shipping and trade treaty between the Free and Hanseatic cities of Lübeck, Hamburg, and Bremen with Brazil, ratified in 1828, was a milestone in this regard; see *Handels- und Schiffahrtsvertrag zwischen den Senaten der freien und Hansestädte Lübeck, Bremen und Hamburg, und Sr. Majestät dem Kaiser von Brasilien, unterzeichnet zu Rio de Janeiro am 17. November 1827. Eine Dokumentation von Herbert Minnemann*, ed. by Albrecht von Gleich (Hamburg: Institut für Iberoamerika-Kunde, 1977).

69 Until 1837, Great Britain and the kingdom of Hanover were ruled in personal union. Article 1 of the German Federal Act of 1815 begins as follows: 'The King of Great Britain and Ireland as the King of Hanover, the King of Denmark as the Duke of Holstein and Lauenburg, and the King of the Netherlands as the Grand Duke of Luxembourg are associated with the German Confederation. They are Princes of the Confederation as all the others too'.

Eduard Beurmann wrote that the people of the city states of Lübeck, Bremen and Hamburg were not overly concerned about the rest of Germany, which they viewed mostly as a market for their goods. Nonetheless, they maintained Germany's trade with the transatlantic world.[70] He added that Hamburg, in particular, would become a global city with daily connections to the East, West, North and South.[71] However, Beurmann considered the patriotism in Hamburg (and generally in Germany) as provincial and apolitical (in the sense of national pretensions). Hamburg would end at its city gates, and — in reference to the circumstances throughout Germany — he (over)stated that it would be easier to get from Germany to America than from Hamburg to Altona.[72]

Conclusions

The distribution via new means of reproduction of the musical scores of Johann Strauss the Elder and Joseph Lanner made dance music popular on a supra-regional level. Strauss, in particular, achieved international fame through touring with his orchestra far from Vienna. His music became known in other European regions soon after being published. Although this fact does not sufficiently explain how the dance was spread, the dissemination of well-known dance music certainly influenced the distribution of Waltz as a dance.[73] However,

---

70 Beurmann, *Skizzen aus den Hanse-Städten*, p. 8.
71 Ibid., pp. 157ff. Another book of interest regarding Hamburg and Altona, and also published in 1836, is a five-hundred-page handbook: Ant. Joh. Heinr. Meyer, *Hamburg und Altona nebst Umgegend. Topographisch-statistisch-historisches Handbuch für Einheimische und Fremde* (Hamburg and Itzehoe: Schuberth & Niemeyer, 1836). As an appendix, Meyer gives 'special notices for foreigners' with all locations of consular offices. These include representations of thirty other states from inside as well as from outside the German Confederation.
72 Eduard Beurmann, *Deutschland und die Deutschen*, vol. 1 (Altona: Johann Friedrich Hammerich, 1838), p. 215: 'Fürwahr man kann leichter von Deutschland nach Amerika gelangen, als von Hamburg nach Altona, und doch wollen wir eine Nation sein'.
73 Apart from the regional dissemination, the seasonal changes were also of importance. In Vienna, for example, dance and dance music boomed during Carnival in February, meanwhile during Passiontide in April and also in the summer season there was comparatively little, as Alice M. Hanson proved on the basis of music impost (Alice M. Hanson, *Die zensurierte Muse. Musikleben im Wiener Biedermeier* (Vienna: Böhlau, 1987), p. 180).

Strauss and some of his colleagues not only played at the balls, but also began to perform music not composed especially for dance. For example, the overtures of contemporary and popular operas were part of the concerts of the so called 'Waltz kings', and Strauss also included the themes of such operas as a reference to his own compositions. Be that as it may, philosophically-oriented writing on music discarded the compositions of the 'Waltz kings' as merely entertaining. Subsequently, dance music (and dance in general) never became a serious part of academic discourse on music history and historiography. However, Strauss was very up to date with developments of his time, so much so that, especially from 1830 onwards, his music had begun to change rapidly with the proliferation of technical innovations.[74]

Strauss's stay in Hamburg in the autumn of 1836 gives an insight into how new forms of supra-regional touring with an orchestra of about thirty musicians was organised partly on the spot when changing dates or prolonging the stay. The newspapers also provide some information about the circumstances of that time, about international affairs, technical innovations, and organisation of balls and cultural events. Studying dance and dance music in other cities, in addition to their supposed places of 'origin', shows that, already in the 1830s, the distribution of music and dance genres was beginning to have an international appearance, first in Europe, and, subsequently, worldwide.

Fig. 10.6 Audio: Eisenbahnlustwalzer, Op. 89 by Johann Strauss the Elder, performed by the Slovak State Philharmonic Orchestra. 'Eisenbahn-Lust-Walzer, Op. 89', 7:35, posted online by Slovak State Philharmonic Orchestra — Topic, *Youtube*, 16 August 2018, https://www.youtube.com/watch?v=q_k2kuhG0BM

---

74 To what extent such industrial changes were reflected in the dynamics of dances newly in fashion may be explored in future studies.

Bibliography

Baasch, Ernst, *Geschichte des Hamburgischen Zeitungswesens von den Anfängen bis 1914* (Hamburg: Friederichsen, de Gruyter & Co. m. b. H., 1930).

Bauer, Elisabeth Eleonore, *Wie Beethoven auf den Sockel kam. Die Entstehung eines musikalischen Mythos* (Stuttgart: Metzler, 1992).

Beurmann, Eduard, *Deutschland und die Deutschen*, vol. 1 (Altona: Johann Friedrich Hammerich, 1838).

——, *Skizzen aus den Hanse-Städten* (Hanau: Friedrich König, 1836), https://reader.digitale-sammlungen.de/de/fs1/object/display/bsb10018583_00005.html

Caeyers, Jan, *Beethoven. Der einsame Revolutionär. Eine Biographie* (Munich: Beck, 2012).

Der Kieler Frieden 1814. Ein Schicksalsjahr für den Norden —The Peace of Kiel 1814. A Fateful Year for the North.—Kielfreden 1814. Et skjebnear for hele Norden [n.a.], ed. by Sonja Kinzler (Neumünster/Hamburg: Wachholtz, 2014).

Dörner, Wolfgang, *Joseph Lanner — Chronologisch-thematisches Werkverzeichnis* (Vienna: Böhlau, 2012).

Echternkamp, Jörg, *Der Aufstieg des deutschen Nationalismus (1770–1840)* (Frankfurt: Campus, 1998).

Erichsen, Jørgen, *Friedrich Kuhlau. Ein deutscher Musiker in Kopenhagen. Eine Biographie nach zeitgenössischen Dokumenten* (Hildesheim, Zürich, New York: Olms, 2011).

Evans, Richard J., *Death in Hamburg. Society and Politics in the Cholera-Years 1830–1910* (Oxford: Oxford University Press, 1987).

Faulstich, Werner, 'Einführung', in *Grundwissen Medien*, ed. by Werner Faulstich, 5th edn (Munich: Fink, 2004), p. 9.

Fuchs, Ingrid, 'Zur Wiener Kammermusiktradition zwischen Schubert und Brahms', in *Brahms' Schubert-Rezeption im Wiener Kontext*, ed. by Otto Biba, Gernot Gruber, Katharina Loose-Einfalt, and Siegfried Oechsle (Stuttgart: Franz Steiner, 2017), pp. 33–49.

Göttsch, Silke, 'Grenzziehungen — Grenzerfahrungen. Das Beispiel Schleswig-Holstein und Dänemark 1800–1860', in *Grenzen & Differenzen. Zur Macht sozialer und kultureller Grenzziehungen*, ed. by Thomas Hengartner and Johannes Moser (Leipzig: Leipziger Universitätsverlag, 2006).

Handels- und Schiffahrtsvertrag zwischen den Senaten der freien und Hansestädte Lübeck, Bremen und Hamburg, und Sr. Majestät dem Kaiser von Brasilien, unterzeichnet zu Rio de Janeiro am 17. November 1827 (Tratado de Comércio e Navegção...) Eine Dokumentation von Herbert Minnemann [n.a.], ed. by Albrecht von Gleich (Hamburg: Institut für Iberoamerika-Kunde, 1977).

Hanson, Alice M., *Die zensurierte Muse. Musikleben im Wiener Biedermeier* (Vienna: Böhlau, 1987); originally published as *Musical Life in Biedermeier Vienna* (Cambrige: Cambridge University Press, 1985).

Hegewisch, Dietrich Hermann, *Über die gegenseitigen Pflichten verschiedener unter Einem Oberhaupte vereinigter Nationen*, 2nd edn (Eckardt: Altona, 1784).

Heine, Heinrich, 'XXXIII' (Paris, 20 April 1841), in 'Lutetia — Erster Teil', http://www.heinrich-heine-denkmal.de/heine-texte/lutetia33.shtml

Hill, Thomas, 'Liebet euer Vaterland über alles. Zur Konstruktion und Wirksamkeit eines Gesamtstaatspatriotismus in der dänischen Monarchie Ende des 18. Jahrhunderts', in *Rund um die Meere des Nordens. Festschrift für Hain Rebas*, ed. by Michael Engelbrecht, Ulrike Hanssen-Decker, and Daniel Höffker (Heide: Boyens, 2008), pp. 131–44.

Hirschbach, Hermann, 'Ueber Beethoven's letzte Streichquartette', *Neue Zeitschrift für Musik*, 11 (1839), 5–6.

Kobylanska, Krystyna, ed., *Frédéric Chopin: Briefe* (Frankfurt am Main: Fischer, 1984; Berlin (GDR): Henschel, 1983).

Linke, Norbert, *Musik erobert die Welt oder Wie die Wiener Familie Strauß die Wiener Familie Strauß die 'Unterhaltungsmusik' revolutionierte* (Vienna: Herold, 1987).

Lyser, Johann Peter, 'Beethoven', in *Beethoven. Zwei Novellen von Johann Peter Lyser und Ernst Ortlepp*, ed. by Paul Bülow (Lübeck: Antäus, 1924), pp. 8–41.

Meyer, Ant. Joh. Heinr., *Hamburg und Altona nebst Umgegend. Topographisch-statistisch-historisches Handbuch für Einheimische und Fremde* (Hamburg and Itzehoe: Schuberth & Niemeyer, 1836).

Miller, Frank, *Johann Strauss Vater. Der musikalische Magier des Wiener Biedermeier* (Eisenburg: Castell, 1999).

Ortlepp, Ernst, 'Beethoven', in *Beethoven. Zwei Novellen von Johann Peter Lyser und Ernst Ortlepp*, ed. by Paul Bülow (Lübeck: Antäus, 1924), pp. 43–72.

Schönherr, Max, and Karl Reinöhl, *Johann Strauss Vater. Ein Werkverzeichnis* (*Das Jahrhundert des Walzers I. Band*) (London: Universal Edition, 1954).

Scott, Derek B., *Sounds of the Metropolis. The 19th-Century Popular Music Revolution in London, New York, Paris, and Vienna* (Oxford: Oxford University Press, 2008).

Suhm, Peter Frederik, *Danmarks, Norges og Holstens Historie i Udtog, til den studerende Ungdoms Tjeneste* (Copenhagen: L. Simmelkjaer, 1776), https://archive.org/details/historienafdanm00suhmgoog/page/n9/mode/2up

Torp, Jörgen, *Alte atlantische Tangos. Rhythmische Figurationen im Wandel der Zeiten und Kulturen* (Hamburg: LIT Verlag, 2007).

——, 'Zur Entwicklungsgeschichte urbaner Popularmusik unter besonderer Berücksichtigung des Tango rioplatense' (unpublished master's thesis, University of Hamburg, 1989).

Voss, Egon, 'Das Beethoven-Bild der Beethoven-Belletristik. Zu einigen Erzählungen des 19. Jahrhunderts', in *Beethoven und die Nachwelt. Materialien zur Wirkungsgeschichte Beethovens*, ed. by Helmut Loos (Bonn: Beethoven-Haus, 1986), pp. 81–94.

Wagner, Richard, 'Eine Pilgerfahrt zu Beethoven', in *Richard Wagner. Ausgewählte Schriften und Briefe*, ed. by Philipp Werner (Frankfurt am Main: Fischer, 2013), pp. 27–53.

Wicke, Peter, *Von Mozart zu Madonna. Eine Kulturgeschichte der Popmusik* (Berlin: Suhrkamp Verlag, 2001).

Wendt, (Johann) Amadeus, *Ueber den gegenwärtigen Zustand der Musik besonders in Deutschland und wie er geworden. Eine beurtheilende Schilderung* (Göttingen: Dieterichsche Buchhandlung, 1836).

Witzmann, Reingard, *Der Ländler in Wien. Ein Beitrag zur Entwicklungsgeschichte des Wiener Walzers bis in die Zeit des Wiener Kongresses* (Vienna: Arbeitsstelle für den Volkskundeatlas in Österreich, 1976).

11. Continuity and Reinvention: Past Round Dances in Present Estonia[1]

Sille Kapper

Introduction

Who needs round dances today, and why? The aim of this chapter is to discuss the meanings and functions of round dances[2] in social and recreational contexts in Estonia, since the nineteenth century, and explore the way in which they gradually turned into a specific practice valued as local or national cultural heritage. The dance forms in question derive from the repertoire of the Estonian-speaking population, who, until the beginning of the twentieth century, lived mainly in rural settings. I shall focus on the use of past round dance forms in modern times — from 1991, when important changes in the entire social and cultural sphere were initiated by Estonia regaining its independence, until 2012,

---

1   This research was supported by ETF (Eesti Teadusfond, Estonian Science Foundation), grant no. 9132.
2   In this contribution, the concept of round dances is based on the minutes of the first meeting of a sub-study group of the study group on Ethnochoreology, *Round Dances — Couple Dances Originating in the 19th Century*, held in Prague on 3–6 April 2003. According to the minutes, the major characteristics of round dances were that 1) one couple can realise a complete version of a dance; 2) couple-turning moves along a circular path; and 3) in couple turning, partners face each other. Waltz, Polka, Schottische and Mazurka were mentioned as focal dance types for the planned research, while regulated (one-melody, sequence) dances were considered as a separate group, adjacent, but connected, to round dances.

when the research project was completed. During the period under study, we witnessed a broad range of different and partially opposed ideologies and identities revealed in the dancing of round dances in Estonia. A Polka or Waltz can be danced because they are perceived as a manifestation of someone's local origin (identity); for a dancer or choreographer the same dances may also mean and express being Estonian (as national identity and ideology). However, these dances can also be chosen by a dancer or a choreographer in order to emphasise some aspects considered characteristic, important, and desired in traditional dancing (ideology) by a particular community or group of dancers (identity), etc. To understand the roots of these numerous possibilities for interpreting round dances in a contemporary society, I shall provide a short summary of the history of round dances in Estonia.

General Outlines of the Historical Background

Round dances conquered the dance floors of Estonian peasants by the end of the nineteenth century,[3] superseding earlier chain dances, older forms of couple dancing and contra dances.[4] The scholarly collection of Estonian folk dances[5] started in 1913[6] and at first, relatively little attention was paid to unregulated round dances. The focus was on

---

[3] Kristjan Torop, 'Kus sai tantsida ja mida tantsiti enne meid', in *Vanad seltskonnatantsud*, ed. by Heino Aassalu, Pill Luht, and Kristjan Torop (Tallinn: Rahvakultuuri Arendus- ja Koolituskeskus, 1997), pp. 8–12 (pp. 10–11).

[4] Rudolf Põldmäe and Herbert Tampere, *Valimik eesti rahvatantse* (Tartu: Eesti Rahvaluule Arhiiv 1938), p. 41.

[5] In order to avoid confusing connotations, I employ the term *traditional dance* instead of *folk dance*, but the latter sometimes appears in quotations and reviews.

[6] The earliest data about Estonians' dancing are found in *Gesta Danorum* by Saxo Grammaticus (1172), followed by medieval chronicles (1584, 1610), and later travelogues (1741, 1819), in which Baltic-Germans emotionally describe local festivities. See Anu Vissel, 'Ülevaade varasematest töödest eesti rahvatantsu kogumisel ja arhiveerimisel Eesti Rahvaluule Arhiivi materjalide põhjal', in *Rahvatantsu uurimine: arhiivid, meetodid*, ed. by E. Lukka (Viljandi: Viljandi Kultuurikolledž, 1991), pp. 54–64 (pp. 54–55). In 1913, Anna Raudkats, the first Estonian scholar specialising in choreology, made expeditions to Kolga rand on the Northern coast and Setumaa in the South-West of Estonia. Her research produced a list of thirty-eight dances (EÜS X 1147/1335). Raudkats herself considered many of them as 'modern salon dances with local names', and did not accord particular importance to this set within the dances listed; Richard Tõnnus, *Anna Raudkats oma ajas* (Tallinn: Eesti Raamat, 1991).

variants of sequence dances and older forms, where possible. Probably one reason for the lack of interest in 'simple' Polkas and Waltzes was their popularity and wide distribution as social dances among different population groups, which encumbered their use on stage. During Estonia's first period of independence between 1918 and 1940, the capacity to build national identity was the main justification for any kind of national research, including folklore studies. As can be detected from contemporaneous comments,[7] folklorists looked particularly for obsolete dance forms. Valuable materials were as old and 'authentic' as possible, preferably without urban influences,[8] and peculiar to 'original'[9] Estonian peasant culture. Round dances, especially their unregulated forms (as opposed to sequence forms) were considered unsuitable for stage presentation, and therefore not worth collecting either.

With the development of technology, film recording of traditional dancing was also made possible from the beginning of the twentieth century, but, due to several reasons, a thorough analysis of collected audio-visual materials only started in 2007.[10] Materials recorded from the small West-Estonian island of Kihnu formed the first collection to be analysed, and it also constitutes an important part of the basic data used in the present study. The statistical composition of analysed film and video clips provides evidence for oral statements often repeated in the archives.[11] 31 of 352 excerpts are classified as Polka and 43 as Waltz, the rest are divided between 44 different dance types (mainly one-melody dances, sequence dances, but also unregulated Schottische and *Labajalg* — to be addressed later in this chapter). While archival

---

7   E.g. 'Ka rahvatants muinsuskaitse alla' [n.a.], *Postimees*, 200 (28 July 1936).
8   It should be noted that urban influences were certainly there. According to folklore collections, many popular dances are said to be 'brought in' by musicians, seamen, remote workers or soldiers. But, unlike many other European countries, there are no (or at least no discovered) references to dancing masters' activities or organised training courses in Estonia before the first period of independence (1920–1939).
9   Meaning here: unique, different from others.
10 The grant project ETF7231 examining 'original choreographic text and performing style of Estonian folk dances on the material of audio-visual recordings' was carried out by researchers from Estonian Literary Museum (Ingrid Rüütel) and Tallinn University (Eha Rüütel, Angela Arraste and Sille Kapper), based on materials from West-Estonian island Kihnu. See also https://www.etis.ee/Portal/Projects/Display/2c23791e-80ab-4a48-b957-79d568798615?lang=ENG
11 'Polka and Waltz were the main dances' as Kristjan Torop has put it in *Viron vakka. 105 virolaista kansantanssia* (Tampere: Suomalaisen kansantanssin ystävät ry., 1991), p. 10.

manuscripts shed light on the end of the nineteenth and the beginning of the twentieth century all over Estonia, the audio-visual recordings used in my study derive from Kihnu in 1931–2009. However, the proportion of round dances seems to be quite similar in both sources. At the same time, unregulated Polka and Waltz dances, although very popular, are not described in published Estonian folk dance collections,[12] which are based on verbal fieldwork notes, mainly from the first half of the twentieth century. This suggests low folkloristic interest in those dance types, but this is explained by the fact that at the time of collecting, round dances were still popular — everybody knew them and so they felt no need to fix or preserve them. Another reason for the lack of interest may be the seeming simplicity of round dance patterns — dances without formation were deemed unsuitable for stage presentation.

Due to the late inception of the scholarly collection of traditional dances in Estonia, we have little information about their choreographic texts before the mid-nineteenth century. Assumptions have been made based on indirect sources such as music, or on better-investigated neighbouring dance cultures like those of the Finnish, Scandinavian (especially Swedish), Russian and also German peoples, because the local upper class in Estonia consisted of Baltic-German nobility. However, researchers[13] have claimed that Estonian peasants probably had more influential cultural contacts with the lower classes of neighbouring countries. This can be seen from the repertory spread and the proliferation of dancing styles that were described as rather simple and having little in common with court dances. For a more nuanced appreciation of round dancing, we have to consider the communication that existed between the Baltic-German nobility and Estonian-speaking peasant communities — in archival manuscripts, there are remarks that refer to their dancing together, although as a rare and exceptional occasion.

---

12 Such as Anna Raudkats, *Eesti rahvatantsud* (Tartu: Postimees, 1926); Põldmäe and Tampere, *Valimik*; Herbert Tampere, *Eesti rahvapillid ja rahvatantsud* (Tallinn: Eesti Raamat 1975); Torop, *Viron vakka. 105 virolaista kansantanssia*.

13 Põldmäe and Tampere, *Valimik*; Kristjan Torop, *Kontratantsud* (Tallinn: Rahvakultuuri Arendus- ja Koolituskeskus, 1995).

Theoretical Background and Some Methodological Aspects

In this article, round dances are addressed mainly within the frameworks of social communication and traditional dancing. I define the latter based on Lauri Honko[14] and Tiiu Jaago[15] as a part of folklore (oral traditions) — a way of dancing or a dance form that exists in variants and occurs within communities. This folkloristic approach is essential when analysing choreographic texts, with which a credible dance study should begin. Looking at verbal descriptions, audio-visual recordings, and live events of round dances danced in Estonia, their individual and communal variability is obvious. In public discourse, the same phenomenon may also be called 'folk dancing', but I would rather avoid this term here because of its vague nature and connotations related to stage performance. I shall mention stage dance later in this article (and the expressions 'national stage dance' and 'stage folk dance' are then used as synonyms) — this is because of the particular situation in Estonia where the position of stage dance is very visible and powerful, leading people to see traditional dancing through the prism of stage folk dance as well.

The social position of traditional dancing is better understood by addressing it as a functional practice, which could be defined by its use of traditional movement elements or patterns for different purposes like ritual or social communication. Following Richard Handler and Jocelyn Linnekin,[16] tradition can be seen as a symbolic representation of the past, inseparable from its present interpretation. I find this approach especially suitable in the case of such an ephemeral phenomenon as dancing, regardless of whether the first, second or third existence of a dance[17] is in question, as we shall see in this chapter.

---

14 Lauri Honko, 'Folklooriprotsess', *Mäetagused*, 6 (1998), 56–84, https://doi.org/10.7592/mt1998.06.honko

15 Tiiu Jaago 'Rahvaluule mõiste kujunemine Eestis', *Mäetagused*, 9 (1999), 70–91, https://doi.org/10.7592/mt1999.09.rhl

16 Richard Handler and Jocelyn Linnekin, 'Tradition: Genuine or Spurious?', *Journal of American Folklore*, 97 (1984), 273–88, https://doi.org/10.2307/540610

17 Andriy Nahachewsky, 'Participatory and Presentational Dance as Ethnochoreological Categories', *Dance Research Journal*, 27/1 (1995), 1–15, https://doi.org/10.2307/1478426

Regina Bendix[18] emphasises the temporal character of the authenticity of traditions and asks who needs them and why. Proceeding from this idea, traditional dancing can also be addressed as a bodily manifestation of identity — either personal or corporate, not necessarily national. People need and use dancing to reinforce or even declare their identity, and identity formation through real bodily activity should be accessible to everybody. In today's Estonia, national identity-building is colourfully expressed in choreographed national dances, widely practised in organised folk dance groups and performed on stages and in stadiums. The individual agency and identity of dancers tends to be suppressed in such cases, and therefore, one cannot really address such dancing as revival or second-existence dance.[19] Traditional dancing in its participatory and social functions, on the contrary, permits and reveals personal identities because it is based on dancers' adherence to norms or rules they have chosen deliberately.

Until about the end of the nineteenth century, traditional dancing was the only way of dancing an Estonian peasant would consider — other opportunities were unknown or at least their practice unthinkable. Nowadays, traditional dance as a style is chosen consciously and purposefully from an immense range of alternatives. Choosing round dances is another step further along the same path, which reveals something about their attitude to traditional dancing, and to traditional culture in general.

Although some data describing local variants of internationally known round dances has existed in Estonian folklore collections since their very beginning, the opportunity to highlight round dances as a special genre and possible expression of identity has emerged only with their gradual falling out of everyday use. The speed of this process has differed regionally throughout the twentieth century. Now we have arrived at a highly interesting situation in which round dances are practised in different, smaller communities, both real and imagined,[20]

---

18 Regina Bendix, *In Search of Authenticity: The Formation of Folklore Studies* (Madison: University of Washington Press, 1997).

19 Please see Felix Hoerburger, 'Once Again: On the Concept of "Folk Dance"', *Journal of the International Folk Music Council*, 20 (1968), 30–32, https://doi.org/10.2307/836068

20 Benedict Anderson's (1983) concept of imagined communities refers to nations as socially constructed and imagined groups of people who never really meet all together. I propose to imagine communities as culturally constructed groups whose

usually in recreational situations, but nevertheless carrying several identity-related meanings or ideologies. Previously, addressing staged folklore and dance folklorism in Estonia[21] and following the examples of Peter Niedermüller[22] and Ingrid Rüütel,[23] I have also referred to such groups as symbolic communities — groups of people sharing common values and expressing them in their choices concerning dance movements and context. In this chapter I have decided to use the term 'imagined communities' to stress the imaginary of dancers' communities as differentiated from real social groups of people.

In dance research, direct participant observation can sometimes contribute more than a critical analysis of recordings. Therefore, much of my data concerning the context and use of round dances nowadays derive from my personal bodily experiences on dance floors, combined with observation and conversations with dancers and musicians. My unstructured fieldwork diary covers about the last eight years of my experience, but my visual and bodily memory as a dancer and dance teacher reaches back to the 1990s. Based on the combination of verbal, visual and embodied data, I shall proceed with my discussion of the main issue of this chapter: the role and position of round dances in Estonian social dance tradition.

Round Dance Types in Kihnu

The memories of elderly people interviewed by dance collectors since the beginning of the twentieth century reach back to the second half of the nineteenth century, even in Kihnu, where systematic dance

---

peculiarities come from, and are expressed in, their dancing. Benedict Anderson, *Imagined Communities: Reflections on the Origin and Spread of Nationalism* (London and New York: Verso, 1983).

21 Sille Kapper, 'Tantsufolklorismist tänases Eestis', in *Tonditosin*, ed. by Mall Hiiemäe and Liina Saarlo (Tartu: Eesti Kirjandusmuuseumi Teaduskirjastus, 2008), pp. 24–52.

22 Peter Niedermüller, 'Central Europe between Tradition and Modernity', in *Tradition and Modernisation. Plenary Papers Read at the 4th International Congress of the Société Internationale d'Ethnologie et de Folklore*, ed. by Reimund Kvideland (Turku: NIF Publications, 1992) pp. 109–21.

23 Ingrid Rüütel, 'Pärimuskultuur postmodernistlikus ühiskonnas — minevikurelikt või taasleitud väärtus?', in *Pärimusmuusika muutuvas ühiskonnas. Töid etnomusikoloogia alalt*, vol. 1, ed. by Triinu Ojamaa and Ingrid Rüütel (Tartu: Eesti Kirjandusmuuseumi etnomusikoloogia osakond, 2002), pp. 165–89.

collection started especially late — the first descriptions derive from 1932, written by local school teacher, historian and musician Theodor Saar (1906–1984).

Kihnu, with its approximately 500 inhabitants and 16.4 km² area, is a small island located in the Baltic Sea. Physical detachment (it lies over 10km from the mainland, and 41km from the nearest city) has shaped the conditions for the preservation of regional differences in Kihnu culture. Among other traditional phenomena present in everyday life today, Kihnu people know their older dance forms well and are always eager to dance when musicians play the suitable tunes. This has made possible a relatively long period of folkloristic documentation, and in this way Kihnu culture constitutes a unique reservoir for a researcher interested in the change in traditions over time, including dancing. Continuous dance practices in Kihnu literally provide tangible data from intangible past times.

Labajalg before and after the Waltz

In the middle of the nineteenth century and earlier, the only dance used for entertainment purposes in Kihnu was *Labajalg*.[24] It is important to discuss *Labajalg* here because it is the direct predecessor of the Waltz in Estonia, and remains closely related to it after the emergence of the Waltz in Estonia. In earlier scholarly literature,[25] *Labajalg* is described as similar to several European 3/4-time couple dances with rather fast

---

24 ERA II 56, 206 (26) and 217 (3) — H. Tampere 1933; ERA II 128, 41 (10) — H. Tampere 1936. Chain dances with *labajalg*-like basic steps were also used in ritual functions, which slowly disappeared during the second half of the nineteenth and the first half of the twentieth centuries, and have sometimes been revived for special occasions later (e.g. SKSÄ-K 23 — P.-L. Rausmaa, I. Rüütel, K. Torop 1987). The ritual function of round dances is not the main topic of this chapter, but I cannot resist mentioning that our 'main dances', Polka and Waltz, have also been used in ritual situations, e.g. bridal dancing at weddings, which used to be graced by the (pre-Waltz) *Labajalg* (Kristjan Torop, *Viron vakka. 105 eesti rahvatantsu* (Tallinn: Eesti Rahvatantsu ja Rahvamuusika Selts, 2008), p. 14). Later, the Waltz or Polka tended to fulfil this function (RKM II 10, 11/104 (2) — T. Saar 1947). The most common dance in this context was the Waltz, and it is also the dance of the bridal couple in contemporary mainland weddings — special wedding Waltz lessons are taught for that purpose, but sometimes newlyweds select their favourite tune to perform the dance to.

25 Põldmäe and Tampere, *Valimik*, p. 41

turning, like the German Dreher or Ländler.[26] Kristjan Torop compares earlier forms of *Labajalg* with the Finnish couple *Polska*.[27] Its basic step combination consists of three supports on the full sole, one on each beat of a bar while the first (or another) beat is usually stressed. Variations in the steps are possible, but this is the basic scheme. Presumably, the same step combination was also used in chain dances and Polonaise-like couple-column dances in older forms of couple dancing, as can be derived from the rather fragmentary descriptions and musical analysis that exist.[28] Estonian data does not reveal much about the partners' hold and movement paths in older couple dancing from the beginning of the nineteenth century or earlier. However, the scarce information available hints at similar traits as old Norwegian couple dancing as described by Egil Bakka:[29] it is likely that older forms of couple *Labajalg* included the improvisational combination of traditional elements, such as holding hands and turning round on the spot (or with very little progression) or travelling along the dance floor without turning (promenade), and they were not accompanied by any special melody.[30] Torop also states that couple-turning on the spot might be characteristic of older couple dances, practised before the contra dance era.[31]

Written analytical descriptions of the nineteenth-century (and later) *Labajalg* in Kihnu[32] do not specify the turning technique other than to say it is 'usual', which in 1936 probably meant executing a full turn during two bars as in the Waltz, Polka, etc. That is why I address *Labajalg* in this chapter, concentrating on nineteenth-century-derived round dances; although *Labajalg* steps and even couple-turning were probably already danced much earlier, in the nineteenth century they intermingled with the round dance technique in which the turning couple moves along

---

26 For a detailed description of these dances see e.g. Aenne Goldschmidt, *Handbuch des Deutschen Volkstanzes* (Berlin: Henschelverlag Kunst und Gesellschaft, 1981), pp. 100–12, 177–86.
27 Torop, *Viron vakka. 105 eesti rahvatantsu*, p. 13.
28 Tampere, *Eesti rahvapillid ja rahvatantsud*.
29 Egil Bakka, 'Dance Dialects: Traces of Local Development or of Processes of Diffusion', *Studia Musicologica Academiae Scientiarum Hungaricae*, 33.1 (1991), 215–29, https://doi.org/10.2307/902445
30 Tampere, *Eesti rahvapillid ja rahvatantsud*; Torop, *Viron vakka. 105 eesti rahvatantsu*, p. 13.
31 Torop, *Kontratantsud*, p. 23.
32 ERA II 128, 39/40 (6–7) — H. Tampere 1936.

a circular path.[33] However, what is noteworthy is that the descriptions from Kihnu mention turning couples progressing in a big circle in a clockwise direction.[34] This was unusual elsewhere in Estonia,[35] but quite widespread in eastern Europe,[36] e.g. Poland or Slovenia.

According to collected data, in Kihnu, couples turning with the *Labajalg* step clockwise or counter-clockwise always moved clockwise in the large circle, until the first decades of the twentieth century. It is quite unusual in other parts of Estonia, and similar data are only derived from the western coastal area (geographically and culturally close to Kihnu).[37] Elsewhere, couple dancing usually meant progressing in the circle counter-clockwise; there are plenty of data about Estonian couple dances, including *Labajalg*,[38] as well as from European social dance tradition. The reasons why clockwise progression was popular in Kihnu remain unclear, but there are colourful memories among the Kihnu people about how counter-clockwise progression first came into fashion approximately after the First World War. The following archival quotation from T. Saar also contains much information about other aspects of *Labajalg*; therefore, let me present it in full:

> *Labajalg* is nowadays played when older women are present, in weddings and christening parties, for example. The younger do not participate much in this dance. [...] Fifteen to twenty years ago, the dancing usually progressed clockwise. Then a change came. Perhaps the new fashion was brought in by men who came back from the [First] World War. In the transition period, usually before dancing, it was agreed in which direction to dance. More 'modern' guys sometimes made others dance counter-clockwise by starting the dashing dance in the opposite direction. Now, clockwise dancing is seen very seldom, and it tends to be danced as a 'joke' by women over thirty because the younger women are not able to follow.[39]

---

33 Bakka, 'Dance Dialects', 266.
34 ERA II 133, 613/4 (137) — T. Saar 1937.
35 Except for some western coastal areas — Tampere, *Eesti rahvapillid ja rahvatantsud*, pp. 62, 159.
36 Personal communication.
37 Tampere, *Eesti rahvapillid ja rahvatantsud*, pp. 62, 159.
38 Ibid., p. 159.
39 ERA II 133, 613/4 (137) — T. Saar 1937, translated from the Estonian by Sille Kapper.

Descriptions lack detail about how this 'dashing dance in the opposite direction' functioned practically. It could not last for long because it is technically impossible (or could cause serious problems) to move simultaneously in opposite directions on the same trajectory. Consultation and agreement were more peaceful options, and, indeed, there were others: in personal correspondence in 2010–2011, Estonian ethnomusicologist Ingrid Rüütel, who has been studying Kihnu culture for more than half a century, also remembered her own experience with two different dancing directions. In 1951, at a dancing party in an old community house in Kihnu there were very many dancers, she said, and therefore, two concentric circles were formed, one of them progressing clockwise and the other counter-clockwise.[40] What makes this information interesting is that in the 1950s, the *Labajalg* had fallen out of fashion. The archival quotation above shows that the *Labajalg* started to disappear from wider use in the second half of the 1930s at the latest. By the 1950s, many new dances had come into use. In 1956, Rüütel and her colleague described twenty-one of them, including the Waltz and the Polka,[41] and by then these new dances were also performed progressing clockwise.[42] Forming two or more concentric circles is a traditional and widespread way of dancing round dances (unregulated as well as sequence forms), but, until now, there has been no data of circles moving in opposite directions.

The last sentence of the quotation is also noteworthy: T. Saar claims that younger people cannot dance progressing clockwise. It really requires some mastery to transform the movement schemas so that the couple can progress clockwise, but probably only because it is an unfamiliar way of moving, at least in the beginning. On film and video recordings there is no evidence of clockwise progression in round dances — now, Kihnu people have generally accepted the standard European and mainland-Estonian way of dancing.

---

40 From the author's personal communication with Ingrid Rüütel.
41 TRÜ EKRK I 9, 387/485 — I. Rüütel and M. Sikk 1956.
42 After reading a draft of this article, Rüütel additionally remembered that the Foxtrot was also danced at the party she described, and that later, in 1955–1956, it was the only dance with random movement paths in the repertoire.

The Polka

Although the women of Kihnu have always been more eager to dance than men, and traditional round dances are usually danced by female couples (see Fig. 11.1),[43] new dances were introduced by men.[44] Due to natural and geographical conditions and historically developed customs, they were usually seamen or, in later times, they at least worked away from home. So, according to folklore collections, the arrival of the Polka can be dated quite exactly; in 1937, eighty-seven-year-old Liis Alas described how, about sixty-three years earlier, Uieda Jõnn brought the Polka from Denmark. There was no Polka in Kihnu before, she said.[45] The Jõnn in question was a ship captain born in 1848, so he was really a young man at that time and travelled a lot, at least on the Baltic Sea. Based on this excerpt and some other similar data, we can conclude that the Polka was brought in from overseas and it has been danced in Kihnu since the last quarter of the nineteenth century.

The Schottische

There is not such exact data about the Schottische coming to Kihnu, but elsewhere in Estonia, and since the 1950s in Kihnu, it has usually been mentioned as of the same period as the Waltz and the Polka. The Schottische is very popular among Kihnu people nowadays, and it is danced not only to traditional music, but also to any suitable rhythm, including pop music. In the usual schema of the Kihnu Schottische, there are some characteristic differences from the versions danced on the mainland, but in recent years the younger people of Kihnu have also started to improvise and use more variants of the Schottische. On the mainland, interested dancers sometimes try to imitate the usual Kihnu version.

---

43 Additionally, a video example of Kihnu women and girls dancing their traditional version of the Polka in July 2016 in Viljandi can be seen here: '20160729 161512 polka', 1:23, posted online by Sille Kapper, *Youtube*, 14 November 2017, https://youtu.be/3Bu5pumjPUU

44 Ingrid Rüütel, 'Kihnu pärimustantsud minevikus ja tänapäeval', *Mäetagused*, 41 (2009), 53–74, https://doi.org/10.7592/mt2009.41.ryytel

45 ERA II 172, 110 (1) — H. Tampere 1937.

The Mazurka

In the existing research data, among Kihnu dances, the Mazurka has only been mentioned once and without any further description.[46] The informant was born in 1871 and knew '*Massorka*' from when she was young, i.e. the end of the nineteenth century. Elsewhere in Estonia there was the *Polkamasurka* — with a basic step consisting of three supports in a bar and down-and-up swings on each support.[47] Herbert Tampere thinks the latter has also intermingled with the *Labajalg*.[48] Maybe some fusion with *Polkamasurka* can be seen in the movement of the only Kihnu *Labajalg* captured on videotape, in which some couples dance with noticeable bounds and rebounds on every beat,[49] but without any typical Mazurka basic step.[50] On the other hand, in this recording the *Labajalg* also very much resembles the Waltz, and only differs in some nuances. This can be explained by the fact that, for the recording, older ladies were asked to demonstrate the *Labajalg* they could remember from their youth, but which was not in active use any more.

The Waltz

The smooth assimilation of the *Labajalg* into the Waltz may be the reason why it is hard to say when the Waltz arrived on the dance floors of Kihnu. Liis Pull, born in 1880, has said that she danced the Waltz when she was young,[51] i.e. the Waltz had arrived at least by the turn of the twentieth century. This is the earliest date we can derive from the folklore collections of Kihnu, but it is extraordinarily when compared to other regions of Estonia, to say nothing about Europe in general. What I mean by the assimilation of the *Labajalg* into the Waltz is mainly the turning technique that allowed couple progression along a circular path, because in the basic step no principal differences actually emerged. The Kihnu Waltz is also danced on an almost full sole and with modest bounds in

---

46 KKI 7, 402 (10) — R. Viidalepp 1948.
47 ERA II 172, 49/50 (19) — H. Tampere 1937.
48 Tampere, *Eesti rahvapillid ja rahvatantsud*, p. 62.
49 SKSÄ-K 23 — P.-L. Rausmaa, I. Rüütel, and K. Torop 1987.
50 For the typical Mazurka basic step, see e.g. Goldschmidt, *Handbuch des Deutschen Volkstanzes*, pp. 199–200.
51 RKM II 27, 487 (7) — A. Strutzkin 1948.

the ankle joint and ball of the foot. In the Kihnu Waltz, the combination of turning motifs and travelling without turning also persist, but instead of promenade-like progression where partners are positioned next to each other, now the closed position is retained, and in progressing the girl usually moves backwards. In progression without turning, the basic steps of the Waltz are usually replaced by walking (one step on the first beat of each bar). Motifs are changed according to the music, usually after each sixteen bars. Based on the analysed audio-visual recordings,[52] the older way of changing motifs was rather unified — when a couple started walking or waltzing (turning), others followed; nowadays different motifs may also be danced. Couples progress in a big circle counter-clockwise, and, although different motifs (turning or travelling without turning) do not have to be performed by all couples at the same time, the progression speed of couples is similar so that it is easy to maintain the circle.

Round Dances as Part of Kihnu Identity

Since the 1980s, there are no more data about clockwise progression in Kihnu dance collections, but progression in a circle has remained, namely in its counter-clockwise form. Furthermore, nowadays the position of couples in a big circle and their progression along a circular path are considered special traits of dancing in Kihnu, and local people present the floor pattern of round dances as peculiar to the dance tradition of Kihnu. Similar statements can also be found in the scholarly literature.

Ingrid Rüütel has described how Kihnu people form their own 'Kihnu circle' around other dancers when dancing together with mainland people.[53] In January 2009 I observed the same in Pärnu Kuursaal, where traditional Kihnu dance tunes were played. Many couples from Kihnu danced the Waltz, Polka and Schottische, as well as sequence forms in a big circle around the others, who did not know those dances and seemingly also did not care much about them. The circle was clearly formed and Kihnu dancers sometimes struggled to maintain it when

---

52 SKSÄ-K 22 (2) — P.-L. Rausmaa, I. Rüütel, K. Torop 1987; ERA, DV 34 (33) — I. Rüütel 1997; ERA DV 615 (1) — I. Rüütel 2007.
53 Rüütel, 'Kihnu pärimustantsud minevikus ja tänapäeval', 59.

those who weren't aware of it had disrupted the pattern. Some mainland couples who tried to join the circle were kindly accepted on the condition that they were able to keep up with the speed of movement.

In August 2003, I documented a similar personal experience in Kihnu. There was a band in a local pub playing pop music and a crowd of tourists were hanging around on the dance floor. Several couples formed of Kihnu girls and young women danced Polkas and Schottisches in a circle around the tourists. I was there with my teenage daughter and we decided to join in. Local dancers did not pay any attention to us.

Based on the above events, my reading, and my personal experience as a dance teacher, I never would have thought that a circular movement path was something peculiar to Kihnu. Rather, I associated it with the turning technique of nineteenth-century-derived couple dances, which succeed best when the couple moves around on a circular path. But another case I observed in July 2010 brought me back to the idea that the floor pattern of round dances can really be regarded as an identity symbol: Kihnu women were teaching some dances, including the Waltz, the Polka and the Schottische, in a festival workshop where their group leader Veera Leas emphasised that Kihnu couple dances are always performed in a circle. What I heard her expressing at that moment was a proud declaration of difference in respect of what is actually a typical feature of internationally known social dances; she wished to identify a peculiarity unique to her own small region, her home.

Round Dances and Dancing Communities in Postmodern Estonia

In contemporary Estonia, oral traditions of dancing are rather fragmented, as is the entire cultural environment. Traditional dance forms are practised in different real and imagined communities with their own peculiarities and unique traits. In the following, I address the use of round dances in a real community (Kihnu) and two imagined communities of dancers (stage folk dancers and dance clubs).

Inhabitants of Kihnu

Fig. 11.1 Women dancing the Polka at a wedding cerimony. Photo by Olev Mihkelmaa (2009), Kihnu, Estonia. © ERA DF 28313.

Veera had every right to say what she did. Nowadays, the island of Kihnu, in addition to its geographical location, has turned into a cultural island within the landscape of Estonian dance tradition. Nowadays the Kihnu dance tradition represents distinctive qualities dissimilar to surrounding areas. The knowledge of round dancing technique, together with the traditional circular movement path, has been retained in Kihnu despite the influence of modern ballroom dances (Foxtrot, Tango, etc) that resulted in the increased popularity of random movement patterns elsewhere. On the Estonian mainland, people started dancing Polka and Waltz along random pathways, which obviously reflected the influence of modern ballroom dances adopted first in towns and, since the 1920–1930s, also taught in villages.[54] Kihnu people continued dancing the Waltz, Polka, and Schottische throughout the twentieth century, thinking of them as local traditional dances (although remembering the common knowledge that they had initially been brought in from outside). The

---

54   Torop, 'Kus sai tantsida ja mida tantsiti enne meid', p. 11.

local forms of those dances also included maintaining the circular movement path. Thus, a former internationally known fashion turned into a local peculiarity, and, thereby, a means of identity expression as well as a useful 'unique' element to be presented to guests and tourists. Local identity is manifested in bodily movement while dancing, and in forming the 'Kihnu circle' anywhere there are enough Kihnu people dancing together.[55] It is also expressed verbally when explaining the Kihnu way of dancing to others, as in the above-mentioned workshop or in my interview with Maria Michelson in 2011.[56]

Fig. 11.2 Women dancing the Waltz 'Sõrmõlugu'. Photo by Anu Vissel (1985), Linaküla village, Kihnu, Estonia. © ERA Foto 14172.

In addition to the steps, the turning technique and the circular travelling on the floor, the dancing of the Kihnu community is quite original in its movement style, which has been characterised by different observers as modest, peaceful and dignified, but also light and lively. For a typical dance hold and dancers' posture, see Figures 11.1, 11.2, and 11.3, and

---

55 E.g. ERA DV 702–704 — I. Rüütel, S. Kapper 2009.
56 Sille Kapper, Interview with Maria Michelson in Kihnu on August 13 2011. Private collection.

also the video example in footnote 43 above. The style is revealed best in round dances when many couples are dancing at the same time;[57] it does not depend much on the dancers' age, but has some connection with individual skill. The Kihnu community is also justified in being proud of their dancing, because such uninhibited circular flow of round dances is based on good body co-ordination and technical skills that many untrained mainland dancers do not possess.

Fig. 11.3 Dancing in Kihnu. Photo by photo by Mikk, TRÜ (1954), Kihnu, Estonia. © ERA Foto 2530.

Stage Folk Dancers

Stage folk dancers[58] are usually able to co-ordinate themselves so that couple-turning in round dances succeeds. But this rule has exceptions, because choreographed national stage dances learned in many hobby groups often do not include a round dance couple-turning technique and therefore, in some cases, little attention is paid to it in group rehearsals.

---

57 E.g. TRÜ EKRK I 9, 387/485 — I. Rüütel and M. Sikk 1956.
58 I use this term in reference to people belonging to organised folk-dance groups and ensembles that meet regularly (once, twice, or three times a week as a maximum) for rehearsals and usually learn their repertoire for performing purposes.

Another reason for the disappearance of round dances from social dance floors is that regular practice or some special training are required to be able to move this way, and even more so if several couples are on the floor: in that case, knowledge of the tradition is needed by a critical number of dancers who can make the circular progression work, as is the case in Kihnu. In national stage dance choreographies, on the contrary, traditional circles are purposefully broken and floor patterns diversified. In Estonia, folk dances were presented on stage for the first time in 1904,[59] and, in the beginning, their form was not changed much. Stylised national stage dance, similar to character dance, was developed in Soviet times and it has been fostered until the present as a special style clearly distinct from traditional dancing. Increasingly sophisticated compositions, thick with different motifs and rich in standardised details, often leave out the turning technique as well as the floor pattern of round dances. Due to this, through national stage dances practised in folk-dance groups, the skill of traditional round dancing technique is not passed on. However, teachers with a special interest in older traditions consciously choose to introduce motifs belonging to traditional dancing, including round dances, and there are also groups who mainly deal with traditional dances or who have interest, time and energy for both styles.

As a result, stage folk dancers (or former stage folk dancers), who through their activity in folk-dance groups know the steps and techniques of round dances, can be imagined as a community in contemporary Estonia. Their dancing style is usually influenced by national stage dance training and is therefore rather different from, for example, Kihnu style, but this does not matter if stage folk dancers use their knowledge and skills in spontaneous dance situations. It is important that in those cases their dancing can be seen as a dual expression of their personal identity: their identity as a skilled dancer and their identity as an Estonian.

Dance Clubs

However, observations of traditional dancing events — e.g. traditional music concerts, traditional dance festivals and workshops or dance club[60]

---

59 Tõnnus, *Anna Raudkats oma ajas*, p. 99.
60 Dance club (Estonian: *tantsuklubi*) is an informal social movement for practising traditional dances mainly derived from Estonian villages at the end of the nineteenth

gatherings — however, show that there are not enough opportunities for practising round dances nowadays (at least, not from the point of view of skilled and interested dancers). The use of round dancing knowledge is impeded by the small number of skilled dancers, which sometimes may turn out to be frustrating. In 2011, a dance student expressed her resentment to me in this way: 'I am frustrated when I dance a normal dashing Polka and then they [other dancers] dawdle in my way'.[61] Therefore, people interested in traditional dancing organise special events, such as dance clubs, where people come together to learn and enjoy old social dance forms they consider traditional. But the acquisition of round dance steps and turning techniques implies some systematic exercise, which is not done in dance clubs. Sometimes, short workshops on different topics are organised, but this does not substitute for regular practising. In dance clubs, there is no formal dance teaching. According to my observations, long-term regular participation may result in knowledge of the round dance turning technique and the skill to practise it, but often it does not. In dance clubs, as a rule, sequence dances — which usually include round dance turning elements during four bars maximum — are popular. This is a manageable amount of turning, easy even for occasional guests. The inability to perform coordinated couple-turning, I suppose, has caused the popularity of a sequence Polka form consisting of heel and toe steps, basic Polka steps moving forward counter-clockwise and girls turning under their partner's arm.[62] This is often danced to any Polka music instead of couple turning.

Dance club guests sometimes consider unregulated round dances boring, which can also be connected to their lack of skills (and thus their lack of enjoyment in the experience of turning). However, this can also be caused by deeper changes in society; traditional forms of round

---

and beginning of the twentieth centuries. The movement started in Estonia in the beginning of 1990s, following the example of Hungarian *táncház*, as opposed to national stage dance. Regular events that always include live music are held in Tallinn and Tartu every two weeks, occasionally in other places.

61   Translated from the Estonian by Sille Kapper.
62   At the end of the nineteenth and beginning of the twentieth centuries, this sequence spread in Estonia under many different names, the most popular of them *papiljonipolka* (Butterfly Polka), but it was usually danced to a specific type of melody only. In Norway, this dance form is known under the name *lettisk polka* (Latvian Polka).

dancing began over one hundred years ago, when the speed of life was different. Nowadays, young people seek kaleidoscopic change on dance floors and elsewhere. Dance club dancers say that sequence forms bring variety. From my observations, I can add that, nowadays, richer and more frequent variation is brought into round dances performed by skilled couples too.[63]

International Round Dances in Local Mirrors: A Kihnu Case and an Estonian Case

The casual atmosphere of dance clubs and other traditional music and dance events allows people to choose their way of dancing and thereby express their attitudes, beliefs, and convictions. The situation on contemporary dance floors in Estonia can be described as postmodern, fragmentary, plural, and playful. Round dances are out of fashion in general, but danced in more or less historical forms in some small communities — the real one of Kihnu and imagined communities of stage folk dancers and dance clubs. To be accurate, unregulated round dances have never been alone on Estonian dance floors. Sequence forms, later modern ballroom dances or improvisational styles, have been danced by turns with round dances. In this way, knowledge and use of unregulated round dances reveal the attitudes, beliefs, and convictions of dancers, i.e. their identity.

The dancing of Kihnu people reveals their respect for past dance forms as part of their local culture and identity. The high value put on local cultural space from inside and outside the island has allowed purposeful safeguarding of past knowledge by teaching children to dance and play music and organising events where traditional dances, including round dances, can be practised, e.g. traditional weddings. It has been an individual and communal choice to preserve round dances, once brought in from outside the island, now taking on the role of local peculiarity. Since the 1970s, the performing activities of the local folklore

---

63   In the following video, a young couple improvises with Estonian *Reinlender* (Schottische). They sometimes consciously break down the traditional four-bar-schema (done by the other couple who joins in later). 'Harju Mehed ja Tarmo Noormaa — Reilender', 8:26, posted online by Tiit Saare, *Youtube*, 7 December 2010, https://youtu.be/WK8O-QN96vQ

group Kihnumua have also contributed to the survival of traditional round dancing that, based on the example of surrounding areas, could have disappeared without conscious learning and preservation.[64] It is interesting that, in contrast to other regions of Estonia, in Kihnu the use of traditional dances has not substantially influenced the dancing style. Based on video recordings and personal observations, I can say that, nowadays, it is rather similar to the style described by Ingrid Rüütel half a century ago.[65] This, once more, indicates a firm reliance on past traditions.

Safeguarding the local variants of round dances, together with other cultural peculiarities, is essential in Kihnu because they now also function as a source of income through the developing tourism industry. Knowledge of dance techniques can be compared here with handicraft skills, which can be of direct use in earning one's living. At the same time, round dances have retained their entertainment function because they are enjoyable and easy when dancers manage the appropriate techniques.

In the rest of Estonia, great interest in past traditions, including dancing, can be observed at traditional music events and workshops, which are enormously popular.[66] I have repeatedly observed how traditional music concert audiences actively and diligently follow the instructions given by musicians when following traditional movements. Unfortunately, round dances cannot be learned this way, because the acquisition of technical skills needs more detailed instruction and regular practice. Figuratively speaking, the music goes forward and, in the case of round dances, the audience cannot catch up with it. Concerts, workshops, dance clubs and even hobby-folk-dance groups have not been able to gather the critical number of skilled round dancers who would change the general situation on the dance floor. This is probably the place to repeat the words of my teacher, Kristjan Torop, that every kind of social dancing is the child of its era, and mechanical transfer into another time period would be impossible.[67]

---

64   Rüütel, 'Kihnu pärimustantsud minevikus ja tänapäeval'.
65   TRÜ EKRK I 9, 387/485 — I. Rüütel and M. Sikk 1956.
66   The statement is based on my participant observations at Viljandi Traditional Music Festival 2010 and 2011, which, with its 20,000 guests, is one of the largest of its kind in the Baltic and Northern countries; see also https://www.folk.ee/en/
67   Torop, 'Kus sai tantsida ja mida tantsiti enne meid', p. 11.

The use of traditional movements and techniques is also inhibited by the fact that music has evolved quickly and often without regard for the needs of dancers: skilled dancers claim that new elaborations of former dance tunes are often uncomfortable or totally unsuitable for dancing older traditional forms due to beat or rhythm irregularities or other added contemporary elements. On the other hand, the number of musicians interested in and trying to make high-quality traditional dance music is slowly growing, because of the obvious need for such music among the dancing audience.

Conclusion

In Estonia, functional use of round dances has moved from real village communities into communities with a special interest in the forms. Here, round dances occur as tradition, repeatedly recreated and reinvented in different ways according to the individual and shared values of the dancers. Past movement material is performed again and again in more or less changing forms, depending on dancing purposes as well as the music, company, surroundings or dancers' personalities. In discussing who needs traditional round dances in Estonia today, and why, generally two prevailing functions can be outlined:

- identity confirmation — conscious reconstruction, presentation and reuse of old forms and styles in order to preserve them as a living practice for posterity and thereby maintain and confirm local identity (e.g. Kihnu);

- amusement — improvisational recreation and reinvention of past patterns for the sake of ecstatic joy from the successful turning and exercise of one's physical, spiritual and intellectual abilities, general entertainment, or just as a pleasant and safe background for conversation.[68]

The use of round dances in any function is possible thanks to knowledge and skills acquired in the community: by growing up in a real local community with this knowledge, like Kihnu, or learning to dance in a

---

68 Personal communication with young skilled dancers between twenty-two and twenty-four years of age, in 2010.

special environment created for that purpose, e.g. a folk-dance group. Skills necessary for performing round dance turning provide dancers with more opportunities to feel joy from dancing, but also make them more demanding in respect to music or other dancing conditions.

As a subsection of the first function, the connection of traditional round dances with national identity can also be seen in Estonia. It can be revealed through the stepping-stones of local identity as in Kihnu, while in dance clubs it is rather hidden behind personal values that are important to young dancers, such as impressive music or communication with friends. Among dance club patrons, the awareness of the foreign origin and international character of social dances often prevents an excessive stress on nationality. From the above-described communities, stage folk dancers certainly appreciate national values the most and quite directly through the stage and stadium performances of choreographed compositions. To some extent, the importance of nationality can also be seen in round dances when stage folk dancers bring their technical abilities and habits into social dancing, such as their use of positions, holds, posture or step versions that are characteristic of the standardised national stage dance style.

The boundaries of communities described in this article are not sharp. Many young stage folk dancers also participate in dance clubs and bring along their knowledge and skills. Boys and girls from Kihnu are often studying or working on the mainland, and also use their knowledge of traditional Kihnu dance forms and dancing skills at traditional music events outside the island. In this way, the role and position of unregulated round dances is different in every person's life. The general similarities and principles that can be observed on dance floors outlined above demonstrate the continuous importance of round dances for many people who have made the conscious choice, or have had the opportunity, to learn these dances.

Bibliography

Archival Sources

ERA = Eesti Rahvaluule Arhiiv [Estonian Folklore Archives], Estonian Literary Museum, Tartu, Estonia.

EÜS = Eesti Üliõpilaste Selts [Estonian Students Society], manuscript collection now preserved in Estonian Folklore Archives, Estonian Literary Museum, Tartu, Estonia.

RKM = Riiklik Kirjandusmuuseum [State Literary Museum], manuscript collection now preserved in Estonian Folklore Archives, Estonian Literary Museum, Tartu, Estonia.

SKSÄ = Suomalaisen Kirjallisuuden Seura, Äänitearkisto [Sound Archives of the Finnish Literature Society], copies preserved in Estonian Folklore Archives, Estonian Literary Museum, Tartu, Estonia.

TRÜ EKRK = Tartu Ülikooli Eesti Keele ja Rahvaluule Kateeder [State University of Tartu, Department of Estonian Language and Folklore], manuscript collection now preserved in Estonian Folklore Archives, Estonian Literary Museum, Tartu, Estonia.

Secondary Sources

Anderson, Benedict, *Imagined Communities: Reflections on the Origin and Spread of Nationalism* (London and New York: Verso, 1983).

Bakka, Egil, 'Dance Dialects: Traces of Local Development or of Processes of Diffusion', *Studia Musicologica Academiae Scientiarum Hungaricae*, 33.1 (1991), 215–29, https://doi.org/10.2307/902445

Bendix, Regina, *In Search of Authenticity: The Formation of Folklore Studies* (Madison: University of Washington Press, 1997).

Handler, Richard, and Jocelyn Linnekin, 'Tradition: Genuine or Spurious?', *Journal of American Folklore*, 97 (1984), 273–88, https://doi.org/10.2307/540610

Hoerburger, Felix, 'Once Again: On the Concept of "Folk Dance"', *Journal of the International Folk Music Council*, 20 (1968), 30–32, https://doi.org/10.2307/836068

Goldschmidt, Aenne, *Handbuch des deutschen Volkstanzes* (Berlin: Henschelverlag Kunst und Gesellschaft, 1981).

Honko, Lauri, 'Folklooriprotsess', *Mäetagused*, 6 (1998), 56–84, https://doi.org/10.7592/mt1998.06.honko

Jaago, Tiiu, 'Rahvaluule mõiste kujunemine Eestis', *Mäetagused*, 9 (1999), 70–91, https://doi.org/10.7592/mt1999.09.rhl

'Ka rahvatants muinsuskaitse alla' [n.a.], *Postimees*, 200 (28 July 1936).

Kapper, Sille, 'Tantsufolklorismist tänases Eestis', in *Tonditosin*, ed. by Mall Hiiemäe and Liina Saarlo (Tartu: Eesti Kirjandusmuuseumi Teaduskirjastus, 2008), pp. 24–52.

Nahachewsky, A., 'Participatory and Presentational Dance as Ethnochoreological Categories', *Dance Research Journal*, 27/1 (1995), 1–15, https://doi.org/10.2307/1478426

Niedermüller, Peter, 'Central Europe between Tradition and Modernity', in *Tradition and modernisation. Plenary Papers read at the 4th International Congress of the Societé Internationale d'Ethnologie et de Folklore*, ed. by Reimund Kvideland (Turku: Nordic Institute of Folklore Publications, 1992), pp. 109–21.

Põldmäe, Rudolf, and Herbert Tampere, *Valimik eesti rahvatantse* (Tartu: Eesti Rahvaluule Arhiiv, 1938).

Raudkats, Anna, *Eesti rahvatantsud* (Tartu: Postimees, 1926).

Rüütel, Ingrid, 'Kihnu pärimustantsud minevikus ja tänapäeval', *Mäetagused*, 41 (2009), 53–74, https://doi.org/10.7592/mt2009.41.ryytel

——, 'Pärimuskultuur postmodernistlikus ühiskonnas — minevikurelikt või taasleitud väärtus?', in *Pärimusmuusika muutuvas ühiskonnas. Töid etnomusikoloogia alalt*, vol. 1, ed. by Triinu Ojamaa and Ingrid Rüütel (Tartu: Eesti Kirjandusmuuseumi etnomusikoloogia osakond, 2002), pp. 165–89.

Tampere, Herbert, *Eesti rahvapillid ja rahvatantsud* (Tallinn: Eesti Raamat, 1975).

Torop, Kristjan, *Viron vakka. 105 eesti rahvatantsu.* (Tallinn: Eesti Rahvatantsu ja Rahvamuusika Selts, 2008).

——, 'Kus sai tantsida ja mida tantsiti enne meid', in *Vanad seltskonnatantsud*, ed. by Heino Aassalu, Pill Luht, and Kristjan Torop (Tallinn: Rahvakultuuri Arendus- ja Koolituskeskus, 1997), pp. 8–12.

——, *Kontratantsud* (Tallinn: Rahvakultuuri Arendus- ja Koolituskeskus, 1995).

——, *Viron vakka. 105 virolaista kansantanssia.* (Tampere: Suomalaisen kansantanssin ystävät ry., 1991).

Tõnnus, Richard, *Anna Raudkats oma ajas* (Tallinn: Eesti Raamat, 1991).

Vissel, Anu, 'Ülevaade varasematest töödest eesti rahvatantsu kogumisel ja arhiveerimisel Eesti Rahvaluule Arhiivi materjalide põhjal', in *Rahvatantsu uurimine: arhiivid, meetodid*, ed. by E. Lukka (Viljandi: Viljandi Kultuurikolledž, 1991), pp. 54–64.

12. The Ban on Round Dances 1917–1957: Regulating Social Dancing in Norwegian Community Houses

Egil Bakka

This chapter aims to contextualise the forty-year ban which the Norwegian Liberal Youth Movement placed on round dances during meetings[1] in the period 1917–1957. I hope to feed into the discussion on the resistance these dances met throughout Europe. The chapter portrays the three largest popular movements in Norway, which were the main agents in relation to popular dance, because they controlled most of the community houses in the country. Since such houses were very much sought after for dancing, the owners had to take a stance on; an attitude which depended on the social climate and the practices and ideologies of each agent. Description of the movements, their houses and their stance on dance will therefore be the main focus of this chapter, combined with historical contextualisation of the dances from their arrival in Norway.

The Agents

The term 'popular movement' is a common translation into English of the Nordic terms *folkerørsle/folkebevegelse*, a phenomenon found in

---

1   The clubs had regular meetings for enlightenment, discussions, and singing, and there was time for games or dances at the end. Here, round dances were banned, but the rules were more liberal for parties. Jan Kløvstad et al., *Ungdomshuset: Eit kultursenter i Bygde-Noreg* (Oslo: Noregs ungdomslag: I kommisjon hos Det norske samlaget, 1986).

all the Nordic countries.² The Swedish researcher Helena Forsås-Scott claims that 'Common to all the popular movements was a desire to rouse people, to organise and transform them and to change their way of life'.³ Norway had several popular movements influencing social dance in the decades before and after 1900; the most important were the movements of lay Christianity, the Liberal Youth Movement and the Labour Movement.

Fig. 12.1 Public summer meetings could attract thousands of listeners to the countryside of sparsely populated Norway. All popular movements used such meetings to spread ideas in the decades around 1900. The author Bjørnstjerne Bjørnson was one of the most popular speakers, even if he did not belong to any of these movements. An audience of over 5,000 attended his speach at Stiklestad in 1882. Photo by Henning Anderson (1882). Public Domain.

The term 'modern' has been used in many ways. In this context, the characterisation of the British writer Peter Child is intended: 'The Modernist movement of the late nineteenth and early twentieth centuries

---

2   Helena Forsås-Scott, *Swedish Women's Writing, 1850–1995*, Women in Context: An International Series (London: The Athlone Pres 2000), p. 18.
3   Forsås-Scott refers to popular movements as 'the temperance movement, the free church, the Social Democratic Party, and the organisation of labour' when discussing Sweden (*Swedish Women's Writing*, p. 18). Her characterisation of popular movements echoes the definition provided in Ulf Himmelstrand and Göran Svensson, *Sverige: Vardag och struktur: Sociologer beskriver det svenska samhället* ([Stockholm]: Norstedts, 1988), pp. 806ff.

constituted a literary and cultural revolution'.[4] This understanding of modernism is mostly used in the fields of arts, but here attempts are made to transfer the term to phenomena of social and political life, more specifically to popular movements.

The dominating genre of social dance in this period was what dance teachers of the nineteenth century called round dances. The specific question dealt with here is how and why round dances were banned from some important arenas in Norway during the period from 1917 to 1957. It concentrates on the period surrounding the ban, and mainly analyses the discourse on social dance in Norway in the first three decades of the twentieth century. This discourse sprang from broad ideological movements, the organisations they formed, and the community houses they built. First, however, I offer a brief introduction to the period when the round dances established themselves in Norway.

A Historical Perspective

Norway was in union with Denmark in the period from 1380–1814. It was a province ruled by the Danish kings in Copenhagen on the outskirts of Europe. There was no royal court and almost no nobility. The Waltz seems to have arrived in the Nordic countries during the last decades of the eighteenth century, during a period when economy and trade were flourishing in Norway. Early in the nineteenth century, the Napoleonic wars broke out. Denmark-Norway tried to stay neutral, continuing its trade with both sides. This resulted in the English blocking off trade on the coasts, which pressured Denmark-Norway into alliance with Napoleon. The peace treaty in 1814 forced Denmark to give up Norway to Sweden. Norway managed to get status as nation with its own constitution, but remained in union with Sweden until 1905.

The arrival of the Waltz and related couple dances do not seem to have attracted much attention from Norwegians. In 1796 and 1797, a newspaper in Trondheim published two articles, in several parts, about dancing. They are critical, but not strongly condemning, of *at Valdse* ('to Waltz/waltzing'). The argument is that the Waltz dislodges other, more

---

4   Peter Childs, *Modernism: The New Critical Idiom* (London: Routledge, 2000), p. 5
    https://doi.org/10.4324/9780203131169

valuable dances such as the Allemande, Minuet and Quadrilles; it has grown too popular, and is sometimes indecent. These ideas are not new or original, but reiterated similar continental discourse. There are no traces, however, of scepticism towards the foreign dance, and the article does not refer to the Waltz as particularly new. The writer states that mature women of a modest background, as well as 'mature ladies of the world', have told him how the Waltz touched them in their younger days. This suggests that the arrival date of the Waltz in Norway should be moved to at least ten or twenty years earlier.[5]

Fig. 12.2 This famous painting represents the moment Norway became an independent nation. A specifically elected national assembly met to write the country's Constitution which was completed on 17 May 1814, since then the National Day of Norway. Oscar Wergeland, *Riksforsamlingen på Eidsvoll 1814*, 1885. 285 x 400 cm. Parliament of Norway Building, Oslo. Wikimedia Commons, Public Domain, https://en.wikipedia.org/wiki/Norwegian_Constituent_Assembly#/media/File:Eidsvoll_riksraad_1814.jpeg

---

5 'En prøve hvorledes noget om dands vel monne smage [5 Parts]', *Trondhjemske Tidender*, no. 3–7 (1796). I thank my colleague Professor Anne Fiskvik for giving me this source. 'Saa skal vi nu ikke mere valdse?' [n.a.], *Trondhjemske Tidender*, 47–49 (1797).

12. Regulating Social Dancing in Norwegian Community Houses

Historians mostly argue that nationalism surfaced in Norway with national romanticism towards the middle of the nineteenth century.[6] At this point, the old couple dances of the peasants, such as *springar* and *halling*, started to be named national dances, but this does not seem to have triggered any critical attitude toward new 'foreign dances'. At least, it is hard to find comments about it in contemporary Norwegian sources.

Fig. 12.3 Old dances — *halling* and *polsk* — in the mountain mining town of Røros. Chapter frontispiece in Edward Daniel Clarke, *Travels in Various Countries of Europe, Asia and Africa*, vol. 10 (London: T. Cadell and W. Davies, 1824), part 3, p. 166. Library of Norwegian Centre for Traditional Music and Dance.

---

6   Mary Hilson, 'Denmark, Norway and Sweden. Pan-Scandinavianism and Nationalism', in *What Is a Nation?: Europe 1789–1914*, ed. by Timothy Baycroft and Mark Hewitson (Oxford: Oxford University Press), pp. 192–209.

In fact, an English traveller, Edward Clarke, wrote one of the most important comments. I cite his remarks from 1799, regarding a ball in the Norwegian capital, Christiania, which is also one of the earliest sources for the Waltz as an established dance in Norway:

> There are public balls on a Sunday evening, once in every fortnight. These are held in a large room belonging to the principal inn; and the ball is followed by a supper. Tickets are given to the different persons as they enter, to regulate their places in the dance; a different set of tickets being distributed for a similar purpose at supper. The dances are, the waltz, which has always the preference, and the common English country-dance: but even in the country-dance the waltz is introduced: indeed it is so great a favourite, that our English dance would probably not be tolerated, but in compliment to the English who may happen to be present. Some of our popular dances were performed by the band, but in so slow and solemn a manner, that the effect became truly ludicrous.[7]

A colonel's wife, born around 1801, reports from her young days in Christiania, the capital of Norway:

> In general there were more original personalities at that time than is seen now, and often they were quite comic. One of them, whose name was Flor, I think, was teacher at the Latin school, a middle-aged man who was very enthusiastic about dancing, in spite of a quite unbecoming appearance. He was the alarm of all ladies, because he used to tap the beat with his big hand at the lady's back. At that time there was waltz in nearly all dances, partly a very slow one, as in English dance, partly 2/4 quick as in *Feier* and *Molinack*, not to forget about *Figaro* which did not have neither beginning nor end. Everybody danced at the same time, and everyone with their favourites, because it was the dance of inclination. It ended the ball and lasted long.[8]

---

7   Edward Daniel Clarke, *Travels in Various Countries of Europe, Asia and Africa*, vol. 10 (London: T. Cadell and W. Davies, 1824), part 3, p. 454, https://babel.hathitrust.org/cgi/pt?id=nyp.33433000631485&view=1up&seq=7

8   Oberstinde Rehbinder, *Carine Mathea Thrane Rehbinder and Nanna Thrane, Barndoms Og Ungdoms Erindringer* (Kristiania: Gyldendal, 1915), pp. 23–24. Translated from the Danish by Egil Bakka. It is worth noting that Ms. Rehbinder is using the term Waltz in accordance with the term's usage in the early nineteenth century, considering also dances in 2/4 to be versions of the Waltz. The dance names based in this understanding stayed on even after the name Polka spread over Europe from Prague via Paris in the late 1840s as shown in Egil Bakka, 'The Polka before and after the Polka', *Yearbook for Traditional Music*, 33 (2001), 37–47, https://doi.org/10.2307/1519629. The description of *Figaro der alle dansar* in Klara Semb, *Norske*

12. Regulating Social Dancing in Norwegian Community Houses

Additionally, the famous Danish ballet master and choreographer, August Bournonville (1805–1879) commented on the Waltz in 1829 with a slightly critical tone:

> I would like to add a few words on the frequent use of the German waltz. Not to mention the violent movement in which it brings the blood and the untidiness it brings about in the clothing, I think, though, that, since the more civilised world distinguishes itself from the lower classes as well as in language, customs and clothes as in pleasures, it should also make its dance a bit less accessible for those whose being and manners cannot give the necessary grace. For I consider it to be impossible in a waltz to distinguish between more or less decency. I will probably find many opponents among the passionate waltzers, but I do not present my opinion as an oracle, I just think that a bit less waltzing at the balls would not hurt.[9]

These sources seem to confirm that the Waltz was already a very popular dance in the first decades of the nineteenth century, at least in the upper classes of the capital cities of Norway and Denmark.[10] Bournonville's voice may have been heard in Norway in matters of dance even in those days, when he was only in his mid-twenties, and dancing masters in Norway might be of similar opinions. It is worthwhile noting that Bournonville seems afraid of criticising the waltzers too harshly, which is why one might propose that it does not reflect any strong critical attitude in his circles in Copenhagen. Rather, it perhaps reflects his international orientation, and stronger critical attitudes towards the Waltz elsewhere in Europe. In turn, the source itself is too early to suggest that his calling the Waltz German, whilst at the same time criticising it, has anything to

---

    Folkedansar. Turdansar (Oslo: Noregs boklag, 1991), p. 215 makes the last sentence about Figaro understandable.

9   Aug Bournonville, *Nytaarsgave for danse-yndere* (Copenhagen: C. A. Reitzels forlag, 1829), p. 122. Translated from the Danish by Egil Bakka.

10 The Waltz, as the earliest representative of the round dances, seems to have been established in all the Nordic capitals around 1800. Cf. Henning Urup et al., ed., *Gammaldans i Norden: Rapport Fra Forskningsprosjektet: Komparativ Analyse av Ein Folkeleg Dansegenre i Utvalde Nordiske Lokalsamfunn* (Dragvoll, Norway: Nordisk forening for folkedansforskning 1988).

do with the slowly rising scepticism in Denmark towards Germany,[11] a scepticism which culminated in armed border conflicts.[12]

Fig. 12.4 E. Lange, *August Bournonville*, before 1879. August Bournonville was a Danish Choreographer and Ballet master at the Royal Theatre in Copenhagen. Royal Library, Copenhagen. Wikimedia Commons, Public Domain, https://commons.wikimedia.org/wiki/File:August_Bournonville_by_E._Lange.jpg#/media/File:August_Bournonville_by_E._Lange.jpg

---

11 See, for instance, Poul Kierkegaard and Kjeld Winding, *Nordens historie* (Copenhagen: H. Hagerup, 1965), p. 2, who claim that there had not been any conscious antagonism between the Danes and the Germans, even in the Southern provinces where there was a border between the two languages, before 1830. The conflicts over the provinces of Schleswig and Holstein resulted in two wars (1847 and 1864).

12 Ibid., p. 205.

It seems that Norwegians received the Waltz and the round dances generally without much reflection on their origin. There is no evidence to support the assumption that they may have been considered as threatening to Norwegian identity or to older, traditional dances in this period. It is striking to note that more than a hundred years passed before anyone singled out the round dances as threatening and banned them. During this period, the round dances spread to most of Norway, with few exceptions. At the beginning of the twentieth century, they dominated in urban as well as rural dance repertoires. There were, however, a few rural districts where they were hardly accepted and of little importance, and some districts where, while they were still on equal terms with older couple dances, they were mostly the dominant genre for young people.[13]

Early Twentieth-Century Building of Community Houses in Rural Norway

In the first two to three decades of the twentieth century, there was an impressive boom in the building of community houses that could act as venues for dancing in Norway. Local groups and clubs belonging to different, more or less national, movements built the houses. This radically changed the situation for social dancing, particularly in the Norwegian countryside. Earlier, most dancing had taken place either out of doors in all kinds of weather, in narrow rooms of private homes, or in improvised locations, such as vacated houses, barns or, in some liberal communities, even the schoolhouses. In the twenty-first century, it can be hard to understand fully what a treat it was for young people to dance in spacious community halls with excellent dance floors. The young people were sheltered from wind and rain and did not need to beg permission from their parents' generation in each case. Community houses open for dancing were exceptions in the Norwegian countryside before 1900.[14]

---

13   Egil Bakka, *Norske Dansetradisjonar* (Oslo: Samlaget, 1978).
14   Ibid., p. 175.

Fig. 12.5 Dance in Vålåskard, a dairy farm hamlet in the mountains between Meldal and Rindal, around 1920. Young people from Løkken and Rindal had set a weekend meeting and dance out of doors at an old meeting and dance place. Photo owned by Ingeborg Isdal Løkken, CC BY-NC.

Community houses were obviously very attractive for young people who wanted to dance, and many of them eagerly participated in the building, even if dancing was not at all given as any official purpose for such houses. There were, however, fierce struggles on the question of dancing in some of the new houses, and they seem to have peaked in the decade around 1920. These struggles are the main topic for this article.

There were two dominant groups of community houses which were, at least in principle, available for dancing. These were the houses of the Liberal Youth Movement, called *Ungdomshus* [Youth Houses], and the houses of the Labour Movement, called *Folkets Hus* [The People's House]. The two movements behind these houses based themselves on strong ideologies, and had many similar characteristics, despite the fact that they were opposing agents in the formation of Norway as a new state. They were also opposing agents in concrete and practical terms in local communities.[15]

---

15 There were also other types of small, rural assembly houses in which dance could take place (for example, those belonging to shooting clubs or temperance lodges), but these are neither numerous enough, nor do they sufficiently represent coordinated strategies, to be examined in more detail here.

There was also an older type of community house that existed in considerable numbers, the *Bedehus* [House of Prayer]. Small, local, informal groups or congregations of devout, often stern Christians built these houses. Dance was unthinkable in the *Bedehus*, but, due to their explicit stance against dance, these houses nonetheless belong in the picture of the struggle about dance in the early decades of the twentieth century.

Fig. 12.6   Svae Bedehus and its congregation at Skiptvedt, 1902. Public Domain.

Fig. 12.7   Dølehalli Ungdomshus Morgedal with members, from *Den Frilynde Ungdomsrørsla. Norigs Ungdomslag i 25 År*, ed. by Sven Moren and Edvard Os (Oslo: Norigs Ungdomslag, 1921), p. 265. Public Domain.

Fig. 12.8 The workers in the mining community of Løkken in front of their Folkets Hus, preparing for the Labour Day procession which unions organized throughout the country. The house was built in 1914, and the picture was probably taken in 1919. Photo by Karl August Berg, Folkets Hus, Løkken (c.1919). Public Domain.

Before discussing the main topic, I must give this picture some more nuances. There were certainly a variety of assembly houses used for dancing in towns and cities, at least from the early nineteenth century. Most of them were probably venues for clubs of the upper classes.[16] Even in the early twentieth century, the upper strata of society had some houses built for their own dances. In regions with relatively sharp class divisions, the leading farmers built their own houses (i.e. Bøndernes Hus in Lørenskog, built 1921),[17] in competition with the houses of the Labour Movement. Large industrial enterprises in small communities also built assembly halls (i.e. Sauda Klubb, built in the 1930s, and Festiviteten in Tyssedal, built 1913). They were mainly for officers who might not be at ease in the houses of the Labour Movement or in a house for everyone in the community. The enterprises may not explicitly have stated any distinction in who could use the house.

---

16   Trygve Wyller, *Det Stavangerske klubselskab og Stavanger by i 150 år* (Stavanger: Dreyers grafiske, 1934), p. 242.
17   'Bøndernes Hus (Lørenskog)' [n.a.], *lokalhistoriewiki.no*, 20 July 2017, http://www.lokalhistoriewiki.no/index.php/B%C3%B8ndernes_Hus_(L%C3%B8renskog)

The conflict over popular dancing took place in the Liberal Youth Movement, and not in the Labour Movement. Nonetheless, the Labour Movement and their houses are an important backdrop against which to understand this conflict, and are thus necessary to provide a full picture of popular dancing in Norway during this period. If we depart from the dance repertoire, all levels of the community shared the round dances. Around 1900, the egalitarian rural communities dominating most parts of the country would additionally still have kept the couple dances, which were older than the round dances. The so-called regional dances, and the very thin layer of the bourgeoisie (the upper class of Norway), would still have a repertoire of contra dances. The lower classes in rural regions with a strong class division, the working classes in the towns, and much of the coastal population, would have used the round dances, practically speaking, as their only repertoire.[18]

Fig. 12.9 Video: *Reinlender*, a round dance popular in Norway, performed at the dance competition at the Landsfestivalen 2013, Løten. 'Reinlender 2 — Landsfestivalen 2013', 3:42, posted online by norsound, *Youtube*, 21 July 2013, https://www.youtube.com/watch?v=cY7WHpd_nvQ

Fig. 12.10 Video: The regional dances of Norway include *springar*, *pols*, *halling*, and *gangar*. This link is a clip showing the *springar* from the region of Valdres, as performed in the National competition in folk music and folk dance, and gives a good impression of what a regional dance could have looked like in the nineteenth century. 'Valdres springar', 2:35, posted online by Lars R Amundsen, *Youtube*, 24 December 2015, https://www.youtube.com/watch?v=Ijq5RYxIGz4

---

18 These rather broad generalisations are based on the author's extensive fieldwork in all regions of Norway in the period between 1966 and 1990, and on the resulting collections at the Sff-sentret, Trondheim. It is also based upon the impression that it took some decades before African-American dances such as Onestep, Twostep, Tango etc. gained any broad importance as social dances in Norway. See for instance Egil Bakka, *Norske Dansetradisjonar* (Oslo: Samlaget, 1978).

The Labour Movement and the People's Houses

In the late 1890s, Labour unions and the Labour Party grew into a Norwegian Labour Movement[19] through complex political and organisational processes. Numerous unions and local clubs experienced problems in finding places for their meetings. To deal with this dilemma, the idea of building houses became obvious. In 1910, the National Labour Union[20] established a fund for supporting the building of local assembly houses,[21] which could offer many local unions a much-needed contribution for this purpose. There is no statistical information available to tell us how many of these houses were built, but a knowledgeable representative for the People House Union in the late 1970s guessed that around 500 such houses might have been built up to then. However, old houses that were later replaced by new houses were also counted in this number. Provisional houses, built by migrant workers during a period of construction work on road or railways who left afterwards, might also be in this number.[22] A monograph on *Folkets Hus* by Harald Berntsen — a historian and political activist on the radical left — names some 250 such houses.[23] This history, alongside other histories of the Labour Movement, speaks about the efforts of building these houses.[24] These histories name the leaders of the work, discuss the financial arrangements involved, and describe how the houses strengthened the social life of the membership. The union activity and political meetings were, of course, a primary aim, but broad cultural activity is also mentioned. The dance parties, which seem to have been perhaps the most regular activity at the weekend, whether it was proceeded by some cultural or political activity or not, are hardly mentioned.[25]

---

19 Ida Blom, Sølvi Sogner, and Gro Hagemann, eds, *Med kjønnsperspektiv på norsk historie: Fra Vikingtid til 2000-Årsskiftet* (Oslo: Cappelen akademisk forl., 2005), p. 461

20 Arbeiderens Faglige Landsorganisasjon.

21 Harald Berntsen, *100 år med Folkets Hus* ([Oslo]: Folkets hus landsforbund,1987), p. 530

22 Bakka, *Norske dansetradisjonar*, p. 170

23 Berntsen, *100 år med Folkets Hus*.

24 For example, Bjarne Jullum, *Folkets Hus 1907–1932: Fagforeningenes Centralkomité, De Centraliserte Fagforeninger, De Samvirkende Fagforeninger 1883–1893–1932* (Oslo: [n.p.], 1932).

25 Ibid., p. xii.

Berntsen counts the stonecutters' community house Spjerøy Folkets Hus at Hvaler in the county of Østfold, as the oldest *Folkets Hus* in Norway.[26] Torsnes Folkets Hus, also built by stonecutters in Østfold, finished in 1902, claims to be the second oldest. A short online article, written to celebrate the one hundredth anniversary of Torsnes Folkets Hus, gives some background information and a lively account of the social life during the early years of the house, unfortunately without precise dating.[27]

A company that brought in stonecutters from Sweden established the stonecutting industry in Østfold in the 1880s. The workers there established their Stonecutter Union in 1896, which, from the beginning, held its meetings in the parish house. One may suspect that there were quite strong tensions between the local farmers and the mostly immigrant stonecutters. In 1910, the community had 360 people connected to the stonecutting industry and 265 to agriculture. This was a typical situation when small communities in Norwegian countryside were being industrialised through mining or large construction work such as building roads, railways or factories. The large influx of immigrants from Sweden or other parts of Norway, often from a proletariat background or liberated from the norms of the stable rural society and inspired by socialism or communism, created a new labour class in rural Norway, and even more in towns and cities.

One of the members of the Thorsnes Stonecutter [Brass] Band has given an account about how the band and the stonecutter community in Torsnes celebrated the First of May in the early twentieth century:[28]

> **First of May** At 5 o'clock in the morning we lined up at Høyda på Holm started playing and marching [...] and at Kråkberget we blew the Internationale and other socialist marches. [...] Then we continued along the dusty road to Folkets Hus. In the fields, the farmers were spreading manure, which was their way of celebrating the day. Outside Folkets Hus, the women served coffee and sandwiches, and sometimes someone might have a tot. Then everybody went home for a few hours before the First of May procession at two o'clock. The Stonecutter Music

---

26   Berntsen, *100 år med Folkets Hus*, p. 19.
27   Willy Olsen and Sverre Holt, 'Jubileumsberetning Folkets Hus Torsnes. Et Faglig, Politisk Og Kulturelt Sentrum Gjennom 100 År. 1902–2002', *Folkets Hus Torsnes*, 2002, http://www.folketshus-torsnes.no/index.php/historie
28   The Band was dissolved in 1938.

led the procession with the Stonecutter banner and a red standard, then came the children and then the grown ups' procession. We may have been 100–150 people who were winding through the small parish. The procession went to the Folkets Hus where there was a speech for the day, community singing and music by the Band [...]. In the evening, we played again. There was a partyat the house until midnight and the Band provided the music, I think mainly the bass drum was excused. We played old time dances, *reinlender*, the Waltz and the Polka [...].[29]

Fig. 12.11 Opening celebration of the Folkets Hus at Torsnes, 1902. Postcard, Torsnes Arbeiderlag. Public Domain.

Even if most available accounts keep the issue of class very low key, some attitudes and hints shine through in the text: heavy drinking and partying among the stonecutters, an emphasis on cultural activity in the *Folkets Hus*, and the comment about farmers spreading manure on the fields as a protest to the celebration of the First of May.

There are few, if any, signs of the Labour Movement having any position on dancing. Dancing was a given phenomenon which the Movement did not seem to have any opinion about, a treasured activity among the membership, which the leaders probably saw neither as politically interesting nor harmful, but which must have been useful to attract members.

---

29   Olsen and Holt, 'Jubileumsberetning Folkets Hus Torsnes', http://www.folketshus-torsnes.no/index.php/historie. Translated from the Norwegian by Egil Bakka.

Dancing — a Problem in *Ungdomshuset*, not in the *Folkets Hus*

The rules for Folkets Hus Høvik in 1909 seem typical for such houses, and the following paraphrase gives an impression of the tone and aims:

> At parties and similar gatherings outerwear, hats, umbrellas and the like should be left at the designated place. Smoking should not take place during lectures, discussions, recitations or performances. Moreover, dancing persons may not use a pipe, cigar or cigarette. Two men are not allowed to dance together.
>
> It is strictly forbidden to drink spirits in the house. Intoxicated persons are not admitted. Persons who repeatedly behave in disturbing or violent ways will be refused admission for up to half a year.[30]

There is reason to assume that the rules were intended to regulate or prevent typical behaviour. Some of them may have been an attempt to improve manners, such as leaving outerwear on when entering. It might not have created great problems that some people kept their outerwear on. Men are reported to have danced with hats indoors, considering 'bare-head' dancing snobbish.[31] The rather lenient restrictions on smoking probably had a similar background, together with rules against spitting indoors.

The rules against more serious problems, such as drinking and unruly behaviour, are more sharply formulated, but they still tolerate# such behaviour at least twice. The prohibition against two men dancing together could be connected to this and meant to stop drunken men. Girls had perhaps refused them, and then they disturbed the dancing by being unruly on the floor. In the many isolated, next to all-male, working places, such as construction sites and fisheries and during military service, it was quite usual for men to dance together, for the purpose of practice and for the pleasure of moving to music.[32]

---

30 Berntsen, *100 år med Folkets Hus*, p. 196.
31 Egil Bakka, 'Samandrag Frå Intervju Om Ålen', in *Gammaldans i Norden: Rapport Fra Forskningsprosjektet: Komparativ Analyse av Ein Folkeleg Dansegenre i Utvalde Nordiske Lokalsamfunn* (Dragvoll: Nordisk forening for folkedansforskning, 1988), pp. 180–201 (esp. pp. 188, 195).
32 Bakka, *Norske dansetradisjonar*.

Rather than representing any homophobic ideas among labourers, the prohibitions could also be a concession to what good considered polite manners.

The radical Labour Movement used slogans such as 'Down with the Throne, the Altar and the Plutocracy'[33] and mostly did not see a need to work for acceptance in religious circles. Their wishes for good manners probably had educational rather than moral roots. Their use of political and cultural activity as a means to promote the educational was central. They saw that the formation and progress of the labourers' culture needed to be based in a knowledge of, and being on level with, existing culture in Norwegian society.[34] Probably leaders saw drinking in particular as a problem for such progress, not least because the Labour Movement had influential members belonging to the temperance movement.[35] It is worth noting, however, that the public discourse of the Labour Movement does not blame dancing for increasing drinking, nor for creating problems for other cultural or political activity.

The folklorist Ørnulf Hodne discusses the particular problem of 'culture' in the Labour Movement. There was hardly any specific 'Labour culture'[36] employed during the 1920s and 1930s. What was available was either the bourgeois culture of the upper class or the folk culture from the countryside. Therefore, elements from those had to be appropriated and adapted to the ideas of the international Labour Movement, based on the concepts of solidarity, community spirit and joint action.[37] There were somewhat spectacular attempts to appropriate folk dance in the capital city around 1920 through communist folk-dance groups for children. The communists belonged in the Labour Movement at that time.[38] One may interpret this as having been successful; individual initiatives and actions came from folk dance instructors who belonged

---

33   Berntsen, *100 år med Folkets Hus*, p. 77.
34   Berntsen, *100 år med Folkets Hus*, p. 79.
35   Øyvind Bjørnson, *På Klassekampens Grunn: (1900–1920)*, ed. by Arne Kokkvoll et al. (Oslo: Tiden, 1990), p. 177.
36   Hodne's use of the term 'culture' here, seems to point towards performative or social practices, such as music, dance, theatre, etc., and not towards an open anthropological understanding, encompassing all human practices. Ørnulf Hodne, *Fedreland Og Fritid: En Mellomkrigsstudie i Noregs Ungdomslag* (Oslo: Novus forl., 1995), p. 35.
37   Hodne, *Fedreland Og Fritid*.
38   Einar Øygard and Johan Austbø, *Folkedansen i 20 aar. 1903–1923* (Ski: Den norske folkeviseringen, 1923).

to the left wing of the Labour Movement. This may be the reason why they sprung up suddenly and disappeared, possibly due to the changing personal circumstances of the leaders. If this was the case, it did not need to have had any deep political roots. On the other hand, when the communists formed their own party in 1923, the split deeply affected the Labour Movement's work for children.[39] The split had already marginalised the communist party during the late 1920s, and it seems that the individuals who had earlier supported the children's movement were on the communist side. This may explain the rapid decline and be an important reason why folk-dance activity did not continue as an important element in the Labour Movement.

Round dances constituted the dominant dance genre within the Labour Movement in the early twentieth century, but there is no evidence that anyone looked upon it as any kind of cultural asset. Books on the history of the Labour Movement mention theatre, choir singing, club newspapers, and similar activities as culture, but not the weekend dance parties in the *Folkets Hus*, which was a traditional activity up into the 1950s.[40]

Ungdomshuset and the Liberal Youth Movement

The Liberal Youth Movement grew from the local youth clubs which shared aims and values. Ivar Blekastad, an eighteen-year-old son of a farmer, initiated the club which has been counted as the first in Sel in Gudbrandsdalen during the winter of 1868/69. He and most of the other pioneers in the movement derived their inspiration directly or indirectly from the teachers' seminars and the folk high school movement. Many young people from the countryside attended these schools and came back to become resources and innovators in their communities. Further new clubs came into being in the 1870s and 1880s, but during the 1890s the development exploded. The local clubs formed regional unions in the early 1890s, and these were the basis for the national organisation which was founded in 1896.[41] The Liberal Youth Movement came

---

39 Hodne, *Fedreland Og Fritid*, p. 72.
40 E.g. Frode Rinnan and Olav Tveten, *Vi Skal Bygge et Folkets Hus: 1937* (Oslo: [n.p.], 1937), and Jullum, *Folkets Hus 1907–1932*.
41 Kløvstad et al., *Ungdomshuset*, p. 15.

from the grassroots and had its strongholds among small farmers and countryside teachers. During its first twenty years, the organisation had four chairmen, all of whom were farmers' sons.

The organisation promoted popular enlightenment and national and rural values. One of its main aims was to build a strong civic society, according to modernistic,[42] liberal values. The clubs built community houses to attract young people to be enlightened through talks or lectures, discussions, recitations, unison singing, playing theatre, and playing games. They could use standard popular dance as an attraction, but, increasingly, they viewed dancing as problematic.[43]

Histories about *Noregs Ungdomslag* [Norwegian Youth Association] stress how Grundtvigianism was the ideological basis for both the Liberal Youth Movement and *Noregs Ungdomslag*, and how these ideas spread through the folk high schools.[44] Grundtvigianism emphasises a joyous Christianity, a sense of the national, of popular culture, and of the spoken word as the optimal kind of communication.

> The founder of the folk high school movement is considered to be N. S. F. Grundtvig (1783–1872) [...] He was not interested in creating an educational system, and he was never able to set up a school according to his ideas [...]. But his lectures on national education inspired others to found folk high schools.[45]

> Grundtvig argued that to be a true Christian, one must first be a full human being. And a human being was someone embedded in a specific cultural and historical tradition. [...] For Grundtvigianism, therefore, the study and celebration of rural folk culture was an integral part of the search for salvation...[46]

---

42   The large popular movements of this time may seem to have had a mostly conservative aspect, building on established values. Historians are divided, however, on whether even the religious revival movements should be seen as mainly representing continuity, or, despite their intention, whether they actually represent change and modernism. Such movements contributed, for instance, to the enlightenment and emancipation in the countryside. Dag Thorkildsen, 'Vekkelse Og Modernisering i Norden på 1800-Tallet', *Historisk Tidsskrift*, 77 (1998), 160–80; Svein Aage Christoffersen, *Moralsk Og Moderne?: Trekk av den Kristne Moraltradisjon i Norge fra 1814 til Idag* (Oslo: Ad notam Gyldendal, 1999), p. 274.

43   Sven Moren and Edvard Os, eds, *Den Frilynde Ungdomsrørsla. Norigs Ungdomslag i 25 år* (Oslo: Norigs Ungdomslag, 1921).

44   Moren and Os, *Den Frilynde Ungdomsrørsla*, p. 2; Kløvstad et al., *Ungdomshuset*, p. 25.

45   Cati Coe, 'The Education of the Folk: Peasant Schools and Folklore Scholarship', *The Journal of American Folklore*, 113 (2000), 20–43, https://doi.org/10.2307/541264

46   Andrew Buckser, 'Tradition, Power, and Allegory: Constructions of the Past in Two Danish Religious Movements', *Ethnology*, 34 (1995), 257–72, https://doi.

Fig. 12.12 Cover of Sven Moren and Edvard Os, eds, *Den Frilynde Ungdomsrørsla. Norigs Ungdomslag i 25 År* (Oslo: Norigs Ungdomslag, 1921). Public Domain.

In the context of this article, the main point of interest is that the Grundtvigian orientation promoted a kind of Christianity that accepted dancing. This enabled two priests to be chairs in *Noregs Ungdomslag*, and a good number of other priests to be prominent members. Halvdan Wexelsen Freihow was the first priest who chaired *Noregs Ungdomslag* 1925–1936.[47] In 1921, he wrote an article where he compares the ongoing struggle about dance to a lawsuit where the Liberal Youth Movement

---

org/10.2307/3773941

47 The second one was Knut Eik-Nes, who was chairman from 1936–1947 (but not functioning under the German occupation).

stands trial. Freihow metaphorically frames the lay preacher as a prosecutor, the stern laity as the jury, and Freihow himself takes on the defence:

> I admit that young people of the Liberal Youth movement are dancing, I admit that drunken people sometimes attend meetings and reunions, but can this serve to prove that the work of the Liberal Youth movement prevents a true Christianity among the young people? If the youth clubs had as a task to teach young people to dance, then would that be the same as preventing true Christianity? If it is, there are many who prevent true Christianity among young people. If the work among young people had as an aim to teach them to drink, then the accuser could have found proof for his accusations.[48]

Freihow accuses the laity of seeing themselves as a kind of Supreme Court in questions of religion and culture, and popular opinion for seemingly accepting that. He ends submitting 'not guilty' as statement for the defence, stressing that: 'The Liberal Youth Movement does not see it as a task to condemn and suppress the joy of life in playful dancing. The movement sees it as a task to do everything it can to help young people play with dancing *without* killing their spiritual and intellectual engagement'.[49]

Freihow's polemic explicitly targets a newspaper article by a named lay preacher, and such articles were manifold in this period. An anonymous writer heavily criticises dance and liberal youth clubs in a small contribution to a local newspaper in 1916. It gives an impression of how the stern lay movement pleads its case of dance as dangerous and sinful. The writer claims:

> Dance is perfect for fostering and nourishing sins against the 6th commandment[50] in thoughts, mind and action. [...] In the Bible 1 John 2:16 one can read: 'Everything in the world — the lust of flesh, the desires of the eyes, and haughty lifestyle — comes not from the Father but is of this world'. Our Saviour says, 'The world loves its own'.[51] This fits dance

---

48 Halfdan Freihow, 'Ikkje skuldig!', in *Den Frilynde Ungdomsrørsla. Norigs Ungdomslag i 25 År*, ed. by Edvard Os and Sven Moren (Oslo: Norigs Ungdomslag, 1921), p. 71. Translated from the Norwegian by Egil Bakka.
49 Freihow, 'Ikkje skuldig!', p. 73.
50 Under the Augustinian division used by Roman Catholics and Lutherans, the sixth commandment refers to the commandment against adultery.
51 This statement is taken from John 15:19.

perfectly. It is the three-headed animal that constitutes the 'desires of the eyes, the lust of flesh, and haughty lifestyle'. Those who are not true converts seek to place the activity of dance into a spacious bag alongside other loved sins under the name of indifferent things.[52]

If a person, for instance on the street, approaches someone of the opposite sex in the same way as during a dance, any decent individual approached would feel it as defamatory, even as a crime for which the person rightfully would deserve punishment. But in the dance clubs it is counted as purity and decency.[53]

It seems clear here that the main problem with dance is the impurity and indecency of a public act of intimacy between man and woman. No distinction is made between kinds of dances, and even singing games were generally forbidden.[54]

According to Freihow, the laity was very influential in many parts of the Norwegian countryside. They also had support from some clergymen of the state church. This was probably an important part of the backdrop for the quite intensive debates in Noregs Ungdomslag about dancing, peaking in the years from 1916 into the 1920s. The religious laity published articles as part of the heavy discourse against both dance and the Liberal Youth Movement in newspapers throughout the country. Sometimes, Norsk Ungdom[55] cited such articles to enable replies in the internal channels of the movement. The opinions about dance as sin hardly found support within the internal debate, but the movement found it important to argue against them.

In 1917, Norsk Ungdom was the arena for particularly intensive debates about the dancing in member clubs of Noregs Ungdomslag. An anonymous contributor wrote, 'If one has followed the work for young people in clubs where many members have an inclination to dance, one will acknowledge that dance is and remains the worst enemy a youth club can get. There is nothing that can overwhelm young people spiritually and culturally more than the dance'.[56] The reason given for

---

52 'Indifferent things' here refers to adiaphora — matters not regarded as essential to faith, but nevertheless as permissible for Christians or allowed in church.
53 'Betydelig fremskrit' [n.a.], Nordlands Avis, 7/4 (1916), 2. Translated from the Norwegian by Egil Bakka.
54 Olaf Aagedal, Bedehuset: Rørsla, bygda, folket (Oslo: Samlaget, 1986), pp. 122, 236.
55 The newsletter of Noregs Ungdomslag.
56 'Dansen i Ungdomslaga' [n.a.], Norsk Ungdom (1921), p. 4. Translated from the Norwegian by Egil Bakka.

this claim was based on experience, 'If there is a discussion, only older members participate. The young people are sitting uninvolved, perhaps making noise, longing for the end so that they can get a dance, even if the questions debated are burning issues, that particularly bear on their situation'. The members who had joined the club in order to dance were not engaged with other activities or issues the organisation had as its main aim. Rather, they were impatiently waiting for the dancing that would end the meeting. In this way they, destroyed all engagement with other issues. Hence, the dance prohibition was intended for meetings and not for parties. The *folkeviseleik* [ballad games] were identified as the most efficient means to eradicate round dances from the meetings. The *folkeviseleik* would still provide the pleasure of movement that young people needed after the meetings, but those individuals who attended for the sole purpose of dancing would no longer disturb the meetings, since they did not care about the *folkeviseleik*.

In a later issue, Hulda Garborg published an article arguing along similar lines. She refers to Martin Luther: 'If vice and sin can be found together with dance, it is not the fault of dance itself, but rather the fault of the evil minds of some of those who dance'. She vehemently attacks the 'new-fangled' dancing as 'vulgar, ugly and of bad taste [...] being poisonous flowers from the most unsound city culture'. She continues: 'Therefore, I think that this kind of dance should be barred by everyone for aesthetic and moral reasons. Unfortunately, I also think that the good round dance needs to be kept away from the liberal youth clubs — for other reasons'.

These clubs had idealistic goals; they were founded to combat brutality, materialism and indifference, and to help young people find their way to a higher cultural life, better self-esteem and stronger national feeling. 'Everything that hampers this must be taken away from the clubs, however good it may be in itself. Long experience shows that the round dance hampers, it destroys fellow feeling and disperses motivation'. She argues that, for dancing to have educational value, it should engage the mind as well as the body. She suggests that the 'song dance' and the 'figure dance' have such qualities; they are serious disciplines that keep dancers alert and have spiritual content. The round dances do not, even if they are pretty and innocent. Garborg probably thought that dances that could be performed without demanding a certain concentration on them were of less educational value.[57]

There were several other articles on dancing in the clubs in 1917. Even if no article argued directly against Hulda Garborg, there is every reason to believe that many members at a local level wanted to dance round dances without restriction. An example from the small community of Sauda is likely representative: a farmer gave the ground for the house, on the condition that the users did not allow round dancing. The house was ready for use in 1915, and a struggle arose soon after. Parts of the membership wanted to dance round dances; not only the song dances and figure dances which rules allowed. At Easter in 1922, the dance faction broke into the house to dance, and there were threats of bringing in the police. The struggle ended when this faction left and built a house of their own some years later. In 1938, the youth club bought the site, and, from then on, allowed round dances at parties, but still not at meetings.[58]

Fig. 12.13 The — at the time — new Ungdomshus (Youth clubhouse) in Sauda, with a dining room in the basement, and a hall for meetings with a small stage and a gallery. *Den Frilynde Ungdomsrørsla, Norigs Ungdomslag i 25 År*, ed. by Sven Moren and Edvard Os (Oslo: Norigs Ungdomslag, 1921), p. 239. Public Domain.

Noregs Ungdomslag held its annual general meeting of 1917 at Voss in western Norway, and Hulda Garborg attended to teach song dance

---

57 Hulda Garborg, 'Dansen i Ungdomslagi', *Norsk Ungdom* (1917), pp. 178–79. Translated from the Norwegian by Egil Bakka.
58 Egil Bakka and Magne Eiesland, *Sauda Ungdomslag 1909–1964. Lagssoge* (Sauda: Sauda ungdomslag, 1964), p. 44.

and to be part of the discussion about the round dances. It seems that the board of the organisation had brought together a strong team to argue for a proposal from the Board: 'The meeting is of the opinion that the round dance ought to be prohibited at ordinary meetings'.[59] The proposal was unanimously adopted.

The struggle over round dances was, however, not won locally, and articles on the issue appeared in the internal channels of *Noregs Ungdomslag*:

> The aim for Norwegian folk dancers is to promote Norwegian folk dancing, not only for use in the youth clubs, but also as a common dance both at home and elsewhere. One of our worst enemies, which we have to fight, are the round dances. The question is, what have we done to tackle this, our worst enemy? There are different answers. Some will reply, 'We are only allowed to dance (round dances) at our club parties'. Others reply, 'The round dances are totally banned in our club'. This may be fine, but, in my mind, good bylaws and decisions in the clubs do not help much as long as each of us [...] do the round dances as soon as the opportunity arises. We often see that people we count among the folk dancers are the most dedicated in keeping alive our worst enemy. Perhaps there would be many who would ask, 'You can't mean that liberal youth should establish a life-time promise against using round dance in our private lives?' No, this is not my intention; I do not think it should be necessary. People always said that the liberal youth are the most alert and intelligent youth. Because of this, I believed that this intelligent youth would see that, if they were to achieve something through their actions, it would just be their private lives, which would be influential. Here, all the folk-dance groups should lead as good examples, so that people can see what a group looks like that is working seriously. Those who want to be pioneers and leaders in cultivating also need to show that they can protect what has already been sown, so that it can grow large and strong.[60]

59　Noregs Ungdomslag, *Norsk Ungdom: Noregs Ungdomslag 1916–1929: Bodstikka: Blad for Noregs Ungdomslag og Noregs Mållag*. Translated from the Norwegian by Egil Bakka. Bjørnar Blaavarp Heimdal, 'Nasjonal Samling Og Den Norske Folkemusikken: Norges Folkemusikken' (unpubished master's thesis, Norwegian University of Science and Technology, Faculty of Humanities, Department of History and Classical Studies, 2012). Translated from the Norwegian by Egil Bakka.

60　Vilfred Moen, 'Svenske hell norske dansar?', *For Bygd og By. Leikarvollen* (1923), p. 270. Translated from the Norwegian by Egil Bakka.

It may be that Hulda Garborg's rather forceful attacks on the modern dances, and, in contrast, her acceptance of round dances, constitute a more urban perspective, while modern dances were not of great importance in the countryside around 1920. *Noregs Ungdomslag* also ruled against a proposition to ban the latter as well, which may seem strange.

The folk-dance subfield made decisions to promote song dance and national dances. In some places, the difference between round dances and national dances would be small. The national dances could be just as dominant and attractive as the round dances, but those leaders who adopted a national folk-dance perspective and were based in large urban clubs may not have understood this at the time. The result was either a ban or lack of interest in the national dances such as *springar, gangar,* and *pols* at the local level, which led to annoyance among the fiddlers who wanted to play the local music, but were forced to learn simple melodies for the national repertoire of figure dances.

Another difference between developments at the national and local level was the term for folk dancing. From the very beginning, Garborg used the term *folkevisedans* [ballad dance] or *songdans* [song dance] for the chain dance used on the Faroe Isles, as well as for the Norwegian version she initiated.[61] Her main follower, Klara Semb, used the terms *songdans* and *turdans* [song dance and figure dance].[62] It is interesting to note that, in spite of this, local leaders in the clubs used the term *folkeviseleik* [ballad game] or, simply, *leik* [games], in which they often included the national repertoire of figure dances. Klara Semb published many of them and they were danced to music. The reason seems patent: there was a clear distinction in the countryside between *leik* [games] and *dans* [dance]. In this distinction, games were considered far more innocent than dance, and were far more acceptable in many contexts. *Leik* quite soon became an important term for the national repertoire of

---

61 *Norske Folkevisor: Med Ei Utgreiding Um Vise-Dansen Av Hulda Garborg*, I, ed. by Hulda Garborg, Nr 8 vols (Oslo: Norigs ungdomslag, 1903), p. 48 s., Hulda Garborg, *Songdansen i Nordlandi* (Kristiania: Aschehoug, 1903)., Hulda Garborg, *Dagbok 1903–1914*, ed. by Karen Grude Koht and Rolv Thesen (Oslo: Aschehoug, 1962)., Hulda Garborg, 'Færøisk Dans', *Dagbladet* (25 January 1902).

62 Klara Semb, *Norske Folkedansar II. Rettleiding Om Dansen* (Oslo: Noregs Ungdomslag, 1922).

song dance and *turdans*, leading to the term *leikarring* for a folk-dance group specialising particularly on song dance and figure dance.

It is possible to understand the argument for *turdans* and song dance rather than round dances in the way they would function in a youth club. Freely improvised couple dances, such as the round dances, allow the dance partners to concentrate on themselves and each other. They do not need to pay attention to others, except for avoiding dancing into other couples. In turn, they could more easily hide flirting or even sexual tensions, and could slip out of the house more easily than in more organised dances. The couple would only feel responsibility to one another, whereas, in a big crowd of dancing couples, each couple would be less available to each other's gaze than when couples formed circles and lines where they could see each other most of the time. The leaders of a club who considered dancing as a tool wanted to create a collective feeling of closeness and cooperation, rather than allowing happy couples to isolate themselves from everyone else in the group. In this way, attention on the group, and alertness to precise and complex patterns that were purported to hold educational value, were both understood as efficient means of maintaining this collective feeling of unity in the group. It could also help the disciplining of unruly and perhaps slightly drunk groups of young people who tried to challenge conventions of 'good' behaviour.[63]

The song dance had even stronger tools for creating a collective feeling of unity in the group, since the unison singing and dancing even aimed to create a shared emotional involvement in the stories told by the text. This shared expression of emotion probably appeared strange in a secular context, since it is reminiscent of religious singing. This is probably why people in the folk music movement scornfully called it 'den heilage dansen' ('the holy dance').

Conclusion

The round dances were about one hundred years old in Norway in the early twentieth century. Dance was generally strongly criticised

---

63   The Cotillion — a mixture of party games and round dances, often organised by ball directors — might have had similar effects, and be promoted by the dancing masters and adults for similar reasons.

in religious circles, and much more so by lay preachers than by the clergymen of the official church. The Labour Movement used them extensively in social life, but did not recognise them at all as having any cultural value or being of relevance for the movement itself. The Liberal Youth Movement had a much more complex relationship to round dances. The movement did not see round dances as harmful or sinful in themselves, but did not recognise them as having any educational or national value. Since it was a genre that nearly all dancing Norwegians knew and enjoyed, occasions for dancing it in the new assembly houses were cherished and yearned for. The leading ideologists in the Liberal Youth Movement found the competition encouraged by round dances in the clubs to be very problematic, and banned it from meetings for forty years, whereas the Labour Movement let it live on without paying it any attention.

Bibliography

Aagedal, Olaf, *Bedehuset: Rørsla, Bygda, Folket* (Oslo: Samlaget, 1986).

Bakka, Egil, 'The Polka before and after the Polka', *Yearbook for Traditional Music*, 33 (2001), 37–47, https://doi.org/10.2307/1519629

——, 'Samandrag Frå Intervju Om Ålen', in *Gammaldans i Norden: Rapport Fra Forskningsprosjektet: Komparativ Analyse av Ein Folkeleg Dansegenre i Utvalde Nordiske Lokalsamfunn*, ed. by Henning Urup, Henry Sjöberg, and Egil Bakka (Dragvoll: Nordisk forening for folkedansforskning, 1988), pp. 180–201.

——, *Norske Dansetradisjonar* (Oslo: Samlaget, 1978).

Bakka, Egil, and Magne Eiesland, *Sauda Ungdomslag 1909–1964. Lagssoge* (Sauda: Sauda ungdomslag, 1964).

Berntsen, Harald, *100 År Med Folkets Hus* ([Oslo]: Folkets hus landsforbund, 1987).

'Betydelig fremskrit' [n.a.], *Nordlands Avis*, 7/4 (1916), 2.

Bjørnson, Øyvind, *På Klassekampens Grunn: (1900–1920)*, ed. by Arne Kokkvoll et al. (Oslo: Tiden, 1990).

Blom, Ida, Sølvi Sogner, and Gro Hagemann, eds, *Med Kjønnsperspektiv på Norsk Historie: Fra Vikingtid til 2000-årsskiftet* (Oslo: Cappelen akademisk forl., 2005).

Bournonville, Aug, *Nytaarsgave for Danse-Yndere* (København: C. A. Reitzels forlag, 1829).

Buckser, Andrew, 'Tradition, Power, and Allegory: Constructions of the Past in Two Danish Religious Movements', *Ethnology*, 34 (1995), 257–72, https://doi.org/10.2307/3773941

'Bøndernes Hus (Lørenskog)' [n.a.], lokalhistoriewiki.no, 20 July 2017, http://www.lokalhistoriewiki.no/index.php/B%C3%B8ndernes_Hus_(L%C3%B8renskog)

Childs, Peter, *Modernism: The New Critical Idiom* (London: Routledge, 2000), https://doi.org/10.4324/9780203131169

Christoffersen, Svein A., *Moralsk Og Moderne?: Trekk av den Kristne Moraltradisjon i Norge fra 1814 til Idag* (Oslo: Ad notam Gyldendal, 1999).

Clarke, Edward Daniel *Travels in Various Countries of Europe, Asia and Africa*, vol. 10 (London: T. Cadell and W. Davies, 1824), https://babel.hathitrust.org/cgi/pt?id=nyp.33433000631485&view=1up&seq=7

Coe, Cati, 'The Education of the Folk: Peasant Schools and Folklore Scholarship', *The Journal of American Folklore*, 113 (2000), 20–43, https://doi.org/10.2307/541264

'Dansen i Ungdomslaga' [n.a.], *Norsk Ungdom* (1921), p. 4.

'En Prøve Hvorledes Noget Om Dands Vel Monne p. [5 Parts]' [n.a.], *Trondhjemske Tidende*, 3–7 (1796).

Forsås-Scott, Helena, *Swedish Women's Writing, 1850–1995*, Women in Context: An International Series (London: Continuum International Publishing, 2000).

Freihow, Halfdan, 'Ikkje Skuldig!', in *Den Frilynde Ungdomsrørsla. Norigs Ungdomslag i 25 År*, ed. by Edvard Os and Sven Moren (Oslo: Norigs Ungdomslag, 1921), pp. 69–74.

Garborg, Hulda, *Dagbok 1903–1914* (Oslo: Aschehoug, 1962).

——, *Norske Dansevisur*, ed. by Karen Grude Koht and Rolv Thesen (Kristiania: Aschehoug, 1923).

——, 'Dansen i Ungdomslagi', *Norsk Ungdom* (1917), pp. 178–79.

——, ed., *Norske Folkevisor: Med ei utgreiding um vise-dansen av Hulda Garborg, I* (Oslo: Norigs ungdomslag, 1903).

——, *Songdansen i Nordlandi* (Kristiania: Aschehoug, 1903).

——, 'Færøisk Dans', *Dagbladet* (25 January 1902).

Hagemann, Gro, *Det Moderne Gjennombrudd: 1870–1905*, Aschehougs Norgeshistorie, B, 9 vols (Oslo: Aschehoug, 2005).

Heimdal, Bjørnar Blaavarp, 'Nasjonal Samling Og Den Norske Folkemusikken: Norges Folkemusikken' (unpubished master's thesis, Norwegian University of Science and Technology, Faculty of Humanities, Department of History and Classical Studies, 2012).

Hilson, Mary, 'Denmark, Norway and Sweden. Pan-Scandinavianism and Nationalism', in *What Is a Nation?: Europe 1789–1914*, ed. by Timothy Baycroft and Mark Hewitson (Oxford, GBR: Oxford University Press, 2006), pp. 192–209.

Himmelstrand, Ulf, and Göran Svensson, *Sverige: Vardag och Struktur: Sociologer Beskriver Det Svenska Samhället* ([Stockholm]: Norstedts, 1988).

Hodne, Ørnulf, 'Fedreland Og Fritid 1920–1939', in *Ungdomslaget: Noregs Ungdomslag 1896–1996*, ed. by Jan Kløvstad (Oslo: Samlaget, 1995), pp. 125–88.

——, *Fedreland Og Fritid: En Mellomkrigsstudie i Noregs Ungdomslag* (Oslo: Novus forl., 1995).

Jullum, Bjarne, *Folkets Hus 1907–1932: Fagforeningenes Centralkomité, De Centraliserte Fagforeninger, De Samvirkende Fagforeninger 1883–1893–1932* (Oslo: [n.p.], 1932).

Kierkegaard, Poul, and Kjeld Winding, *Nordens Historie* (København: H. Hagerup, 1964–1965).

Kløvstad, Jan, et al., *Ungdomshuset: Eit Kultursenter i Bygde-Noreg* (Oslo: Noregs ungdomslag: I kommisjon hos Det norske samlaget, 1986).

Moen, Vilfred, 'Svenske Hell Norske Dansar?', *For Bygd og By. Leikarvollen* (1923), p. 270.

Moren, Sven, and Edvard Os, eds, *Den Frilynde Ungdomsrørsla. Norigs Ungdomslag i 25 År* (Oslo: Norigs Ungdomslag, 1921).

Noregs Ungdomslag, *Norsk Ungdom: Medlemsblad for Noregs Ungdomslag Undertittel 1916–1929: Bodstikka: Blad for Noregs Ungdomslag Og Noregs Mållag*.

Oberstinde Rehbinder, Carine Mathea Thrane Rehbinder, and Nanna Thrane, *Barndoms og Ungdoms Erindringer* (Kristiania: Gyldendal, 1915).

Olsen, Willy, and Sverre Holt, 'Jubileumsberetning Folkets Hus Torsnes. Et Faglig, Politisk Og Kulturelt Sentrum Gjennom 100 År. 1902–2002', *Folkets Hus Torsnes*, 2002, http://www.folketshus-torsnes.no/index.php/historie

Øygard, Einar, and Johan Austbø, *Folkedansen i 20 Aar. 1903–1923* (Ski: Den norske folkeviseringen, 1923).

Rinnan, Frode, and Olav Tveten, *Vi Skal Bygge et Folkets Hus: 1937* (Oslo: [n.p.], 1937).

Ropeid, Andreas, 'Bedehuset Og Bygda', in *Bedehuset: Rørsla, Bygda, Folket*, ed. by Olaf Aagedal (Oslo: Samlaget, 1986), pp. 114–24.

'Saa skal vi nu ikke mere valdse?' [n.a.], *Trondhjemske Tidender*, 47–49 (1797).

Semb, Klara, *Norske Folkedansar. Turdansar* (Oslo: Noregs boklag, 1991).

——, *Norske Folkedansar II. Rettleiding Om Dansen* (Oslo: Noregs Ungdomslag, 1922).

Thorkildsen, Dag, 'Vekkelse Og Modernisering i Norden på 1800-Tallet', *Historisk Tidsskrift*, 77 (1998), 160–80.

Urup, Henning, Henry Sjöberg, and Egil Bakka, *Gammaldans i Norden: Rapport Fra Forskningsprosjektet: Komparativ Analyse av Ein Folkeleg Dansegenre i Utvalde Nordiske Lokalsamfunn* (Dragvoll: Nordisk Forening for Folkedansforskning Dragvoll, Norway, 1988).

Wyller, Trygve, *Det Stavangerske Klubselskab og Stavanger by i 150 År* (Stavanger: Dreyers grafiske, 1934).

13. Dance and 'Folk Devils'[1]

Mats Nilsson

This chapter will discuss how new dances, especially when danced by young people, tend to be seen as a negative and even evil influence by elder members of society. By framing the discussion with the use of the concepts of 'moral panic' and 'folk devils' by the British sociologist Stanley Cohen and those influenced by his work, I want to place the Waltz and other couple dances as just one example of how social reactions create folk devils out of new dance forms in different historical contexts.

The Waltz 'In and Out'

In June 2010 the Swedish Crown Princess Victoria married Prince Daniel, and at the wedding party they started the dancing with a Waltz.[2] In 200 years, the Waltz has gone from being an immoral popular dance to one accepted throughout the whole of society, and accepted by all as the prime wedding dance.

Fig. 13.1 Video: Crown Princess Victoria and Prince Daniel of Sweden's Wedding Waltz (*bröllopsvals*), 19 June 2010, Sveriges Television AB. 'Victoria & Daniel of Sweden's Royal Wedding Waltz/Bröllopsvals', 4:15, posted online by 2x7, *Youtube*, 21 June 2010, https://www.youtube.com/watch?v=xLk977Ktaus

---

1 This chapter is a revised and updated version of an article published in Swedish in Kerstin Gunnemark and Magnus Mörck, eds, *Vardagslivets fronter* (Göteborg: Arkipelag, 2006).

2 *Det kungliga bröllopet 19 juni 2010*, dir. By Lars Bjalkeskog (Nordisk Film, 2010).

Establishing the date that Waltz dancing became popular in Sweden is difficult, if not impossible; there are too few sources. However, in 1785 it was at least noted by an anonymous author under the pseudonym G. F. Koskull as a fashion among the gentry:

> [As to] the Waltz, the earlier fashions we have got from abroad, but this figure we have learned from our own farmers; nobody that has been in the countryside any time during spring or summer can have missed how the people, especially the youth, amuse themselves by laying down in the green grass, preferably on a small hill, always two and two, one above the other, holding each other with the arms and throwing their legs around each other, and in this formation they roll or waltz down the hill. This has previously been a game, but the gentry today has developed it as something serious; it has been introduced into the Contra dance, and is done to music. The formation is nearly the same and is executed in the same way, nota bene: in dance it is done upright. The lady and the man take each other with one hand around the waist, the other hands hold each other, press each other as hard as they can to each other, and turn around in a circle, always so that the man has a knee between the lady's thighs, which must keep them apart, otherwise the Waltz shall not work. Whether a lady is strong or weak, and whether she can stand a stronger or softer Waltz, is something a sensible man shall decide.[3]

One of the other traces of the Waltz is the name 'väggadans', which means something like 'dancing along the walls', following the inside walls of the house. It is mentioned in 1809 in southern Sweden, in a source that tells us that people danced around the room in a circle when dancing the Waltz, instead of on the spot like one of the Polska forms that had been more common previously.[4] One example of the reaction towards this novel dance comes from an anonymous writer, who wrote in a Turku[5] newspaper in 1801:

> If you, my lady, want to avoid embarrassment, then stay away from the dances that put you in danger. The Waltzes are such a group, not only because their circular movements are the most harmful: they are also the most indecent and immoral. I want to ask any male if he can have the same respect as before for a girl when he has seen her Waltzing? Even

---

[3] Henry Sjöberg and Anita Etzler, *Folkets danser* (Stockholm: Brevskolan, 1981), p. 136. Translated from the Swedish by Mats Nilsson

[4] Ibid., p. 137.

[5] Turku was at the time a largely Swedish-speaking town and capital town of the eastern part of Sweden, in south-western Finland.

less can he who waltzed with her have any respect for her. It was well done by Goethe, when he let Werther say that, whatever will happen with love, the girl who he loves should never waltz with someone else.[6]

The Waltz, and later the Polka, became the popular dances of the nineteenth century and replaced the older Polska and the Minuet. In his book, which has the expressive title *Decorum of the Minuet, Delirium of the Waltz*, Eric McKee gives examples to show how bad the new Waltz, as both dance and music, was seen to be by parts of the society in the beginning of the nineteenth century.[7] A hundred years later in the early twentieth century, around 1920, Waltz and Polka forms had to compete with jazz (both dance and music) as the most popular genre among those who danced, especially the youth. And there was also a debate around the good and bad elements of this new fashion from America. According to numerous sources, the young lost sight of proper morality by taking part in, and performing, these 'negroid mating games' or 'devilish rites'.[8] The targets here were the American music and dance that became popular around 1900, as well as the advent of jazz in Sweden during the 1920s and its popularity in the dance pavilions of the 1930s. During the 1990s we can detect the same moral reasoning about young people's leisure and the dance events that have widely come to be called 'raves'.[9]

---

6   Petri Hoppu, 'Folkdansande Eros', *Folkdansforskning i Norden*, 34 (2011), 10–16 (at 10). Translated from the Swedish by Mats Nilsson.

7   Eric McKee, *Decorum of the Minuet, Delirium of the Waltz. A Study of Dancemusic Relations in ¾ Time* (Bloomington, IN: Indiana University Press, 2012), p. 118, https://doi.org/10.2307/j.ctt2005r6k. See also Mark Knowles, *The Wicked Waltz and Other Scandalous Dances. Outrage at Couple Dancing in the 19th and Early 20th Centuries* (Jefferson, NC: McFarland, 2008) for more examples.

8   Jonas Frykman, *Dansbaneeländet. Ungdomen, populärkulturen och opinionen* (Stockholm: Natur & Kultur, 1988) p. 91. See also the discussion in Alexander Agrell, *Hotet från jazzen. En studie av motstånd mot jazzmusik* (Lund: Etnologiska institutionen, 1984); Johan Fornäs, *Moderna människor. Folkhemmet och jazzen* (Stockholm: Norstedts, 2004); Göran Larsson, 'Onestep & Jumpa: om moralisk panik i 1910talets Sverige', in *Uppsatser i svensk jazzhistoria*, ed. byAlf Arvidsson (Umeå: Institutionen för etnologi, 1998), 8–35; Gösta Rosén, *Kriget om den moderna dansen* (Stockholm: Harriers bokförlag AB, 1952), and Erik Walles, *Jazzen anfaller* (Stockholm: Natur och Kultur, 1946).

9   Michael Axelsson, *Ravekultur. En studie om ravekulturens gemenskapsbildning och den rörliga platsens fasta punkt* (Stockholm: Etnologiska institutionen, 2004); Henrik Edberg, *'De kommer för lätt undan'. En jämförelse mellan moralisk panik i 1960talets England och 1990talets Sverige* (Göteborg: Etnologiska institutionen, 1996); Mikael Eivergård, *Hotad moral — en studie av 1930 och 1940talens debatt om ungdomens*

'Folk Devils' as Targets

Morality has to do with feelings and opinions, panic with an uncontrolled reaction, while 'the others' and devils tend to describe what one dislikes. This is how one might briefly summarise theories about moral panic, which are a reaction on a social level and not only on an individual level. It is not just one person, or a couple, whose anxiety about something creates emotional panic, but rather a fear which spreads to large parts of society. This fear singles out other groups or unique events as a harmful threat to the entire society.

Since medieval times (and maybe earlier) dancing has been some sort of folk devil — a behaviour practised by ordinary people that the rulers and elite classes dislike. The combination of body, movement and morality has been an issue for those who do not take part in these activities, especially adults versus the youth. It is said that Augustine of Hippo, who died in 430, formulated his dislike for dancing thus:

> It is better to take care of your fields than to dance on Sundays. The dance is a circle, where the devil is in the middle and every movement of the dance is a leap to meet him in hell.[10]

New dances and new fashions seemed to trigger opinions about dancing. John of Münster wrote in 1594 about the new and 'indecent' dance Volta:

> Nowadays everybody in Germany only wants to dance the Gaillard. Especially there is a new, indecent dance named the Volta, which takes its name from the French word *voltiger*, meaning to fly around in whirls. In that dance the dancer takes the lady with a jump, and she also advances towards him, forced by the music, and he seizes her in an improper place, where she has a piece of wood, and he throws the lady and also himself so high up in the air, so high above the floor, that the onlooker believes

---

nöjesliv (Uppsala: Etnologiska institutionen, 1987); Peter Nilsson, *Hon dansade som en skadskjuten kråka. En uppsats om rave och massmedia* (Göteborg: Etnologiska institutionen, 1997); Evalotta Sandberg, *Rave och media* (Stockholm: Institutet för folklivsforskning, 1998), and Stefan Thungren, *Raveelländet. Debatten om ravefester som moralisk panik* (Stockholm: Institutet för folklivsforskning, 1998); Elisabeth Tegner, 'Dans i stormens öga', in *Drömmar och strömmar — om att tolka ungdomars värld*, ed. by Mohamed Chaib (Göteborg: Daidalos, 1993), 65–69.

10   Cited in Mats Rehnberg, 'Från svärdsdans till menuett', in *Det glada Sverige: Våra fester och högtider genom tiderna*, vol. 2, ed. by Gösta I. Berg (Stockholm: Natur och Kultur, 1948), pp. 133–82 (p. 170). Translated from the Swedish by Mats Nilsson.

that the dancers will not be able to come down again without breaking arms and legs.[11]

If moral panic amounts to a spate of moralising that has deteriorated into panic, the folk devils are the group of people, or the activity they engage in, that become targets in this process. Young people's dancing for pleasure seems to be a constantly latent field of moral panic over time. The dances and dance events themselves are then the folk devils that are believed to ruin young people.

Panic does not always arise, but moralising about pleasure dancing (or bar dances, dance pavilions, discotheques, raves, etc.) is apparently a continuous undercurrent in our society. In these dance environments, dangerous things can happen, especially connected with (alcohol and/ or narcotic) drugs, and with the physical encounter between human bodies.[12] And if dancing and physical bodies are not dangerous, at the very least they do not constitute pure or fine culture. For instance, in an article in *Göteborgs-Posten* about a danceband trip by boat, the headline read 'The ape stage, round trip'.[13] Even some of our very well-known and popular performers, such as Hasse & Tage, uphold the image that many of us have of pleasure dancing. In the monologue *Stadslollan* [The City Wench], performed by Lena Nyman, the 'wench' gets pregnant as soon as she sets a foot in the 'boondock' barn dance.[14] In another of their conversations, Hasse & Tage allow the punkrocker Trindeman Lindeman to reveal why dance music exists: if it did not, the whole dance floor would be impounded for disorderly conduct.[15] The implication is that what one does on the dance floor becomes, with music, more or

---

11   Ibid., pp. 160–61
12   Christina Carmbrant, 'Olaglig ravfest i kyrkolokal. Tre unga greps — flera olika sorters droger i beslag', *Göteborgs-Posten* (16 October 2000), p. 9; Rasmus Malm, 'Regisserad jakt på droger', *Dagens Nyheter* (2 November 2000), part B, pp. 1, 4; Ebba Malmström, '26 unga greps vid razzia mot ravefest. Polisen tog stora mängder narkotika i beslag', *Göteborgs-Posten* (27 Nov 2000), p. 11, and Jan Nyman, 'Världarnas krig', *Göteborgs-Posten* (10 December 2000), p. 11.
13   Frida Boisen, 'Apstadiet tur och retur. Om en rock'nrollkryss till Norge och tillbaka', *Göteborgs-Posten Aveny* (3 March 2000), [n.p.].
14   Hans Alfredsson and Tage Danielsson, '1973: Stadslollan. Monologue with Lena Nyman', in 'Glaset i örat på Berns', *Guldkorn från Hasse & Tages Revyer* (Svenska Ljud/Sonet Grammofon AB, 1998) [on CD].
15   Hans Alfredsson and Tage Danielsson, '1979: Punkrockare Trindeman Lindeman', in 'Under Dubbelgöken på Berns', *Guldkorn från Hasses & Tages Revyer* (Svenska Ljud/Sonet Grammofon AB, 1998) [on CD].

less what one otherwise does in bed. My point here is not that Hasse & Tage are extreme; on the contrary, they only express prevailing norms, which is why we laugh when we recognise ourselves in their incisive formulations. Similarly, there are examples of pictures in which dance is represented as something superficially calm and innocent, but when one folds the picture in a certain way the real subject emerges — sex.[16]

Today the folk devils probably have a greater opportunity to defend themselves, and argue in speech and writing, than ever before in history. The perspectives of the dancers and participants, and a 'defence' of rave and disco, appear for instance in student essays.[17] Here one's own participation and understanding allow one to use the theories about moral panic as a defence against the attacks of the moralists. Those who are subjected to moralising cast back the objections by asserting that 'it is simply moral panic' (compare also Thornton below). Even pair dances, such as the Foxtrot, Tango, and Salsa, are explained and defended by their performers nowadays.[18] There are also examples of an alleged panic being undiscernible except from a Stockholmer's middleclass media perspective. When going to the countryside, outside the capital, many people did not realise there was any panic about dancing.[19]

---

16 Ulf Palmenfelt, *Folkhumor i fotostat* (Stockholm: Prisma, 1986), p. 85.
17 Lotta Björkman, *'Go with the flow'. En studie av rumslighet, rörelse och tidlöshet* (Lund: Etnologiska institutionen, 1996); Anna Cecilia Weschke, *Nattklubbens själ* (Göteborg: Etnologiska institutionen, 1993), and Kajsa Wiklund, *Saturday night fever. En studie av dans, agerande och kommunikation på diskodansgolvet* (Lund: Etnologiska institutionen, 1997). Cf. also Maria Pini, 'Cyborgs, Nomads and the Raving Feminine', in *Dance in the City*, ed. by Helen Thomas (London: Macmillan, 1997), 111–29, https://doi.org/10.1057/9780230379213_7
18 Sonia Abadi, *Milongan — omfamningarnas basar* (Stockholm: CKM media AB, 2003); Johan Borghäll, *Salsa! Och livet i Havanna. Om musiken i dansen och dansen i musiken* (Stockholm: ICA bokförlag, 2001); Birgitta Holm, *Pardans* (Albert Bonniers Förlag, 2004); M. A. Numminen, *Tango är min passion* (Jyväskylä: Alfabeta, 1999); Sam Savander, *Dans, inte bara en sexjakt. En deltagares analys av umgängeskulturen* (Skelleftehamn: Artemis, 1997); Kerstin Thorvall, *Nödvändigheten i att dansa* (Stockholm: Bonnier pocket, 2002), and Liisa Ängquist, 'Är det du eller jag som för'. *En etnologisk studie av några generella drag av sällskapsdansens förändring under de senaste femtio åren* (Umeå: Etnologiska institutionen, 1996).
19 Anna Wennerlund, *En förförd ungdom? Om nöjeslivet och moralisk debatt i 1940talets Karlstad* (Göteborg: Etnologiska institutionen, 1995); Chatarina Wiklund, *Om dessa backar kunde tala! Berättelserna om Fällforsen, Övre Norrlands största danshak* (Umeå: Etnologiska institutionen, 1997); and Eva Helen Ulvros, *Dansens och tidens virvlar. Om dans och lek i Sveriges historia* (Lund: Historiska media, 2004).

Moral Panic — Morality in Panic?

The concept of moral panic was not coined by Stanley Cohen in 1972, but rather by his colleague Jock Young. An article by Young in 1971 discusses the general anxiety caused by statistics over the growth of drug abuse, and states that 'the moral panic over drugtaking results in the setting up of drug squads', which in turn causes an increase of drug related arrests.[20] It was, however, Cohen who in 1972 introduced the concept to a wider public in his book *Folk Devils and Moral Panics: The Creation of Mods and Rockers*. During the 1960s, rumours flourished about what transpired when two youth groups as different as Mods and Rockers met on the beaches at the English resort of Brighton. When Cohen subsequently investigated what allegedly happened and what he could establish to have occurred, great differences emerged. It was when he described these differences, and how they could be disseminated, that he gave shape to the idea of moral panic as well as to folk devils.

For Cohen and his younger colleague Kenneth Thompson,[21] the key element in a moral panic is a series of events or phenomena that generate each other — or, even better, a spiral of events and actions that finally lose their force and die out.[22] First, someone or something is defined as a *threat to fundamental social values or interests* by somebody else, usually called a *moral entrepreneur*. The threat is then depicted in an easily recognisable form by *mass media*, which in turn contributes to a *rapid build-up* of the public interest in what happened. Authorities and *opinionmakers* begin to get involved. Next, the panic *disappears* without visible traces as easily as it arose, or else it results in *social changes* of some kind, such as a new law. The actual cause of the panic seldom disappears, despite the panicked moral activities. An alternative formulation is that a moral panic occurs when the public, via mass media, is alarmed with the help of entrepreneurs, those moral crusaders who hound the authorities for more social control and moral rules resting on an absolute ethic. The

---

20 Quoted in Kenneth Thompson, *Moral Panics* (London and New York: Routledge, 1999), p. 7.
21 Stanley Cohen, *Folk Devils and Moral Panics: The Creation of the Mods and Rockers*, 3rd edn (New York: Routledge, 2002), p. 9, and Thompson, *Moral Panics*, p. 8.
22 Thompson, *Moral Panics*, p. 6.

actions of moral crusaders (entrepreneurs) can be seen as symbolic of social dissatisfaction among certain groups or classes in society.[23]

The threat that the moral crusaders experience or observe, and the culprits they blame, become evil *folk devils*.[24] These stimulate strong feelings of righteousness, primarily among the moralising groups themselves. The literature about moral panic often concerns itself with morality among the deviants — as well as how and why the panic arises. My own interest as an ethnologist is really in the panic's 'victims' and what or who they are, or how they reason. For example, what is it in dance and music that threatens? And, perhaps most importantly, how do the folk devils themselves, or rather the people who perpetrate the devilry, experience the questioning of their morality and their activities? These issues are confronted much less extensively in the literature. Moral panic has two characteristics on which everyone seems to agree. It concerns a social group's worries over the behaviour of another group or category of peoples, at the same time as there is a growing degree of enmity toward the indicated group, which is seen as a threat to the social order. Thompson points out another common feature: that panic implies some measure of inconstancy and disproportionality.[25] Here panic means 'generalised fears and anxieties of a large part of the population'.[26] Moral panic arises when the official picture of, or the press reaction to, a deviant social or cultural phenomenon 'completely lacks proportion regarding the true threat that exists'. In addition, Cohen notes that there is a periodic tendency to identify and create folk devils as scapegoats (in his case, Mods and Rockers), whose activities are viewed by hegemonic groups (the moralists) as evidence of an internal social breakdown.[27] This suggests that the creation of moral panic is a part of these groups' method of exercising power.

Moral panic, then, is collective in its performance and behaviour. It is relatively spontaneous, volatile, ephemeral, impetuous, extra-institutional, and short-lived, arising in situations where clear definitions

---

23 Ibid., p. 13.
24 Cohen, *Folk Devils and Moral Panics*, pp. 2–3.
25 Thompson, *Moral Panics*, p. 9.
26 Philip Jenkins, *Intimate Enemies. Moral Panics in Contemporary Great Britain* (New York: Aldine de Gruyter, 1992), p. 4.
27 John Springhall, *Youth, Popular Culture and Moral Panics. Penny Gaffs to GangstaRap, 1830–1996* (London: Macmillan, 1998), pp. 4–5.

or explanations and patterns of action set by the mainstream culture are lacking. The episodic character of these panics distinguishes moral panic from other actions by, for example, more long-lived political or environmental groups. This distinction in is often considered important by scholars.[28] However, it is difficult to see that political or environmental groups *themselves* would be excluded as moral entrepreneurs. The distinction between moral panic and these other actions ought to lie precisely in whether we are dealing with longer activities which surround moral or other issues, but which are not themselves panicked; or whether we are dealing with a moral/political opinion that creates a panic among influential groups in society.

According to Sarah Thornton, a British researcher in youth culture and media, moral panic is the culmination and fulfilment of young people's cultural goals, in the sense that negative news coverage baptises and confirms transgression as a desired immoral act. Moral panic is, for example, one of the few marketing strategies open to relatively anonymous, late modern instrumental dance music. The tabloid press is in many ways essential to the British youth movement — it helps to delimit the subcultures, at the same time as it differentiates them from the mainstream culture. Positive judgements are the kiss of death. To be misunderstood in the mass media is often an aim, and not an effect, of the youth culture's search for identity.[29] Thornton adds:

> 'Moral panic' is a metaphor which depicts a complex society as a single person who experiences sudden groundless fear about its virtue [...] its anthropomorphism and totalization mystifies more than it reveals. It fails to acknowledge competing media, let alone their disparate reception by diverse audiences. And its conception of morals overlooks the youthful ethics of abandon.[30]

As for counterattacks, some researchers' critiques of moral panic contain as a clarifying concept the very notion that it has become a simple, sociological excuse or an insult to throw back at the social reactions which surround, for instance, football hooligans and welfare freeloaders

---

28 Thompson, *Moral Panics*; Jenkins, *Intimate Enemies*; Erich Goode and Nachman Ben-Yehuda, *Moral Panics. The Social Construction of Deviance* (Oxford: Blackwell, 1996).
29 Sarah Thornton, 'Moral Panic, the Media and British Rave Culture', in *Microphone Fiends Youth Music, Youth Culture*, ed. by Andrew Ross and Tricia Rose (London and New York: Routledge, 1994), pp. 176–92.
30 Ibid., p. 184.

in our time.³¹ Scientific concepts spread into everyday language and their usage, significance and meanings are changed, as social science and daily life constantly influence each other.³² This dual hermeneutics implies that moral panic has become clearly loaded with ideology, and is more of a polemical than an analytical concept.³³

Mass media, as much as the concept of moral panic, is thus employed by both sides — the moral entrepreneurs and the folk devils. To the former, media are a way of spreading their message and creating moral panic, but also a way of trying to affect and alter what causes the panic. Folk devils, the other party in the struggle for interpretive priority, defend themselves by claiming vulnerability to moral panic. But the moralists (and probably also their victims) tend to exaggerate the media's ability to influence behaviour in people who are less educated than they are, at least according to John Springhill. The mass media play a double role, since in addition to being interlocutors for both parties in a moral struggle, they can be, through their news coverage and journalism, a source of moral panic.³⁴

Ignorance at a Distance — Morality and Power

The moral field revolves in two overlapping spheres: official and non-official. When they are articulated together, a moral panic may arise, though it need not.³⁵ Rumours belong to the nonofficial sphere, and their life resembles that of moral panic in many ways.

> Rumour begins somewhere, is set in motion and multiplied, and starts to circulate. The process expands and reaches a high point, then declines and splits into lesser sources of rumour. Finally, it usually ceases completely — or is laid latently in the collective memory for the future.³⁶

---

31 Jenkins, *Intimate Enemies*, p. 8. Compare also *Godmorgen världen*, Sveriges Radio P1, 13 February 2005; and *Kulturnytt*, Sveriges Radio P1, 23 March 2005, where the reactions to the accusation of 'child pornography' towards a children theatre project shown at the University College of Film, Radio, Television and Theatre were rejected as 'mere moral panic'.
32 Antony Giddens, *Modernitetens följder* (Lund: Studentlitteratur, 1996), p. 22, and Mats Nilsson, *Dans — kontinuitet i förändring. En studie av danser och dansande i Göteborg 19301990* (Göteborg: Etnologiska föreningen i Västsverige, 1998), p. 39.
33 Thompson, *Moral Panics*, p. 10.
34 Springhall, *Youth, Popular Culture and Moral Panics*, pp. 158–59.
35 Thompson, *Moral Panics*, p. 6.
36 Jean-Noël Kapferer, *Rykten. Världens äldsta nyhetsmedium* (Stockholm: Norstedts, 1988), p. 8. Translated from the Swedish by Mats Nilsson.

Jean-Noël Kapferer sees rumour as a collective consultation, and refers to the sociologist Tamotsu Shibutani's definition of rumour as 'the group's common exploitation of its intellectual resources to find a satisfying explanation of the event'.[37] Kapferer summarises this with the formula R=B*O, where R is the rumour, B is significance for the group, and O is lack of clarity. It is easy to perceive that insignificant events or people are not subjected to rumours, or that no rumours arise if everything is unambiguous and clear. Yet, how often does this really apply?

Thus, one angle of approach is to assume that fears and anxiety are what create rumours (and legends) as well as moral panics. The rise of rumours, legends, travellers' tales and similar narratives is almost always rooted in ignorance about what they describe. When we recount and discuss things we do not know very much about — they might be called 'the unknown', and what we seldom encounter, 'the unusual', or what we cannot understand or control, the 'uncontrollable' — we move in the uncertain borderland where belief and knowledge are inseparable.[38]

All industrial countries have periodic outbreaks of moral panic. This is a hallmark of modernity and of late or postmodernity. Rapid social changes and growing social pluralism increase the potential for value conflicts and lifestyle confrontations, which entail moral enterprises to defend or assert a group's values against others. It happens in the public arena where the media offers opportunities for reinforcement and articulation of fears and demands for social control and regulation to defend one's own values.[39]

> The very fact of a recurring cycle might suggest not so much a persistent irrationality or media induced 'panic', but rather the expression of fundamental contradictions in relations between classes and generations. We should give more emphasis to the *continuity* of the apprehension and loathing of 'modernity' which such fears represent and the specificity of the various constituencies, populist, conservative and fundamentalist, from which they emerge [...] Unfortunately, because of modernity theory's emphasis on dramatic change, its proponents tend to underestimate continuities between preindustrial and urbanindustrial popular culture.[40]

Cohen points out that there is a periodic tendency to identify and create folk devils (such as Mods and Rockers) whose activities are regarded

---

39 Thompson, *Moral Panics*, p. 11.
40 Springhall, *Youth, Popular Culture and Moral Panics*, p. 159.

by some groups in society as signs of internal social collapse.[41] When a moral panic arises, it revives dormant stereotypes or folk devils. They linger on as latent motives and are activated when a diversion from other social problems is needed.[42] Moral panics thus regenerate the dominant and established system of values in a period of anxiety and crisis, while folk devils provide a necessary external threat in the dichotomy between social anxiety and interest groups' policies.[43] As a comparison, the folklorist William R. Bascom considers the overall function of folklore to be an important factor for a society's survival and a culture's stability through time.[44] Outbreaks such as moral panic can therefore be seen as a collective safety valve, and the stereotypes of folk devils as a part of the eternal folklore.

Changes in society often cause anxiety in large groups of citizens. The deficiency in awareness and knowledge of new conditions and technologies creates insecurity and aversion. Relevant here are theories about modernisation and globalisation, where it is precisely change that creates insecurity.[45] Moral panic is connected with a fear of new technology alongside elaborated forms of popular culture. Ever since the early 1800s, commercial forms of entertainment have been demonised by some groups in society — those who think they have superior knowledge to others.[46] What is culturally 'over there' but is physically close, which we know little about despite its being nearby, is sometimes experienced as threatening. Our anxiety and ignorance then easily lead to moral panic in the face of these devils, or diabolical phenomena. My thesis about the causes of moral panic and the creation, or rather activation, of folk devils (stereotypes) is that they have to do with cultural distance and inadequate knowledge of the phenomena that each of us now and then demonises in an attempt to wield power. The lack of knowledge refers mainly to our lack of experience of what we moralise about, at least in the same emic sense as those who are subjected to moral lectures.

---

41 Cohen, *Folk Devils and Moral Panics*.
42 Springhall, *Youth, Popular Culture and Moral Panics*, pp. 5, 14.
43 Jenkins, *Intimate Enemies*, p. 7.
44 William R. Bascom, 'Four Functions of Folklore', in *The Study of Folklore*, ed. by Alan Dundes (Englewood Cliffs, NJ: PrenticeHall Inc., 1965), pp. 279–98.
45 Zygmunt Bauman, *Globalisering* (Lund: Studentlitteratur, 2000), pp. 39 and 43.
46 Springhall, *Youth, Popular Culture and Moral Panics*, p. 159. Compare with Pierre Bourdieu, *Kultursociologiska texter* (Lidingö: Salamander, 1986) and his concept 'distinction'.

13. Dance and 'Folk Devils'

The moralist seldom, if ever, meets, in their own arena, the people and phenomena that they react against. The indirect wielding of power by the moralist is due to deficient experience and typically a position on the fringes of real power. One feels threatened but cannot protect oneself and does not know how. Hence, one tries to make the real powers do something, to save oneself the confrontation with immorality, and thus evade an encounter face-to-face with the folk devils.

The dilemma is that, to avoid panic and 'meaningless moralising', we must relativize and question certain claims about what, sometimes with good reason, we dislike. We must examine our own 'centric' attitudes (whether they involve ethno, socio-, or chronocentrism, or the like) and values. Are all young people at a rave on drugs? Why are they attracted there? What is in fact bad and immoral, and from whose perspective? Why do we think computer games, casinos, 3Gmasters, or cell phones are dangerous? Is the creation of folk devils about a genuine fear of technology, more conscious ideological dissociation, or purely moral issues?

Fig. 13.2 *A Drunken Party with Sailors and Their Women Drinking, Smoking, and Dancing Wildly as a Band Plays*. Reproduction of an etching by C. H., c. 1825, after George Cruikshank. Wellcome Collection, CC BY 4.0, https://wellcomecollection.org/works/y4vwqhg7

Back to Dance

To conclude, youth culture in general — and, especially, where dance is concerned — has been, and continues to be, a target for moral issues and rumours from older people. But in the twenty-first century does it cause moral panics as Cohen describes them, or are they more of a 'moral dislike' that doesn't escalate to panic?

I think there is a little more tolerance towards dance today. There are more dance genres and older people dancing themselves today than there were fifty years ago. Middle-age dancing, and dancing as a hobby, have become genres of their own, parallel to more youth-dominated club dancing. So called *dansbandsmusik* (closely related to country and western music), a relatively large and widespread type of music to which people in their mid-fifties and over still dance the Jitterbug and Foxtrot in amusement parks and elsewhere, generally has a low status among the cultural elite as well as musicians and musicologists.[47] But it does not create moral panic.

Dance courses are a relatively modern phenomenon, at least for the public at large. My thesis is that these courses are a way of handling the morally difficult aspects of dancing and body exposure, and of institutionalising and disarming the dangerous borderland in which pleasure dancing in a public hall occurs. Here the interest, notably among women, now seems to be in oriental dances,[48] Salsa,[49] or Tango.[50] So, maybe the moral panic entrepreneurs have left the dance field and are now concerned with the internet and computer games, which seem to be the new folk devils. However, there might be a potential moral panic concerning dance in the rather new phenomena of pole dancing (dancing on a pole as in a sex club), especially when there are courses

---

47 Mats Trondman, 'Självbedrägeriets och misskännandets princip. Till kritiken av dansbandskulturen', *Mardrömmar och önskedrömmar. Om ungdom och ungdomlighet i nittiotalets Sverige*, ed. by Fredrik Miegel and Thomas Johansson (Stockholm and Stehag: Symposion, 1994), pp. 177–212.

48 Magnus Berg, 'Orienten på en höft', in *Där hemma, här borta. Möten med orienten i Sverige och Norge*, ed. by Åsa Andersson, Magnus Berg and Sidsel Natland (Stockholm: Carlssons, 2001), pp. 145–222; Karin Högström, *Orientalisk dans i Stockholm, Femininiteter, möjligheter och begränsningar* (Stocholm: Stockholms universitet, 2010); Maria Kihlstenius, *Längtan till kvinnlighet. En studie av svenskor på kurs i orientalisk dans* (Stockholm: Institutet för folklivsforskning, 1996), and Hanna Särborn and Cecilie Mykkeltvedt, *Orientalisk dans. Snusk eller konst?* (Göteborg: Etnologiska institutionen, 1993).

49 Britt Ramström, *Livets krydda. Salsadansare i 1990talets Göteborg* (Göteborg: Etnologiska institutionen, 1998).

50 Birgitta Holm, *Pardans*.

for children from six years of age. I have not seen any public reaction that has become a big business at the time of writing, but since there are courses and exercises for young children there is fuel for a spark of moral indignation that could become a fire when it comes to pole dancing.

In light of the examples mentioned above, I see the Waltz as just one dance form through history that older people and the authorities disapproved of when it was new. In the beginning of the nineteenth century, couple dances like the Waltz and the Polka were new and provocative for the older generations, since young men and women were physically very close when dancing — and they could not be controlled in the way that was possible, for instance, in the Minuet or contra dances. After a while, the Waltz became the conventional and morally accepted way to dance. Early in the twentieth century, jazz dancing and the Foxtrot became the folk devils and the immoral dances.

Bibliography

Secondary Sources

Abadi, Sonia, *Milongan — omfamningarnas basar* (Stockholm: CKM media AB, 2003).

Agrell, Alexander, *Hotet från jazzen. En studie av motstånd mot jazzmusik* (Lund: Etnologiska institutionen, 1984).

Arvidsson, Alf, ed., *Uppsatser i svensk jazzhistoria* (Umeå: Inst för etnologi, 1998).

Axelsson, Michael, *Ravekultur. En studie om ravekulturens gemenskapsbildning och den rörliga platsens fasta punkt* (Stockholm: Etnologiska institutionen, 2004).

Bascom, William R, 'Four Functions of Folklore', in *The Study of Folklore*, ed. by Alan Dundes (Engelwood Cliffs, NJ: PrenticeHall Inc., 1965), pp. 279–98.

Bauman, Zygmunt, *Globalisering* (Lund: Studentlitteratur, 2000).

Berg, Magnus, 'Orienten på en höft', in *Där hemma, här borta. Möten med orienten i Sverige och Norge*, ed. by Åsa Andersson, Magnus Berg, and Sidsel Natland (Stockholm: Carlssons, 2001), pp. 145–222.

Björkman, Lotta, *'Go with the flow'. En studie av rumslighet, rörelse och tidlöshet* (Lund: Etnologiska institutionen, 1996).

Borghäll, Johan, *Salsa! Och livet i Havanna. Om musiken i dansen och dansen i musiken* (Stockholm: ICA bokförlag, 2001).

Bourdieu, Pierre, *Kultursociologiska texter* (Lidingö: Salamander, 1986).

Cohen, Stanley, *Folk Devils and Moral Panics: The Creation of the Mods and Rockers*, 3rd edn (New York: Routledge, 2002).

Edberg, Henrik, *'De kommer för lätt undan'. En jämförelse mellan moralisk panik i 1960talets England och 1990talets Sverige* (Göteborg: Etnologiska institutionen, 1996).

Eivergård, Mikael, *Hotad moral — en studie av 1930 och 1940talens debatt om ungdomens nöjesliv* (Uppsala: Etnologiska institutionen, 1987).

Fornäs, Johan, *Moderna människor. Folkhemmet och jazzen* (Stockholm: Norstedts, 2004).

Frykman, Jonas, *Dansbaneeländet. Ungdomen, populärkulturen och opinionen* (Stockholm: Natur & Kultur, 1988).

Giddens, Antony, *Modernitetens följder* (Lund: Studentlitteratur, 1996).

Gunnemark, Kerstin and Magnus Mörck, eds, *Vardagslivets fronter* (Göteborg: Arkipelag, 2006).

Goode, Erich, and Nachman BenYehuda, *Moral Panics. The Social Construction of Deviance* (Oxford: Blackwell, 1996).

Holm, Birgitta, *Pardans* (Stockholm: Albert Bonniers Förlag, 2004).

Hoppu, Petri, 'Folkdansande Eros', *Folkdansforskning i Norden*, 34 (2011), 10–16.

Högström, Karin, *Orientalisk dans i Stockholm, Feminiiteter, möjligheter och begränsningar* (Stockholm: Stockholms universitet, 2010).

Jenkins, Philip, *Intimate Enemies. Moral Panics in Contemporary Great Britain* (New York: Aldine de Gruyter, 1992).

Kapferer, Jean-Noël, *Rykten. Världens äldsta nyhetsmedium* (Stockholm: Norstedts, 1988).

Kihlstenius, Maria, *Längtan till kvinnlighet. En studie av svenskor på kurs i orientalisk dans.* (Stockholm: Institutet för folklivsforskning, 1996).

Knowles, Mark, *The Wicked Waltz and Other Scandalous Dances. Outrage at Couple Dancing in the 19th and Early 20th Centuries* (Jefferson, NC: McFarland, 2008).

Larsson, Göran, 'Onestep & Jumpa: om moralisk panik i 1910talets Sverige', in *Uppsatser i svensk jazzhistoria*, ed. by Alf Arvidsson (Umeå: Institutionen för etnologi, 1998), 8–35.

McKee, Eric, *Decorum of the Minuet, Delirium of the Waltz. A Study of DanceMusic Relations in ¾ Time* (Bloomington, IN: Indiana University Press, 2012), https://doi.org/10.2307/j.ctt2005r6k

Nilsson, Mats, *Dans — kontinuitet i förändring. En studie av danser och dansande i Göteborg 19301990* (Göteborg: Etnologiska föreningen i Västsverige, 1998).

Nilsson, Peter, *Hon dansade som en skadskjuten kråka. En uppsats om rave och massmedia*. (Göteborg: Etnologiska institutionen, 1997).

Numminen, M. A., *Tango är min passion* (Jyväskylä: Alfabeta, 1999).

Palmenfelt, Ulf, 'Det femuddiga hexagrammet. Ryktesspridning och häxtro i Drömtågets spår', in *I spåren efter Drömtåget*, ed. by Håkan Lahger, Kenneth Andersson, and Olof Wallgren (Stockholm: Gidlunds & Riksutställnningar, 1994), pp. 48–64.

——, *Folkhumor i fotostat* (Stockholm: Prisma, 1986).

Pini, Maria, 'Cyborgs, Nomads and the Raving Feminine', in *Dance in the City*, ed. by Helen Thomas (London: Macmillan, 1997), 111–29, https://doi.org/10.1057/9780230379213_7

Ramström, Britt, *Livets krydda. Salsadansare i 1990talets Göteborg* (Göteborg: Etnologiska institutionen, 1998).

Rehnberg, Mats, 'Från svärdsdans till menuett', in *Det glada Sverige: Våra fester och högtider genom tiderna*, vol. 2, ed. by Gösta I. Berg (Stockholm: Natur och Kultur, 1948), 133–82.

Rosén, Gösta, *Kriget om den moderna dansen* (Stockholm: Harriers bokförlag AB, 1952).

Sandberg, Evalotta, *Rave och media* (Stockholm: Institutet för folklivsforskning, 1998).

Savander, Sam, *Dans, inte bara en sexjakt. En deltagares analys av umgängeskulturen* (Skelleftehamn: Artemis, 1997).

Selberg, Torun, *Nostalgi og sensasjoner. Folkloristik perspektiv på mediekulturen* (Åbo: Nif, 1995).

Sjöberg, Henry, and Anita Etzler, *Folkets danser* (Stockholm: Brevskolan, 1981).

Springhall, John, *Youth, Popular Culture and Moral Panics. Penny Gaffs to Gangsta-Rap, 1830–1996* (London: Macmillan, 1998).

Stattin, Jochum, *Från gastkramning till gatuvåld. En etnologisk studie av svenska rädslor* (Stockholm: Carlssons, 1990).

Särborn, Hanna, and Cecilie Mykkeltvedt, *Orientalisk dans. Snusk eller konst?* (Göteborg: Etnologiska institutionen, 1993).

Tegner, Elisabeth, 'Dans i stormens öga', in *Drömmar och strömmar — om att tolka ungdomars värld*, ed. by Mohamed Chaib (Göteborg: Daidalos, 1993), 65–69.

Thomas, Helen, *Dance in the City* (London: Macmillan, 1997).

Thompson, Kenneth, *Moral Panics* (London and New York: Routledge, 1999).

Thornton, Sarah, 'Moral Panic, the Media and British Rave Culture', in *Microphone Fiends. Youth Music, Youth Culture*, ed. by Andrew Ross and Tricia Rose (London and New York: Routledge, 1994), pp. 176–92.

Thorvall, Kerstin, *Nödvändigheten i att dansa* (Stockholm: Bonnierpocket, 2002).

Thungren, Stefan, *Raveeländet. Debatten om ravefester som moralisk panik* (Stockholm: Institutet för folklivsforskning, 1998).

Trondman, Mats, 'Självbedrägeriets och misskännandets princip. Till kritiken av dansbandskulturen', in *Mardrömmar och Önskedrömmar. Om ungdom och ungdomlighet i nittiotalets Sverige*, ed. by Fredrik Miegel and Thomas Johansson (Stockholm and Stehag: Symposion, 1994), pp. 177–212.

Ulvros, Eva Helen, *Dansens och tidens virvlar. Om dans och lek i Sveriges historia* (Lund: Historiska media, 2004).

Walles, Erik, *Jazzen anfaller* (Stockholm: Natur och Kultur, 1946).

Weschke, Anna Cecilia, *Nattklubbens själ* (Göteborg: Etnologiska institutionen, 1993).

Wennerlund, Anna, *En förförd ungdom? Om nöjeslivet och moralisk debatt i 1940talets Karlstad* (Göteborg: Etnologiska institutionen, 1995).

Wiklund, Chatarina, *Om dessa backar kunde tala! Berättelserna om Fällforsen, Övre Norrlands största danshak* (Umeå: Etnologiska institutionen, 1997).

Wiklund, Kajsa, *Saturday night fever. En studie av dans, agerande och kommunikation på diskodansgolvet* (Lund: Etnologiska institutionen, 1997).

Ängquist, Liisa, 'Är det du eller jag som för'. *En etnologisk studie av några generella drag av sällskapsdansens förändring under de senaste femtio åren* (Umeå: Etnologiska institutionen, 1996).

Newspaper Articles

Boisen, Frida, 'Apstadiet tur och retur. Om en rock'nrollkryss till Norge och tillbaka', *Göteborgs-Posten Aveny* (3 March 2000), [n.p.].

Carmbrant, Christina, 'Olaglig ravfest i kyrkolokal. Tre unga greps — flera olika sorters droger i beslag', *Göteborgs-Posten* (16 October 2000), p. 9.

Malm, Rasmus, 'Regisserad jakt på droger', *Dagens Nyheter* (2 November 2000), part B, pp. 1, 4.

Malmström, Ebba, '26 unga greps vid razzia mot ravefest. Polisen tog stora mängder narkotika i beslag', *Göteborgs-Posten* (27 November 2000), p. 11.

Nyman, Jan, 'Världarnas krig', *Göteborgs-Posten* (10 December 2000), p. 11.

Radio Programmes

Godmorgen världen, Sveriges Radio P1, 13 February 2005.

Kulturnytt, Sveriges Radio P1, 23 March 2005.

Compact Disks

Alfredsson, Hans and Tage Danielsson, '1973: Stadslollan. Monologue with Lena Nyman', in 'Glaset i örat på Berns', *Guldkorn från Hasse & Tages Revyer* (Svenska Ljud/Sonet Grammofon AB, 1998) [on CD].

——, '1979: Punkrockare Trindeman Lindeman', in 'Under Dubbelgöken på Berns', *Guldkorn från Hasses & Tages Revyer* (Svenska Ljud/Sonet Grammofon AB, 1998) [on CD].

DVDs

Det kungliga bröllopet 19 juni 2010, dir. By Lars Bjalkeskog (Nordisk Film, 2010).

14. Nostalgia as a Perspective on Past Dance Culture in Finland

Helena Saarikoski

My ongoing study concerns a late development of the dances that form the subject matter of this book. Sometime in the mid- to late nineteenth century, local groups of young Finnish men in rural villages started to organise dances for their own amusement, so that they could invite girls of their age to have fun with them. In contrast to older popular dance culture, they danced couple dances, and they danced for their own amusement and as a leisure activity, not only as a ritual on designated occasions. This phenomenon in Finland was a modern development. Rural working-class people adopted and arranged the dances as an expression of a new autonomous youth culture, a new romantic idea of marriage, and a new kind of leisure culture, or popular culture.

Unlike music, which was always played to accompany dances and written by named musicians, composers and lyricists, the dances were considered of common creation, known and danced by everyone. From the very beginning, these dances were also considered exotic novelties, arriving from foreign countries and big cities far away from Finland, whether in Central Europe, North or South America, or elsewhere.[1] A young person typically wanted to master the dances that formed the local repertoire à la mode, so as to be able to take part in youth culture, on local dance floors.

In 1991, a collection of manuscripts was gathered by the National Museum of Finland (NMF), written by elderly people recollecting their

---

1   Helena Saarikoski, '"Taian tantsihin ruveta". Tanssikulttuurin muistomerkki 1800-luvun alkupuolen Vienasta', in *Tanssi tanssi: Kulttuureja, tulkintoja*, ed. by Helena Saarikoski (Helsinki: Finnish Literature Society, 2003), pp. 119–45.

dancing youth. These written memories formed the research material for my study. The material on pavilion dances is extensive and consists of approximately four thousand standard pages, from 543 respondents. Of this amount, roughly a quarter is defined as the research material proper in my study, according to the criteria of its being a personal experience narrative or a narrative of specific events from participants' point of view.[2] The respondents, who were mostly elderly people by the time of the inquiry, were asked to talk about dances and dancing at pavilions in their youth. The narrated events took place between 1910 and 1970. After two decades of discos triumphing over couple dances as the amusement of choice for young people, the couple dance culture had come to be considered as a 'vanishing folk tradition', a suitable subject for an inquiry by the Museum. The inquiry produced unique material for cultural dance research: a large collection of vernacular writings by ordinary people, describing their own dancing, in the form of personal experience narratives.[3] To approach dancing and dance events via such narratives, I developed a narrative-ethnographic method of source criticism. Such narratives of days gone by are deeply embedded in contemporary discourses concerning and defining the subject matter. I looked at the respondents' personal experiences on past dance floors, as they were framed and shaped in the discursive realm of the narrating time.

The Dances and Dance Culture

New couple dances became popularised in Finland in successive waves of dance and music culture: first, in the 1840s, the Waltz, and later the Tango, the Foxtrot, *Humppa* (two-step), and, finally, rock 'n' roll dances. Forms of longer duration such as the Polka and the Schottische and, to an extent, the Mazurka, were practised along with the new ones. The dances were introduced in Finland largely by professional dance

---

2   I explored these criteria in two methodological articles based on a preliminary sample study. Helena Saarikoski, 'Tanssi kirjoituksena, kirjoitus tanssina', *Elore*, 17.2 (2010), 4–9, https://doi.org/10.30666/elore.78872, http://www.elore.fi/arkisto/2_10/saarikoski_2_10.pdf; and Helena Saarikoski, 'Menneisyyden ruumiinkokemusten tutkiminen kirjoitetuissa aineistoissa', in *Tekstien rajoilla*, ed. by Sami Lakomäki et al. (Helsinki: Finnish Literature Society, 2011), pp. 117–36.

3   Sandra Stahl Dolby, *Literary Folkloristics and the Personal Narrative* (Bloomington, IN: Indiana University Press, 1989).

teachers and as part of the social customs of the elite.[4] The dance forms, however, soon became assimilated into popular dancing and the dances themselves were arranged and developed into local variants by common people.[5]

Throughout the twentieth century until the 1980s, the couple-dance forms, or simply *dances*, were an everyday and common form of socialising for young people in Finland. From the late nineteenth century to the beginning of the twentieth century, the dancing events of the youth in rural villages developed into a regular institution, in connection with a new kind of autonomous youth culture and the early developments of modern leisure culture.[6] The rural dance institution was characterised by dance events organised on a weekly basis by local people — first, by young men in a village, and, later, by the nascent civic societies, the local youth societies, labour societies, sports clubs, and so on. Small dance stages (literally, *tanssilava* in Finnish) or temporary roofed dance venues (also called *paviljonki* in Finnish) were built for summer dances by local young people, to be their meeting places for amusement and socialising. From the first decades of the twentieth century onwards, local civic societies built their own houses (*talo*, lit. 'house', or *seurantalo*, 'society's house') which were also to serve as dance places. A temporary dance floor, or an open-air stage for dancing, could also be built just for one occasion, for example, for wedding dances or for St John's Eve, or Midsummer dances.[7] The new dances were accompanied by local musicians; often there was only one musician playing the fiddle or the accordion.

---

4   E.g. for the Waltz, Petri Hoppu, *Symbolien ja sanattomuuden tanssi* (Helsinki: Finnish Literature Society, 1999), p. 203; referring to Gunnel Biskop, 'Om borgerligt valsande före 1840', in *Kring tiden. Etnologiska och folkloristiska uppsatser*, ed. by Anna-Maria Åström and Ivar Nordlund (Helsingfors [Helsinki]: Society for Swedish Literature in Finland, 1991), pp. 86–96.

5   For France, cf. Eugen Weber, *Peasants into Frenchmen* (Stanford: Stanford University Press, 1976), pp. 368–69, and pp. 446–51.

6   Matti Sarmela, *Reciprocity Systems of the Rural Society in the Finnish-Karelian Culture Area* (Helsinki: Academia Scientiarum Fennicae, 1969), pp. 128–50.

7   Aila Nieminen, '"Tanssilava, järvi ja hanuri". Lavatanssit Suomessa vuosisadan vaihteesta 1960-luvun loppuun asti' (unpublished MA thesis in ethnology, University of Jyväskylä, 1993), pp. 30–35. 'Helismaa ja kumppanit juhannuskeikalla', 5:35, posted online by Jukka Lindfors, *YLE*, 8 September 2006, https://yle.fi/aihe/artikkeli/2006/09/08/helismaa-ja-kumppanit-juhannuskeikalla (the singer Reino Helismaa and others on a St John's Eve gig; a TV documentary film of the artists and the festivities in north-eastern Finland, 1948).

Fig. 14.1 View from the Punkaharju State Hotel down to the beach towards the ship jetty and bandstand. Postcard (unknown author), c.1905. The Finnish Forest Museum Lusto, image from the Nuutti Kanerva Collection. Wikimedia Commons, Public Domain, https://commons.wikimedia.org/wiki/File:Valtionhotellin_laivalaituri,_Valtionhotellin_tanssi-_ja_soittolava,_circa_1905_PK0059.jpg?uselang=fi#file

Nowadays, the popular couple-dance genre has a particular name: the Pavilion Dance Culture, named after the specific type of light building that was erected for dancing; these Finnish dance pavilions were important venues for the dances discussed in this book. Pavilion dancing (Finnish *lavatanssit*) is a popular hobby, and the dance forms are undergoing a minor revival in today's Finland.

The 1970s saw the popularisation of the 'loose' dance (*irtotanssi* in Finnish) — so called by dancers who were used to couple dancing, since in the 'loose' dance there was no dance frame uniting the couple, and indeed no strict pairing of couples on the floor at all. The dance audience became divided along generational lines; younger people went to discos while the elderly still went dancing at pavilions and society houses.[8] Dance music was assigned to two different genres, *dance* and *rock*, and bands specialised in one or the other (even if individual musicians could move quite smoothly between each genre).[9]

Practically all young people danced, in spite of hostile attitudes to dance perpetuated by sectarian Lutherans. Parents usually allowed their youngsters to go dancing anyway, because, after confirmation, it was considered the right of young people to do so. Going dancing was conventional when looking for a girlfriend or a boyfriend. Most older couples, the parents of those who are now middle-aged, met each other at a dance event. This is often evoked as the shared foundation for the nostalgia that is felt towards this form of dance culture and dance music in the consciousnesses of present-day Finns.

The overwhelming majority of ordinary dancing Finnish people (that is, nearly all Finns) learnt to dance by means of imitation, invention and peer guidance. In historical sources, we may trace and date the arrival of specific dance forms via known mediators, such as dance teachers or artists. However, to trace the 'arrival' of a dance in the life of any individual dancer, the beginnings of waltzing or tangoing in any

---

8   Sini Kuha, 'Tanssilavat, konvat ja discot nuorten areenana 1960-luvun Jyväskylässä', in *Tanssilavan luona. Huvielämää Jyväskylän Ainolassa*, ed. by Henna Mikkola (Jyväskylä: Minerva, 2005), pp. 55–72. 'Dansholmen, Tolkis FBK', 12:45, posted online by The Archive of the Finnish Broadcasting Company, *YLE*, 26 October 2011, https://areena.yle.fi/1-50228262 (dances at the pavilion of Dansholmen, Tolkis VFB; a TV documentary film of dances in the South coast of Finland, 1966).

9   Sven-Erik Klinkmann, *Från Wantons till Wild Force* (Stockholm: Gidlunds, 2010), pp. 354–83.

particular body and in the lives of specific individuals, we have to look for different kinds of sources: oral history and other unconventional sources of grassroots history.

On the basis of an inquiry that also provided the material for my own study, Aila Nieminen has described the overall choreography of pavilion dances at the level of culturally shared knowledge of dancing customs and etiquette:

> To start with, lines or groups of women and of men faced each other on opposite sides of the floor, waiting for the music to begin. At the first tunes, the men rushed towards the women to choose and catch the one they wanted to dance with. Dance couples were formed usually by a man asking a girl for a dance, according to set turns of asking for men and for women; the *women's turn* or *asking* came later in the evening and was shorter than the men's. Customarily, there was no good reason to refuse a dance, except a man's overt drunkenness (there is no traditional rule concerning a drunken woman, since, before the mid-1960s, it would have been hard to imagine such a sight at public dances). Two women could occasionally decide to dance, for several customarily acknowledged reasons, whereas it was usually not acceptable to dance in a male-male couple, or so-called ox couple.[10]

Each couple danced turning around its own axis. At the same time, the entire dancing crowd also progressed counter-clockwise around an (imagined or real) central pole of the dance floor. The twofold turning around was a new bodily protocol,[11] first introduced with the Waltz in the mid-nineteenth century. Acquiring the skill was not easy for the dancers who were used to the more static models of earlier social dances.[12]

The dancers' step pattern does not necessarily follow the musical rhythm — actually, it is claimed that the Finnish audience dances to the words and not to the music.[13] Finnish dance music is always sung in Finnish, and the dance itself is characterised by inhibited emotional expression. At a dance event, it is thus the song lyrics that most clearly

---

10 Nieminen, '"Tanssilava, järvi ja hanuri"'. All translations in this chapter from the Finnish are by Helena Saarikoski.
11 Judith Hamera, *Dancing Communities* (London: Macmillan, 2007), p. 32, https://doi.org/10.1057/9780230626485
12 Hoppu, *Symbolien ja sanattomuuden tanssi*, pp. 202–04.
13 Klinkmann, *Från Wantons till Wild Force*, p. 346.

express the emotions involved. Different couples on the floor can follow a different pattern to the same music. In practice, the identity of a dance, or dance type, like the Tango, Foxtrot or Two-Step, is more likely to be found in the music than in the dancers' movements.[14]

It was during the first decades of this modern popular culture of weekly public dance events that Finland gained independence, after little more than a century of Russian rule of the north-western province, the Grand-Duchy of Finland.[15] Finland declared independence after the October Revolution in December 1917. The declaration was followed by a civil war in the spring of 1918. With far-reaching societal and cultural consequences, the country was divided into two warring parties, the working-class Red Guards and the victorious White Guards. The trauma of the civil war was evident in the dance culture, as well as everywhere in Finnish society; the dance venues were divided according to the owner's affiliation to one or other of the two parties. For example, a sports club belonged either to the working class or to the bourgeois central organisation, and some of the dancers also felt obliged to choose their dancing venues accordingly.

An old cultural divide was — and, to an extent still is — felt between the Finnish- and Swedish-speaking Finns in the coastal area where neighbouring villages or even houses may belong to different language areas.[16] The dance audience was divided between the pavilions of each language group and so were dance music and bands. The dance music played by Swedish-speaking bands was influenced by the Swedish country-like *dansbandsmusik* and the musicians had frequent contact with

---

14 Cf. Nieminen, '"Tanssilava, järvi ja hanuri"', the appended observation report; dance types are identified solely on the basis of music and no attention is paid to dancers' movements in this respect.
15 Before 1809, areas that today belong to Finland were known, since ancient times, as the eastern province of Sweden.
16 At the end of 2010, there were nearly 300,000 Swedish-speaking Finns, or 5.5 % of the total population of nearly 5.5 million (*Statistics Finland*, http://www.stat.fi/index_en.html). Alongside Finnish, Swedish has the status of an official national language. The Swedish-speaking population is not evenly distributed regionally. While the so-called *Svenskfinland*, or Swede-Finland, is more of a cultural concept than a regional one, there are still two Swedish-speaking areas on the South and West coasts of Finland. Åland Islands, south-west from mainland Finland is an autonomous area with Swedish as the only official language.

Sweden, the United Kingdom and even further abroad.[17] The Finnish dance music evolved more into a genre of its own, characterised by the largely romantic-nostalgic *Schlager*-type texts, always sung in Finnish, and the overwhelming popularity of Finnish Tango music. While many individuals were bilingual, the dance organisers, the venues and the music did not straddle the divide, and it was always a little adventure to take a dance trip to a pavilion of the other language group.

The religious, political, and ethnic divides created some of the historic differences that emerged and became embodied in the popular dance culture, intertwined with the more readily evident generational and gender differences and identities.

The 1920s in Finland were characterised by a modernist impulse. Besides jazz, Tango was introduced as an exotic dance from the New World. Bigger dance pavilions were built to gather larger audiences. In turn, these groups ran the fundraising of the organising civic societies and also provided for a more professional entertainment business, based on starring vocalists. Larger dance bands were established which travelled across smaller or larger areas, and thus standardised the music played on dance occasions.[18] This modernisation thrust was connected to technical innovations such as the bicycle, which enabled people to make longer trips to dance events, and the radio and gramophone was within every person's reach.[19] Still, the overwhelmingly agrarian structure of society did not change to any remarkable degree. Indeed, Finland remained agrarian and rural until the late 1960s, the age of the Great Migration to towns and to Sweden in search of jobs in industry and in services.

---

17 Klinkmann, *Från Wantons till Wild Force*; Anna-Maria Nordman, *Takt och ton i tiden. Instrument, musik och musiker i svenskösterbottniska dansorkestrar 1920–1950* (Åbo [Turku]: Åbo Akademi University Press, 2003).

18 Marko Tikka and Toivo Tamminen, *Tanssiorkesteri Dallapé. Suomijatsin legenda 1925–2010* (Helsinki: Finnish Literature Society, 2011).

19 Saara Tuomaala, 'Polkupyörällä pääsee. Suomalaisen maalaisnuoruuden siirtymiä 1920–1940-luvuilla' in *Nuoruuden vuosisata*, ed. by Sinikka Aapola and Mervi Kaarninen (Helsinki: Finnish Literature Society, 2003), pp. 355–72; Tiina Männistö-Funk, 'Säveltulva kaupungissa — Gramofonimusiikki uudenlaisena kaupungin äänenä ja makukysymyksenä Helsingissä 1929', *Ennen ja nyt*, 3–4 (2008), http://www.ennenjanyt.net/?p=272

During the Second World War in Finland,[20] public dances and dancing in general were forbidden, as part of the moral mobilisation of the so-called home front, in support of the warring eastern front.[21] The wartime dance prohibition from the central government was met with local resistance. Indeed, the prohibition was not obeyed; people danced during the war, but it had to be done in secrecy.

Fig. 14.2 Dances on the stage of Käpylä VPK, Helsinki, 1945. Photo by Väinö Kannisto. Helsinki City Museum, CC BY 4.0, https://www.helsinkikuvia. fi/search/record/?search=tanssi&page=14

After the war, the prohibition was abolished by the end of the 1940s; this led to an unforeseen blossoming of public dances as a highly popular amusement activity of the new leisure culture. The 1950s and 1960s saw what can be called the golden age of popular couple dance culture.

---

20 The Second World War in Finland proceeded in four phases called the Winter War (1939–1940), the Interim Peace of 15 months, the Continuation War (1941–1944) and, finally, the Lapland War, from September 1944 to April 1945, when according to a separate peace treaty with the Soviet Union (1944) the German troops had to be forced out of the country.
21 Sakari Pesola, 'Tanssikiellosta lavatansseihin', in *Rillumarei ja valistus. Kulttuurikahakoita 1950-luvun Suomessa*, ed. by Matti Peltonen (Helsinki: Suomen Historiallinen Seura, 1996), pp. 7–18; the Finnish war-time dance prohibition is considered unique, at least on a European scale.

From the 1960s onwards, the new rock 'n' roll and Disco-based forms of youth culture meant that the popularity of dance pavilions and of couple dances in general declined.[22] This diminishment, which seemed to amount almost to a total disappearance of couple dance culture, was at its most severe towards the end of the 1980s, by the time of the inquiry that produced the narrative material for this study. From the now-dominant city perspective, pavilion dances came to be considered an old-fashioned and weird pastime for elderly people in the countryside, if they were considered at all.[23]

Perhaps with the coming of age of a generation that possesses their parents' and grand-parents' nostalgia toward pavilion dances, the degrading label has given way to a new vogue for pavilion dances, which are now conceived primarily as a dance genre and no longer as a socialising instrument for small communities. Today, there are hundreds of large dance pavilions and society-house floors that are of national significance in Finland, as well as all the smaller pavilions, the dance restaurants, and the night-clubs. Going out to enjoy an evening of couple dances is a popular hobby among many other dance hobbies, and it shows no sign of disappearing.[24]

Ethnographic Approach to Archived Material

Of the popular variants of the Tango, the Finnish Tango is especially famous and Finland possesses one of the most outstanding Tango cultures outside Argentina. The Finnish Tango, like its Argentinian cousin, was developed by ordinary people and became one of their embodied passions of choice.[25] But the Finnish Tango developed into a very different mood and style of both dancing and music.[26] According

---

22 Kuha, 'Tanssilavat, konvat ja discot', pp. 67–72.
23 'Dansholmen, Tolkis FBK', https://areena.yle.fi/1-50228262
24 Juha Laine, 'Suomalaisten nuorten tanssilavakulttuuri — modernia kansankulttuuria?' (unpublished Master's thesis, University of Jyväskylä, 2003); Kerkko Hakulinen and Pentti Yli-Jokipii, *Tanssilavakirja. Tanssista, lavoista ja lavojen tansseista* (Helsinki: AtlasArt, 2007).
25 See, e.g., M. A. Numminen, *Tango on intohimoni* (Helsinki: Schildts, 1998), pp. 5–6; for Argentina, cf. Marta E. Savigliano, *Tango and the Political Economy of Passion* (Boulder, CO: Westview Press, 1995).
26 *Tuomari Nurmio — stadilaista tangoa etsimässä*, dir. by Tahvo Hirvonen (Pettufilmi Oy, 2009).

to a comparative perspective, these differences could be put to use to reveal the differing mentalities of the two peoples. The dance forms could be read as modes of representation and decoded in terms of their representative relationship to the social realities beyond dance.[27]

From an ethnographic perspective, however, the research questions revolve more around the presentation and self-presentation in dance of and by the dancers than around representation. Dancing is seen as an embodied performance practice in which people present themselves to themselves and to each other, as they see themselves through their dancing. The realities studied are not external to dance, but are seen to emerge in the dancing itself.[28]

I take what I term a narrative performance perspective on the written material, as contrasted to an empiricist, or so-called recovery perspective.[29] The writers are not innocent reporters of past event, but they consciously create stories of their own life history, and, as a means of social action, take part in current discussions.[30]

To exemplify my approach, I present the following excerpt of the material in which the respondent describes first how she learned to dance when she was sixteen, in a wedding party, at the end of the 1920s, and then discusses dancing in her youth more generally. The dances took place in Antrea, a small rural parish in southern Karelia near Vyborg, then the second largest city in Finland.

> Refreshments first, then dancing began, and there was a band from Vyborg. Our neighbour's son asked me to dance, [...]. I won't come, I said, I can't dance, this Tuomas he said, now tonight I'll teach you to

---

27 Susan Leigh Foster, 'Choreographies of Gender', *Signs: Journal of Women in Culture and Society*, 24.1 (1998), 1–33, https://doi.org/10.1086/495316
28 E.g. John McCall, *Dancing Histories. Heuristic Ethnography with the Ohafia Igbo* (Ann Arbor: Michigan University Press, 2000), https://doi.org/10.3998/mpub.15520
29 See Natalie Zemon Davis, *Fiction in the Archives* (Cambridge: Polity Press, 1987).
30 Richard Bauman, *Story, Performance, and Event* (Cambridge: Cambridge University Press, 1986), https://doi.org/10.1017/cbo9780511620935; Jerome Bruner, 'Life as Narrative', *Social Research*, 54.1 (1987), 11–32; Richard Bauman and Charles L. Briggs, 'Poetics and Performance as Critical Perspectives on Language and Social Life', *Annual Review of Anthropology*, 19.1 (1990), 59–88 (at 62–66), https://doi.org/10.1146/annurev.an.19.100190.000423; Eric E. Peterson and Kristin M. Langellier, 'The Performance Turn in Narrative Studies', *Narrative Inquiry* 16.1 (2006), 173–80, https://doi.org/10.1075/ni.16.1.22pet; Michael Bamberg, 'Stories: Big or Small. Why Do We Care?', *Narrative Inquiry* 16.1 (2006), 139–47, https://doi.org/10.1075/ni.16.1.18bam

dance. And as it happened, he asked me to every piece. At first, I stepped on his feet and also on other dancing couples' feet and all the time had to apologise to whoever's feet I stepped on. After a few hours of these dancing lessons I then got the rhythm and learned the swing of it. By the end of the evening also boys I did not know, wedding guests, came to ask me, and that is how dancing began in my life. The Tango was the first dance I learned. My second dance was the Waltz.

I enjoyed lively movement and speedy goings-on. I was a slim and tall lassie, and agile too with a reasonably good sense of rhythm, so I always had great fun. I loved the Schottische and the Polka and the Waltz, dances with speed and action. I had three regular Schottische partners [one was my cousin, and one was a former classmate, and the third was a family friend of my younger uncle's]. [This last one] used to go to dances in the Youth Association's and the Lottas' and the Civil Guard's[31] social evenings and in the summer to pavilion dances, when he did not have to go to work. He was a good dancer, not lacking speed. All these three men had a similar style of dancing Schottische so that you only touched your partner with your fingertips and kept a distance of stretched arms during the hops, and when the whirling part began, they stormed around and around. Whenever the sound of the Schottische started, one of these three boys, anyone, the quickest, would run from the other side of the hall to ask me to dance, and we would go around at top speed as there were not so many dancing couples on the floor.[32]

The meaning of the dances to the dancers emerges and can therefore be studied in the narrative material. Dances become firmly embedded in their historical, cultural and ethnographic contexts and in the emotional and conceptual meanings given to them by the dancers. Meanwhile, the dance itself is not easily separated from the dancers, or the respondents, nor is it described objectively or according to universal descriptive traits that depart from the narratives. Bodies and movements are described in detail, such as the way the dance was first learned stepping on other dancers' feet, as in this account, and the way the Schottische was danced by the particular partners and divided into the choreographic aspects of the *hops* and the *whirling part*. By accumulating such detailed

---

31 The Lotta Svärd and the Civil Guard were voluntary auxiliary paramilitary organisations, the former for women. Both organisations were disbanded and forbidden in 1944, by the Allied Commission.
32 Antrea, previously Eastern Finland; NMF:K37/504. Referring to the archived material, a place name is followed by NMF = National Museum of Finland; K37 = Manuscript collection 37 (1991), Pavilion Dances; 504 = identifying the respondent.

descriptions, the embodied practices become articulated conceptually, in the discursive realm. But this will amount to a culture-specific conceptualisation of the moving bodies and the embodied practices, to a description of the dances as experienced by the dancers; and not to an objective description.

Nostalgia as Emotion and as Narrative Device

Nostalgia is commonly defined as an emotion: longing for the past or something other which is unreachable.[33] The next quote reveals itself to be nostalgic immediately, from the first intuition. My question is, how to analyse explicitly an emotion in a text? How to make the written text speak out in an emotional voice?

> I think the dancing trips of today's youth are different altogether. I suppose they'd go out there wearing whatever, although the make-up is always flashy. A dance band must be renowned and have a glamorous vocalist. Who would these days twirl around on a cosy wooden floor of the little workers' or societies' house, accompanied by the gaffer next door? Or on a small, uncovered stage in an alder thicket, circled by gnats. Or walk her bicycle on a wood-path fertilised by the cows. The youth today wouldn't care for or have the time to listen to the cheep of the bird in the night, not that they'd hear it from the noise. And surely, they wouldn't laugh at the summer rain on the saddle of their bicycle coming home from a dancing trip. We, the fortunate elderly, had the chance to experience that in our youth, and I too feel like a lucky girl; despite the wartimes, I experienced many merry trips.[34]

In order to analyse emotions, I see as necessary a dialogue between the supposed writer and myself as the reader. There is no emotion in a written text as such, in the paper and ink, so to speak, and there is no emotion in research without the personal involvement of the researcher with the people she is studying. With written materials, the dialogue and the involvement must be established by methods of reading. In order to make the analysis of emotion more explicit, I therefore describe my personal and emotional reactions to this piece of text and try to clarify the path I took in interpreting it.

---

33 E.g. Karin Johannisson, *Nostalgia. En känslans historia* (Stockholm: Bonnier, 2001).
34 Forssa, South-Western Finland; NMF:K37/666.

When I first read this passage, to tell the truth I felt quite irritated. The text is full of stereotypes of the 'good old times' which, as we all know, never existed in the first place. I felt offended as a reader since I realised that she had written with a reader precisely like me in mind, representing 'today's youth' or younger people as compared to her. She is considerably older than I am, maybe some fifty years, and with totally different generational experiences of the amusements of our youth. I think it is this condescending attitude toward other people's (my own) experiences that I first read into the text and that annoyed me.

My next reaction was to name this piece of text a *nostalgia piece*, or more exactly, *the* nostalgia piece, in the material I had read through by that point in time. This naming, as I reflect on it afterwards, is equivalent to granting a conscious attitude to the writer. The text is not an outcome of an innocent longing for the remembered past. It was the writer's intention precisely to create a nostalgic piece of writing in response to this inquiry. Here I am entering into a dialogue with the supposed writer, as I see her in her text.

In order to understand this text, I then looked for shared grounds for understanding. Of these, nostalgia is the self-evident one. Nostalgia can be seen as largely defining the research subjects of folkloristics and ethnology in the context of modernisation, in the (for the most part) nostalgic discourse of 'disappearing' traditions of agrarian society that must be preserved in the archives and museums and saved by the researchers. The inquiry itself has set the stage for nostalgia as a mood to recount this 'disappearing tradition'.

Looking at nostalgia as a narrative device, there is of course the juxtaposition of the here and now with the object of nostalgia. What is interesting is the amount of highly patterned images and motifs in this small piece of text. Stereotypes of 'today's youth' are contrasted with an idealised picture of past dance trips. It is only in the last lines of the story that the teller refers to her own experiences as the source of this utopia. There are several specific markers of the good old times, and the less good times of the present: for instance, busy and noisy modernity, again a stereotyped image; noisy both aurally and visually, in the *flashy* make-up and the *glamorous* vocalist. While the story itself is individually crafted and presented as an autobiographical narrative, the writer relies heavily on culturally shared images and notions as the authoritative sources of her text.

The next aspect I noticed was that besides nostalgia there is considerable irony in the story. The reasons for happiness, and for feeling lucky to experience all the gnats and cow fertiliser, cannot be taken at face value as expressions of pathetic nostalgia. They are left enigmatic, without further explanation of the narrator's intentions. The ironic motives, however, do not contest the goodness of the good old times. The irony points at the understanding of the supposed reader: the writer is challenging the interpretive imagination of the reader she has had in mind. She has engaged in a dialogue with her imagined reader, and, in my interpretation, I am engaging in continuing this dialogue, now with the imagined writer or author of the text.

As a possible interpretive frame, I suggest what I have termed a narrative of guts, Finnish *sisu*. The Finnish notion of *sisu* (literally, 'the inner', 'the innermost') conveys endurance and courage, inner moral strength, but also hard work to reach a goal, and it is part of Finnish self-understanding, a trait attributed to Finns in particular as *the Finnish Sisu*. *Sisu* has been explicated as being an *ethos of toughness*, verbalised as: 'Life is hard; we have to manage it; we have managed it; we are proud of that'.[35]

My suggestion is that in her story the narrator gives content to and animates, or embodies, the notion of Finnish *sisu*. Within this interpretive frame, I can find a common ground for understanding between my 'life-world' and that of the narrator's, and comprehend the happiness she is claiming. Even if I myself might not identify with the ethos of *sisu* in the way it is expressed in this text, the ethos provides an interpretive frame within which the text becomes intelligible to me; or, to put it more simply, as a native of Finnish culture I can understand what the text is about if it is about *sisu*.

The motives and contents of such a small story reveal themselves to be highly culturally specific. My initial discomfort with this text arose, in the first place, from the time difference between the narrated world and my own life-world, estranging me from the narrated past and from its idealisation as well. From that distance, the text could be

---

35 Matti Kortteinen, *Kunnian kenttä. Suomalainen palkkatyö kulttuurisena muotona* (Helsinki: Hanki ja jää, 1992), p. 63.

approached and made familiar by means of some more general cultural models: the interpretive frames of nostalgia and that of Finnish *sisu*. The former represents, in the first place, a reflective awareness as the researcher of the discourses in which the research is embedded. The latter is admissible as contextualisation in Finnish culture at large. In this interpretation of mine, the popular imagination that was communicated by the narrative was not the goodness of 'the good old times and cosy places in the countryside' as such, but that there is something *Finnish* that is worth remembering and that continues in spite of the changing times.

The narrative in this reading constructs Finnish self-understanding or, one could also say, national identity. Since this is precisely the aim of such traditional collections, and since the writer could be seen to be responding to such a call in the inquiry, one might ask whether there are no other discourses or attitudes discernible in the material than the ordered national-romantic nostalgic gaze at the remembered past.

Fig. 14.3 Illustration of the 'Open air dancing' entry on the Living Traditions wiki, hosted by the National Museum of Finland at the Pyhäsalmi dance pavilion, Northern Ostrobothnia region, Finland. Open air dancing is included in the list of Finnish Intangible Cultural Heritage. Photo by Sari Hovila (2011), CC BY 4.0, https://wiki.aineetonkulttuuriperinto.fi/wiki/Tiedosto:Pyh%C3%A4salmi.jpg

Cultural Heritage: An Alternative Perspective to Nostalgia

Finnish folklorist Jyrki Pöysä suggests that cultural heritage ought to be considered as a new perspective on the research subject of folkloristics and ethnology, differing from nostalgia, which dominated much earlier research.[36] I explore his suggestion here by presenting one more excerpt from my research material and by comparing and contrasting the two perspectives.

The narrator of this second excerpt first talks about the dances right after the Second World War, and then of how she learned to dance, as a child, before the war. In the course of her narrative, she describes a local revival of the dance pavilion culture after the war, and we can see that this revival or reconstruction was based on the memories that the young people had of their childhood and the local dance culture that existed before the war.

> I'm of the war-time youth; turned seventeen when the racket of war was over. The Fritz burned down my home, about three km from downtown Tornio, and half of the houses in Yliraumo, too.[37] The house of the Youth Society was left standing, fortunately. After all the commotion was over, we had a cleaning bee at the society house, there was no shortage of labour, and the bee dances have really stayed with me.[38]
>
> We had lived through a time of anxiety, but the young had the will to live and hopes for the future, so we started to organise social evenings with all kinds of amusement: plays, old dances, courses on folk dance, and in the end, we had an hour-and-a-half of dancing. This Youth Society really was an important site for recreation in the area; in almost every event there was a full crowd of people, and hardly any disorder at all. I only remember that the Raumo boys were jealous of the Karelia boys, of whom there were many in the neighbourhoods, and many marriages,

---

36   Jyrki Pöysä, 'The Performative Nostalgia of Work', paper presented in the IV Spring School of Finnish Folklore Society, Helsinki, 15 May 2009.
37   During the Lapland war (1944–1945), the civil population, of ca. 170,000, was evacuated to more southern parts of Finland and partly to Sweden. The German troops, forced to withdraw by the Finnish, used scorched-earth tactics.
38   'Cleaning bee' refers to a gathering of people who volunteer for communal work — here, to clean the society house. Similarly, 'bee dances' refer to the dances held by this collective gathering.

> too, were settled between these immigrants and the locals.[39] All my siblings were involved in the society, and we all danced.
>
> I remember, when I was a child, my parents would go out and my sisters rolled the rugs aside and the gramophone started to play, and the dance started. Back then girls and boys mingled differently from nowadays; there was a larger circle of friends. Because I was the youngest (of eight siblings), I soon learned all the dances and the songs, and I still remember them.[40]

There are elements of nostalgia in the story; for instance, the emphasis on the communality of the dancing young people of the village. Although the narrated events, especially the setting of the story, are extremely emotional and anxiety-laden, there are not many direct expressions of this at the textual level. Instead, the expressions referring to 'remembering' can be read as pointing to affective moments.

There is a double movement of orientations or time perspectives in the narrated time: to the past, in childhood memories, and to the future, because the war is over and the time of peace has arrived with its new hopes and possibilities. There is not as much nostalgia for the past as there is action to build a desired future. The exact point in time of the narration is irrelevant to the narrated time, except that the telling is posterior to the events related, since the story is about something remembered. In contrast, in the first text I discussed, the reference point of the narrated past is always in the present of narrating, in the oppositional present.

Both nostalgia and irony are reflective, conscious attitudes taken in the narrative present towards the narrated world. So, the perspective of cultural heritage is, indeed, tantamount to an economic aspect of profiting, more or less metaphorically speaking, from past history. The two perspectives have in common the selective valuing of the past, with the power dynamics of who can say what is valued and how and to what ends.

Nostalgia means a view according to which there is no return to the good old times, except in memories — it criticises or deplores the present,

---

[39] The inhabitants of the areas that Finland had to cede to the Soviet Union were evacuated and resettled in Finland. The resettlement of a population of 450,000, representing nearly 15% of the whole Finnish population at the time, did not proceed without conflicts at the local level.

[40] Alatornio, Northern Finland; NMF:K37/569.

but with little constructive alternative perspective. In contrast, creating a cultural heritage involves selecting and screening ideas, items and traits from the past in order to construct a future of a desired or planned kind. In an item that is defined as belonging to cultural heritage, there is some productive value invested for the present and for the future. While nostalgia involves a politics of emotions and remembering, cultural heritage refers in a complicated way to an economy of traditions and lore.[41]

Concluding Remarks

The collection of the pavilion-dance material was part of an ethnological project that was pan-European. The aim was to collect detailed information on every aspect of agrarian culture before the so-called vanishing traditions disappeared from living memory. The new narrative approach to these materials leaves aside the myriad facts, and with them an understanding of the producers of this material as 'informants'; it considers them instead as storytellers, or conscious form-givers to their past, and so a whole range of new kinds of knowledge becomes available.

A narrative evaluation of the materials enables a focus on what the respondents reveal in their dialogue with the archives: on the life experiences as they are articulated and presented in the stories and on the meanings given to the experiences and events by the narrators, or the people studied themselves.

There is no reach 'beyond' the narratives that form the research material, to the 'authentic' or 'unspoiled' experience of pavilion dances. According to the definition of experiences presented in this chapter, experiences are created by the very act of narrating. The phenomenon of pavilion dances as an entity in itself, as it can be discerned in the material, was created by the dialogue of the archive with the respondents and in a larger contemporary context, a dialogue defined by the prevailing nostalgic gaze backwards in time to this dance culture and to forms of agrarian and urban culture of the twentieth century.

---

41 Petja Aarnipuu, *Turun linna kerrottuna ja kertovana tilana* (Helsinki: Finnish Literature Society, 2008).

Narratives, as contrasted with facts, are always already contextualised in discourses. Besides nostalgia, which can be considered the dominant discourse defining much of the research subject under ethnological inquiry, I have explored the alternative and complementary discourse of cultural heritage, as it can be seen to be expressed in the research material. Other discourses that are present in the material — for example, popular resistance against the many ways of condemning dancing — are not touched upon in this chapter. Both nostalgia and cultural heritage are powerful discourses in research; the collected written and oral histories add to these kinds of discourse. Discerning and analysing the discourses that govern the material are important means of reflection and source criticism in research, but they are also a method in their own right. Discourses cannot be separated from the study of the dances that are defined and narrated in them.

Bibliography

Aarnipuu, Petja, *Turun linna kerrottuna ja kertovana tilana* (Helsinki: Finnish Literature Society, 2008).

Bamberg, Michael, 'Stories: Big or Small. Why Do We Care?', *Narrative Inquiry*, 16.1 (2006), 139–47, https://doi.org/10.1075/ni.16.1.18bam

Bauman, Richard, *Story, Performance, and Event: Contextual Studies of Oral Narrative* (Cambridge: Cambridge University Press, 1986), https://doi.org/10.1017/cbo9780511620935

Bauman, Richard, and Charles L. Briggs, 'Poetics and Performance as Critical Perspectives on Language and Social Life', *Annual Review of Anthropology* 19.1 (1990), 59–88, https://doi.org/10.1146/annurev.an.19.100190.000423

Biskop, Gunnel, 'Om borgerligt valsande före 1840', in *Kring tiden. Etnologiska och folkloristiska uppsatser*, ed. by Anna-Maria Åström and Ivar Nordlund (Helsingfors [Helsinki]: Society for Swedish Literature in Finland, 1991), pp. 86–96.

Bruner, Jerome, 'Life as Narrative', *Social Research*, 54.1 (1987), 11–32.

Buckland, Theresa Jill, 'Dance, History, and Ethnography: Frameworks, Source, and Identities of Past and Present', in *Dancing from Past to Present: Nation, Culture, Identities*, ed. by Theresa Jill Buckland (Madison: The University of Wisconsin Press, 2006), pp. 3–24.

'Dansholmen, Tolkis FBK', 12:45, posted online by The Archive of the Finnish Broadcasting Company, *YLE*, 26 October 2011, https://areena.yle.

fi/1-50228262 [Dances at the pavilion of Dansholmen, Tolkis VFB; a TV documentary film of dances in the South coast of Finland, 1966].

Davis, Natalie Zemon, *Fiction in the Archives* (Cambridge: Polity Press, 1987).

Foster, Susan Leigh, 'Choreographies of Gender', *Signs: Journal of Women in Culture and Society*, 24.1 (1998), 1–33, https://doi.org/10.1086/495316

Hakulinen, Kerkko, and Pentti Yli-Jokipii, *Tanssilavakirja. Tanssista, lavoista ja lavojen tansseista* (Helsinki: AtlasArt, 2007).

Hamera, Judith, *Dancing Communities* (London: Macmillan, 2007), https://doi.org/10.1057/9780230626485

'Helismaa ja kumppanit juhannuskeikalla', 5:35, posted online by Jukka Lindfors, *YLE*, 8 September 2006, https://yle.fi/aihe/artikkeli/2006/09/08/helismaa-ja-kumppanit-juhannuskeikalla [The singer Reino Helismaa and others on a St John's Eve gig; a TV documentary film of the artists and the festivities in North-eastern Finland, 1948].

Hirvonen, Tahvo, dir., *Tuomari Nurmio — stadilaista tangoa etsimässä* (Pettufilmi Oy, 2009).

Hoppu, Petri, *Symbolien ja sanattomuuden tanssi. Menuetti Suomessa 1700-luvulta nykyaikaan*. (Helsinki: Finnish Literature Society, 1999).

Johannisson, Karin, *Nostalgia. En känslans historia* (Stockholm: Bonnier, 2001).

Klinkmann, Sven-Erik, *Från Wantons till Wild Force. Nya sound i en gränsstad* (Stockholm: Gidlunds, 2010).

Kortteinen, Matti, *Kunnian kenttä. Suomalainen palkkatyö kulttuurisena muotona* (Helsinki: Hanki ja jää, 1992).

Kuha, Sini, 'Tanssilavat, konvat ja discot nuorten areenana 1960-luvun Jyväskylässä', in *Tanssilavan luona. Huvielämää Jyväskylän Ainolassa*, ed. by Henna Mikkola (Jyväskylä: Minerva, 2005), pp. 55–72.

Laine, Juha, 'Suomalaisten nuorten tanssilavakulttuuri — modernia kansankulttuuria?' (unpublished Master's thesis, University of Jyväskylä, 2003).

Lehtipuro, Outi, 'Voiko perinnettä kerätä? "Maailman suurin kansanrunousarkisto" ja kansanrunoudentutkimus toistensa haastajina', in *Tutkijat kentällä*, ed. by Pekka Laaksonen et al. (Helsinki: Finnish Literature Society, 2003), pp. 13–33.

McCall, John, *Dancing Histories. Heuristic Ethnography with the Ohafia Igbo* (Ann Arbor: Michigan University Press, 2000), https://doi.org/10.3998/mpub.15520

Männistö-Funk, Tiina, 'Säveltulva kaupungissa — Gramofonimusiikki uudenlaisena kaupungin äänenä ja makukysymyksenä Helsingissä 1929', *Ennen ja nyt*, 3–4 (2008), http://www.ennenjanyt.net/?p=272

National Museum of Finland (NMF), *K37 Lavatanssit*, compiled by Aila Nieminen (Helsinki: Ethnological Archive of the National Museum of Finland, 1991).

Nieminen, Aila, '"Tanssilava, järvi ja hanuri". Lavatanssit Suomessa vuosisadan vaihteesta 1960-luvun loppuun asti' (unpublished MA thesis in ethnology, University of Jyväskylä, 1993).

Nordman, Anna-Maria, *Takt och ton i tiden. Instrument, musik och musiker i svensköserbottniska dansorkestrar 1920–1950* (Åbo [Turku]: Åbo Akademi University Press, 2003).

Numminen, M. A., *Tango on intohimoni* (Helsinki: Schildts, 1998).

Pesola, Sakari, 'Tanssikiellosta lavatansseihin', in *Rillumarei ja valistus. Kulttuurikahakoita 1950-luvun Suomessa*, ed. by Matti Peltonen (Helsinki: Suomen Historiallinen Seura, 1996), pp. 7–18.

Peterson, Eric E., and Kristin M. Langellier, 'The Performance Turn in Narrative Studies', *Narrative Inquiry* 16.1 (2006), 173–80, https://doi.org/10.1075/ni.16.1.22pet

Pöysä, Jyrki, 'The Performative Nostalgia of Work', paper presented in the IV Spring School of Finnish Folklore Society, Helsinki, 15 May 2009.

Saarikoski, Helena, 'Menneisyyden ruumiinkokemusten tutkiminen kirjoitetuissa aineistoissa', in *Tekstien rajoilla. Monitieteisiä näkökulmia kirjoitettuihin aineistoihin*, ed. by Sami Lakomäki et al. (Helsinki: Finnish Literature Society, 2011), 117–36.

——, 'Tanssi kirjoituksena, kirjoitus tanssina', *Elore*, 17/2 (2010), 4–9, https://doi.org/10.30666/elore.78872, http://www.elore.fi/arkisto/2_10/saarikoski_2_10.pdf

——, '"Taian tantsihin ruveta". Tanssikulttuurin muistomerkki 1800-luvun alkupuolen Vienasta', in *Tanssi tanssi: Kulttuureja, tulkintoja*, ed. by Helena Saarikoski (Helsinki: Finnish Literature Society, 2003), 119–45.

Sarmela, Matti, *Reciprocity Systems of the Rural Society in the Finnish-Karelian Culture Area: With Special Reference to Social Intercourse of the Youth* (Helsinki: Academia Scientiarum Fennicae, 1969).

Savigliano, Marta E., *Tango and the Political Economy of Passion* (Boulder, CO: Westview Press, 1995).

Stahl Dolby, Sandra, *Literary Folkloristics and the Personal Narrative* (Bloomington, IN: Indiana University Press, 1989).

Tikka, Marko, and Toivo Tamminen, *Tanssiorkesteri Dallapé. Suomijatsin legenda 1925–2010* (Helsinki: Finnish Literature Society, 2011).

Tuomaala, Saara, 'Polkupyörällä pääsee. Suomalaisen maalaisnuoruuden siirtymiä 1920–1940-luvuilla', in *Nuoruuden vuosisata. Suomalaisen nuorison historiaa*, ed. by Sinikka Aapola and Mervi Kaarninen (Helsinki: Finnish Literature Society, 2003), pp. 355–72.

15. A Twenty-First Century Resurrection: The *Potresujka*, the Croatian Polka Tremblante

Tvrtko Zebec

This chapter investigates a particular kind of Polka that entered the field of popular culture and generated extraordinary enthusiasm as late as the twenty-first century. The round dances were mostly neglected by ethnographic research on dance during the twentieth century, as we see in several of the chapters in this book (see Chapters Two, Seven, and Eleven) that focus on different countries, and this was also the case for Croatia. Polka dancing was present in Croatia throughout the twentieth century, and from the 1970s it was recognised in some regions as having the value of a traditional dance. From that time and to the present day we see an extraordinary resurrection of popularity for one particular Polka form, the *potresujka*, in the broader region around and in the city of Rijeka. The portrayal of this resurrection will try to explore several questions about how a dance from the early nineteenth century experiences a revival that is taken up and spread by modern media.

Participation in the work of the Sub-Study Group on round dances — nineteenth-century-derived couple dances — is a particularly inspiring undertaking. It has prompted ethnographic dance research that had been neglected in Croatia for some years. Nineteenth-century Central European couple dances were of little interest to Croatian ethnochoreologists for a long period. After the formal shaping of the discipline in Croatia in the early 1950s, Vinko Žganec, Ljelja Taš, and Ivan Ivančan conducted in-depth research into the dances of the villagers, which were generally regarded as a reflection of national pride and identity. Such a stance coincided with the dominant theoretical, cultural and historical aims of the ethnology of that time, which resulted largely from the ideological orientation of the *Hrvatska seljačka stranka* [Croatian Peasant Party]. That political party, like similar examples in Europe, advocated shaping national cultural identity to distinguish the Croats from the uniform, universal, 'civilisational' progress that was emerging from Central European urban centres.

Seljačka sloga [Peasant Harmony] — the cultural, educational and charitable cooperative, driven by the populist ideology of the Peasant Party — attempted to inspire self-confidence in the peasants, to gradually enlighten them, and to introduce them to national political life. Folklore festivals were mirrors of cultural policy and places for public presentations of recognised national practice. This process was one-sided — from urban to rural, from intelligentsia to peasantry — wherein the aristocracy and intellectuals 'became aware of and discovered folk traditions and the life of "simple" peoples'.[1] As Max P. Baumann further asserts: 'The outsider ideology of emancipation through literacy and the aesthetisation of old traditions created a new dependency: the subordination to musical practices, aesthetics and performance concepts from the hegemonic culture of the upper classes'.[2]

Couple dances — the Polka, *valcer*, the Mazurka, *čardaš*, *šotiš*, *tango*, *fokstrot* and the like — were not readily accepted at the festivals organised by *Peasant Harmony* during the late 1930s, since they showed the influence of urban and non-Croatian centres.[3] Even when they were later performed at festivals as an exception to the rule, they were not favourably evaluated. The analysis of the repertoires of groups that appeared long after the first *Peasant Harmony* festivals — at the

---

1   Max P. Baumann, 'Folk Music Revival: Concepts between Regression and Emancipation', *The World of Music*, 38 (1996), 71–86 (at 72).
2   Baumann, 'Folk Music Revival', p. 77.
3   In a similar way, in the 1920s and 1930s in Sweden, the Swedish Foxtrot was the local answer to American Jazz (cf. K. O. Edström, 'From Schottis to Bonnjazz: Some Remarks on the Construction of Swedishness', *Yearbook for Traditional Music*, 31 (1999), 27–41, https://doi.org/10.2307/767971) and manifested resistance to American influence.

International Folklore Festival in Zagreb (since 1966) — shows that these dances were rarely seen on the stages of festivals right up until the 1980s.[4]

At the same time, from the end of nineteenth century one could find, parallel with their own tradition, fireman brass bands and tambura and jazz orchestras, as well as dance masters and their schools, especially in the smaller cities. They played music and danced all the European modern dances during dance evenings, events and weddings, but only for fun as a social gathering and not for the stage.

The Polka in Croatia

The Polka was adopted and accepted, we could say *naturalised*, in Croatia soon after its appearance in Central European ballrooms and dance salons in the second part of the nineteenth century.[5]

It was accepted in diverse ways in the different parts of Croatia. We can ascertain just how popular the Polka was by observing the strong criticism levelled against it on the part of traditionalists, who wrote about a craze for the Polka and the Waltz among the youngsters in the north-western part of Croatia in the mid-nineteenth century.[6] They describe how these dances are done in mixed pairs in which partners danced very close to each other, and did so with a lot of passionate turns. They also state these new kinds of dances should be fought against, in order to protect and preserve traditional dances and national melodies (see Chapter Nine in this volume).

---

4   Stjepan Sremac, 'Smotre folklora u Hrvatskoj nekad i danas', *Narodna umjetnost: hrvatski časopis za etnologiju i folkloristiku*, 15 (1978), 97–114 (at 109); Tvrtko Zebec, 'Dance Research in Croatia', *Narodna umjetnost: hrvatski časopis za etnologiju i folkloristiku*, 33 (1996), 89–111 (at 111); Tvrtko Zebec, 'Development and Application of Ethnochoreology in Croatia', *Međunarodni simpozij 'Muzika u Društvu'*, 6 (2008), 138–52 (at 140).

5   'Polka and *polkomanie* in the Bohemia of the 1830s and 1840s was firstly a manifestation of the energy of the young dynamic bourgeoisie, profiting from all features that could help to build the national identity and finally result in the creation of the national state' (Daniela Stavělová, 'Polka jako Český národní symbol', *Český lid*, 93.1 (2006), 3–26 (at 3)). See also Chapter Five in this volume.

6   Kuhač and other members of the Enlightenment movement promoted national values as opposed to foreign ones. See Franjo K. Kuhač, *Južno-slovjenske narodne popijevke*, vol. 3 (Zagreb: Tiskara I litografija C. Albrecht, 1880), pp. 319–20.

Even stronger reaction came from the moralists in the Catholic Church — especially the Blessed Ivan Mertz during the 1920s.[7] He was generally in favour of the promotion of the traditional dances as they were mirrors of the people's spirit. While he accepted artistic dance, such as classical ballet, he maintained that 'Modern, mixed dances are something else. We still do not have formal bans against that kind of dance from the pontiffs'.[8] Concomitantly, he ordered young people to abandon these types of dances. A parish priest called Leopold Jurca wrote a manuscript in Istria in 1950, largely following Ivan Mertz's line of thought. In that extensive work about dance and morality, Jurca proudly concluded that, after fifteen years of work, he had succeeded in exterminating such dance types in his parish, recommending the same to other priests in the neighbourhood.[9]

Comparing the Waltz and the Polka, the following observation could be made in accordance with the superficial urban opinion: that the Waltz is an urban tradition (everybody knows it from Vienna as the *Wiener walzer*), while, in contrast, the Polka is regarded as a dance from the countryside (see Chapter Nine in this volume).

While tensions grew among traditionalists concerning the integration of the Polka into the Croatia dance scene, the Polka was being danced in a very vigorous fashion all over Croatia. Thus, Ivan Ivančan wrote that it was reliably known that bourgeois couple dances from Central Europe (such as the Polka, the Mazurka, *mafrina*, *cotić* (*schottisch*), *varsovienne* and the like) had a lively influence on the members of the Austro-Hungarian Monarchy.[10] He did not do detailed research into those dances, but mentioned them as a newer tradition, and regularly referred to them in research localities in Istria and in later research in Dalmatia. He speaks of them having many spins and turns in the couple dance around a circle, with the presence of the *capobalo*, a dance leader. This characteristic social role came to these areas from the Alpine region, just

---

7   The Blessed Ivan Merz — a Croat from Banja Luka in Bosnia (1896–1928) — was a philosopher who was beatified by Pope John Paul II in 2003 at his birthplace. He finished his studies in Vienna, Paris, and Zagreb, and his thoughts and discussions are accepted in the Catholic Church as strong moral messages. See Ivan Merz, *Katolici i novi plesovi* (Sarajevo: Kaptol Vrhbosanski, 1926), p. 13.
8   Kuhač, *Južno-slovjenske narodne popijevke*, pp. 319–20.
9   Leopold Jurca, *Ples u vjerskom, ćudorednom i socijalnom pogledu* (Pazin: [n.p.], 1950).
10 Ivan Ivančan, *Istarski narodni plesovi* (Zagreb: Institut za narodnu umjetnost, 1963), p. 9.

as the accordion did (particularly the *botunara*).[11] Ivančan refers to the Polka as one of the most widely disseminated dances, still popular at the time of his field research in the 1960s, with the comment that it reached certain regions more quickly and others more slowly, even after World War Two.[12]

We also know, for example, that people from the central Croatian region of Lika used to use the word *Polkati* — to dance[13] — for dancing in general. Simplicity and adaptability were significant reasons for the dynamic spread of the Polka — a Polka step or refrain could be introduced into a Quadrille,[14] but also into different traditional dances, even into circle-dance formations. There are a lot of traditional dances in Croatia (the *drmeš* and especially the *kolo* circle dance in Slavonia and all over Croatia) where the Polka step replaced some other steps from the older traditional layer in the same 2/4 time and, with different accenting, even changed the performance style of particular dances.[15]

The *Potresujka*, a Local *Polka Tremblante*

A number of different variants of the Polka are known all over Croatia. We can find a special style of Polka dancing that involves a strong trembling movement, such as the French *Polka tremblante* (shaking the whole body with strong vertical movement and small steps) under its

---

11   *Botunara* derives from the word *botuni* — buttons — since it did not have a classic keyboard. It is also known as the *trieština*, since it was purchased in Trieste. Other instruments involved included an ensemble of stringed instruments — a violin and a *bajs* [a contrabass] — along with a clarinet and a trombone. Ibid., p. 23.

12   Conclusions on that historical period, however, can only be superficial and incomplete, since Ivančan did not supply detailed analyses of the historical, social, political and economic context, nor did he consider migration from neighbouring areas, which was particularly complex in Istria.

13   Ivančan, *Istarski narodni plesovi*, p. 48.

14   Libby Smigel, 'Minds Mad for Dancing: Polkamania on the London Stage', *The Journal of Popular Culture*, 30 (1996), 179–207 (at 198), https://doi.org/10.1111/j.0022-3840.1996.00197.x

15   Daniela Stavělová also writes about similarities between the *třasák* and Polka (see Chapter Five in this volume). Egil Bakka explains that the 'two measure turning Polka' type is a usual element in many West European folk dances and, at the same time, is a traditional dance in itself. On Norwegian examples in the countryside, he explains different names for the same dance — *hamborgar, skotsk, hoppvals* and *galopp* — as older names, before the Polka, which stayed on in use; Egil Bakka, 'The Polka before and after the Polka', *Yearbook for Traditoinal Music*, 33 (2001), 37–47 (at 38–39), https://doi.org/10.2307/1519629

local name — the *potresujka* or *potresuljka*.[16] This is found in the regions in the hinterland of the city of Rijeka (Croatia's major harbour city), comprising *Kastavšćina* (the region surrounding the small town of Kastav), *Liburnija* (the region surrounding the town of Opatija), and, a little higher in the mountains, at Grobnik and in *Grobinšćina* (the region which is also called the 'Grobnik Alps') (see Fig. 15.1).

However, it is interesting to note that Ivančan did not mention the *potresujka* in his research in the immediate vicinity of Istria, or anywhere else in Croatia. Along with the most frequently mentioned Polka, in Istria he noted the *denči* dance with the same rhythmic pattern as the Polka, then the *krajc-Polka* (*Kreuzpolka*) as a derivation from the Polka with crossing of the arms, and the *špic-Polka* (*Spitzbaumpolka*), a Polka in which the partners in the dance threaten each other from time to time with raised admonishing fingers. Although he mentioned dances from Mune and the *Kastavšćina* area, where the *potresujka* is danced today, Ivančan made no mention of that dance in the 1960s. He did not do research in *Liburnija* or *Grobinšćina*. Stjepan Sremac, who carried out research in Gorski Kotar and the Littoral near Rijeka during the 1980s, was more interested in studying the Croatian *tanac* dance, and did not mention the *potresujka* at all.[17]

Alemka Juretić wrote about the *potresujka* from the *Grobinšćina* area in 2004.[18] She stated that the *potresujka* was danced there from the end of the nineteenth century. The local folk recall that an unknown merchant had taught it to the villagers. They performed it until World War Two, when it was abandoned along with other dances and not danced until its renewal during the 1970s. Juretić established a performance group in her village, Gornje Jelenje, in 1978 and the *potresujka* has also been performed on stage with other dances since then. It was allocated the value of a traditional dance, although it was still not seen at the *International Folklore Festival* in Zagreb at that time, which would have been an indication of its ratification by experts, mirroring the paradigm of public cultural policy.

---

16 See Fig. 15.3.

17 Stjepan Sremac, *Pričanja iz života, Običaji i druga folklorna građa Križišća i Hrvatskog primorja: kazivanja Josipa Juričića 1978.–1980. u Zagrebu* (Zagreb: Dokumentacija Instituta za etnologiju i folkloristiku, 1980).

18 Alemka Juretić, *Grobnički luštrini* (Jelenje: Katedra Čakavskog sabora Grobinšćine, 2004).

According to more recent research in the *Kastavšćina* area, where the *potresujka* is very popular today, interlocutors claim that the *potresujka* was already being danced by their grandmothers, their *none*.[19] This also permits us to locate its importation there to the first half of the twentieth century. It is believed that the trading connections between the inhabitants of Rukavac, Mune and Žejane with neighbouring Slovenia, Austria and Italy also influenced the adoption of this lively and trembling performance style. It is said that the *potresujka* is the modern term for the *potresuja* dance, which was also called the *pojka po strainski* (the foreign Polka). Use of the latter name was ostensibly intended to attract interest and draw the largest number of visitors possible to the Sunday entertainment events held at the inns and in front of the churches on Sundays and feast days.

After the *potresujka* was recognised on the local stages as being 'traditional' and a part of popular heritage at the end of the 1970s, it took almost three decades for it to impose itself once again as part of contemporary life — this time throughout the entire region and in a much more intensive manner. Although it had not been forgotten as a local tradition in the meantime, it nonetheless needed media support to receive public recognition. One particular musician who played the *trieština* accordion learnt to play the *potresujka* melody from an older musician in the village. He said of its beginnings in the *Grobinšćina* area that 'It was born here with the music!'[20]

The new wave of public recognition of the *potresujka* was also linked with the music. The performance of the song 'Potresujka' by Ivana Marčelja and Tomi Krešević at the *Melodije Kvarnera* Festival in 2004 made this music and dance more popular again (see the example on YouTube).[21] They were awarded second prize at that festival, but also ranked high on the hit-parades of the local radio and TV programmes.

Two years later it was said that the same singer, Ivana Marčelja, 'with a special voice and perfect local Chakavian dialect has quickly become one of the favourites in and around the "Chakavian capital (Rijeka)"'.[22]

---

19 Ivana Sajko, 'Potresujka kao pokazatelj identiteta' (unpublished graduate thesis, Odjel za etnologiju i antropologiju, Zadar, 2010), p. 9.
20 Ibid.
21 See Fig. 15.6.
22 'Melodije Istre i Kvarnera (MIK) 2006, Finale, Rijeka, June 24, 2006' [n.a.], *Istrian Experience*, http://www.istrianexperience.com/mik06/mik06-program.

She performed at the *Melodije Istre i Kvarnera* Festival with the song, 'Boća i bulin', again in a lively Polka rhythm. *Potresujka* popularity continued and we can read about the festival in 2008: '[...] and to the delight of the audience the *potresujka* came spontaneously into the program once again'.[23]

The *potresujka* has become very popular during Carnival celebrations and at weddings. One can even find headlines in newspapers during the last several years saying: 'The potresujka is "in" again!', or 'As Rio de Janeiro has samba, in Rijeka you will dance 'potresujka', a local entertaining dance, the only one of its kind in the world!'[24]

We can see how the *potresujka* has become a notable part of people's identity nowadays through the work of seventh grade primary school pupils. Stella Paris,[25] a student at a school in Čavle, wrote a poem entitled 'A Grobnik Postcard', which, in the Chakavian dialect, recited important images of her native place and, of course, mentioned the *potresujka* as one of the most important symbols of Carnival events:

> A small place where everyone knows everyone.
> Where children play, and grandmammas tell stories.
> Below the town the Ričina flows. Everyone knows of it.
> It's like some fine lady. Oh, our dear Ričina!
> A church stands on the hill, beside it a fort counts the stars.
> The school in the middle from times long past, that is our town's famous trio.
> The masks are always here, and the potresujka is danced.
> All the people are merry, in good humour and full of courage.
> Our tiny Grobnik Town, a place of blessed peace.
> You just look at it and it touches your heart.[26]

---

htm; for audio, see 'BOĆA I BULIN — IVANA MARČELJA', 3:06, posted online by Križišćan1993, *Youtube*, 5 January 2012, https://www.youtube.com/watch?v=Xhcvt9cpW6M

23 'Welcome to My Impressions of Melodije Istre i Kvarnera a Festival with Soul: Kostrena — *Potresujka* on the Grass' [n.a.], *Istrian Experience*, http://www.istrianexperience.com/mik08/kostrena.htm

24 Mašenka Vukadinović, 'Doživjeti osebujni grad / Experience a peculiar town', *Welcome to Rijeka*, 6 (June, 2012), pp. 8–15 (at p. 10), https://www.htz.hr/sites/default/files/2012-05/HR_EN-Welcome-to-Rijeka-2514.pdf

25 Stella Paris, 'Grobnička kartulina', *Gmajna*, 9 (2008), p. 18, https://www.cavle.hr/home/wp-content/uploads/2014/07/Gmajna_9.pdf

26 Translated from the Croatian by Nina H. Antoljak.

Since 2008, there have been workshops and courses teaching the *potresujka* not only in the *Liburnija*, *Kastavščina* or *Grobinščina* areas, but also in the broader region of the Croatian Littoral (*Hrvatsko primorje*) and in Istria, even in towns in the more southern part of the Primorje coastal area such as Novi Vinodolski.

The *potresujka* has become as popular as the Salsa and some dance teachers of the *potresujka* have become very popular as well, through teaching these dance courses. In local online news we read about the *potresujka* dance course (held at the *Hangar* Social Club in Matulji) organised by the Tourist Board, with sixty participants on the first Saturday of teaching and double that number during the second term.[27] They came from different places in Istria and the Primorje, even from neighbouring Slovenia. A dance teacher stressed the significant possibilities for improvisation where 'each dancer could give something of his/her own, after learning the basic steps'; just as each village has developed something unique in its collective style of *potresujka* dancing.[28] At the end of the course each dancer is eligible to receive 'a prestigious autochthonous dancer diploma'.[29] The courses are usually announced and organised during the weekends in December, as preparation for the Carnival dance evenings. During these evenings, and particularly at the end of Carnival on Shrove Tuesday, the participants have to complete certain assignments and publicly show their competence. One of these assignments is to make a paper flower, and the other is to dance the *potresujka* in front of a 'jury', which selects the winners.[30] In the 2009 Carnival contest, *potresujka* dance ability became the most important condition in choosing 'the best Carnival girl' in Matulji. She 'should be more than 18 years old, she should dance the *potresujka*, drink a glass of wine, make a paper Carnival-flower, sing Carnival songs, corrupt the jury and drive a Carnival puppet around in the wheelbarrow'.[31]

---

27 See 'Škola potresujki' [n.a.], *Tzmatulji*, https://tzmatulji.hr/dogadanja/skola-potresujki/. In December 2010, the dance course 'Matuljska škola potresujki' was organised for the sixth time with the same dance teacher, Dean Jurdana, at the same place by the same organiser! See http://moja.opatija.net/najave.asp?id=4959

28 'Škola potresujki', https://tzmatulji.hr/dogadanja/skola-potresujki/

29 Ibid.

30 'Matulji', *Hrvatski karnevalist*, 5 (May, 2007), p. 24, http://www.karnevali.hr/wp-content/uploads/2018/12/karnevalist5.pdf

31 For example, the award was 5000 kuna — roughly 650 dollars — in 2009 on the election of 'the best Carnival girl' (see http://www.opatija.net/hr/najave/najpusna-djevojka-2009-01310).

Together with a lot of positive comments and cordial invitations to dance the *potresujka*, as well as frequently expressed knowledge of the *potresujka* as one of the main conditions in choosing a boyfriend, some negative reactions in online blogs also reveal the vital presence of the *potresujka* in the contemporary life of Rijeka and its surroundings. There are young people who do not like this type of music and dance and they are very critical of this well-established activity enjoyed by a huge part of the population, often popularised by the local media.

The popularity of the Polka, the local *potresujka*, continues to grow in the broader region of Istria and Kvarner (the Quarnero Bay).

Fig. 15.1 The Istrian Peninsula and the Kvarner (Quarnero Bay). Detail of Map from CIA World Factbook 2009. Wikimedia Commons, Public Domain, https://commons.wikimedia.org/wiki/File:Croatia_Transportation. jpg#/media/File:Croatia_Transportation.jpg

An example of interweaving of dance into the play *Potresujkom po Čehovu* [Through Chekhov with the *potresujka*] shows how the *potresujka* became the main connecting element in the dramaturgy, linking four single-act dramas by Anton Pavlovich Chekhov. The director/producer Serđo Dlačić (from the city of Rijeka) together with the choreographer

Đurđica Kunej (from Zagreb) linked this dance with the great Russian writer. They found it very appropriate and attractive to show some grotesque situations coloured by Chekhov's well-known irony and rhythm, integrating them with this lively local dance, popular during the Carnival and at wedding parties. They merged the ironical context of famous, 'global' and highbrow literature and the universal wedding theme with the rural, local context of small places. Members of the amateur 'JAK' theatre company performed these dramas.[32] The director of Chekhov's plays in Mali Lošinj told me that, just as in other small places in Rijeka's surroundings, the *potresujka* 'with its lively and frisky tempo can find a way to wake up the whole body' and, with the love story often mentioned in discussions about that dance, could lead the partners into bed just as in Chekhov's single-act plays. The *potresujka*, which has become well-known through the festivals and media in Rijeka and its surrounding areas in recent years, has been very well accepted in Mali Lošinj as well.

In this way, the stage became a place where the *potresujka*, through its characteristic embodiment, could be used to express local experiences in order that the audience might better understand the universal feelings that Chekhov wrote about and dramatised. Theatre audiences, largely in Mali Lošinj, have enjoyed watching this form of staged Polk — the *potresujka* — known in their broader neighbourhood of the Quarnero Bay as something domestic and traditional. Just as in London one hundred and fifty years ago, 'the couple dance as a *divertissement* in larger works or, as an *entr'acte*, became a vehicle for exhibiting the virtuosity of local stars, so the Polka was easily featured in this way'.[33] And as for this kind of stage presentation of the Polka in London in the 1840s, where 'the Polka itself assured the theatres of attracting the throngs', in Mali Lošinj, 'audiences have responded, then, not so much to the virtuoso qualities of a theatricalised Polka as to the recognisable signs of dance fashion onstage' at the beginning of twenty-first century.[34] Exactly the same process happened again, this time in Mali Lošinj. Turning the

---

32 The JAK acronym was chosen in honour of the Croatian writer and collector of oral tradition, Josip Antun Kraljić (1877–1948), who was born on the island of Krk and died in Mali Lošinj. He was a well-known patriot who worked for many years as a teacher in Istria and at Mali Lošinj.
33 Libby Smigel, 'Minds Mad for Dancing', p. 199.
34 Ibid.

Polka's popularity to his own use, the playwright/director adopted the *potresujka* dance into scenes reflecting and making fun of contemporary, but also universal, social practices.[35]

Fig. 15.2 Nikola Šubić (Shuba), poster for *Potresujkom po Čehovu*, 2008. Reproduced with author's permission, all rights reserved, http://www.mi3dot.org/gallery/original/20280/

Finally, we can turn to the musical accompaniment and the instrumental aspect. The accordion and trombone are the most important symbols of *potresujka* music and dance. This connects us again with the Alpine influences of brass bands, but also with a perception about ourselves in connection with our neighbours from the Northwest — the Slovenians and Austrians.[36] What does this look like as a perception of Alpine culture in Grobnik — the highest part of Rijeka's hinterland mountains — also called 'Grobničke Alpe [Grobnik Alps]' among the local inhabitants? *Polka/potresujka* music and dance, the *jodlanje* [yodelling] style of singing, *dinderl* costumes, accordions, trombones, sausages, strong and

---

35 See Fig. 15.7.
36 See Fig. 15.8.

fat men, and so on. Thus, integration continues on not only on a local or regional level, but on a higher transnational, even international, level.[37]

In the meantime, after three years, the Slovenian version of Ivana Marčelja and Tomi Krešević's *potresujka* melody appeared. Titled and performed in Slovenian, in keeping with the first verse *Hej mala, opala*, there is no mention of *potresujka* in the text. The video clip on YouTube is designated as 'turbofolk Slovenia'.[38] In the context of that and other similar Slovenian performances by Werner and Brigita Šuler, it is somewhat easier to understand the negative comments on the part of the younger Rijeka population, who do not like that type of music and the Polka rhythm, or the *potresujka* adapted to new conditions and the taste of the broad population. On the other hand, it is interesting to observe how identity is shaped and modified under various conditions. It is evident that the broader Littoral region is very close in music and dance taste to neighbouring Slovenia and Austria, where the traditional forms of dance music masterfully penetrate into contemporary music and dance trends.

Conclusion

We can monitor the journey of the Polka through the story of its local version — the *potresujka* — which shows us how some expressions in dance can progress from being local and national to being transnational, and can be accepted once again as being local, but in a different, new

---

37 See Fig. 15.9. Singing about 'musica Alpina' in the Latino and Cubana rhythm combining English and Spanish text with yodelling and brass band instruments, the accordion, and some elements of Austrian traditional costumes, the Global Krayner group (an Austrian jazz-folk band), produced a real mixture of cultures during their performance at the Eurovision Song Contest, when representing Austria in 2005 in their first international success. Shall we try to find local, regional, or national, Austrian-Krayner elements in their performance, or should we look at the mixture of different styles, genres, and rhythms gathered together producing some kind of global musical fusion? This kind of tension is expressed firstly in their name; the stage could accept both, and integration could be constructed and interpreted from different points of view and discourses. This kind of Cosmopolitan Karawanken beat and their unconventional, catchy Salsa-Polka-Pop tune 'Y Asi' warrant much more investigation.

38 See Fig. 15.10. Turbofolk is the term that has been used for the pop-folk music style in Serbia and other countries of the Balkans since the 1990s — often with negative connotations, as 'cheap' trash.

and transformed context and form. Such expressions can exist for a long time as something that perseveres, and then, the next moment, can explode again into a kind of mania — like the *Polkamania* or the *potresujkamania* in the local, but also in the regional context. They can also be accepted and presented as traditional, old and prestigious ways in which to interpret universal values, connecting local and global layers of art, high and low culture, dance and literature, along with philosophy and fun. Through different kinds of production, the Polka fulfilled the function of integrating these different layers.

Additional Video Resources

Fig. 15.3 Video: Presentation of Croatian folk dances in a performance of couple dances. 'Jadranka Pilčić-Zlatko Franović: Potresuljka (Grobinščina)', 3:09, posted online by dusanmusic1, *Youtube*, 11 June 2013, https://www.youtube.com/watch?v=Md3jaV2GkSQ

Fig. 15.4 Video: 'bela nedeja-kastav 2014 — pumpa band — škola potresujke', 11:20, posted online by valter pecman, *Youtube*, 4 October 2014, https://www.youtube.com/watch?v=p14Kd3hDI8E

Fig. 15.5 Video: 'Potresujka-Mirela i Zub.MTS', 1:25, posted online by biba121212, *Youtube*, 29 February 2012, https://www.youtube.com/watch?v=24YniJPnP7o

Fig. 15.6 Video: 'Ivana Marčelja i Tomi Kresevič, Potresujka', 3:01, posted by Zoran Ventin, *Youtube*, 21 January 2014, https://www.youtube.com/watch?v=k2T6wwvv3rA

Fig. 15.7 Video: 'Potresujkom po Cehovu', 5:14, posted online by etnokor, *Youtube*, 15 April 2009, https://www.youtube.com/watch?v=1Xxd4bygisY [the dancers in this video do not use the typical step pattern that distinguishes the *potresujka* from the ordinary Polka]

Fig. 15.8 Video: 'Linda Gizdulic, Grobnicke Alpe', 4:16, posted online by Marin1975, *Youtube*, 31 March 2008, http://www.youtube.com/watch?v=sg1RFKgMxes

Fig. 15.9 Video: 'Global Kryner — Y Asi — Austria 2005', 3:06, posted online by primadonna11, *Youtube*, 8 November 2006, http://www.youtube.com/watch?v=9VdFY6vFiU0

Fig. 15.10 Video: 'Hej mala opla — Werner in Brigita Šuler', 3:03, posted online by Brigita Šuler, *Youtube*, 12 June 2007, https://www.youtube.com/watch?v=z8KV-KdY0ds&feature=related

Bibliography

Egil, 'The Polka before and after the Polka', *Yearbook for Traditional Music*, 33 (2001), 37–47, https://doi.org/10.2307/1519629

'BOĆA I BULIN — IVANA MARČELJA', 3:06, posted online by Križišćan1993, *Youtube*, 5 January 2012, https://www.youtube.com/watch?v=Xhcvt9cpW6M

Baumann, Max P., 'Folk Music Revival: Concepts between Regression and Emancipation', *The World of Music*, 38 (1996), 71–86.

Edström, K. O., 'From Schottis to Bonnjazz: Some Remarks on the Construction of Swedishness', *Yearbook for Traditional Music*, 31 (1999), 27–41, https://doi.org/10.2307/767971

Ivančan, Ivan, *Narodni plesni običaji u Hrvata* (Zagreb: Hrvatka matica iseljenika, 1996).

—— *Istarski narodni plesovi* (Zagreb: Institut za narodnu umjetnost, 1963).

Jurca, Leopold, *Ples u vjerskom, ćudorednom i socijalnom pogledu* (Pazin: [n.p.], 1950).

Juretić, Alemka, *Grobnički luštrini* (Jelenje: Katedra Čakavskog Sabora Grobinšćine, 2004).

Kuhač, Franjo K. *Južno-slovjenske narodne popijevke*, vol. 3 (Zagreb: Tiskara I litografija C. Albrecht, 1880).

'Matulji', *Hrvatski karnevalist*, 5 (May, 2007), p. 24, http://www.karnevali.hr/wp-content/uploads/2018/12/karnevalist5.pdf

'Melodije Istre i Kvarnera (MIK) 2006, Finale, Rijeka, June 24, 2006' [n.a.], *Istrian Experience*, http://www.istrianexperience.com/mik06/mik06-program.htm

Merz, Ivan, *Katolici i novi plesovi* (Sarajevo: Kaptol Vrhbosanski, 1926).

Paris, Stella, 'Grobnička kartulina', *Gmajna*, 9 (2008), p. 18, https://www.cavle.hr/home/wp-content/uploads/2014/07/Gmajna_9.pdf

Sajko, Ivana, 'Potresujka kao pokazatelj identiteta' (unpublished graduate thesis, Odjel za etnologiju i antropologiju, Zadar, 2010).

Škola potresujki' [n.a.], *Tzmatulji*, https://tzmatulji.hr/dogadanja/skola-potresujki

Smigel, Libby, 'Minds Mad for Dancing: Polkamania on the London Stage', *The Journal of Popular Culture*, 30 (1996), 197–207, https://doi.org/10.1111/j.0022-3840.1996.00197.x

Sremac, Stjepan, *Pričanja iz života, Običaji i druga folklorna građa Križišća i Hrvatskog Primorja: Kazivanja Josipa Juričića 1978.–1980. u Zagrebu'* (Zagreb: Dokumentacija Instituta za etnologiju i folkloristiku, 1980).

—— 'Smotre folklora u hrvatskoj nekad i danas', *Narodna umjetnost: hrvatski časopis za etnologiju i folkloristiku*, 15 (1978), 97–114.

Stavělová, Daniela, 'Polka jako Český národní symbol', *Český lid*, 93.1 (2006), 3–26.

Vukadinović, Mašenka, 'Doživjeti osebujni grad / Experience a peculiar town', *Welcome to Rijeka*, 6 (June, 2012), pp. 8–15, https://www.htz.hr/sites/default/files/2012-05/HR_EN-Welcome-to-Rijeka-2514.pdf

'Welcome to My Impressions of Melodije Istre i Kvarnera, a Festival with Soul: Kostrena — *Potresujka* on the Grass' [n.a.], *Istrian Experience*, http://www.istrianexperience.com/mik08/kostrena.htm

Zebec, Tvrtko, 'Development and Application of Ethnochoreology in Croatia', *Međunarodni simpozij 'Muzika u Društvu'*, 6 (2008), 138–52.

—— 'Dance Research in Croatia', *Narodna umjetnost: hrvatski časopis za etnologiju i folkloristiku*, 33 (1996), 89–111.

List of Illustrations

Chapter 1

Fig. 1.1 Video: 'Vals og Folkedanslaget Springar`n sin avslutning i HD format', 7:08, posted online by Svein Arne Sølvberg, *Youtube*, 12 May 2010, https://www.youtube.com/watch?v=LolpphyIWS8 7

Fig. 1.2 Victor Gabriel Gilbert, *The Ball or an Elegant Evening*, c.1890. Wikimedia Commons, Public Domain, https://commons.wikimedia.org/wiki/File:Une_soir%C3%A9e_%C3%A9l%C3%A9gante_par_Victor_Gabriel_Gilbert_(A).jpg 7

Fig. 1.3 Video: 'Klapptanz', 1:20, posted online by Stefan Ziel, *Youtube*, 17 August 2009, https://www.youtube.com/watch?v=aJ6CVIAn5u0 8

Fig. 1.4 *The Hombourg Waltz*, 1818. Coloured engraving, British Cartoon Prints Collection (Library of Congress). Wikimedia Commons, Public Domain, https://upload.wikimedia.org/wikipedia/commons/1/1d/The_Hombourg_waltz%2C_with_characteristic_sketches_of_family_dancing_LCCN2006688900.jpg 8

Fig. 1.5 Photo from Bangsund, Norway, 1981. Photo by Egil Bakka, CC BY 4.0. 9

Fig. 1.6 Video: 'Woher kommt der Zwiefache? Verzwickter Tanz', 12:00, posted online 27 February 2016, *BRMediathek*, https://www.br.de/mediathek/video/woher-kommt-der-zwiefache-verzwickter-tanz-av:584f862a3b467900119cdb27 11

Fig. 1.7 Aquatint, 117 x 18.5 cm. From John Dean Paul, *Journal of a Party of Pleasure to Paris in the Month of August, 1802* (London: Cadell & Davies, 1802). Wellcome Collection, CC BY 4.0, https://wellcomecollection.org/works/stggecfr 12

Fig. 1.8 Eadweard Muybridge, *A Couple Waltzing*, colour lithograph presented in a phenakistoscope, 1893. Wikimedia Commons, Public Domain, https://commons.wikimedia.org/wiki/File:Eadweard_Muybridge%27s_phenakistoscope,_1893.jpg 13

Fig. 1.9   Video: 'Pardans runddans. Hamborgar og vals. Kvalik. 15
Vestlandskappleiken 2015', 5:52, posted online by
Jostedalsvideo, *Youtube*, 11 October 2015, https://www.
youtube.com/watch?v=C2ZQAIyYWe8&feature=youtu.be

Fig. 1.10 Video: 'Snoa', 1:49, posted online by Folkdance Noa-am, 15
18 March 2018, *Youtube*, https://www.youtube.com/
watch?v=_RXbbAeqXuE

Fig. 1.11 Video: 'Aelixhir — Atelier de Dreischrittdreher avec Ralf 15
Spiegler', 2:48, posted online by Lionel Thomas, 14 August
2013, https://youtu.be/qPxHcmGEpRY?t=81

Fig. 1.12 Video: 'Powolniak', 1:24, posted online by Dom Tańca, 16
12 January 2013, *Youtube*, https://www.youtube.com/
watch?v=Vy3mxGQBhiM

Fig. 1.13 Video: 'Hambo', 1:16, posted online by Skansens Folkdanslag, 16
Youtube, 9 October 2013, https://www.youtube.com/
watch?v=fif8Zt1ir70

Fig. 1.14 Video: 'Sff: Ami og Håkon Dregelid — Vossarull', 1:59, posted 17
online by Norwegian Centre for Traditional Music and Dance,
Trondheim, *Youtube*, 15 June 2011, https://www.youtube.com/
watch?v=f3c4mUeMFCEor

Fig. 1.15 Video: 'Ture i svejtrit, Vals+ — MVI 1892', 15:58, posted online 17
by Jørgen Andkær, *Youtube*, 28 October 2016, https://www.
youtube.com/watch?v=iaN37z6cbXk

Fig. 1.16 Johann Christian Schoeller, *Der große Galopp von Joh. Strauß*, 18
1839. Copper engraving. Wikimedia Commons, Public Domain,
https://commons.wikimedia.org/wiki/File:Strauss_I_-_
Wiener_Scene_-_Der_gro%C3%9Fe_Galop.jpg

Fig. 1.17 G. Munthe, *En Østlandsk St. Hansaften*. Lithograph from Chr. 19
Tønsberg, *Billeder af Norges Natur og Folkeliv* (Christiana:
Tønsberg, 1875). Owned by Egil Bakka, CC BY 4.0.

Fig. 1.18 Video: 'Slangpolska från Skåne', 2:26, posted online by Steve 21
Carruthers, *Youtube*, 5 May 2010, https://www.youtube.com/
watch?v=Ces253nl19U&t=63s

Fig. 1.19 Video: 'Polsdans fra Finnskogen 1', 2:55, posted online by Atle 21
Utkilen, *Youtube*, 23 August 2015, https://www.youtube.com/
watch?v=hB1RJaVBBRk

Fig. 1.20 Video: 'Polonez Gimnazjalny 2015', 15:16, posted by Telewizja 22
internetowa Gminy Nadarzyn, *Youtube*, 28 May 2015, https://
www.youtube.com/watch?v=3zVnVaGiQv0

Fig. 1.21 Video: 'HälsingeHambon Final 2010', 4.50, posted online by 22
meriksson84, *Youtube*, 30 August 2010, https://www.youtube.
com/watch?v=nJYwODr8700&list=RDnJYwODr8700#t=28

List of Illustrations 435

Fig. 1.22   Video: 'Leiv Fåberg og Johanna Kvam. Hamborgar', 2.37, posted online by Jostedalsvideo, *Youtube*, 28 November 2015, https://www.youtube.com/watch?v=kGenW4UV2vs   22

Chapter 2

Fig. 2.1   Project meeting in the Nordic Association of Folk Dance Research at the Finnish Literature Society in Helsinki, 2002. Photo by Esko Rausmaa, CC BY 4.0.   30

Fig. 2.2   The publications resulting from the project *Gammaldans i Norden*, 1988. Photo by Egil Bakka, CC BY 4.0.   32

Fig. 2.3   Title page of Johann Wolfgang von Goethe's *Die Leiden des jungen Werthers*, Part 1 (Leipzig: Weygand, 1774). Wikimedia Commons CC BY 3.0, https://commons.wikimedia.org/wiki/File:-1-_Die_Leiden_des_jungen_Werthers._Erstdruck.jpg   33

Fig. 2.4   [Anonymous, possibly Marcus Gheeraerts,] *Queen Elizabeth I Dancing La Volta with Robert Dudley, Earl of Leicester*, c.1580, Wikimedia Commons, Public Domain, https://commons.wikimedia.org/wiki/File:Robert_Dudley_Elizabeth_Dancing.jpg   36

Fig. 2.5   Video: 'Contrapasso Historical Dance Ensemble: Volte (Lavolta)', 1:34, posted online by Contrapasso E., *Youtube*, 19 February 2012, https://www.youtube.com/watch?v=AvaGvUoor1E   37

Fig. 2.6   Video: 'Coronation Banquet — Elizabeth Dance', 2.44, posted online by gozala00, *Youtube*, 16 May 2007, https://www.youtube.com/watch?v=5rXpNtXNOrI&feature=youtu.be   37

Fig. 2.7   The Allemande. From Simon Guillaume, *Almanach dansant ou positions et attitudes de l'Allemande* (Paris: Chez l'auteur rue des Arcis, 1769). Wikimedia Commons, Public Domain, https://commons.wikimedia.org/wiki/File:Guillaume_Almanach.jpg   40

Fig. 2.8   Daniel Hopfer, copper engraving, c.1500. Wikimedia Commons, Public Domain, https://commons.wikimedia.org/wiki/File:Kulturbilder_489.JPG   43

Fig. 2.9   George Cruikshank, *The Drunkard's Children. Plate I*, 1848. Wellcome Collection, CC BY 4.0, https://wellcomecollection.org/works/utfd99fy   44

Chapter 3

Fig. 3.1 Alexander Altenhof, *Europe in 1812: Political Situation before Napoleon's Russian Campaign*. Wikimedia Commons, CC BY 3.0, https://commons.wikimedia.org/wiki/File:Europe_1812_map_de.png 55

Fig. 3.2 Theeuro, *Location Map of Armenia Within Europe*, 2010. Image by Egil Bakka, based on Wikimedia Commons, Public Domain, https://commons.wikimedia.org/wiki/File:Europe_map_armenia.png 56

Chapter 4

Fig. 4.1 Postcard, 1901. Wikipedia, Public Domain, https://de.wikipedia.org/wiki/Datei:200_Jahre_Preussen.jpg 66

Fig. 4.2 Anna Dorothea Lisiewska, *Portrait of a Princely Family*, c.1777. oil on canvas, National Museum in Warsaw. Wikimedia Commons, Public Domain, https://commons.wikimedia.org/w/index.php?title=File:Lisiewska_Portrait_of_a_Princely_family.jpg&oldid=237421193 67

Fig. 4.3 An engraving by J. Fr. Bolt of a painting by J. C. Dähling, *Die Gartenlaube* [The Garden Arbor], 1883. Wikimedia Commons, Public Domain, https://commons.wikimedia.org/wiki/File:Die_Gartenlaube_(1883)_b_785.jpg 68

Fig. 4.4 Heinrich Anton Dähling, *Friedrich Wilhelm III and His Family*, 1806. Wikimedia Commons, Public Domain, https://commons.wikimedia.org/wiki/File:Friedrich_Wilhelm_III._und_seine_Familie.jpg 69

Fig. 4.5 Anton von Werner, *Coronation of Wilhelm I as Emperor of Germany in Versailles*, oil on canvas, Otto-Von-Bismarck-Stiftung, 1885. Wikimedia Commons, Public Domain, https://commons.wikimedia.org/wiki/File:Anton_von_Werner_-_Kaiserproklamation_in_Versailles_1871.jpg 70

Fig. 4.6 Postcard, 1912. Wikimedia Commons, Public Domain, https://commons.wikimedia.org/wiki/File:Kaiser_Wilhelm_II_Familie_main35.jpg 71

List of Illustrations 437

Fig. 4.7 Adolph von Menzel, *Das Ballsouper* [Dinner at the Ball], oil on canvas, Alte Nationalgalerie, 1878. Wikimedia Commons, Public Domain, https://commons.wikimedia.org/wiki/File:Adolph_Menzel_-_Das_Ballsouper_-_Google_Art_Project.jpg 73

Fig. 4.8 Video: 'Martín y Soler: Una cosa rara (opera completa)', 2:45:45, posted online by Classicus Musicalis, *Youtube*, https://www.youtube.com/watch?v=TtSFzFoUCoc&t=8251s 74

Fig. 4.9 Josef Kreutzinger, *Porträt der Familie des österreichischen Kaisers* [Portrait of the Family of the Austrian Emperor], c.1805. Oil on canvas. Wikimedia Commons, Public Domain, https://commons.wikimedia.org/wiki/File:Josef_Kreutzinger_-_Kaiserliche_Familie.jpg 76

Fig. 4.10 Engraving after Richard Cosway, *The Italian Castrato Singer Luigi Marchesi*, 1790. National Portrait Gallery, London. Wikimedia Commons, Public Domain, https://commons.wikimedia.org/wiki/File:Luigi_Marchesi.jpg 77

Fig. 4.11 Wilhelm Gause, *Hofball in Wien*, 1900. Historisches Museum der Stadt Wie. Wikimedia Commons, Public Domain, https://commons.wikimedia.org/wiki/File:Wilhelm_Gause_Hofball_in_Wien.jpg 78

Fig. 4.12 James Gillray, *Monstrous Craws, at a New Coalition Feast*, 1787. Etching with aquatint. Wikimedia Commons, Public Domain, https://commons.wikimedia.org/wiki/File:Monstrous_craws,_at_a_new_coalition_feast.jpg 80

Fig. 4.13 Thomas Phillips, *Portrait of Lord Byron in Albanian Dress*, 1813. Oil on canvas. Government Art Collection at the British Embassy, Athens. Wikimedia Commons, Public Domain, https://commons.wikimedia.org/wiki/File:Lord_Byron_in_Albanian_Dress_by_Phillips,_1813.jpg 81

Fig. 4.14 George Cruikshank, *Merry-Making on the Regent's Birthday*, 1812. Wikimedia Commons, Public Domain, https://commons.wikimedia.org/wiki/File:Merry_making_on_the_regents_birth_day,_1812_LCCN2003689159.tif 84

Fig. 4.15 George Cruikshank, *Longitude and Latitude of St Petersburgh*, 1813. Wikimedia Commons, Public Domain, https://commons.wikimedia.org/w/index.php?search=Waltzing+at+Almacks%2C+George+Cruikshank+&title=Special%3ASearch&go=Go#/media/File:Almack%27s_Longitude_and_Latitude.jpg 85

Fig. 4.16 Carle Vernet, a depiction of a couple dressed in French formal court styles, 1973. Image scanned by H. Churchyard from Blanche Payne's *History of Costume* (New York: Harper & Row, 1965), Wikimedia Commons, Public Domain, https://commons.wikimedia.org/wiki/File:1793-1778-contrast-right.jpg 86

Fig. 4.17 John Cassell, *Sans Culottes dancing the Carmagnole*, 1865. Image from *Cassell's Illustrated History of England, Volume 5* (London, Paris, & New York: Cassell Petter & Galpin, 1865), p. 613. Wikimedia Commons, Public Domain, https://commons.wikimedia.org/wiki/File:P613_SANS_CULOTTES_DANS_THE_CARMAGNOLE.jpg 87

Fig. 4.18 Ivan I. Terebenev, etching, Bodleian Library, 1979. Wikimedia Commons, CC BY 4.0, https://commons.wikimedia.org/wiki/File:Bodleian_Libraries,_Russians_teaching_Napoleon_to_dance-_Napoleon_Bonaparte_premier_consul_s%27est_rendu_%C3%A0_Notre_Dame_pour_y_entendre_la_Saint.jpg 90

Fig. 4.19 Gerhard von Kügelgen, *Dorothea, Princess of Lieven*, 1801. Oil on canvas. Private collection. Wikimedia Commons, Public Domain, https://commons.wikimedia.org/wiki/File:Gerhard_von_K%C3%BCgelgen_-_Portrait_of_Princess_Dorothea_von_Lieven_(1801).jpg 92

Fig. 4.20 Gerhard von Kugelgen, *The Emperor Paul I with his Family*, oil on canvas, Pavlovsk State Museum, 1800. Wikimedia Commons, Public Domain, https://commons.wikimedia.org/wiki/File:Family_of_Paul_I_of_Russia.jpg 94

Fig. 4.21 Dmitry Nikolaevich Kardovsky, *Ball at the Assembly Hall of the Nobility in St Petersburg*, 1913. Wikimedia Commons, Public Domain, https://commons.wikimedia.org/wiki/File:Ball_at_20s_by_Kardovsky.jpg 94

Fig. 4.22 Johann Peter Krafft, *Declaration of Victory After the Battle of Leipzig, 1813*, 1839. Oil on canvas. Deutsches Historisches Museum. Wikimedia Commons, Public Domain, https://commons.wikimedia.org/wiki/File:1839_Krafft_Siegesmeldung_nach_der_Schlacht_bei_Leipzig_1813_anagoria.JPG 95

Fig. 4.23 Video: 'Polonaise (Pushkin Ball 2011)', 4:51, posted by Khasanov1988, *Youtube*, 19 October 2011, https://www.youtube.com/watch?v=o3e1OH1BpjA 97

Fig. 4.24 Jean Godefroy, after Jean-Baptiste Isabey, *Delegates of the Congress of Vienna*, 19th c. Numbers added by Maciej Szczepańczyk. Wikimedia Commons, CC BY 3.0, https://commons.wikimedia.org/wiki/File:Congress_of_Vienna.PNG 97

Fig. 4.25 Forceval, *The Congress*, 1814–1815. Vinck Collection, National Library, Paris. Wikimedia Commons, Public Domain, https://commons.wikimedia.org/wiki/File:Forceval-Congr%C3%A8s_de_Vienne_1814-15.png 98

Chapter 5

Fig. 5.1 Polka, watercolour from Petr Maixner, published in the ethnological journal *Český lid* 12 (1903), p. 93. All rights reserved. 108

Fig. 5.2 *Maděra* in the collection of folk dances from Josef Vycpálek, *České tance* (Praha: B. Kočí, 1921), p. 105, CC BY. 123

Fig. 5.3 *Maděra cpálek* in the collection of folk dances from Josef Vycpálek, *České tance* (Praha: B. Kočí, 1921), p. 106, CC BY. 124

Fig. 5.4 'The Russian Polka Double-Polka' in the collection of folk dances from Josef Vycpálek, *České tance* (Praha: B. Kočí, 1921), p. 106, CC BY. 125

Fig. 5.5 'The Double-Polka' in the collection of folk dances from Josef Vycpálek, *České tance* (Praha: B. Kočí, 1921), p. 94, CC BY. 126

Fig. 5.6 *Tramlam-Polka* in the collection of folk dances from Josef Vycpálek, *České tance* (Praha: B. Kočí, 1921), p. 107, CC BY. 127

Fig. 5.7 *The Bartered Bride*, Royal Opera House programme, 10 December 1998, p. 25. Wikimedia Commons, Public Domain, https://commons.wikimedia.org/wiki/File:Bohemian_Polka.jpg#/media/File:Bohemian_Polka.jpg 130

Fig. 5.8 *La Polka enseigné sans maître par MM. Perrot et Adrien Robert* (Paris: Aubert, 1845), p. 10. Private archive of Dorota Gremlicová, all rights reserved. 131

Fig. 5.9 'Pas bohémien', *La Polka einseignée sans maître par MM. Perrot et Adrien Robert* (Paris: Aubert, 1845), p. 58. Private archive of Dorota Gremlicová, all rights reserved. 132

Fig. 5.10 J. Raab and Mlle Valentine dancing Polka at the Théâtre Ambigu Paris. Private archive of Dorota Gremlicová, all rights reserved. 133

Fig. 5.11 Portrait of Jan Neruda by Jan Vilímek from *České album, sbírka podobizen předních českých velikánů* (V. Praze: Jos. R. Vilímek, [n.d.]). Wikimedia Commons, Public Domain, https://commons.wikimedia.org/wiki/File:Jan_Vil%C3%ADmek_-_Jan_Neruda.jpg#/media/File:Jan_Vil%C3%ADmek_-_Jan_Neruda.jpg 135

Fig. 5.12   Polka, from a booklet describing the dance *Česká Beseda* 137
(*Česká beseda*, ed. by J. Fiala, J. Prokšová-Evaldová, M. Malá, J.
Vokáčová, and H. Livorová, p. 10), CC BY.

Fig. 5.13   Polka, from a booklet describing the dance *Česká Beseda* 138
(*Česká beseda*, ed. by J. Fiala, J. Prokšová-Evaldová, M. Malá, J.
Vokáčová, and H. Livorová, p. 6), CC BY.

Fig. 5.14   Bedřich Smetana, *La Fiancée vendue. Avant Scène Opéra No. 248* 141
(Paris: Premières Loges, 2008). Wikimedia Commons, Public
Domain, https://commons.wikimedia.org/wiki/File:Bartered
BridePianoReduction.jpg#/media/File:BarteredBridePianoRe
duction.jpg

Fig. 5.15   Video: 'Česká polka — finale Česká Lípa dupen 2012', 1:37, 143
posted online by Lenka čermáková, *Youtube*, 22 April 2012,
https://www.youtube.com/watch?v=oYiaywtlQxU

Fig. 5.16   Video: 'Polka', 14:35, posted online by An000b, 144
Youtube, 24 October 2011, https://www.youtube.com/
watch?v=LiIxtj0wtcA

Chapter 6

Fig. 6.1   Excerpt from music for *Reydowak* by Ch. W. Schiessler, 156
published in his *Carnevals-Almanach für das Jahr 1830* (Prague:
C. W. Enders, 1830), http://kramerius.nkp.cz/kramerius/
MShowMonograph.do?id=24112. Josef Vycpálek, *České tance*
(Prague: B. Kočí, 1921), p. 47.

Fig. 6.2   IZdeněk Míka, *Zábava a slavnosti staré Prahy* (Prague: 157
Nakladatelství Ostrov 2008), p. 128.

Fig. 6.3   Video: 'Stanford at Spoleto Festival: Winner's Redowa', 2:08, 159
posted online by Jason Anderson, *Youtube*, 17 July 2011,
https://www.youtube.com/watch?v=fzSRDv3f0-8

Fig. 6.4   'The Redowa Waltz: A new Bohemian waltz as danced in the 160
Parisian saloons and taught by Monsieur Jules Martin', c.1846.
Jerome Robbins Dance Division, The New York Public Library
Digital Collections, Public Domain, https://digitalcollections.
nypl.org/items/9fae00f0-3386-0131-f0f9-58d385a7bbd0

Fig. 6.5   Video: '"Česká Beseda" — Vystoupení skupiny "Beseda" Jitky 161
Bonušové — Beroun 23/03/13', 14:51, uploaded by Ludmila
Sluníčková, *Youtube*, 27 March 2013, https://www.youtube.
com/watch?v=Pmrh_0uhLX8

List of Illustrations 441

Fig. 6.6   V. R. Grüner, 'Carneval in Prague', c.1829. Zdeněk Míka, 166
          Zábava a slavnosti staré Prahy (Prague: Nakladatelství Ostrov,
          2008), p. 123.
Fig. 6.7   Zdeněk Míka, *Zábava a slavnosti staré Prahy* (Prague: 170
          Nakladatelství Ostrov 2008), p. 128.

Chapter 7

Fig. 7.1   Pollencig József, *Grosser Ball bey Sv. Kőnigh Hoheit de Palatins Ofen* 200
          den 11ten Februar 1795 [Great Ball held by His Royal Highness
          of Palatine], 11 February 1795. Paper and gouache, 282 x 408
          mm. Szépművészeti Múzeum, Budapest, Index number: 1930–
          2188. Image courtesy of Szépművészeti Múzeum.
Fig. 7.2   Unknown artist, *Bál a kis Redoute-ban* [Ball in the small 201
          Redoute], c.1830. Coloured lithography. Historical Museum,
          Metropolitan Gallery in Budapest. Image courtesy of Budapesti
          Történeti Múzeum.
Fig. 7.3   Max Felix von Pauer, *Pest-Budai bál* [Ball in Pest-Buda]. Paper 202
          and ink, 110 x 16 mm. Metropolitan Szabó Ervin Library of
          Budapest (FSZK). János Jajczay, *Pest-Budai figurák a múlt század*
          30-as éveiből. Max Félix Pauer rajzai a Fővárosi Könyvtárban
          (Budapest: Stadtbibliothek, 1941), pp. 9–10. Image courtesy of
          Fővárosi Szabó Ervin Könyvtár, Budapest.
Fig. 7.4   Unknown artist, *Tánciskola* [Dance school], 1845–1846. 204
          Lithography. Historical Museum, Metropolitan Gallery in
          Budapest. Ignácz Nagy, *Magyar titok* [Hungarian secret] (Pest:
          Hartleben Konrád Adolf, 1845–1846), p. 258. Image courtesy of
          Budapesti Történeti Múzeum.
Fig. 7.5   A playbill of the opera *Hunyadi László* composed by Ferenc 205
          Erkel, 'father' of the Hungarian national opera. Textbook
          written by Béni Egressy. The opera was premiered in the
          National Theatre in Pest, in 1844. The original playbill belongs
          to the collection of the Széchenyi István State National Library.
Fig. 7.6   The Polka Mazur, on the front-page of the publication with 207
          musical notes, 1864. 150 x 90 mm. Kränzchen-Souvenir,
          Polka Mazur für pianoforte von kapellmeister Josef Dubez (Pest:
          Rózsavölgyi & Comp., 1862). Image courtesy of the Library of
          the Liszt Ferenc Music Academy, Budapest.

Fig. 7.7   Pálóczi Horváth Ádám, *Ó és új mintegy Ötödfélszáz énekek, ki magam csinálmánya, ki másé* [450 Old and New Songs, Composed by Myself and Others] (Budapest: Akadémiai Kiadó, 1953), pp. 172–73 (notes) and 528–29 (lyrics).   208

Fig. 7.8   Pálóczi Horváth Ádám, *Ó és új mintegy Ötödfélszáz énekek, ki magam csinálmánya, ki másé* [450 Old and New Songs, Composed by Myself and Others] (Budapest: Akadémiai Kiadó, 1953), pp. 173 (notes), 529 (lyrics).   210

Fig. 7.9   Pálóczi Horváth Ádám, *Ó és új mintegy Ötödfélszáz énekek, ki magam csinálmánya, ki másé* [450 Old and New Songs, Composed by Myself and Others] (Budapest: Akadémiai Kiadó, 1953), pp. 131 (notes), 265 (lyrics).   211

Fig. 7.10   Réthei Prikkel Marián, *A magyarság táncai* [Dances of Hungarians] (Budapest: Stúdium, 1924), pp. 232–33.   213

Fig. 7.11   Georg Emmanuel Opitz (1775–1841), *Táncoló Magyarok* [Dancing Hungarians], early nineteenth century. Paper, gouache, 478 x 361 mm. Magyar Nemzeti Múzeum, Történeti Képcsarnok T. 7136. Image courtesy of Magyar Nemzeti Múzeum.   221

Fig. 7.12   Márk Rózsavölgyi, *Első magyar társas tánc* [First Hungarian Social Dance]. From Szentpál Olga, *A csárdás* (Budapest: Zeneműkiadó, 1954), p. ix.   223

Fig. 7.13   Lajos Kilányi, *Andalgó* [Promenade], 1844. Image copied from Szentpál Olga, *A csárdás* (Budapest: Zeneműkiadó, 1954), p. 32.   225

Fig. 7.14   *Palotás* [For the Palace], composed by Bertha Sándor (1843–1912) (Budapest: Khor & Wein könyvnyomdája, 1864). Lithograph, 31 x 26 cm. Liszt Ferenc Zeneművészeti Egyetem Könyvtára, 50.471.   229

Chapter 8

Fig. 8.1   *Valček s prestopanjem* [Waltz with shift steps], 2003. © Institute of Ethnomusicology ZRC SAZU. Drawing by Mirko Ramovš.   246

Fig. 8.2   *Valček z menjalnim korakom* [Waltz with the change step], 2003. © Institute of Ethnomusicology ZRC SAZU. Drawing by Mirko Ramovš.   247

Fig. 8.3   *Drseči valček* [the sliding Waltz], 2003. © Institute of Ethnomusicology ZRC SAZU. Drawing by Mirko Ramovš.   249

List of Illustrations 443

Fig. 8.4 *Poskočni valček* [gambolling, springing Waltz], 2003. © Institute of Ethnomusicology ZRC SAZU. Drawing by Mirko Ramovš. 250

Fig. 8.5 Third variant of *dvokoračni valček* [two-step Waltz], 2003. © Institute of Ethnomusicology ZRC SAZU. Drawing by Mirko Ramovš. 251

Fig. 8.6 Photo by Danilo Škofič (1962). Wikimedia Commons, Public Domain, https://commons.wikimedia.org/w/index.php?search=Maturantski+ples+&title=Special%3ASearch&go=Go#/media/File:Maturantski_ples_v_Mariboru_1962_(5).jpg 253

Fig. 8.7 Video: 'MATURANTSKA PARADA — 2014 — QUADRILLE PARADE', 6:36, posted online by Tomaz Ambroz, *Youtube*, 28 May 2014, https://www.youtube.com/watch?v=QoSOpu4Y58w 254

Chapter 9

Fig. 9.1 Video: 'Veterani KUD-a Croatia – "hrvatsko salonsko kolo"', 7:50, posted online by fudooo01, *Youtube*, 7 May 2017, https://www.youtube.com/watch?v=OA9D5Zt94HQ; and 'Goran Knežević-Hrvatsko salonsko kolo, FA Ententin, 1. FFK — Zagreb, 2003', 7:48, posted online by Goran Knežević, *Youtube*, 21 July 2013, https://www.youtube.com/watch?v=J8LOIffuy_0 258

Fig. 9.2 Dragutin Weingärtner, *Meeting of the Croatian Parliament, 1848*, 1885. Wikimedia Commons, Public Domain, https://commons.wikimedia.org/wiki/File:Dragutin_Weing%C3%A4rtner,_Hrvatski_sabor_1848._god.jpg 260

Fig. 9.3 Dance programs preserved at the Museum of the City of Zagreb, with permission from the Zagreb City Museum. 265

Fig. 9.4 Video: 'Dani grada Karlovca 2012 (07-3): Rođendanski bal — valcer', 13:24, posted online by MaPisKA047, *Youtube*, 13 August 2012, https://www.youtube.com/watch?v=-wH873n5EU4 278

Fig. 9.5 Video: 'Valceri, Polke i druge špelancije 2016', 1:18:08, posted online by Hrvatska radiotelevizija, *Youtube*, 7 July 2017, https://www.youtube.com/watch?v=pnhihJ7Lab0 279

Chapter 10

Fig. 10.1　Josef Kriehuber, *Johann Strauss the Elder*, 1835. Lithograph. Wikimedia Commons, Public Domain, https://commons.wikimedia.org/wiki/Category:Johann_Strauss_I#/media/File:Strau%C3%9FVaterLitho.jpg　285

Fig. 10.2　Johann Poppel, *Das Stadttheater in Hamburg* (after C. A. Lill), published by Berendschenschen Buch & Kunsthandlung, Hamburg, c.1842. Wikimedia Commons, Public Domain, https://commons.wikimedia.org/wiki/File:Hamburg_Stadttheater_c1842.jpg　290

Fig. 10.3　Charles Wilda, *Der Ball*, 1906. Wikimedia Commons, Public Domain, https://commons.wikimedia.org/wiki/File:Charles-Wilda_Joseph-Lanner-und-Johann-Strauss_1906.jpg　297

Fig. 10.4　Wilhelm E. A. von Schlieben, Map of Hamburg (in the East) and Altona/Ottensen (in the West) in 1833, https://www.christian-terstegge.de/hamburg/karten_umgebung/files/1833_neue_geographie_300dpi.jpeg. Image courtesy of Christian Terstegge, Public Domain.　305

Fig. 10.5　Jacob Petersen, *The Steamship Frederik den Siette*, 1838. Landesmuseum, Schleswig, Germany. Wikimedia Commons, Public Domain, https://da.wikipedia.org/wiki/Jacob_Petersen_(maler)#/media/Fil:Ship_Frederik_den_Siette_by_Jacob_Petersen.jpg　308

Fig. 10.6　Audio: 'Eisenbahn-Lust-Walzer, Op. 89', 7:35, posted online by Slovak State Philharmonic Orchestra — Topic, *Youtube*, 16 August 2018, https://www.youtube.com/watch?v=q_k2kuhG0BM　312

Chapter 11

Fig. 11.1　Photo by Olev Mihkelmaa (2009), Kihnu, Estonia. © ERA DF 28313.　332

Fig. 11.2　Photo by Anu Vissel (1985), Linaküla village, Kihnu, Estonia. © ERA Foto 14172.　333

Fig. 11.3　Photo by photo by Mikk, TRÜ (1954), Kihnu, Estonia. © ERA Foto 2530.　334

Chapter 12

Fig. 12.1 Photo by Henning Anderson (1882). Public Domain. 344
Fig. 12.2 Oscar Wergeland, *Riksforsamlingen på Eidsvoll 1814*, 1885. 285 x 400 cm. Parliament of Norway Building, Oslo. Wikimedia Commons, Public Domain, https://en.wikipedia.org/wiki/Norwegian_Constituent_Assembly#/media/File:Eidsvoll_riksraad_1814.jpeg 346
Fig. 12.3 Edward Daniel Clarke, *Travels in Various Countries of Europe, Asia and Africa*, vol. 10 (London: T. Cadell and W. Davies, 1824), part 3, p. 166. Library of Norwegian Centre for Traditional Music and Dance. 347
Fig. 12.4 E. Lange, *August Bournonville*, before 1879. Wikimedia Commons, Public Domain, https://commons.wikimedia.org/wiki/File:August_Bournonville_by_E._Lange.jpg#/media/File:August_Bournonville_by_E._Lange.jpg 350
Fig. 12.5 Photo owned by Ingeborg Isdal Løkken, CC BY-NC. 352
Fig. 12.6 Svae Bedehus and its congregation at Skiptvedt, 1902. Public Domain. 353
Fig. 12.7 *Den Frilynde Ungdomsrørsla. Norigs Ungdomslag i 25 År*, ed. by Sven Moren and Edvard Os (Oslo: Norigs Ungdomslag, 1921), p. 265. Public Domain. 353
Fig. 12.8 Photo by Karl August Berg, Folkets Hus, Løkken (c.1919). Public Domain. 354
Fig. 12.9 Video: 'Reinlender 2 — Landsfestivalen 2013', 3:42, posted online by norsound, *Youtube*, 21 July 2013, https://www.youtube.com/watch?v=cY7WHpd_nvQ 355
Fig. 12.10 Video: 'Valdres springar', 2:35, posted online by Lars R Amundsen, *Youtube*, 24 December 2015, https://www.youtube.com/watch?v=Ijq5RYxIGz4 355
Fig. 12.11 Postcard, Torsnes Arbeiderlag (1902). Public Domain. 358
Fig. 12.12 Cover of Sven Moren and Edvard Os, eds, *Den Frilynde Ungdomsrørsla. Norigs Ungdomslag i 25 År* (Oslo: Norigs Ungdomslag, 1921). Public Domain. 363
Fig. 12.13 *Den Frilynde Ungdomsrørsla, Norigs Ungdomslag i 25 År*, ed. by Sven Moren and Edvard Os (Oslo: Norigs Ungdomslag, 1921), p. 239. Public Domain. 367

Chapter 13

Fig. 13.1 Video: 'Victoria & Daniel of Sweden's Royal Wedding Waltz/ Bröllopsvals', 4:15, posted online by 2x7, *Youtube*, 21 June 2010, https://www.youtube.com/watch?v=xLk977Ktaus   375

Fig. 13.2 *A Drunken Party with Sailors and Their Women Drinking, Smoking, and Dancing Wildly as a Band Plays.* Reproduction of an etching by C. H., c. 1825, after George Cruikshank. Wellcome Collection, CC BY 4.0, https://wellcomecollection.org/works/y4vwqhg7   387

Chapter 14

Fig. 14.1 Postcard (unknown author), c.1905. Image from the Nuutti Kanerva Collection. Wikimedia Commons, Public Domain, https://commons.wikimedia.org/wiki/File:Valtionhotellin_laivalaituri,_Valtionhotellin_tanssi-_ja_soittolava,_circa_1905_PK0059.jpg?uselang=fi#file   398

Fig. 14.2 Photo by Väinö Kannisto (1945). Helsinki City Museum, CC BY 4.0, https://www.helsinkikuvia.fi/search/record/?search=tanssi&page=14   403

Fig. 14.3 Photo by Sari Hovila (2011), CC BY 4.0, https://wiki.aineetonkulttuuriperinto.fi/wiki/Tiedosto:Pyh%C3%A4salmi.jpg   410

Chapter 15

Fig. 15.1 Detail of Map from CIA World Factbook 2009. Wikimedia Commons, Public Domain, https://commons.wikimedia.org/wiki/File:Croatia_Transportation.jpg#/media/File:Croatia_Transportation.jpg   426

Fig. 15.2 Poster for *Potresujkom po Čehovu*, 2008, with the permission of the author Nikola Šubić (Shuba), all rights reserved, http://www.mi3dot.org/gallery/original/20280/   428

Fig. 15.3	Video: 'Jadranka Pilčić-Zlatko Franović: Potresuljka (Grobinščina)', 3:09, posted online by dusanmusic1, *Youtube*, 11 June 2013, https://www.youtube.com/watch?v=Md3jaV2GkSQ	430
Fig. 15.4	Video: 'bela nedeja-kastav 2014- pumpa band- škola potresujke', 11:20, posted online by valter pecman, *Youtube*, 4 October 2014, https://www.youtube.com/watch?v=p14Kd3hDI8E	430
Fig. 15.5	Video: 'Potresujka-Mirela i Zub.MTS', 1:25, posted online by biba121212, *Youtube*, 29 February 2012, https://www.youtube.com/watch?v=24YniJPnP7o	430
Fig. 15.6	Video: 'Ivana Marčelja i Tomi Kresevič, Potresujka', 3:01, posted by Zoran Ventin, *Youtube*, 21 January 2014, https://www.youtube.com/watch?v=k2T6wwvv3rA	430
Fig. 15.7	Video: 'Potresujkom po Cehovu', 5:14, posted online by etnokor, *Youtube*, 15 April 2009, https://www.youtube.com/watch?v=1Xxd4bygisY	430
Fig. 15.8	Video: 'Linda Gizdulic, Grobnicke Alpe', 4:16, posted online by Marin1975, *Youtube*, 31 March 2008, http://www.youtube.com/watch?v=sg1RFKgMxes	430
Fig. 15.9	Video: 'Global Kryner — Y Asi — Austria 2005', 3:06, posted online by primadonna11, *Youtube*, 8 November 2006, http://www.youtube.com/watch?v=9VdFY6vFiU0	430
Fig. 15.10	Video: 'Hej mala opla — Werner in Brigita Šuler', 3:03, posted online by Brigita Šuler, *Youtube*, 12 June 2007, https://www.youtube.com/watch?v=z8KV-KdY0ds&feature=related	430

Contributor Biographies

Egil Bakka is Professor Emeritus of Dance Studies at the Norwegian University of Science and Technology, and former Director of the Norwegian Centre for Traditional Music and Dance. He built a full teaching program in Ethnochoreology at NTNU, and, in collaboration with six other universities, he developed two international Masters programs — NoMAds (Nordic Master in Dance Studies) and Choreomundus (International Master in Dance Knowledge, Practice, and Heritage) – which he coordinated. His latest publications include 'Theorizing and De-Theorizing Dance' (2018) and 'Museums, Dance, and the Safeguarding of Intangible Cultural Heritage: "Events of Practice" – A New Strategy for Museums?' (with Tone Erlien, 2017).

Theresa Jill Buckland is Professor of Dance History and Ethnography, Department of Dance, University of Roehampton, London. Her edited books include *Dancing from Past to Present* (2006) and *Folklore Revival Movements in Europe post 1950* (with Daniela Stavělová, 2018). She is also the author of *Society Dancing*: *Fashionable Bodies in England 1870–1920* (2011).

László Felföldi is a Professor of the Department of Ethnology and Cultural Anthropology, University of Szeged, Hungary. He is the former head of the Department of Folk Dance in the Institute of the Hungarian Academy of Sciences, and the Co-Founder of Choreomundus.

Dorota Gremlicová is Professor of Dance Studies at the Academy of Performing Arts in Prague, Czech Republic. She is a dance historian, choreologist, pedagogue, and dance critic specialising in theatrical dance. Her books include *Stopy Tance*: *Taneční Prameny a Jejich Interpretace* [Traces of Dance: Dance Sources and their Interpretation] (2007) and *Tanec a společnost* [Dance and Society] (2009).

Sille Kapper is Associate Professor of Folk Culture (Folk Dance) at the Baltic Film, Media, Art and Communication School, Tallinn University, Estonia. She has been a practising dance teacher since 1986, and since 2014 the Artistic Director of the Estonian Folklore Ensemble Leigarid. In 2013 she completed her PhD at the Estonian Institute of Humanities with a dissertation on 'Changing Traditional Folk Dance: Concepts and Realizations in Estonia 2008–2013'. Her research focuses on past and present traditional dances, and on the folk dance movement, including its recreational dimension and Estonia's standard stage folk dance. She is actively involved in the Estonian Song and Dance Celebrations; is a board member of CIOFF-Estonia; a folk dance mentor at the Estonian Folk Dance and Folk Music Association; and a council member of the Union of Estonian Dance Education and Dance Artists.

Ivana Katarinčić has worked at the Institute of Ethnology and Folklore Research in Zagreb, Croatia, since 2005. Her articles have been published in scientific and professional journals and books. Her scholarly work has been promoted through active participation at international conferences in Croatia and abroad. Ivana is a member of the International Council for Traditional Music (ICTM) as well as the Croatian National Committee of the ICTM. She is an Editor of the journal *Narodna umjetnost: Croatian Journal of Ethnology and Folklore Research*.

Rebeka Kunej is Assistant Professor and Research Fellow at the Research Centre of the Slovenian Academy of Sciences and Arts, Institute of Ethnomusicology. She is the author of *Štajeriš: podoba in kontekst slovenskega ljudskega plesa* [The Štajeriš: The Form and Context of a Slovenian Folk Dance] (2012) and the co-author of *Music from Both Sides* (2017).

Iva Niemčić is Research Associate and Director (2019–2023) of the Institute of Ethnology and Folklore Research (IEF) in Zagreb, Croatia. In 2007, she obtained her PhD from the University of Zagreb with a dissertation on *Dance and Gender*. Niemčić is the author of *Lastovski poklad. Plesno-etnološka studija* [Lastovo Carnival. Dance Ethnology Study] (2011).

Mats Nilsson is Associate Professor in Ethnology at the Department of Cultural Sciences, University of Gothenburg, Sweden. His main research field centers on dance and the discourse about dance through time and space. He teaches fieldwork methodologies and ethnological perspectives at all levels of university education. Mats is also a dance teacher specialising in folk and old-time dances. As a member of folk dance groups he has toured in Europe, Peru, Malaysia, and Japan.

Helena Saarikoski is Adjunct Professor of Folklore and Women's Studies, University of Helsinki. She is a Helsinki-based folklorist, specialising in youth and women studies and ethnographic studies of popular culture.

Daniela Stavělová is Director of Research in Ethnomusicology and Ethnochoreology at the Institute of Ethnology of the Czech Academy of Sciences, and Associate Professor in Dance Studies of the Academy of Performing Arts in Prague, Czech Republic. Her research focuses on ethnochoreology, dance anthropology, historical records of the traditional dance, nationalism and revival.

Jörgen Torp received his PhD in Systematic Musicology from the University of Hamburg, Germany, in 2007. He is author of *Alte atlantische Tangos*: *Rhythmische Figurationen im Wandel der Zeiten und Kulturen* [Old Atlantic Tangos: Rhythmic Figures through Different Ages and Cultures] (2007), a book focusing on aspects of various forms of tangos on both sides of the southern Atlantic around and before 1900. Jörgen's research interests include studies in music and dance. For more than thirty years he has been a member of the ICTM (International Council for Traditional Music) and, for more than twenty-five years, a member of the ICTM Study Group on Ethnochoreology.

Anne von Bibra Wharton teaches ballroom and world dance traditions in the Dance Department at St. Olaf College in Minnesota. She has served as Secretary of the ICTM Study Group on Ethnochoreolgy and as an editor for multiple study group proceedings. Among her research interests are continuity and change in social dance forms in the Franconian region of Germany, which include many round dances.

Tvrtko Zebec is a Senior Researcher and, since 2019, Deputy Director at the Institute of Ethnology and Folklore Research, Zagreb, which he headed from 2011–2015. Zebec is also Honorary Professor and Visiting

Scholar at Choreomundus, Chair of the Publication Committee and member of the Board of the ICTM Study Group on Ethnochoreology, and Artistic Director of the Zagreb Folklore Festival.

Index

Aachen 286, 308
Abonnentenbälle 305
abroad 58, 88, 128, 161, 169, 201, 226, 228, 376, 402
accessibility 322, 349
accordion 144, 397, 421, 423, 428–429
advertisement 270, 295, 306
aesthetic rules 111
African-American dances 1, 39, 54–56, 58–59, 355
  prohibition of 39
agency 322
agrarian culture 402, 408, 413
Alas, Liis 328
Alexander I, Emperor of Russia 67–68, 85, 91–97, 100, 102
Allemande 20, 38, 40, 86, 88, 346
Almack's 82, 85, 91, 99
Altona 283–284, 287, 289–290, 305–306, 309–311
Altonaer Nachrichten. See *Königlich priviligirte Altonaer Adreß-Comtoir-Nachrichten*, newspaper
Amadé Theatre 263–264
Amazonia 113
America 275, 311, 377, 395
Americas, the 1–2, 73, 107
Amsterdam 286
anachronism 75
Anglaise 20
anthropology 110
anthropomorphism 383
antipathy 80
Antofagasta 274–275
Antrea 405–406
Antwerp 286
Apollosaal 289–292, 294, 296
Apollo-Soirée 298
Apollo-Theater 298
appropriation 91, 360
Arbeau, Thoinot 36
Argentina 404
aristocracy 19, 34, 45–46, 74, 83, 86, 91, 93, 96, 99–101, 119, 165, 179, 181, 190, 198–199, 201, 226, 259, 261, 268, 272, 418
  liberal 218
  multi-ethnic 216
Arraste, Angela 319
arts 67, 93, 153, 165, 197, 215–216, 345
assembly houses 60, 352, 354, 356, 371
  fund for building of 356
Association of Dance Teachers in Hungary 217
Athenaeum, periodical 198
audience 4, 182, 280, 292, 294–295, 338, 400–401, 424, 427
Augsburg 286
Augusta of Saxe-Weimar-Eisenach, Queen Consort of Prussia 72
Augustine of Hippo 378
Australia 2
Austria 89, 97, 153, 227–228, 241, 243, 309, 423, 429–430
Austrian
  Absolutism 227
  dances 38
  Empire 152–153, 173, 177, 215, 222, 230, 233, 241
  identity 274

Monarchy 153, 164, 195
Restoration 153
Austro-Hungarian Empire 64, 215
   dissolution of 241
Austro-Hungarian Monarchy 228, 420
   countries of 228
   court of 65, 74
authenticity 111, 275, 319, 322, 413
autobiography 408

Bach, Johannes Sebastian 41, 262, 281–282
bajs 421
Bakka, Egil 54, 119, 325, 421
Balett lexikon 187
Balkans 60, 429
ball 4, 11, 32, 39, 55, 65, 68, 71–76, 78, 83, 86, 88, 94–98, 112, 116, 118, 120–122, 134, 152, 157, 167–168, 190, 199, 218, 226, 228, 257, 260–262, 266–272, 274, 277–278, 289–290, 293, 295, 297, 304–306, 312, 348–349
   as act of representation 71
   European 273
   graduation ball 278
   house ball 304
   in Budapest 188
   in Christiana 348
   invitation card to 157
   location of 308
   lower-middle-class 203
   masked ball in Zagreb 273
   masquerade (redoute) 304
   most prevalent dance at 273
   organisation of 312
   picnic ball 304
   private 153
   public 153, 158, 163, 304, 348
   Schnackerlballs 304
   seasonal 290
   society ball 304
ballet 35, 38, 45–46, 98, 224
ballet comedy 182
ballet dancers 279, 306

ballroom 6, 16–17, 39, 45, 96, 98, 151, 161, 184–185, 190, 201, 216, 228, 231, 235, 257, 267, 270, 273–274, 419
   etiquette 119
   fashion 157
ballroom dancers 114, 279
ballroom dances
   national 220
ballroom dancing 16, 39, 45, 58, 98–99, 115, 119, 121, 161, 218–219, 226, 228, 231, 240, 277, 279
   development of 277
   modern 332, 337
   regulated 219
   schools 278
   traditional 233
   urban 228, 276
Baltic Sea 309, 324, 328
Banja Luka 420
barn dance 379
Barthes, Roland 112
Bascom, William R. 386
Baumann, Max P. 418
Bavarian dances 20
Bedehus. *See* community house: *Bedehus*
Beethoven, Ludwig van 300–302
   reception of 303
   successor to Mozart 302
behaviour 171, 378, 382, 384
   gendered 232
   public 165, 172–173
   regulation of 359
   uncontrolled 169, 359
Belgium 286
Belgrade 129
Bellermann, Johann Joachim 93
Bendix, Regina 322
Berens, Conrad 298
Bergenser 20
Berlin 64–65, 68, 71, 100, 285, 309
Berntsen, Harald 357
   Folkets Hus 356
Berzsenyi, Dániel 190–192, 196
Beseda 120, 134, 136. *See also* Česká Beseda

besedy 122
Beurmann, Eduard 295, 311
Bible 364
Biedermeier period 307
Biedermeier style 153, 165
Bie, Oskar 5, 18, 37, 74
Bismarck, Otto von 70
Bjørnson, Bjørnstjerne 344
Blanchett, Cate 36
Blekastad, Ivar 361
body 378–379
   activity of 322
   co-ordination of 334
   exposure of 388
   new bodily protocol 400
Bogunović, Marko 268, 275
Bohemia 107, 116, 121, 129, 134, 149, 151–152, 156, 162–163, 165, 167, 286, 419
Bohemia, newspaper 149–152, 154, 156, 168, 172
Bohemian intellectuals 153
Bohemian musician 199
Bohemian society 164, 170, 172
bolcar 240, 247–248
Bombay 300
Bøndernes Hus 354
Bonn 286
Boricatánc 178
Borovský, Karel Havlíček 120
Börsen-Halle: Hamburgische Abend-Zeitung für Handel, Schiffahrt und Politik, newspaper 288
botunara 421
Bourbon Restoration 101
bourgeois 46, 68, 88, 91, 93, 173, 186, 230, 401
   couple dances 420
   culture 164, 360
      establishment of 153
   fashion dances 187
   new bourgeois 171
   petit-bourgeois 204

   social dances 187
   society 171
bourgeoisie 34, 41, 63, 93, 134, 165, 355, 419. *See also* middle class
   dominance of 215
   round dances 98
Bournonville, August 349–350
brass band 296, 306, 357, 419, 428
Bratřic, Jan Jeník z 159
Braun, Rudolf 45, 70, 72
Brazil 8, 310
breath
   shortness of 232
Bremen 286, 292, 310–311
Brighton 381
Brno 287
Bronn, Wilhelm 168–169
   Kalobiotik 168–169
Brunswick 83, 286, 291
Brussels 286
Buckland, Theresa Jill 45, 72
   Society Dancing: Fashionable Bodies in England 1870-1920 45
Budapest 303
Byron, Lord 79–82, 84, 102, 155, 172
   'The Waltz' 79, 155, 172

Caeyers, Jan 303
Calliot, Antoine 86, 101
Căluş 179
čamara 114, 136
Canthal, August Martin 298
capobalo 420
Carinthia 248
Carnival 132, 149–150, 156, 224, 261, 267, 269, 286, 311, 424–425, 427
   in Zagreb 266
   Shrove Tuesday 425
Caroline of Brunswick, Queen Consort of the United Kingdom 83
cartoon 79
Casino 264, 266
Catherine the Great, Empress of Russia 92, 100

Catholic Church 261, 420
Čelakovský, F. L 113
celebrity 95, 199
Cellarius, Henri 118, 131–132, 161, 184
cell phone 387
censorship 74, 165, 218
Central Labe Region 116
Česká Beseda 134, 137–139, 161–163, 276, 278
Česká Včela 122, 128
chain dances 46, 318, 325, 369
Chakavian dialect 423–424
character dances 35, 45, 335
Charintia 250
Charkov, Ukraine 118
Charlotte of Mecklenburg-Strelitz, Queen Consort of the United Kingdom 79, 82
Chekhov, Anton Pavlovich 426
Childers, William 84
child pornography 384
Chopin, Frédéric 41, 304
choreographer 222, 224, 226, 275, 318, 349, 426
choreographic structure 107, 113, 115–117, 120, 122, 138–139
choreography 47, 125, 159, 180–181, 217, 219, 275–276, 335, 400
  Hungarian style 220
  structured 140
choreology 318
Chotek, Count Karel 154
Christian 11, 18, 24, 37, 60, 242, 300, 305, 353, 362, 365
Christiania 348
Christianity 344, 362–364
  acceptance of dance by 363
Christmas Eve 262
chronocentrism 387
circle dances 260, 266, 268, 273, 421
  Croatian 268, 273
City Council hall 261
Civil Guard 406
clarinet 421
Clarke, Edward 348

classes (social) 4, 22, 47, 119, 139, 181, 261, 382. *See also* aristocracy, bourgeoisie, lower class, middle class, upper class
  class distinction 34, 43, 47, 354–355
  communication between 320
  issue of 358
classes (social) 109
classification of dances 9
clergy 272, 365, 371
closeness 370, 419. *See also* intimacy
clothing 86, 120, 349
  pseudo-folk 114
club
  local 356, 361
  urban 369
coexistence 257
Cohen, Stanley 375, 381–382, 385, 388
  Folk Devils and Moral Panics: The Creation of Mods and Rockers 381
Cologne 286
commandment, 6th 364
communication 110, 216, 340, 362
  ritual 321
  social 321
communism 357, 360–361
communities
  imagined 322–323, 331, 337
  liberal 351
  local 3, 59, 186–187, 277, 352
  rural 355
community hall 351
community houses 327, 343, 345, 351, 352, 353, 357, 362
  Bedehus 353
  building of 351
competition 17, 59, 101, 226, 354–355
composer 57, 118, 284, 299–301, 306, 395
composers
  foreign 271
computer game 387–388

concerts 154, 285–287, 289–291, 295–297, 300, 306–308, 312, 335
　location of 308
construction work 357, 359
Consulate period (1799-1804) 88
contamination 111
continuity 385
　representation of 362
contra dances 19, 46–47, 58, 88, 192, 204, 211, 213, 226, 318, 355, 389
　era before 325
　French Contradance 89–90
Convict Hall 153, 157
cooperation 370
Copenhagen 345
Coralli, Eugène 118, 129, 131
Coronelli, Pietro 270, 275
Correspondent Staats und Gelehrte Zeitung des Hamburgischen unpartheiischen Correspondenten, newspaper 287, 291–292, 307
Cossack 211, 213
costumes 73, 110, 131, 201, 203, 267–268
　folk 114, 129
　Hungarian 218
　international 202
　traditional 429
　traditional 8
Cotillion 78, 157, 159, 181, 187, 192–193, 265, 269
Coulon, Eugène 161
country dances 93
countryside 57, 67, 240, 244–245, 253, 344, 351, 357, 360–362, 365, 369, 376, 380, 404, 410, 420–421
couple-column dances 325
couple dances 1, 15, 34, 60, 163–164, 192, 200, 213, 218, 228, 235, 239, 265, 268, 272–273, 276, 280, 318, 324–326, 345, 347, 351, 355, 370, 375, 389, 396, 399, 404, 406, 420, 427, 430
　as leisure activity 395
　criticism of 220
　fashionable 182
　foreign 265, 267, 272

　golden age of 403
　improvised 370
　in Hungary 186
　mixed 235
　nineteenth-century 181–184, 186–188, 216–217, 230, 331
　Norwegian 325
　origin in folk dances 265
　regulated 192, 220, 226
　traditional 180, 279
　two-part 222
　unregulated 226
　urban 273
couples
　female 328
　male 359
　　prohibition of 359, 400
　mixed pairs 419
　no strict pairing of 399
　older 278, 399
couple-turning.　　See movements:couple-turning
court circles 73, 79, 91
court dances 91, 100, 320
　court Waltz 72
court in Vienna 74, 78
court life 65, 100
crime 44, 76, 365
Croatia 53, 58, 60, 257, 259, 261, 264, 268–269, 272, 274–278, 417, 419–422, 426
Croatian 58, 179, 259, 261, 264, 266, 269–270, 276, 278–280, 421, 427
　ballrooms 257
　Banate 259
　dances 277
　　folk dances 279
　　Polka. *See potresujka*
　dance tradition 277, 420
　diaspora 276
　expatriates 258, 274
　identity 267, 274
　language 259–260, 267
　national colours 266

national revival 257, 259–260, 264.
    See Illyrian movement
  Sabor 259
  spirit 260
Croatian National Theatre 279
Croatian Radiotelevision Symphony
    Orchestra 279
Cruikshank, George 387
Crum, Dick 275
Csárdás 9, 57, 178–179, 182, 184, 198–199,
    208, 218, 226–228, 230–233, 277
  as dance of freedom 227
  as Hungarian national dance 181, 219
  as Hungarian response to round
    dances 178
  as national symbol 227
  name 222, 226
      origin 219
  origin of 186
  unregulated form of 199
cultural asset 361
cultural change 173, 187
cultural climate 178
cultural goals 383
cultural heritage 317, 411–414
cultural text 110
culture
  hegemonic 418
  leisure 395, 397, 403
  mainstream 383
  popular 383, 395, 401, 417
  subculture 383
  traditional 111, 235, 322
Czech
  ball 120–121, 153, 158
  character 114
  choreography 276
  culture
      revival of 113
  dance master 217
  dances 18–19, 56–57, 107, 110, 112–
    116, 120, 126–128, 134–135, 162–165,
    168, 182, 221, 276
      folk dances 108–109, 158, 182

folk costume 128
folk songs 118, 142, 154
identity 112–115, 136
intellectuals 114, 118, 154
lands 35, 107, 109, 114–115, 117, 122,
    129, 132, 153, 158–159, 164, 166, 168
language 120, 152
minorities 276
musician 217
mythology 114, 154
nation 112, 128, 134, 136
    in Prague 153
national culture 57, 143
nationalism 119
nationalistic circles 276
national movement 109, 111–113, 152,
    154, 158, 164
national symbol 109–110
patriotism 109, 112, 114–115, 120–121,
    138, 143, 158
patriots 123
people 108–109, 114, 123
Polka 108, 128, 142–143
    origin of 107, 114, 121, 140
semi-Czech 121
society 109, 113, 165
tradition 114, 121
values 108, 143
Czech Academy of Sciences 107
Czech Republic 53, 57, 107, 109, 278
Czerwinski, Albert 195

daguerrotype 307
Dalmatia 259, 420
dance 259, 360, 377
  as female activity 65
  as indicator of national character 225
  as sin 364–365, 371
  as social duty 4
  as symbol 110
  attitudes towards 43, 55, 60, 64–65,
    101, 343, 399
  conventions 4–5, 115, 142–143, 164
  criticism of 27, 42, 60, 90, 99, 259, 364

from religious circles 371
discourses on 149
fashionable 42, 58, 156, 182, 194, 196, 217, 226, 280
Hungarian
  rivalry with foreign dances 178
manner of 152, 171
  as expression of moral character 171
negative aspects of 149
negative influence of 375
new 5–6, 34–35, 42–43, 57, 59, 73, 93, 99–100, 122, 232, 235, 327–328, 375, 397
  as national symbols 55
  fashionable 119
  prohibition of 73
  resistance to 57
popular 17, 343, 349, 355, 362, 375, 395, 397, 402
positive aspects of 149
power of 45, 111
quickness of 151–152, 170, 172
role in political life 257
social significance of 153
traditional 16, 46, 59, 178, 194, 219, 222, 230, 233, 275, 318–319, 321–322, 332, 335–337, 351, 417, 420–422, 429
  social position of 321
dance clubs 331, 335–337, 340
dance concept 3–4
dance culture 183, 222, 233, 240, 320, 395–396, 399, 401–404, 413
  local 411
dance drama 217
dance events 4, 34, 45, 58, 132, 153, 157, 165, 168, 187–188, 218, 226, 254, 258, 260, 295, 337, 377, 396–397, 399–400, 402
  eighteenth-century 259
  local 129
  public 401
dance fashion 155, 164, 166, 214, 217, 427
  Western 235

dance floors 22, 93, 253, 280, 318, 323, 325, 329, 331, 337–338, 340, 351, 379, 396–397, 400
  crowded 253
  Estonian 337
  European 5
  local 395
  public 11
dance formations 19, 58, 93, 138, 257
dance forms 2–3, 5, 31, 37, 42, 45–46, 59, 164, 177–179, 181, 187, 210, 230–231, 239–240, 304, 317, 331, 336, 375, 397, 399
  as mode of representation 405
  obsolete 319
  older 324
  past 337
  traditional 336
  unregulated 319
dance game 252
dance genre 6, 30–31, 60, 107, 284, 322, 371, 388, 399, 402, 404
  dominant 361
  urban 284
dance halls 42, 72, 116, 139, 143, 159, 172, 257, 260, 263, 287
dance historian 12, 15, 17, 20, 27, 35–36, 42, 46, 74, 184, 187, 195
dance history 5, 9–10, 16, 27, 38–41, 45, 53, 56, 58, 60, 64, 99, 101, 156, 184–185, 187, 213, 217, 233, 241, 389, 400
dance master 4–6, 10–12, 15–16, 20, 27–28, 31–34, 37, 39, 42–43, 46–47, 55, 86, 88, 93, 100, 118, 161, 168, 180–181, 184–185, 187–188, 205, 209, 217, 228, 232, 234, 243, 349, 370, 419
  foreign 220
  Hungarian 222
  manuals 1, 15–16, 27, 31–32, 47, 161, 163–164, 167
  'wandering' 181
dance music. *See* music:dance music
dance musician 40, 299

dance names 3–4, 10–11, 20–21, 35, 46, 78, 113, 116, 119, 127, 180, 212, 271, 348
dance notation. *See* choreology
dance palace 190
dance paradigm 5, 10, 13, 16, 19, 31, 100, 232
 nineteenth century 178
dance party 3–4, 6, 40, 84, 240, 244
dance performers 199
dance practices 67
dance programmes 157–158, 163, 265, 271
dance repertoires 29, 34, 45, 57, 59, 83, 158, 267–268, 271, 277, 317, 355, 418
 Hungarian 177–178
 international 220
 in Zagreb 266
 local 3, 395
 new 10
 rural 28, 252, 351
 spread of 320
 traditional 179
dance salons 419
dance schools 30, 240, 205
 curriculum 58, 163
 for children 72
dance teachers 59, 88, 99–100, 270, 290, 306, 345, 399, 425
 professional 269, 397
dance tradition 63, 239, 326, 330
 Estonian 332
 Kihnu 332
dance type 3–4, 6, 10, 15, 28, 57–58, 182, 317, 319–320, 401, 420
 local 3
 new 222
 regional 3
 traditional 179
dance venues 40, 258, 261, 399, 401–402
 appropriate 258, 272
 improvised 351
 outdoors 59

 pavilions 59, 377, 379, 399, 401–402, 404, 411
 public 262–263
 society houses 399
 temporary 397
dancing crowds 56, 58–60
dancing king 46, 64
dancing practices 149–150
dancing queen 46, 64
dancing ruler 46, 64
Danica, newspaper 258, 266–267, 270–272
Daniel, Prince of Sweden 375
Danish dances 16
Danish king 97
dansbandsmusik 388, 401
Da Ponte, Lorenzo 74
Darmstadt 286
Daul, Florian 42
Davi Ćiro 275
death 82, 88, 151, 168, 263
 danger of 168, 170
decency 149, 155
democracy 119
denationalisation 227
denči 422
Denmark 30, 308–310, 328, 345, 349
Denmark-Norway 345
Deperis, Alojzije 269
depoliticisation 227
Der Freischütz, newspaper 288, 290, 293, 297
Desrat, Gustave 37
Desrat. Gustave 37
Deutscher 20, 157–158, 168
Deutscher Tanz 40
Diabelli 296
diaries 27, 78, 109
diaspora 58
Directory (1795-99) 86
discos 396, 399, 404
dissemination 1–2, 16, 19–20, 22, 31, 35, 37, 47, 57–58, 60, 93, 100, 121–122, 139, 179–180, 230, 233, 242, 270, 274, 284, 336, 344, 348, 362, 307

distinction 13, 121
Divattáncok 181
Dlačić, Serđo 426
Dlouhý, František 163
Dörner, Wolfgang 299
Double-Polka 125–126, 138
Dragoner, Albert 270
dramaturgy 426
Drehen 11, 13–16, 100
Dreher 11, 14–17, 21, 100, 325
Dreischrittdreher 14–16
Dresden 286
drinking 43, 54, 84, 358–360, 364, 370, 387
drmeš 421
Drottningholm Court Theatre 74
drseči valček 248–249
drug abuse 381, 387
Dubez, Johann 207
Dupavá 114
Duren 286
Düsseldorf 286
dvojni valček 251
dvokoračni valček 245, 248
Dvoransko Kolo 275

Eberty, Felix 68–69
Eccosaise-Waltzer 20
economic autonomy 259
economy 45, 196, 345
Ecossaise 14, 20, 69, 107, 159, 187, 210, 213
education 60, 65, 121, 185, 241, 258, 360, 362, 366–367, 370–371, 418
Egey, Klára B 184
Eisenbahnfest 309
Elberfeld 286
Elbe River 309
Elbpavillon 298
elderly people 59, 323, 375, 395–396, 399, 404
Elizabeth I, Queen of England 36, 46
Ellrich, August 194–195
Elsner, Josef 304
emancipation 136, 273, 362, 418

female 121, 273
embourgeoisement 216, 227, 230
embrace 163, 169, 171, 200, 230, 280
emotion 407
  analysis of 407
  politics of 413
  shared expression of 370
English 5, 12, 19–20, 47, 83, 101, 300, 348, 381
  dances 5, 12, 98, 212
enlightenment 343–344, 362, 418
Enlightenment, the 215
entertainment 110, 120, 235, 261–262, 264, 298, 303–304
entrance fees 296
Erben, Karel Jaromír 117–118
Esmeralda 122–123, 127
Estonia 53, 59, 317–324, 326, 328–329, 331–340
Estonian
  identity 335
  mainland 332
  national identity 318
  peasant culture 319
Estonian Interwar Independence (1918-40) 319
Estonian Literary Museum 319
Estonian Restoration of Independence (1991) 317
ethnocentrism 387
ethnochoreological 41
ethnochoreologists 57
  Croatian 417
Ethnochoreologists 239
ethnochoreology 110
ethnographic data 240
ethnography 185
ethnologist 54, 243
ethnology 411, 418
etiquette 42, 45, 67–68, 75, 164, 268, 400
Europe 312, 349, 417
  Central Europe 46, 60, 235, 395, 419–420
    courts 63

courts in 64
urban centres 418
courts in 36, 53, 99, 101
Eastern Europe 235
Western Europe 28, 46
Eurovision Song Contest 429

facial expressions 110
factories 357
Faistenberger 304
famous 91, 284, 298, 404
fan 271
farmers 134, 354, 357–358, 361–362, 376
Faroe Isles 30, 310, 369
fashion 1, 5, 17, 44, 47, 58, 63–64, 85, 149, 161–162, 183, 194, 219, 259, 280, 312, 376, 307
national 260
new 326
Viennese 264
fatherland 310
fear 152, 378, 383, 386–387
articulation of 385
Felföldi, László 9, 22, 54–55, 57, 276
Ferdinand I, Emperor of Austria 75, 77, 244
Ferdinand V, King of Bohemia 115
Festiviteten 354
feudalism 259
fiction 33–34, 44, 109, 114
figure dances 369
film 2, 6, 36, 319
Fink, Monika 39
Der Ball 39
Finland 29–30, 53, 59, 376, 395–397, 399, 402–406, 411–412
independence 401
Finnish
civil war 401
dances 320
Finnish Tango 402, 404
language 401–402
self-understanding 409
sisu 409–410
Fire Brigade's Festivity 254

fisheries 359
Fletcher, Margaret 195
fokstrot 418
folk culture 100, 111, 277, 360, 362
as ideological concept 111
definition of 277
folk dance 13, 28–30, 35, 38, 45, 47, 59–60, 63, 73, 114, 123–124, 127, 140, 179, 183, 219, 239–240, 243–244, 251, 265, 267, 271–272, 274, 276, 278, 300, 318, 320–322, 335, 355, 360, 368–369, 411
coexistence with foreign couple dances 272
collectors 28, 54–55, 59
Estonian 319
groups 7–8, 250, 334–335, 338, 340
for children 360
manuals 29, 47
movement 30, 35, 59–60, 73
Norwegian 368
pioneers 28
revival 54–56
Slavic 267, 275
vague nature of term 321
folk dancers 59, 279, 331, 334–335, 337, 340
folk devils 59, 240–241, 375, 379–382, 384–389
creation of 382
dance as folk devil 379
folkerørsle/folkebevegelse ('popular movement') 343–345, 362
Folkets Hus 352, 354, 357–359, 361
folkevisedans [ballad dance] 369
folkeviseleik 366, 369
folk high schools 362
folklore 321, 386
staged 323
folklore festivals 277
folklore group 338
folklore studies 319
folklorisation 186
folklorists 54, 319
folk motifs 142
folk music 300

folk songs 269
folk tradition 142, 278, 396, 418
foreign 60, 150, 177, 180, 182, 184, 193–195, 257, 259–260, 265, 267, 419
foreign countries 121
foreign dances 63, 93, 178, 183–184, 186, 193, 196, 220, 270, 347
foreign influence 57, 121
foreign influences 55, 111, 121, 261
Forsås-Scott, Helena 344
Foxtrot 1, 54, 58, 327, 332, 380, 388–389, 396, 401, 418
Francaise 73, 78
Francia Tánc (French dance) 181
Francis I, Emperor of Austria 75, 77, 95
Francis Joseph I, Emperor of Austria 76, 78, 262
Frankfurt am Main 286
Frederica Louisa of Hesse-Darmstadt, Queen Consort of Prussia 65
Frederick the Great, King of Prussia 65
Frederick William III, King of Prussia 67–68
Frederick William II, King of Prussia 65–66
Frederick William II, Prussia 67
freedom 68, 153, 155, 165, 172–173, 195, 227, 261, 301. *See* freedom
Freihow, Halvdan Wexelsen 363–365
French
 court 86, 90
 dances 5, 19–21, 35–37, 126, 181–182, 191, 198, 204–205, 212, 234
  acceptance of 216
French Revolution 86–88, 101, 153, 215
Friedrich Wilhelm III, King of Prussia 75
Friedrich Wilhelm III of Prussia 67
friss 222
Frisska 179
Fülöp Jákó, Imets 214
Furiant 140

Gallopade 118, 121, 136, 138

Galop 17–18, 20, 69, 72, 107, 119, 128, 142, 152, 157–159, 162, 168, 181–182, 184, 187, 192, 218, 226, 265, 298
Galop-Waltz 17, 20
gambling 43
Gammaldans i Norden 32
gangar 355, 369
Garborg, Hulda 366–367, 369
Garde-Chambonas, Count 96
gas lighting 306–308
Gautier, Théophile 119
Gavotte 88
Gawlikowski, Philippe 162
gender 402
George III, King of the United Kingdom 79–80, 82
George I, King of Great Britain and Ireland 79
George IV, King of the United Kingdom 80, 82–84
German
 administrators 244
 companies 263
 courts 46, 65, 79, 83, 98–100
 culture 114
 dance masters 217
 dances 5, 8, 10, 12, 13, 14, 15, 16, 19, 20, 21, 35, 37, 39, 42, 43, 46, 65, 74, 79, 83, 93, 100, 101, 128, 179, 181, 182, 191, 193, 209, 212, 233, 243, 244, 307, 310, 320. *See also* Bavarian dances
  folk dances 12–13
  rejection of 216
 dance songs 213
 lands 10, 42–43, 65, 79
 language 83, 100, 120, 152, 241
German Confederation 305, 309–311
Germanophobia 80
Germany 19, 31, 33, 36, 53, 58, 64, 79, 82–83, 93, 99–100, 102, 129, 173, 302, 307–308, 311, 350, 378
gestures 110, 114
Gigue 98
globalisation 386
Gluck, Christoph Willibald 154

Goethe, Johann Wolfgang von 33–34, 39, 68, 171, 377
  Die Leiden des jungen Werthers 33, 171
Goldschmidt, Aenne 12–13
Gornje Jelenje 422
Gorski Kotar 422
Göteborgs-Posten, newspaper 379
grace 73, 82, 151–152, 169, 349
Great Britain 286
Great Migration
  age of 402
Greenland 310
Gremlicová, Dorota 18, 54–55, 57
Grobinšćina 422–423, 425
Grobnik 422, 424
Grobnik Alps 422, 428
Grobnik Postcard 424
Grundtvigianism 362–363
Grundtvig, N. S. F. 362
Gudbrandsdalen 361
Gugerli, David 45, 70
Guilcher, Jean-Michel 90
Gvadányi, József 188, 190
György, Pálfy 187
gypsies 128, 130, 199, 217

Hablawetz 304
Habsburg Monarchy 211, 220, 227, 241, 259
  anti-Habsburg 179, 198, 212, 216
Hague, The 286
Halle 286
halling 347, 355
Hambo 16, 21–22
Hamborgar 21–22, 119
Hamburg 21, 53, 58, 119, 283–284, 286–298, 301, 305–312
  newspapers 291–292
Hamburger Waltz 14
Hamburska 16, 20–21
Hanau 286
Handler, Richard 321
Hanover 286, 291–292, 308, 310
Hansen-Löve, Aage Ansgar 91, 93
Haraszti, Emil 184

Harburg 309
Harmoniemusik 306
harmony 173
Harring, Harro 150, 152, 155
Haslinger 296
Hasse & Tage 379–380
Haydn, Joseph 39, 41, 300–301
health 42–43, 54, 60, 63–64, 97, 149–151, 167–168, 172, 297
  endangering of 169
  women's health 63, 101
Hegel, Georg Wilhelm Friedrich 154
Hegewisch, Dietrich Hermann 310
Heidelberg 286
Heikel, Yngvar 29
Heilbronn 286
Heine, Heinrich 155, 303
Heller, Ferdinand 134
Helmke, Eduard Friedrich David 20, 35
helstaten 310
Hennig, G. 306
Herder, Johann Gottfried 111
heroism 192
Hess, Remi 36
Heydt, Eduard von der 72
Hilmar, F. M. 122–123, 127–128, 138, 142
Hippollitus 129
Hirschbach, Hermann 302–303
historiography 64, 173, 312
history. *See* dance history
Hitler, Adolf 39
Hodne, Ørnulf 360
Hofer, Tamás 187
Holland 291
Holstein 310
Holy Alliance – Prussia, Austria and Russia 153
Homeland War 275
homophobia 360
Honko, Lauri 321
Hoppvals 119
Hopsanglaise 11
Hopwaltz 14
Horák, Jiří 118

Horvatsko Kolo 271–274
Houpavá [Swing Dance] 121
Hradec Králové region 113, 115, 117
Hrvatska seljačka stranka 418
Hrvatsko Kolo 268–269
Hufeland, Christoph Wilhelm 167
Hulán 114
human rights 173
humour 79, 297
Humppa (two-step) 396
Hungarian
  aristocracy 209
  choreography 276
  dance companies 182
  dance culture 183, 186, 233
    historical trajectory of 234
  dance masters 180, 181, 217, 228
  dances 57, 177, 179, 183, 191, 195, 211, 218, 220, 222. *See also* Csárdás
    ballroom dances 228
    character of 226
    folk dances 186
    national 181, 184, 192, 194, 219, 222
    national characteristics 183
    social dances 216
    unregulated 195
  democratic revolution 222
  history 222
  identity 216, 219
  kingdom
    subordination to the Austrian Empire 215
  language 197, 218
  middle classes 218
  national culture 216
  nationalist movement
    radicalisation of 222
  noblemen 216
  poet 191
  political elite 227
  resistance to foreign dances 183
  soldiers 179
  songs 212

Hungarian Ethnographic Lexicon 187
Hungarian Society 264
Hungary 22, 53, 57, 97, 127, 177–178, 180–183, 185–187, 191, 194–196, 199, 203, 207, 209, 213, 215–218, 222, 226–227, 230, 232–235, 241
Hvaler 357

Iceland 30, 310
iconography 39
identity 318, 322, 333, 337, 402, 424. *See also* national identity
  formation 322
  local 333, 339
  personal 335
identity symbol 331
ideology 111, 122, 230, 232, 318, 323, 343, 345, 352, 362, 371, 384, 387, 418
Ilirske narodne novine, newspaper 258
Illyrian
  ideology 264, 267
  masked balls 267
  movement 257, 259, 261, 265, 272, 274, 276
  music 266
  musicians 269
Illyrian National Hall 264
Illyrians 257, 259–260, 263–264, 267–268
immorality 42, 101
Imperial Continental Gas Association (ICGA) 308
imperialist 46
Incroyables et Merveilleuses 86
indecency 54
inns 272, 423
Institute of Ethnomusicology 239, 244–247, 249–251
Intangible Cultural Heritage 39
intelligentsia 112–113, 115, 171–173, 240, 418
internet 388
intimacy 34, 63, 151, 165, 171–172, 266, 365
irony 409, 412
irtotanssi 399

Israeli 15
Istria 259, 420–422, 425–427
Istrian Peninsula 426
Italian dances 5
Italy 241, 423
Ivančan, Ivan 417, 420–422
Ivancich Dunin, Elsie 275

Jaago, Tiiu 321
Jacobins 88
Janáček, Leoš 140
Jastrebarsko 272
jazz 54, 377, 389, 402, 429
Jiříkovo Vidění [Jiřík's Vision] 121
Jitterbug 388
Jizera Region 116
John, Archduke of Austria 243
John of Münster 378
Jõnn, Uieda 328
Josephine, Empress Consort of France 89
Jospeh II, Holy Roman Emperor 74
Jota 182
Jungmann, Josef 164
Jurca, Leopold 420
Juretić, Alemka 422
Jysk på næsen 16

Kalliwoda, Johann Wenzel 301
Kalup 113
Kanásztánc (swineherd dance) 178
Kapferer, JeanNoël 385
Kaposi, Edit 184–185
Kapper, Sille 54, 59, 319
Karelia 405
Karlsruhe 286
Károly, Balla 192, 194, 218
Kastav 422
Kastavščina 422–423
Katarinčić, Ivana 54–55, 58
Kattfuss, Johann Heinrich 11
Katzenstein, J. 306
Kegelquadrille 158
Kehraus 159
Keringő 217, 228

Kiel 306
Kihnu 319–320, 323–335, 337–340
  circle 333
  couple dances 331
  culture 324, 327, 337
    regional differences in 324
  dance forms 340
  identity 330, 337
  Waltz 329
Kihnumua 338
Kilányi, Lajos 180, 224–225
Kínai Tánc 182
Kinetography Laban 245
King of Hanover 79
Kinizsi, Pál 192
Klemm, Bernhard 162
Knowles, Mark 43
  The Wicked Waltz and Other Scandalous Dances: Outrage at Couple Dancing in the Nineteenth and Early Twentieth Centuries 43
Koblenz 286
Kodály, Zoltán 185
Kohl, George Johann 195
Kolo. See Hrvatsko Kolo; See Narodno Kolo; See Salonsko Kolo; See Slavonsko Kolo
Kolomejka 179
Komoly Kettős 182
Komzak, Karel 139
Königlich priviligirte Altonaer Adreß-Comtoir-Nachrichten, newspaper 288, 290, 304, 306
Kontradanz 190
Kopidlno near Jičín 122
Koprivnica 272
Körmagyar 179
Körtánc 180, 219, 222, 226
Körvonat Táncok 228
Koskull, G. F. 376
Kostelec nad Labem 122
Kozák Kettős 182
Krajina 259
Krakovianka 182

Krakowiak 20, 113
Krčelić, Baltazar Adam 259
Krešević, Tomi 423, 429
Križevci 272
Kuhač, Franjo 268, 273, 275, 419
Kumpania 179
Kunej, Đurđica 427
Kunej, Rebeka 53, 57
Kunz, Thomas Anton 159
Kuretić, Bogdan 271
Kvarner (Quarnero Bay) 426
Květy 109, 122, 128, 132

Labajalg 324–327, 329
    as predecessor of the Waltz in Estonia 325
    assimilation into the Waltz 329
    steps 325–326
Labitzky, Joseph, Bohemian Waltz-King' 300
labour class 357
Labour Day 354
Labour Movement (Norwegian) 344, 352, 354–356, 358, 360–361, 371
    history of 361
Labour Party (Norwegian) 356
Lachner, Franz 307
LADO ensemble 279
laity 364–365, 371
Lakatos, Sándor 217
Lamb, Lady Caroline 85
l'ancien régime 41, 86, 98, 101
Landaris 179, 214
Ländler 11, 38, 86, 157–158, 179, 325
    as basis for Waltz 86
Landsfestivalen 355
Länger, Christian 168
Langer, Josef Jaroslav 109, 113, 117, 169–170
Lanner, Joseph 39, 41, 76, 297, 299, 301, 304, 306, 311
    newest Waltzes by 298–299
Laudová, Hannah 116
lavatanssit 399
Leas, Veera 331

leik 369
leikarring 370
Leipzig 286, 307
leisure time 235
Lejtő 211, 213
Leopold, Siniša 279
Liberal Youth Movement (Norwegian) 60, 343–344, 352, 355, 361–365, 371
Liburnija 422, 425
Lidové noviny 140
Liège 286
Lieven, Dorothea 85, 91
lifestyle 365, 385
    change in 344
life-world 409
Lika 421
Lindhorst, J. H. C 306
Lindpaintner, Peter Josef von 301
Linke, Norbert 285–286, 303
Link, Karel 134, 161–162, 168
Linnekin, Jocelyn 321
Linz 169, 286
Lisinski, Vatroslav 268
List, Friedrich 309
Litomyšl county 115
Ljubljana 244, 254, 309
Løkken 352, 354
London 64, 79, 85, 91, 132, 226, 427
Lord Castlereagh 98
Lørenskog 354
Lotta Svärd 406
Louise of Mecklenburg-Strelitz, Queen Consort of Prussia 65, 67–70, 92, 102
Louis XIV, King of France 46
lower class 6, 10, 16, 32, 34, 41, 43, 45–47, 74, 87, 100, 119, 178, 185, 320, 349, 355
Lübeck 309
Lumbye, Hans Christian 300
Lunga 179
Lutheranism 399
Luther, Martin 366
Lyser, Johann Peter 301

Maácz, László 184
Macura, Vladimír 112–113

Mädel, Ernst Chr. 11
Maděra 122–125, 127, 132
　origin of 127
Magedburg 286
Magyar Nemes Tánc 182
Magyar Tánc 179, 220
Magyar táncművészeti lexikon 187
Mainz 286
Maixner, Petr 108, 114
Malá Strana 157
Mali Lošinj 427
manners 82, 264, 349, 359–360
　good 150
Mannheim 286
Marčelja, Ivana 423, 429
Marchesi, Luigi 75
Maria Anna of Savoy, Empress Consort of Austria and Queen Consort of Hungary 75
Maria Carolina of Austria, Queen Consort of Naples and Sicily 75
Maria Feodorovna, Empress Consort of Russia 93
Maria Theresa of Naples and Sicily, Holy Roman Empress 75
Marolt, Tončka 239
Martin, György 185–186, 233
Marx, Adolf Bernhard 300
Massorka 329
Masur 19–20
Maturantska parada 254
Mazur 93, 98, 193, 198
Mazurka 1, 3, 16, 18, 56–58, 91, 93, 159, 181–182, 187, 208, 214, 217, 226, 228, 233, 243, 265, 271–273, 317, 329, 396, 418, 420
　portrayal of 188
McKee, Eric 41, 377
media 129, 217, 222, 283–284, 380–386, 389, 391, 423, 426–427
　print 217
　tabloid press 383
meetings 120, 134, 142, 343, 356–357, 364, 366, 368, 371
　public 344

Meldal 352
Memel 67–68
memoirs 27, 71, 78, 96, 109
memory 44, 59, 123, 323, 396, 411–412
　collective 384
Mendelssohn, Felix 307
mentality
　change in 173
　different 405
Menuett 194–195
merchants 203
merendy 122
Mertz, Ivan 420
metaphor 136, 159, 383
metre 14, 31, 38, 41–42, 142, 159, 161
　triple metre 277
　two-bar hypermetre 41
Meyerbeer, Giacomo 294–295, 298
Michelson, Maria 333
middle class 152, 169, 171, 190, 198, 203, 218, 226, 263, 267, 268. *See also* bourgeoisie
　multi-ethnic 179
　urban 181
Midsummer dances 397
migration 179, 216, 421
Milan 226
military 95, 110, 165, 292
　bands 138
　music 298, 301
　service 359
Minitelu 179
Minuet 20, 34, 41, 46, 69, 73, 82, 88, 91, 93, 98, 159, 195, 209–210, 213, 265, 346, 377, 389
modern dances 187, 369, 419
　prohibition of 369
modernisation 386, 408
modernism 344–345, 362
modernity 385, 408
Módi Táncok 181
Mods 381–382, 385
Monaco 89
monarchy 100

moral 377
moralisation 379–380, 387
morality 11, 43, 54, 59–60, 63–64, 82, 85, 90, 99, 101–102, 149, 165–169, 171–172, 241, 360, 366, 377–378, 381–384, 387–389, 403, 409, 420
moral panic 59, 240–241, 375, 378–388
　concept of 381
　creation of 384, 388
Morelly, Franz 299, 304
Mosonyi, Mihály 226
motive types 31
　on-the-spot 31
　promenade 31
　resting 31
　special 31
　turning 31
movements 2, 4, 11, 21, 123, 159, 162, 164, 195, 203, 225, 323, 352
　alternative turning 164
　arm movements 158
　bent knee 248
　changing step 125, 131–132, 138, 143
　characteristic 3, 5–7, 10, 13, 28, 41, 45, 57, 114, 117, 156, 159, 162–163, 222, 226, 231–232, 248–249, 268, 280, 318, 325, 328, 340, 352
　circular path 6–7, 9, 60, 317, 326, 329–333, 335, 376
　clockwise 245, 247, 249–250, 253, 326–327
　counter-clockwise 203, 231, 245, 249–250, 252, 326–327, 330, 400
　couple-turning 6, 8, 14–15, 17, 42–43, 140, 317, 325, 334, 336
　heel-tip step 131, 138, 143
　hops 406
　jumping 162, 190
　one-measure turning 13
　pas de Basque 162
　prolonged first step 161
　rapid turning 15, 32, 54
　reversing 72
　shift steps 245–246
　sliding of the tip of the toe 161
　traditional 338–339
　trembling 421
　trembling knees 251
　triple basic step 191
　turning 6–11, 14, 16–17, 21, 59–60, 83, 119, 140, 162–163, 165, 195, 201, 232, 248, 251, 253, 280, 317, 325–326, 329, 331, 333–336, 340, 400
　two-measure turning 13
　unfamiliar 327
　waltzing 8, 10–13, 15–16, 47, 74, 131, 376, 399
　wave-like movement 280
　whirling 11, 167, 169, 190–191, 231, 406
Mozart, Wolfgang Amadeus 39, 41, 154, 300–301
muhe pobujat 250
mulcertanc 251
Müller, Anton 154–156, 159, 167–169, 171–173
Mune 422–423
Munich 155, 226, 286, 307
Munster 286
Muraj, Aleksandra 273
Musard, Philippe 300
music 4, 13–14, 27, 40–41, 46, 58–59, 67, 74–76, 86, 96, 98, 107–108, 110, 117, 119, 122–123, 127, 134, 136, 139, 156, 158, 167, 182, 184, 186, 195–196, 199, 215, 218, 222–224, 226, 231, 234, 251–252, 259, 268, 271, 273, 275, 278–279, 283–284, 294, 296, 299, 311–312, 320, 328, 330–331, 336–337, 339–340, 355, 359–360, 369, 376–378, 395, 400, 402, 404, 419, 423, 429
　dance music 41, 197, 208, 213, 216, 231, 293, 300–301, 303, 306, 311, 379, 383, 399–401, 429
　　traditional 339
　Finnish Tango 402
　live performances of 284
　national 142, 193
　rural 283
　traditional 338

urban 283–284
Waltz music 283–284, 287, 303
international spread of 289
musical compositions 140
musical programme 290
musical scores 156, 158, 188, 231, 299, 307
reproduction of 311
music history 213, 302–303, 312
musicians 319, 324, 388, 395
local 293
rural 244
touring 284
music journalism 295
mythology 37, 57, 108, 112, 115, 122, 143. *See also* Czech: mythology
definition of 112

Nagy, Ignácz 204
Nahachewsky, Andriy 274–275
Napoleon 86, 88–90, 95, 101, 209–210, 241, 345
reign of 86, 90, 100
Napoléon du quadrille 300
Napoleonic wars 55, 67, 91, 153, 165, 173, 307, 345
Narodne novine, newspaper 258
Narodni dom 270
Narodno Kolo 266–269
as symbol of unity of South-Slav peoples 267
later known as *Salonsko Kolo* 267
nation 20, 28, 35, 64, 111–112, 121, 135, 155, 165, 170
national awareness 260
national consciousness 111, 128, 134, 139, 143
awakening of 259
national costumes 197, 216, 218
national dances 35, 57, 98, 101, 108, 114, 178–179, 190, 196, 198, 234, 241, 260, 270, 276, 347, 369
guides to 140
lack of interest in 369
prohibition of 369

promotion of 369
National Day of Norway 346
national education 362
National Hall 264
national heritage 109
national identity 128, 135–136, 142, 252, 258, 275–276, 318–319, 340, 410, 418–419
building of 322
national independence 215
nationalism 17–18, 20, 35, 39, 58, 60, 64, 98, 101–102, 109, 112–113, 120–122, 139, 164, 179, 191, 230, 257, 260, 262, 265, 272, 274–276, 309–310, 319, 322, 335–336, 340, 347, 362, 366, 404, 418–419, 429
National Labour Union 356
national memory 234
national movement 64, 109, 112, 122, 134, 152
National Museum of Finland 395, 410
national promotion 112, 120
national replacement 178
national revival 136
national romanticism 347
national self-confidence 241
national self-identification 234
national spirit 264
national symbols 55
National Theatre 182
Nejedlý, Zdeněk 108–109
Német 179
Nemzeti Tánc 179
Neruda, Jan 134, 136, 139
'O taneční hudbě' [On Czech Dance Music] 139
Neruda, Josef 122
Neue Polka 128
Neue Zeitung und Hamburgische Adreß-Comtoir-Nachrichten, newspaper 288, 291–293, 297, 299, 302, 308–309
newspapers 27, 44, 54, 57, 58, 91, 109, 136, 149, 151, 152, 156, 168, 194, 231, 241, 244, 258, 266, 287, 288, 290, 292, 294, 296, 297, 298, 304, 306, 307,

308, 345, 361, 364, 365, 376, 424.
  See also *Bohemia*, newspaper; See
  also *Prager Zeitung*, newspaper
  German 150
New Year's Eve 279
Niedermüller, Peter 323
Niemčić, Iva 54–55, 58
Nieminen, Aila 400
Nilsson, Mats 54, 59
Nimra 122
nobility 34, 78, 179, 230, 234–235, 259, 272, 345
  local 179
  lower 190
Nordic Association for Folk Dance Research 29
Nordic Association of Folk Dance Research 30
Nordic countries 16–17, 29, 31, 100, 119, 344–345
Noregs Ungdomslag 360, 362–363, 365, 367–369
Norlind, Tobias 185
Norsk Ungdom 365
Norway 3, 7, 9, 15, 21–22, 29–30, 53, 60, 119, 310, 336, 343–349, 351, 355, 357, 370
  formation of 352
  independence 346
Norwegian dances 16–17
  regional 355
Norwegian Labour Movement 356
Norwegian Youth Association. *See
  Noregs Ungdomslag*
nostalgia 39, 56, 59, 63, 73, 101, 395, 399, 402, 404, 407–414
  as narrative device 408
  definition of 407
Novák, Arne 134
Novi Vinodolski 425
Nuremberg 286
Nyman, Lena 379

Obkročák 114
October Revolution 401

Odzemok 179
Offenbach 286
Oldenburg 286
one-melody dances 8
Onslow, George 301
Opatija 422
Opava (Troppau) 153
opera 38, 161, 306, 312
Opitz, Georg Emmanuel 221
oral traditions 321
orchestra 96, 158, 200, 269, 285–287, 289, 291–296, 298–299, 304, 311–312, 419
Ortlepp, Ernst 301–302
Ortolani, Pietro 274
Osnabruck 286
Østfold 357

Paar, Eduard von 76
Palacký, František 120, 154
Palm Sunday 262
Pálóczi, Horváth Ádám 208, 210–213
Palotás 228–229, 234, 276
panic 54, 378, 379, 380, 381, 387. *See
  also* moral panic
paradigm 5–6, 10, 14–15, 19, 33, 42, 46, 177, 422
Paris 12, 17–18, 57, 64, 85, 89, 118, 126, 128–129, 131–132, 137, 226, 286, 294, 300, 307, 424
Paris Opera 131
Pärnu Kuursaal 330
Passau 286
patriotic flavour 271
patriotism 82, 109, 112–116, 119–120, 128, 132, 136, 138, 142, 158, 179, 196, 222, 257, 260, 263, 266, 269, 310–311
  regional 108, 143
Patterson, Arthur 195, 199
Pauer, Max Felix von 202–203
Paul I, Emperor of Russia 94
pavilion. *See* dance venues:pavilions
Pavilion Dance Culture 399
pavilion dances 396, 399, 404, 406, 413
  choreography of 400
paviljonki 397

Pavlicová, Martina 118
Peasant Harmony. See Seljačka sloga
peasantry 4, 34, 43, 46, 178, 183, 186, 194, 219, 228, 239, 267, 318–320, 322, 347, 418
Pejaković, Stjepan 269
pemišvalček 248
performance 405
personality 76, 101, 152
Pesovár, Ernő 185, 187, 222, 233
Pesovár, Ferenc 186
Petrinja 272
playbill 205
Playford 47
pleasure 115, 167
poet 117, 119, 150, 190, 194, 196, 212
Pohl, Josef 163
Poland 100, 107
pole dancing 388–389
police 213, 367
Polish
  dances 16, 18–19, 21, 35, 93, 98, 101, 113, 128, 165, 181–182, 186, 232, 234, 326
    acceptance of 216
    national dances 18–19
  revolutionary movement 113
political activity 165
political autonomy 259
political circumstances 232
political climate 149
political conservatism 153
political demonstration 230
political elite 216–217
political life 134, 264, 345
political meaning 57
political satire 79
political turmoil 258, 260, 274–275
politics 37, 45, 102, 110, 218, 303
Polka 1, 3, 11, 15, 17, 18, 20, 21, 35, 38, 42, 56, 57, 59, 60, 73, 75, 107, 108, 109, 112, 113, 114, 115, 116, 117, 118, 119, 121, 122, 123, 125, 126, 127, 128, 129, 131, 132, 133, 134, 136, 137, 138, 139, 140, 142, 143, 144, 162, 163, 181, 182, 184, 187, 214, 217, 226, 227, 228, 233, 240, 243, 245, 252, 265, 267, 269, 270, 271, 272, 273, 276, 277, 278, 279, 317, 318, 319, 324, 325, 327, 328, 330, 331, 332, 336, 348, 358, 377, 389, 396, 406, 417, 418, 419, 420, 421, 422, 426, 428, 429. *See also* Czech: Polka
  arrival of
    in Kihnu 328
  as cultural product 57, 143
  as Czech national dance 35
  as Czech national symbol 57
  as French dance 131
  as Prague Waltz 118
  as rural tradition 420
  criticism of 419
  definition of 120
  dissemination of 421
  early 128
  'folk' Polka 108
  in Croatia 419
  in London 427
  in Paris 119, 129
  in triple time 18
  king of 139
  'national' Polka 108
  origin of 107, 109, 113, 117, 122, 129, 143
  popularity of 417, 428
  portrayal of 188
  'shaking' Polka 60
  steps 125, 336
  unregulated 320
Polka, La 131
Polkamasurka 329
Polka Mazur 207–208
Polka tremblante 142, 421
polkomanie 419
Pollencig, József 201
Polonaise 20–22, 58, 78, 91, 93, 96–97, 157, 325
pols 355, 369
Polsdans 21
Polska 21, 35, 325, 376–377

Polska/Polskdans 21
polythetic classification 5, 9
popularity 38, 60, 67, 91, 109, 157–158, 161, 169, 180, 184, 231, 234–235, 270–271, 277–278, 280, 311, 319, 332
popular movement. *See folkerørsle/ folkebevegelse* ('popular movement')
ports 188, 283
position 340
   face to face 8, 200, 246
   old 253
   ordinary 248, 253
   side by side 201–202
   Walzer 200
poskočni valček 249–250
post-modernity 385
posture 333, 340
   curved body 234
   'deli', 'daliás', 'délceg' 234
potpourris 294
potresavka 246
potresujka 417, 421–429
   popularity of 424, 426
Potresujkom po Čehovu 428
Powers, Richard 159
Powolniak 16
Pöysä, Jyrki 411
Pozor, newspaper 270
Prager Zeitung, newspaper 149–150, 154
Prague 17–18, 115–116, 118, 120, 128–129, 132, 139, 149, 152, 154–158, 165–166, 168–170, 259, 286, 297, 317, 348
   ballrooms 162
Prague University 154
Pressburg 220
priests 363
Primorje 425
Priviligirte wöchentliche gemeinnützige Nachrichten von und für Hamburg, newspaper 288, 290–293, 296, 298–299, 304, 306
Procházka 139
Proksch, Josef 154
promenade 325

prostitution 43
protocol 67
Prussia
   French occupation of 69
Prussian court 65, 67, 69, 72–73, 91, 94
public 11, 39, 42, 88, 112, 131, 133–134, 151, 153–154, 157–158, 163, 165, 171–173, 188, 193, 198, 222, 244, 254, 260–264, 270, 297, 304, 321, 348, 360, 365, 381, 385, 388, 400–401, 403, 418, 422–423
public dances 400, 403
   prohibition of 403
public life 151, 165, 172–173
Puget, Loïsa 307
Puigni, Caesar 182
Pull, Liis 329
Punkaharju State Hotel 398
purger dances 261

Quadrille 71, 78–79, 84, 134, 136–138, 158, 161, 163, 181, 192–193, 198–199, 208, 224, 242, 265, 269, 271, 273, 346, 421
   national 161
   portrayal of 188
   salon 275
Quarnero Bay 427
questionnaire 243–244

Raab, Johann 128–129, 131–133
Raikes, Thomas 84
railway 307, 309–310, 307
Rakovac, Dragutin 269
Ramovš, Mirko 239, 279
Raudkats, Anna 318
realisation 3–5, 31
Red Guards 401
Redowa 18, 57, 152, 158–159, 162, 182
Regensburg 286
Reichert, Adam 161
Reign of Terror 88
reinlender 355, 358
Reinöhl, Karl 285–286, 289, 304
rejdování 163–164
rejdovat, Czech verb 164

religious circles 360
religious lay movements 54
research methodology 27
Réthei, Prikkel Marián 183, 213–214
revival period 112
revolution 100, 153, 165, 173
 cultural 345
 in Poland, 1830 153
 literary 345
 suppressed 216
Revolutions of 1848 153
Reydowaczka 157, 159, 162–163
Reydowak 149–150, 152, 155–163, 168–169
 criticism of 152
Rheinlender 17
Ričina 424
Rieger, František Ladislav 120
Ries, Ferdinand 302
Rijeka 417, 422–424, 426, 428–429
Rindal 352
Rockers 381–382, 385
rock 'n' roll 58, 396, 404
Roić, Gjuro 274–275
Romanian 179
Romanian dances 38
Romani people 129
Romanticism 230, 300
Romberg, Andreas and Bernhard 301
Ronström, Owe 4
Røros 347
Rotterdam 286
round dances 1–2, 5–7, 9–10, 13–14, 16–17, 19, 22, 27–31, 35, 39, 42–43, 47, 53–60, 63–64, 78, 93, 100–101, 177, 228, 230, 232, 239, 317–318, 320–323, 325, 330–331, 334–340, 345, 351, 355, 361, 366–371, 417
 acceptance of 46, 74, 79, 82, 99, 101–102, 161, 226, 232, 280, 351, 369, 418
 accompaniment to 179
 criticism of 27
 definition of 6, 54, 178
 disappearance of 335
 European 230–231

 function of 317, 324, 338–339
 history of in Estonia 318
 Hungarian counterpart to 178
 Hungarian response to 178
 in Hungary 182
 in Slovenia 239
 local revival of 56
 migration of 10
 nineteenth-century 230–231
 origin of 10, 35, 100
 preservation of 55
 prohibition of 56, 60, 65, 343, 345, 351, 366–368, 371
 reception of 2, 4, 10, 33–34, 41–44, 56–57, 60, 64–65, 84, 101, 177–178, 232
 rejection of 54–55, 60, 121, 232, 259
 resistance to 57
 spread of 351
 technique 325
 traditional 328, 340
 unregulated 7, 318, 327, 336–337, 340
Royal Burg Theatre, Vienna 74
Rózsavölgyi, Márk 222
Rukavac 423
rulers 64, 96, 98, 101
Rull 16–17
rumour
 definition of 385
rural 46, 117, 119, 128, 135, 139, 159, 215, 235, 239–240, 252, 271–272, 274, 277–278, 284, 317, 355, 357, 395, 397, 402, 418, 427
 values 362
Russian
 court 78, 91–93, 100
 dances 98, 320
 Polka 125, 132
Russian Waltz 20
Ruthenian 179
Rutscher 17
Rüütel, Eha 319
Rüütel, Ingrid 319, 323, 327, 330, 338
Ruyter, Nancy Lee Chalfa 275–276
Rychnov region 123

Saarikoski, Helena 54, 56, 59
Saar, Theodor 324, 326–327
Saint Leon, Arthur 182
Saint Petersburg 64
Salmen, Walter 39
salon dances 267
Salonsko Kolo 58, 257, 267–268, 271, 274–276, 279
  as patriotic response to Waltz 257
  survival of 257
  symbol of Croatian national identity 275
Salsa 380, 388, 425
salvation 362
Sándor, Bertha 229
sans-culottes 87–88
Saphir, Moritz Gottlieb 304
Sauda 367
Sauda Klubb 354
Saxo Grammaticus 318
Saxony 173
scepticism 65, 83, 136, 346, 350
Schiessler, Sebastian Willibald 155, 158–159
  Carnevals-Almanach 158
Schindler, Anton 302
Schleifer 11
Schlußdeutsch 157
Schneider, Karl 153
Schnellwalzer 159
Schönherr, Max 285–286, 289, 304
Schönwald, Andreas 42
Schottische 1, 3, 11, 17, 20, 100, 317, 328, 330–332, 337, 396, 406
  arrival of
    in Kihnu 328
  unregulated 319
Schottky, Julius Max 151–152, 155–156, 167–173
Schreger, Christian Heinrich Theodor 11
Scott, Derek B. 283
  Sounds of the Metropolis 283
Scottish dances 20
Seghidiglia 75

self-expression 173, 220
self-presentation 405
Seljačka sloga 418
Seljačka Sloga 277
Semb, Klara 369
sequence dances 319
Serbian 179
servants 34, 203
Setumaa 318
seurantalo 397
sexual promiscuity 54
Shibutani, Tamotsu 385
shooting range 261, 263–264
singing 68, 111, 113, 121, 179, 252, 343, 358, 361–362, 365, 370
  prohibition of 365
Skiptvedt 353
Skočná 114, 140, 142
Skotsk 119
Slangpolska 21
Slavic
  balls 272
  dances 5–6, 19, 56–57, 182
  ideas 114
  identity 274
  lands 19, 259
  peoples
    unity of 267
  traditions 114
Slavonia 421
Slavonsko Kolo 268–269, 271–273
Slezáková, Anna Chadimová 122
Slovakian 178
Slovanka 114
Slovenia 53, 57, 239–241, 245, 248, 279, 326, 423, 425, 429
  eastern regions 248
  southern regions 247
  western regions 246
Slovenian
  dances 57, 239, 242–243, 252, 429
  lands 241
  language 241
  population 240

Slovenian National Awakening 241
Slovenian Research Agency 239
Smetana, Bedřich 57, 109, 117, 134, 140, 142, 154
  The Bartered Bride 109, 130, 140–142
smoking 359, 387
Snoa 15–16
social activities 134, 165
social breakdown 382
social change 173, 216, 230, 381, 385
social collapse 386
social context 41, 44, 119, 258
social control 381, 385
social dance gatherings 253
social dances 2–4, 6, 12, 30, 38, 46, 60, 65, 91, 101, 156–157, 162–163, 179, 181, 183, 185, 187, 198, 218, 222, 226, 233, 254, 264–265, 267, 270, 275, 278, 319, 326, 331, 335, 338, 340, 344–345, 355, 400
  criticism of 278
  cross-cultural features of 185
  Estonian 323
  European 260
  in Prague 162
  origin of 38, 122
Social Democratic Party 344
social equality 34
social event 116
social gatherings 261
social interaction 110
socialism 357
social life 34, 95, 101, 139, 168, 171, 182, 196, 201, 222, 227–228, 235, 258–259, 262–263, 275, 345, 356–357, 371
social meetings 120
social pluralism 385
social realities 405
social rules 110
sociocentrism 387
socio-cultural 109–111, 119, 232
socio-cultural conditions 111
Sokol 134
soldier dances 179
soldiers 203, 240, 272, 319

Soler, Vicente Martín y 74
songdans 369
Sorell, Walter 99
šotiš 418
Sottis 228
Sousedská 114
Spanish dances 20
Spanyol Tánc 182
Specht, Bernard 168
speed. *See* tempo
Sperl 287
Spjerøy Folkets Hus 357
Spohr, Louis 301
sports clubs 397
springar 347, 355, 369
Springdans 16
Springhill, John 384
Sremac, Stjepan 274, 277, 422
Sreznevsky, Ivan Izmail 109, 118–119
Staats und Gelehrte Zeitung des Hamburgischen unpartheiischen Correspondenten, newspaper 287, 290
Stadslollan 379
Stadttheater 289–290, 294, 296–297
stage dances 187, 265, 321, 334–336
stage performances 181
štajeriš 246, 251
  ritual function of 252
State Ballet Institute in Budapest 184
Stavělová, Daniela 35, 54–55, 57
steamship 307, 309
Steirisch 179
steps
  simple 253
  sliding 242
stereotypes 63, 101, 113, 386, 408
Stiklestad 344
St John's Eve 397
stonecutters 357–358
St Petersburg 85, 94
Strasbourg 34
Strauss family 39

Strauss the Elder, Johann 41, 58, 76, 285–299, 301, 303–304, 306–307, 311–312
   Die Nachtwandler (Op. 88) 295
   Eisenbahn-Lust-Walzer (Op. 89) 309
   international fame of 286
   Philomelen-Walzen (Op. 82) 295
   reception in Hamburg 287
   Taglioni-Walzer (Op. 110) 287
   Waltzes
      dissemination of 307
   Waltz-king 292–293
   Waltz virtuoso 291
   Walzer (à la Paganini) (Op. 11) 296
   Walzer-Guirlande 295
Strauss the Younger, Johann 299
Stuttgart 286
Styria, Duchy of 243
Styrian 208–211, 243, 246, 251–252
Sulzer, Johann Georg 154, 171
summer dances 397
Supreme Court 364
survey. *See* questionnaire
Šuštar, Marija 239
Sváb Tánc 182
Svejtrit 16–17
svikt 14
Svoboda 139
Sweden 15–16, 21, 29–30, 53, 59, 74, 344–345, 357, 376–377, 402, 411, 418
Swedish
   dances 16, 21, 29, 35, 95, 320, 401
   language 376, 401
   symbol 113–114, 119–120, 122, 136–137, 139–140, 216, 219, 275
      ideal symbol 111
      national 57, 109, 115, 140, 142–143, 230
   symbolic meaning 115, 172
Szabolcsi, Bence 184
Széchenyi, István 196–197
Széklers 179, 214
Szentpál, Olga 184, 225
Szőllősy Szabó, Lajos 181, 222

Tallinn University 319

talo 397
Tampere, Herbert 329
Tango 1, 4, 54, 58, 73, 241, 332, 355, 380, 388, 396, 401–402, 404, 406, 418
tanssilava 397
Tarantella 182, 198
Társalgó 180, 219
Taš, Ljelja 417
Tatzelt, Vilmos 207
taverns 88, 272
technological change 307, 312, 386
   fear of 387
temperance movement 360
tempo 14, 54, 119, 123, 152, 162, 169, 406
   di Marcia 132
   free 125, 142
   increasing 140
   marching 138
Tescher, ballet master 306
theatre 263, 360–362
Théâtre Ambigu Paris 133
theatre dancers 180
theatre dances 16, 60
theatres 217
   private 217
   rivalry between German and Hungarian 217
Thompson, Kenneth 381–382
Thornton, Sarah 380, 383
Thyam, Johann 289
Tirol 179, 214
Tissot, Victor 195
Tomek, Václav Vladivoj 109, 117
Töpfer, A. C. 306
Tornio 411
Torop, Kristjan 319, 325, 338
Torp, Jörgen 39, 54, 58, 287
Torsnes 357
Torsnes Folkets Hus 357–358
tradesmen 203
tradition
   as symbolic representation of the past 321
   transgression 383

transport 116, 285, 307, 309. *See also* railway; *See also* steamship
Transylvania 214, 226
Třasák 113, 117–118, 122, 126
  name origin 117
Třesovice 117
Triebensee, Joseph 158
Trieste 242, 269, 309, 421
trieština 421
trombone 421, 428
Trondhjemmer 20
tuberculosis 136, 168
Turbofolk 429
turdans 369–370
Turkey Trot 73
Turku 376
Túr Táncok 228
Two-Step 401
Tyl, Josef Kajetán 109, 116, 120–121, 123, 127, 153
typological category 239
Tyrolienne 18
Tyssedal 354

Ukrainian dances 38
Ulm 286
Umek, Ivan 242–243
  Moderniplesalec 242
  Slovenski plesalec 242
Una Cosa Rara 74
Ungdomshus 352, 359, 367
unions 228, 356, 361
United Kingdom 402
unity 370
upper class 6, 17, 22, 28, 32, 38, 43, 47, 58, 63, 74, 83, 100–102, 320, 349, 354
  culture 360, 418
urban 22, 115, 181, 198, 216, 220, 228, 235, 240, 252, 257, 267, 271–274, 276–277, 283, 319, 369, 385, 413, 418, 420
  dance 257
utopia 408

Vahot, Imre 197–198

Vålåskard 352
valc 239
valček 239, 242, 245, 252
  angleški 240
  dunajski 240
  počasni 240
valček s prestopanjem 245–246
valček z menjalnim korakom 245, 247
valcer 240, 245, 418
Valdres 355
Valentine, Mlle 133
Valtserish 190
Vályi, Rózsi 184
Varaždin 270, 272
Varaždinec, Horvat 270
variations 4, 14
Varsovienne 20
Vary, Karlovy 300
venues. *See* dance venues
Verbunk 178, 220, 222
Veszter, Sándor 181
Victoria, Crown Princess of Sweden 375
Victoria Louise, Princess of Prussia 70–72
Victoria of Saxe-Coburg-Saalfield, Princess 79
Victoria, Queen of the United Kingdom 79, 82
Vienna 38–39, 64–65, 70, 74–75, 77–79, 100, 153, 190, 194, 199, 207, 224, 226, 259, 271–272, 286, 299, 302, 306, 311, 420
  Court Military Council in 259
Vienna Congress 67, 70, 75, 77, 95, 98, 153, 173
Viennese Waltz 20, 40, 72, 158, 240, 253
  branding of 39
  German associations of 266
  heritagisation of 39
  hostility towards 266
Vigadó 180
violin 421
Vitányi, Iván 184
Vlastimil 120
Volta 36–37, 378

as predecessor of Waltz 38
Voltseris 190
Voss, Egon 301
Voss (Norway) 367
Voss, Rudolph 11, 14, 17
Voss, Sophie von 91
Vranyczany, Ambroz 270
Vrhovac, Maksimilijan 263
Vukotinović, Ljudevit 266–267, 269
Vyborg 405
Vycpálek, Josef 123, 125, 158

Wagner, Richard 301–302
Waldau, Alfred 134, 160
Waltz 1, 3, 7, 8, 11, 12, 13, 14, 15, 17, 19, 20, 21, 27, 33, 34, 35, 38, 40, 41, 42, 44, 46, 57, 59, 63, 64, 65, 67, 69, 72, 74, 75, 76, 78, 79, 82, 83, 84, 85, 86, 89, 91, 92, 93, 96, 99, 100, 101, 107, 115, 118, 119, 121, 140, 152, 157, 158, 159, 162, 163, 164, 168, 169, 171, 184, 187, 195, 199, 208, 214, 225, 226, 227, 233, 239, 240, 241, 242, 243, 244, 245, 246, 247, 248, 249, 251, 252, 253, 257, 258, 265, 266, 267, 269, 270, 271, 272, 273, 274, 276, 277, 278, 279, 280, 284, 285, 294, 295, 304, 317, 318, 319, 324, 325, 327, 328, 329, 330, 331, 332, 333, 348, 349, 351, 358, 375, 376, 377, 389, 396, 397, 400, 406, 419, 420. *See also* Viennese Waltz
  arrival of 241–242, 257, 279, 345–346
  as folk dance 239
  as foreign dance 115
  as mark of adultery 242
  as model of elegance 241
  as urban tradition 420
  as wedding dance 252, 375
  attacks on 82
  Bohemian 248
  bolcar 247–248
  choreological aspects of 245
  condemned at the French court 90
  considered immoral 240
  considered inappropriate 72–73, 76
  criticism of 266, 280, 349
  drseči valček 248–249
  early development of 284
  foreign 142
  German 349
  golden age of 254
  indecency of 346
  in duple time 14, 17, 21
  in Estonia 324
  in triple time 14
  longevity of 258
  moral acceptance of 389
  oldest form of 245
  origin of 36, 38, 240–242, 244, 266, 351
  persecution of 242
  podrsan valček 248
  popularisation of 102
  popularity of 266, 346
  portrayal of 188
  poskočni valček 249–250
  potresavka 246
  prohibition of 46, 65–66, 69–70, 72–76, 79, 98–100, 102
  quick 157
  reception of 33, 89, 349
  resistance to 100, 241
  sliding 248, 253
  social life of 171
  spread of 257
  survival of 257
  two-step 245, 248, 251, 253
  unregulated 320
  variations 251
  with change step 245, 247–248, 252–253
  with shift steps 245–247, 252
Waltz kings 312
Walzen 10–11, 13–16, 34, 100, 244
walzen, German verb 240
Walzen und Drehen 10–11, 15, 34
Walzer 3, 13–14, 194–195, 198, 226, 244, 271, 298
Wanzenböck 304
War II 239
Warschauer 20

wedding dances 397
weddings 252, 278, 324, 326, 332, 337, 419, 424
Wegeler, Gerhard 302
Wendt, Johann Amadeus 300–301
Wergeland, Oscar 346
White Guards 401
Whitsuntide 262
Wiesbaden 286
Wilhelm II, King of Prussia and Emperor of Germany 71–73, 76
Wilhelm I, King of Prussia and Emperor of Germany 67, 70, 72
William II, Prussia 70
William IV, King of the United Kingdom 82
Witzmann, Reingard 40
Der Ländler in Wien 40
Wobeser-Rosenhain, August von 306
Wolfram, Richard 38
workers 134, 356–357
workshops 335, 338
World War I 241, 244, 326
World War II 59, 70, 150, 240–241, 245, 268, 274, 403, 411, 421–422
Wurzburg 286

Yaraman, Sevin H. 41
Revolving Embrace: The Waltz as Sex, Steps, and Sound 41
Year of the Waltz 84
Young, Jock 381
young people 34, 71, 76, 326, 337, 351–352, 361–362, 364–366, 375, 377, 379, 383, 387, 396–397, 399, 411–412, 419–420, 426
youth clubs 364, 368, 397
local 361
youth culture 383, 388, 395, 397, 404
youth movement. *See also* Liberal Youth Movement
Norway 60
Youth Society (Finnish) 411
youth versus adults 378
Ypsilanti, Alexander 155
Yugoslavia, Socialist Federal Republic of 241

Zagreb 257, 259–260, 263, 270, 272, 419
aristocracy in 272
dance halls 263, 265
Harmica 261
newspapers
eighteenth-century 258
nineteenth-century 258
nobility 259
ruling classes 259
social life 260, 262
Zagreb City Museum 265, 271
Zagreb Marksmen Society 263, 266
Zebec, Tvrtko 29, 54, 56, 60
Žejane 423
Žganec, Vinko 417
Zweischrittdreher 13, 15–16
zwiefacher 10

About the Team

Alessandra Tosi was the managing editor for this book.

Adèle Kreager performed the copy-editing and proofreading.

Anna Gatti designed the cover using InDesign. The cover was produced in InDesign using Fontin (titles) and Calibri (text body) fonts.

Francesca Giovannetti typeset the book in InDesign. The text font is Tex Gyre Pagella; the heading font is Californian FB. Francesca created all of the editions — paperback, hardback, EPUB, MOBI, PDF, HTML, and XML — the conversion is performed with open source software freely available on our GitHub page (https://github.com/OpenBookPublishers).

This book need not end here...

Share

All our books — including the one you have just read — are free to access online so that students, researchers and members of the public who can't afford a printed edition will have access to the same ideas. This title will be accessed online by hundreds of readers each month across the globe: why not share the link so that someone you know is one of them?

This book and additional content is available at:

https://doi.org/10.11647/OBP.0174

Customise

Personalise your copy of this book or design new books using OBP and third-party material. Take chapters or whole books from our published list and make a special edition, a new anthology or an illuminating coursepack. Each customised edition will be produced as a paperback and a downloadable PDF.

Find out more at:

https://www.openbookpublishers.com/section/59/1

Like Open Book Publishers

Follow @OpenBookPublish

Read more at the Open Book Publishers BLOG

You may also be interested in:

Denis Diderot 'Rameau's Nephew' – 'Le Neveu de Rameau'
A Multi-Media Bilingual Edition

M. Hobson. Translated by K.E. Tunstall and C. Warman. Music researched and played by the Conservatoire National Supérieur de Musique de Paris under the direction of P. Duc

https://doi.org/10.11647/OBP.0098

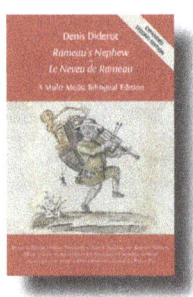

The Juggler of Notre Dame and the Medievalizing of Modernity. Volume 1
The Middle Ages

Jan M. Ziolkowski

https://doi.org/10.11647/OBP.0132

Tellings and Texts
Music, Literature and Performance in North India

Francesca Orsini and Katherine Butler Schofield (eds)

https://doi.org/10.11647/OBP.0062

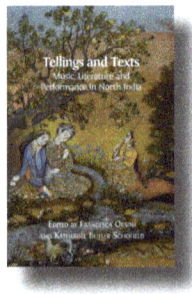

www.ingramcontent.com/pod-product-compliance
Lightning Source LLC
Chambersburg PA
CBHW062024290426
44108CB00025B/2775